Exiting the Cold War, Entering a New World

Daniel S. Hamilton and Kristina Spohr
Editors

Paul H. Nitze School of Advanced International Studies
Johns Hopkins University

Daniel S. Hamilton and Kristina Spohr, eds., *Exiting the Cold War, Entering a New World.*

Washington, DC: Foreign Policy Institute/Henry A. Kissinger Center for Global Affairs, Johns Hopkins University SAIS 2019.

Supported by

DAAD   Deutscher Akademischer Austauschdienst
        German Academic Exchange Service

Funded by

Federal Foreign Office

Front cover images used with permission.

Distributed by Brookings Institution Press.

Foreign Policy Institute and Henry A. Kissinger Center for Global Affairs
Paul H. Nitze School of Advanced International Studies
Johns Hopkins University
1717 Massachusetts Ave., NW
Washington, DC 20036
Tel: (202) 663-5880
Email: transatlantic@jhu.edu
http://transatlantic.sais-jhu.edu
https://www.fpi.sais-jhu.edu/
https://www.kissinger.sais-jhu.edu

ISBN: 978-1-7337339-5-3

Contents

Part III: Freedom and Its Discontents

Part IV: Reflections

Acknowledgments

This book explores how and why the dangerous yet seemingly durable and stable world order forged during the Cold War collapsed in 1989, and how a new order was improvised out of its ruins. It is an unusual blend of memoir and scholarship that takes us back to the years when the East-West conflict came to an end and a new world was born.

In this book, senior officials and opinion leaders from the United States, Soviet Russia, Western and Eastern Europe who were directly involved in the decisions of that time describe their considerations, concerns, and pressures. They are joined by scholars who have been able to draw on newly declassified archival sources to revisit this challenging period. All were able to exchange perspectives and offer comments at an authors' workshop at Johns Hopkins SAIS on May 8, 2019—the 54th anniversary of the end of World War II in Europe.

This project has been conducted by the Foreign Policy Institute and the Henry A. Kissinger Center for Global Affairs of Johns Hopkins University's School of Advanced International Studies (SAIS), specifically our program on "The United States, Europe and World Order."

We are particularly grateful to the German Academic Exchange Service (DAAD) and the Federal Foreign Office (AA) for their support of our postdoctoral program and related activities, including this project.

We would also like to thank our colleagues Francis Gavin and Christopher Crosbie, Director and Associate Director, respectively, of the Henry A. Kissinger Center for Global Affairs at Johns Hopkins SAIS, and Carla Freeman, Director of the SAIS Foreign Policy Institute.

A special note of thanks goes to our Program Coordinator Jason Moyer, who has been tireless in his support of us and our postdoctoral fellows and made countless efforts to ensure the success of this project. We express particular gratitude to Margaret Irvine—the cover designer—and our copy editor Peter Lindeman for converting the manuscript so quickly into this book.

The views and opinions expressed are those of the authors, and do not necessarily reflect those of any institution or government.

Daniel S. Hamilton
Kristina Spohr
September 2019

Introduction

Daniel S. Hamilton and Kristina Spohr

An old world is collapsing and a new world arising; we have better eyes for the collapse than for the rise, for the old one is the world we know.
—John Updike

The late 1980s and early 1990s were not history's end, but they certainly were history's hinge. Over forty years of Cold War conflict a widespread view had to come to prevail that the competition between East and West would simply continue, that Germany and Berlin would remain split, and that the Soviet Union and its empire would continue to exist. Although many courageous souls sought to overcome these divisions and the injustices they represented—sometimes at the cost of their freedom or their lives—this mindset took root in capitals and societies across much of the world, and two generations of people planned their futures on the hard rock of the Berlin Wall itself—on the assumption that that Wall, and the world it represented, was here to stay.

Then surprisingly, without warning, the Iron Curtain opened, the Berlin Wall fell, and the crisp, clean lines of the Cold War turned into the abstract colors of a Jackson Pollock painting. Leaders and experts on both sides of that vanishing divide suddenly found themselves superbly trained to deal with a world that no longer existed.

Two chief catalysts for change took center stage. The first was a new Soviet leader with a new political vision. Mikhail Gorbachev, in charge of the Union since 1985, understood that the Soviet system was in deep crisis. His solution—economic *perestroika* and political *glasnost* at home, together with "new thinking" in Soviet approaches to world politics—mesmerized audiences at home and abroad. Gorbachev was intent on implementing his reforms to save socialism and the Soviet Union itself. In the end he proved to be less wizard than sorcerer's apprentice. After having unleashed changes of historic scope, he proved not only unable to contain them but was ultimately swept away by them.

Gorbachev shared the stage with a vast and diverse assemblage of people who began to lose their fear—the priests and the pastors, the dockworkers and the intellectuals, the many thousands of people who jumped into their Skodas, Ladas and Trabants and took to the streets of Gdansk, Budapest, Prague, Leipzig, Bucharest and other central and eastern European cities in the late 1980s with essentially one message: "We want to return to Europe"—to be part of a Europe to which they had always belonged, and yet had been prevented from joining after World War II because of where the Red Army had stopped in the summer of 1945.

Together, these center stage actors shook the continent and its institutions. Behind the scenes, however, deeper currents were accelerating pressures for change as well. The information revolution in particular was empowering and revitalizing open societies and economies even as it was bypassing and undermining the secretive and relatively closed Soviet system. As David Gompert recounts in this volume, by the time Mikhail Gorbachev appeared on the world's stage, the Soviet Union was proving itself unable to either create or withstand information technology, falling badly behind its competitors, over-spending on its military, and increasingly illegitimate with its population.

The symbolic moment that captured the drama and power of these forces was the opening of the Berlin Wall on the night of November 9, 1989.

Here, in what had been the cockpit of the Cold War for four decades, the new freedom evoked the possibility that new forms of European unity could meet the coming century's looming challenges. Yet even as the Iron Curtain finally rusted through, it became apparent that post-Cold War Europe would not be undivided. As the military-ideological division of the continent wound down, economic and social divisions between East and West ramped up. Within the East, long-suppressed ethnic and national conflicts reappeared. Even as old lines were being erased, new lines were being drawn, and even older lines were reemerging.

This symbiosis between new divisions and new allegiances changed the frames of reference through which societies had grown accustomed to viewing change and stability in Europe.

The division of Political Europe into free and totalitarian societies stopped running along the familiar East-West divide. The East bloc dissolved into a political archipelago of islands of openness and repression.

Nationalist Europe burst again on the scene as nationalities on the periphery of Western consciousness—Ukrainians, Estonians, Latvians, Lithuanians, Serbs, Armenians, Slovaks, Slovenes, Croats—stole the thunder and the headlines from more traditional concerns. The West's mental map of Europe could no longer end at the Elbe. Hungarian-Romanian hostilities, national-ethnic conflicts in Yugoslavia, Baltic cries for independence, and bitter clashes bordering on civil war in Armenia and Azerbaijan sent a clear message: Marxism-Leninism did not overcome 19th century ethnic divisions among East Europeans; they were merely bottled up by the heavy hand of Soviet power. In such a situation, future Sarajevos appeared more likely than future Munichs, in the sense that conflicts erupting out of a string of unexpected events involved a variety of powers seemed more likely than conflict due to cold, premeditated calculation on the part of a single nation bent on conquest.

Economic Europe witnessed growing unity within the West and growing divisions between East and West, and particularly within the East. As the European Community continued to integrate, the Eastern economic bloc, COMECON, disintegrated. The challenges facing Eastern Europe were so daunting that reforms in the East seemed likely to further impoverish the same proletariat that had already suffered so greatly from the bankruptcy of socialist economics. At the same time, Western business, financial and technology leaders had long turned their gaze to a new front in global competition, not with the Soviet Union but with Japan, which at the time was touted as the coming hegemon of the "Pacific Century."

Throughout most of the 20th century the nature of European order was a linchpin of global order. The transformation of European order and of the geo-ideological East-West conflict thus also affected key allies on the continent's edge, as Cengiz Günay describes in his article on Turkey, and had significant impact on the nature of the "global Cold War," as John-Michael Arnold outlines in his essay on how the Bush administration sought to engineer democratic transition in Nicaragua and cope with chaos in Afghanistan. Moreover, the collapse of Soviet power allowed former clients around the world to assert themselves as so-called 'renegade' states. Even after the Kuwait War of 1990–1, the problem of Saddam Hussein's Iraq remained unresolved, and Kim Il-sung's North Korea, with its secret nuclear weapons program, now became a particular headache.

In short, during this dramatic period tendencies toward integration and disintegration coexisted uneasily. The hope that humankind was entering a new age of freedom and sustained peace competed with the dawning recognition that the bipolar stability of the Cold War era was already giving way to something less binary and more dangerous.[1]

The story our authors tell is of men and women struggling to understand and control the new forces at work in their world, and exploring a range of often-conflicting options in an effort to manage events, impose stability and avoid war.[2] Lacking road maps or shared blueprints for the future, they adopted an essentially cautious approach to the challenge of radical change—using and adapting principles and institutions that had proved successful in the West during the Cold War. This was undoubtedly a diplomatic revolution, but conducted—paradoxically perhaps—in a conservative manner.

The measures adopted to stabilize post-Wall Europe were essentially conservative in the sense that they made use of pre-existing, Western institutions and structures, rather than custom-designing new ones to meet the exigencies of a new era.

The most prominent example was Germany. The German Question posed a huge challenge because of the country's problematic place in Europe, its centrality to the origins of two world wars and its subsequent position as the cockpit of the Cold War. Yet nowhere did domestic and international diplomacy interact to produce swifter and more impressive results than in the unification of Germany. Faced with the choice of joining two equal halves of Germany to form a new entity via Article 146 of the Federal Republic's Basic Law, or simply acceding to the Federal Republic via Article 23 of the Basic Law, the East German people chose the latter course, preferring to take on the constitution, penal code, political system and currency of the FRG rather than to embark on yet another German venture into the unknown. Internationally, faced with a choice between a neutral united Germany obliged to none, or a united Germany anchored in Western structures, the

Soviet Union and Germany's Western partners agreed to the latter, a more predictable and conservative course.

German unification, therefore, was the catalyst to conserve and then modify two key alliances of the West during the Cold War—NATO and the European Community. Despite the efforts of some European statesmen—notably Mikhail Gorbachev, François Mitterrand and Hans-Dietrich Genscher—no new pan-European architecture was created to embrace the two halves of the continent and incorporate Russia into a shared security structure. The Helsinki 1975 Conference on Security and Cooperation in Europe (CSCE) appeared to some to possess the potential to become such a structure, but it was never converted into an operative security organization. The attractions of a Europe reunified under the aegis of an ever-closer European Union and secured by a reinvented NATO were simply too strong.

The Cold War denouement was a largely peaceful process, out of which a new global order was created through international agreements negotiated in an unprecedented spirit of cooperation. It was a remarkable period. Yet the Cold War settlement also left challenges unattended and planted the seeds of later challenges to come.

The Bush administration was overwhelmingly focused on peacefully managing the Cold War's end and moving to design a "new Europe and a new Atlanticism," as U.S. Secretary of State James Baker put it. Much was achieved. Yet by the time the Bush administration came to an end in early 1993, two states—the Soviet Union and Yugoslavia—had dissolved into no less than twenty new countries in Eurasia. The future of violent conflict in Europe seemed likely to stem more from the explosive disintegration of states rather than from disagreements among them.[3] The Bush Administration and its partners had begun the process of updating and reorienting Euro-Atlantic architecture to the challenges of a new era, but the relationship between the various institutions was left unclear, as was the process of potential membership.

The violent break-up of Yugoslavia, the the disintegration of the Soviet Union and the subsequent series of conflicts between and within some of the new states on the periphery of the former USSR presented an especially daunting challenge for peace and stability in the rest of Europe. Indeed, the splintering of Yugoslavia had raised fears of what Gorbachev himself called the 'Balkanization' of the Soviet Union in the fall of 1991.[4]

What if anarchy and mass migration spread? What if ethnic strife turned violent or even into warfare? Washington was particularly anxious about the fate of the Soviet nuclear arsenal—from 1992 scattered between Russia and three other newly independent post-Soviet republics.

It soon became apparent that the EU and the CSCE lacked the mechanisms and institutional capabilities to prevent, suppress or mediate the conflicts arising in this broad era. NATO alone had the structures and forces to engage in such tasks, but many of its members did not have the will to do so, and NATO had not acted "out of area" before. Watching the Yugoslav tragedy unfold, Secretary Baker famously declared "we ain't got no dog in that fight." With nations at odds as to what action to take and America initially leaving the ball in "Europe's" court, by early 1993 NATO appeared to have turned into a bystander, more misalliance than alliance.[5]

The changing domestic context in the United States was also crucial. Despite President Bush's masterful orchestration of the unification of Germany within NATO, the peaceful end of the Cold War, victory in the Persian Gulf war, and the establishment of constructive relations with Yeltsin's post-Soviet Russia, enough voters believed he had taken his eye off the ball on problems at home to elect a new President committed to domestic renewal and "the economy, stupid." The mood was decidedly inward-looking; there was talk of a peace dividend and retrenchment from global exertions. A new case would have to be made by a new American President for continued U.S. engagement in Europe.

In retrospect, the deficiencies of the international settlement that ended the Cold War are now obvious. China, which had not been involved, went its own way after Tiananmen, seeking in the long term to challenge the United States (and Russia) with its own brand of communist capitalism. Meanwhile, festering conflicts, the unravelling of arms-control agreements, the sclerosis of international institutions, the emergence of powerful authoritarian regimes and the proliferating threat of weapons of mass destruction (WMD) were just some of the unforeseen consequences of design flaws in the new order improvised with such haste and ingenuity by the shapers of world affairs in 1989–92.[6] That is why—now more than ever—we need to understand its origins and troubled birth.

Notes

1. For the mood at the time, see Daniel Hamilton, "As Europe Sheds Its Old Lines, Others Form," *Los Angeles Times*, October 22, 1989.

2. See Kristina Spohr, *Post Wall, Post Square: Rebuilding the World after 1989* (London/New Haven: HarperCollins and Yale University Press, 2019/2020); cf. Philip Zelikow and Condoleezza Rice, *To Build a Better World: Choices to End the Cold War and Create a Global Commonwealth* (New York: Twelve, 2019).

3. For considerations at the time, see William H. Hill, *No Place for Russia: European Security Institutions Since 1989* (New York: Columbia University Press, 2018), p. 67ff.

4. Jason Burke, "Signs of "Balkanization" seen in Soviet Union," *Christian Science Monitor*, August 10, 1991.

5. Hill, op. cit., p. 68.

6. See Henry Kissinger, *World Order* (London: Penguin Books, 2015).

Part I

Moving Out of Bipolarity

Chapter 1

U.S. Soviet Policy in the Cold War's Last Years

Thomas W. Simons, Jr.

One of the questions that continues to hang over the Cold War battlefield thirty years after the smoke lifted is why the United States did not do more to "help Gorbachev" in those last years, when he was so obviously ushering in amazing changes for the better in Soviet policies, in U.S.-Soviet relations, and in international relations generally.

A large part of the answer is that the question simply did not arise for most U.S. policymakers. The reason had to do with a U.S. policy approach to the Soviet Union that had been put in place through years of arduous internal struggle within the U.S. Government. It was a struggle that dated back to the beginning of the Reagan administration in 1981, long before Gorbachev came to office in March 1985. It was made more acute by the President's distaste for struggle itself and disinclination to arbitrate disputes, but the issues were serious enough to start with. During the Cold War U.S. internal infighting about policy toward the Soviet Union usually had less to do with the Soviet Union itself than with the United States, with whether we had the strength and virtue to stand up to the Soviet threat, and then, after détente and Watergate and Vietnam, the question loomed larger than ever.

The stakes could seem very high: to many participants, they were engaged in a struggle for the American soul. The weapons used could be correspondingly low: cunning abounded, and exile sometimes resulted. But the policy approach fashioned in painful battle by the time Gorbachev came to office had something in it for all major American stakeholders and had achieved something like consensus support in government, including the President, and in political and public opinion. Its integrity seemed more important than any single policy goal. And it also precluded steps designed to influence Soviet domestic politics one way or another, i.e. like steps to "help Gorbachev."

I was probably the U.S. official involved the longest in Soviet policy during this period: from 1981 to 1985 as Director of the Office of

Soviet Union Affairs (SOV) in the State Department's European and Canadian Affairs Bureau, under Assistant Secretaries Lawrence S. Eagleburger, who had brought me there, and Richard Burt, and under Secretaries Alexander Haig and George P. Shultz. I then served from 1986 to 1989 as the Bureau's Deputy Assistant Secretary responsible for relations with the Soviet Union, Eastern Europe, and Yugoslavia, still under Shultz and then under Assistant Secretary Rozanne L. Ridgway.

As a mid-level official, I was not privy to a lot of high-level policy-making, but that also protected me from some of the viciousness (although I still remember an incoming Reagan administration appointee's comment on one of our drafts: "Well, well, well, this could have been written in Moscow"). Or I might have learned about a decision at one remove, and only after the body-slamming on the floors above ceased for the night. But I assumed, it turned out correctly, that I was the most senior official dealing with Soviet affairs who could meet with anyone, right or left, without being penalized: hence I could brief ex-Governor Jerry Brown before a trip to Moscow to polish his presidential credentials, or travel to Princeton at George Kennan's invitation to check out a speech he intended to make to the Committee for East-West Accord criticizing the administration. (At the Committee's head table, Kennan's former Moscow boss Averell Harriman, whom I also knew, sat down beside me and whispered hoarsely, "Who the hell are these people?" I explained that they were honest folk opposed to current policy.)

The Reagan administration was also the first in years to have no competing Soviet expert at the Secretary's ear, like Helmut Sonnenfeldt under Kissinger or Marshall Shulman under Cyrus Vance. I was so centrally located in the policy apparatus that even if I was not engaged in every gearbox, my view of what was going on (once I learned the main points) was uniquely comprehensive, and it elevated as the years passed. I was the U.S. notetaker at the last Reagan-Gorbachev session at Reykjavik, which broke up without result. During the 1988 Moscow Summit, I was with Reagan beside the Tsar Cannon in the Kremlin when he was asked about "the Evil Empire," as he had labeled the Soviet Union in 1983. He replied "that was another time, another era;" the hair stood up on the back of my head.

In this essay I would like to describe the emergence of the U.S. policy approach that explains why for most U.S. policymakers the question of "helping Gorbachev" never even came up.

Milestones Along the Way

Probably the clearest way to follow the process it is to point to the milestones along the way.

During Alexander Haig's eighteen months as Secretary of State the Reagan administration's priorities were economic recovery (via tax cuts) and rearmament; in foreign affairs it wished to reestablish U.S. world leadership. To do so it needed to follow through on the earlier 1978 NATO dual-track decision responding to Soviet deployment of intermediate-range nuclear forces (INF) against our European allies: if negotiations on INF with the Soviets were unsuccessful by the end of 1983, we would deploy our own. Both European and American opinion also required continued negotiations with the Soviets on strategic nuclear weapons.

This meant the Reagan administration was stuck with an arms control agenda not of its making; otherwise it had very little incentive for active engagement with the Soviet Union. Some preferred and others (like me) understood the preference for waiting until economic recovery and rearmament were well underway before seriously returning to the table.

In the meantime, public and allied pressure for arms control produced two startling U.S. negotiating proposals from President Reagan: in November 1981, to eliminate INF entirely ("the zero option"); and in March 1982, to reduce strategic ballistic missiles by 50% (requiring disproportionate Soviet cuts because they had more of them). These proposals appealed to Reagan's instinct for boldness, and they appealed both to those who suspected (or hoped) the Soviets would never accept them and those (like me) who welcomed the structure they helped give the superpower relationship. But it was also an article of faith that we had to get away from the "arms control-centered agenda" favored under Carter (and Nixon and Kissinger before him), and since we were stuck with some arms control anyway, Haig himself preferred to give priority on the agenda to so-called "regional" issues, hotspots like Afghanistan and Southern Africa and especially Central America, where the Soviets were expanding their influence and threatening U.S. interests.

I was devoted to Al Haig. He had very good policy instincts, and as a former NATO Supreme Commander he totally understood that America's position in the world depended heavily on its alliance relationships. This set him apart from players who were very impatient with Europe and whose unilateralist inclinations were restrained only by the need to be different from President Jimmy Carter, who had left U.S.-European relations under some pretty dark clouds.

I also admired Haig for (figuratively) throwing his body in front of tanks to keep sound policy practice alive during that first heady year of the Reagan administration. We in SOV supported him in that as he prepared for the traditional meeting with Soviet Foreign Minister Andrei Gromyko during the UN General Assembly session: I remember going out on the street to get nuts because the UN Mission that lent us one of its many ambassadors' offices was ill-equipped to supply them. I was with him the next June in New York for another Gromyko meeting, when he abruptly announced his resignation. His special assistant Woody Goldberg told me afterward that Haig had been in high office so long he did not know how to make a telephone call himself. Ever after, in his retirement working for United Technologies, he would greet me at parties with an affectionate "you old scoundrel."

But Haig was also very Kissingerian, and this was not an asset when dealing with the Soviets under Reagan. It may have helped keep him robust in fighting those who wanted to replace diplomacy with ideology, but it hurt when he tried to explain things in Kissingerian terms that did not come naturally to him—he was at his most pungent and accurate when he sounded like he was in a golf club locker room— and I think it may also help explain why he was so hesitant about talking to the Soviets about human rights.[1]

One of the issues that had brought Kissinger low was his insistence that human rights were subordinate to issues of war and peace—"human rights too," as he grumbled—and Haig really had trouble talking about them with Gromyko or handing over the lists of divided families or Jewish refuseniks that we put into his briefing books. He would have someone else do it, usually our newly-arrived Moscow Ambassador Arthur Hartman, who came home for the meeting, and since the Soviet position was still that these were internal Soviet affairs, it could not have helped Hartman's running-in as ambassador. When Haig summed up his last Gromyko meeting for the President, he defined "our full agenda" as "regional security, military security, human rights and other bilateral issues.[2] Human rights, in other words, were still (just) a bilateral issue.

The first milestones were thus the work of George Shultz. During the first year after he replaced Haig as Secretary in June 1982, his main preoccupations were the Middle East and fashioning a resolution of the imbroglio over the Soviet gas pipeline to Western Europe that had helped eject Haig: it involved intricate negotiations both internally and with our European allies, and it ended only at the Williamsburg Summit in May 1983. (For the rest of his tenure Shultz kept the Williamsburg table, built with the imbedded names of the world leaders in attendance, in his private conference room on the 7th Floor.) As he learned and scouted the policy landscape, Shultz was very careful in approaching the arms control and Soviet Union minefields. But one of his early acts was to redefine our agenda for Soviet relations: in preparing for his first meeting with Gromyko at the UN that September, he separated human rights from bilateral issues and put it at the head of his presentation.

That came as no real surprise: at Westminster that June Reagan had delivered one of his most powerful speeches, mainly on democracy and freedom, but including human rights, and in discussing Soviet affairs with Haig and Shultz he repeatedly returned to cases like the Jewish refusenik Anatoly Shcharansky and the Siberian Pentecostalist families holed up in our Moscow Embassy since 1978. It was only later, when Reagan's diary was published, that we learned that before that first meeting with Gromyko, Reagan had told Shultz it was okay to talk about a summit, but we would need action first on items like permitting Jews to emigrate and letting the Pentecostals go.[3]

At the time, though, Shultz had simply reordered his talking points: speaking explicitly on behalf of the President, he put human rights first. And when Gromyko groused that surely these were tenth-priority issues compared to the arms race and reducing arms, Shultz replied that he was disappointed, for "the U.S. view of the world depends on how people are treated."[4] The exchange marked the emergence in practice of what became the U.S. "four-part agenda" for U.S.-Soviet relations:

human rights, arms control, regional matters, and bilateral issues. And that was the first milestone.

As we prepared Shultz for this initial encounter with a senior Soviet in that summer of 1982, the policy machinery was also engaged in two other exercises that bore on the emerging shape of the U.S. approach. One was contingency planning for our response to Brezhnev's approaching demise. In our discussions there was rapid agreement that we knew too little about the inner workings of Soviet leadership politics to try to play favorites or tailor what we did to unknowable prospects. The second exercise was development of an overall Soviet policy document, to be enshrined in a National Security Decision Directive (NSDD) signed by the President. The President's Soviet affairs advisor, Harvard Professor Richard Pipes, was determined that, in addition to our traditional goals of containing Soviet expansionism and negotiating agreements that were in our interest, the document include language about encouraging Soviet domestic change. Most of the tension in the exercise was over how strong that language should be. In the end it was quite mild—"to promote, within the narrow limits available to us, the process of change." When the document emerged as NSDD 75 the next January, however, just as Pipes returned to Harvard, it explained the point Shultz had made to Gromyko as a national policy judgment: "The U.S. recognizes that Soviet aggressiveness has deep roots in the internal system."[5]

Shultz attended Brezhnev's funeral in November 1982 with Vice President Bush (and me, among a plane full of others), and in the aftermath the Soviets moved quickly to propose renewal of dialogue. Shultz in turn proposed a review of all our agreements still in force with their Ambassador Anatoly Dobrynin (which I prepared with his senior aides) and scheduled it for February 15, 1983.

Washington was awash in studies of how to deal with the Soviets under Brezhnev's successor, former KGB chief Yuri Andropov. At one point, on January 13, after sitting through another meeting, Reagan confided to his diary that he "Found I was wishing I could do the negotiating with the Soviets—they cant (sic) be any tougher than (Paramount Studios head) Y. Frank Freeman & (Columbia Pictures head) Harry Cohen" (with whom he had negotiated on behalf of the Screen Actors Guild; "Cohen's" name was actually Harry Cohn).[6]

Shultz cannot have known of Reagan's wish, but he was a close student of Reagan—his prospects as Secretary of State depended on having the confidence of one of our most mysterious Presidents—but he probably suspected. For he then took advantage of a chance White House dinner *à quatre*, with just the two couples present, to suggest bringing Dobrynin over to see Reagan. Reagan accepted and held to it despite internal White House opposition. There, in his first meeting ever with a senior Soviet, even before turning to overall relations and arms control, Reagan started with the Pentecostals in our Moscow Embassy, urging permission for them to go abroad and promising not to crow if they did.[7] A bit mystified and a bit suspicious, the Soviets decided on a response which we took to be positive, and there followed five months of intricate back and forth (in which I was heavily involved) until, in July, the last family member left the USSR. Reagan did not crow. As Shultz pointed out in his memoir, Reagan's first successful negotiation with the Soviet Union was over a human rights issue.[8] That was the second milestone.

The third milestone also had its serendipitous side. We now had the makings of an agenda for dealing with the Soviets, but no overarching rationale of the kind required to maintain public and political support for any major policy approach. Meanwhile, Shultz' Mideast preoccupations had obliged him to postpone previously scheduled testimony on U.S.-Soviet relations before the Senate Foreign Relations Committee, and it was now rescheduled for June 15, 1983. He paid careful attention to this testimony, and as part of his preparations, the previous month he had "reviewed for the president where we stood on each of the items in our four-part agenda."[9] But the intention was to inform and lay out the makings of a strategy, rather than break new ground. Given this opening to ambiguity, the next day the Soviet beat reporters for the two newspapers mostly read in Washington, Don Oberdorfer of *The Washington Post* and Phil Taubman of *The New York Times*, wrote diametrically opposed interpretations of what Shultz had meant to convey: Oberdorfer heard a "new hard-line note," Taubman a "conciliatory tone."[10]

Les Gelb, Taubman's boss at *The New York Times*, called me to ask sardonically what my boss had actually said; so, in putting together the press guidance with Shultz, we had to decide. And what we decided was that after two-plus years in office, our new "realism" and recovered "strength" vis-à-vis the Soviets had proceeded to the point where it was time for "dialogue." And that was a third milestone.

That summer of 1983 then saw a mini-thaw in U.S.-Soviet relations, as both sides loosened up and took small steps, inside and outside the ongoing arms control negotiations, to move things forward. As an example on our side, Shultz went to the President directly for a decision—blocked for months by guerrilla warfare from the White House staff—to propose negotiations on our bilateral cultural agreement and opening new consulates in Kiev and New York. He got it: Ronald Reagan was ready to negotiate with the Soviet Union in 1983; he was not waiting for a more amenable Soviet leadership to emerge.

This mini-thaw came to an abrupt end, for a while, at the turn of August and September, when the Soviets shot down Korean Airlines flight 007, with 269 people aboard. But even as we led world outrage at the slaughter of innocent civilian air travelers, Reagan sent our strategic arms negotiators back to Geneva, against the advice of conservatives, including Defense Secretary Weinberger, who were recommending everything from expelling Aeroflot (which we did) to seizing all Soviet assets. And he did so even before returning to Washington from a California vacation. The message was that arms control negotiations were in the U.S. national interest, and should be pursued short of truly catastrophic reasons to abort.

The rest of that "hot autumn" was devoted to the struggle over deploying U.S. INF in Europe; absent a negotiated solution, we deployed; and it was the Soviets who walked out of all arms control negotiations. The effect was to put us into the 1984 U.S. election year. Presidential election years are times for stocktaking rather than bold new policies. But the message had been given, and that was the fourth milestone.

At the end of the summer Pipes was finally replaced as Reagan's Soviet affairs advisor by the dean of Foreign Service Soviet experts, Jack F. Matlock, Jr. (who went on to finish his career as U.S. Ambassador to Moscow, his fourth assignment there, in the USSR's very last years). He had been named earlier, but was limited to intermittent spells at the White House until he could leave his post as U.S. Ambassador to Czechoslovakia, which helped account for the rambunctiousness of his NSC staff subordinates while he was away. Matlock restored some order to the NSC approach and some harmony to the U.S. Government approach, and he instituted what amounted to little seminars for Reagan on Russian culture and history, with scholars like Suzanne Massie and Professor Nina Tumarkin of Wellesley. Reagan was a man who thought symbolically and expressed himself most easily in parables, and these sessions made Russia and Russians real for him, probably for the first time in his life. In our presidential system that made a difference to policy. I was told that new National Security Advisor Robert (Bud) McFarlane had asked his Northern Virginia church congregation to pray for Massie on one of her Moscow trips.

On the policy side, election year 1984 opened with a January 17 speech by the President on U.S.-Soviet relations, inspired and (probably) mainly drafted by Matlock. The three great goals of 1981 had been reached, Reagan announced: "we halted America's decline. Our economy is now in the midst of the best recovery since the 60's. Our defenses are being rebuilt, our alliances are solid and our commitment to defend our values has never been more clear." So, he continued, it was time for dialogue: "We must and will engage the Soviets in a dialogue that will serve to promote peace in the troubled regions of the world, reduce the level of arms and build a constructive working relationship."[11]

This was not quite the four-part agenda (for Matlock too had spent part of his coming of age under Kissinger). Human rights were in the speech, as "Another major problem in our relationship." But the speech's agenda had only three parts, and in laying out the elements of the third, the "constructive working relationship," human rights reverted to a bilateral issue: "Respecting the rights of individual citizens bolsters the relationship; denying those rights harms it. Expanding contacts across borders and permitting a free exchange of information and ideas increase confidence...Peaceful trade helps..." But, as the Washington saying goes, it was good enough for government work. And the whole was to go forward under the familiar (Shultzian) three principles of "realism, strength, and dialogue," and it was capped by the kind of musing on the hopes of ordinary American and Soviet people—Ivan and Anya and Jim and Sally—that Reagan had reached for (without the names) in his first handwritten message to Brezhnev from the hospital after he was shot in March 1981.[12]

The speech summed up and registered the results of three years of uphill struggle to arrive at a sensible, sustainable U.S. policy toward the other superpower, this time as policy enunciated by President Reagan himself. Shultz was known to complain that Washington was not one damned thing after another but the same damned thing over and over again, but unruly as we are, when the President announces policy at this level the battlers down below tend to fall in line. And that was the fifth milestone.

General Secretary Andropov died the next month, on February 9, and for the rest of 1984 until our election, the Soviets licked their wounds and struggled with their succession, for the Brezhnev crony who followed Andropov, Konstantin Chernenko, was also old. Watching Andropov's funeral from our Spaso House residence in Moscow while Bush, Shultz, and Ambassador Hartman waited in Red Square, I commented to CIA analyst Bob Blackwell that the four top men on Lenin's mausoleum were probably 300 years old, and calculating mentally, he confirmed that they were exactly that, for an average age of 75. Born in 1938, I no longer consider that so old, but then it was, and for Soviets too. With arms control negotiations in abeyance, we used that election year to pile the U.S.-Soviet table with proposals for new or renewed or renegotiated agreements in the other three parts of the four-part agenda; they would be there if and when the icepack broke. And I made sure the four-part agenda itself became a staple of our public affairs material on U.S.-Soviet relations.

As the election approached, Shultz accepted an invitation to speak at the opening of a new RAND/UCLA Soviet studies center in California, and he used the speech to provide the ideological capstone to the first term's Soviet affairs policy achievement. It was not easy going: as we and others in the Department picked at draft after draft, he finally stopped sending drafts for comment and wrote the finished speech himself, because there was something specific he wanted to say and do. He wished to put to rest the notion of linkage that Nixon and Kissinger had made the centerpiece of our Cold War diplomacy, the idea that issues should be mixed together and played off against each other. "If applied rigidly," Shultz said gently, "it could yield the initiative to the Soviets, letting them set the pace and the character of the relationship."[13] It had lingered among practitioners ever since, and Shultz wished to replace it with something less vulnerable and more sustainable, within the framework of "realism, strength, and dialogue" which the President had reaffirmed that January.

"We do not seek negotiations for their own sake," Shultz told his listeners:

> We negotiate when it is in our interest to do so. Therefore, when the Soviet Union acts in a way we find objectionable, it may not always make sense for us to break off negotiations or suspend agreements. If those negotiations or agreements were undertaken with a realistic view of their benefits for us, then they should be worth maintaining under all but exceptional circumstances. We should not sacrifice long-term interests in order to express immediate outrage … Over the longer term, we must structure the bargaining environment to our advantage by modernizing our defenses, assisting our friends, and showing we are willing to defend our interests. In this way we give the Soviets more of a stake, in their own interest, in better relations with us across the board … A sustainable strategy must include all the elements essential to a more advantageous U.S.-Soviet relationship. We need to be strong, we must be ready to confront Soviet challenges, and we should negotiate when there are realistic prospects for success.

Shultz's RAND/UCLA speech was our sixth milestone.

After Reagan's landslide reelection November 6, it took the Soviets eleven days to propose "new negotiations with the objective of reaching mutually acceptable agreements on the whole range of questions concerning nuclear and space weapons," and a January meeting between Gromyko and Shultz to kick them off.[14] On Thanksgiving Day, November 22, I came into the office with John Tefft (who would go on to retire as Ambassador to Moscow in 2017) to finish off the joint statement announcing that the meeting would take place in Geneva January 7 and 8, 1985. I noted with pleasure that in explaining it to the press Bud McFarlane introduced the four-part agenda on his own, without talking points from us: it had become an integral, almost unconscious part of American policy. A new era had begun.

Chernenko died in March, so I had a third trip to Moscow with the Vice President and Shultz. The joke was that on the wall of the Andrews Air Force base office responsible for Presidential and other VIP flights, a sheet listed Brezhnev, Andropov, and Chernenko one after the other, under the notation "You die, we fly," and with plenty of room below. After meeting with Gorbachev, Bush and Shultz reported to Reagan that we were dealing with a different kind of Soviet leader. And we were ready.

The Gorbachev Years

U.S.-Soviet relations during the Gorbachev years were no picnic. They began in uncertainty, and uncertainty never entirely disappeared. The story of the 1980s in East-West relations was not one of steady progress, but of lurching from the worst of times, which included something like a close call in the 1983 Able Archer affair, a U.S. exercise the Soviets feared was a prelude to attack, to the best of times with Gorbachev.[15] It was no wonder that gears ground: while successful practice gradually fortified trust and confidence on both sides, the way forward was never smooth.

Starting with traditional secrecy on the Soviet side and traditional skepticism on ours, it took years for us to learn to take Gorbachev at his word. His radical arms control proposals of January 1986, including the proposal to eliminate nuclear weapons that now bulks larger in the historiography because of what transpired at Reykjavik that October, seemed to us at the time to be a rehash or enhancement of Soviet ideas that dated back to the 1950s: a kind of election platform *after* his March 1985 "election," perhaps, but not the kind of negotiating proposals we had to deal with seriously.

In these Gorbachev years, new Soviet domestic policy concepts followed each other in refreshing but somewhat bewildering succession: "new thinking," *perestroika*, then *glasnost*. They certainly inflected Soviet negotiating positions, but it was hard to tell how at any given moment. There were times when relations slowed almost to a pre-Gorbachev pace, for instance between Geneva in late 1985 and Reykjavik in October 1986. Later on, I was with Shultz in Moscow in 1987 on the day Foreign Minister Shevardnadze announced that an INF treaty would not be enough to justify a Washington summit (the subtext was that something on strategic defense or SDI would also be required). Shultz was at his impassive best in response, and before long, an INF-only summit was back on. We found out only later that the hiccup followed a Yeltsin-Ligachev blowup in the Central Committee.[16]

It was thus easier, but also seemed more sensible, for us to continue avoiding speculation on Soviet motives and infighting—although there was plenty of it around—and to keep our focus on concrete Soviet negotiating positions. It is true that for most policymakers that meant Soviet positions in arms control. Not only did old habits of thinking die hard, but it was still the fact that there was really only one goal— avoiding nuclear war—that was shared by the elites of two superpowers who competed in every other vital respect.

I was therefore only slightly taken aback when my boss Rick Burt, himself an arms control expert, let drop that he had no memory of Reagan's meeting with Dobrynin in February 1983; it was now two years later, in 1985, before he went off to be Ambassador to Bonn. (He returned in 1989 as President George H.W. Bush's strategic arms negotiator.) But I was convinced that given recent U.S. history and politics, the way détente had died, the way Reagan had succeeded Carter, the only path back to arms control was through the more innocent-sounding broad agenda I had helped George Shultz invent. As the gears ground us forward from epoch to epoch, it was the critical lubricant.

Compared to relations in the first Reagan term, of course, the Gorbachev years *were* a picnic—incrementally, the "worst of times" transmuted into a period of substantial accomplishment achieved through negotiation on an expanding agenda at an increasingly steady pace. Both sides could be proud of the seriousness and skill they brought to this joint accomplishment. Together, they brought the Cold War that had absorbed so many of mankind's energies and resources since World War II to a peaceful conclusion.

Yet there were costs. They were mainly costs at home for Gorbachev, and as confusion there proliferated and resources dwindled and opposition mounted, continued progress in U.S.-Soviet relations became ever more important to him. But there were no comparable costs to us: we negotiated intensely and in good faith, but also, as Mark Twain once put it, buoyed by the "calm confidence of a Christian with four aces." We liked and admired Gorbachev, but we saw no reason to go the extra mile he increasingly felt he needed from us.

I was in the UN General Assembly hall in December 1988 when Gorbachev announced a reduction of half a million Soviet troops and equipment cuts in Eastern Europe that made the "Brezhnev doctrine," the Soviet commitment to keep other Communist regimes in power, unenforceable. I was electrified; it was a fabulous moment. But afterward I was also with Gorbachev, Reagan, and President-elect Bush on Governors Island as Gorbachev tried to get Bush to sign on to everything he and Reagan had accomplished together, and got only a weak last toast to show for it. Nothing came easily. And of course a dust-up with our German allies over short-range missiles, the Communist implosion in Eastern Europe, German reunification, and the Soviet collapse were all still to come.

To be sure, we had grown somewhat complacent: we were so used to nice surprises that seemed to be validate our policy of negotiating from strength that if good things kept coming, why change? But it was also because we changed administrations in what turned out to be mid-stream. At the Governors Island meeting, Bush was reluctant to pledge continuity because he was determined to keep his powder dry, to be his own man in Soviet policy. That hesitation carried into his Administration as well. I also chaired the study groups set up in the spring of 1989 on U.S.-Soviet and U.S.-East European relations: they ended with versions of previous policy, but they extended into the summer, and that had the effect of putting U.S.-Soviet relations on hold at a turbulent time in Soviet politics: the Congress of Peoples' Deputies, issuing from amazing partially contested elections, met that March. By the time we were ready again, East European developments—power-sharing and then a Solidarity-led government in Poland—absorbed most of our energies and resources for months to come; in November the Berlin Wall fell, and German reunification heaved itself onto the agenda. When we reengaged, at Malta in December, the words were fine, but there was very little more than that left over for Gorbachev.

I would argue, however, that the main reason why the question of "helping Gorbachev" went unanswered was because it was never asked, and that it was never asked because there was no room for it in the U.S. policy approach that had achieved a consensus satisfactory to all major Washington stakeholders and to U.S. political opinion, after years of struggle, by the end of Reagan's first term. It was not controversial during the 1984 election campaign, the acid test in U.S. politics. It was based on the Shultzian concept that the two superpowers should define their key interests to each other, and continue to confront each other where those interests clashed, but continue to negotiate, based on those interests, when they did not. It kept us at the negotiating table(s) despite setbacks in one or another area. But it gave us no reason to adjust positions depending on the vagaries of a Soviet political system which we would always understand only imperfectly, "as through a glass, darkly." All we needed to know about "where the Soviets were" we would learn at the negotiating table; we were merely curious about the rest. It had taken time for the concept to permeate U.S. policymaking toward the Soviet Union. But by the time Gorbachev was entering his vale of tears in the late 1980s, it had; and none of us involved in the process saw any reason to change in order to reward him for moves he obviously judged to be in the Soviet interest, or he would not have made them. That is the story I have tried to tell.

Notes

1. *Foreign Relations of the United States 1981-1988*. Vol. III *Soviet Union* January 1981-January 1983 (Washington, D.C., United States Government Publishing Office, 2016), No. 209, p. 682. Hereafter FRUS 81-3.

2. FRUS 81-83, No. 188, Tab B, p. 625.

3. Douglas Brinkley, ed., *The Reagan Diaries Unabridged* (New York: Harper Collins, 2009), Vol. I, p. 157, cited in FRUS 81-83, No. 216, p. 715 n2.

4. George P. Shultz, *Turmoil and Triumph. My Years as Secretary of State* (New York: Charles Scribner's Sons, 1993), pp. 122-23.

5. FRUS 81-83, No. 260, p. 862.

6. Brinkley, op. cit., p. 188, cited in FRUS 81-83, No. 259, p. 861.

7. See Dobrynin's account in Anatoly Dobrynin, *In Confidence* (New York Times Books/Random House, 1995), pp. 218-20.

8. Shultz, op. cit., p. 171.

9. Ibid., p. 275.

10. https://timesmachine.nytimes.com/timesmachine/1983/06/16/issue.html?action=click&contentCollection=Archives&module=LedeAsset&region=ArchiveBody&pgtype=article; and Shultz, op. cit., p. 277.

11. https://www.nytimes.com/1984/01/17/world/transcript-of-reagan-s-speech-on-soviet-american-relations.html.

12. FRUS 81-83, No. 46, pp. 116-8.

13. Shultz, op. cit., pp. 487-90.

14. Cited in Ibid, p. 500.

15. See Robert E. Hamilton, "ABLE ARCHER at 35: Lessons of the 1983 War Scare," Foreign Policy Research Institute, December 3, 2018, https://www.fpri.org/article/2018/12/able-archer-at-35-lessons-of-the-1983-war-scare/. Thanks to James Dobbins for highlighting this point at our May 8, 2019 workshop at SAIS.

16. On this episode, see Pavel Palazchenko, *My Years with Gorbachev and Shevardnadze: The Memoir of a Soviet Interpreter* (University Park, PA: The Pennsylvania State University Press, 1997), pp. 72-76.

Chapter 2

The Endgame of the Reagan Doctrine: Democratic Transition in Nicaragua and Chaos in Afghanistan

John-Michael Arnold

Introduction[1]

This chapter examines what happened, during the waning years of the American-Soviet struggle, in two conflicts that were part of the "global Cold War."[2] In both Afghanistan and Nicaragua throughout the 1980s, Soviet-supported Marxist regimes had fought American-aided insurgencies. The United States' support to the Afghan and Nicaraguan guerillas was central to what became widely known as the "Reagan Doctrine," a term coined by columnist Charles Krauthammer in 1985 and which he defined as "overt and unashamed American support for anti-Communist revolution."[3]

While President Reagan became associated in many people's minds with the American counter-offensive against Marxist regimes, it fell to Reagan's vice-president and successor in the Oval Office, President George H.W. Bush, to preside over the endgame of the "Reagan Doctrine." The following analysis demonstrates three major things about the Bush administration's record in that regard. First, in the midst of continuing competition with the Soviet Union, the Bush administration wanted settlements to the wars in Nicaragua and Afghanistan, preferably with the departure of the Soviet-aligned governments in those countries. Second, during the Bush administration's term—which ran from January 1989 until January 1993—there was a narrowing of ideological differences between the superpowers when it came to "regional conflicts," with Mikhail Gorbachev's Soviet Union sharing similar ideas to the United States about the need for political settlements and even democratic elections as the way to end proxy wars. Third, despite a reduction in superpower ideological competition and efforts to reach mutual American-Soviet understandings—most notably in regard to

Afghanistan—a narrowing of superpower differences was not enough to guarantee a cessation of all regional conflicts. While the war in Nicaragua concluded with a political settlement and a democratic transition in 1990, the war in Afghanistan raged on, leaving the country to become a failed state and the source of new post-Cold War threats.

After providing an overview of American support to the anti-communist insurgencies in Afghanistan and Nicaragua, the heart of this chapter examines the Bush administration's policy approach towards the two countries and shows how events in them played out in markedly different ways. The conclusion reflects upon why the Nicaraguan and Afghan wars followed distinct trajectories during the closing stages of the Cold War.

An Overview of American Support to the Afghan and Nicaraguan Insurgencies

By the close of the 1970s, as Hal Brands writes, "the Cold War was frequently feared to be tilting in Moscow's direction, amid a major Soviet military buildup and a string of Kremlin advances—and American defeats—in the Third World."[4] The year 1979 was truly disastrous for the United States.[5] In January, the American-aligned Shah of Iran was deposed by a revolution. In July, the Marxist-Leninist Sandinista National Liberation Front seized power in Nicaragua by overthrowing another U.S. ally, Anastasio Somoza Debayle, whose family had ruled that country repressively since 1936. In November 1979, Iranian hardliners took 52 Americans hostage in Tehran. On December 24, the Soviet Union invaded Afghanistan. The Kremlin embarked on that venture to change the leader of the People's Democratic Party of Afghanistan (PDPA) and more broadly to shore up the party's rule.[6] The communist PDPA had seized power in an April 1978 coup but, by the following year, its position was imperiled by widespread domestic opposition and infighting between its own factions.[7]

Several days after Soviet forces entered Afghanistan, U.S. President Jimmy Carter signed a covert action "finding"—an approval required by American law for such operations—that authorized the CIA to "provide lethal military equipment either directly or through third countries to the Afghan opponents of the Soviet intervention in Afghanistan."[8] By the time Carter left office in January 1981, the United States had provided the Afghan resistance with approximately $30 million, in nominal dollars, of military assistance.[9] The CIA provided weapons and materiel to Pakistan's Inter-Services Intelligence agency (ISI), who passed them along to the Afghan mujahedin.[10] That anti-Soviet resistance movement was a fragmented one; seven political leaders were based in Peshawar, Pakistan, while numerous commanders led the war effort in Afghanistan.[11]

Under Ronald Reagan, the years between 1981 and 1984 saw the United States contribute a steadily increasing quantity of weaponry and other support to the mujahedin. The year 1985 was a watershed, however, because from then on the United States dramatically ramped up both the scale and the technological quality of its assistance.[12] Overall, from December 1979 until the USSR's departure from Afghanistan in February 1989, the United States provided around $2 billion in support to the mujahedin, in nominal dollars, equivalent to over $4 billion today.[13] One reason why the Afghan resistance received so much material aid was because the effort enjoyed bipartisan and wide-ranging support among U.S. policymakers and politicians.

The same was not true of the Reagan administration's support for the Nicaraguan contras, which precipitated a huge political fight in Washington D.C. In their successful quest for power in Nicaragua, the Sandinistas had benefitted from Cuban assistance. They had also allied with a broad coalition that was drawn from across Nicaraguan society and that included private sector representatives as well as moderate political groups that opposed the Somoza regime.[14] Once in power, the Sandinistas pushed many members of that coalition aside.[15] Additionally, they began providing arms to Marxist guerillas in El Salvador.[16] On December 1, 1981, President Reagan authorized the CIA to aid an armed opposition movement, writing in his diary that "we're proceeding with covert activity in Nicaragua to shut off supplies to the Guerillas in El Salvador."[17] Initially, the anti-Sandinista rebels—who became known as the "contras," short for *contrarevolucionarios*—numbered only around 500 fighters, most of whom were former soldiers from Somoza's military.[18]

The Reagan administration's goals expanded over time. In September 1983, the president stipulated, as part of a new covert action "finding," that American support for the contras would continue until the Sandinista regime demonstrated "a commitment to provide amnesty and nondiscriminatory participation in the Nicaraguan political process by all Nicaraguans."[19] Meanwhile, the contras' ranks also grew; by 1987, they had around 18,000 fighters, compared to the 70,000-strong Sandinista army.[20] Reflecting their numerical inferiority, the contras waged an insurgency. They used camps in Honduras, from where they could deploy into Nicaragua to conduct guerilla operations, and the United States provided them with weapons and training suited to that style of warfare.[21]

From late 1982 onwards, the U.S. Congress took numerous votes on whether to continue aiding the contras. In 1984, congressional opponents of supporting the rebels—led by Representative Edward Boland, a Democrat and chairman of the House Intelligence Committee—passed a ban on helping the contras. President Reagan signed it into law because it was attached to a critically-important piece of legislation.[22] After the president's November 1984 re-election, Reagan's administration began efforts to persuade Congress to rescind the prohibition, including by linking the contras' war with those of other anti-communist insurgencies. In his February 6, 1985 State of the Union address, Reagan declared that:

> We must not break faith with those who are risking their lives—on every continent, from Afghanistan to Nicaragua—to defy Soviet-supported aggression and secure rights which have been ours from birth.[23]

Several weeks later, Secretary of State George Shultz delivered a speech in which he argued that the United States had a "moral responsibility" to support "popular insurgencies against communist domination."[24] Peter Rodman, who served in Shultz's State Department, later noted that the president's and secretary of state's remarks represented "an attempt to get the glow of the popular cause (the Afghans) to rub off onto the unpopular one (the Contras)."[25] Within that context, in April 1985, Charles Krauthammer coined the term "Reagan Doctrine."[26]

In June 1985, Congress voted to restore aid to the contras—albeit of an expressly non-lethal form. The decision followed a good Republican performance in the 1984 elections, which frightened some politically-vulnerable Democrats into backing the contras, as well as increasing evidence about the Sandinistas' repression and close links to the USSR.[27] One year later, in June 1986—following Sandinista military operations against rebel camps inside Honduras and after concerted lobbying by the administration—Congress even approved a resumption of lethal aid, totaling $70 million, to the contras.[28]

The administration's Nicaragua policy, however, soon became mired in scandal. After a series of press revelations, in late November 1986 the U.S. attorney general made a stunning announcement. Earlier that year, while a congressional ban on lethal assistance was still in effect, Lieutenant Colonel Oliver North of the National Security Council (NSC) staff had funneled some proceeds from secret arms sales to Iran to the Nicaraguan rebels.[29] In the aftermath of the "Iran-contra" scandal and the 1986 elections—when Democrats won control of both legislative chambers—Congress would never authorize additional lethal support to the contras. The insurgents did benefit, however, from the military assistance that had been passed in 1986 prior to the scandal and that aid allowed them to prosecute their war with renewed vigor during late 1986 and 1987.[30]

By the late 1980s, the wars in both Afghanistan and Nicaragua were strategically deadlocked. American aid to the insurgents contributed to those stalemates, but it was far from the sole cause.[31] Those battlefield deadlocks, combined with burgeoning superpower cooperation towards "regional conflicts," helped set the stage for important agreements in 1988.[32] In early February of that year, the U.S. House of Representatives voted down an administration proposal to give the contras new aid. At the time of that vote, a Central American peace effort led by Costa Rican President Oscar Arias seemed to be making headway and the Democrat-controlled House was not about to fund further military efforts.[33] Consequently, the contras were left seriously short of supplies and in March 1988 they entered into a ceasefire.[34] For their part, the Sandinistas signed that measure because, although they were still receiving aid from the Soviet bloc, that assistance was lagging behind Nicaragua's economic requirements.[35] After the ceasefire, the U.S. Congress voted new non-lethal aid to the contras; its purpose was to hold the contras together, in an attempt to ensure that the Sandinistas entered into a permanent settlement and allowed free-and-fair elections.[36]

Meanwhile, the Soviet Union's leadership was committed to a with-drawal from Afghanistan from late 1986 onwards, having concluded that it could not win a military victory there. As General Secretary Mikhail Gorbachev described the matter at a Politburo meeting in No-vember 1986: "we have been fighting in Afghanistan for already six years. If the approach is not changed, we will continue to fight for an-other 20-30 years."[37] The Soviet exit subsequently unfolded over a pe-riod that exceeded two years—in Artemy Kalinovsky's phrase, it was "a long goodbye."[38] In April 1988, the Soviet Union accepted the Geneva Accords, under which it would depart, and by February 15, 1989 all of its forces had left Afghanistan.

While the 1988 agreements related to Nicaragua and Afghanistan constituted important steps in de-escalating the global Cold War, they did not settle what longer-term political arrangements would ex-ist in those countries. Of particular importance to the United States, when the Reagan administration left office on January 20, 1989, Sovi-et-aligned regimes remained in power in both Nicaragua and Afghan-istan, led by Daniel Ortega and Mohammad Najibullah respectively.[39] The incoming American administration of President George H.W. Bush would endeavor to produce lasting settlements in those countries, preferably ones that included the departure of the incumbent regimes.

The Bush Administration and the Finale of the Reagan Doctrine

The Endgame in Nicaragua

Secretary of State James Baker's prepared talking points for the first Cabinet meeting of the Bush administration, held on January 23, 1989, included a section on Central America. The first point simply read: "Decade of frustration." The section noted that the contras' non-lethal aid, passed by Congress after the March 1988 ceasefire in Nicaragua, would run out by the end of March 1989. Baker was due to tell the Cabinet that "in a sense, we may have an opportunity because the pres-ent result is so unsatisfactory" and he added the comment "work with Congress" to his talking points by hand.[40]

In mid-February 1989, at a meeting of Central American leaders—the latest stage in Oscar Arias' peace process—the Sandinista president of Nicaragua, Daniel Ortega, promised to hold presidential and legislative elections by February 25, 1990 and to allow external election observers into the country.[41] The same agreement also called for the demobilization of the contras. Consequently, American congressional supporters of the rebels worried that they would have to disband, only to see the Sandinista regime renege on its promises.[42] President Bush stated publicly that he was determined to avoid that outcome.[43]

Secretary Baker, alongside Assistant Secretary of State for Inter-American Affairs Bernard Aronson, engaged in painstaking talks with Congress to forge a bipartisan approach towards Nicaragua. Baker later wrote the following about the challenging dynamics the administration faced on Capitol Hill:

> The diehards on the right wanted to force a vote on military aid, calculating that its preordained failure would give them an excuse to blame the liberals for the death of democracy in Nicaragua. They viewed the very idea of a bipartisan approach as a secret ploy by the President and me to appease the Sandinistas. Conversely, the liberals thought it was nothing less than a plot to save the contras through some semantic trickery.[44]

Following three weeks of onerous negotiations, on March 24, 1989, the administration and congressional leaders announced a "Bipartisan Accord" on Central America. Among its provisions, the United States would give the contras $66 million in non-lethal aid during the period between then and the Nicaraguan elections in February 1990.[45] The contras had to refrain from offensive military operations, otherwise they risked losing that aid.[46]

The essence of this bipartisan approach was coercive diplomacy in pursuit of democracy. The United States would help to hold the contras together as a cohesive movement, thereby keeping the pressure on the Sandinistas to hold a free-and-fair vote. American policy included an implicit threat: if the Sandinistas failed to permit a real election, the contras would still exist and might be able to resume their war. At the beginning of May 1989, the Bush administration spelled out the strategy in National Security Directive 8, which stated that:

> We will maintain as far as possible the Nicaraguan Resistance as a
> viable entity. The Resistance should not be demobilized and vol-
> untarily reintegrated into Nicaraguan society unless democratic
> conditions have been established which guarantee their physical
> safety and safeguard their political rights.[47]

The prospect of a competitive election was enhanced in June 1989
when fourteen political parties from among Nicaragua's unarmed opposition—organizationally distinct from the armed contras—established the Nicaraguan Opposition Union (UNO) and united behind a
single presidential candidate: Violeta Chamorro.[48]

Chamorro was the publisher of the opposition newspaper *La Pren-
sa*, a role she had inherited following the political assassination of her
husband Pedro Joaquín Chamorro, whose murder in January 1978 had
helped catalyze widespread protests against Somoza.[49] When the Sandinistas initially took power in July 1979, Violeta Chamorro had been
one of the moderates who entered government with them, but she resigned in 1980 out of dismay with the Sandinistas' radical trajectory.[50]

In September 1989, President Bush signed National Security Directive 25 (NSD 25), which clarified U.S. policy towards the Nicaraguan
elections. The directive stated that "there shall be <u>no covert</u> assistance
to political or other groups in Nicaragua in the upcoming election
campaign [emphasis in original]." At the same time, the U.S. was to
work for a genuine democratic election through open means. As NSD
25 put it:

> The Department of State shall undertake a vigorous overt pro-
> gram to support a free and fair election process. Every effort will
> be made, consistent with U.S. law, to assist the democratic oppo-
> sition to compete effectively with the Sandinista regime [emphasis
> in original]."[51]

In his memoir, James Baker recalled some of the ways in which the
State Department carried out this instruction. For example, the department "convinced the Congress to provide voter registration and other
support through the National Endowment for Democracy" and Baker explained that the State Department "pressed the OAS, the United
Nations, the Carter Center, the European Union, and many others to
flood Nicaragua with election observers."[52]

While the United States worked for a democratic election in Nicaragua, the Soviet Union also encouraged the Sandinista government to allow such a process to take place.[53] This Soviet stance was driven in significant measure by the views of Mikhail Gorbachev. As Svetlana Savranskaya elaborates, from 1988 onwards Gorbachev's overriding objective regarding regional conflicts was to resolve them.[54] In the Soviet Union itself, Gorbachev introduced meaningful—even if not completely open—elections and they took place in March 1989. As William Taubman emphasizes, "the Soviet regime was transformed when mostly free elections were held for the first time in more than seven decades, and a genuine, functioning parliament replaced the rubber-stamp Supreme Soviet."[55]

Consistent with the introduction of elections at home, the Soviet Union incorporated the same process into its conceptual approach for settling conflicts in the "Third World." This was a key way in which American and Soviet views regarding regional conflicts began to converge in the final years of the Cold War, even while the two sides remained aligned with their own preferred parties on the ground. Pavel Palazhchenko, a contributor to this volume who was an aide and interpreter to both Gorbachev and Soviet Foreign Minister Eduard Shevardnadze, later wrote in his memoir that "I am not sure whether he [American Secretary of State James Baker] knew how much pressure the Soviet Union was putting on the Sandinista government in Nicaragua to hold a really free and clean election and to accept its outcome."[56]

When election day arrived in Nicaragua on February 25, 1990, several thousand foreign observers were at work in the country and they played a critical role in ensuring the integrity of the process.[57] Turnout was around 86% and 54.7% of voters cast their ballot for Violeta Chamorro, while only 40.8% did so for the Sandinista candidate, Daniel Ortega.[58] The next day, President Bush spoke with Oscar Arias and told him that "UNO's victory is also your victory and a victory for the peace process." The American president remarked that "there is no need for the contras to be fighters any more."[59]

Daniel Ortega transferred power peacefully to Violeta Chamorro in April 1990. Despite all of the political divisiveness in Washington D.C. over the previous decade, the United States had witnessed, in the end, a democratic election in Nicaragua and the Sandinista regime's exit.

The costs of attaining that outcome had been very high, most especially for the people of Nicaragua—tens of thousands of lives had been lost during the 1980s—and also, to a lesser extent, for the American political system. The American deputy national security advisor at the time, Robert Gates, later summed up the result: "The United States had not won in Nicaragua. The Sandinistas just lost."[60]

The Endgame in Afghanistan

Regarding Afghanistan, the Bush administration set out its policy through National Security Directive 3 (NSD 3), which was issued on February 13, 1989, two days before the last Soviet soldier left Afghan soil. NSD 3 established the following objective:

> With the departure of Soviet forces, the United States should encourage the establishment of a stable Afghan government, representative of and responsive to the Afghan people. We should support a peaceful political succession that will promote the reconstruction and recovery of Afghanistan and the return of Afghan refugees from neighboring countries.[61]

NSD 3 indicated that the United States wanted to see Mohammad Najibullah's regime leave office. At the time, it was widely assumed that the Afghan government's remaining days would be few in any case. A CIA intelligence assessment from October 1988 had reported that "the Afghan regime probably will collapse within six to 12 months following the departure of Soviet forces from Afghanistan."[62] In late February 1989, Pakistan's foreign minister, Yaqub Khan, told President Bush that "the resistance would soon tear apart the existing Afghan government."[63] Many senior Soviet officials also doubted the Afghan leader's staying power after the Soviet troop departure.[64]

Predictions of a rapid military victory for the mujahedin, however, were shattered in March 1989 when they suffered a debacle during their attempt to take Jalalabad. Anne Stenersen notes that it was the mujahedin's "first attempt to seize a major city from the Afghan Communist regime."[65] As former CIA analyst Bruce Riedel explains, the battle showed that "the mujahedin were simply not ready to conduct a conventional military siege against an enemy with artillery, tanks, Scud missiles, and air power."[66] The Afghan regime remained well-armed because, even though the USSR had removed its ground troops, it continued to supply the regime with a bountiful supply of weaponry.[67] Meanwhile, the United States continued to work with Pakistan to provide significant military aid to the mujahedin.[68]

The United States also tried to achieve the Afghan regime's departure by engaging in discussions with the Soviet Union regarding a political settlement. During a September 1989 Oval Office meeting with Soviet Foreign Minister Eduard Shevardnadze, President Bush said that "we should be able to find a solution to the Afghan problem."[69] Shevardnadze subsequently held two days of meetings with Secretary of State Baker close to the latter's ranch in Wyoming. At the conclusion of those meetings, as part of a joint statement, the U.S. and USSR said:

> The two sides agreed on the need for a political settlement in Afghanistan on the basis of national reconciliation, one that ensures the peaceful, independent, and nonaligned status of Afghanistan. While their approaches differ over how to translate these principles into reality, they, nevertheless, agreed that a transition period is required, as well as an appropriate mechanism to establish a broad-based government.[70]

At the Malta summit meeting, on December 3, 1989, Shevardnadze proposed addressing the situation in Afghanistan by working towards "free elections to be monitored by the UN."[71] President Bush indicated that the mujahedin would not accept any political settlement that failed to change Afghanistan's leader. As Bush put it:

> Najibullah is a major hang-up. About that the resistance groups are united. They all say that reconciliation is impossible with him there.[72]

When Secretary Baker visited Moscow in early February 1990, he again stressed to Gorbachev that the United States wanted a political settlement in Afghanistan. But Baker also explained that "we really have limited influence on the Mujahaddin."[73] American influence upon the mujahedin was constrained, at least in part, because the resistance groups were receiving significant support from other sources, notably including Saudi Arabia and Pakistan.

Baker argued that, if an arrangement could be found that would culminate in Najibullah's departure, then that could help to get the mujahedin, Pakistan, and Saudi Arabia to support such a political process.[74] In response to Baker's comments, Gorbachev expressed a sense of exasperation with Afghanistan, commenting: "maybe we ought to just let them boil in their own juices." Baker agreed: "we have a saying in America," he exclaimed, "that we don't want any cheese we just want out of the trap."[75]

In early March 1990, Pakistan's ISI supported a coup attempt against Najibullah. It was launched by defectors from the PDPA regime and supported by mujahedin fighters from Gulbuddin Hekmatyar's faction. Najibullah quashed the coup within two days.[76] Two weeks after that, on March 20, 1990, James Baker and Eduard Shevardnadze met again. During the part of their conversation that addressed Afghanistan, the American secretary of state returned to the theme of elections, remarking that:

> It occurs to me that there may be some common ground on the issue of elections—though the circumstances in Afghanistan are not the same as they were in Namibia or in Nicaragua. I would be interested at some point in hearing your ideas on how you see elections working in Afghanistan. I know that in constructing a process that at some point we would get to the issue of whether Najib would take part as a candidate in the elections. We've never said someone ought not to run for office—we would never exclude anyone from running for office. But we don't think we can produce the Mujahaddin in a process where Najib could still be in power. That is not a political position—that is really just a statement of reality.[77]

Later in the conversation, Baker offered a suggestion for how to handle Najibullah's political future:

> What would you think of the idea of asking him [Najibullah] to abide by the results of elections, go along with it, but have him agree that he would not run in the first election, but he would be eligible for any election after that. There could even be a PDPA candidate in that first election.[78]

The Soviet foreign minister was not impressed, replying that "I think that we could talk to Najib but it wouldn't get us very far if we were to talk to him in a fashion that you suggested."[79] Secretary Baker sent a cable to President Bush the same day giving him a readout of the discussion. Baker recounted what he had told the Soviet foreign minister about the practicality of holding UN-supervised elections in Afghanistan and Baker added an additional comment for Bush's consideration:

> I said the mujahedin would never accept it if Najib could run in he [sic] elections. It was not a case of being right or wrong, this was simply the reality. He asked if we would think more about the elections approach. Frankly, I have got to say, there is something paradoxical and indefensible about us opposing elections that are free and fair. If the mujahedin won't participate in such elections, how can we justify continued support for them?[80]

President Bush recognized that his secretary of state had fastened upon a problem and he wrote a comment in the margin next to Baker's observation. Bush's comment simply read: "Brent?? good point."[81]

When he met with Gorbachev at Camp David on June 2, 1990, Bush told the Soviet leader that, regarding Afghanistan, "we would like to cut loose" and Bush asked "how does Najilbah [sic] feel about elections?" Shevardnadze responded that "he favors a Nicaragua-type solution, with a group charged with developing elections." At an abstract level, a political solution modelled on Nicaragua should have been appealing to the United States given the democratic transition achieved there. In response to Shevardnadze's comment, Secretary Baker gave general approval to the approach, but again explained how the mujahedin posed an impediment:

> It is difficult for us to argue against the Nicaraguan model. Our problem is with the Resistance. We need something for them to show that elections would be fair, that supervision would be neutral, and that the outcome would be observed. What about Najibullah taking a head of state role during this period to demonstrate that a transition authority would conduct the election and provide security.[82]

In response to a query from Gorbachev, Baker clarified that what he had in mind was Najibullah serving as a type of "interim acting president during the election" with "something less than full authority." Gorbachev responded: "we must think about it."[83]

With discussions about a political settlement having failed to influence events on the ground appreciably, the Bush administration focused increasingly on how to "cut loose" from Afghanistan. During the fall of 1990, American State Department official Robert Kimmitt worked with the Soviet ambassador in Washington D.C. to negotiate an agreement under which both the U.S. and the USSR would cease arming their respective Afghan partners—a step that was termed "negative symmetry."[84] The plan was for Shevardnadze and Baker to announce such an agreement when they met in December 1990. In the end, however, Shevardnadze declined to agree to a date by which Soviet and American weapons supplies would have to cease.[85] Vladimir Kriuchkov, head of the KGB, almost certainly opposed a negative symmetry agreement and Shevardnadze was probably also tepid about such a deal because he believed that Najibullah should not be forced out of power.[86]

As another strand of its efforts to extricate itself from involvement in Afghanistan, from mid-1990 onwards the United States allowed the United Nations to play the foremost role in trying to reach a political settlement.[87] On May 21, 1991 the UN Secretary General, Pérez de Cuéllar, released a five-point framework for achieving a settlement. The plan called for a ceasefire in Afghanistan, the cessation of outside military support to combatants, and the organization of "free and fair elections, in accord with Afghan traditions."[88]

Following the failure of the August 1991 coup attempt in the Soviet Union—which was led by Kriuchkov and supported by other strong backers of the Najibullah regime—the USSR's Afghan policy shifted once more.[89] The United States and the USSR now returned to discussions about a negative symmetry agreement and, in mid-September 1991, Soviet Foreign Minister Boris Pankin and Secretary Baker announced that both powers agreed to "discontinue their weapons deliveries to all Afghan sides," with the mutual cessation going into effect by January 1, 1992. The same statement called for the UN to "work with the Afghans to convene a credible and impartial transition mechanism whose functions would include directing and managing a credible electoral process."[90]

By the start of 1992, the Soviet Union had ceased to exist, the United States had ended its aid to the mujahedin, and the UN was now responsible for trying to effect a political settlement in Afghanistan.

But, among the mujahedin's political leaders, there was hardly much enthusiasm for taking part in a UN-overseen political process.[91] Pakistan also had little time for the UN effort. Peter Tomsen, who served as the Bush administration's special envoy to the Afghan resistance, explains how Pakistan's prime minister, Nawaz Sharif, who entered office in November 1990, agreed with his military's preference for seeking a victory in Afghanistan through the forces of mujahedin leader Gulbuddin Hekmatyar. At the same time as backing that approach, Sharif was, in Tomsen's words, "disingenuously endorsing the UN political settlement process."[92]

Having lost critical pillars of support for his regime within Afghanistan, Najibullah fled the presidential palace in mid-April 1992 and sought refuge at the UN compound in Kabul.[93] For the next several years, the various parts of the mujahedin movement pursued power by waging war against one another, leading Afghanistan to become a failed state.[94]

The Taliban movement emerged in late 1994. It swept across Afghanistan and it seized control of Kabul in September 1996. The movement's leader, Mullah Mohammed Omar, had been a mujahedin commander during the 1980s, but many Taliban fighters had not been part of the anti-Soviet resistance. Instead, the Taliban's ranks included numerous war orphans and former PDPA personnel.[95] Its ascendancy was propelled by the movement's success in imposing order within the territory it held.[96] Support from Pakistan also contributed to the Taliban's strength.[97] Once it had achieved power, the Taliban regime provided sanctuary to an extremist with audacious ambitions: Osama Bin Laden. Having participated in the anti-Soviet war—mainly as a financial backer of the resistance—Bin Laden had founded the al-Qaeda organization in 1988 and then left Afghanistan in 1990 to return to his homeland, Saudi Arabia.[98] In 1991, Bin Laden moved to Sudan, where he remained until May 1996 at which point Sudan's government evicted him as a result of international pressure.[99] After that, the Taliban offered a safe haven to Bin Laden. Afghanistan became the headquarters of al-Qaeda, which demonstrated its global reach through bombings of the American embassies in Kenya and Tanzania in 1998, its attack against the USS Cole in 2000, and the atrocities of September 11, 2001.[100]

Conclusion—Why did the Nicaraguan War End While the Afghan Conflict Raged On?

The George H.W. Bush administration's strategies towards Nicaragua and Afghanistan were similar; the United States continued to provide support to rebels as part of an effort to secure political settlements that would see the incumbent governments leave power. Additionally, as shown above, by the time the Bush administration was in office, the Soviet Union, like the United States, saw a role for elections in the settlement of civil conflicts. Notwithstanding that narrowing of ideological differences between the superpowers, the Nicaraguan war culminated in a democratic transition in February 1990, while the conflict in Afghanistan continued and produced considerable chaos. What accounted for the distinct outcomes?

We can identify multiple factors that combined to produce the divergent results. Regarding Nicaragua, after a decade of heated political debate in Washington D.C., from 1987 onwards there was very little chance that Congress would ever approve any more lethal support for the Nicaraguan insurgents. At the same time, however, there was bipartisan backing for helping the contras to hold together as a means to pursue democratic elections in Nicaragua.[101] The Nicaraguan contras were also very dependent on American support. Thus, after Congress refused to provide them any additional lethal assistance, they were left with little choice but to enter a ceasefire.

The endgame in Nicaragua, and the democratic transition it produced, was also critically shaped by the regional peace plan spearheaded by Oscar Arias, who made democracy a major component of that process. Additionally, there was a viable unarmed opposition in Nicaragua and it managed to coalesce behind an effective candidate, Violeta Chamorro, who believed in a democratic process. As political scientists Erica Chenoweth and Maria Stephan demonstrate, when armed rebellions are victorious they often do not lead to democratic governance, including because insurgents often continue to practice the violent and exclusionary strategies to which they have become accustomed.[102] The existence of a credible and *unarmed* opposition in Nicaragua, in addition to the contras, contributed to the democratic transition that occurred.

On the other side of the conflict, the dire state of the Nicaraguan economy by the late 1980s created incentives for the Sandinista leader, Daniel Ortega, to accept a ceasefire in 1988 and to permit elections in 1990; allowing such a process offered a way to end American support to the contras for good. Under Mikhail Gorbachev, the Soviet Union was also encouraging the Sandinistas along the same path. Furthermore, Ortega probably believed that he could win the 1990 election, which turned out to be a fateful miscalculation.

Afghanistan was a very different war and myriad factors combined to produce a much less satisfactory endgame to the Reagan Doctrine in that country. In contrast to American support for the contras, U.S. support to the mujahedin was politically uncontroversial while Soviet forces were in Afghanistan. After the USSR exited Afghanistan, some American legislators began to question the wisdom of continuing to aid the mujahedin.[103] Despite the voicing of such sentiments, however, there was never a political groundswell to cease aid to the mujahedin rapidly in the aftermath of the Soviet withdrawal. Unlike what happened with the contras, therefore, U.S. domestic politics never applied a strong restraint against continued military action by the insurgents. Additionally, the mujahedin's strongest backers in the United States made very clear that they opposed any negotiated settlement that countenanced Najibullah's continuation in office.[104] Furthermore, in contrast to the Nicaraguan insurgents, the mujahedin were less dependent on American aid. They also received support from Pakistan and Saudi Arabia, which meant that the United States' ability to control the mujahedin's actions was, in any event, weaker than in the case of the contras.

The United States' partners in the Afghanistan operation also had goals that were very different to American ones during the endgame. Various mujahedin leaders had no interest in entering into a negotiated political settlement with Najibullah; instead, they preferred to pursue power for themselves and to use violence to attain it, against opponents both within and outside the mujahedin movement. Pakistan had its own strongly-held interests, foremost of which was to put a reliably pro-Pakistan government in control of Afghanistan. In the period after the Soviet troop withdrawal, even while the highest levels of the American and Soviet governments were discussing a potential political settlement in Afghanistan, Pakistan prioritized installing its most-favored mujahedin leader, Gulbuddin Hekmatyar, in power through force. As

Peter Tomsen later wrote, the Soviet exit from Afghanistan produced a "fundamental shift in Pakistan's Afghan policy from a defensive to an offensive strategy."[105]

Overall, many factors accounted for the divergent outcomes in Nicaragua and Afghanistan at the Cold War's end. Several of those determinants were integral to local and regional dynamics, rather than related to the interactions between the two global superpowers. Consequently, although a growing alignment of ideas between the U.S. and USSR about how to defuse the global Cold War helped to end the Nicaraguan war, the same development was insufficient to stop the conflict in Afghanistan. Among the tragedies of internationalized civil wars is that outside involvement can exacerbate their intensity and increase the bloodshed they cause. Yet another tragedy is that even a thawing of relations between outside competitors will not necessarily guarantee the end of such wars.

Notes

1. I thank my SAIS colleagues, as well as other contributors to this volume, for the helpful feedback I received on an earlier draft. This chapter builds upon case studies of the United States' support to the Afghan and Nicaraguan insurgencies in the author's doctoral dissertation. See John-Michael B. Arnold, "Supporting Rebellion: Liberal Democracy and the American Way of Proxy War" (Ph.D., Princeton University, 2018).

2. The term "global Cold War" was coined by Odd Arne Westad. For his detailed history of how the Cold War competition was waged across the "Third World," see Odd Arne Westad, *The Global Cold War: Third World Interventions and the Making of Our Times*, Kindle Edition (Cambridge; New York: Cambridge University Press, 2005).

3. Charles Krauthammer, "The Reagan Doctrine," *Time*, Vol. 125, No. 13 (April 1, 1985). In late 1985, President Reagan also gave his approval for the supply of lethal assistance to the UNITA rebels in Angola. For an excellent overview and analysis of the policy-making process in the various "Reagan Doctrine" cases, see James M. Scott, *Deciding to Intervene: The Reagan Doctrine and American Foreign Policy* (Durham, NC: Duke University Press, 1996).

4. Hal Brands, *Making the Unipolar Moment: U. S. Foreign Policy and the Rise of the Post-Cold War Order* (Ithaca, NY: Cornell University Press, 2016), p. 2.

5. Ibid., p. 1.

6. Bruce O. Riedel, *What We Won: America's Secret War in Afghanistan, 1979-89* (Washington, DC: Brookings Institution Press, 2014), pp. 22–23.

7. For a good overview of the background to the Soviet intervention in Afghanistan, and the rationale for the Soviet decision to intervene, see Rodric Braithwaite, *Afgantsy: The Russians in Afghanistan, 1979-89*, Kindle Edition (Oxford; New York: Oxford University Press, 2011), pp. 37–81.

8. "Finding Pursuant to Section 662 of the Foreign Assistance Act of 1961, As Amended, Concerning the Operations in Foreign Countries Other Than Those Intended Solely for the Purpose of Intelligence Collection," December 28, 1979, in Folder 'SCC 240—Iran/Afghanistan, 12/28/79,' National Security Council Institutional Files (H Files), 1977-81, Box 107, Jimmy Carter Presidential Library.

9. Scott, op. cit., p. 34.

10. Riedel, op. cit., p. 63.

11. Scott, op. cit., pp. 41–42.

12. Riedel, op. cit., pp. 117–22; Alan J. Kuperman, "The Stinger Missile and U.S. Intervention in Afghanistan," *Political Science Quarterly* 114, no. 2 (1999): 219–63.

13. Scott, op. cit., pp. 34–35; "CPI Inflation Calculator," accessed April 18, 2019, https://www.bls.gov/data/inflation_calculator.htm.

14. William M. LeoGrande, *Our Own Backyard: The United States in Central America, 1977-1992* (Chapel Hill, NC: University of North Carolina Press, 1998), pp. 17–32.

15. Stephen Kinzer, *Blood of Brothers: Life and War in Nicaragua* (Cambridge, MA: Harvard University David Rockefeller Center for Latin American Studies, 2007), p. 79.

16. As one example of the U.S. government's assessment that the Sandinistas were arming guerillas in El Salvador, see "Memorandum, Nicaragua-Cuba: Support of Central American Revolutionaries," 28 September 1979, CIA National Foreign Assessment Center, in Folder 'Nicaragua: 7-9/79,' Records of the Office of the National Security Advisor, Country Files (NSA 6), Box 56, Jimmy Carter Presidential Library.

17. "Finding Pursuant to Section 662 of the Foreign Assistance Act of 1961, As Amended, Concerning the Operations in Foreign Countries Other Than Those Intended Solely for the Purpose of Intelligence Collection," December 1, 1981, Signed by President Ronald Reagan, https://www.brown.edu/Research/Understanding_the_Iran_Contra_Affair/documents/d-all-45.pdf; Ronald Reagan, *The Reagan Diaries*, ed. Douglas Brinkley (New York: HarperCollins, 2007), p. 52.

18. Duane R. Clarridge, *A Spy For All Seasons: My Life in the CIA* (New York, NY: Scribner, 1997), p. 200.

19. "Finding Pursuant to Section 662 of the Foreign Assistance Act of 1961, as Amended, Concerning Operations Undertaken by the Central Intelligence Agency in Foreign Countries, Other Than Those Intended Solely for the Purpose of Intelligence Collection," September 19, 1983, https://nsarchive2.gwu.edu//NSAEBB/NSAEBB210/1-Reagan%20Finding%209-19-83%20(IC%2000203).pdf.

20. "National Intelligence Estimate, Nicaragua: Prospects for Sandinista Consolidation," August 1987, Available from CIA CREST, pp. 4 & 6, https://www.cia.gov/library/readingroom/docs/CIA-RDP89M00699 R00220179000 8-1.pdf.

21. Clarridge, op. cit., pp. 199–202; Abigail T. Linnington, "Unconventional Warfare in U.S. Foreign Policy: U.S. Support of Insurgencies in Afghani-

stan, Nicaragua, and Iraq from 1979-2001" (Ph.D., Fletcher School of Law and Diplomacy (Tufts University), 2013), pp. 174–78.

22. LeoGrande, op. cit., pp. 343–46.

23. Ronald Reagan, "Address Before a Joint Session of the Congress on the State of the Union," February 6, 1985, https://www.presidency.ucsb.edu/documents/address-before-joint-session-the-congress-the-state-the-union-5.

24. George P. Shultz, "America and the Struggle for Freedom." Address before the Commonwealth Club of California in San Francisco. Re-Printed in State Department Bulletin, April 1985. (Washington, DC: U.S. G.P.O., February 22, 1985).

25. Peter W. Rodman, *More Precious than Peace: The Cold War and the Struggle for the Third World* (New York: C. Scribner's Sons, 1994), pp. 270–71.

26. Krauthammer, "The Reagan Doctrine."

27. LeoGrande, op. cit., pp. 426–28; Robert Kagan, *A Twilight Struggle: American Power and Nicaragua, 1977-1990* (New York: Free Press, 1996), pp. 373–85.

28. Robert A. Pastor, "The War Between the Branches: Explaining U.S. Policy Toward Nicaragua, 1979-89," in *Public Opinion in U.S. Foreign Policy: The Controversy over Contra Aid*, ed. Richard Sobel (Lanham, MD: Rowman & Littlefield, 1993), p. 232.

29. Jack Nelson and Eleanor Clift, "Poindexter Resigns, North Is Fired: Leave as Meese Says Contras Got Iran Arms Funds: Not Fully Informed About Initiative, Reagan Asserts," *Los Angeles Times*, November 26, 1986, http://articles.latimes.com/1986-11-26/news/mn-15596_1_shipment.

30. Linnington, op. cit., pp. 211–12; Kagan, op. cit., pp. 523–26.

31. In Afghanistan, the Red Army faced a formidable insurgency that was highly-motivated, enjoyed significant popular support, and made adept use of the country's terrain. In Nicaragua, the Sandinista's own policies bred considerable opposition among many peasants, who buoyed the contras' ranks. See Lester W. Grau and Ali Ahmad Jalali, "Conclusion," in *The Other Side of the Mountain: Mujahideen Tactics in the Soviet-Afghan War, 10th Anniversary Edition* (Quantico, VA.: U.S. Marine Corps, Studies and Analysis Division, 2005); Scott, op. cit., p. 155.

32. For an examination of the Soviet Union's policies towards the "Third World," and the increased emphasis placed upon resolving "regional conflicts" from 1988 onwards, see Svetlana Savranskaya, "Gorbachev and the Third World," in Artemy M. Kalinovsky and Sergey Radchenko, eds., *The End of the*

Cold War and the Third World: New Perspectives on Regional Conflict (London; New York: Routledge, 2011).

33. LeoGrande, op. cit., pp. 530–32.

34. Kinzer, op. cit., p. 368.

35. As a CIA analysis from June 1988 reported, reviewing the previous decade, "while Soviet Bloc aid has increased, it has not kept up with Managua's needs." See "Nicaragua: Prospects for the Economy," 24 June 1988, CIA, Available from CIA CREST," p. 1, https://www.cia.gov/library/readingroom/docs/CIA-RDP04T00990R000100650001-9.pdf.

36. LeoGrande, op. cit., p. 539; Kagan, op. cit., pp. 595–96.

37. "Minutes of the Communist Party of the Soviet Union (CPSU) Central Committee Politburo Meeting," November 13, 1986 (Excerpt), Available from the Wilson Center, Digital Archive, http://digitalarchive.wilsoncenter.org/document/111599.

38. Artemy M. Kalinovsky, *A Long Goodbye: The Soviet Withdrawal from Afghanistan* (Cambridge, MA: Harvard University Press, 2011).

39. Najibullah was previously known as Mohammad Najib, but having become president of Afghanistan in 1986 he subsequently added "ullah" to his last name in an effort to demonstrate his religiosity. See Peter Tomsen, *The Wars of Afghanistan: Messianic Terrorism, Tribal Conflicts, and the Failures of Great Powers*, vol. 1st ed. (New York: PublicAffairs, 2011), p. 227.

40. James Baker Talking Points for January 23, 1989 Cabinet Meeting, JAB Notes from 1/23/89 Cabinet Meeting (First Meeting of Bush Administration), James A. Baker Papers, Box 108, Folder 1, Public Policy Papers, Department of Rare Books and Special Collections, Princeton University Library.

41. Lindsey Gruson, "Latin Presidents Announce Accord on Contra Bases," *The New York Times*, February 15, 1989, http://www.nytimes.com/1989/02/15/world/latin-presidents-announce-accord-on-contra-bases.html.

42. Kagan, op. cit., p. 633.

43. George H.W. Bush, "Remarks on Afghanistan and a Question-and-Answer Session With Reporters," February 16, 1989, https://www.presidency.ucsb.edu/documents/remarks-afghanistan-and-question-and-answer-session-with-reporters.

44. James Addison Baker, *The Politics of Diplomacy: Revolution, War, and Peace, 1989-1992* (New York: G.P. Putnam's Sons, 1995), p. 53.

45. Kagan, op. cit., p. 638.

46. To make that stipulation credible, four committees in Congress were granted the right to review the implementation of the plan in November 1989, and any one of them would have been able to halt further non-lethal aid to the contras at that time. LeoGrande, op. cit., p. 555.

47. "National Security Directive 8, May 1, 1989, U.S. Policy Toward Nicaragua and the Nicaraguan Resistance," Available from George H.W. Bush Presidential Library, https://bush41library.tamu.edu/files/nsd/nsd8.pdf.

48. Robert A. Pastor, *Not Condemned to Repetition: The United States and Nicaragua* (Boulder, CO: Westview Press, 2002), p. 233.

49. Scott, op. cit., p. 153.

50. Pastor, *Not Condemned to Repetition*, op. cit., p. 233.

51. "National Security Directive 25, U.S. Policy Toward the February 1990 Nicaragua Election," Available from George H.W. Bush Presidential Library, September 22, 1989, https://bush41library.tamu.edu/files/nsd/nsd25.pdf.

52. Baker, *The Politics of Diplomacy*, op. cit., pp. 59–60.

53. LeoGrande, op. cit., p. 558.

54. Savranskaya, op. cit., pp. 30–35.

55. William Taubman, *Gorbachev: His Life and Times* (New York: W.W. Norton & Company, Inc, 2017), p. 427.

56. Pavel Palazhchenko, *My Years with Gorbachev and Shevardnadze: The Memoir of a Soviet Interpreter* (University Park, PA: Pennsylvania State University Press, 1997), p. 171.

57. Pastor, *Not Condemned to Repetition*, op. cit., p. 258.

58. LeoGrande, op. cit., p. 562.

59. Memorandum of Telephone Conversation Between President Bush and President Oscar Arias of Costa Rica, February 26, 1990, Available from the George H.W. Bush Presidential Library, https://bush41library.tamu.edu/files/memcons-telcons/1990-02-26--Arias.pdf.

60. Robert Michael Gates, *From the Shadows: The Ultimate Insider's Story of Five Presidents and How They Won the Cold War*, vol. 1st Touchstone ed. (New York: Touchstone, 1997), p. 436.

61. "National Security Directive 3," February 13, 1989, Available from George H.W. Bush Presidential Library, https://bush41library.tamu.edu/files/nsd/nsd3.pdf.

62. "Afghanistan: Regime Military and Political Capabilities After the Soviet Withdrawal," October 1988, CIA Directorate of Intelligence, p. iii, https://www.cia.gov/library/readingroom/docs/CIA-RDP89S01450R000500510001-6.pdf.

63. Memorandum of Conversation, President's Meeting with Prime Minister Benazir Bhutto of Pakistan, February 24, 1989, 4:51-5:22 p.m., American Ambassador's Residence, Tokyo, Japan, Available from George H.W. Bush Presidential Library, https://bush41library.tamu.edu/files/memcons-telcons/1989-02-24--Bhutto.pdf.

64. Artemy M. Kalinovsky, "The Failure to Resolve the Afghan Conflict, 1989-1992," in Artemy M. Kalinovsky and Sergey Radchenko, eds., *The End of the Cold War and the Third World: New Perspectives on Regional Conflict* (London; New York: Routledge, 2011), p. 140.

65. Anne Stenersen, *Al-Qaida in Afghanistan* (Cambridge University Press, 2017), p. 22.

66. Riedel, op. cit., p. 129.

67. Barnett R. Rubin, *The Search for Peace in Afghanistan: From Buffer State to Failed State* (New Haven: Yale University Press, 1995), p. 29.

68. Scott, op. cit., p. 35.

69. Memorandum of Conversation, Meeting with Eduard Shevardnadze, Foreign Minister of the Soviet Union, September 21, 1989, 2:00 p.m.-3:05 p.m. EDT, The Oval Office, Available from the George H.W. Bush Presidential Library, https://bush41library.tamu.edu/files/memcons-telcons/1989-09-21--Shevardnadze.pdf.

70. "Joint Statement by U.S. Secretary of State James Baker and Soviet Foreign Minister Eduard Shevardnadze, September 23,1989," Reprinted in Department of State Bulletin, November 1989, Volume 89, Number 2152.

71. Memorandum of Conversation, Bush–Gorbachev, Second Expanded Bilateral Meeting, Malta, 4:35 p.m.—6:45 p.m., December 3, 1989, Document No. 85, in Svetlana Savranskaya and Thomas Blanton, *The Last Superpower Summits: Gorbachev, Reagan, and Bush: Conversations That Ended the Cold War*, National Security Archive Cold War Readers. (New York: Central European University Press, 2016).

72. Ibid.

73. Memorandum of Conversation by United States Department of State, Meeting between Secretary Baker, President Gorbachev, Foreign Minister Eduard Shevardnadze, Friday February 9, 1990, 1:00pm-3:00pm, The Kremlin, Moscow, Mandatory Declassification Review (MDR) Case No. M-2017-12668, Doc No. C16449222.

74. Ibid.

75. Ibid.

76. Tomsen, op. cit., pp. 361–63.

77. Memorandum of Conversation between Secretary Baker and Eduard Shevardnadze, Prepared by U.S. Department of State, Meeting on March 20, 1990, 6:00pm—9:30pm, Windhoek, Namibia, Available from the National Security Archive, https://nsarchive2.gwu.edu//dc.html?doc=5752902-National-Security-Archive-Doc-18-Memorandum-of.

78. Ibid.

79. Ibid.

80. I am very grateful to Thomas Blanton, director of the National Security Archive, for telling me about the existence of this cable. "Memorandum for the President," Sent via Cable, From James A. Baker III to George Bush, March 20, 1990, Subject: My Meeting With Soviet Foreign Minister Shevardnadze, Folder 'Special Separate USSR Notes Files, Gorbachev Files,' OA/ID 91126-006, Brent Scowcroft Collection, Bush Presidential Records, George HW Bush Presidential Library.

81. Ibid.

82. All the quotes are from the following document: Memorandum of Conversation, Bush–Gorbachev, Final Private Meeting, Camp David, June 2, 1990, 11:15 a.m.—12:59 p.m., and 3:00 p.m., Document No: 102, in Savranskaya and Blanton, *The Last Superpower Summits*, op. cit.

83. Ibid.

84. Tomsen, op. cit., p. 425.

85. Rubin, op. cit., p. 109.

86. Kalinovsky, *A Long Goodbye*, op. cit., pp. 194–95.

87. Tomsen, op. cit., p. 397.

88. Ibid, p. 435.

89. Rubin, op. cit., p. 111.

90. "US-Soviet Joint Statement on Afghanistan," Released in Moscow on September 13, 1991, in US Department of State Dispatch, Bureau of Public Affairs, September 16, 1991, Volume 2, No. 37.

91. Tomsen, op. cit., p. 463.

92. Ibid, p. 435.

93. Kalinovsky, *A Long Goodbye*, op. cit., pp. 206–8.

94. Rubin, op. cit., p. 125.

95. Tomsen, op. cit., p. 533; Kalinovsky, *A Long Goodbye*, op. cit., p. 211.

96. David B. Edwards, *Before Taliban: Genealogies of the Afghan Jihad* (Berkeley: University of California Press, 2002), p. 239.

97. Tomsen, op. cit., pp. 535–41.

98. National Commission on Terrorist Attacks upon the United States, *The 9/11 Commission Report: Final Report of the National Commission on Terrorist Attacks Upon the United States* (Washington, D.C.: U.S. G.P.O., 2004), pp. 56–57.

99. Ibid, pp. 57 & 63.

100. Ibid, pp. 68–70, 190–91, 348–50.

101. Kagan, op. cit., pp. 723–24.

102. Erica Chenoweth and Maria J. Stephan, *Why Civil Resistance Works: The Strategic Logic of Nonviolent Conflict*, Columbia Studies in Terrorism and Irregular Warfare. (New York: Columbia University Press, 2011), pp. 205–16.

103. See, for example, Representative Lee Hamilton's comments at the following congressional hearing: Hearing before the Subcommittees on Europe and the Middle East and Asian and Pacific Affairs of the Committee on Foreign Affairs, House of Representatives, March 7, 1990, United States Policy Toward Afghanistan (U.S. Government Printing Office, 1990).

104. Scott, op. cit., pp. 74–75.

105. Tomsen, op. cit., p. 322.

Chapter 3

Superpowers Walking a Tightrope: The Choices of April and May 1990

Philip Zelikow and Condoleezza Rice

This essay zeroes in on just a couple of months during some tumultuous years. It is a phase, in the spring of 1990, that happened after the initial diplomatic engagements following the opening of the Berlin Wall and before some of the final deals started emerging during the summer and autumn of 1990.

We chose to focus on these two months, in our contribution to this volume, precisely because this phase—and these choices—have received relatively little notice. It was, however, an extraordinarily delicate and difficult phase in which progress could well have collapsed—but did not.

Just to help readers set the scene: The East German elections of March 18, 1990 decided, in effect, that a unification of Germany would take place soon and it would take place as a West German annexation of the East. March 1990 was a decisive pivot for Germany's "internal" unification process.

What diplomatically were called the "external" aspects of unification remained unsettled. These "external" aspects included more than half a million foreign troops deployed in the two Germanies under rights that dated back to the powers the victors had given themselves as occupiers in 1945. There had never been a German peace treaty that wrapped up and put aside those old powers.

Though it is difficult for 21st century readers to comprehend, in early 1990 Germany was still the most heavily militarized area of real estate on the entire planet. To put the scale of militarization then into some perspective, consider that the absolute peak of massed ground warfare on the European continent had been in late 1944, as enemy armies closed in on Germany from every direction. In 1990 there were more than twice as many tanks deployed in Europe then had been there in late 1944. And in 1990 there were thousands of nuclear weapons deployed around Europe too.

Countries, above all the Soviet Union, had deployed such colossal forces for the Cold War confrontation and to manage Germany. In the tough spring 1990 diplomacy over the future of Europe, the United States, the West Germans, and their allies all listened to and worked on addressing reasonable Soviet concerns. At the top of that list was the question about how to manage future German power.

Related to this was the question of Germany in NATO, the main stumbling block to getting a final settlement for Germany. By May 1990 progress in the nuclear and conventional arms control efforts was also stalled practically across the board. In April, the Soviets had walked back understandings reached months earlier; Soviet Foreign Minister Eduard Shevardnadze was being joined in the arms control negotiations by top Soviet marshals.

The Two Other Crises of Spring 1990

To this unpromising situation, two more issues had to be factored in that were not part of the German question. One was a crisis everyone knew about. The other was a crisis almost no one knew about.

The crisis everyone knew about was the most serious challenge to the future of the Soviet Union that had arisen so far. Lithuania had declared its independence from the Union in March 1990. Gorbachev authorized military maneuvers in the republic, deployed additional troops there, confiscated private weapons and disarmed the local national guard, seized printing presses and Communist party property, and imposed economic sanctions—including a cutoff of oil and natural gas.

Privately, Gorbachev was feeling overwhelmed. In February, in a down moment, he had mused to Chernyaev about being ready to leave office. In April, grappling with Lithuania, he had the impulse of cancelling all his upcoming meetings with foreigners, even an upcoming summit with U.S. President George H.W. Bush (though he soon changed his mind).

There was a strong camp that called on Gorbachev to uphold the Soviet Union, to crush the Lithuanians, and set an example. Analysts can argue about whether a "Chinese solution" was still truly feasible in the Soviet Union. In the spring of 1990, we think it still was, maybe for the last time.

Such a Soviet move would not have been able to stop with Lithuania. In essence, it would have been the point where Moscow said: "Enough!" A full crackdown would probably have extended to other emergency measures, diplomatic defiance, a financial confrontation with Western creditors, and the reestablishment of a 'socialism in one country' kind of philosophy.

Gorbachev might have been tempted to lead such a counterrevolution. But then he would say, to Chernyaev, that a full crackdown on the republics might mean putting 100,000 people on trial. "We would be going back to 1937,"[1] he concluded, alluding to the peak of Stalin's "great terror."

For that, Gorbachev had no stomach. Instead, he tried an economic blockade of Lithuania. He had expected a popular revolt against Lithuania's breakaway leaders. That did not happen. To his diary, Chernyaev confided, "He [Gorbachev] does not have a Lithuania policy, just pure ideology of power not to allow the breakup of the empire."[2]

Meeting in Bermuda on April 16, Bush and UK Prime Minister Margaret Thatcher compared notes on what Bush called Gorbachev's "dilemma." Both agreed the situation was getting worse. Thatcher judged that "the military is no longer on Gorbachev's side."[3]

Bush said that "if Gorbachev doesn't get out of the Baltic dilemma, I can't do business with him.... We have come so far, but there is a danger we could slide back into the dark ages."

Gorbachev's partial crackdown in Lithuania in April and May filled the American press with calls for a strong reaction from the United States. Bush noted to his diary that he was in "almost a no-win situation, and I keep hoping that Gorbachev will recognize the disaster this will bring him internationally." Bush asked visiting senators what they suggested he should do; they had no answers to offer.

Seeing French President François Mitterrand in Florida only three days after his April meeting with Thatcher, Bush sought the French leader's advice. Mitterrand urged patience and negotiations. "Gorbachev has inherited an empire. It is now in revolt. If the Ukraine starts to move, Gorbachev is gone; a military dictatorship would result."

After an internal debate among his advisers, Bush decided to freeze plans to normalize trade relations with the Soviet Union until the Soviets lifted their economic blockade of Lithuania and resumed dialogue. He personally drafted a letter to Gorbachev on this. The Senate voted its own resolution with the same conclusion.

Meanwhile, Bush indirectly put pressure on the Lithuanians to soften their stand and come to the table. He encouraged an initiative from Mitterrand and West German Chancellor Helmut Kohl. The French and German leaders wrote to the Lithuanians and urged them to "suspend" their independence declaration and resume negotiations.

The Franco-German work was backed by a similar message delivered to the Vilnius leadership by a senior Republican senator, Richard Lugar, acting with the help of U.S. Secretary of State James Baker. Bush and European leaders met with the Lithuanian prime minister in early May. Negotiations resumed; tensions calmed—for a while. Gorbachev (and Bush) stayed on their tightropes. Bush said privately at the time: "I don't want people to look back 20 or 40 years from now and say, 'That's where everything went off track. That's where progress stopped.'"[4]

Lithuania was the *public* crisis. The *secret* crisis was at least as serious. In October 1989 a Soviet defector had contacted the British government. By the spring of 1990 Thatcher, Bush and a few of their advisers had to make some very difficult choices.

In 1969 the American government had decided to shut down its biological weapons (BW) program; the British had done so ten years earlier. Both governments had concluded that such horrifying weapons were not militarily useful. The Soviet government also said it did not need them. In 1972 the superpowers led the way in signing the Biological Weapons Convention (BWC), which entered into force in 1975, to ban the development, production, or stockpiling of any such weapons. It was a historic agreement, eventually signed by more than a hundred countries.

During the 1980s the U.S. had raised concerns about some possible Soviet BW research, because of an apparent suspicious 1979 outbreak of anthrax in the city of Sverdlovsk. But the Soviets heatedly denied the allegations. By the end of the 1980s, most opinion among people who followed the issue had swung in favor of the Soviet story of a public health problem from contaminated meat.[5]

Very few U.S. or British analysts still followed BW issues. The U.S. national security community still regarded BW as militarily useless. It worried a little, but not too much, about a Soviet BW program.

The Soviet defector who had come to the British in October 1989 had been the head of a key lab in what, he secretly revealed, was a very advanced and active BW program—extensive, extremely secret, and entirely illegal under the BWC. The program was not only manufacturing large quantities of BW for battlefield use; it was producing about a dozen different kinds of biological weapons: quantities of anthrax, smallpox (a disease the world health community thought had just been eradicated at last), pneumonic plague, and more. Sophisticated methods for weaponizing the viruses had been developed for possible strategic use in missiles to kill large numbers in a faraway enemy population. Active work was underway to develop viruses resistant to antibiotics (and also work to immunize Soviet soldiers).

At first, as these details were digested in early 1990 in the British and American intelligence agencies, the analysts could not quite believe what they were hearing. The Soviet BW program was worse than anything they had even imagined.

The agencies then did extensive work to verify as many details of the defector's account as they could from other intelligence sources. Verifiable details of the account checked out. But the agencies could not get into the sites to be sure or learn more. (It turned out that the defector had been truthful. In fact, the program was more elaborate than even he knew. The head of the whole BW program defected to the United States in 1992.)[6]

In April and early May 1990, at the very same time they were dealing with the Lithuanian crisis, Bush and Thatcher and their top aides were deliberating about what they should do about this startling information about the enormous, clandestine Soviet biological weapons program. They could not even be sure that Gorbachev and Shevardnadze were aware of all these details.

It is actually rather astonishing, but true, that Bush and Thatcher seriously wondered whether the top leaders of the Soviet Union even knew about such a large and incredibly dangerous scientific and military program. This is a question no one would have ever asked when Leonid Brezhnev or Yuri Andropov were running the Soviet Union. (In fact, Gorbachev and Shevardnadze did know something about this program. The defection of the lab director had been promptly reported straight to the Politburo.)

If what the U.S. and British leaders now knew was made public, it would have been a shock and a sensation. To ordinary citizens, the revelation of such a hitherto secret Soviet arsenal would have been much scarier than anything going on in places like Lithuania. It is hard to imagine what would have happened to all the diplomatic work about Germany, arms control agreements, and everything else that, at that moment, was still so up in the air.

Thatcher and Bush and their top aides considered this. They assumed that, if confronted in such a public and embarrassing way, the Soviet government would instantly go into a full defensive mode and deny everything. Evidence about later Soviet behavior reinforces their supposition that denial would have been the order of the day. In such a public confrontation, the American and British leaders could not see how they would be able to get the program shut down—which was their most important objective—while also preserving a relationship with Gorbachev.

On the other hand, if they did *not* make what they knew public, the leaders might later be faulted for not having called public attention to the danger. And there was also a danger that the information might leak.

Thatcher and Bush together decided to keep the shocking discoveries about the clandestine Soviet biological weapons program as secret as they possibly could. Bush authorized a briefing for a small number of members of Congress. There were no leaks.[7]

Bush and Thatcher decided they would present the concerns to Gorbachev and Shevardnadze, in the hope that the Soviet leadership would secretly solve the problem, and do so in a way that U.S. and British experts could then verify. On May 14 and 15, the U.S. and British ambassadors in Moscow made carefully prepared and coordinated presentations about their concerns to Chernyaev and the deputy foreign minister, Alexander Bessmertnykh. The two Soviets did not appear to know anything about the program.

According to Bessmertnykh's record of the meeting, the American ambassador (Jack Matlock) emphasized that the two governments wanted to try to solve this problem "without additional fuss." They "do not intend to raise the given question in a confrontational context and do not intend to make it public …. We are absolutely not interested in burdening our relations with a new problem on the eve of the most important negotiations at the highest levels."

In Moscow a couple of days later, Baker had decided he would deliver the BW message personally, to stress its significance. He made time for a substantial private discussion about the apparent BW program in person with Shevardnadze.

When Gorbachev came to Washington, Bush too decided to raise it personally. He waited until they were at Camp David and then pulled Gorbachev aside for a private discussion of the issue. Bush would raise it again at later summit meetings. Thatcher also personally raised the issue with Gorbachev during her trip to Moscow in June 1990 (her last as prime minister).

The immediate reactions from Gorbachev and Shevardnadze were defensive. They displayed little knowledge (this was only partially truthful) and promised to check into it. Gorbachev pushed back, saying that his government thought that the United States also had such a BW program. He offered to set up a program of mutual inspections and site visits.

The U.S. pursued that, a process that continued into 1991 with more top secret, high-level exchanges. The Soviets discovered the U.S. was telling the truth. By contrast, the U.S. inspectors discovered more Soviet cover-ups.

Gorbachev himself had already begun encountering prolonged difficulties in completely shutting down this program, difficulties he never fully solved. The issue would pass to his successor in 1992.[8]

At the time Bush, Baker, Scowcroft, Gates, and Thatcher wrote their memoirs, the details of what they and their intelligence agencies had known were still secret. Therefore, none of those memoirs discuss the BW issue, the many high-level discussions about it with the Soviets, or the choices the U.S. and British leaders had to make. (We have not seen evidence that the BW program details were shared at this time either with the West Germans or the French.) The historical literature therefore has so far not touched on this topic and the way it intersected with everything else that was going on.

While this secret crisis was unfolding, the top leaders might compartmentalize the concern, putting it in a sort of mental safe, just as the secret information itself was compartmented and so closely held. But the leaders did not forget about the Soviet BW program.

Even if left unstated, this was the kind of concern that might come to mind in a discussion about giving the Soviet government large-scale economic assistance. The U.S. leaders knew that some key members of Congress—who would have to act on any such request—also had this knowledge.[9]

Go Ahead on Germany Without Soviet Agreement?

In April and May 1990, the Americans took seriously the Soviet threat to decouple Germany's internal unification from the external issues. Moscow was threatening to maintain occupation powers and leave hundreds of thousands of Soviet troops in Germany, to be maintained at German expense (per East German-Soviet agreements that the Soviets insisted would remain in force).

The Americans quietly discussed contingency plans in which the U.S., Britain, and France would give up their occupation rights when Germany unified, even if the Soviets did not. In early May 1990, the two of us wrote that the Soviets "must know that, after a given date, the West will declare the game over, devolve their own Four Power rights, and deploy legal arguments to the effect that all Four Power rights—including the Soviets'—have now lapsed." Moscow and Gorbachev would then have the unpopular task of insisting to the German people that they alone retained the right to stay in a newly united and democratic German state.[10]

Kohl had come to a similar conclusion. Unification had to go ahead. Foreign policy, he told the visiting British foreign secretary, was like mowing grass for hay: you had to gather what you had cut in case of a thunderstorm.[11]

Yet the Americans and West Germans sought more creative ways to address Soviet concerns without such a blunt, dangerous, confrontation. Their ideas would use the institutions of the new Europe.

First, they stressed NATO and NATO's integrated military command. They had decided against a "French" solution for Germany.

The stock, cutesy quote, constantly repeated, and attributed to Lord Ismay, is that the purpose of NATO was to "keep the Russians out, the Americans in, and the Germans down." This is clever. It is not really right.

The basic genius of the European constructions was to temper all the old national conflicts in a wider political community. The old European Coal and Steel Community, a precursor of the European Community, included the vital industrial resources of France as well as Germany. NATO, then, was similar to the European Community, later the European Union, in that it was not just a control mechanism—it was a different kind of political and economic and even military community. The political community worked because its members were free and democratic.

Like other NATO members, West Germany did not have truly independent armed forces. It was not singled out; this was the situation of all NATO member forces in the integrated military command. All of them were assigned to NATO's command structures, so that the higher command and staff echelons were international. By retaining full German membership in NATO, the German military remained enmeshed in this international military structure.

NATO was also a key factor on the question of German nuclear weapons. Before Germany agreed to join the Non-Proliferation Treaty in 1969, governments had been arguing for ten years about whether Germans needed nuclear defenses. West Germans had their share of national pride and felt very threatened by Soviet military power. The renunciation of nuclear weapons finally made sense to them because of the NATO alliance. The West Germans could point to the assurance of British, French, and—above all—American nuclear defense. For the systems in Europe, American nuclear defense was coordinated through NATO.

The other big constraint on the Germans would be the planned Conventional Forces in Europe (CFE) treaty. The West Germans and Americans were happy to limit a future German army, but only if and when other national armies in Europe were limited too.

After the first CFE treaty was concluded in 1990, it would limit alliance totals of military equipment and U.S. and Soviet stationed manpower. These would not necessarily limit *German* force size. The plan was that in the next round of CFE talks all countries would accept national manpower ceilings too. The Germans would then have national limits along with everybody else.

The Soviets did not want to wait for the 'next' CFE treaty after this one. The governments worked out a compromise solution, with some particular help from the American side. The plan would still be that all the CFE countries would accept such limits. Rather than be silent and noncommittal until that future agreement was signed, the West Germans would lean forward and simply make a unilateral political statement about the ceiling they planned to adopt in that future negotiation.

Thus, Germany would have committed itself to a future ceiling. But it would still stick to the plan that such a ceiling would only be binding when all the other CFE parties went along and joined in accepting limits too. The solution had another key virtue: it kept the pressure on the Soviets to come to agreement on the current CFE treaty and get that done in 1990, a very difficult task.[12]

This plan worked. The Germans made their commitment. They picked a total ceiling of 370,000 on the active duty strength of their armed forces. This was a meaningful reduction. In 1988 West German armed forces alone were about 490,000 strong; East German forces numbered about another 170,000. So, in theory, upon unity the combined German armed forces would be about 660,000 strong, and the Germans were pledging to cut them back to no more than 370,000, along with all the other CFE limits on military equipment.

The Germans complied with these limits, at great expense. The Germans ended up destroying nearly 11,000 items of major military equipment at a cost of about $5 billion.[13]

As planned, the CFE treaty was signed alongside the Paris Summit of the Conference on Security and Cooperation in Europe (CSCE) summit in 1990. Also, as planned, the follow-on agreement (CFE 1A) was concluded alongside another CSCE summit, in Helsinki, in 1992. It added the binding national ceilings on troop strength for all of the other 29 countries that then were parties to the agreement (as by then the Soviet Union had broken up).[14]

German forces remained in NATO's integrated military command. This, plus the use of 'annexation/takeover' as the vehicle for unification, helped settle Germany's nuclear weapons status as well.

The old Federal Republic of Germany's acceptance of the Non-Proliferation Treaty in 1969 remained binding on unified Germany. The Two Plus Four Treaty (the Final Settlement with Respect to Germany) reaffirmed Germany's non-nuclear weapons commitment. Further, since the Western approach would not allow American forces to be stationed in the former territory of East Germany (the "special military status"), that area thus also became a nuclear-weapons-free zone as well.

In the spring of 1990 the West Germans and Americans had put together a serious and adequate package of assurances about how to address future German military power. These reassurances were probably more important to Moscow than the NATO membership issue itself. Germany's NATO membership was essential to this control concept. It, along with the planned CFE arms control system, allowed such controls to make lasting sense for the Germans.

In Moscow in May, Baker and his aide, Robert Zoellick, had started using and sharing a set of 'nine points' to summarize all the ways that the West was already addressing, or moving to address, Soviet concerns. These points, frequently reiterated, had real substance. And the United States, West Germans, and their allies followed through on every one of these points.[15]

All these agreements have been taken for granted for a long time. Yet it is worth remembering how much these understandings are intertwined with other structures, like CFE and NATO. If the wider structures disintegrate, long-entombed questions about German security, and the security of others, will return to Europe.

Kohl made another visit to Washington on May 17 to coordinate again with Bush before Gorbachev arrived in Washington two weeks later. Amid the meetings, the German and American leaders broke away for a more private discussion. Bush and Kohl had a private talk, practically alone.

Quietly sitting together in the Oval Office, Bush asked Kohl for his honest opinion about the core question: Did the German public want the American troops to stay, if Soviet troops left, as Bush thought they should?

Bush acknowledged the "isolationist" tendencies on both sides of the Atlantic. "It would be understandable," he said, "if [the German people] didn't want U.S. troops."

Kohl's answer was twofold. "The U.S. troop presence is related to NATO. What sort of NATO would it be, leaving U.S. troops aside? If the U.S. left, NATO would vanish and there might be only CSCE." Where would be the security, including for countries like Norway or the smaller states?

Second, Kohl added, even if the Soviet Union withdraws, "it is still in Europe. If the U.S. withdraws, it is 6,000 kilometers away. That is a big difference."

Looking at the future of Europe even beyond the year 2000, Kohl foresaw the Americans staying in Europe. If the Europeans allowed the Americans to leave, it would be "the greatest defeat for us all. Remember Wilson in 1918," he said, referring to the failure to keep the United States engaged in Europe after World War I.

Kohl became emotional. Trained in history, Kohl felt deeply about issues and places of national memory. Looking ahead to his next visit to the United States, in a few weeks, he and Scowcroft had already made plans to tour Arlington Cemetery, a resting place for the remains of many American soldiers, sailors, and marines.

George, he said, don't worry about those who draw parallels between U.S. and Soviet forces. We will push this through. We'll put our political existence at stake for NATO and the political commitment of the United States in Europe.[16]

Germany was not alone in such beliefs. Almost all the NATO member governments positively liked the alliance. Led by some with especially positive experiences and views among key ministers, like Norway or the Netherlands, the smaller governments felt enlarged and empowered by being part of a larger whole.

Therefore, it is a bit disorienting for us to read contemporary scholarly arguments about these years, accounts perhaps a bit colored by knowledge of what happened after 1990 and 1991, that see in this diplomacy an offensive American master plan to attain "preeminence" or "hegemony" in Europe (or some other imperious-sounding term currently in academic fashion). It should be apparent by now just how complex transatlantic and European power relationships were, and still are even now.

In 1989 and 1990, Bush was planning a gradual but large *downsizing* of the American military and U.S. defense spending, a plan he announced in August 1990 (a historic announcement that coincided, by astonishing happenstance, with Iraq's invasion of Kuwait). With the world changing and the tide of American presence in Europe going out, the Bush administration was trying to anchor a diminished but still reassuring military presence and ensure that America remained a European power. In that sense the administration felt defensive, not expansive.

In 1989-90 the United States was coming off a large national debate about U.S. decline and the powerful surge of economic nationalism so remarked upon by American and foreign observers. A core issue—as Bush opened up about so candidly to Kohl—was whether, and how, the United States would maintain a major presence in Europe at all. On this point, U.S. leaders were extremely attentive to European views and currents of European opinion, none more important than those in West Germany.

In this context, the true consensus position emerging during the spring and summer of 1990 was neither to abolish the alliances nor to extend them. It was a mix.

Unnerved by Moscow's April 1990 crackdown against Lithuania, the East Europeans were rapidly losing interest in retaining any defense alliance with Moscow at all. The West Europeans wanted to keep the alliance they had. Dangers did seem to have diminished for the moment, so there was no pressing need to create any new alliances.

What was pressing in the spring of 1990 was a widely shared sense of *uncertainty* about the future. On May 4, 1990, Bush used a commencement address in Oklahoma to discuss the need for a new kind of NATO, with a new strategy. He apologized to the graduating college students for dwelling on such a seemingly faraway topic.

The new mission, Bush explained, would be much more political. As for the military side, as Bush put it, "our enemy today is uncertainty and instability."[17]

That phrase seemed like a vague hedge. It was. It also turned out to be an accurate prediction.

Few, if anyone, predicted in May 1990 that NATO allies would face two wars just in the next year. One would arise in the Middle East: Iraq's August 1990 invasion and conquest of neighboring Kuwait. The other, for which the storm clouds were already gathering, was a set of wars that arose in the Balkans, as the disintegration of Yugoslavia led to wars that began in 1991.

The Soviet threat seemed to be gone. But new sorts of conflicts and dangers were already on the edge of bursting into flame. In April 1990 the Soviet government was placing an embargo on breakaway Lithuania and the threat of violence was obvious.

Leaders liked and generally trusted Gorbachev. But they were already looking beyond him.

For instance, by 1990 Kohl and Mitterrand were as close as cousins, or even brothers, including the occasional flareups. Meeting with Kohl at Mitterrand's country home in Latche near the southwest coast of France on a chilly, windy day in January 1990, the two men talked about what might come next in Moscow.

"The Gorbachev experiment will still go on for a certain time," Mitterrand predicted. "What will come after, if he fails? "Ultras!" Mitterrand said, answering his own question. "Not Communists, but a tough military dictator." If the military won, Mitterrand thought they would stick with liberalization of the economy. "But the nationalist elements would stand strong in the foreground. Blood would flow in Georgia and other parts of the Soviet Union."[18]

Conjectures like these were common in 1990. They were one reason why the existing allies valued their defense link to America.

Worries like these were also a reason to try to help Gorbachev stay in power. It was why Bush, Kohl, Mitterrand, Thatcher, and others all worked hard to find a way to help Gorbachev with the issue of Germany staying in NATO.

How to Help Gorbachev?

For his part, by May 1990 there was no doubt Gorbachev was interested in getting significant economic assistance for the Soviet Union. The Soviet desire for economic assistance surfaced at last when Shevardnadze spoke with Kohl in Bonn on May 4. It was getting hard for the Soviet government to borrow money to import goods, especially food. Their existing creditors (in Western Europe and Japan) would not make new loans.

Shevardnadze asked the West German government for help. Kohl was determined to help as much as he could.

Without informing his cabinet (but telling Genscher), Kohl contacted leaders of two major West German banks. He sent his national security advisor, Horst Teltschik, with the bankers to Moscow, in secret, to explore the Soviets' needs and possible responses.[19] The Soviets asked for a credit line of DM 20 billion (about $12 billion) guaranteed by the West German government. The West German government could not back up that kind of loan.

Teltschik met directly with Gorbachev, who again linked the credit issue to continuation of his overall program of economic reform and *perestroika*. But Gorbachev was not interested in compromising on the security issues involving Germany. They at least agreed that Kohl would come back to the Soviet Union in the summer and visit Gorbachev in his home region, the Caucasus.

When Kohl met with Bush in Washington a few days later, the Soviet request for money was at the top of his agenda.[20] Kohl said his government could guarantee about $3 billion in loans. He hoped the U.S. would guarantee some more.

Bush would not do it. He was still walking his tightrope. He had tried not to be too tough about Lithuania. But with the Lithuanian crisis not yet settled, adding more Soviet debt, without real Soviet economic reform, did not make sense to him. The secret biological weapons crisis (which we believe Kohl did not know about) could have been in the back of Bush's mind too, but we do not know.

Kohl urged Bush to change his mind.

But Bush stood firm. He did not think the Soviets could repay big new loans under their current circumstances.

Kohl still disagreed. He urged Bush to help Gorbachev, not wait for him to be overthrown.

Did Kohl think that there would be a military takeover? Bush asked.

Yes, said Kohl, by a civilian group backed by the military. He urged Bush again to think about the upcoming summit. Gorbachev needed to be able to stand beside the American president as an equal.

Bush promised to treat Gorbachev as an equal, moving forward on political relations and arms control. But the United States would not give Gorbachev money, not unless the Soviets changed their policy toward Lithuania.

The issue of economic assistance was left there for Bush to ponder as the U.S.-Soviet summit approached. Meanwhile, Baker was meeting with Shevardnadze, then Gorbachev, in Moscow.

The meetings did not go well. Baker made little headway with Gorbachev, but did deploy the set of nine assurances about managing Germany and changing NATO, which Zoellick had drafted and tried out earlier in the day.

For weeks, Chernyaev had privately urged Gorbachev to stop what he called this "nonsense," this "false patriotism of the masses," and adjust his position on NATO and not "again miss the train." Gorbachev, however, still seemed adamant.[21]

Gorbachev moved the conversation with Baker to his agenda. He challenged the Americans' real intentions toward the Soviet Union, given the clashes over issues such as Lithuania and Germany.

Then, just as Kohl had expected, Gorbachev presented to Baker the same kind of request for money that he had made to the West Germans. Gorbachev said he needed $20 billion in loans and credits to overcome a significant funding gap over the next few years. The United States had to be involved, at least symbolically, in the loan effort. The next few years would be critical in easing the transition to a market economy.

Baker could offer Gorbachev little encouragement. It was hard to justify spending U.S. taxpayers' money if the Soviets were still subsidizing the Cubans and economically squeezing the Lithuanians. Baker was essentially making the same points Bush had made to Kohl, in Washington, the day before.

Reflecting on this meeting in a message back to Bush, Baker's leading impression was that Gorbachev was clearly feeling squeezed and would probably react strongly to any action that compounded his political difficulties at home. "Germany definitely overloads his circuits right now."

It was one thing for the U.S. and the Soviet Union to no longer be enemies. It was still another long road for the U.S. to actually consider giving the Soviet Union large sums of money.

First, the United States at this point did not even have normal trade relations with the Soviet Union, something which Bush could not do alone. Any such deal would require support from the U.S. Congress, controlled by the opposing Democratic party. U.S.-Soviet trade relations were not yet even on the level the U.S. had with China (normal status, but temporary, up for renewal each year).

Next, someone would have to make a case about what the money was for—how it would actually be spent. After that, Bush would have to persuade the Congress, then embroiled in a taut battle with Bush over his determined efforts to move back toward balancing the budget, that the United States should appropriate large sums of money to a Soviet government that, on the surface, still seemed to be in pretty good shape and was devoting an enormous part of its economy to its military-industrial complex and massively subsidizing governments like those in Cuba and North Korea.

After Baker returned from Moscow, Scowcroft laid out, in a very closely held memo, what he thought was the emerging "strategic choice" for Bush. This was the first time the Soviet Union had asked for help in this way from Western governments. "The decision," Scowcroft wrote, "is not in essence about aid to Soviet economic reform—the chance that we can turn the Soviet economy around is a slim one indeed."

"This is—and you should view it as such—a strategic choice about whether economic assistance is a direct and expeditious means by which to secure the victory of the West in the Cold War by obtaining the unification of Germany in NATO and the withdrawal of the Soviet military from Central and Eastern Europe."

On that question, Scowcroft thought that a big investment, even $20 billion, was worth considering. "Some will say that we would be paying for what the Soviets will have to do anyway—leave Eastern Europe and Germany." But Scowcroft explained how difficult things could get. The Soviets "could make Central Europe a tense place for the next few years—years that are critical to the solidification of the Western gains of the recent period."

It was true that the money to the Soviets might be wasted. It "would probably be spent on a quick infusion of consumer goods to blunt the impact of half-hearted economic reform measures."

Nor would Congress support help "while the Soviet Union spends $15 billion a year to arm its client states—$5 billion in Cuba alone—and continues to strangle the Lithuanian independence movement." But the U.S. had to concentrate on the most important problems, even if such an understanding about assistance would be a gamble on both sides.[22]

Free to Choose

Mitterrand did not like to lean on Gorbachev. When he journeyed to Moscow to meet again with the Soviet leader, in late May, about a week after Baker left, the French president's tone was more philosophical. He threw in his weight on the German freedom to make the choice of alliances for themselves. "I do not see," Mitterrand told him, "how to forbid united Germany from choosing its alliances as agreed in Helsinki."[23]

The notion of Germans debating about NATO was not idle theory. In election campaign after election campaign, anyone who had followed German politics that year, West or East, could see that their political leaders—West or East—were offering a full menu of options.

Free to choose: the Soviet government had said it agreed with that principle when it was codified in the Helsinki CSCE Final Act of 1975. This had always been an argument that had stuck with Gorbachev, resonating as it did so strongly with his other political principles.[24]

By the end of May, as Gorbachev contemplated his trip to the United States, he faced a turning point in the course of East-West relations and *perestroika*. The stakes in continued cooperation with the West were enormous. Gorbachev and Shevardnadze had stated both publicly and privately that their first priority was domestic reform. That meant cutting military expenditures and avoiding the distraction of a major international crisis.

In the spring of 1990 the Soviet Union appeared to be resigned to the failure of its policy in Eastern Europe. A long document prepared by the Central Committee staff spoke matter-of-factly about the changed political and ideological face of Eastern Europe. The analysis warned Soviet leaders that they currently had no policy to respond to this situation. There was a vacuum, and the West was filling it.

The USSR was withdrawing with "no rational explanation, with no regard for the immense material and spiritual investment that we made there." The policy guidance grasped at straws. There was still a chance to strengthen the Soviet cultural presence, interest in the Russian language, and so forth. The Central Committee staff even suggested to a leadership desperately short of hard currency that a new policy in Eastern Europe might require a certain financial investment. "We should not economize," the staff told their impoverished leaders, "because this is a matter of capital for the future."[25]

The fact remained, however, that Soviet policy in Eastern Europe—premised on the potential for reformed communism—was dead. Germany and Lithuania, however, were a different matter.

The division of Germany and Soviet dominance of its eastern half could be considered the most important achievements of half a century of Soviet foreign policy. This Soviet emplacement in the heart of Europe was the highest and last remaining measure of meaning from the vast sacrifices endured during the Great Patriotic War. Now the West and NATO were threatening to overrun this bastion of Soviet power. It seemed inconceivable that the USSR could submit supinely to such a reverse. Gorbachev's own political survival could be jeopardized by such a concession, and Gorbachev would face a full congress of the Soviet Communist party in July.

Gorbachev tried new economic reforms. On May 24 Prime Minister Nikolai Ryzhkov announced a major new economic reform program, to include liberalizing prices. This would sharply increase the cost of food. The price of bread would triple. A wave of panic buying and public unrest followed. Gorbachev addressed the nation on television on May 27, pleading for calm.

The economic reform measures were eventually rejected by the Supreme Soviet before they could take effect. And, as if to underscore Gorbachev' beleaguered political situation, on May 29 the Russian legislature chose Boris Yeltsin as its president despite Gorbachev's opposition.

Kohl called Bush just before Gorbachev arrived in Washington. Again, Kohl pressed on U.S. money for the Soviets.

But Bush had decided against the kind of $20 billion "strategic choice" that Scowcroft had invited him to consider. There was just too much against it. There were the problems with how the money would be used.

Also, though this was a seemingly technical detail, too time-consuming to explain in top-level meetings, there was a crucial issue of different legal authorities and institutions. Under its laws the West German government had much more scope to offer government-guaranteed loans to support its country's exports than was (or is) the case in the U.S. government.[26] Bush and Baker had trouble seeing how to get the federal government to guarantee loans on this sort of scale, and certainly not while Lithuania (and the BW program) were still unresolved.

It would be hard enough just to try and normalize trade relations. As Gorbachev was arriving, Bush had just been going through a very hard battle with the Congress over his decision to renew normal trade with China for another year.

So, Bush did not expect any breakthroughs with Gorbachev. He hoped to at least maintain forward progress.[27]

In this essay, we will not go through the details of the Bush-Gorbachev summit discussions, including the famous meeting on May 31 in which Gorbachev matter-of-factly agreed that Germany should be free to choose its alliance status.

What is worth recalling again is that, the next day, the discussions came back to whether to sign a U.S.-Soviet trade agreement. Bush had checked views around his administration and on Capitol Hill. Opinions were divided, but Baker recommended going ahead with the deal.

Bush agreed. Gorbachev's apparent move on Germany probably contributed to the president's decision to help the beleaguered Soviet leader.

Moving from Washington to the presidential retreat at Camp David, for more relaxed and private discussions, privately, Bush raised the concerns about the discovery of the Soviet biological weapons program. Gorbachev was defensive and promised to look into it.

Gorbachev raised the question of economic aid, of U.S. government-guaranteed loans. Bush said that he wanted to help but needed to see more economic reforms, movement on Lithuania, and a reduction of subsidies to Cuba. Progress on Germany would also create the right political climate for Bush to seek money from the Congress.

Bush did pledge that the G-7 would consider a broad multilateral assistance program, including substantial credits. They would do this at the Houston summit in July 1990, to be held right after the NATO summit in London.[28]

None of the reporters at the post-summit press conference appeared to notice the significance of Bush's press statement mentioning Gorbachev's agreement that Germany was free to choose its alliance status. Nor did American officials call attention to it. They sensed that Gorbachev had finally turned a corner in his approach to the German Question, but the situation was tentative and shaky. Indeed, later in June, Shevardnadze continued to present a doctrinaire line in the discussions about Germany.

Bush carefully reported on his press statement in phone calls to Kohl, Thatcher, and Mitterrand. He did not dramatize the concession. He instead emphasized the need to follow up with a successful NATO summit in July.

None of the other leaders appeared, at least at first, to grasp the significance of the Soviet move; none even inquired about it. (Teltschik, however, noted that this was "a sensation.") Mitterrand did remark shrewdly that Gorbachev would be counting on achieving his security objectives through West Germany's domestic politics.

Bush then followed up with written messages. Again, Bush's tone was cautious: "We, of course, will have to see whether this reflects real flexibility in the Soviet position."[29]

But, as Chernyaev recalled, the Americans were correct to take the exchange on Germany's right to choose very seriously. When asked later when the Soviet Union agreed to membership of a united Germany in NATO, Chernyaev "unhesitatingly" answered, "On May 30, at the Soviet-American summit in Washington."[30]

Conclusion

In this chapter we just offer a snapshot of one phase in a remarkable story. It is a phase in which, to the outside world, no great events occurred.

But recall again what Bush said to Rice and others that spring: "I don't want people to look back 20 or 40 years from now and say, That's where everything went off track. That's where progress stopped."

Progress did not stop. The superpowers walked the tightrope. They found a way through the new crises over Lithuania and biological weapons. Though the United States could not see any economic aid panacea for the Soviet Union's problems in the spring of 1990, the United States did move forward on normalizing economic relations, for the first time, with its former Cold War enemy. The United States and its allies did craft solutions for the core Soviet security concerns about Germany. The solutions used the institutions of the Cold War and the institutions of the new Europe coming into being.

Notes

1. Anatoly Chernyaev Diary, trans. Anna Melyakova & ed. Svetlana Savranskaya, 1990, entries for 22 & 30 Apr, pp. 25, 27, from National Security Archive online (hereinafter cited as Chernyaev Diary).

2. Ibid.

3. This summary and the following exchanges draw from Rice's recollections; George Bush & Brent Scowcroft, *A World Transformed* (New York: Knopf, 1998), pp. 222-29 (for quotes from April meetings with Thatcher and Mitterrand); James A. Baker, III with Thomas DeFrank, *The Politics of Diplomacy: Revolution, War, and Peace 1989-1992* (New York: G.P. Putnam's, 1995), pp. 239-44; Frédéric Bozo, *Mitterrand, The End of the Cold War, and German Unification*, trans. Susan Emanuel (New York: Berghahn, 2009), pp. 240-41. "I don't want people to look back …," Don Oberdorfer, *The Turn: From the Cold War to a New Era, The United States and the Soviet Union, 1983–1990* (New York: Simon and Schuster, 1991), p. 404 (from Oberdorfer interview with Rice).

4. The use of Lugar as an intermediary arose from an American debate about whether the United States should pressure the Lithuanians to go along with the German and French initiative. Robert Gates, Robert Blackwill, and Rice were opposed, arguing that Washington should not leave its fingerprints on an effort to dissuade the Baltic states from seeking independence. Scowcroft, Baker, and Dennis Ross, however, believed that the Americans could send an "indirect" message to the Lithuanians that they wanted to see a resolution.

5. On the historical evolution of conventional wisdom about the Sverdlovsk issue up to this point, see Michael Gordin, "The Anthrax Solution: The Sverdlovsk Incident and the Resolution of a Biological Weapons Controversy," *Journal of the History of Biology*, vol. 30 no. 3 (1997): 441-80. When Gordin wrote this article, he did not know about the information that Soviet leaders of the BW program had already provided, from late 1989 onward, to the U.S. and British governments.

6. The first key defector, in October 1989, was Vladimir Pasechnik. Later there were other defectors and sources. The head of the Soviet BW program, and Pasechnik's supervisor, was Ken Alibek. In 1989 Alibek joined in the cover-ups, external and internal. In 1992 Alibek defected to the United States. He has since published a memoir about his work and his defection: *Biohazard* (New York: Random House, 1999). The best overall account of the Soviet biological weapons issues is now Milton Leitenberg & Raymond Zilinskas with Jens Kuhn, *The Soviet Biological Weapons Program: A History* (Cambridge: Harvard University Press, 2012). For more on the origins of the program, see Raymond

Zilinskas, *The Soviet Biological Weapons Program and Its Legacy in Today's Russia* (Washington: National Defense University Occasional Paper 11, July 2016); see also the valuable narrative in David Hoffman, *The Dead Hand* (New York: Doubleday, 2009), pp. 327-57. The Soviet program leaders, like Alibek, appear to have assumed that the U.S. and British also had large clandestine BW programs. They were profoundly shocked when they learned, including through Soviet site visits in the U.S., that this was not true and that the Americans and British had actually complied with the BWC.

The 1990s-era memoirs, including that of the U.S. ambassador, Jack Matlock, leave out any discussion of these BW issues. The British ambassador in Moscow, Rodric Braithwaite, another contributor to this volume, published his memoir in 2002, after the Soviet defector identities and information had been made public, and he gave some information about this. See Rodric Braithwaite, *Across the Moscow River: The World Turned Upside Down* (New Haven: Yale University Press, 2002), pp. 141-43, but at that time Braithwaite did not feel able to discuss many of the other details that have since come out.

7. Some British officials apparently wanted to publicize all that was known and have a public confrontation with the Soviet government. Bush and Thatcher, and their top aides, did not agree. See the sifting of some of the evidence on this in Leitenberg & Zilinskas, op. cit., pp. 582-92 and their notes.

8. For the Matlock-Bessmertnykh discussion, Ibid., pp. 594-95. Leitenberg & Zilinskas have the best summary of the subsequent developments, including a substantial analysis puzzling over Gorbachev's handling of this issue. Ibid., pp. 595-630. They are mistaken on a small factual point; they date the first Baker-Shevardnadze discussion of the BW issues on May 2; in fact, these discussions were on May 17, after the initial demarches at the lower-level. Hoffman did the initial reporting on Gorbachev's recollection of the first Bush-Gorbachev discussions of the BW problem. See *The Dead Hand*, op. cit., pp. 350-51.

9. We believe the intelligence discoveries were briefed to the congressional "Gang of Eight," which would include the leaders of both parties in the House and the Senate, as well as the chair and ranking minority member of the House and Senate intelligence committees.

10. Rice and Zelikow to Blackwill, "Two Plus Four: The Next Phase," 10 May 90. U.S. documents cited without an archival location were reviewed by Zelikow in the early 1990s, before they were archived; Zoellick also made notes for himself around the same time, in his office files. He had discussed the issue with the West Germans and previewed it for Baker back in March. On that and also the difficult legal issue that would be confronted, effectively forcing the U.S. to adopt the kind of arguments that the Soviets had used in the 1950s during the Berlin crisis, see Philip Zelikow & Condoleezza Rice, *Germa-*

ny Unified and Europe Transformed: A Study in Statecraft (Cambridge: Harvard University Press, 1995), pp. 246, 448 n. 9.

The British government disagreed internally on whether it was willing to let Four Power rights terminate. But Foreign Secretary Hurd and his team in London had about the same position as the Americans. They pushed back hard against concerns voiced in Number 10 and from their ambassador in Bonn, and insisted that the British should let their rights lapse when Germany unified. See Weston to Wall, 18 May 90, answering Powell to Wall that day, reacting to Bonn 634, "German Unification: The Timetable Accelerates," 17 May 90, in *Documents on British Policy Overseas, Series III:* vol. VII, *German Unification 1989-1990*, edited by Patrick Salmon, Keith Hamilton & Stephen Twigge (London: Routledge, 2010) (hereinafter cited as *DBPO-German Unification*), pp. 390-94; see also the earlier Foreign Office analysis by Hurd's policy planner, Robert Cooper, on "The Soviet Veto in the Two plus Four Talks," 6 Apr 90, in ibid., pp. 371-72.

11. On the Hurd-Kohl meeting, see Teltschik, *329 Tage*, p. 235; Bonn (U.S. embassy) 15540, "Hurd's May 15 Visit to Bonn," 16 May 90.

12. On the details of this diplomacy, with the approach effectively settled among the Americans and West Germans in June 1990, see Zelikow & Rice, op. cit., pp. 239, 267-68, 274-75, 306-07, 308, 323, 333.

13. On the eventual scale and cost of German CFE compliance, Celeste Wallander, *Mortal Friends, Best Enemies: German-Russian Cooperation after the Cold War* (Ithaca, NY: Cornell University Press, 1999), pp. 104, 110.

14. CFE 1A was more formally called the Concluding Act of the Negotiation on Personnel Strength of Conventional Armed Forces in Europe, signed in Helsinki in July 1992. In that agreement Germany reduced its ceiling to 345,000. France, which had about three-quarters of Germany's population, had a ceiling of 325,000. With nearly double Germany's population, Russia was granted a disproportionately large ceiling of 1.45 million, more than four times the German total. Ukraine, with about one-third the population of Russia, was granted a ceiling of 450,000.

15. The nine points were:

(1) limiting the Bundeswehr in CFE II [as mentioned in the text, this pledge was made in 1990 without waiting for CFE II];

(2) accelerating negotiations about short-range nuclear forces [Bush jumped over the negotiations in September 1991 with a unilateral withdrawal of practically all such weapons, which Gorbachev reciprocated];

(3) ensuring that the Germans would not develop, possess, or acquire either nuclear, biological, or chemical weapons [this was done in the Final Settlement];

(4) keeping NATO forces out of the GDR for a transition period [also done, with further details discussed in Soviet-West German talks];

(5) developing a transition period for Soviet forces to leave the GDR [worked out between West Germans and Soviets];

(6) adapting NATO politically and militarily [accomplished both in word and deed in 1990 and 1991];

(7) getting an agreement on the Polish-German border [also done in 1990];

(8) institutionalizing and developing CSCE [done in the 1990 Charter of Paris and the 1992 Helsinki CSCE summit, with solid Soviet, then Russian, participation]; and

(9) developing economic relations with the Germans, while ensuring that GDR economic obligations to the USSR would be fulfilled [also worked out between the Soviets and Germans].

As Baker recalled, "Gorbachev took copious notes as I went through the list and made clear he approved of it very much." Where Gorbachev still balked at that time, in mid-May, was the acceptance of a unified Germany in NATO. James Baker, *The Politics of Diplomacy*, op. cit., pp. 250-51.

Citing "insights from international relations theory," Joshua Itzkowitz Shifrinson has argued that the U.S. made "informal assurances" not to extend NATO and that it made a "false promise of accommodation" of Soviet interests. The promise was false, he asserts, because, in 1990, the U.S. and its allies hoped to preserve NATO and because, in 1990, the door to possible future NATO enlargement was "left ajar." Thus, "the United States was insincere when offering the Soviet Union informal assurances against NATO expansion." "Deal or No Deal? The End of the Cold War and the U.S. Offer to Limit NATO Expansion," *International Security*, vol. 40 no. 4 (2016): 7, 40, 34, 38.

The context of the "left ajar" quote provides a more accurate snapshot of U.S. views not only in 1990, but also onward until 1993, after the Soviet Union had disintegrated. At the end of October 1990 Zelikow briefed Gates on the state of play, in the European Strategy Steering Group, on the question of: "Should the US and NATO now signal to the new democracies of Eastern Europe NATO's readiness to contemplate their future membership?"

Zelikow reported that, "All agencies agree that East European governments should not be invited to join NATO anytime in the immediate future. There is general satisfaction with the way the State paper ended up handling the issue of Eastern Europe [page numbers]. However, OSD [Cheney's civilian aides] and State's Policy Planning Staff (and possibly Zoellick) would like to keep the door ajar and not give the East Europeans the impression that NATO is forever a closed club." The rest of State preferred to just be "inscrutable," treating the issue "as premature and not on the table, while of course reserving our options as the political situation in Europe evolves." Zelikow through Gompert & Kanter to Gates, "Your Meeting of the European Strategy Steering Group," 26 Oct 90, pp. 4-5, Wilson files, Bush Library.

This reserved stance was precisely the approach that had animated the April 1990 Zelikow/Rice proposal to invite the Soviet Union and all other Warsaw Pact states to send "diplomatic liaison missions" to NATO, a U.S. proposal that NATO leaders adopted in July 1990, accepted by all the Warsaw Pact countries, and which then led to the 1991 creation of the North Atlantic Cooperation Council that included all those states, including the Soviet Union.

There were no agreements to scuttle or settle NATO's future contours, one way or another. The American sources, which we know well, do not say different. Perhaps more to the point, the other governments so centrally involved, like the Soviet and West German governments, also did not believe at the time that they had struck such an agreement, formally or informally. Those who did the work were professionals who knew what they were agreeing to, or not.

Bush, Baker, Kohl, and Genscher actually worked conscientiously and in good faith to accommodate Soviet and Russian security concerns. Those looking for informal assurances meant to accommodate such concerns can readily find them. They are the list of nine assurances Baker so carefully enumerated to Gorbachev in May 1990. This list was circulated and discussed among allied governments. It was repeatedly stressed in the subsequent diplomacy that led to the Final Settlement signed in September 1990.

16. Kohl-Bush memcons, Washington, 17 May 90, Bush Library; Horst Teltschik, *329 Tage: Innenansichten der Einigung* (Berlin: Siedler, 1991), pp. 236-39; *Dokumente zur Deutschlandpolitik: Deutsche Einheit Sonderedition aus den Akten des Bundeskanzleramtes 1989/90*, research supervision from Klaus Hildebrand & Hans-Peter Schwarz with Friedrich Kahlenberg of the Bundesarchivs, edited by Hanns Jürgen Küsters & Daniel Hofmann (München: R. Oldenbourg Verlag, 1998) (hereinafter cited as *DzD-Einheit*), pp. 1126-27 (in which the record of the three meetings run together). The small discussion seeking the "honest opinion" was just with Bush, Kohl, Scowcroft, Teltschik, and the interpreters (the 10-1130 meeting). For that meeting the American record is more detailed than the German one, although the essence of the exchange is clear in both.

17. Bush address, Oklahoma State University, 4 May 90, Bush Library.

18. Kohl-Mitterrand memcon, Latche (near the coast, in the French Pyrenees), 4 Jan 90, *DzD-Einheit*, p. 685.

19. The account that follows is drawn from Horst Teltschik, *329 Tage*, op. cit., pp. 221, 226–228, 230–235.

20. The discussion that follows is drawn from Ibid., pp. 237–238; Bush-Kohl memcon, 17 May 90, Bush Library.

21. For the Zoellick-Ross drafted presentation on Germany which Baker took into his meeting with Gorbachev, see briefing paper, "One-on-One Points: Gorbachev Meeting," n.d. For Baker's summary to Bush on his meeting with Gorbachev, see Secto 7015 (from Moscow), "Memorandum for the President: Moscow, May 18," 19 May 90. For Chernyaev's vehement private dissent, see Chernyaev diary 1990, 5 May, op. cit., p. 29.

22. Scowcroft to Bush, "A Strategic Choice: Do We Give Aid to the Soviet Union?", 25 May 90, in Rice files, Soviet Union/USSR Subject Files, US-USSR Soviet Relations (2), Bush Library. The memo was drafted principally by Rice, working with Blackwill and Gates. It was highly classified at the time and handled outside of the normal paperwork system.

23. Quoted in Bozo, *Mitterrand*, op. cit., p. 253.

24. The language appears in "Principle I" of the "Principles Guiding Relations between Participating States" in "Basket I" of the Helsinki Final Act of 1975, dealing with security questions: "They [the participating states] also have the right to belong or not to belong to international organizations, to be or not to be a party to bilateral or multilateral treaties including the right to be or not to be a party to treaties of alliance; they also have the right to neutrality." Within the American government, Zoellick had seized on this principle, months earlier, as a way to strengthen the West's position since the CSCE document, though not legally binding, was one of the few bodies of principles clearly agreed to by both sides.

25. Central Committee staff to members of the Politburo, "O svazi otnosheniyakh c vostochnym-evropa," May 1990, in Center for the Storage of Contemporary Documentation (TsKhSD),Moscow.

26. The German government has long had relatively broad authorities to guarantee export-related loans, combined (not coincidentally) with close relationships between top government and banking leaders. An example is their "Hermes cover" program. In the U.S. government the strongest export credit guarantee authorities are confined to agricultural exports. The G-7 governments could help fund and persuade more loans to the Soviet Union by the international financial institutions, led by the IMF. This would require Soviet membership in the IMF, a process which began getting underway, precariously, in late 1990, and would then lead to setting policy conditions in order to get credit.

27. See Bush & Scowcroft, *A World Transformed*, op. cit., pp. 276-78.

28. Based on our understanding of the discussion at the time. As far as we know, there is no written record of the Bush-Gorbachev side discussions at Camp David about credits or about biological weapons.

29. See Teltschik, *329 Tage*, op. cit., pp. 255–258; Bush-Kohl and Bush-Thatcher telcons, 3 Jun 90, Bush-Mitterrand telcon, 5 Jun 90, Bush Library. The written messages were sent out on June 4. Bush did tell both Kohl and Thatcher about the private discussions of credits and economic aid. The letter to Thatcher did not mention Bush's discussion of the biological weapons problem with Gorbachev. Some of those discussions were handled directly between Scowcroft and Charles Powell. Thatcher kept up to date on the BW issue. She followed up on the subject with Gorbachev when she went to Moscow later that month.

30. Zelikow interview with Chernyaev, Moscow, January 1994; Hannes Adomeit, "Gorbachev, German Unification, and the Collapse of Empire," *Post-Soviet Affairs*, 10 (August–September 1994): pp. 197, 229 n. 28.

Chapter 4

The Soviet Collapse and the Charm of Hindsight

Rodric Braithwaite

Those on the spot always get some things wrong: memory later betrays them. Those who subsequently try to disentangle the story always miss part of the context. In politics, perceptions and emotions are as important as reason. The theme of what follows is that we cannot understand the causes and consequences of the Soviet collapse unless we take every account of its deep roots in the past and the strong emotions that accompanied it. It is of course imprudent, or even impertinent, for foreigners to pontificate about how "most Russians" think or feel. But it is an essential part of the story.

In this deliberately personal account I attempt to recreate how the collapse looked to me at the time and in the aftermath, drawing on a detailed diary, my reporting to London, and on later writings.

I. How it Looked at the Time

A Kind of Democracy

Poland shows the way

I witnessed two attempts to bring a kind of democracy to the communist world. The Polish experiment of the late 1950s and the Soviet experiment of the late 1980s are now largely forgotten or ignored. Both are significant for the history of the time, and for an understanding of the events of today.

In October 1956 the Poles expelled their Soviet advisers, abolished the collective farms, allowed people to travel abroad, and gave a degree of freedom to the press. They were encouraged by Khrushchev's denunciation of Stalin, and driven by a combination of patriotism, a liberal faction inside the Party, and an alliance between students and workers. When I arrived in Warsaw in February 1959 the secret police were still demoralized. We had almost complete freedom to make Polish friends. Even the communists among them talked about such hitherto taboo subjects as the Soviets' massacre of Polish officers at Katyn, their betrayal of the Warsaw Rising, the ruthless way they had imposed their rule in Eastern Europe.

Our friends hoped that Poland would lead the way to a social-democratic communism they could live with. But as my wife Jill and I left Warsaw in Summer 1961, they told us sadly that their achievements would wither unless their "neighbors" to the East changed in fundamental ways. They watched aghast as the Russians suppressed reform in Hungary in 1956 and Czechoslovakia in 1968. But they did not give up. In the late 1970s students, workers and intellectuals formed a new alliance in the Solidarity movement. Martial law in 1981 failed to snuff it out. By autumn 1988 Solidarity was maneuvering towards a power-sharing deal with the communists.

The East Europeans were unconvinced when, at the 19th Conference of the Soviet Communist Party in June 1988 Gorbachev clearly indicated that they could find their own way: "The imposition from outside, by any means, let alone military force, of a social system, or a way of life, is a dangerous trapping [доспехи] of the past." Even in Poland formal negotiations between communists and opposition began only after the Soviet elections of March 1989 demonstrated that the "neighbors" were indeed changing. The Poles held free elections in June, the communists were comprehensively defeated, and Poland formed the first non-communist government in the bloc. By the end of 1990 the other countries of Eastern Europe had followed, and the bloc dissolved.

The Russians Catch Up—Slowly

By the time I arrived in Moscow in September 1988, Gorbachev had launched a whirlwind of political reform. The press was transformed, almost scurrilous in its attacks on public abuse though still careful to spare the top leadership. Nothing, it seemed, was sacrosanct. The Chairman of the State Bank remarked to me that October: "I'm a Party member of forty years standing. But I don't see how we can have proper guarantees as long as the Party has a monopoly of power." My official drivers, Sasha and Konstantin, freely criticized Gorbachev to me in private (I naturally assumed that both reported on our conversations to the authorities. After the Soviet collapse Konstantin told the Russian press that for seventeen years he had reported to the KGB on successive British ambassadors).

History became a national obsession. People joked that the Soviet Union was a country with an unpredictable past. Individuals burrowed in hitherto closed archives to reveal the details of Stalin's crimes. Almost everyone, after all, had lost friends and relatives under his brutal regime. Now at last they could find out what had happened to them, and discuss their fates in public without fear of the consequences.

In his chapter in this volume, Roderic Lyne describes the emotional reaction of audiences at *Krutoi Marshrut*, the dramatized version of Evgenia Ginsburg's memoir of the gulag, which premiered in March 1989. After one performance the young son of a Russian friend of ours had nightmares in which he heard the women prisoners screaming as they were beaten by the guards. Such memories do not go away: *Krutoi Marshrut* is still running in Moscow.

Some thought that the process of uncovering the past was going too far: it was becoming impossible for people to take pride in their country's history. Others thought it was not going far enough. In December 1988 I called on Yuri Afanasiev, the Rector of the State Historical Archives Institute, and an organizer of the massive street demonstrations which followed. He was firm: the process was still entirely inadequate. It would not be complete until Lenin and the Revolution as well as Stalin had been demythologized. Afanasiev accepted that Gorbachev could not simply set the myths aside: that would give his enemies a lever against him. But any attempt to ban the public debate would now be harder to impose. There would be resistance and probably bloodshed.

It seemed like Warsaw all over again, a place where one could live and work and talk almost as if it were a normal country. It was a time of exhilarating hope, but also of deep apprehension. Like Afanasiev, most of our friends worried that Gorbachev's experiment could end in bloodshed and civil war: fears exacerbated by the massacre on Tiananmen Square in Peking in June 1989, and the bloody end to the Communist regime in Romania the following December. It was hard for any of us to keep a proper sense of detachment: Jill and I found ourselves emotionally committed to Gorbachev, and I may have been less than fair to his rival, Yeltsin, in consequence.

It had not been like that when we lived in Khrushchev's Moscow in the 1960s, still largely closed to us despite his attempts at reform. Then too there was hope. Khrushchev understood that something needed to be done about the obvious and growing weaknesses in the Soviet system. He permitted a genuine though limited economic debate. But his ill-considered remedies failed to deliver. In October 1964 he was overthrown without warning by a combination of the barons in the Party, the army, and the KGB. *Pravda* reported laconically that he had asked to be relieved of his duties "in view of his advanced age and the deterioration of his health."

Under Khrushchev's successor Brezhnev the Soviet Union enjoyed nearly two decades of apparent domestic stability and international success. But the weaknesses ran deep. Sakharov told Brezhnev in 1970 that unless the "bureaucratic, ritualistic, dogmatic, openly hypocritical, and mediocre style" that governed Soviet life were replaced by "democratization, with its fullness of information and clash of ideas," the Soviet Union would become a second-rate provincial power. In 1974 the Chairman of the State Planning Committee warned that the economy was in serious trouble. A decade later the Soviet Union was in seventy-seventh place in the world for per capita consumption.[1]

Such facts could not be ignored. In March 1985 the Politburo chose Gorbachev—young, energetic, effective, and apparently orthodox—to put things right.

But Gorbachev had more radical ideas, many rooted in the debate which flourished briefly under Khrushchev. He believed that the economy was being strangled by bureaucratic central planning. Defense expenditure was a crippling burden. It would have to be reduced. That would only be possible if the Cold War, hideously dangerous in itself, could be brought under control.

Gorbachev spoke with unprecedented frankness and at first people flocked to hear him. But his initial policies were rooted in the Soviet past. The economy continued to decline. People increasingly complained that he was doing nothing to halt it.

Then in 1988 he set out on what amounted to a revolution in Soviet politics. Soviet elections had been mere rituals: electors voted in droves for the only available candidate lest they be penalized at work. He now persuaded the Party that new elections should be held at which voters could choose freely between at least two candidates for each post. There would be restrictions: for example, seats would be reserved for the Central Committee, academicians, and others. (This is, of course, a gross simplification of Gorbachev's complicated proposals).

The intense campaigning which followed involved lively public meetings, noisy TV debates, dirty tricks, and other trappings of genuine democracy. We attended a rally in support of Gorbachev's critic Yeltsin, who was standing for a large Moscow constituency. It mustered perhaps forty thousand people carrying nationalist flags and banners attacking the Party. One slogan was "Bread and Freedom," the traditional cry of Russians on the verge of rebellion.

The vote took place peacefully on March 26, 1988. The results were spectacular. One in four of the powerful Obkom (Regional) Party Secretaries were defeated. The local leaderships in Moscow, Leningrad and Kiev were massacred. Senior military commanders lost the seats they had always held by right. Yeltsin was elected by four fifths of the voters in his seven million strong constituency. By contrast Gorbachev was only elected by the six hundred-odd members of the Central Committee. His political legitimacy began to crumble.

"It was not," I told London, "a genuine democratic election as we understand it. The overwhelming majority of the candidates came from one party, the Communist Party. In one constituency in four there was only one candidate... Yet the election has aroused genuine public interest and participation in the political process unprecedented since the 1920s."[2]

The Congress of People's Deputies opened on May 25, 1988. The deputies relentlessly lambasted the leadership, including Gorbachev himself. They accused the Party of corruption, the government of gross mismanagement. They called the invasion of Afghanistan a shameful crime and assailed the KGB for murder and torture. The proceedings were broadcast live. For two weeks people were glued to their TV sets and transistors. The national economy suffered accordingly.

The euphoria soon dissipated as the economy continued to spiral downwards and strikes spread across the country. But people were still determined to make their voices heard. Tens of thousands demonstrated against the Party's political monopoly: Konstantin and Jill marched with them. The communists yielded. In March 1991 the constitution was changed. Political pluralism was no longer illegal.

A kind of fragile democracy had arrived, thanks not least to the sustained pressure of ordinary people. But the gloom and apprehension continued: one Russian friend told us after the annual Victory Parade in May 1991 that the anniversary of the victory over Nazi Germany was the only occasion on which the Soviet people could still feel happy and proud of their history.

The Failing Economy

Gorbachev never got a grip on the economy. He took advice from good economists, but may not have fully understood it, and took no decisive action because he feared that a botched reform would simply lead to widespread hardship. The unreformed Soviet economy began to enter free fall. Even basic commodities failed to reach the shops. By the autumn of 1990 there was a real surge of sympathy among ordinary people in the West for their counterparts in the Soviet Union—though most Russians still do not believe that. Dutch TV organized a charity telethon to produce food. Private citizens in Britain collected a million books for Soviet libraries. Western governments organized technical aid programs and arranged to supply food directly to Soviet consumers. Bypassing the central Soviet government, which they regarded as incompetent and corrupt, they sent teams of monitors to check that the aid was reaching its destination. Some of the monitors were former or current soldiers: inevitably the Russians suspected they were spies. Soviet ministers forced themselves through gritted teeth to accept these conditions with gratitude. But by 1992 the Commander of the Northern Fleet, Admiral Gromov, was asking the Norwegians to supply his sailors with humanitarian aid.[3] Humiliation could go little further.

Even under these conditions, Western aid was not always efficiently distributed or gratefully received. We spent a night in May 1992 as guests of Father Oleg, an ill-disciplined priest who had been exiled by his bishop to a muddy parish north of Moscow. Oleg told us that there had been a great local scandal over aid brought in by the Germans, who had thrown sweets to the local children and then filmed them scrabbling over the handfuls. Aid from Exeter in Britain turned out to consist of flea-ridden old clothes. The only successful operation was when a French group sent the aid to Oleg directly, and he was able to distribute it through the parish. Such stories multiplied in the Russian press, and were naturally resented.

As Soviet finances spiraled out of control in 1991, Gorbachev pressed the Americans and the rest of the Group of Seven (G-7) for money to plug the gap. The G-7 consists of the major capitalist countries, Canada, France, Germany, Italy, Japan, Britain and the United States, whose leaders meet annually to discuss political and economic questions. Although the Japanese and to some extent the Americans were initially opposed, the British, who held the chair, successfully pushed for Gorbachev to be invited to the G-7 meeting in London in July 1991. Prime Minister John Major sent a senior British Treasury official beforehand to explain to Gorbachev that the G-7 could not help him effectively until his government adopted a plausible plan of economic reform. There would be no money on the table in London. If he asked for it, he would be rebuffed: a political humiliation. He ignored the advice and sent his own senior official to London to promote his case on the British media. The G-7 leaders turned him down just the same. They sugared the pill with a vague promise to facilitate Russian access to advice from the World Bank and the International Monetary Fund: bricks without straw which all concerned had to present as a success.

The coup took place within weeks of Gorbachev's return from London. A few days after it failed, he called me into the Kremlin late at night. Still clearly in a state of shock from his experiences in the Crimea, he told me that the country was on the brink of financial collapse. It needed $2 billion new credits in the next two-three weeks, the rescheduling of its debt, and urgent help with food and pharmaceutical supplies. The West had spent $100 billion on the Gulf War that spring: now he was asking it to make a small insurance payment against the failure of his reforms and a return to the aggressive Soviet Union of the past. I could only tell him what he had already heard in London: no money without a viable plan. It was a harsh line but, I still think, inevitable. John Major repeated it a few days later, when he became the first Western politician to visit Moscow after the coup.

By January 1992, however, Yeltsin was in charge of Russia, and his Deputy Prime Minister Gaidar was trying to implement a courageous reform program. He too asked for financial support: $13 billion. My American colleague Bob Strauss and I sent eloquent telegrams to our governments, pointing out that the G-7 condition had now been met, and that we should come up with the money. Our advice was ignored: the Americans argued that they were having their own economic problems and that Congress would inevitably oppose the request.

Encouraged by Britain's apparently greater sympathy for Russia's plight, Gaidar then asked the British to sponsor its application for membership of the IMF and the World Bank. I and my Treasury colleagues from London found ourselves in the bizarre situation of sitting with Gaidar in the former offices of the Central Committee of the Communist Party of the Soviet Union, coordinating tactics to get around continued opposition from the Americans and others. We succeeded. On April 2 the Moscow press announced the "Sensational success of the Russian Government: Russia will ... be accepted into the IMF."[4]

The previous day President Bush had finally announced a $24 billion aid package, backed by other G-7 countries. It was less generous that it looked, because much of it consisted of repayable loans already promised.

It didn't work. By the end of 1992, as he had predicted, Gaidar had lost his job and inflation was approaching 3000%. Army officers, doctors, teachers and pensioners went unpaid for months at a time. Factory workers were paid, if at all, in kind not cash: we saw women workers lined up along one of the main roads out of Moscow trying to sell carpets produced by their factory, some carrying pornographic designs. Old ladies sold their family possessions on the sidewalks in the capital. Russian newspapers reported that conscripts in the navy had died of malnutrition.[5]

The Lurch to the Right

It was always obvious, not least to Gorbachev himself, that unless he was cautious and lucky he might easily go the way of Khrushchev.

In January 1989 Sakharov told the German press that Gorbachev was about to be overthrown. I wrote to London that Gorbachev's political and economic difficulties were piling up. He might have to trim his policies. We might have no advance warning of his fall. Russian nationalists, backed perhaps by the military, might attempt to reassert national discipline, and imperial power. A return to repression or even bloodshed was not impossible. The ascendency of these people would nevertheless be nasty and brutish, but short. The underlying reasons for change would not go away. Eventually reform would have to be resumed. The Foreign Office thought I was too complacent.

Rumors of coups continued to succeed one another, stoked by sensational reporting in the West. In autumn 1990 troops maneuvered around the capital, for reasons never satisfactorily explained. Two disaffected army officers publicly called Gorbachev a traitor. Fifty-three senior deputies to the Congress called for Presidential rule to hold the Union together. The head of the KGB warned that the CIA was trying to disrupt the economy. The forces of law and order, he said with menace, would prevent chaos and anarchy.

Russia's liberals increasingly switched their support to Yeltsin. Gorbachev began to lose his closest allies. He sacked his liberal interior minister. His foreign minister Shevardnadze resigned, and warned of impending dictatorship. Gorbachev recruited replacements from among the reactionary barons of the KGB, the army, and the Party.

Under their influence, he put increasing pressure on the obstreperous Balts, who had been massively demonstrating for independence since 1988 at least.[6] In January 1991, Soviet special forces killed thirteen people in Vilnius. The liberal press in Moscow bitterly blamed Gorbachev. He must have known, I told London. Either he had backed the attack, or he had acquiesced in an initiative of the reactionaries, or he had lost control. But he could not escape the responsibility.

Two months later Yeltsin called a massive demonstration to demand that Gorbachev step down. Gorbachev banned it. Troops massed on the Moscow streets. Bloodshed seemed imminent. Gorbachev blinked and withdrew the soldiers. He then tried to regain the political center. But his authority declined still further.

Gorbachev's priority was now to get the Union republics to agree to a treaty to preserve the Union. But the Ukrainians, the Balts, and the Caucasians were adamantly opposed to any hint of federalism. The hard men were opposed to any weakening of centralized rule. Gorbachev maneuvered desperately between them to find a text that would gain general support.

His time had run out. On August 18 conspirators from the Party, the army, and the KGB—the combination that had overthrown Khrushchev—put him under arrest in his Crimean holiday home, moved tanks into Moscow, and formed an emergency administration.

Their coup turned into a fiasco. They failed to arrest Yeltsin, who defied them from the Russian government building, the White House. His supporters flocked in their thousands to defend him: they included my two official drivers and my wife. Perhaps because Gorbachev had allowed them to think independently, the soldiers and secret policemen were divided among themselves. Unwilling to shed blood, they lost their nerve and withdrew the tanks.

Gorbachev returned to Moscow. But it was Yeltsin who won the game. Throughout the autumn he ruthlessly whittled away at Gorbachev's authority. He claimed until the last, perhaps genuinely, that he wanted some kind of Union to survive. But he had long been exploring—perhaps as a lever against Gorbachev—a draft treaty between the Slav republics, Russia, Ukraine, and Belarus. On December 8, 1991, without warning, he, the Ukrainian leader Kravchuk, and their Belarus colleague Shushkevich met to declare that the Soviet Union had ceased to exist. On Christmas Day 1991 Gorbachev resigned and we watched from the embassy window as the Soviet flag was replaced over the Kremlin by the flag of Russia.

Ironically, in attempting to preserve the Union the conspirators had accelerated its final collapse.

The End of Empire

Once the idea of national independence takes hold it is almost impossible to eliminate, as the British discovered in the last decades of their empire. Gorbachev's loosening of political constraints enabled the republics to express their discontent with Russian rule.

These trends were visible to domestic and foreign observers alike. Soon after my arrival I wrote myself a note: "We are witnessing the breakup of the last great European empire...The key could be the Ukraine. It has remained comparatively—and ominously—quiet so far. If it is now on the move, the consequences could be grim indeed."

Ukraine was slower off the mark than the Balts. But its eventual defection sealed the fate of the Soviet experiment. In autumn 1988 it was still run by Volodymyr Shcherbytsky, a hardline disciplinarian. Soon Gorbachev ejected him for someone more flexible. Before our eyes hitherto orthodox Ukrainian Communists began to shift their views. The foreign minister and the ideology secretary told a visiting British minister in January 1989 that Ukrainians wanted autonomy, but no more. But the nationalists with whom we dined that evening talked of outright independence.

That summer thousands of demonstrators carrying the Ukrainian national flag picketed the Supreme Soviet in Kiev and denounced the Party leadership. I asked Konstantin if it was a revolution or only a rebellion. The people are just getting into practice, he replied. In July 1989 the Supreme Soviet passed a Declaration on Ukrainian Sovereignty, for the time only symbolic.

In September 1990 we visited Lvov, in fiercely nationalist Western Ukraine. The nationalists had taken control. One of them asserted that an independent Ukraine would reject the unpleasant Ukrainian tradition of anti-Semitism. I was skeptical, but he was right. Ukraine now has a Jewish President and a Jewish Prime Minister.[7] The local communists, by contrast, were thoroughly demoralized, huddling in a couple of rooms that they had been allowed to keep in the palatial former Party Headquarters. At the end of October student demonstrators forced the resignation of the Ukrainian prime minister.

By March 1991 Kravchuk, the self-confident new Chairman of the Supreme Soviet, still claimed to favor the Union. But he and his colleagues were already determined that it should be their kind of Union, where the Republics controlled their own resources, and delegated only the most limited powers to the center.

After the failure of the coup against Gorbachev, the Ukrainians announced that their country would become independent in December 1991. Throughout that autumn they refused to cooperate in talks with Russia on long-term political and economic links. The Union was doomed.

Yeltsin had publicly supported the Balts during their struggles against Moscow, and he quickly recognized their sovereignty. Immediately after the coup he called in the European ambassadors to meet Lennart Meri, Estonia's new foreign minister and later its president. Meri and his family had been deported to Siberia in 1940, but survived. He told us with much emotion that he had always opposed the Soviet regime, but had never abandoned his admiration for the Russian people, whose sufferings he had shared and whose culture was an integral part of his life. It was a moving occasion and seemed like a good omen.

But Yeltsin's handling of Ukraine was more scratchy. The coup was barely over before the Russians started quarrelling with the Ukrainians—over Crimea, the disposal of the Black Sea fleet, the division of responsibility for Soviet debt. They threatened to raise frontier issues. The Ukrainians accused them of old-fashioned imperialism. Yeltsin sent his people to Kiev to soothe things down: but he himself was making similar remarks in private.

Our Russian friends were increasingly distressed. Gorbachev's diplomatic adviser Anatoly Chernyaev, wise and liberal, told me that though Russia might be going through a bad time, the reality was that in a decade or so, Russia would reassert itself as the dominant force in its own huge geopolitical area. If the Ukrainians were too provocative—over Crimea for example—Yeltsin (whom Chernyaev did not admire) would have to assert Russia's position, perhaps even with force. As a Russian, Chernyaev could not imagine a future in which Ukraine and Russia were separated.

Chernyaev's feelings were widely shared. Gorbachev, Yeltsin and the Kazakh leader Nazarbaev all said in private that they believed something like the Union would eventually be reconstituted. One acquaintance said that the breakup of the Union profaned a thousand years of Russian history: no Russian could accept it. Others repeated an entrenched Russian view that the Ukrainians and their language were merely a peasant version of Russian. The Russian parliament condemned the cession of the Crimea by Khrushchev to Ukraine in 1954 as unconstitutional. A young couple told us they strongly agreed: Crimea had always belonged to the Russians, or perhaps to the Tatars, but never to the Ukrainians. In early January I warned the Prime Minister's office in London—with deliberate exaggeration, to make a point—that war between Russia and Ukraine was not impossible.

The conflict between Russia and Ukraine that blew up two decades later had very deep roots.

II. The Charm of Hindsight

Despite the passage of time and the accumulation of new documentary material, there is still no consensus on the reasons for the Soviet collapse. Was the collapse inevitable? Could it have been averted by a more competent or ruthless Soviet government? How far was it the result of intense political and economic pressure from the Americans? Could better Western policy have eased Russia's path into the "Western" community, or were the later antagonisms between Russia and the West unavoidable?

Some argue that the Soviet Union could have staggered on, perhaps for decades. Others argue that the collapse was foreseeable and foreseen. Despite her reputation as an Iron Lady, Margaret Thatcher was one of those who believed that the Soviet Union's days were numbered.[8] One reason for Western failure to foresee the collapse was the systematic tendency of Western intelligence estimates to exaggerate the military and economic prowess of the Soviet Union, its stability, and the aggressive intentions of its leaders. Few, including myself, foresaw the timing of the collapse when it finally came.[9]

Such questions will never be finally resolved. We are, after all, still arguing about the reasons for the decline and fall of the Roman Empire.

Western Policy

The negotiations between the West and the Soviet Union in its last five years were not exchanges between equals. By the early 1980s the Soviet Union was suffering from imperial overstretch, domestic decay, and technical backwardness even in the military sphere, while its arch-rival, the United States, was richer and politically more resilient, had more powerful and widely-flung military forces, and an array of cooperative allies. Marshall Ogarkov, the Soviet Chief of Staff, lamented, "We cannot equal the quality of US arms for a generation or two. Modern military power is based on technology ... we will never be able to catch up ... until we have an economic revolution. And the question is whether we have an economic revolution without a political revolution."[10]

On the Western side the negotiations were driven by the Americans and the Germans, whose interests were directly involved. The British and the French played a lesser part, though they influenced the discussions within the Western alliance. Margaret Thatcher's role has been somewhat exaggerated in British myth. But she took a well-informed interest in Soviet affairs even before she became Prime Minister, she was very active in supporting dissidents in Eastern Europe and the Soviet Union throughout the 1980s, she was one of the first to recognize that Gorbachev was an unprecedented factor in Soviet politics, and she was important as a link between Moscow and Washington at times when they were failing to communicate. Indeed, she developed something of an attachment to Gorbachev the man. In autumn 1988 George Bush Senior and Michael Dukakis were contending for the presidency of the United States. When I called on Margaret Thatcher that September before leaving for Moscow as ambassador, she remarked, "If Dukakis wins the election, Gorbachev will be my only friend left." Her international influence declined after 1989, partly because of her politically illiterate opposition to German reunification. But she remained an active supporter of Gorbachev and his project even after she left office.[11]

President Reagan, too, recognized Gorbachev's quality early on. After being a vocal and effective opponent of Soviet policy, he underwent an epiphany in the winter of 1983-84. He realized that the Russians really were afraid of American aggression and that the nuclear confrontation was intolerably dangerous. Helped by Margaret Thatcher's perceptions, and perhaps by the first-hand insights of Oleg Gordievsky, a Soviet double agent who had been working for the British, he concluded that something needed to be done, and that Gorbachev was the man with whom he could do it.[12]

But others in Washington and London saw Gorbachev as merely a more cunning version of his predecessors, not to be trusted. In December 1988 Gorbachev announced to the United Nations that the Soviet Union would withdraw a significant number of its troops from Eastern Europe, including six tank divisions and assault bridging units which had particularly worried the Western military. It was stunning evidence of his willingness to move. But it was initially dismissed as just another communist trick by senior security advisers to the incoming President, George H. W. Bush, such as Brent Scowcroft and Robert Gates.[13] As late as April 1989 the CIA judged that the Soviet Union would be the main threat to American security for the next two decades.[14]

Such attitudes led to a temporary but damaging hiccup in the relationship between Russia and America. The new President suspected Reagan might have gone too far in his relationship with Gorbachev.[15] On taking office in January 1989 he imposed a pause to allow for a thorough policy review. By April, Gorbachev's diplomatic adviser Anatoly Chernyaev told me that his boss was deeply worried about the prolonged silence from Washington. He was comforted by the knowledge that Margaret Thatcher, at least, genuinely wanted Gorbachev to succeed and was prepared to say so in pubic.

The relationship between Bush and Gorbachev recovered. At their summit meeting in Malta in December 1989 they developed a spirit of cooperation which enabled them to negotiate effectively on the central issues of arms control and German reunification.

Reagan and his successors naturally pursued America's interests relentlessly. They also genuinely tried to spare Russian susceptibilities and help Russia become a cooperative member of the world community, peaceful and prosperous.

But after the Soviet Union had collapsed Bush sounded a damaging note of triumphalism in his State of the Nation speech January 1992: "By the grace of God, America won the cold war.... A world once divided into two armed camps now recognizes one sole and preeminent power, the United States of America. Bill Clinton, who later developed a close relationship with Boris Yeltsin, also misspoke himself from time to time. At a meeting in the Hague in 2014, Obama slightingly called Russia a mere regional power.[16] Such incidents may seem comparatively trivial to outsiders. But they helped to feed a settled belief among many Russians that, whatever they claimed to the contrary, the Americans aimed to diminish or even destroy their country. Whether the feelings were justified or not is barely relevant: as always, they fed the politics.

German Reunification and NATO Enlargement

The Americans and the Germans led the negotiations over German reunification with tact, though the Germans occasionally irritated their allies by dealing directly with the Soviet Union: naturally enough, since their interest was by far the greatest. The Americans were determined that a reunited Germany should become a full member of NATO, an ambitious goal. Soviet officials warned us that ordinary Russians remembered the German invasion and would turn against Gorbachev and his reforms. But ordinary Russians to whom we talked, such as my driver Sasha, saw nothing odd about Germans coming together half a century after the end of the war. In August 1990 two cheerful Russian lorry drivers in Weimar—still part of East Germany—told us that they had been living there for four years. Life in East Germany had been pleasant enough: but it would get a lot better now that the locals would have a chance to get themselves organized.

Agreement was reached in September 1990, after a last-minute row over wording about the deployment of Allied forces into former East Germany. Some German officials concluded that Margaret Thatcher, unhappy at the prospect of German reunification, had given their British colleague private instructions to disrupt the treaty. The evidence is slight.[17]

This was the beginning of the subsequent bitterness over NATO enlargement. During the negotiations for reunification and later the Russians were given vague oral assurances by senior Western leaders that NATO would not enlarge. Gorbachev's Russian critics accuse him of feebly failing to get a written commitment.

The record of who said what to whom is well documented.[18] The Russians got no commitment in writing, and have never claimed otherwise. Although Gorbachev's critics say it was weak of him not to insist, the Western allies would never have agreed to bind their hands formally for the future.

But ambiguous things were said by Western politicians, both in private and in public. During the negotiation of the agreement on German reunification some constructive ambiguity was perhaps inevitable. Afterwards the need to jolly the Russians along was less pressing. By the end of 1990 the President of newly independent Czechoslovakia was already arguing strongly for enlargement. I was present when, in response to a question, the British Prime Minister reassured his Soviet interlocutors in the spring of 1991 that there was no intention of enlarging NATO. That statement was true at the time it was made.

Still, it is not surprising that the Russians were upset when Western intentions changed in the mid-1990s and the enlargement process began. Their decades-old ambition to create a pan-European security system in which they would be equal members was rebuffed. Attempts to mollify them by offering forms of association with NATO that fell short of full membership were unsuccessful.

They were equally disconcerted by NATO's bombing of Serbia in 1999, which they saw as an illegal attack on a small sovereign European country, not sanctioned by the United Nations nor justified by Serbian ethnic cleansing of Kosovo (Legal advisers in major European foreign ministries were also uneasy about the legal justification for the bombing).[19] They worried that their own country might be next. They were not soothed by the subsequent Western air campaigns in Iraq and Afghanistan.

Some in the West believe that no assurances were given, and that Yeltsin at least acquiesced in the enlargement. They argue that the Russian reaction has been artificially stoked up by Russia's leaders for their own purposes. Here too the record is clear enough. Yeltsin was erratic and inconsistent. On a visit to Poland in 1993 he did indeed say that he understood Poland's desire to join NATO.[20] But he drew back. He warned Clinton that Russia would be humiliated by the expansion of NATO, and asked him to hold back from bombing Serbia, commenting prophetically that "our people certainly from now have a bad attitude with regard to America and with NATO." That is indeed what happened in the event.

NATO enlargement and the events surrounding it inevitably colored subsequent Russian policy making. Enlargement was, however, all but inevitable. The veteran American diplomat George Kennan and others predicted serious damage to Russia's reform effort and to its relations with the West. But NATO countries, for reasons of domestic politics as well as international policy, could hardly refuse membership to newly independent Eastern European countries who still feared Russian aggression, fears that were reinforced by subsequent Russian bullying of the Baltic states and attacks on Georgia and Ukraine.

Aftermath

The dramatic events in Moscow and elsewhere in 1988-91 showed that Russians were well able to take to the streets in pursuit of political objectives. They did not need the later "color revolutions" in Tbilisi and Kiev to show them the way. But like previous Russian leaders, Putin feared what Pushkin had called the mindless and pitiless Russian mob[21] He remembered the lesson and mixed carrots and sticks to ensure that no color revolution took place in Moscow.

The Soviet collapse was followed by a decade of economic misery and political dysfunction. Western experts with ill-adapted theories and little practical experience showered the Russians with inadequate advice about how to dismantle a Communist economy of continental scale. People later wondered why Poland was able to manage economic change fairly smoothly, while Russia was not. The answer lies partly in Russia's vastly greater size, its lack of any recent free market experience, and the fact that the communist system in Russia was imposed by the Russians on themselves, whereas in Poland it was a comparatively recent alien import, more easily disentangled and jettisoned.

The net result was that many Russians became deeply suspicious of Western democratic and economic ideas, convinced that their country had been brought low not by its own weaknesses, but by the intrigues of domestic traitors and foreign spies.

The sense of humiliation over NATO enlargement and resentment over Ukrainian independence were reignited when NATO suggested that Ukraine should join NATO. Among the motives which led Putin to annex Crimea and destabilize eastern Ukraine was the prospect that Sevastopol, a major Russian naval base with a glorious place in Russian history and sentiment, might find itself on NATO territory.

Putin's action was condemned in the West as illegal and it cast an inevitable chill. Russia's vulnerable neighbors concluded that its intentions were as malign as ever. NATO deployed troops to support its eastern members. Europe and America imposed sanctions. Russia and its friends accused the West of double standards and provocative overreaction. But if Putin's advisers had not warned him of the likely Western response, they were not doing their job.

Russia today is attempting with some success to reassert its place in a world increasingly dominated by more powerful competitors. Russia's geographical size and position, the determined ingenuity and resilience of its people, and the growing sophistication of its armed forces are obvious and continuing assets. Its comparatively small population and economy are not.

Gorbachev: An Assessment

Gorbachev has been criticized for excessive caution, for lacking a strategy, and for letting himself be out-negotiated by the West. But he faced an unprecedented task: to reform a complex and authoritarian politico-economic structure in the grip of a deep crisis, while negotiating an equitable deal with a superpower rival which held many of the cards. He himself argued that there could be no simple blueprint for rejuvenating the Soviet system. Instead he claimed to set out broader strategic lines which pointed in the right direction.

No one has come up with convincing alternatives. Doing nothing was no answer. Disarray within the system had probably already gone too far to permit a disciplined "Chinese" alternative—tight one-party control over a new kind of state-dominated capitalism. An attempt to preserve the Warsaw Pact and hold the Union together by force was probably well beyond the Soviet government's strength, and would have risked civil war and an international conflagration.

Gorbachev made many mistakes. But his record is defensible. Future generations may judge him more kindly.

The Geopolitical Catastrophe

As the Soviet Union collapsed, we in the Moscow embassy wondered if feelings of humiliation among the Russians could lead to the rise of a revanchist right-wing regime, as it had in Germany after Versailles. Would such a regime exploit the Russian minorities who now found themselves living abroad, as Hitler had exploited the Sudeten Germans? It did not seem impossible, though we hoped otherwise.

In subsequent years a controversy has arisen in the West: did the Russians have legitimate grounds for their sense of humiliation, or were they being manipulated by the government for its own domestic and international political purposes? Commentators especially picked up on Putin's remark in 2005 to parliament that "[T]he collapse of the Soviet Union was a [or the] major geopolitical disaster of the century."[22] Despite his failure to mention other even greater geopolitical catastrophes, such as Hitler's aggression and the Holocaust, Putin was not calling for a return to Stalinism. Indeed, he subsequently remarked to German television: "People in Russia say that those who do not regret the collapse of the Soviet Union have no heart, and those that do regret it have no brain.[23]

But the events Putin went on to list—the loss almost overnight of the Soviet Union's international position, the collapse of the country's institutions and its military, economic and social welfare systems, the impoverishment, the unemployment, and in some cases the near famine—were real enough. However the Russian government may subsequently have exploited them, the events surrounding the end of the Soviet Union were indeed perceived as a humiliation even by our Russian friends who had always been opposed to Communism.

Many Russians have retreated into a defiant nationalism. They exalt Stalin and strong leadership, though few would like to see the reconstitution of the Gulag. But there is no reason to think that their current political system, however much one may dislike it, will lurch towards the excesses of full-blown Nazism or Stalinism.

The Matter of Democracy: A Misplaced Optimism?

On leaving Moscow in May 1992, I wrote: "I do not think it is an act of mindless optimism to look forward to a future in which Russia has developed its own form of democracy, no doubt imperfect unlike those which have sprung up elsewhere, but still a vast improvement on what has gone before.[24]

Today that may look incautious. Some—Russians as well as foreigners—argue that democracy is not the Russian way, that reform in Russia has always failed, that Russia has authoritarianism and empire "in its genes." That is pseudo-science. Countries are indeed conditioned by their geography and history. But they also respond to circumstance. Genes have nothing to do with it.

When the Soviet Union collapsed, Russians hoped that they could now live in what they called a "normal" country, a hope many of us shared. Russia has indeed become open and prosperous as never before. But it has returned to a form of authoritarianism, and is again at odds with the West, with opportunities missed on both sides. It seems unlikely that Russians will soon look to the West for a model. The possibility of "normality"—to be defined by the Russians themselves, not by foreigners—nevertheless remains. Other countries have successfully tackled an unpromising legacy. There is no compelling reason why Russia should not do so too.[25]

Notes

1. Sakharov's letter is in Stephen F. Cohen, ed., *An End to Silence: Uncensored Opinion in the Soviet Union* (New York: W.W. Norton, 1984). See also Rodric Braithwaite, *Across the Moscow River: The World Turned Upside Down* (New Haven: Yale University Press, 2002), p.128.

2. Braithwaite R, Telegram to London, Monday, 27 March 1989.

3. According to the Norwegian ambassador in Moscow (diary entry 24 February, 1992).

4. *Nezavisimaya Gazeta*, Moscow, April 2, 1992.

5. I take these details from memory. But there is plenty of supporting evidence in contemporary newspapers and memoirs.

6. My embassy colleagues travelled regularly to the Baltic states to keep in touch with the opposition leaders, and Baltic politicians regularly met British ministers in our embassy in Moscow. But for legal reasons I was unable to visit the Baltic states myself, because we did not recognize the Soviet annexation of 1940. That changed once the Baltic states regained their independence in late 1991.

7. According to a recent Pew Research Center survey Ukraine is the least anti-Semitic country in East Europe and the former Soviet Union. The most anti-Semitic is Armenia.

8. Thatcher's views about the likely collapse of the Soviet Union are briefly described in Rodric Braithwaite, "Gorbachev and Thatcher," in I. Poggiolini and A Pravda, eds., *Journal of European Integration History*, vol. 16, no 1, 2010.

9. I discuss the reasons why Western intelligence analysts systematically overestimated Soviet capabilities in "Chapter 9: Know your Enemy," in Rodric Braithwaite, *Armageddon and Paranoia: The Nuclear Confrontation* (London: Profile Books, 2017).

10. V. Zubok, *A Failed Empire* (Chapel Hill, NC: University of North Carolina Press, 2007, pp. 277, 30).

11. Braithwaite, *Gorbachev and Thatcher*, op. cit.

12. Ibid.

13. Scowcroft was the President's National Security Adviser from January 1989 to January 1993. Gates was Deputy Director of the CIA from 1986 until March 1989, and then Deputy National Security Adviser.

14. US Government National Intelligence Estimate, April 1989, Cold War International History Project, at https://chnm.gmu.edu/1989/ items/ show/349.

15. Braithwaite, *Gorbachev and Thatcher*, op. cit.

16. *The Guardian*, March 25, 2014, at https://www.theguardian.com/ world/2014/mar/25/barack-obama-russia-regional-power-ukraine-weakness

17. Klaus-Rainer Jackisch, "An einem runden Tisch mit scharfen Ecken," Deutschlandfunk, October 3, 2005, https://www.deutschlandfunk.de/an-ei-nem-runden-tisch-mit-scharfen-ecken.724.de.html?dram:article_id=98285. John Weston, the British official, gives his version at pp. 466-471 of the volume of British documents on German Unification 1989-1990, P. Salmon, ed., London 2012.

18. Rodric Braithwaite, "NATO enlargement: Assurances and Misunderstandings," European Council on Foreign Relations, July 7, 2016; "NATO Expansion: What Yeltsin Heard," National Security Archive Briefing Book #621, Washington, DC, March 16, 2018; "The Clinton-Yeltsin Relationship in Their Own Words," National Security Archive Briefing Book #640, Washington, DC, October 2, 2018; William J. Burns, *The Back Channel* (London: PenguinRandomHouse, 2019) pp. 91-2, 105-8.

19. Private information.

20. *New York Times*, August 26, 1993.

21. From Pushkin's short novel *The Captain's Daughter*, which all Russians have read.

22. Since Russian lacks the definite and indefinite articles the original can be translated both ways. The Russian text is at http://www.kremlin.ru/acts/ bank/36354.

23. Interview with German television channel ARD and ZDF, May 5, 2005. English text at http://en.kremlin.ru/events/president/transcripts/22948.

24. Braithwaite R, Despatch to FCO, "The Obsession with Russia," May 17, 1992.

25. I have used a version of these two final paragraphs in a review of *The Russia Anxiety* by Mark Smith (to be published London July 2019) in the London-based journal *History Today*.

Chapter 5

The End of the Cold War:
A View From the Trenches

Roderic Lyne

I was an intermittent foot-soldier in the vast army of Western officials dealing with the Cold War and its aftermath. Many fine treatises
have been written about the strategic dimensions and leading actors of
the Cold War. This is not such a treatise. It is simply the personal view
of an eyewitness who served for about twenty years in the trenches
between 1971 and 2004.

1989 and the Momentum of Change in Four Dimensions:
Perestroika, Politics, Nationalities, Eastern Europe

1989, Gorbachev's fifth year as leader, was when *perestroika* came to
a head. It was also the year when the forces of change which he had
unleashed, inside the USSR and the Warsaw Pact, ran away from him
and developed unstoppable momentum.

To a foreign diplomat or journalist, what was happening in Russia
was extraordinary and exciting. To Russians, it was extraordinary—and
to most rather frightening. Old certainties were disappearing. They
didn't know where their country was heading. Almost every day events
were occurring which they, and we, had not expected to see in our lifetimes. Let me start with a small example.

In March of 1989, my wife and I were in a Moscow theatre to see
a dramatized version of Yevgenia Ginzburg's account of her time in
the gulag, *Krutoi Marshrut*. Ginzburg's book had been published in the
West in 1967,[1] part of the *samizdat* literature seeping out of the Soviet Union. It had made a deep impression on me as an undergraduate
student.

A year earlier, Vladlen Dozortsev,[2] the editor of a small-circulation
monthly literary journal in Latvia called *Daugava*, had told me that he

was beginning to publish *Krutoi Marshrut* chapter by chapter to test how far he could get before the Soviet authorities stopped him. He wasn't stopped, and within a year the ice had melted to the point where this subversive work could be placed on public view in Moscow.

On the streets outside the theatre, the election campaign for the Congress of People's Deputies was in full swing: over four thousand candidates competing in 1500 constituencies in the first partially-free general election held in the Soviet Union (partially free, because a further 750 seats had been reserved for the Communist Party and affiliated organizations).

When the curtain fell at the interval, no one in the packed audience moved for some minutes. There was no applause. As we looked around, many of the audience were in tears, reliving the past experiences of their own families. The same happened at the end of the play. Because to admit that one's family had included an "enemy of the people" was taboo, few of those weeping had appreciated the extent to which others had shared their suffering, even years after Khrushchev's de-Stalinization.

The Soviet Union was to last for another 21 months, and few in that audience would have predicted its dissolution; but, if *Krutoi Marshrut* could be put on stage, and individuals could compete freely for election on differing platforms, there was no doubting the profundity of the change under way to the communist system.

*   *   *

The Soviet Union and the Warsaw Pact were held together by force. Gorbachev removed the force. He never intended to dismantle the USSR and the Warsaw Treaty organization, but he aspired to change them into voluntary organizations which would work more effectively by consensus and the rule of law than through coercion.

1989 was both the peak of Gorbachev's achievements as a reformer and also the point where he became mired in his own contradictions.

Within the Soviet Union, overlapping battles were being fought over the economy, democratization, and the relationships between the constituent parts of the Union. On the USSR's periphery, communist rule and Soviet hegemony were coming into question. Merely to keep abreast of these four dimensions as an observer was demanding; to lead and control them, as Gorbachev was trying to do with a relatively small team, turned out to be almost impossible.[3]

It was the failure of the Soviet economy which had induced the Politburo to elect Gorbachev, desperately hoping that a young and dynamic leader could turn it around. A neon slogan on a power station by the Moscow River used to proclaim, quoting Lenin,[4] that "Communism is Soviet power plus the electrification of the whole country." The electrification of this vast territory had indeed been a huge achievement. But the most significant achievement of communism was to bankrupt a country with by far the world's largest stock of natural resources and, most importantly, a country with exceptional human resources and talent—in all areas of science and technology, in culture and the arts.

On my first visit to the Soviet Union in 1961, I stood on Gorky Street to watch the triumphal return of the second cosmonaut, German Titov. I admired Moscow's historic and grandiose architecture and exploited its fine public transport system. I also queued for the most basic foodstuffs; observed people who almost universally were poorly clothed and badly fed; and peered into communal housing and ramshackle hovels where families lived, often three generations to a room. In the villages outside, living standards were even lower. It did not take an economist to see that the command economy wasn't working. When I returned in the 1970s and 1980s, there were marginal improvements, particularly in housing, but Russia's living standards had fallen even further behind the developed world. The USSR's civilian needs were being sacrificed to the gargantuan demands of its military machine.

Gorbachev was the only Soviet leader to tell his people the truth about the economy: their socialist state was not catching up with the West. As more Western images seeped into the country, the message was reinforced in unexpected ways. A live TV debate screened with a British independent channel featured advertisements for succulent meat and gravy marketed as dog food; a Soviet film intended to highlight Western decadence showed a Russian girl, lured into prostitution in Sweden, driving in a smart car to a supermarket laden with goods unseen in her own country. These small insights had a riveting effect.

Gorbachev's initial approach was to try to modernize and "accelerate" the command economy, rather than to attempt radical restructuring: "For some time we indeed hoped to overcome stagnation by relying on such 'advantages of Socialism' as planned mobilisation of reserve capacities, organisational work, and evoking conscientiousness and a more active attitude from the workers."[5] He then tinkered at the edges with small experiments in private enterprise, such as "cooperative" restaurants. As a lifelong socialist, however, he could not bring himself to make the big leap into private property and market economics advocated by his more liberal advisers. His critics complained that he was trying to cross an abyss in small steps.

Democratization became the second dimension of Gorbachev's struggle. From the outset he had encouraged greater openness through *glasnost*. The resistance that Gorbachev encountered to economic reforms, however, convinced him of the need for more fundamental changes to dismantle the top-down command system. He came to recognize that economic, political and constitutional reforms were inseparably linked.[6]

In the summer and autumn of 1988 Gorbachev fought his way through the 19th CPSU Conference and past heavy opposition from the Party's old guard to secure agreement for a reconstructed Supreme Soviet, to be chosen by an elected Congress of People's Deputies.

In 1989 Gorbachev's experiment with democracy was put into operation. Beginning with the selection of candidates for the Congress of People's Deputies in January, moving into elections in March and April, and sessions of the Congress of People's Deputies and the reformed Supreme Soviet from May to December, the experiment ran through the year and effectively beyond the President's control, breaching (although not yet breaking) the Communist Party's monopoly of power.

As with his economic reforms, Gorbachev was not able to make the final leap. He had alienated much of the Communist Party, from which some of his key advisers were departing. He had allowed Boris Yeltsin back into the political arena, making the running with non-communists such as Andrei Sakharov (until his death in December 1989). But the Party was still Gorbachev's political base, and he dared not leave or demolish it: "I can't let this lousy, rabid dog off the leash. If I do that, all this huge structure will be turned against me."[7]

The third dimension of internal change was what used to be called "the nationalities question." The coexistence within one country of over a hundred national and ethnic groups had theoretically been resolved with the establishment of the Soviet Union in 1922 as a purportedly federal state, enlarged in 1939 with the annexation of the three Baltic states. Stalin had used extreme force to suppress dissenting national groups, including forced deportations. From the West, it was hard to assess the extent of ethnic tensions within the USSR, not least because 90% of Soviet territory was off limits to foreigners and visits to the other 10% were tightly controlled by the organs of security. We were aware of the deep longing of the Balts for the return of their freedom, but the superficial appearance was that the other nationalities incorporated for far longer in the Soviet and Russian empires had settled for their lot and in some cases were benefiting from it. That said, I recall a perceptive analysis written in the late 1970s by an expert in the Foreign Office's Research Department[8] which argued that the nationalities question could boil over if the Stalinist lid was ever lifted off the saucepan.

Starting in 1987, steam was escaping from the saucepan. Protests grew in the Baltic states, Ukraine and Georgia, and conflict between Armenians and Azeris erupted in Nagorno-Karabakh in February 1988. By the end of 1988, Popular Front movements had been established in each of the Baltic republics, and a campaign for independence was also under way in Georgia. In April 1989 Soviet troops, acting in panic and under local command, killed two dozen unarmed demonstrators in the Georgian capital. Early that year, Rukh, which was to develop as an independence movement, was founded in Ukraine.

Gorbachev was slow to appreciate the risk of nationalist unrest. He sought to conciliate the nationalities, not coerce them. Anatoly Chernyaev has recorded Gorbachev's (remarkable) conclusions following a Politburo discussion of the Baltic states in May 1989: "we have to learn to communicate with them ... If we hold a referendum, not one of the three republics, even Lithuania, will walk out. What we need to do is bring Popular Front leaders into government, give them positions in the administration ... in general we must keep thinking how to transform our federation or else everything will really fall apart ... Use of force is out of the question."[9]

In September Gorbachev told Thatcher that a Plenum of the CPSU had decided to "create mechanisms...to remove tensions from inter-ethnic relations without interfering with the basic interests of individuals, nationalities, and society in the economic, cultural and other spheres. Otherwise inter-ethnic tensions could bury *perestroika*."[10]

Once again, the processes he had facilitated ran beyond Gorbachev's ability to direct them. In regional elections in 1990, the CPSU lost control of six Union Republics—the three Baltic republics, Armenia, Georgia and Moldova. Lithuania and Estonia declared independence in March and Latvia in May. All six republics boycotted the referendum of March 1991 to approve Gorbachev's new Union Treaty, designed to consolidate the Soviet Union as a looser, voluntary federation. By September, after the failed coup in Moscow, the Baltic states had achieved internationally recognized independence and membership in the UN; and in December a referendum in Ukraine produced a majority for independence in every region, including Crimea. The pot had boiled over. Nationalist movements had buried not just *perestroika*, but the Soviet Union.

The developments on the USSR's periphery that we were observing from Moscow from 1989 were a no less dramatic fourth dimension.

The year began—optimistically—with the end of the Soviet Union's ill-fated military involvement in Afghanistan (although President Najibullah's Soviet-backed regime hung on until April 1992, outliving the USSR). General Gromov led the last troops out on February 15, 1989. Gorbachev (as we have since learned) had resisted pressure to deploy a fresh brigade in January, and then to mount air strikes in March, in breach of the 1988 Geneva accords. Chernyaev records him as arguing that "I won't permit anyone to trample the promise we made in front of the whole world."[11]

The invasion of Afghanistan had been recognized as a strategic error. The view from Moscow towards Central and Eastern Europe was different. These were countries integrated militarily and economically into the Soviet bloc. Soviet control was expensive to maintain, but seen as vital to strategic defence. We had watched Soviet tanks crush Hungary in 1956 and Czechoslovakia in 1968.

Nonetheless, in his speech to the UN of December 1988, Gorbachev announced that the USSR would withdraw six armored divisions from the GDR, Czechoslovakia and Hungary by 1991. He stressed freedom of choice and refraining from the use of force in international affairs. Both his message and his rhetoric differed sharply from Soviet orthodoxy, and were rightly acclaimed.

Three months later Gorbachev set out the principles of relations with socialist countries as "unconditional independence, full equality, strict non-interference in internal affairs, and rectification of deformities and mistakes linked with earlier periods in the history of socialism."[12] For all his fine words, we assumed that, whatever licence they were given in their internal affairs, the East Europeans would have to remain within the constraints of the Warsaw Treaty; and that the Soviet Union would retain its large military presence in the GDR and a tight grip on that country. I do not think that any of us in the Embassy would have conceived in December 1988 that within twelve months the Soviet leadership would have allowed Communist regimes to collapse throughout the Warsaw Pact area, the Berlin Wall to be breached and the Iron Curtain to be eroded.

Gorbachev's refusal to licence the use of force will stand eternally to his credit. It allowed new post-Communist leaders such as Lech Wałęsa in Poland and Václav Havel in Czechoslovakia to assume power peacefully and democratically. A small vignette: in early 1990, Havel visited Moscow as the new President of Czechoslovakia. The political counsellor at the Czechoslovak Embassy came to me in a panic to ask if the British could provide contact details for the reformers and ex-dissidents whom Havel was asking to meet. He also sought a crash course on how to report on the policies and internal affairs of the Soviet Union—previously off limits for Warsaw Pact diplomats.

The End of the Cold War—and of the Soviet Union

When Gorbachev came to power in 1985, there were few expectations in the West that he would make dramatic changes to the Soviet system[13] or the USSR's foreign policy. Fears were expressed that, by revitalizing the Soviet economy, he would make the Soviet Union a stronger opponent.

From 1987, this initial caution was progressively replaced in Western Europe by a desire to work with Gorbachev, notably on the part of
Margaret Thatcher and Helmut Kohl. The caution was reciprocated
on the Soviet side. Politicians, officials and generals in both East and
West were putting out feelers, but struggled to move beyond deeply
ingrained suspicions and the fear of being tricked.[14] Chernyaev records
that as late as Gorbachev's meeting with Thatcher in April 1989 he was
striving to convince a skeptical Gorbachev that "Thatcher was genuinely well-meaning toward us" and helping *perestroika*, notwithstanding
years of hostility between the UK and the USSR.[15]

Ronald Reagan had followed a similar course, reviving détente and
arms control negotiations through five summit meetings with Gorbachev between 1985 and 1988; but the U.S./Soviet relationship went
cold when George H. W. Bush succeeded Reagan in January 1989.
Bush's closest advisers had reverted to the idea that Gorbachev was
potentially more dangerous than his predecessors and persuaded the
President to hold off meeting Gorbachev while the U.S. administration reassessed its policy. Bush changed his view in mid-year and met
Gorbachev on a ship off Malta in December 1989, less than one month
after the fall of the Berlin Wall. Gorbachev told Bush that the USSR
was ready to cease considering the United States as an enemy; Bush
assured Gorbachev of his support for *perestroika* and readiness to give
concrete assistance.

This effectively brought Bush into line with the Western Europeans.
The West would support Gorbachev. So long as he could maintain his
position and hold off his hard-line opponents, the Cold War was over.
A great deal of work remained to be done to implement this funda-
mental realignment of relations and, especially, to resolve the status of
Germany and its relationship to NATO; but, by September 1990, the
Two Plus Four Treaty had been signed, leading to the reunification of
Germany on October 3, 1990. The six remaining Warsaw Pact states
declared the end of their alliance in February 1991, and it was formally dissolved on July 1. The final chapter saw the discrediting of the
Communist Party and the KGB in the failed coup of August 1991, the
supplanting of Gorbachev by Yeltsin from his power base as President
of the Russian Republic, and the dissolution of the Soviet Union in
December.

My account has focused heavily on Gorbachev and events within the Soviet Union because the ending of the Cold War was a by-product rather than the central purpose of the upheaval in the USSR. The Cold War ended because of the unravelling of a system, an ideology and an empire. The West claimed "victory" (President George H. W. Bush declared, "It's a victory for the moral force of our values. Every American can take pride in this victory"[16]), but it was the peoples of the Soviet Union and the Warsaw Pact countries who ended the Cold War by overthrowing Communism. That the Cold War ended when it did, and how it did, was due, not to Ronald Reagan, but to Mikhail Gorbachev, and to the legacy of the failing system which he inherited and tried to reform.

Gorbachev knew that the Soviet Union needed relief from the pressure of the superpower competition with the United States. He knew that it was becoming harder to sustain both the USSR's dominance of Eastern Europe, especially with Poland and the GDR becoming deeply indebted to Western lenders, and the Soviet ability to project power globally and subsidize allies such as Cuba. He therefore worked to achieve a more harmonious relationship with the West and to reduce armament levels, but by reinvigorating the economy he aspired to maintain the Soviet Union's status as a Great Power with a socialist model of development, protecting its zone of influence as the head of an alliance of neighbors. Had he achieved his vision of a "Common European Home," I believe it would have been on a basis of peaceful coexistence rather than full integration.

The Aftermath: Russia and the "West" Since 1991— Is the Cold War Really Over?

There is a myth, assiduously propagated and widely believed in Russia, that the West plotted the breakup of the Soviet Union, and then set out to humiliate, weaken and even dismember the Russian Federation through the 1990s and beyond.

Vladimir Putin has given voice to this sense of victimhood on many occasions, in progressively more direct terms, even to the extent of comparing the West to Hitler. In 2004 he complained that "It is far

from everyone in the world that wants to have to deal with an independent, strong and self-reliant Russia."[17] By 2007 he was claiming that

> Some, making skilful use of pseudo-democratic rhetoric, would
> like to return us to the recent past, some in order once again to
> plunder the nation's resources, and others in order to deprive our
> country of its economic and political independence. There has
> been an increasing influx of money from abroad being used to
> intervene directly in our internal affairs ... Some are not above
> using the dirtiest techniques, attempting to ignite inter-ethnic and
> inter-religious hatred in our multiethnic and democratic country.[18]

Announcing the annexation of Crimea in March 2014, Putin said
that: "the infamous policy of containment, led in the eighteenth, nineteenth and twentieth centuries, continues today. They are constantly
trying to sweep us into a corner." When the USSR had broken up,
Russia "was not simply robbed, it was plundered."[19]

In December of the same year, speaking of the 1990s and early
2000s, Putin declared that:

> the support for separatism in Russia from across the pond, includ-
> ing information, political and financial support provided by the
> special services, was absolutely obvious and left no doubt that they
> would gladly let Russia follow the Yugoslav scenario of disinte-
> gration and dismemberment ... It didn't work ... Just as it did not
> work for Hitler ... who set out to destroy Russia and push us back
> beyond the Urals.[20]

He later accused the West of controlling a whole series of "color
revolutions:" "the real masterminds were our American friends. They
helped train the nationalists, their armed groups, in Western Ukraine,
in Poland and to some extent in Lithuania. They facilitated the armed
coup."[21]

It was after the 2004 Beslan massacre, shockingly mishandled by
Russian security forces, that Putin (and his adviser Vladislav Surkov)
first made the ludicrous accusation that the West was supporting
Chechen terrorism. It has been repeated by Putin's close associate and
former colleague from the Leningrad KGB, General Nikolai Patrushev, Secretary of the Russian Security Council, who claimed that in
Chechnya, "extremists and their adherents were supported by the US

and British intelligence services, as well as allies in Europe and the Islamic world."[22] In the same interview, Patrushev asserted that the Soviet collapse had been the result of a plot by Zbigniew Brzezinski to undermine the economy and dismember Russia. In a press conference of December 2014 Putin declared: "After the fall of the Berlin Wall and the breakup of the Soviet Union, Russia opened itself to our partners. What did we see? A direct and fully-fledged support of terrorism in the North Caucasus. They directly supported terrorism ... this is an established fact."[23]

From a different angle, Russian liberals and some Western commentators have argued that the 1990s were a "lost opportunity for institutionalising cooperation" and that the chance should have been kept open for Russia to join the European Union and possibly also NATO.[24]

Did the West seek to precipitate and exploit the breakup of the Soviet Union? Did we try to sweep Russia into a corner?

My impression was the opposite. The overriding preoccupation of Western policy from 1989 onwards was to support (but not try to direct) a peaceful transition and minimize the huge potential risks to European and international stability from the Soviet collapse.

This was an argument used by Margaret Thatcher against the reunification of Germany when meeting Gorbachev in September 1989: "We do not want the unification of Germany. It would lead to changes in the post-war borders, and we cannot allow that because such a development would undermine the stability of the entire international situation and could lead to threats to our security. We are not interested in the destabilization of Eastern Europe or the dissolution of the Warsaw Treaty either."

Nor would we interfere in internal processes in Eastern Europe and spur decommunization. She added that President Bush had asked her to tell Gorbachev that "the United States would not undertake anything that could threaten the security interests of the Soviet Union, or that could be perceived by Soviet society as a threat."[25] Concern about the risks to stability led President Bush, like Margaret Thatcher, to support Gorbachev's proposed Union Treaty, providing for a decentralized federation combining "greater autonomy with greater voluntary interaction," in his much-criticised speech to the Ukrainian parliament on August 1, 1991.[26]

The Soviet collapse presented the West with a formidable list of headaches and challenges. First among them was to ensure that the USSR's vast arsenal, including some 35,000 nuclear weapons as well as stockpiles of chemical and biological weapons, remained under secure control, and that Soviet adherence to arms limitation and non-proliferation agreements was maintained. This was a prime reason for accepting the Russian Federation as the legal successor state to the USSR and for transferring the USSR's seat at the UN and Permanent Membership of the UN Security Council directly to Russia (whereas the other new states emerging from the Union, except for Ukraine and Belarus, were required to apply for membership). Negotiations then took place to arrange the transfer of nuclear weapons to Russia from Ukraine, Kazakhstan and Belarus, culminating in the Budapest Memorandum of December 1994 in which security guarantees were given to these three states by Russia, the United States and the UK. The United States provided practical and financial assistance in the dismantling of stockpiles under the Cooperative Threat Reduction Act (better known as the Nunn-Lugar program) which widened into a multinational initiative under the G7, and which lasted until 2015. By 1997 the United States had sent 33,000 fissile material containers to Russia. The G7 program contributed around a billion dollars to the construction of a plant in the Urals to decommission chemical weapon agents.

Control of weaponry, however, was only one element of a daunting agenda confronting Western policy-makers as the Soviet Union dissolved. Russia was reeling from the loss of nearly half of the USSR's population. The Russian economy was in deep distress as shock therapy was applied to make the transfer from socialism to the market. In 1992 inflation in Russia reached an annual rate of 2,300%. Fourteen other new states, with a combined 140 million people, had emerged as independent, self-governing entities—with no preparation, ill-defined borders, interdependent economies and security arrangements, mixed populations, and (with the exception of the Baltic states) little recent history of nationhood. There were fears of regional conflict and mass migration across the European continent. In Central and Eastern Europe, six former members of the Warsaw Pact and CMEA comprising 110 million people, with a stronger history of nationhood, were struggling to convert and develop their economies and establish sustainable democracies. While their transformation was remarkably peaceful, in the former Yugoslavia Serbia, Croatia and Bosnia were at war for the first half of the decade. Coping with war in the Balkans became the top priority for European governments and NATO, diluting their attention to developments to the East.

The resources of Western governments, the EU, NATO, the UN (especially in Bosnia) and other multinational organizations were stretched to the utmost. As the head of the Foreign Office department dealing with the former Soviet Union, I was constantly asked to submit briefings on different possible scenarios. Our most optimistic projection was that somehow the region would "muddle through" without a major catastrophe. I recall the Director for Defence and Intelligence looking at one of my papers and saying that the only answer was to get under the bedcovers with a bottle of whisky.

As it turned out, the former Soviet empire did better than to muddle through the aftermath of the Cold War. However imperfect and variable the process and the results, all of these states began to function, and—except in the former Yugoslavia—with very low levels of conflict. The primary actors were the peoples of the countries themselves, but very substantial help was given from outside—by the EU, the IMF, the IBRD, the EBRD, and national governments, including through technical assistance programs. As late as 2003, my own government was spending around £50 million a year on technical assistance programs in Russia ranging from educational reform, regional administration, agricultural development, combating HIV/AIDs and tuberculosis to the retraining of military officers for civilian life (under the latter program we assisted some twenty thousand officers to find new careers).

None of this—and a thousand more examples could be quoted, especially of the efforts made by Western companies to build cooperation and investment in Russia—supports the narrative that the West's objective was to weaken, undermine and isolate Russia. Russian attitudes to Western help were ambivalent. As the progeny of a Great Power, the Russian people did not want to be in receipt of charity or to be patronized, but in every sector they were keen to form partnerships and to absorb modern practices previously denied to them. They were eager to attract foreign investment: in Putin's words, "Russia is extremely interested in a major inflow of private, including foreign, investment. This is our strategic choice and strategic approach."[27]

Some have argued that the West should have done yet more to help Russia (for example, that the inherited Soviet debts should have been wiped off the slate), but that is a different point.

What about the argument that we could and should have gone further to integrate Russia into Western structures in the 1990s? This was not a question of will so much as one of feasibility.

The Group of Seven (G7), being not an organization but a club with an annual meeting, had the flexibility to start inviting, first Gorbachev (to the 1991 London Summit) and then Yeltsin to sessions tacked onto its meetings. Putin pressed for full membership, although Russia was not one of the world's eight largest economies; it was granted when Washington wished to reward him for support over Afghanistan after 9/11.

The European Union, as an organization tightly defined by treaty and its "acquis," had less flexibility. It was able, with some difficulty then and now, to incorporate former members of Comecon because of their size (Poland being the largest, at 38 million), because their economies could be turned around fairly rapidly with substantial EU help, because they established acceptable standards of democracy and the rule of law (from which there has been some backsliding), and because they were keen to accept the conditions of membership. None of these factors applied to Russia. Russia has never sought EU membership. It is inconceivable that Russia would buy into the acquis or accept subordination to qualified majority voting even if it reached the point of meeting the economic and democratic criteria for membership. The EU therefore adopted the approach of seeking to build cooperation with Russia progressively in as many areas as possible (articulated, for example, in the Partnership and Cooperation Agreement of 1997 and the "Road Maps for the Four Common Spaces" of 2005), against the declared and ambitious objective of trying to create a strategic partnership.[28] Until Russia and the EU found themselves in conflict over Ukraine, the Russian government did not treat the enlargement of the EU as hostile or threatening to its interests. In 2004, Putin spoke positively of the accession to the EU of the three Baltic states and four former Warsaw Pact members (Poland, Hungary, the Czech Republic and Slovakia): "The expansion of the European Union should not just bring us closer geographically, but also economically and spiritually … This means new markets and new investment. Generally it means new possibilities for the future of Greater Europe."[29]

Much ink has been expended on the question of who said what to whom about the future of NATO in the frantic times leading up to the end of the Soviet Union. These semantic debates seem to me to miss the three central points.

First, Russia has never asked to join NATO or shown any serious desire to do so;[30] is not within sight of meeting the criteria; could not, hypothetically, adapt its armed forces to the requirements of the Alliance within decades; and would not accept the pooling of sovereignty and subordination to NATO command, but would insist on the power of veto over NATO decisions.

Second, far from seeking to provoke, "encircle" or threaten Russia, NATO sought to implement enlargement in a cautious and deliberate way which would not destabilize relations with Russia. A twin-track policy was adopted of developing closer relations between NATO and Russia in parallel with preparing to admit applicant states which manifestly met NATO's criteria. A critical step was the Russia-NATO Founding Act, signed by President Yeltsin in Paris on May 27, 1997 on the explicit understanding that NATO was on the path to enlargement. As Yeltsin explained to the Russian people, "Any split is a threat to everybody, and that is why we opted for talks with NATO. The task was to minimize the negative consequences of the North Atlantic alliance's expansion and prevent a new split in Europe…We trust each other more and have begun to get to know each other really well … there will be a new peaceful Europe, not divided into blocs."[31] This cleared the way for the eventual accession to NATO in 1999 of the Czech Republic, Hungary and Poland—eight years after they had applied.

The Russians froze their relationship with NATO in response to the bombing of Belgrade in 1999, but it was then unfrozen less than a year later by Vladimir Putin, one of whose first decisions as acting President was to invite NATO Secretary General George Robertson to Moscow. The twin-track approach resumed.

In 2002, NATO upgraded the NATO-Russia Council at a summit with Putin in Rome. Like Yeltsin before him, Putin then publicly acquiesced in the further enlargement of NATO (to include the three Baltic states and Bulgaria, Romania and Slovakia), notwithstanding the objections of his generals.[32] Where NATO went wrong was at the 2008 Bucharest Summit, when the George W. Bush administration sought to put Ukraine and Georgia on the path to membership—neither country being in a condition to join, no consensus within the Alliance, and with the certainty of triggering a violent Russian reaction. While Chancellor Merkel succeeded in blocking this outcome, a compromise communique was adopted which faced, absurdly, in two opposing directions and placed incendiary matter in the hands of Russian hard-liners.

The third, and most fundamental, point is that what separates Russia from "the West" is not NATO, per se, but irreconcilable views of the sovereignty of the states now on Russia's periphery and formerly within the Russian and Soviet empires. To the West, the sovereignty of these member states of the United Nations is paramount. They must be free to determine their own affiliations without threat or coercion, and Russia should respect its formal pledges in numerous international agreements to respect their independence, sovereignty and territorial integrity. The Russian view is that these countries (above all Ukraine and Belarus) have been closely linked to Russia historically and through myriad personal and economic connections, form Russia's security perimeter, must be recognized as within Russia's sphere of strategic interests[33] or "zone of influence," and not be permitted to form affiliations deemed to be contrary to Russia's interests. Russia claims the former Soviet Union as its "Near Abroad," as part of its value system, and as the home to Russian "compatriots," who (like expatriates of many countries) have chosen not to return to the motherland but over whom the motherland still asserts rights and responsibilities. In the Russian view, these countries enjoy limited rather than complete sovereignty.[34]

The expansion of NATO is a proxy for the sovereignty dispute. It is this which has led to Russia's deepening confrontation with the United States and the leading actors of Western Europe since the Orange Revolution in Ukraine of 2005, the Bucharest Summit and Georgian war of 2008, and especially since the ouster of Viktor Yanukovych, the annexation of Crimea and Russia's intrusion into eastern Ukraine five years ago. It is a confrontation which would have arisen, sooner or later, with or without the enlargement of NATO; which long antedates the present Kremlin regime; which is underpinned by Russia's self-image as a "Great Power" with satellites; and which no longer requires the physical occupation of territory. It has been well described by Keir Giles:

> Russia is content to exert control remotely, including organising state capture without any military intervention at all. This attitude is related to the permanent and persistent belief throughout history that Russia's land borders present a critical vulnerability and that, in order to protect itself, Russia must exert control far beyond them ... Russia demands a veto over security arrangements within its self-declared sphere of influence.[35]

It is misleading to label this a "new Cold War." The present situation differs in so many respects: it is not a war between ideologies; it is not a bipolar global struggle between two superpowers; Russia is not threatening to expand into Central and Western Europe; the Russian Federation is not the Soviet Union.

Nevertheless, we are dealing with the *legacy* of the Cold War. Russia hankers after a variant on the Yalta and Potsdam understandings under which, during the Cold War, the West *de facto* accepted Soviet control of the territories behind the Iron Curtain. Behavior and attitudes in the current confrontation have inevitably been influenced by Cold War DNA. Most of the leading figures in Russia and the countries of the former Soviet Union, and many of their Western counterparts, were in their late twenties or thirties when the Soviet Union collapsed (Putin was 37 when the Berlin Wall was breached, serving far from *perestroika* and *glasnost* in Dresden). They had been born and brought up, and their outlook formed, in the Cold War (which is not to say that they all—or we, for I am of this generation—remained life-long Cold Warriors). Not only the mentality but also some of the structures and doctrines of the Cold War remain, adapted to a greater or lesser degree: the Russian General Staff, the GRU, the successor organisations to the KGB, and (necessarily) elements of NATO. The Cold War embedded in both East and West an "enemy image" which has yet to be dispelled, and which leads to mutual paranoia.

I witnessed a cameo of this paranoia in 2003. Vladimir Putin's state visit to the UK, the first by a Russian leader for a century and a half, marked a high spot in the warm relationship which had developed between the Putin and Blair administrations. At around the same time, a British court of law rejected a patently unsound Russian request for the extradition of a Chechen political representative (and former theatre director), Akhmed Zakayev—a man who the Russians themselves had previously declared not to have "blood on his hands." Shortly afterwards, the British government had no choice, on judicial grounds, but to grant asylum to Putin's critic, Boris Berezovsky. The Russian government demanded the return of Zakayev and Berezovsky. I was told that they could not understand why Mr Blair's government had taken these hostile "political" decisions. My efforts to explain that, in the UK, the government did not control the courts cut no ice with the Kremlin. I suspect that the Russian intelligence agencies were telling Putin that his friend Blair (for whatever reason) had betrayed and humiliated him. General Patrushev, then the head of the FSB, told me bluntly that, if we did not send Zakayev and Berezovsky back, we could expect "reciprocal measures."

These duly arrived in the form of raids on the offices in Moscow and other cities of the British Council by leather-jacketed security agents, who stole computers and detained and interrogated staff. The British Council ran libraries and cultural and educational programs in fifteen centers across Russia, as an important part of our policy of building closer relations, and greatly to the benefit of the Russians. It was an entirely open organization, employing mainly Russian nationals; but the KGB and its successor, the FSB, had always been hostile to the Council, presumably seeing the spreading of enlightenment and Western values as subversive. The paranoid reaction to a false analysis of legal decisions in the UK—a knee-jerk from the Cold War—did material damage to Russia, and began a downward spiral in relations with the UK which has continued to this day (notably with acts of murder and attempted assassination carried out on British soil).

To conclude, for about seventeen years, from 1987 to 2004, Russia and the West were on broadly convergent courses. There were disagreements and points of serious tension (notably the wars in former Yugoslavia and Chechnya in the 1990s), but significant progress appeared to have been made towards the erasure of the dividing lines in Europe and in Russia's closer association with Western organizations, reaching a high point when Russia became a full member of the G-8 in 2002. Russia's attitude to integration, however, was ambivalent. It wished to have a seat at all the top tables, but even more strongly aspired to act as an independent Great Power with a cluster of subservient neighbors, not constrained by international law or the rules of any club it might have joined. On this, the post-Cold-War integration foundered.

Vladislav Surkov (perhaps seeking to provoke, as is his wont) has described this as "the conclusion of Russia's epic journey towards the West, the ending of numerous fruitless attempts to become part of Western civilisation, to inter-marry with the 'good family' of European nations" and the precursor to "100 years of geopolitical solitude."[36]

Many in Russia would share this pessimistic view, though I do not. I doubt if recent history would have been greatly different under any other likely successor to Boris Yeltsin. Putin's strength has rested in large part on his ability to reflect and enhance the perceptions of his countrymen about Russia's identity and place in the world.

Russian history has followed a cyclical pattern, with periods of Westernization and emulation of Europe alternating with introverted, socially and spiritually conservative nationalism.[37] At some point, though perhaps not for another decade, the present cycle of xenophobic nationalism and alienation from the West will be subsumed by a renewed desire to modernize. Russia will enter a new phase of development. The Cold War generation will have gone. New leaders will need to plot Russia's course—as a huge country which wishes to be an independent power, but with a diminishing population and a backward economy, overshadowed by a much more powerful and assertive neighbor in China. NATO does not encircle Russia; but under the slogan of One Belt, One Road, China is investing heavily in countries on Russia's periphery, from Central Asia all the way around to Belarus. This will pose some awkward choices for Russia's future leaders. The perception of the West as an enemy, seemingly interred by the events of 1989 to 1991 but resurrected by the Putin administration, may well change.

Notes

1. Published in Russian by Arnoldo Mondadori Editore, Milan 1967, and in English, entitled *Into the Whirlwind* by Collins/Harvill, London 1967.

2. Vladlen Dozortsev was taken by his mother as a child to Riga, following the arrest of his father, a Party member, in a Stalinist purge. He became a successful playwright and a liberal supporter of Latvian independence, joining the Latvian Popular Front on its first day and becoming an influential member of its governing board and a member of the post-Independence parliament. As an ethnic Russian, he then found himself classified as a non-citizen and joined the People's Harmony faction, lobbying for the rights of non-citizens long resident in Latvia.

3. The policy overstretch was well illustrated by Chernyaev's observation that: "Even in the most dramatic moments, even in the period of German reunification, [foreign policy] took up only five or six percent of the considerations of Gorbachev and the Politburo, of their time and their nerves." Quoted in William Taubman, *Gorbachev: His Life and Times* (New York: Simon and Schuster, 2017), pp. 465-466.

4. VI Lenin, *New Internal and External Position and the Problems of the Party*, 1920.

5. Mikhail Gorbachev, *Memoirs* (New York: Doubleday, 1996), p. 217.

6. As Gorbachev explained to Margaret Thatcher in their meeting in Moscow on September 23, 1989, "How can you reform both the economy and politics without democratizing society, without *glasnost*, which incorporates individuals into an active socio-political life?" National Security Archive/Archive of the Gorbachev Foundation.

7. Gorbachev to Chernyaev, 11 June 1990. Quoted in William Taubman, op. cit. p. 519.

8. Martin Nicholson, later to serve as Minister-Counsellor at the British Embassy in Moscow.

9. Anatoly Chernyaev, foreign policy adviser to Gorbachev, *My Six Years with Gorbachev*, English edition (Philadelphia: Pennsylvania University Press, 2000), p. 227.

10. National Security Archive/Archive of the Gorbachev Foundation.

11. Chernyaev, op. cit., p. 208.

12. Quoted in Odd Arne Westad, *The Cold War: A World History* (London: Allen Lane, 2017) p. 586.

13. *New York Times* editorial, March 13, 1985: "Continuity, caution and consensus characterize a system revolutionary in doctrine but deeply conservative in practice. Whatever his ambitions, Mr. Gorbachev is unlikely soon to make waves." *The Times* (London), March 12, 1985: "It will take years for a shake-up in party organisation to have any real effect, to judge by President Andropov's failures. The Gromyko-Ponomarev line in foreign policy will continue at Geneva and other East-West negotiations."

14. One example of this suspicion was a story fed to Gorbachev by the KGB and apparently believed by him that a special CIA group had been set up to discredit him. See Taubman, op. cit., pp. 470 and 474.

15. Chernyaev, op. cit., pp. 221-2; and Chernyaev's diaries, 1972-91, published as *Sovmestniy Iskhod* by ROSSPEN, Moscow, 2008, pp.788-9.

16. Television broadcast by President Bush, December 25, 1991.

17. President Putin's Address to the Federal Assembly, May 26, 2004.

18. President Putin's Address to the Federal Assembly, April 26, 2007.

19. Address in the Kremlin by President Putin, March 18, 2014.

20. President Putin's Address to the Federal Assembly, December 4, 2014.

21. TV documentary on Crimea broadcast on the "Rossiya" channel, March 14, 2015.

22. *Rossiiskaya Gazeta*, October 15, 2014.

23. Press conference, December 18, 2014.

24. See Westad, op. cit., pp. 618 and 623.

25. National Security Archive/Archive of the Gorbachev Foundation.

26. https://bush41library.tamu.edu/archives/public-papers/3267

27. President Putin's Address to the Federal Assembly, April 25, 2005.

28. The EU's Common Strategy on Russia, 1999, looked towards "Russia's return to its rightful place in the European family in a spirit of friendship, cooperation, fair accommodation of interests and on the foundations of shared values."

29. Annual address to the Federal Assembly, May 26, 2004.

30. Yeltsin played around with the idea in conversation, but also acknowledged to Vice President Gore that Russia was too big to join NATO. See Timothy J. Colton, *"Yeltsin: A Life"* (New York: Basic Books, 2008), p. 269.

31. Boris Yeltsin, radio address, May 29, 1997. Quoted in Leon Aron, *Boris Yeltsin: A Revolutionary Life* (New York: HarperCollins, 2000), p. 667.

32. At a joint press conference with the NATO Secretary General in Brussels on November 11, 2002, Putin said that, if cooperation continued to develop and NATO continued to transform in a way that corresponded with Russia's security interests, Russia could consider "a broader participation in that work." He hoped that enlargement would not undermine the military stability and security in the common European space.

33. President Putin: "we see the CIS area as the sphere of our strategic interests." Address to the Federal Assembly, May 16, 2003.

34. To justify Russia's conflict with Georgia in 2008, Defense Minister Serdyukov said that Georgia was part of Russia's "zone of influence" while Foreign Minister Lavrov spoke of Russia's "historically conditioned mutually privileged relations" with its ex-Soviet neighbors.

35. Keir Giles, "Moscow Rules," Chatham House and Brookings 2019, p. 26.

36. *Russia in Global Affairs*, April 2018.

37. Well analyzed by Professor Iver B. Neumann in "Russia's Europe, 1991-2016: inferiority to superiority," *International Affairs*, Chatham House, Vol. 92, No. 6, November 2016.

Chapter 6

Bonfire of the Vanities: An American Insider's Take on the Collapse of the Soviet Union and Yugoslavia

David C. Gompert[1]

Setting the Stage

As the Cold War ended, the Berlin Wall was demolished, and Central and Eastern Europeans freed themselves from communism, the demise of both the Soviet Union and Yugoslavia would be just a matter of time. Yet, the stunning speed of events left Western policy-makers, not to mention Eastern ones, in catch-up mode. Each of these two multi-national communist states was held together by autocratic rule, thuggish security services, and ideological vanity. The glue had gotten brittle, owing to economic failure, pervasive cynicism, and heightened public awareness of how badly living conditions compared with those in the West, and it gave way when last-ditch efforts at reform only fed demands to discard communism altogether.[2]

The bonfire of communism in the Balkans and Eurasia caught the U.S. administration of George H. W. Bush pretty much by surprise. The strategic goals of the United States at the time were clear and steady enough: end East-West confrontation, spread liberty, and extend the Western liberal order. The Gulf War of 1990 underlined the potency and value of American leadership and, dare to say, the prospect of unipolarity. However, even as Berliners danced on the Wall, the swiftness and extent of revolution in the East were not anticipated.

As if a pause button could be pressed on the rush of change in the East following German unification, the United States and its European partners shifted attention to adapting their institutions to the end of the Cold War. Toward the end of 1990, they began debating in earnest the future of NATO, the rationale for U.S. troops in Europe, the nature of a "European pillar" of the Alliance, the next phase of European political and economic integration, and the mission of the Conference on Security and Cooperation in Europe (CSCE). The Atlantic allies were not braced for the approaching crash of communism's multinational states.

When it dawned on the Bush administration that developments in the East were out of control, its lofty notion of a whole, free and peaceful "Euro-Atlantic community" was made to compete with heightened anxiety over the dangers of havoc, conflict, mass migration, and loose nuclear weapons. At the same time, there was no interest in seeing communism endure. As secessionism intensified in Yugoslavia and the Soviet Union, U.S. policy-makers had one foot on the accelerator and one on the brakes, as well as (mixed-metaphor alert) a left-hand/right-hand problem.

While concerned about the potential for violence in the communist East, Western policy-makers were lulled by the fact that the revolutions until then in Central and Eastern Europe had on the whole been of the velvet variety.[3] Internal support for the old regimes melted away, as did their politicians. The Soviet leadership under Mikhail Gorbachev had become too concerned for the Union's own survival to continue the policy of using force to save communism in neighboring states: The "Brezhnev Doctrine," invoked to justify military intervention since the Czech Spring of 1968, had been replaced by the "Sinatra Doctrine," which allowed any country wishing to leave Soviet orbit to "do it my way."[4]

Still, the Soviet Union and Yugoslavia in 1991 were different than Poland, Hungary and Czechoslovakia (which would soon break in half without much hassle, let alone bloodshed). It could be assumed that Belgrade and Moscow would use force to prevent secession by any republic. Also, each state had several republics with minorities of the most powerful nationality, Serbs and Russians respectively, supplying kindling for civil war in the event of breakup.[5]

Within three years of the fall of the Wall, both states had gone out of existence, one peacefully and the other in a paroxysm of killing. While Yugoslavia's mayhem, ethnic cleansing and mass murder were horrific on their own terms, Western governments observed that similar flammable materials existed in the Soviet Union, made far more dangerous by the deployment of nuclear weapons in Ukraine, Belarus and

Kazakhstan. Yet, the breakup of the Soviet Union in December 1991 proved to be remarkably well-ordered. The reasons for this contrast are worth examining.

Events leading to the collapse of Yugoslavia and of the Soviet Union, as well as the violence in one and the absence of violence in the other, were largely beyond the control of the United States and its European partners. Whether things could have been different had the Atlantic allies been more proactive, purposeful and coordinated is unknowable, but doubtful. As we will see, the United States and its NATO allies reacted more jointly to the break-up of the Soviet Union than to the break-up of Yugoslavia. The hypothesis here is that events were governed by the character, outlooks and actions of peoples and leaders of these states, with Western allies often ambivalent or at odds, capable at most of nudging events by saying how they might react to steps taken by actors in the East.

In addition to geopolitics, important principles of international law were at issue in both Yugoslavia and the Soviet Union. The right of self-determination was in tension with the prohibition of unilateral (non-consensual) change of international borders. Relatedly, Western states were generally respectful of the norm against interference in the internal affairs of recognized sovereign states. In the end, though, such precepts did not determine Western policy. Support for self-determination was accepted insofar as peoples used democratic means to escape undemocratic rule. As for non-interference, there were ample grounds for forcible humanitarian intervention in Yugoslavia, whereas intervening in the Soviet Union, still a superpower, was never under consideration. In both cases, the policies of the United States and its European allies were dictated by constraints of feasibility and hard-headed calculations of interests.

Even as the United States lacked the means to manage the demise of communism's two multilateral states, its domestic politics and bureaucratic misalignments hindered policy-making. Americans of Croatian descent urged taking Zagreb's side, whereas Serbs had no such lobby.[6] Support within the United States for Baltic independence, waiting fifty years for this moment, brooked no delay. There was zero domestic affinity for the Soviet Union. President Bush's proclivity toward restraint in both cases did not go down smoothly at home. The State Department and the Defense Department pulled in different directions in both cases (for reasons and in ways detailed below), handicapping efforts by the National Security Council (NSC) to broker policy. Meanwhile, the West Wing of the White House was not convinced that being proactive was politically wise in either case. Thus, the inherent limits of U.S. influence in the Balkans and Eurasia were reinforced by presidential prudence and political contention.

If the United States neither caused Yugoslavia to break up violently nor enabled the Soviet Union to break up peacefully, what did?

Yugoslavia

Serbia had been the cradle of World War I. After the war, the "Union of South Slavs" was organized out of Balkan fragments of the Austro-Hungarian and Ottoman empires. The founding agreement among Serbs, Croats and Slovenes was for the most part voluntary, though the victorious allies pressed hard for it in hopes of stabilizing this ethnic crazy-quilt. Serbia, having been a state, had the upper hand in negotiations and named Aleksander I to head a constitutional monarchy. There ensued feuding and skirmishing among Croatian fascists, Serbian royalists, and communists, which burst into civil war during World War II, until communist strongman Josip Broz Tito put a lid on it.

In view of Tito's central role in controlling the South Slavs, the U.S. Government drew up contingency plans for what might follow his death, anticipating civil war and possible Soviet invasion to end Yugoslav independence. Yet, for ten years following Tito's death in 1980, Yugoslavia held together: a new rotating presidency functioned more or less well, interspersed nationalities lived more or less harmoniously, and the monster of ethnic warfare remained in the closet.

As communism buckled elsewhere in Central and Eastern Europe, however, Serbian leader Slobodan Milošević and Croatian leader Franjo Tuđman, among others, ditched that discredited ideology in favor of ultra-nationalism. As a way of saving themselves politically, they dredged up ancient grudges and stoked enmity among ethnic groups.[7] The Yugoslav case suggests that diverse ethno-sectarian peoples can co-exist unless incited to hate by demagogues.

As Serb-Croat tensions increased, Slovenes plotted to remove themselves from undemocratic Serb-dominated Yugoslavia and to follow the trail toward Western freedoms and institutions blazed by their Central European neighbors. With 90% of its population ethnic Slovene and only 2% Serb, Slovenia had less to fear from Serbia than did Croatia and Bosnia-Herzegovina, with their large Serb populations. Yet, it became apparent, including to Western governments, that Slovenia's secession would trigger a Croatian decision to bolt. With over a half-million Serbs in Croatia (of 4.7 million people), and Croat nationalism whipped up by Tudman, there was a high potential for sectarian violence between Roman Catholic Croats and Greek Orthodox Serbs. Croatian independence would in turn make it difficult if not dangerous for other republics, especially Bosnia and Herzegovina, with its million ethnic Serbs, to stay inside a rump Yugoslavia increasingly dominated by Serbs and governed by an autocratic Serb nationalist. Though with few Serbs—but many Albanians—Macedonia would also break free. Domino Theory may not have applied to Indochina, but it described the disintegration of Yugoslavia.

Anticipating this scenario, the European Community (EC)—on course to become the European Union (EU), in adjusting to German unification with deeper economic and political integration—insisted on taking the lead in handling the Yugoslav crisis. Such European hubris coincided with a French-led effort to create an EC-based alternative to NATO. Yugoslavia was seen in Paris and at EC headquarters as a chance to exercise newfound EC unity and clout. The U.S. Government, which was more alarmed than European governments were of Yugoslav dangers, was only too glad to defer, thinking the Europeans would either succeed or, by failing, be reminded of the importance of American leadership.[8]

In early 1991, the administration of George H. W. Bush was wrapping up a spectacularly successful war to liberate Kuwait from Iraq and, with the president's approval rating hovering at 90%, hesitant about getting drawn into another, far riskier conflict. With history in mind—deep Balkan enmities, Nazis' difficulty in gaining control of Yugoslavia, and U.S. experience in the quagmire that was Vietnam—Bush, Secretary of Defense Dick Cheney, Secretary of State James Baker, and Chairman of the Joint Chiefs of Staff Colin Powell opposed military intervention in what seemed to be a lost cause. The administration defended its hands-off posture publicly by explaining that Yugoslavia's rows were too complicated, immutable, and removed from U.S. vital interests to warrant U.S. involvement.

Washington was right to see the Europeans as naïve about Yugoslavia's chances and their ability to exert unified and effective influence. For one thing, Germany was predisposed to recognize the independence of both Slovenia and Croatia, mainly for domestic political reasons, whereas the UK and France were hesitant. Recall that the British and French had had reservations about German unification, whereas that same experience turned Germans into cheerleaders of self-determination. In the event, all would follow Germany's lead in order to avoid a rupture that would derail the move toward a more common European foreign policy.

Predictably, European diplomacy was no match for the secessionist momentum of Slovenia and Croatia. So, on the eve of Slovenia's declaration of independence, Secretary Baker visited Yugoslavia to warn against unilateral secession and urge pursuit of a middle ground, e.g., a loose confederation proposed by Macedonia and Bosnia. Baker's appeal for Yugoslavs to avoid abrupt and complete dissolution was based on the American assessment—correct, as it turned out—that Yugoslavia's disintegration was sure to be bloody, given the nationalist baiting of unprincipled politicians, the aim of Milošević to create a "Greater Serbia," and the potential for civil war where large Serb minorities lived. A 1990 CIA analysis showed that if Yugoslavia disintegrated into its constituent states, half the population would be left as minorities in the "wrong" place. Critics of Baker's plea for Slovenia and Croatia to postpone independence overlook the fact that the prospect for a peaceful breakup of Yugoslavia was a mirage.

As forces of secession gathered strength, the EC offered sizeable emergency assistance and debt relief on the condition that the Yugoslav republics settled their differences peacefully and consensually. Given conditions in Yugoslavia, the European aid package was dead on arrival, and economic intervention was abandoned. Worse yet, EC mixed-signals regarding unilateral pursuit of independence by Slovenia and Croatia—Germany in favor, France and the UK against—aggravated Yugoslav divisions. The United States, once a source of economic aid to anti-Soviet Yugoslavia, formally suspended its support when fighting erupted and violence began to spread. Against the centrifugal forces of Yugoslavia, neither offers nor denials of economic assistance had any effect.

In late 1990, 88% of Slovenes voted in favor of independence, which was declared the following June. Serb-dominated Yugoslav armed forces under Milosevic's control made only a perfunctory, unsuccessful effort to thwart Slovenian independence. But they reacted ferociously when Croatia promptly followed suit. With Serb militias inside Croatia taking the lead, that republic burst into flames.

Certain American officials, including Deputy Secretary of State Lawrence Eagleburger and his protege and friend at the NSC (this author), argued that NATO military intervention—if only U.S. air strikes—might stop the killing in Croatia and its spread to Bosnia, Macedonia and eventually the Serbian province of Kosovo. They reasoned that the appearance of U.S. air power could be enough to persuade the Serbs to back off and permit independence, and that if the United States had any chance to nip Yugoslav warfare in the bud, it was early in the fighting.[9] Their superiors and Pentagon colleagues, however, felt the United States should not intervene in the Balkans—indeed, should never intervene anywhere—unless it decided in advance that it was prepared to escalate as needed to win. To these opponents, entering the Yugoslav war could prove open-ended, costly and unsuccessful.

Meanwhile, ethnic hatreds throughout Yugoslavia ignited the worst violence and forced human relocations in Europe since World War II. In Bosnia, Serbs targeted Croats and Muslims. Once leaders injected nationalist venom, people who had been living side-by-side now engaged in vendettas for acts committed generations ago. The demographic mixing-bowl of Bosnia made it all the more incendiary. Milošević, having become torch-bearer of Serb nationalism and pride, had no incentive to restrain Serbian militias, especially when it became obvious, early on, that NATO would not intervene and that he would keep control of the Yugoslav People's Army (JNA).

A 40,000-strong UN peacekeeping force (UNPROFOR) was formed, mainly with European contingents, and inserted into Bosnia. But it could barely keep relief supplies flowing, much less stop the fighting and atrocities. Peacekeepers could not keep peace that the parties themselves rejected. It is conceivable that if UN forces in Bosnia had had rules of engagement and armaments permitting use of force—peacemaking instead of peacekeeping—killing might have been less. But the Europeans sought no such mandate.

Hope for peace further dimmed when the EC, cued by Germany, recognized Slovenia and Croatia as independent in December 1991. By April 1992 Bosnia held a referendum, seceded and had its independence recognized by the Atlantic allies. Yet contrary to what the German Chancellor Kohl and Foreign Minister Genscher had wished, independence did not safeguard Croatia and Bosnia from descending further into war or stopping Milošević's relentless and worsening aggression. Western recognition contributed nothing to deterrence, as Europeans and Americans did nothing to back it up. There was grousing in Washington, London and Paris about Berlin's eagerness to recognize breakaway independence knowing that its allies, not Germany, would be the enforcers.

Even after President Bush proclaimed at the 1992 Helsinki CSCE summit that the United States would do "whatever it takes" to stop the bloodshed, the United States did not use force. Without the United States, the Europeans lacked the will and ability to stop the fighting in Yugoslavia even if they could agree to do so. As things got worse in the Balkans, Washington and most Americans (per Gallup polling) did not believe that U.S. interests at stake in the fighting or the fate of Yugoslavia warranted a protracted, and unpromising war, lacking public support. The case for intervening to salvage the credibility of NATO and U.S. leadership was not convincing enough.

Meanwhile, at NATO's 1991 fall summit, the United States proposed a post-Cold-War "New Strategic Concept" for the Alliance: to preserve stability and, as needed, keep peace in the emerging "Europe whole and free."[10] Of course, NATO's failure to stop the violence in Yugoslavia flew in the face of this concept. Questions about NATO's continued relevance resurfaced, though these were answered subsequently by the Clinton administration's use of airpower against Serbia (and some years later by the Alliance's stalwart response to the 9/11 attacks).

George H.W. Bush paid a political price for his hesitation to support the independence of Yugoslavia's seceding states, particularly where Croatian-Americans were concentrated and activated. Bill Clinton, his

Democratic opponent in the 1992 election, denounced Bush's inaction. But, as noted, the American public at large was hardly clamoring for a military intervention. And, with the U.S. economy in recession in 1992, opinion shifted against a president who seemed more attuned to foreign than domestic affairs. Bush's achievements in the Gulf War and in supporting East European liberation did not help his reelection prospects; intervention in Yugoslavia would at best have amplified criticism that he was inattentive to problems at home.

The instinctive wariness of U.S. leaders was complicated by the divergent views of the State Department and the Defense Department. State, concerned about the credibility of U.S. leadership and relevance of NATO, post-Cold-War, argued behind the scenes for U.S. activism if not military intervention. Pentagon E-Ring civilians and brass were strongly opposed, exercising a veto in effect because the NSC was in no position to push for intervention over the objections of a military establishment that had just liberated Kuwait with minimal casualties.[11]

One cannot exclude that the United States and its allies might have been able to prevent the violent break-up of Yugoslavia by acting early. However, that presumes that they could have foreseen the magnitude of horrors to come if they did not act. The longer the United States delayed, the harder it became for those who favored intervention to claim that it would succeed. And it was never obvious what U.S. forces' objectives would be or whom they would fight if sent in. Bush, Baker, Cheney, and Powell and Co. were staunch believers in having clear war aims.

The Soviet Union

Unlike Yugoslavia, the Soviet Union was formed by conquest—first by Red Army invasion, then by Stalin's edict. For much of its history, the USSR was maintained by force and relocation, combined with central control of republic governments by appointing and propping up Soviet hacks. Communism was imposed and with time became entrenched, as fewer and fewer Soviet citizens knew anything else. Again, unlike Yugoslavia, no other Soviet nationality had the wherewithal to challenge Russian domination (as Croats challenged Serbs). Even as uprisings spread through its satellite states, the Soviet Union's domestic status quo held. Even with its economy in a tailspin and democratic dissidence on the rise, in Russia as elsewhere, neither revolution nor dissolution appeared inevitable, much less imminent.

Starting with the Kremlin's 1981 decision not to intervene against Poland's Solidarity uprising, followed by Gorbachev's attempt at reforms, acceptance of German unification, and withdrawal from Afghanistan and then from Eastern Europe, the main goal of Soviet leaders was to save the Soviet Union, and themselves.[12] They were helpless in preventing decomposition, however, due to inexorable political-economic decay. Toward the end, Gorbachev was on the defensive both from hard-liners, who despised reform, and Russian president Boris Yeltsin, who demanded democratization and free markets—thus, the end of communism.

The end came more dramatically than anyone expected. The abortive coup against Gorbachev in August 1991 by old-line party and military bosses exposed not only his political weakness and but also that of the very figures and forces opposing him. Gorbachev may have been rescued by Yeltsin during the attempted coup, but the "Center" was finished.

Even as the United States and its European allies cheered the coup's failure and democracy's brighter prospects in the Soviet Union, they had misgivings: Would the Soviet Union's disintegration turn bloody, as Yugoslavia's had?[13] Would elements of the Red Army use force against secessionists? Would turmoil cause a tsunami of refugees? Would the Soviet Union's huge, far-flung arsenal of nuclear weapons remain under firm, accountable control? How large would the bill for economic aid be? Would food distribution fail and hunger follow?

The Bush administration's proactive role in German unification within NATO, followed by its Gulf War victory, raised expectations that the United States would take the lead in the more momentous process of Soviet disintegration. Moreover, the stakes were higher in the Soviet case than they were in Yugoslavia. Would Washington, despite the perils, insist on independence for peoples who sought freedom—something it had done grudgingly in Yugoslavia? At the same time, apprehensions about instability, control of nuclear weapons, and implied aid obligations held back Washington—and London and Berlin and Paris and Brussels. Although Bush's handling of the collapse of communism in Europe and then of the Soviet Union was his most important legacy prior to the coup, he had been criticized at home for tardiness in recognizing Baltics' independence and for his "Chicken Kiev" speech warning Ukraine against "suicidal nationalism" and saying that "freedom is not the same as independence."

As the Soviet Union started to split at the seams, the highest priority of American diplomacy was to build arrangements to control nuclear weapons, which it eventually did. In addition, Bush and Baker stressed with their Soviet counterparts the special importance of finding a graceful path for independence, or something resembling it, for the Baltic states. This reflected domestic U.S. politics and appreciation that the nationalities most likely to fight and die for freedom from Soviet rule were the Balts. Whether Washington's entreaties dissuaded Moscow from using massive force to prevent Baltic secessionism is unknown. Anyway, the most dangerous corner of the Soviet Union did not erupt in violence.

The Bush administration did offer economic support of sorts, though that also was fraught with internal contradiction: how to assist materially without propping up a failed system. Washington helped organize emergency distribution of food, though it was clear to those of us involved at the time that the only sustainable solution to food distribution was creation of markets. In addition, the Departments of State and Treasury supported reformers in planning the shift from central planning.[14] But leading reform economist Grigory Yavlinsky, who authored a 500-day transition plan, lost out to party heavies (e.g., Yevgeny Primakov), and Gorbachev's ignorance of how markets work left reformers to twist in the wind. Some Americans—even Richard Nixon!—called for massive aid, but the government rightly argued that that would be a colossal waste without transition, which aid could actually delay.

After the failed coup of August 1991, the end of the Soviet Union came quickly. Ukraine promptly declared independence from the USSR, and there was nothing the remnants of the Soviet state could do about it. In December, Russian president Boris Yeltsin called George Bush to inform him that he and Ukrainian president Leonid Kravchuk had agreed that both states would immediately leave the Soviet Union. Of course, Russia's departure meant the Soviet Union's extinction. In a

dazzlingly creative career move, Yeltsin promoted himself by eliminating his boss's job, which required eliminating the Soviet Union. When
Bush asked what would happen to his friend Mikhail, Yeltsin explained
that he would be out of work but otherwise fine. Bush thanked Yeltsin
for the heads-up. Without fuss, Gorbachev resigned at Christmas and
turned out the lights.

What followed was nothing like the warfare then engulfing Yugoslavia. The Union dissolved along the boundaries of its republics, albeit with some sporadic fighting over certain territorial disputes, namely
Ossetia, Abkhazia and Nagorno-Karabakh. The Red Army was intact
but demoralized, its top leaders having been implicated in the farci-
cal coup attempt. Moreover, whereas Serbia opposed with force other
republics' secession from Yugoslavia, Russia in the end took the lead
in precipitating the breakup of the Soviet Union. Former Soviet Republics, except the Baltics, formed a Commonwealth of Independent
States (CIS) around Russia. (Recall that the attempt to reconfigure Yugoslavia as a confederation had failed, leaving no ties at all among the
warring ex-republics.) Creation of the CIS, with Russia the unques-
tioned leader, quelled fears of what would happen to Russian minorities in other independent states. Russia would not need to use force
to protect fellow Russians, as Serbia felt it had to do when Croatia
and Bosnia broke away with some one-and-a-half million ethnic Serbs.
Russians were not attacked in Ukraine, Kazakhstan, or anywhere else,
including the Baltic states.

Western concern about control of Soviet nuclear weapons stationed
outside Russia was allayed by U.S. intelligence reporting that officers
in the chains of command of all such weapons were all Great Russians.
In addition, Russia was recognized as the sole successor-custodian of
Soviet nuclear weapons, and non-proliferation assurances were secured
from other former republics. Force was never needed to secure the
Soviet arsenal.

With President Bush setting the tone, U.S. policy-makers reacted
cautiously and tactically as the Soviet Union self-destructed. One false
step, they feared, could ignite a conflagration with nuclear risks. They
walked a fine line between discouraging reckless unilateral moves toward independence, which could strengthen hard-liners in Moscow,
and encouraging those who sought freedom. In the end, U.S. officials

exhaled when the Soviet Union's dissolution proved peaceful, given what could have been.

As in the Yugoslav case, the State Department and the Defense Department (DoD) were of two minds regarding the disintegration of the Soviet Union, but their positions toward the latter were a mirror-image of those toward the former. Simply put, doves and hawks swapped sides. DoD policy-makers, taking what they said was a strategic view, saw such opportunity in the demise of the USSR that they argued for unqualified support for secessionist republics, breakage be damned. State argued for promoting a soft landing, as well as for not alienating Soviet transition leaders or giving ammo to remaining hard-liners. Although U.S. domestic politics, still anti-Soviet, resonated with the Pentagon's view, the President was cautious—more so than he had been toward German unification in 1989 or the Gulf War in 1990. Having sided with Defense in the Yugoslavia case, Bush sided with State in the Soviet case—and with restraint in both cases. His hallmark of prudent pragmatism prevailed as the Soviet Union crashed. Although he never bullied his advisors and agencies with his own views—preferring instead to foster debate, options and consensus—the President's views set the tone and limits of U.S. policy.

Comparison

Why was the breakup of Yugoslavia violent and that of the Soviet Union not? They were comparable in political structure and multi-national composition, and both were bulwarks against forces of democracy. Yet one exploded and the other more or less petered out. Although important situational differences can be found, two differences—both internal to these states—stand out: attitudes of people and qualities of leaders.

Great Russians were largely disliked by other nationalities and in other republics of the USSR. Often, Russian minorities and functionaries had power and perks indigenous peoples did not (unless they were lackeys of Moscow). Moreover, the Soviet Union came into being largely through conquest and imposition of the conqueror's ideology. It was sustained for three-quarters of a century by central power, security services with tentacles everywhere, appointment of local leaders beholden to Moscow, and a massive Red Army that the Center was liable to use. While there was a long history of animosity between Russia and other nationalities, Russians and Ukrainians had common racial roots ("Rus"), common culture, and general affinity. Also, Stalin's terror was not discriminatory: even during the worst of his purges, forced collectivization, mass relocations, show trials and executions, Russians were not spared.

Soviet cohesiveness, imposed at first, was reinforced by World War II. Soviet defense against and then defeat of Nazi Germany was both unified and unifying. Most peoples rallied to the Soviet cause, cheered Soviet victories, supplied soldiers and casualties, and saw Stalin, the Georgian, as a hero. Although German forces got some support from non-Russian partisans, the Red Army that defeated them was multinational.

Yugoslavia went through no such "Great Patriotic War." Quite the opposite: pro-Nazi Croatian fifth column (Ustashe) and anti-Nazi Serbian partisans (Chetniks) tore at each other lustily during World War II. What German troops did in Yugoslavia was mild compared to the unspeakable atrocities Croats and Serbs committed against each other. While it is true that Croats and Serbs, as well as other nationalities, lived together in relative quietude under Tito and in the years after his death, it did not take much dog-whistling by Milošević and Tuđman for killings to resume, often in revenge.

Yugoslavia's fault lines were essentially religious—Orthodox, Roman Catholic, and Muslim. There are only minor if any racial (Slavic) or linguistic (Serbo-Croatian) variations. Although historically religious differences are often compounded by political and/or economic grievances (think Lebanon, Northern Ireland, Iraq, and lately Yemen and Syria), Yugoslavia is not the first place, nor will it be the last, where whipped-up religious fervor motivates extreme violence. Where Eastern Orthodoxy and Islam brushed up against each other in the Soviet Union, the former had, and has, the upper hand (think Chechnya). That there was no dominant religion in Yugoslavia made it inherently more unstable and more violent than the Soviet Union.

If Yugoslavia's nationalities were more predisposed toward violence than those of the Soviet Union, the same can be said about their respective leaders. Generally speaking, Milošević, Tuđman and other Yugoslav despots were not interested in stability—indeed, they feasted on conflict. In contrast, Soviet transitional leaders dreaded the destabilization of the Soviet space, and they made clear to Western counterparts their desire that change be peaceful. The Soviet Union's ethnic problems had largely been settled, though often brutally, through internal and external wars, purges, gulags, and mass dislocations. With minorities (e.g., Muslims and Armenians) living on the fringes, the Soviet Union was largely segregated, except where Russians lived outside of Russia. Nothing had been genuinely resolved in Yugoslavia, leaving ethnic problems to fester and tempting leaders to exploit these problems for their own power.

Leaders matter, even when their days are numbered. Indeed, handling failure and transition can test a leader's moral principles differently but no less stressfully than can power. As communism's two multi-national states were on their last legs, Soviet leaders conducted themselves for the most part responsibly and humanely. Gorbachev tried his level best to make the Soviet state authentically legitimate and viable via *perestroika* and *glasnost*, and he revoked the Brezhnev Doctrine and worked to end the Cold War. When it was clear that these moves were too little too late—indeed, had released a revolutionary genie—he ordered the use of force reluctantly and sparingly. For tactical reasons—in hopes of saving reform—he accepted the return of hardliners in the fall of 1990, which led foreign minister Eduard Shevardnadze to resign.[15] Once the Soviet Union was formally dissolved in later 1991, Gorbachev resigned with dignity. He has since then been a voice of moderation and paragon of statesmanship, though still an avowed socialist.

Though he could have, Gorbachev did not order a full-bore Red Army offensive to crush dissidents, satellite states, separatists or republics that were abandoning his beloved Union. He could have incited Great Russians in and out of Russia to use force against other nationalities, but he never did. Unlike his Yugoslav contemporaries, Gorbachev did not embrace and exploit nationalism as communism failed. Indeed, he was anti-nationalist.

Paradoxically, Milošević, a Serb loyalist, was ready to use force to preserve multi-national Yugoslavia, but Gorbachev, a Soviet loyalist, was *not* ready to use force to preserve multi-national Soviet Union. One explanation is that Milošević was motivated by a nationalist vision of a "Greater Serbia" alloyed with concern for the safety of fellow Serbs stranded in seceding states, not by some attachment to the Yugoslav state per se. Milošević was also ruthless, egoistic, and quick to deflect blame. On trial in The Hague, he showed no hint of remorse for Serb atrocities.

In contrast, Gorbachev's allegiance was to the Union—the history, the ideology, the Soviet ideal—not to Russia or Russians. Gorbachev had a romantic view of the Soviet Union. As a devout communist of mixed Russian-Ukrainian descent, he regarded the Union as organic, transcendent and, ideally, voluntary. Using force to save it should not be necessary, or else it would shatter the Soviet ideal to which he clung. In any case, he found the use of force repellent. Gorbachev had spent most of his career on domestic affairs, far from the organs of Soviet hard power. He was a relentless reformer, and he stridently supported Khrushchev's de-Stalinization. Being a true child of the Soviet Union, Gorbachev had neither a vision of Greater Russia nor a fear of what would become of fellow Russians living in seceding states—again, Ukrainians and Russians had lived side-by-side peaceably for centuries and fought side-by-side to repel the Nazis.

In any case, force was a less practicable option for Gorbachev than for Milošević, especially after the failed coup had sapped his authority and discredited the army's leadership. Once Ukraine left the USSR right after the failed coup, it was too late for Gorbachev to hold the state together with force. Recall that the Red Army depended heavily on non-Russian soldiers and officers, and Ukrainians were integrated into combat forces.

Gorbachev's foreign minister, Eduard Shevardnadze of Georgia, played an especially principled role. A Soviet career success-story, like Gorbachev, Shevardnadze knew nonetheless that sweeping change was coming, perhaps better than Gorbachev did. He explained in 1990 to his American counterpart, James Baker, that he would not resist change provided it did not lead to "catastrophic destabilization," and he assured Baker that Moscow would not use force against those peoples and countries that wished to leave communism and Soviet rule.[16] The Shevardnadze-Baker relationship was critical in managing the end of the Cold War, the Warsaw Pact, and the Soviet Union. Shevardnadze counselled against the use of force, and he resigned when Gorbachev reluctantly turned to hardliners in late 1990.[17]

Then there is Boris Yeltsin, another alumnus of the Soviet system. For all his flaws and failures, Yeltsin neither fomented Russian unrest in former non-Russian republics nor called out the security forces to crush opposition. He may have ruled ineffectively, but he ruled more or less democratically. Like Gorbachev, he maintained a rapport with George H. W. Bush, and his foreign minister, Andrey Kozyrev, stressed cooperative relations with the West (much to the dismay of Russian nationalists and revanchists). Outgoing and transitional Soviet leaders had a sense of history, humanity and decency.

Compare these Soviet figures to those of Yugoslavia, especially Slobodan Milošević (compared to whom Tuđman was mild). Milošević instigated ethnic cleansing of non-Serbs in Bosnia and elsewhere, and he condoned if not inspired such atrocities as the murder of eight thousand Bosnian Muslims at Srebrenica. He was the author of genocide, for which he was brought to justice in The Hague, where he died in prison. Milošević's associates in Bosnia, notably Radovan Karadžić and Ratko Mladić, were the ones with fresh blood on their hands; both were tried for genocide and war crimes. One European statesman opined to a U.S. diplomat that Yugoslav leaders "are all killers." Another added, "they are all liars."[18] Both comments ring true to this author.

The diplomacy of President Bush and Secretary Baker neither caused violence in Yugoslavia nor prevented it in the Soviet Union. But they were more directly and continually engaged in contacts with their Soviet counterparts than with Yugoslav leaders, which is understandable given the enormous risks of collapse of a superpower. Other than Baker's unsuccessful visit in 1990, the only substantive contact either had with Yugoslav leaders was when Bush met in 1992 with Bosnian president Alija Izetbegović, who appealed, in vain, for American help to stop the holocaust in Bosnia. Those who met with Milošević during the crisis, including this author, knew that presidential diplomacy would have had no real effect. Left to leaders who wholesaled hate, the peoples of Yugoslavia resorted to violence to avenge acts of earlier generations, as Western leaders, diplomats and armies watched.

In both cases, the caution of "Bush 41" shaped U.S. policy. Gone was the boldness he had shown during German unification in 1989 and Kuwait's liberation in 1990. But those cases were comparatively easy and well aligned with U.S. domestic politics. The breakup of Yugoslavia and, all the more, of the Soviet Union involved daunting complexities and presented huge risks. Given what we knew then, it is hard to argue that the policy of non-intervention in either collapsing communist state was wrong at its core.

Epilogue

What became of former Yugoslavia and former Soviet Union thirty years on could be viewed as surprising. Following NATO intervention, peace agreement, and removal and war-crimes prosecution of Serbian leaders, each ex-Yugoslav state went its own way. Most of them experienced economic recovery and adopted democracy. Croatia, Montenegro and Slovenia have become NATO members. Bosnia and Herzegovina, North Macedonia and Serbia are members of the Partnership for Peace. Croatia and Slovenia are EU members, and North Macedonia, Montenegro and Serbia are official candidates for membership. The EU has recognized Bosnia and Herzegovina and Kosovo as potential candidates. All have signed Stabilization and Association Agreements with the EU. At present, none of the Balkan's territorial disputes or inter-ethnic flashpoints seems capable of re-igniting war.

Given that Yugoslavia broke apart violently while the Soviet Union did so peacefully, it is ironic that what was the latter is now mired in conflict. Some of those conflicts, such as in the Caucasus, have been ethno-territorial. Some have had religious undercurrents, such as in Central Asia. But the worst have been caused by Russian revanchism. Prior to Vladimir Putin, Russia's economy sputtered, investors stayed away, oligarchs flourished, democracy frayed, and the military deteriorated; but at least Russia did not threaten its ex-Soviet neighbors. Under Putin, democracy has been deep-sixed, old oligarchs have been replaced by Putin's new ones, the economy has improved—owing to high oil and gas prices (not to investment)—and the military has been rebuilt. Under Putin, Russia has threatened or attacked a number of ex-Soviet states: Georgia was invaded and effectively partitioned; Crimea was taken; Ukrainian territory and sovereignty are under assault; and the Baltic states look anxiously to NATO for protection. A common theme is Russia's intent to protect Russians residing outside of the motherland, if not to expand the motherland or even to re-assemble the Soviet Union. The conflict that did not occur when the Soviet Union disintegrated—when Russia did not try to control the former Soviet space by force—is now occurring wherever Putin see a chance.

Russia's economy is now in a prolonged funk, thanks to deflated prices of oil and gas, lack of investment, and Western sanctions. Yet its belligerent foreign policy and reliance on threats and force persist. Although Russia may not be able to finance such an expansive external strategy indefinitely, Putin finds it useful if not essential to continue trying in the interest of rallying patriotic support despite poor domestic conditions. While post-Soviet violence was delayed for two decades, there is no sign that it will end soon—not while Russia is ruled by a man who lacks the humanity of the Soviet Union's last leaders.

Notes

1. The author wishes to thank Raymond Seitz, Robert Hutchings and Robert Zoellick for their inputs to this chapter.

2. For an excellent and efficient explanatory narrative, I recommend Robert L. Hutchings' *American Diplomacy and the End of the Cold War* (Washington, DC: Woodrow Wilson Center Press and Johns Hopkins Press, 1997).

3. Romania was the exception, and violence there was brief and limited to the execution of the communist dictator.

4. Coined by Soviet Foreign Ministry spokesman Gerasimov on October 25, 1989, though first explained by Gorbachev to the UN General Assembly in December, 1988.

5. About 2 million Serbs lived in other Yugoslav republics, and 15 million Russians lived in other Soviet republics.

6. It is estimated that Croatian-Americans number 500,000 to one million; Serbian-Americans are only a small fraction of that.

7. Apart from anti-Croat sentiment, Serbs saved their deepest, racial, and sectarian animosity for ethnic Albanians of Kosovo Province, whose separatism was seen as a desecration of fallen Serb heroes at the Battle of the Field of Blackbirds six hundred years earlier—a point Milošević found to have political traction.

8. In early 1990, the United States called for NATO to take up the Yugoslav crisis. The French reaction was to claim that the United States was exaggerating the problem in order to demonstrate the importance of NATO.

9. This argument surfaced around the time of Serbian bombardment of the treasured Adriatic city of Dubrovnik in October of 1991.

10. Rome NATO Summit, 1991.

11. President Bush's National Security Advisor, Brent Scowcroft, was to become a role model in part because he did not permit his staff to make policy on its own.

12. At a meeting of Soviet leaders during the Polish crisis, then-KGB chief Yuri Andropov said, "Even if Poland falls under the control of Solidarity, so be it...We must be concerned above all with our own country." Mark A. Kramer, Working Paper No. 1, from the Cold War History project, cited in David Gompert, et al., *Blinders, Blunders, and Wars* (Washington, DC: RAND, 2014).

13. Bush administration officials also could not forget the 1989 crushing of democratic forces in Tiananmen Square.

14. Treasury's push for Soviet debt refinancing proved unhelpful by taking the focus off of internal transition to markets.

15. Author was present at a conversation between Bush and Gorbachev during which the Soviet leader explained that Baltic separatism put him under heavy pressure to lean toward a hard line, though he intended to make this temporary.

16. Hutchings, op. cit., p. 71.

17. Shevardnadze returned as foreign minister of the Soviet Union for the final month of its existence.

18. Thanks to Raymond Seitz, then-ambassador to the Court of St. James, for this telling anecdote.

Part II

The German Question

Chapter 7

Gorbachev and the GDR

Daniel S. Hamilton

The German Democratic Republic (GDR) was the illegitimate off-spring of the Cold War, in the words of one writer, the "state that can-not be."[1] Even after forty years of separate existence, the GDR never became a nation; it was never seen as a legitimate state by its own people, by West Germans or even by its own superpower patron, the Soviet Union.[2]

The illegitimate nature of the East German regime proved to be an incurable birth defect. It was also a characteristic that distinguished East Germany from its socialist neighbors. Unlike Polish, Hungarian or Czechoslovak rulers, the GDR regime could not fall back on distinct national traditions or a sense of historical continuity binding its citizens to its leaders. The Finnish diplomat Max Jacobson captured the essence of the GDR's precarious position:

> The GDR is fundamentally different from all other Warsaw Pact members. It is not a nation, but a state built on an ideological concept. Poland will remain Poland, and Hungary will always be Hungary, whatever their social system. But for East Germany, maintaining its socialist system is the reason for its existence.[3]

As J.F. Brown put it, "history has been full of nations seeking statehood, but the GDR was a state searching for nationhood."[4]

This lack of legitimacy afflicted the regime during the entire 40-year existence of the East German state. Without legitimacy, the regime could never consolidate its internal authority or its external stability. The imperative to gain legitimacy on each front—at home, from the West, and from the East—became the driving force behind the regime's policies. Yet the requirements to do this on each front were mutually exclusive. Full legitimacy would have been conferred by the West only if the GDR had transformed itself into a democratic state, which would then be relatively indistinguishable from the Federal Republic of Germany (FRG). Legitimacy in the eyes of the East German people would

145

have meant the right to travel, to free expression and free elections, and greater material well-being. These conditions were not only unacceptable to the East German regime, they would have posed a fundamental challenge to the Soviet Union. Full legitimacy was unlikely to come from an imperious ally who viewed the GDR as little more than war booty, the largest chunk of German flesh and soil that the Soviet Union had been able to command in return for the deaths of untold millions of Soviet citizens at the hands of the Nazis during World War II. In Soviet eyes, the purpose of the GDR was to keep Germany divided and partially under Soviet control, and to guarantee Soviet influence in European developments.

Brezhnev and the GDR

As the westernmost outpost of the East, the clamp of stability on the restless Soviet empire, the hinge of Soviet power in Europe, and the Soviet Union's most important economic partner, the GDR was critical to Soviet external and internal policies.[5] In the summer of 1970, Soviet leader Leonid Brezhnev made this view brutally clear to Erich Honecker, who at the time was the heir apparent to Walter Ulbricht, the GDR's hard-line leader:

> The GDR is an important post for us, for the fraternal socialist countries. It is the result of the Second World War, our acquisition, obtained with the blood of the Soviet people. I told you already once before that the GDR is not just your affair, but ours together ... After all we have troops in your country. Erich, I'm telling you frankly, don't ever forget it: without us, without the Soviet Union, its power and strength, the GDR cannot exist. Without us there is no GDR.[6]

Brezhnev's discussion with Honecker took place as rifts appeared between Soviet and GDR assessments of East-West détente in the early 1970s. From Walter Ulbricht's perspective, relaxation of East-West tensions, particularly West German leader Willy Brandt's new *Ostpolitik*, were dangerous attempts to undermine his efforts to build socialism at home and bolster the GDR's position in the East, thereby forcing its eventual acceptance by the West. His foreign minister, Otto Winzer, fumed that Brandt's "change through rapprochement" was nothing more than "aggression on felt slippers."[7] Ulbricht stuck to a maximalist position: de jure recognition of the GDR; an end to West Berlin's ties to the FRG; no easing of people-to-people contacts; and a combative intensification of the ideological struggle to prevent greater West German influence in the GDR.

The Soviet approach to détente was based on a different assessment of the relative opportunities and risks involved. Economic pressures and related demands for technological development were pushing the East toward greater reliance on the West for highly valued goods, technology, credits and markets. Brezhnev clearly recognized the seditious possibilities inherent in the new *Ostpolitik*. Nevertheless, the risks seemed tolerable given Bonn's offer of de facto recognition of the GDR and the territorial status quo in Europe. Moscow overruled Ulbricht's opposition, yet warned its allies that vigilance was still required. Moscow remained firm in its position that the German Question had been resolved and reaffirmed the Four Power status of Berlin, which provided Moscow with a lever of influence over all of Germany. The Kremlin brushed aside Ulbricht's demand that the GDR have a direct role in any settlement of Berlin's status. Some progress in German-German ties was also in Soviet interests since these developments, if gradual and controlled, promised to contribute to the political stability and economic survival of Moscow's key ally in Eastern Europe. The pull of German-German ties was also seen as a means for the Soviet Union to seek greater influence over the Federal Republic, less in the sense of a direct bid for German neutrality and more in terms of anticipatory compliance by the Federal Republic with Soviet desires related to selected issues, a kind of "preventive good behavior" that might lead to a less active FRG within the West.

Ulbricht's continued obstreperousness in foreign policy, coupled with his assertiveness on matters of Marxist doctrine, in which he presented himself more as teacher than student, rankled the Soviet leadership. His intransigence was even more irksome given that his ambitious economic program was collapsing and his domestic power base was unraveling.[8] In the end, Brezhnev worked with Honecker to engineer Ulbricht's ouster as party first secretary in early May 1971.

During Erich Honecker's entire tenure as leader of the East German regime, he would be preoccupied with managing the openness generated by relaxation of East-West tensions in ways that could enhance, rather than disrupt, domestic stability. Whereas Ulbricht had been hostile to détente, Honecker sought to limit its domestic impact while using the process to advance stability at home, promote the GDR's indispensability in the East, and bolster its legitimacy in the West. Honecker's rule was predicated on the notion that the GDR could manage German division and its own inherent illegitimacy by sustaining a series of precarious balances: between exposure to the West and insulation from it; between loyalty to the East and latitude within it; and between domestic viability and control. What appeared to be a relatively stable, even rigid, European order rested, in fact, on a number of delicate balances, each of which had to be sustained to compensate for the abiding absence of legitimacy in the GDR.

Over time, economic ties to the Federal Republic became the umbilical cord that nurtured Honecker's ambitious domestic economic and social program. The GDR began to rely on German-German trade as a stop-gap to overcome production bottlenecks or protect against short-term economic disturbances. At the same time, Honecker was careful to reaffirm and strengthen East German ties to its patron power, the Soviet Union. The GDR enhanced its position as Moscow's most important economic and strategic ally. The East German economy continued to deliver valuable machinery, chemicals and other industrial products, and provided an essential military contribution.[9] Having chafed under their second-class status for so long, GDR leaders relished the chance to act as Moscow's loyal agents, castigating Eurocommunists for ideological deviation, aligning themselves behind Kremlin policies, and supplying military and technical training as well as sophisticated weaponry to key Soviet clients in the Middle East, Latin America, and Africa.[10] In the eyes of the regime, a higher international profile would enhance the GDR's prestige and visibility around the world and at home. Honecker also realized that any latitude he might have to pursue more specific GDR state interests would derive from his utility to Moscow. Support for the Soviet economy, the Soviet military alliance, and Soviet global adventures might allow some greater maneuvering at home and vis-a-vis the West. The more indispensable the GDR was to the Soviet Union, the more leeway it would have.

These efforts also coincided with Soviet interests. From the Soviet point of view the very process of détente required a high degree of bloc discipline. Although the Soviets had pushed the GDR regime toward a more conciliatory stance toward Bonn in the early 1970s, Moscow remained interested in a status-quo policy regarding the German Question. The Soviet Union's principal stance was that the network of East-West agreements concluded in the early 1970s—the 1970 Moscow Treaty, the 1971 Quadripartite Agreement on Berlin (which the USSR and the GDR continued to try to apply only to West Berlin), the treaties between the FRG and its eastern neighbors (including the GDR), and the 1975 Helsinki Final Act—constituted a "settlement" of the post-World War II European territorial and political order. In the Soviet view, these agreements constituted legal and political recognition by the FRG that the German Question was irrevocably closed. Any attempt to reopen it was ipso facto "revanchism" and a danger to peace. Conversely, continued adherence to these agreements, as Moscow and East Berlin interpreted them, was a precondition for continued good relations.[11]

Thus, despite improved West German-Soviet relations and some initial hopes in Bonn, for years there was no "Soviet card" for Bonn to play in its relations with East Berlin. Some in Bonn began to argue that any attempts to pressure East Berlin, even if initially successful, could prove counterproductive in the long run by destabilizing the East German leadership and unnerving Moscow. Bonn was interested in internal liberalization in the GDR, but not to the point of political upheaval which, it was feared, could lead to unpredictable and possibly violent consequences on the front line of the Cold War. Richard Löwenthal summed up what he called the "silent consensus" in Bonn:

> unless there were a major change in the nature and policy of the Soviet regime that would open the door to basic transformation of the Soviet bloc in Eastern Europe, no change in the status of East Germany could occur. Even in that case, the consequence would be a rapprochement rather than a reunification of the two German states. Short of such a basic change in Soviet policy, even a major crisis in East Germany would be most unlikely to provoke active West German intervention because such intervention would not only be contrary to the international commitments assumed by West Germany, but might also lead to its physical annihilation by the Soviets.[12]

The Lull Before the Storm

As the motorcade glided up to the squat black Chancellery building in Bonn, what from a distance appeared to be a harmonious sea of black, red and gold circling the Chancellery courtyard was transformed upon closer inspection into the colors of German division. A hammer and compass within a garland of wheat, the symbol of East German sovereignty, was imposed on every other black-red-gold tricolor. The flags hung limply in the wan Rhineland sunshine as the leader of East Germany stepped from his limousine onto a red carpet. The West German Chancellor welcomed his guest with a stiff handshake and the gray-uniformed *Bundeswehr* band struck up the anthems of the two states. As the discordant sounds of German division rang out, the two men standing uneasily at attention seemed to have become frozen caricatures of the states they represented: a wooden Erich Honecker, resolute yet conveying a hint of frailty; and a huge, hale and hearty Helmut Kohl.

Honecker's visit to Bonn in September 1987 was the first by an East German leader to West Germany. It was marked by a variety of conflicting positions and ambivalent images that appeared simultaneously to dilute and harden the 38-year-old partition of the country. The man who supervised the building of the Berlin Wall, the symbol of German division, was now standing next to a man who held eventual German unity to be a sacred constitutional and moral obligation. For Honecker, the visit was a triumphant affirmation that Bonn accepted the sovereignty and legitimacy for which East Berlin had struggled for so long. For Kohl, the visit was proof that his efforts to deepen the cohesion of the nation were bearing fruit.

This tension characterized the entire five-day trip. Honecker declared that "socialism and capitalism are as incompatible as fire and water;" Kohl insisted that the "unity of our nation is our goal." Honecker evoked the common responsibility of both German states to ensure that "war never again emanate from German soil;" Kohl gave his visitor a tongue-lashing about the order given to East German border guards to shoot on sight anyone attempting to escape to the West.

Despite Kohl's efforts during the visit to convey the enduring unity of the nation, the ceremonial honors bestowed on Honecker all appeared to confirm its division. At the same time, Honecker's strident affirmations of this division seemed to be undermined by his visit to his own dingy Saarland hometown of Wiebelskirchen—a testament to the very personal ties that continued to unite Germans across the barbed-wire border. When Honecker drove to Dachau, one of Nazi Germany's most terrible concentration camps, and laid a giant wreath of red roses before a wall inscribed with the words "Never Again," he validated the deep bonds of obligation imposed on both German states by a common history.[13]

Honecker's visit to Bonn in 1987 was the most visible ratification of the tacit consensus that had come to govern intra-German detente. It was less a breakthrough than a benchmark of the progress that had been reached over the 17 years since Willy Brandt's visit to the East German city of Erfurt in 1970 had ushered in a new era of German-German ties. Each German state remained a loyal member of its respective alliance, yet both had built a relatively extensive network of relations across the Iron Curtain. German-German cooperation had expanded beyond a tense and narrow tradeoff of East German political concessions for West German economic concessions to incorporate cultural exchanges and cooperation on energy, environmental, scientific and transportation matters.

In retrospect, this period of budding German-German cooperation was but the lull before the storm. Yet at the time, Honecker's visit was the most concrete signal yet to most observers that the German Question had been transformed from the issue of reunification in a unitary German state to the more practical issue of how German-German reassociation might affect the East-West balance in Europe. "The unification of Germany is not on the agenda in the historically anticipated future," the Polish government newspaper *Rzeczpospolita* declared on the eve of Honecker's visit. Neither, of course, was the demise of communist Poland. Yet gathering forces of change were to prove the "historically anticipated future" wrong on both accounts, and with breathtaking speed.

The Eroding Pillars

By the time of Honecker's visit, the pillars of the regime's rule in the GDR were eroding. Yet the extent of the damage was not clear to the rulers or the ruled. The ascension of Mikhail Gorbachev to power in Moscow not only unleashed a new dynamic in the Soviet Union, it clarified and accelerated two other important factors shaping the historical forces at the heart of the Cold War in Central Europe. The GDR, the Soviet Union's key strategic and economic partner, formerly the most active protagonist of socialist conformity in Eastern Europe, quickly emerged as the strongest proponent of individuality. This dynamic was compounded in turn by a new, complex triangular relationship between Moscow, East Berlin and Bonn that transformed the German Question. These currents of change, together with Gorbachev's own agenda for reform, produced a voluble potion that was to recast the balance of European and global power.

The German Democratic Republic, no longer a child of the Cold War, remained a 38-year old political adolescent. Outward manifestations of self-assertion were motivated by more deep-seated feelings of insecurity, which in turn were aggravated by a veritable volte face in the behavior of its guardian power. An excessively intransigent Soviet Union suddenly became a dangerously reformist Soviet Union. Soviet subsidies reversed themselves into Soviet demands. As the rest of COMECON slid into economic disaster and the domestic GDR economy began to falter, German-German ties provided the only source of external relief. At the same time, the GDR could not afford to stray too far from the Soviet fold, for the limited latitude it enjoyed resulted from its utility within its Eastern alliance. Drifting too close to West Germany would further erode the regime's chronically weak domestic legitimacy and forfeit Moscow's support for continued German-German ties. While Bonn was supporting the GDR economically, the seditious effects of détente, marked by increased travel and communications, had only increased the attractiveness of the West. A relatively cohesive Western alliance faced an increasingly diffuse Eastern alliance.

While Moscow continued to support East Berlin's position on the finality of the German Question, it was undermining it politically and economically. East Berlin's refusal to acknowledge, let alone resolve, the inherent contradiction between its abiding political rigidity and the imperative of economic modernization was bankrupting the country. Dealing with detente with the West, *glasnost* from the East, and disaffection at home required an impossible dexterity in turning the spigots of power that were at the heart of Honecker's complex balancing act.

Gorbachev and the German Question

The deterioration and eventual rejuvenation of Soviet foreign policy was related to a prolonged triple succession crisis prompted by the death of three General Secretaries of the Communist Party of the Soviet Union in less than three years. "I can't get down to business with Soviet leaders," President Ronald Reagan complained. "They keep dying on me."[14]

In March 1985 relatively young and highly energetic Mikhail Gorbachev emerged as the new leader of the Soviet Union. He promptly set out to rouse his country from the lethargy associated with its prolonged leadership crisis. Gorbachev had "iron teeth," Andrei Gromyko noted approvingly; the veteran Soviet foreign minister hoped the new leader would be able to convince audiences at home and abroad that the Soviet Union was again a dynamic force to be reckoned with in world affairs. Gorbachev intended to do just that, but hardly in the way Gromyko had expected. One of the new General Secretary's most significant early acts was to bump Gromyko up to the ceremonial presidency and thus out of the Foreign Ministry he had dominated for decades. Eduard Shevardnadze, a Gorbachev ally and a Georgian with little foreign policy experience, was appointed Foreign Minister in July 1985.

Concerned with stagnating economic performance, deteriorating social conditions and relative isolation in foreign affairs, and buffeted by pressures from a new, educated, urban social strata that came of age in the late 1970s and early 1980s, Gorbachev advanced a triad of reforms in domestic and foreign policy. He initiated a major campaign for domestic economic and social "restructuring"—*perestroika*; pushed for a new transparency and self-critical attitude—*glasnost*—within the Soviet state and Soviet society; and proclaimed a "new thinking" in the Soviet approach to international affairs.

The spectacle of an energetic, reform-minded Soviet leader was a daily fascination for audiences at home and abroad who had grown accustomed to a plodding and heavy-handed group of old men in the Kremlin. Yet despite Gorbachev's vigorous image, the early stage of his tenure, which lasted until the fall of 1986, was characterized by a confusing mélange of old and new thinking. On the one hand, he issued tantalizing proclamations about human rights and human values. At the Central Committee plenary in April 1985, for instance, he spoke out for "civilized relations between states based on true adherence to the norms of international law." This was followed by a speech before French parliamentarians on October 3, 1985 in which he praised Europe as "a cradle of spiritual values" and stressed that the Soviet Union attributed "greatest importance" to human rights. After his first meeting in November with President Reagan, Gorbachev emphasized that every people had the "right to choice...the choice of their system, their methods, forms and friends ... If one does not recognize that, I don't know how one can shape international relations."[15]

On the other hand, there was continuing evidence of old thinking, such as Gorbachev's report to the 27th Party Congress of the Communist Party of the Soviet Union (CPSU) on February 25, 1986, in which he charged that the main dangers to peace emanated from the West. Even his toughest rhetoric, however, was modified by references to global interdependence and the resultant need for cooperative rather than competitive "peaceful coexistence."[16]

Early contradictions were apparent in Moscow's European policies. In the fall of 1985 Gorbachev spoke for the first time in public at some length about the "European House," an initial indication that arms control initiatives were to be only the beginning, and not the end, of his foreign policy reforms, and that for the first time a Soviet leader would not be reluctant to link arms control to human rights concerns.[17] Despite such images of cooperation and isolated pronouncements about a "socialist commonwealth" and new notions of "socialist internationalism," it was unclear whether the Kremlin was prepared to risk a fundamental redefinition of its relations with its East European neighbors. Traditionally, Moscow wanted regimes that were economically and politically viable but whose policies and domestic systems came under broad Soviet control. The abiding tension between these two goals led to periodic eruptions. By the mid-1980s Eastern Europe had entered a period of economic and political change marked by a conjunction of destabilizing elements, including economic decline, open social unrest and the dwindling appeal of ideology, all against the backdrop of highly uncertain leadership succession issues in various countries. For many observers, it appeared that the added impact of the winds of reform from the Soviet Union itself could so aggravate these processes that things would get out of control. Scholars were comparing Gorbachev with Khrushchev, wondering whether he would become so preoccupied with internal problems that he would miss the signs of impending turmoil in Eastern Europe until it would be too late.[18] The optimal mixture of alliance cohesion, internal autonomy, and controlled opening to the West was quickly becoming the unresolved and ultimately unresolvable equation in Soviet-East European relations.

Gorbachev reflected this ambivalence. While he tolerated more individual expression of national interests in Eastern Europe and was careful to stress "their autonomy in their internal affairs," at the same time Moscow urged more "efficient" economic integration among the COMECON states and raised its expectations of East European economies. The resulting push-me pull-you policies promoted individualism on the one hand and increased demands for tighter bloc efficiency on the other. Yet economic cooperation among the COMECON nations remained indifferent. Although the Soviets were keen on stepping up COMECON integration, the economic interests of the East European countries led them to look westward. In addition, Gorbachev remained tied to elements of the Brezhnev Doctrine. In Poland on June 30, 1986 he declared that "socialist achievements" could never be reversed, nor could this or that country be ripped out of the socialist community. Any other policy, he added, would mean "challenging not only the will of the people, but the entire postwar order and, as a final consequence, peace."[19]

In sum, despite a fresher rhetorical approach to differences within the socialist camp, there was no indication, as 1986 ended, that Moscow would abandon its traditional twin goals of viability and control in Eastern Europe. While the degree of diversity and experimentation in Eastern Europe was remarkable by postwar standards, the parameters of permissible political reform and national autonomy ultimately remained undefined. The "Gorbachev Doctrine" vis-a-vis Eastern Europe had neither been formulated nor tested. While Gorbachev was clearly prepared to sacrifice some control for greater viability, it seemed unlikely at the time that he would risk too much in this regard. The benefits of a somewhat more dynamic Eastern Europe appeared to be insufficient to risk a revival of such crises as in the GDR in 1953, Hungary in 1956, Czechoslovakia in 1968, and Poland in 1980/81. And a serious future eruption in Eastern Europe, so the common wisdom, would certainly reverberate in Moscow.

The limits of new thinking seemed most clear in Moscow's position on the German Question. Despite rumors and eager talk in the West, there was little indication until 1989 that "new thinking" would lead to any Soviet initiative regarding a new framework for the German Question. Upon entering office Gorbachev did little to change the Brezhnev position on the closed German Question and general Soviet foreign policy toward the two German states. There were only vague and superficial hints of change in the "principal stance" of the Soviet Union toward the German Question, a position supported fully by the GDR. During the interlude between Brezhnev's death in 1982 and the first two years of Gorbachev's tenure, the Kremlin's ties with Bonn, its major European partner during the heyday of détente, were in the deep freeze.

Honecker had been acquainted with Gorbachev since the 1960s and did not believe him to be a radical reformer.[20] Gorbachev, for his part, had been struck by Honecker's willingness to buck Moscow's hard line during the early 1980s with his call for "damage limitation" in the wake of the stationing of the INF missiles. During their first serious encounter as general secretaries of their parties on May 5, 1985, both appeared keen to reconfirm their close ties and present an image of unity on all major issues, particularly on the eve of the 40th anniversary of the end of World War II.[21] Any West German hopes for new flexibility were quickly dashed by the uncompromising language of the final communique, which stated that both leaders "firmly rejected any concept regarding an 'open German question'." Internally, Gorbachev told his advisors that while the GDR was "stronger" than the other east European countries, "it could never withstand a union with the FRG."[22] The orthodox Soviet position was so strong, in fact, that Gorbachev rejected Honecker's plan to visit the Federal Republic, did so again when the two leaders met in Moscow during the 27th Party Congress of the CPSU on February 26, 1986, and did so a third time in East Berlin for the 11th Party Congress of the SED in April 1986. "We were resentful of his playing games with the West Germans," recalled Shevardnadze's chief aide Sergei Tarasenko.[23]

First signs of serious conflict between Honecker and Gorbachev became apparent in the fall of 1986. Two weeks before the two leaders met in Moscow, West German Foreign Minister Hans-Dietrich Genscher had traveled to the Soviet capital to revive the tenuous relationship between Bonn and the Kremlin. While the West Germans detected no sign of change in the Soviet position on the fundamentals of the status quo, a new flexibility was apparent in Moscow's view of both German-German ties and the West German-Soviet relationship.[24]

New Thinking

When Honecker arrived in Moscow, Gorbachev made it clear that he was ready to redefine the West German-Soviet relationship as part of his concept of the European House. One had to be careful of the West Germans, the Soviet leader said, but for "peace in the world and for the development of Europe this triangle of USSR-GDR and FRG has extraordinary weight."[25] While Honecker was somewhat wary of the new warmth evident in the West German-Soviet relationship, he welcomed Soviet efforts to reinvigorate détente, and was pleased now that it was clear that nothing stood in the way of his visit to Bonn.

The East German leader reserved his harshest words for what he believed to be a much more significant challenge: *glasnost*. Soviet artists and writers were telling their East German colleagues to "overthrow their generals," Honecker charged angrily. "Political deviants in the GDR could quickly use this to their advantage." He demanded that Gorbachev reign in such comments. "It is important for us to have to fight on one and not on two fronts," he fumed.

The battle had been joined. By the turn of the year Soviet diplomats were circulating word that Hans Modrow, the SED party chief in Dresden, was considered favorably by Kremlin reform circles and was Gorbachev's candidate eventually to replace Honecker. KGB Vice-Chairman Kryuchkov visited Dresden in 1987 to discuss reform proposals with Modrow. The East Berlin gerontocracy was further distressed by Gorbachev's pronouncement to the Central Committee of the CPSU in January 1987: "We need democracy as we need the air to breathe." Honecker promptly told Anatoly Dobrynin that what Moscow did at home was its own business.[26]

During 1987 and 1988 Moscow sought to recapture the gains of Soviet-West German detente that had languished during the previous five years, although Gorbachev was unnerved when Chancellor Kohl compared his public relations talents to those of Nazi propaganda chief

Josef Goebbels. Moscow focused on Bonn's stand on arms control negotiations, seeking to persuade West Germany that it was not in German interest to modernize short-range nuclear weapons. The Kremlin also courted the SPD and the anti-nuclear opposition. During this period Moscow also focused much more clearly on the potential role West German trade and investment could play in ensuring the success of Gorbachev's ambitious program of economic reform.

The Kremlin made it clear, however, that a "new page" in relations with Bonn could only be based on the political and territorial status quo in Europe. Gorbachev clung to the "reality" of two German states and was not prepared to acknowledge the continued existence of one German nation, as he indicated in his discussion with German President Richard von Weizsäcker on July 7, 1987. There were two German states with different socio-political systems and differing values, he said. This was the reality. "What will happen in a hundred years will be decided by history...No other approach is acceptable." For the time being, he warned, "one should proceed from the existing realities and not engage in incendiary speculations."[27]

1988 was the turning point, as Gorbachev himself has acknowledged. When he came to power in 1985, he believed he could work through the party-dominated bureaucracy to implement his agenda for reform. But the Communist Party apparatchiks upon whom he was relying to push through change stood to lose most from it and therefore resisted.[28] There was little movement. "By the beginning of 1988," Gorbachev recalls, "it became clear that the efforts to implement the reforms - primarily the efforts toward radical economic reforms—were foundering on the political structures, on the regime itself, on the prevailing property relationships. That was the point when it became clear to me that we were in a systemic crisis and that the system itself would have to be transformed."[29]

A shake-up of revolutionary proportions was launched. Gorbachev and Shevardnadze now went beyond such earlier isolated statements as "no single party has a monopoly on the truth" and that socialism had "no model to which all must orient themselves" by renouncing the Brezhnev Doctrine itself. In a Soviet-Yugoslav declaration in mid-March 1988, both states declared that neither intended to "force others to comply with its views on the development of societies" and that each rejected "any threat and use of force and interference in the or internal affairs of other states."[30]

Behind the scenes, deeds followed words. The Soviets privately made it clear to Hungary's beleaguered communist party boss, János Kádár, that he could no longer count on Soviet support in the event of a major internal crisis. Kádár was replaced in May 1988 by Károly Grósz, a Gorbachev admirer who received complete Soviet support for further political and economic liberalization in Hungary, including the implementation of a multi-party system.[31]

At the 19th All-Union Party Conference in Moscow on June 28, 1988, Gorbachev declared that a key element of new thinking in foreign policy was the concept of freedom of choice. "We are convinced of the universality of this principle," he proclaimed. "In this situation, outside imposition of a particular social order, a particular way of life or a particular policy—by whatever means, not to mention military ones—is a dangerous rudiment of a bygone age...to resist freedom of choice means to oppose the objective course of history itself."[32]

For the first time Gorbachev spoke not of getting more out of the old system, but of "radical reform." Later that year he announced what he called a "blowing up" of the old political system: freer elections, a full-time working parliament, more powers to the local councils, or soviets, all of which were intended to shift power away from the bureaucracy.[33]

Hungary was not the only country that appeared to be free to pursue its own course. Reform-minded forces in Poland also gained new room for maneuver. In September 1988 Nikolai Shishlin, a Gorbachev adviser from the Central Committee, told *Le Monde* that Moscow had abandoned the Brezhnev Doctrine. The Kremlin, he said, no longer had a "right of veto" in Polish internal affairs. Other Soviet officials indicated they would not be overly concerned if *Solidarność* reemerged. Soviet reform circles were openly calling for "an evolutionary path between the neo-Stalinist, centralized bureaucratic 'socialist' system in the East, and the pluralist, social democratic, market-oriented 'capitalist' system in the West."[34]

Gorbachev's ultimate goal was a more humane and productive socialism, not the end of socialism itself. Leading circles in Moscow seriously considered whether an explicit bargain should be offered to the east European "allies:" in exchange for a pledge by the east European regimes to remain socialist, Moscow would drastically reduce, and perhaps even withdraw, its military forces.[35]

A bitter battle was simultaneously underway within the Soviet bureaucracy regarding German policy. For years the Third European Department of the Ministry of Foreign Affairs, led by Alexander Bondarenko, had been the guardians of Soviet orthodoxy on the German Question. Nicknamed "the Berlin Wall" by their own colleagues, the German experts in the Foreign Ministry had made a career out of defending the status of Berlin and Moscow's rights regarding Germany as a whole from any and all challengers. "German problems were isolated" from other areas of foreign policy-making, recalled Shevardnadze's aide Tarasenko. "They had a special status and were under the authority of a close-knit company" within the bureaucracy. For decades they had enjoyed a privileged position under the watchful eye of Foreign Minister Gromyko, who prided himself on his own knowledge of and steadfastness on German issues, and who did not hesitate to punish Soviet diplomats who did not toe his rigid policy line in this area. A further bureaucratic division of labor in Moscow complicating German policy was that relations with socialist countries, including the GDR, traditionally fell under the purview of the International Department of the Central Committee, led by Valentin Falin, former Soviet Ambassador to Bonn.

The Third European Department was "stonewalling on everything," Tarasenko recalls. "They saw their role as spoilers." By 1987, with relations with East Berlin increasingly tense and ties to Bonn still in limbo, even Moscow's German experts realized that changes were necessary—up to a point. They understood better than Gorbachev or Shevardnadze that the GDR's economic and political position was not what it seemed, and that closer economic ties between Bonn and East Berlin were inevitable to prevent the GDR from slipping into "Polish conditions."[36] They were eager to open a new chapter in Moscow's relations with Europe's economic powerhouse—the Federal Republic of Germany. At the same time, they were resentful that East German insecurities hampered fuller bilateral ties between Moscow and Bonn.

That there was little serious consideration of any fundamental change in the basic status quo was made clear by an explosive meeting in the fall of 1987. Upon assuming office Shevardnadze formed academic advisory councils as a mechanism to discuss unconventional ideas. Vyacheslav Dashichev, a controversial department head at the Institute for the Economics of the Socialist World System, was made Chairman of the Advisory Council for the socialist states. In April 1987 Dashichev continued his heretical ways with a 26-page paper on the German Question, which he presented to an Advisory Council meeting on November 27, 1987.[37] In the paper Dashichev examined a wide range of possibilities in the future evolution of the German Question, including the continuation of the two German states; confederation or unification based on the principle of neutrality; and a unified German state integrated into the Western alliance. That Dashichev would reject option three right away was hardly controversial. But he unleashed a storm of controversy by arguing for option two—a unified, neutral Germany—instead of the status quo. The existing situation was disadvantageous to Soviet interests, Dashichev claimed. It could only prolong Cold War confrontation and the economic burdens of empire. The real cause of East-West confrontation, he argued, was German division. As long as the key to the solution of the German Question was in Moscow's hands, the Kremlin should use it to unlock new possibilities for a new relationship between Germany and the Soviet Union that could significantly advance Soviet interests. If it didn't, he predicted, unification would occur regardless of Soviet wishes.

Even in the prevailing atmosphere of "new thinking," Dashichev had broken a long-standing taboo. He was accused of "political sins" and all copies of his paper were ordered destroyed. Sergei Tarasenko commented on the reaction by the senior leadership at the time: "We heard about his early paper and were in general agreement with his position, but the basic attitude then was still 'if it ain't broke, don't fix it.' We were distracted by many problems. We didn't see that Germany was broken, and so we didn't try to fix it. In our gut we knew that sooner or later there would be a problem, but it seemed far enough away so we were not preoccupied with it."[38]

Dashichev persisted in his efforts. In a May 18, 1988 article in *Liturnaya Gazeta* he presented a comprehensive critique of Soviet Cold War policies. Blind Soviet adherence to a status quo policy in Europe, he argued, was damaging Soviet interests by imposing inordinate economic burdens on the country and isolating it from the rest of the world. The Cold War had resulted in an intolerable militarization of Soviet society. The only way to change this was to change the Soviet position vis-à-vis the division of Germany and Europe, which was the true source of East-West antagonism. He again proposed various solutions to the German question, including a neutral confederation. This was followed by his highly publicized remark in June 1988 that the Berlin Wall was a relic of the Cold War and would disappear under more favorable political circumstances. A virulent response, most likely drafted by Honecker himself, appeared the very next day in *Neues Deutschland*, the official communist party newspaper. Soviet Foreign Ministry spokesman Gennady Gerasimov was forced to disavow Dashichev's remarks.[39]

New Winds of Change

As these debates continued, Bonn and Moscow struggled to revive their own relationship after five frosty years. Shevardnadze visited Bonn in January 1988 and Genscher visited Moscow in July to prepare a visit by Chancellor Kohl to Moscow in October.

New momentum was clearly apparent. At the summit German business executives and Soviet representatives signed 16 agreements on economic cooperation and a consortium of German banks approved a credit of 3 billion Deutschmark (DM). The two governments signed a cultural agreement that had been in the deep freeze since 1973 as well as an environmental agreement that had also been on hold for years because of persistent differences whether and how such agreements would include West Berlin. For the first time since World War II the defense ministers of the two countries met for an exchange of views. Outside the wintery Kremlin walls the temperature was -6°C, but inside Gorbachev announced that "the ice had been broken." In advance of the summit Bonn officials looked hard for signs that Moscow might be willing to reconsider its "principal position" on the German Question and the situation of Berlin.

During the summit the Chancellor was so insistent on both issues that Gorbachev chose to respond in public with the toughest of various responses that had been prepared for him in advance by the Foreign

Ministry's "Berlin Wall." The present situation was the result of history, the Soviet leader declared. Any attempt to "force the pace of events through unrealistic policies," he warned, was an incalculable and even dangerous undertaking." He did not object to Bonn including West Berliners in its international activities, but the West Germans had to realize that "the special status of the city remains unshakable." Quoting Goethe, he admonished Kohl that "nothing is as dangerous for the new truth as old mistakes."[40]

Privately, however, there were clearer hints that the Soviet position was changing. "All the possibilities to overcome the phenomenon of the 'Iron Curtain' have not yet been exhausted," Shevardnadze told the West German delegation. Both sides agreed to explore these possibilities in advance of a visit by Gorbachev to Bonn in the summer of 1989.[41]

Among the East European regimes, responses to Soviet debates on the nature and scope of *perestroika*, *glasnost*, and "new thinking" were mixed. While Hungary and Poland joined the Gorbachev course, Romania openly scorned the Kremlin's initiatives, and in Czechoslovakia and Bulgaria the leadership was paralyzed. For East Berlin, however, Gorbachev's calls for reform threatened to undermine the GDR's very rationale for existence as an "antifascist, socialist alternative to the Federal Republic,"[42] in the words of Otto Reinhold, one of the party's leading theoreticians. If the GDR introduced reforms a la Gorbachev, it would lose its socialist identity and be only a poor copy of the Federal Republic. Under such circumstances pressures for reunification would grow and the GDR would eventually be swallowed up by its economically more powerful sister state. Hence, the regime felt it had to resist taking any steps, however, small, down the slippery slope of reform.

The GDR regime differentiated its response to Gorbachev's triad of reform by supporting "new thinking" wholeheartedly in broad terms, while hoping thereby to gain some margin of maneuver, particularly in German-German relations and to retain some influence over Moscow's own *Deutschlandpolitik*; interpreting *perestroika* narrowly to mean simply economic restructuring, which the GDR then sought to dismiss by pointing to the relative success of its centralized command economy; and rejecting *glasnost* outright by building new walls to shelter its society from the fresh winds blowing from the East.

Perestroika and the East German Economy

A key to the GDR's maneuvering room internally and externally was how well it could maintain its reputation as socialism's economic work-horse. Viewed from East Berlin, *perestroika* looked like a prescription for disaster rather than a solution to the GDR's problems. While acknowledging that the *Soviet* economy was in need of massive reforms, they denied that this was true for the GDR. "Many of the changes in the Soviet Union are already routine in the GDR," Honecker sniffed.[43] Kurt Hager, secretary of the Central Committee and chief ideologue of the SED, presented Gorbachev's domestic reform policies as nothing more than interior decorating, a cosmetic touch-up for which the GDR had absolutely no need. "If your neighbor would re-wallpaper his apartment," he asked rhetorically, "would you also feel compelled to repaper your apartment?"[44]

The relative economic success of the GDR did in fact give the leadership some breathing space, particularly given the quite incoherent nature of Gorbachev's own plans for economic reform. The GDR, East German officials argued, enjoyed the highest standard of living, the highest economic productivity, the strongest and the steadiest growth in COMECON. The GDR was the largest supplier of machines and consumer goods within COMECON. It was the Soviet Union's most important trading partner. For most of the other COMECON countries the GDR was the second most important trading partner after the Soviet Union. The GDR population of less than 17 million produced more than its 37 million Polish neighbors. COMECON countries looked to the West, if possible, to secure leading technology, but when left to their own resources, they looked to the GDR. In fact, GDR officials argued, the Soviets themselves counted on the GDR economy to make important contributions to the long-overdue modernization of the Soviet economy. GDR officials were particularly keen to distance themselves from Soviet economic reforms also because they found that Gorbachev's efforts at COMECON efficiency would chain the GDR to its uncompetitive partners and drag down east German standards of living. Thus, while their minimum goal was to limit the impact of the Soviet debate on the GDR, their maximum goal was to exploit Moscow's higher tolerance for east European autonomy by diversifying their economic ties.

Given this position, GDR officials could be relatively secure that there would be little chance of Soviet pressure to undergo an East German version of *perestroika*. Soviet officials confirmed this view. "We thought Honecker's position was strong, we were convinced the GDR was a bulwark of socialism composed of good solid socialists," recalled Tarasenko.[45] Throughout this early period the new Soviet leadership still had an unrealistic picture of the GDR's economic achievements. Warnings about the real situation from other Politburo members were ignored. "We were so busy with our own problems," recalled Vyacheslav Kochemasov, the Soviet ambassador to East Berlin, "we left the GDR to its fate."[46]

Behind this façade of superior economic performance, however, lay a grimmer reality. Honecker's commitment to consumerism and prestige-oriented technology-driven growth had bankrupted the GDR economy. Growth had eased under the weight of growing subsidies, sagging investments, flagging productivity and poor export performance. By 1985 the economy had eroded so badly that the regime has forced to assign up to 55,000 soldiers to work each winter in coal mining, aluminum, and chemical factories even though it refused to ease up on its high standards of defense readiness. This led to increasing morale problems and contributed to the inner erosion of the National People's Army (NVA).[47]

The gap between official propaganda and reality on the streets had become so wide that in 1987 and 1988 the SED was forced to concede openly for the first time since 1971 a clear failure to achieve the targets of the plan, even though this had been true for some time and the Politburo had been falsifying the data on a regular basis. For the average East German, official proclamations of "social rights" rang increasingly hollow when medicine was unavailable, housing remained problematic, the wait for a Trabant automobile or a telephone connection was 12-15 years, and social status was dependent partially on who had access to hard currency.[48]

Official recitations of the GDR's economic achievements compared to its COMECON partners also overlooked one significant fact: for most East Germans, the yardstick of progress was the alternative German state, the Federal Republic of Germany, rather than any of the GDR's Eastern neighbors. Yet despite its position as the most productive socialist economy and its favored access to Western technology, goods and finance through the special German-German channel, the gap in performance and living standards with the FRG widened steadily. Western estimates at the time consistently overestimated the GDR's economic capabilities. Productivity in the GDR was about one-third the level in the FRG. Per capita purchasing power in the GDR was at least 60% behind the West German level. Even more significant than quantitative comparisons, however, was the fact that the growing number of GDR visitors to the FRG were now able to experience first-hand the gap in living standards and the possibilities of a modern social market economy.[49]

In the face of these massive economic challenges, the regime was running on borrowed time and borrowed money. By 1987 the GDR's net foreign debt had climbed to 34.7 billion valuta marks. Domestic economic policy had been reduced to managing scarcity and securing sufficient infusions of quick cash from the West simply to meet the interest payments on its growing mountain of debt.[50]

In sum, by the late 1980s much of the Honecker regime's hard-fought internal and external achievements were being undermined by the GDR's precarious economic situation. Economic performance was no longer able to compensate for its lack of internal and external legitimacy. The fundamental dilemma for the regime was that in the new global economy economic development could not be commanded from above. Technological innovation, creativity, modern communications and information flows were essential to the GDR's own goals of intensive and extensive growth. Yet this presumed a degree of openness and decentralized authority the SED was unwilling to tolerate for fear of political destabilization. The regime was caught between the consequences of greater openness as a precondition for competitiveness and the equally unnerving alternative of stagnation on the front lines of the East-West divide. In short, economic pressures were directly related to the political pressures facing the regime, which in turn were being aggravated by a far more disturbing aspect of the fresh winds blowing from the East—*glasnost*.

Abgrenzung to the East

During the 1970s and 1980s, East Berlin responded rather successfully to West German attempts at "change through rapprochement" with its own policies of "change through *Abgrenzung*"—a policy of carefully controlled opening that maintained the party's control over society. Now, in a remarkable turn of events, the GDR's leadership was faced with a similar challenge of openness; this time, however, the challenge was coming from its own superpower patron, the guarantor not only of East Germany's external security but also of the regime's internal authority. Bewildered, yet skeptical that Gorbachev's reforms would succeed or, for that matter, that Gorbachev himself would remain in power, Honecker attempted to ride out the storm with a stopgap version of *Abgrenzung*, directed this time at the East yet derived from the same fear that unsettling ideas could loosen the regime's precarious grip on its own society.

Fearful that its own population might contract *glasnost* fever, the regime cracked down harshly on internal dissent. It also took active defensive measures to insulate East German society from the provocative ideas now coming from Moscow. Media restrictions were tightened; the internal Soviet debate was censored, and the notion of individual paths to socialism was promoted.

Nonetheless, the mixture of years of détente with the West and now *glasnost* from the East was forcing change on three fronts simultaneously— the West, the East, and from within.

New Thinking and the GDR

Internal retrenchment was accompanied by external activism. GDR officials sought to compensate for their rejection of *glasnost* and *perestroika* at home by embracing Soviet proclamations of "new thinking" abroad, which promised to reduce East Berlin's military costs and grant the GDR greater autonomy to advance its interests in the German-German relationship.

The initial focus of Soviet "new thinking" was in the field of arms control. A variety of new initiatives by Gorbachev reflected arguments Honecker himself had used in 1983-1984 against Moscow's hard-line

positions at the time. Thus, the GDR supported the military security
aspects of "new thinking" wholeheartedly, primarily out of GDR state
interests rather than blind allegiance to the Soviet Union. GDR officials echoed their Soviet colleagues by explaining that the imperative
of "new thinking" in foreign policy was defined out of the "logic of the
atomic age" with the purpose of avoiding a "nuclear inferno."[51] Given
the economic strains facing the regime, one motivation for GDR support for new thinking was to reduce the burden of defense spending on
the economy. Next to the Soviet Union the GDR's defense spending
was the highest in the Warsaw Pact, both in absolute and per capita
terms and in relation to national income.[52]

Yet "new thinking" could only extend so far. The regime made it
clear that "cooperative peaceful coexistence" would not erase the dividing line between socialism and capitalism but provided "the framework
condition for peaceful contest between the two different systems and
is, at the same time, the major prerequisite for both sides to exist according to their own needs and to do things their own way."[53] In other
words, such a condition would bolster the position of the GDR as an
accepted member of the interstate system.

The regime had greater difficulties with Gorbachev's growing emphasis on respect for human rights as the basis for a new international order. East German officials stuck to their traditional position that
peace between societies (read: full acceptance of the GDR) "is the
prerequisite for any human right and its implementation." In addition, they relativized such political rights as free expression and travel,
placing them on a par with social rights and even vaguely defined be
"cultural" rights. "We do not discriminate between more or less as important rights," declared Max Schmidt, Director of the Institute for
Politics and Economics. "Any claim to exclusiveness by one side would
be counterproductive, not to speak of attempts to pervert the human
rights issue to a lever of discrediting and eventual elimination of the
system opponent."[54]

The Home Front

At the time of Honecker's 1987 visit to Bonn, it appeared from the
outside that the regime had proven itself able to contain pressures for

change: it had garnered a more legitimate standing from Bonn; it had wrested a degree of maneuverability from its superpower patron; and it appeared to be maintaining its domestic balance rather successfully due to a combination of repression and carefully calibrated doses of openness. Dissidents were either isolated internally, by being sentenced to jail or confined to the shelter of the Church; or were isolated externally, through emigration or expulsion.

Upon closer inspection, however, the overall effect of the regime's doses of openness was similar to that of splashing water on a hot stone in a sweathouse: it only made the atmosphere hotter. Easier emigration, greater possibilities for travel to the West, the rehabilitation of significant figures and epochs in German history, the greater maneuvering room granted to the Church, and support of "socialist" consumerism were all designed to build down domestic dissatisfaction. Yet they served to create higher popular expectations that were inflamed by the regime's economic mismanagement and ideological rigidity. Thus, just as the regime was faced with growing pressures of détente from the West and *glasnost* from the East, it found itself confronted with an equally challenging situation at home.

The GDR dissident population, torn between those seeking emigration to the West and those preferring to stay and press for reforms at home, remained one of the smallest, least vocal, and most isolated in the Soviet bloc until 1987. Moreover, on the whole east German dissidents continued to seek an "improvable socialism," whereas most of their counterparts in other East European countries sought to overturn it. Gorbachev's assumption of power in the Soviet Union and dramatic changes in Poland and Hungary accelerated the efforts of East German opposition groups to transcend single issue themes such as the environment, peace or the Third World and demand fundamental political reforms that would lead to "improvable socialism." "Gorbachev was our source of hope and we viewed him as a secret ally," said activist pastor Friedrich Schorlemmer. "The situation is exactly the reverse of 1945," noted maverick communist intellectual Jürgen Kuczynski in his diary on March 3, 1987. "Then at the top close allegiance to the SU and down below hate in the population. Today at the top true anti-Sovietism, down below enthusiasm for Gorbachev."[55]

By early 1989 a different kind of solidarity had become apparent within the East German population. Whereas in the past the divergent goals of those seeking to change the system and those seeking to escape it through emigration had dissipated the strength of domestic opposition, the two now joined to form a new critical mass of unrest in the population that started alarm bells ringing within the SED leadership. East German writer Monika Maron commented at the time that the realization had slowly dawned that "the Emperor has no clothes, and the latest fashions from Moscow are simply too revealing."[56]

Spurred by dramatic events in 1989, the diverse currents of domestic dissent that had been gathering force over the preceding months and years coalesced into the revolutionary movement that ultimately would sweep the SED from power. Yet these strands of opposition, in and of themselves, were too weak to be much more than the kindling wood of revolution. The sparks came from external events. They did hollow out sufficiently the SED's claims of legitimacy, however, so that when the GDR's external framework collapsed, its brittle interior immediately shattered.

The Pot Boils Over

Erich Honecker's thin voice quavered with fury and bewilderment. "The Wall," he fumed, "will still be standing in 50 or even 100 years... That is quite necessary to protect our Republic from thieves, not to mention those who are prepared to disturb stability and peace in Europe."[57]

Honecker was supporting his Wall so vociferously because he had his back up against it. At first glance, Honecker's shrill defense was directed at challenges made by Western leaders in January 1989 at the closing ceremonies of a marathon two-year meeting of the Conference on Security and Cooperation in Europe (CSCE). The Vienna CSCE meeting had just produced an agreement promoting East-West trade and safeguarding a broad range of human rights, including freedom of travel and emigration. The Vienna accord pledged the 35 signatory nations, including the GDR, to "respect fully the right of everyone... to leave any country, including his own, and to return to his own country."[58] The retiring U.S. Secretary of State, George Schultz, used the Vienna meeting to issue a blunt challenge to Moscow and East Berlin:

tear down the Wall. The Cold War would not be over, Schultz declared, as long as the Wall remained standing. It remained, he said, the "acid test" of improved East-West relations.[59]

During the Wall's 27-year existence Honecker had grown accustomed to Western bluster. That was not his primary concern. His real message of defiance had been directed at the much more palpable and threatening challenge posed by his own patron power, the Soviet Union. The long-simmering feud between Moscow and East Berlin had now boiled over into public. "We didn't build this Wall—this is not our Wall," Aleksandr Yakovlev, one of Gorbachev's key advisers, declared a few days before. Asked to comment on the Wall, Shevardnadze said that it was a question for the two Germanys to decide, but hinted that in Moscow's view, it was time for a change. "When the Wall was built," Shevardnadze ruminated, "there were most likely reasons for it. One must see whether these reasons are still there." Oskar Fischer, the East German Foreign Minister, was indignant. The factors that led to the construction of the Wall, he snapped, still existed. Shevardnadze was undeterred. In an expansive mood, he leveled his sights on his East German ally in his closing remarks to the Vienna conference. "The Vienna meeting," he declared, "has shaken the Iron Curtain, has weakened its rusty bars, has torn new holes and sped its corrosion."[60]

In response to Yakovlev's remarks, SED Politburo member Werner Krolikowski sniffed that he "never listened to Yakovlev in his life and wasn't about to now." His colleague Günter Schabowski, himself married to a Russian, proclaimed to anyone who would listen that "everything the Russians do is nothing but manure and cheese." Given Gorbachev's embattled position at home and the sluggish progress of *perestroika*, Honecker remained skeptical that the Soviet leader would remain in power. He continued to pin his hopes on Gorbachev's conservative opponents in the Politburo while rejecting any suggestion that the GDR itself was in need of fundamental reforms.

One year earlier the Honecker regime had agreed to grant its citizens a right *to apply to leave* the GDR. This was not the same as agreeing to the right to leave, and authorities could still decide whether to approve an application. Such a step was part and parcel of Honecker's *Abgrenzung* policies—limited concessions that remained under state control. By the time of the CSCE Vienna meeting in January 1989, however, this limited step was insufficient, and the GDR came under pressure from both East and West to sign the Concluding Document. Honecker was intent on circumventing such pressures.

Honecker's brazen attitude was on full display in a private meeting on January 5, 1989 with Yuri Kashlev, the head of the Soviet CSCE delegation. The GDR could not accept two points in the final draft of the Vienna document, Honecker said. The first dealt with granting CSCE observer groups access to average citizens. "We all know what is concealed behind so-called Helsinki observer groups," Honecker declared. "This would mean legalization of counterrevolutionary activities." The second point was a clause that would further legitimize West German demands that the minimum daily currency exchange requirement be abolished. The GDR would not veto the final document, Honecker told his guest, but if these two points were not dropped, Kashlev was asked to convey to "comrade Gorbachev that the GDR would not honor the two points." The GDR, he reminded his guest with more than a hint of *Schadenfreude*, was a "quiet island" compared to Poland, Hungary, Czechoslovakia, Estonia, Lithuania, Azerbaijan, Armenia and Georgia.[61] Stasi chief Erich Mielke ordered his colleagues to block implementation of the Concluding Document wherever possible.[62]

During the first four years of Gorbachev's tenure, Moscow had tolerated Honecker's obstreperousness for various reasons. First, the GDR's role as Moscow's leading economic partner played an important role in Gorbachev's own calculations for reform in the Soviet Union. Second, the GDR's critical position as one of two German states on the front lines of the ideological divide and the clamp of stability on a more fluid, fragmented Soviet empire imposed some caution on impulsive reformers. Third, the GDR remained a powerful symbol among the Soviet people of the Soviet victory over German fascism. Fourth, Gorbachev continued to be preoccupied with his reform efforts at home. Finally, Gorbachev and Shevardnadze did believe in and adhered to the policy of non-interference they had been proclaiming.

As 1988 came to an end, however, so did Soviet patience. The Wall and the man who built it were becoming embarrassing anachronisms in the age of *glasnost* and *perestroika*; they were damaging the credibility of Gorbachev's entire program of reform. Gorbachev was anxious to move ahead with a new approach to international relations that had little room for walls of concrete and barbed wire, automatic guns, and shoot-to-kill orders. "We felt we could not hinge our policy on Honecker," recalled Shevardnadze's key aide Sergei Tarasenko. "He would be a passing leader. We were ready to proceed in our own way whether it pleased him or not."[63]

In his speech to the United Nations on the morning of December 7, 1988, Gorbachev declared that in an age of global mass communications, "the preservation of any kind of 'closed' society is hardly possible." Then, in a signal about Soviet intentions toward Eastern Europe, Gorbachev declared that "all of us, and first of all the strongest of us, have to practice self-restraint and totally rule out any outward-oriented use of force." He went on to say that "the principle of freedom of choice is a must" for all nations, a universal principle that "knows no exceptions." In other words, East European regimes could no longer rely on Soviet military intervention to keep them in power. They would be responsible for sustaining their own legitimacy and viability. To underscore his position, Gorbachev issued a stunning announcement: the Soviet Union would undertake massive unilateral military cuts, including the withdrawal of 6 tank divisions and other forces from the GDR, Czechoslovakia and Hungary, which amounted to about 10% of Soviet armed forces and much higher percentages of the most threatening Soviet forces in Central Europe.

These cuts had been under discussion in Moscow for more than a year between Gorbachev and his military establishment. Earlier that year, in a Warsaw Pact meeting in July, Gorbachev had proposed a unilateral cutback of 70,000 men in the GDR, Czechoslovakia and Hungary, but the proposal was blocked by those regimes. That same month the Soviet General Staff was instructed to begin work on a bigger cutback. Several events during the fall, including a September shakeup in the Politburo in which the influence of the conservatives was reduced, were important in making the cutbacks possible.[64]

In Moscow's secondary elite, the debate over German policy continued. At the end of 1988 Vyacheslav Dashichev was invited to make a brief presentation to the Central Committee's senior advisers on European policy. He repeated his heretical position that the division of Germany hurt, rather than helped, Soviet interests. Valentin Falin, Chief of the International Department of the CPSU Central Committee, exploded with rage, shouted that the Cold War had been unleashed by the United States, began a rambling response and then abruptly left the room.[65]

Dashichev refined his views in a paper dated April 18, 1989 that was presented to Shevardnadze and most likely also read by Gorbachev. The East-West confrontation had damaged the Soviet Union badly, he argued, and could not be overcome without a solution to "the German Question." Dashichev criticized the "ideological primitivism" of the GDR regime, based as it was "on force against its own population," and derided Honecker's assertion that the Berlin Wall would still be standing in 100 years as "absurd." Only radical reforms could bring the GDR out of the dead end in which it now found itself. This would lead to a "revolutionary rapprochement between both German states" and thereby "defuse the German question" which could "open prospects for the creation of a confederation of both German states...or a unification on the condition that the security of all the countries of Europe would be guaranteed. One cannot conceive of a common European home without overcoming the division of Germany in its present form," he concluded, although he added a cautionary note: "It is very important that this process take place under conditions of internal and external stability."[66]

Lightning Strikes

By 1989, a mutually reinforcing confluence of accelerating change abroad and deepening disillusionment at home was transforming the East German situation fundamentally. Cumulative changes emanating from the West, the East and at home were causing the triple high wire upon which Erich Honecker had conducted his delicate balancing act for eighteen years to wobble badly. During the mid-to-late 1980s the Soviet tides of change in particular had been carving channels in which the issues at the heart of the Cold War in Europe were now flowing with gathering speed. The quickening pace of events was creating its own dynamic, generating a heady sense of anticipation that was soon to transfix, and ultimately transform, the continent.

Anticipatory gusts began to blow in from Poland and Hungary. Despite seven years of suppression by Poland's martial law regime,

Solidarność retained its resonance throughout Polish society. General Jaruzelski's regime, buffeted by gales of economic crisis and political illegitimacy, initiated discussions with *Solidarność* leaders in early February. Arduous roundtable talks followed, resulting in legalized status for *Solidarność* in April. The communists agreed to free elections for a new upper house of the Polish parliament, on the condition that they and their traditional parliamentary allies would continue to control the more powerful lower house.[67]

The Hungarian path of reform, in contrast to that in Poland, had been charted by the party itself. These efforts had progressed far enough that on February 11 the Hungarian Central Committee endorsed, with Soviet approval, the idea of a multiparty system. On March 14, the Hungarian government took a little noticed yet fateful step by becoming the first East European state to accede to the 1951 Geneva Convention and 1967 Protocol relating to the status of refugees (under which states agreed not to expel refugees or return them to their homeland if they would face persecution there). The Protocol obligated Hungary, alone in the East bloc, not to force refugees to return home. On May 2, Hungarian soldiers began to tear down the twin barbed wire fences and electronic fortifications along Hungary's 260 km border with Austria.[68] By the end of the year, the government announced, the Iron Curtain between Austria and Hungary would completely vanish.

These actions unnerved East Berlin, which had signed a treaty with Budapest in 1968 that committed each country to prevent each other's citizens from crossing into a third country without specific permission from the home government. In their discussions with East German officials, the Hungarians downplayed the significance of these steps. The actions were intended only to build down the more inhumane aspects of the border installations, Budapest argued. Hungarian officials continued to prevent east Germans from fleeing to Austria. But this was an untenable long-term position, and the reformist leaders in Budapest knew it.

The GDR leadership clearly underestimated the magnitude of the Hungarian action. Honecker preferred to focus on the annual spectacle of hundreds of thousands of East Germans marching for socialism during the traditional May 1 parades than on the increasingly real prospect that those same masses, given the opportunity, would turn their backs on socialism in a flash, risking their livelihoods and even their lives in a headlong dash through the now-porous Hungarian border to the West.

There were also darkening clouds at home. The first thunder claps were heard in Leipzig on January 16 and again on March 13, when hundreds of young people protesting the right to free expression and to emigration took to the streets after regular peace services in the Nikolai Church. Throughout the spring, the Stasi provided the leadership with an unvarnished picture of popular concerns: housing and infrastructure problems, environmental damage, an overbearing bureaucracy, consumer shortages, problems with drinking water, limited opportunities to travel. Even "progressive" (i.e. loyal party) forces, it was reported, were concerned that "the general mood among broad segments of the population has noticeably deteriorated."[69] Rather than acknowledge the need to introduce reforms, however, the regime stepped up its means of reprisal.[70]

Lightening finally struck on May 7 when independent monitoring groups produced hard evidence that local elections had been manipulated by the regime. Instead of backing down, the regime responded with a new crackdown. Over one hundred protesters were detained in Leipzig. Yet this only fanned popular outrage. Over five hundred people demonstrated in Leipzig on May 8 to protest the elections and the detentions of the previous day. A subsequent demonstration scheduled for June 7 in East Berlin was disrupted by state security forces. In a sign of growing sophistication and organization, the demonstrators quickly regrouped and arranged services the next day in the Gethsemane Church that attracted 1,500 people.[71] The communal elections made clear that popular dissatisfaction had reached broadly throughout the population and the people were losing their fear. Popular outrage over the elections had infused new life into the opposition groups. By June 1, over 160 opposition groups—most of them still weakly organized— existed throughout the GDR.[72]

The polarization of the East German internal scene was sharpened further by external developments in June as a cascade of unprecedented events hammered the ideological foundations of the communist world. The stark contrast between the situation in the GDR and in neighboring Poland was brought home on June 4, when pro-*Solidarność* candidates won overwhelming victories in elections for the Polish Parliament. In Hungary, roundtable talks between regime and opposition were about to begin. On June 27, the Hungarian and Austrian foreign ministers gathered near Sopron to cut away the border of barbed wire separating their two countries—a symbolic act opening the Iron Curtain. On the other side of the world, the Chinese army launched a bloody suppression of a peaceful student demonstration in Tiananmen, Beijing's Square of "Heavenly Peace."

The Open Wound

For the Honecker regime, the seemingly inexorable moves in Poland and Hungary toward democracy and pluralism raised the spectre of encirclement and isolation by reformist states. The SED Central Committee responded by denouncing the changes in Hungary, lashing out at Dresden party chief Modrow, who had been drawing greater domestic and international attention as the one prominent reformer within the party, and moving energetically to form a rejectionist front by forging closer ties with reactionary communists in Czechoslovakia, Romania, China and Albania. On June 8 Egon Krenz offered a resolute defense of the Tiananmen Square massacre, and the East German parliament approved an official statement supporting the actions of the Chinese government. This was followed on June 19 by an official visit by Foreign Minister Oskar Fischer to isolated hard-line Albania, the first visit of a Warsaw Pact foreign minister to Albania since it broke its alliance with Moscow in 1961.

The frosty relations between East Berlin and Moscow stood in stark contrast to the thaw evident in relations between Moscow and Bonn. Honecker was now not only being challenged by Gorbachev directly regarding the nature and development of socialism, he feared being outflanked by an improved Soviet-West German relationship that might sacrifice East German interests. Such fears were fanned by intense speculation inside and outside of Germany that Gorbachev would soon signal a dramatic turn in Soviet policy on the German Question.

Expectations of such a change were heightened by Gorbachev's state visit to the Federal Republic in June. The visit heralded a new stage of Soviet *Deutschlandpolitik* that aimed to strengthen Soviet ties to the

Federal Republic, Europe's economic dynamo and Moscow's most important Western economic partner.

In anticipation of Gorbachev's visit to Bonn, West German officials conducted intense discussions with their Soviets counterparts in an effort to win Soviet endorsement of a common document that would lock in earlier Soviet statements about self-determination, human rights, and freedom of choice. The Joint Declaration of the two states, signed by Gorbachev and Kohl on June 13, did in fact reflect elements of new thinking and fundamental principles of the Western community of values. In addition to the aim of securing peace, both states affirmed the "right of all peoples and states to freely determine their destiny." Both states described their "primary task" as "overcoming the division of Europe," a goal to be reached through the construction of "a European Peace Order, a common European home in which the USA and Canada also have their place." The building blocks of a new "Europe of Peace and Cooperation" included "unconditional observance of...peoples' right to self-determination" and "realization of human rights." Kohl, beaming with delight, called it a "sensational" accord.[73] The Soviet Union had endorsed the right to self-determination—which the West Germans had always declared to be the core of the German Question—in an official declaration together with the Federal Republic.

In his meetings with Gorbachev, Kohl used the pledges inherent in the Declaration to press his guest on the German Question. German partition remained an "open wound," he declared. "The feeling of belonging together is unbroken among Germans in east and west." At their October 1988 encounter in Moscow, Gorbachev had sharply refuted Kohl's references to the German Question. The division of Germany was a product of a specific history, Gorbachev had said, and to change it at that time would be "an unpredictable and even dangerous undertaking." This time he was less categorical. While cautioning against deepening existing difficulties and alluding to "certain realities" and "obligations," he observed that "nothing is eternal in this world," and said that the Berlin Wall could be removed as soon as the conditions that had led to its construction no longer existed. "I do not see a particularly big problem here," he added.[74] During the entire visit Gorbachev mentioned the GDR, his most important strategic and economic partner, only peripherally.

These intriguing new turns were balanced by more familiar statements on Berlin and on state sovereignty. While the visit did not result in any breakthroughs on the German Question, there were clear signs that major Soviet rethinking was under way. While Soviet Foreign Ministry officials continued to reiterate the dangers of a new German *Reich*, others, particularly those close to Gorbachev and Shevardnadze, were expressing different views. They spoke of Soviet interests being better served by a "reassociated" Germany tightly integrated into a broader European political and economic community than by the maintenance of an artificial division of Europe in which one German state remained threatened by chronic domestic upheaval.[75]

The GDR regime was acutely sensitive to the Gorbachev visit. Officials avoided any reference to "self-determination." The East German media featured the distant Chinese crackdown on dissent far more prominently than the Gorbachev visit next door.

In subsequent weeks Gorbachev reaffirmed the principles to which he had agreed in Bonn despite vigorous objections by hardline states. At a tense meeting of the political advisory committee of the Warsaw Pact, Romania called for military intervention to suppress the reforms in Poland. In the end, however, reformist forces carried the day. On July 7, the Warsaw Pact joined Gorbachev in a public repudiation of the Brezhnev Doctrine: "Any interference in internal affairs, any attempt to restrict the sovereignty of states, whether by friends and allies or other states, is unacceptable."[76] The hardliners went home in disarray, but the battle was not over.

Meeting Shevardnadze in Paris on July 29, U.S. Secretary of State James Baker said that U.S. support for the reform process in Poland and Hungary was not an attempt "to create problems for the Soviet Union." Serious problems would arise, however, if Moscow were to use force to stop the development of peaceful change. U.S. officials were particularly keen to ascertain the Soviet threshold of tolerance should the East German state start hemorrhaging. Shevardnadze answered U.S. concerns in Paris and in a subsequent meeting in September with Secretary Baker in Jackson Hole, Wyoming by stating that the use of force to stop the reforms in Eastern Europe "would be the end of *perestroika*." He insisted that these reforms were not a threat. "The pace, the movement, the process" in those countries was up to them, Shevardnadze told Baker.[77]

Despite these momentous changes and hints of more to come, consensus opinion among experts in and out of governments in East and West was that neither the GDR nor the Soviet Union could afford my fundamental change in their "principal stance" toward the German Question. While Washington and Bonn welcomed the pronouncements ostensibly undermining the Brezhnev Doctrine, Gorbachev's rhetoric had not been put to a practical test, and some skeptics wondered whether the GDR might be exempt from such proclamations. The end of the Wall, so the mainstream argument, would shatter the modicum of domestic legitimacy garnered painfully by the GDR regime over the past 40 years and immediately question communist rule. The GDR was the keystone of the Warsaw Pact, the chief economic and strategic partner of the Soviet Union. Its disruption, it was argued, would accelerate the destabilizing elements already discernible in the East and ultimately deal a shattering blow to the Soviet system itself— certainly an unacceptable consequence even for Gorbachev. Thus, evidence of Soviet and East German "new thinking" in various areas of international affairs, particularly security relations, had not yet extended to the core issues at the heart of the German Question, nor, did it seem to most analysts at the time, was there much prospect of this occurring in the foreseeable future. U.S. views were conveyed through an editorial in the *Washington Post*:

> If there is anything that could incite Soviet military intervention, it would be instability in East Germany. That's why there is a tacit but powerful agreement among Western politicians and governments, including the West Germans, that for the present East Germany's status needs to remain as it is.[78]

This "tacit agreement" actually extended much further, embracing most of the east German opposition and the Moscow reformists as well. All had pinned their hopes on a gradual, stable East German evolution toward "improvable socialism." Georgy Shakhnazarov, Gorbachev's chief advisor on Eastern Europe, said that the Poles and Hungarian could "do what they want," but that the GDR was "a special case," although not one that Gorbachev would have to worry about anytime soon.

Most East German dissidents agreed. "The Wall seemed stable," recalled Friedrich Schorlemmer. That summer, at a German-German forum on the "European House," he said, "I don't believe it appropriate to erect a pan-German room in this house, but rather two rooms separated by a sliding door. I see our chance in speaking with one voice while remaining in two states."[79]

There was also no indication that any leading West German politician believed that the division of Germany could soon be ended. While Kohl and the CDU remained committed to reunification as a declaratory principle, it was not part of operational policy.[80]

Skeptics could also point to the lack of a reformist faction within the upper echelons of the SED. Some leadership changes were thought possible at the next party conference, which had been brought forward from 1991 to May 1990, but when Honecker finally did depart the scene, the likelihood seemed great that he would be replaced by an East German Chernenko, not an East German Gorbachev.

Finally, most Western leaders harbored deep doubts whether Gorbachev would remain in power. The CIA reported in May 1989 that the Soviet situation was so volatile that Gorbachev had only a 50% chance of surviving the next few years unless he stepped back from his reform policies. Given his tenuous situation it was practically inconceivable that he would be prepared to sacrifice East Germany. According to this broad consensus, any overt moves by the West toward reunification, or any attempt by the East to impose a "Chinese solution" on domestic unrest would represent an intolerable exacerbation of tensions on the most sensitive border in the world.

"Almost everyone agrees to that prudent proposition," the *Washington Post* commented, "except, of course, the people who live in east Germany." The challenge was to find ways to accommodate "these entirely legitimate aspirations of the East Germans without bringing in the Soviet tanks."

The Make-Or-Break Point for the Brezhnev Doctrine

By August the situation in the GDR was transformed dramatically by a series of synergistic developments. Honecker had collapsed at the

Warsaw Pact Summit in July, underwent gall bladder surgery and was not to return in any significant way until September. With the advent of summer vacation, the trickle of East Germans who had been escaping via Hungary's open border turned into a gushing stream. Hundreds of would-be emigrants jammed West German missions in Budapest, Warsaw and Prague, forcing them to close their doors. East German dissenters were emboldened to emerge from the shelter of the Church; there was a sudden proliferation of independent opposition groups throughout the GDR.

These developments were being monitored carefully in Moscow. Valentin Falin told Soviet political leaders in mid-August that the SED leadership itself was to blame for the growing exodus, and that it was "powerless and perplexed" as its citizens continued to leave. He warned that popular dissatisfaction "will, in a relatively short time—by spring of next year at the very latest—lead to mass demonstrations which would be very difficult to control."[81]

The emergence of a *Solidarność*-led government in Poland in late August was the make-or-break point for the Brezhnev Doctrine, the real-life challenge that would test Gorbachev's rhetoric of reform. Hard-line communist resistance still could have prevented the formation of a non-communist government.

Eduard Shevardnadze was vacationing on the Black Sea. His aide, Sergei Tarasenko, had received an urgent early morning call from Moscow and relayed the message to the foreign minister, who was sunning himself on the beach. Romania's Ceausescu was demanding decisive military action against *Solidarność*, and was offering to host an emergency Warsaw Pact meeting to approve the intervention. "Others," he said, shared his view. For the next few hours Shevardnadze and his close aides sat on the beach and discussed the situation. There would be no intervention, Shevardnadze declared. The Polish predicament could not be resolved by military force. But "from now on" Moscow would have to accept the consequence of losing eastern Europe.[82]

Ceausescu's demands were rebuffed. On August 22 Gorbachev spent 40 decisive minutes on the telephone urging Polish Communist Party first secretary Mieczysław Rakowski to convince his comrades to join the *Solidarność*-led government in the interest of national unity.[83]

The emergence of a non-communist government in Poland further accentuated the GDR regime's problems. Whereas the communist Polish government had been circumspect in its commentary on the internal situation in the GDR, members of the new government headed by Tadeusz Mazowiecki openly urged the GDR to undertake reforms. Mazowiecki and Foreign Minister Krzysztof Skubiwszewski remained relatively cautious in their approach toward the issue of German unification, but other leading members of *Solidarność*, such as Bronislaw Geremek, Adam Michnik and Lech Wałęsa, took a much more positive attitude, arguing that it would be hard to deny the Germans the very right of self-determination that *Solidarność* had been fighting for in Poland. By mid-October Wałęsa was calling the division of Germany "illogical" and stated that it could be overcome through the reunification of Europe.[84]

Statements such as these galvanized the east German opposition and sent a shudder of anticipation through the populace. As a 35-year-old worker exclaimed, "Think of *Solidarność*. Back then we never would have thought that they would accomplish anything. Now they're sitting in the government. Watch out, now it's going to happen here."[85]

"The Most Difficult Decision of My Life"

The next dramatic development came when Hungarian Prime Minister Nemeth and Foreign Minister Gyula Horn, after meeting secretly in late August with Kohl and Genscher in Bonn, decided that on September 10 they would break Hungary's treaty with the GDR, which pledged that Hungary would return East Germans attempting to escape to the GDR, and open permanently its western border to the East Germans. "It was the most difficult decision of my life," Horn recalled.[86] He flew to East Berlin on August 31 to deliver the news. GDR Foreign Minister Oskar Fischer stammered that Horn was blackmailing the GDR and accused him of "treason." Horn called Fischer a "blockhead" and flew back to Budapest.[87]

The Hungarian decision was doubly significant due to the lack of Soviet reaction. Before making his fateful decision, Horn had asked his deputy minister, László Kovács, to sound out the Soviet reaction should Hungary let the East Germans go. "We didn't specify, but we hinted,"

said Kovács. "The Soviets did not object."[88] Horn in fact waited to inform the USSR until the day before the action was taken. The GDR, of
course, had informed the Soviets earlier. But the Soviets swung behind
the Hungarian decision. Furious GDR attempts to call an emergency
Warsaw Pact meeting fell apart due to Soviet reluctance.[89]

The GDR regime's cataleptic response to these developments was
not only due to intransigence or old age. It also reflected a lack of viable
options. Otto Reinhold, one of the SED's chief theorists, defined the
true dilemma succinctly:

> The key question…is what one might call the socialist identity of
> the GDR. In this question it is quite obvious that there is a funda-
> mental difference between the GDR and other socialist countries.
> They all had already existed as states with capitalist or half-feudal
> orders before their socialist transformation. Their statehood was
> therefore not primarily dependent on the societal order. This is
> not so for the GDR. It is only conceivable as an antifascist, as a
> socialist state, as a socialist alternative to the FRG. What right to
> exist could a capitalist GDR have next to a capitalist FRG? None,
> of course.[90]

According to this definition of East German identity, which was
shared by many regime leaders, any true reforms, however well inten-
tioned, would mean the beginning of the end of the GDR. Even in its
40th year of existence, the GDR continued to draw its identity from
the confrontation with the political, economic and social system of the
FRG. This had always been fragile. In the wake of the dramatic changes in the Soviet Union, Poland and Hungary it had become even more
so. The Politburo's inflexibility could thus not be attributed solely to
incompetence or senility: it went to the heart of the GDR's very existence as a state. "Socialism in the colors of the GDR," said Reinhold,
was "an essential expression of our national identity."[91]

By September 22 over 120 east Germans had sought refuge on the
grounds of the FRG Embassy in Warsaw and over 900 had done so in
Prague. Unsanitary conditions forced the Embassy in Warsaw to close.
The non-communist government in Warsaw announced that East
Germans would not be forced to return to the GDR. The hard-line
communist government in Prague, in contrast, closed its border with
Hungary to east Germans attempting to escape.

Still in convalescent care, Honecker reasserted command from his sickbed. He authorized negotiations with Bonn to resolve the situation in the FRG embassies in Warsaw and Prague. Genscher also pressed Shevardnadze, who showed some understanding for the situation and agreed to press East German Foreign Minister Oskar Fischer and Czech Foreign Minister Jaromir Johanes for a "quick solution" for the embassy refugees. In the end, East Berlin agreed to let the refugees head west in special trains on the condition that they pass through the GDR, from which they would be formally "expelled" for disloyalty—an empty face-saving gesture.[92]

The solution to the refugee problem in Warsaw and Prague had also been preceded by contacts between Kohl and Gorbachev. Gorbachev let the East Germans know that he would not go to East Berlin to attend ceremonies marking the 40th anniversary of the GDR, which were to take place little more than one week away, if there were the danger of his being implicated in the refugee drama. He had already had that experience during his June visit to China, which had been eclipsed by pro-democracy demonstrations in Tiananmen Square and their brutal suppression soon thereafter. Gorbachev told his aides that he was "disgusted" with Honecker's "inept" handling of the refugee issue.[93]

To Honecker's horror, the refugee drama did not end. As soon as the refugees had left the embassies in Warsaw and Prague, thousands more arrived. Despite efforts by the Czech police to seal off the West German embassy grounds after the last refugees had left for the West, by the very next evening another 350 seeking to escape had arrived in Prague. In Warsaw another 200 arrived. The very next day, October 3, over 3000 refugees had again ensconced themselves on the embassy grounds in Prague. Hundreds more stormed the embassy grounds during the afternoon.

Honecker again agreed to allow all the refugees to leave yet at the same time slapped a visa requirement on GDR citizens seeking to travel to Czechoslovakia, the last country to which East German citizens could travel freely. In 1988 more than 4 million East Germans had vacationed in Czechoslovakia and several millions more crossed the border regularly on business. Although East German authorities called the ban a "temporary measure," it appeared to foreshadow a longer-term crackdown.

The Wall was now complete--to the East and the West. The country that called itself a democratic republic had finally become a prison for its people.

The situation had become dramatic. In a series of secret meetings in the fall of 1989, officials tasked with monitoring the GDR's economic health had come to a stunning conclusion. The regime's rosy public presentations of GDR economic strength belied the fact that export targets had not been met since 1982, and if the target was not met for the current fiscal year, the GDR would "become insolvent already in 1989." In 1988 the GDR's entire national income increased by only 11 billion east marks, whereas the interest payments alone on the state's Western debt were DM 5 billion—the equivalent of 20 billion east marks.[94] Yet consumed by domestic political upheaval, neither Honecker nor his top lieutenants responded to these warnings.

"He Who Comes Too Late Will Be Punished By Life"

Buffeted by internal pressures, the Honecker regime was now to receive another twist of the screw from its patron power, the Soviet Union.

For Mikhail Gorbachev, the GDR had been transformed from the bastion to the ballast of socialism. Arriving for the GDR's 40th anniversary on October 7, Gorbachev was determined to give his East German hosts a clear message.

Honecker clearly was wary of the visit. On his motorcade route into the center of East Berlin, Gorbachev was greeted only by thin lines of selected welcomers waving plastic East German and Soviet flags that had been issued for the occasion. After attending a ceremony in memory of Soviet war dead and victims of the Nazis at Treptow Park, Gorbachev moved into a nearby crowd. "The Berliners welcomed Gorbachev as a savior," Shevardnadze later remarked. He was quickly surrounded by cries of "Gorbi! Gorbi" and "We are staying here!"

"Don't panic. Don't get depressed," he replied reassuringly. "We'll go on together, fighting for socialism. Be patient." Throughout his visit

Gorbachev remained a model of public diplomacy and outward courtesy. Asked whether he thought the situation in the GDR was dangerous, he replied, "Alongside our problems in the Soviet Union, there is no comparison. *Perestroika* would not have begun if it had been suggested to us from outside." And then in a carefully worded message he was to repeat throughout his visit, he proclaimed, "I think that dangers exist only for those who don't grasp the situation, those who don't react to life. We know our German friends have the ability to learn from life, to make changes." In response to questions by Western reporters, he said "whoever picks up the impulses generated by society and shapes his policies accordingly should have no fear of difficulties."[95]

Honecker and Gorbachev then proceeded to East Berlin's Palace of the Republic, where they were scheduled to give major speeches marking the 40th anniversary. Each speech was the subject of intense speculation. Would Honecker now use the occasion, with Gorbachev at his side, to signal that reforms would be undertaken, that the message of the streets and from Moscow, Budapest and Warsaw had been heard? The answer was a resounding *Nein*. In a speech full of empty slogans and self-congratulatory phrases, Honecker addressed none of the serious challenges facing his regime. As thousands streamed out of the country and as massive demonstrations and violent altercations erupted outside the Palace of the Republic, Honecker spoke of a "trusting discussion in the cities and the countryside."[96]

Honecker's dismal performance outraged the East German population as well as members of the party itself. It was another example that the GDR had been transformed, in Schabowski's words, "from the bastion of Marxism-Stalinism to the bastion of Marxism-Senilism."[97] Modrow added bitterly that "there was never a more unrealistic and hypocritical speech in the GDR as Honecker's address."[98] The speech served to convince other SED senior leaders that Honecker had completely lost touch with reality and that changes at the top were imperative if an explosion was to be avoided.[99]

Gorbachev then stepped to the podium. In clear, measured tones, he stressed the challenges and necessities of reforms throughout the socialist world. He referred directly to Ronald Reagan's appeal two years earlier to tear down the Berlin Wall without explicitly rejecting it. He stressed the sovereignty of the GDR, but by so doing sought to distance himself from the Wall:

> One has even heard the call: Let the USSR remove the Berlin Wall! Then we will at last believe in its peaceful intentions...our Western partners must proceed on the understanding that matters affecting the GDR are decided not in Moscow, but in Berlin.

Gorbachev's statement not only underscored East German sovereignty, it made the point that the rules of the game had changed: the East Germans were on their own and could not count on the Soviets to bail them out. Gorbachev had pulled the plug on the East German leadership, leaving them little choice but to embark on a reform course. Standing only a few blocks from the Wall, Gorbachev promised that as East-West rapprochement progressed, "all walls of enmity, estrangement, and distrust between Europeans will fall." The speech was a careful yet clear rebuke of the Honecker regime and an appeal for reforms in the GDR.[100]

Gorbachev repeated his message more bluntly the next morning in a tense one-on-one talk with Honecker in Niederschönhausen Palace.[101] This was followed by a meeting with the Politburo in which Gorbachev again pressed for change. He appealed both to the gerontocratic leadership's incessant hunger for legitimacy as well as their deeply rooted feelings of superiority vis-a-vis their Eastern allies. "The German Democratic Republic is our primary partner and ally," Gorbachev proclaimed. It was precisely East Germany's economic success, he argued, that would "permit you to restructure more easily." He then pressed home the point:

> I can assure you it is not an easy thing to pass a resolution regarding political changes...Courageous times await you, courageous resolutions are required...a good deal of sausage and bread is not everything. People then demand a new atmosphere, more oxygen, a new breath, particularly for the socialist order...A human being needs the appropriate material conditions, but at the same time he needs the corresponding intellectual atmosphere in society. I believe it is very important not to miss the moment and to pass up any chance...If we remain behind, life will punish us immediately. Our experiences and the experiences of Poland and Hungary have convinced us: if the Party does not react to life, it is condemned.

In his response, Honecker directly rebuked Gorbachev's admonition for change, stubbornly reiterating yet again his time-worn litany of self-congratulatory praises. He even went so far as to cite Friedrich Engels' remarks at the grave of Karl Marx, "where," according to Honecker, "he is known to have said that man first needs something to eat, to clothe himself, and to live. As he said this he of course did not underestimate the intellectual problems that we have to solve even today." The SED, concluded Honecker, had already chosen the correct answer: "to continue the policy of continuity and renewal...we are the party of innovators."[102]

After Honecker was finished, he looked around the room. Everyone was silent. Gorbachev quietly looked up and down the table. Finally, he turned to one of his Soviet colleagues, uttering nothing more than an incredulous "Tsss!" and, with a final, piercing glance into the lifeless faces of the Politburo, abruptly stood up and marched out of the room.[103]

That night, as the Leipzig Thomas Church's Men's Choir sang Bach's cantate *Frieden sei im Lande* for the assembled dignitaries in East Berlin's Palace of the Republic, 3,000 people on the other side of the Spree river chanted "We are the people!" and "Gorbi, help!" Reality and façade stood face to face. The regime wanted to celebrate 40 years of the GDR; the people want to celebrate 200 years of the storming of the Bastille. As the rulers sought to demonstrate the achievements of socialism in East Berlin, the ruled preferred to demonstrate for "Democracy, now or never!" in Berlin, Leipzig, Plauen, Jena, Potsdam, Karl-Marx-Stadt, Magdeburg, Ilmenau, Arnstadt, and other cities in the largest demonstrations to that point since 1953.

As the Stasi beat down the demonstrators and the melee on the streets turned ugly, Gorbachev left the official festivities directly for the airport. Back in Moscow, he declared on Soviet television that he had found many "fiery supporters of *perestroika*" in the GDR. To underscore Gorbachev's anger and impatience, Gennady Gerasimov repeated Gorbachev's phrase that "he who comes too late will be punished by life."[104]

Despite the regime's escalating use of force, over the next two days protesters chanting "Gorbi, Gorbi" and "Democracy, now or never" demonstrated across the GDR. Tensions peaked on October 9 in

Leipzig. Faced with tens of thousands of demonstrators, in the end the regime backed down from its threatened use of force. Various Soviet sources have stated that the Kremlin had issued a directive to General Snetkov, Commander of the Western Group of Soviet Forces, not to intervene in such events under any circumstances. Military units were to remain in their garrisons and not engage in any military exercises; military personnel and their families were not to leave their military installations—a clear sign that the renunciation of the Brezhnev Doctrine was real, not rhetorical.[105]

The weight in the Politburo had clearly shifted away from Honecker's hard line. On October 13 the National Defense Council issued Secret Order 9/89, which explicitly prohibited the use of deadly force against the demonstrators.[106] The same day, all the demonstrators who had been arrested were released. The regime also agreed that the approximately 1,000 refugees in the West German embassy in Warsaw would be allowed to leave for the West, without the previous stipulation that they travel over GDR territory.[107]

On October 17 Honecker was deposed and replaced by Egon Krenz, who immediately announced prospects for more liberalized travel regulations, more open media and a more self-critical discussion of domestic problems with broader elements of society. Krenz quickly demonstrated, however, that he was less reformer than renovator—certainly not the Mikhail Gorbachev of East Germany. He continued to seek to control the pace of change while maintaining the leading role of the party and isolating democratic opposition groups. Krenz's glimmers of *glasnost* reflected no overarching plan for a viable socialist GDR; they simply reflected his attempt to buy time and find alternative channels of control. True pluralistic reforms were equated in his mind with the end of the GDR as a separate country; a reformed GDR would have no inner rationale to distinguish itself from West Germany.

Krenz's promises of reform, however, did little to mollify popular fury. Throughout the rest of October and early November hundreds of thousands of people from across the GDR marched peacefully to demand democracy and free elections, ending the power monopoly of the communist party, legalizing independent political groups, tearing down the Berlin Wall, and committing to the rule of law and freedom of the press. Notably, there were no calls for reunification.[108]

Meanwhile, on October 23, Shevardnadze again declared that the Soviet Union recognized freedom of choice for all countries, including those in the Warsaw Pact. Two days later, Soviet Foreign Ministry spokesman Gennady Gerasimov declared that the Brezhnev Doctrine had been exchanged for a new and far more humorous doctrine. "You know the Frank Sinatra song 'My Way'?" he asked stunned reporters. "Hungary and Poland are doing it their way. We now have the Sinatra Doctrine."[109]

By mid-October, Krenz's economic advisers now presented him with truly devastating news: the GDR was essentially bankrupt. "Stopping the debt alone," they concluded, "would require a reduction in living standards in 1990 of 25 to 30 percent and would make the GDR ungovernable." The only way out, they contended, was "fundamental change" toward a "socialist planned economy oriented to market conditions," coupled with a grand German-German bargain in which Bonn would provide a DM 3 billion credit in exchange for a pledge by East Berlin that "the conditions could be created still in this century to render the nature of the border between the two German states, as it exists today, superfluous."[110] GDR emissaries held confidential discussions with West German officials in Bonn to see what the West Germans might be prepared to give the East German regime in exchange for greater political liberties in the GDR and "de facto unlimited travel between the two German states." On October 26 Krenz pitched the deal to Helmut Kohl personally in a phone call. Kohl was noncommittal; West German officials felt that Krenz's negotiating position was weakening by the day.[111]

On November 1 Krenz flew to Moscow to consult with Gorbachev. The Soviet leader had little sympathy for the GDR's problems. Honecker had believed himself to be "the number one in socialism, even in the world," Gorbachev exclaimed. "He no longer saw what was really happening." Gorbachev also harbored deep doubts that Krenz would be able to pull the GDR out of chaos. His advisors viewed Krenz as a "transitional solution," and preferred Hans Modrow or even Markus Wolf, the long-time head of the GDR's intelligence services.[112]

Krenz knew of Gorbachev's doubts, yet he was reluctant to embrace the Soviet leader's admonition to "get rid of any unnecessary problems that hinder you," perhaps because he understood quite well what the full consequences would be. The party was prepared "to look the truth in the eye," Krenz said unconvincingly. He was afraid that if the full truth about the desolate economic situation was revealed, "it could unleash a shock with devastating consequences." [113] Gorbachev himself was unnerved by Krenz's depiction of the GDR's economic woes, particularly since the GDR was Moscow's largest trading partner, and Gorbachev was consumed by the Soviet Union's own economic challenges.

The two discussed East Berlin's relations with Bonn. Krenz indicated that he was considering further opening of travel opportunities for GDR citizens, but only if they had a passport, a visa, and could demonstrate they could pay for their travel. Gorbachev responded that extensive contacts between the people in both German states could not be prevented, one simply had to be able to control and channel them. [114]

This was precisely the goal behind a new travel regulation that the GDR authorities were drafting. [115] The regime touted it as a comprehensive revision; the reality was that those seeking to travel would still need to apply for permission, they would still need a passport (which most citizens did not have), and the government could still deny applications for a range of opaque reasons.

An initial version of the draft law was released on November 6. The public denunciation was thunderous. The legal committee of the East German parliament, normally a rubber-stamp for party decisions, took the unusual step of rejecting the law. Bewildered, the regime attempted to focus on the most urgent question: that of emigration.

On November 7 GDR Foreign Minister Oskar Fischer met in East Berlin with Soviet Ambassador Vyacheslav Kochemasov and his deputy Igor Maximychev, informing them that the regime was considering a new exit, or hole, on the German-German border (not in Berlin, which was subject to Four-Power control) to facilitate emigration by East Germans to West Germany without them having to go through Czechoslovakia. Fischer asked for Soviet "opinion" on the plan.

The Soviet embassy concluded that what it called the "hole variant" was simply a further example of Krenz's weakness and confusion. Kochemasov reached Shevardnadze, who responded that if Krenz thought such a solution was possible, Moscow would probably not register objections. He told Kochemasov, however, that the Foreign Ministry in Moscow should still review the idea—after the major Soviet holidays of November 7 and 8—before giving Krenz an official reply.[116]

The same day, East German emissary Alexander Schalck-Golodkowski met with officials in Bonn in an attempt to secure more than 10 billion DM in exchange for a vague promise to open the Wall.[117] West German officials demurred. Kohl had a different bargain in mind. On November 8, he announced to the West German Bundestag that if the GDR government wanted Bonn's support, it would have to agree to free elections.

As of the morning of November 9, Krenz had still not heard back from Moscow. Meanwhile, four mid-level officials from the GDR Interior Ministry and the Ministry for State Security formulated yet another draft travel law, this time addressing not only permanent emigration but also temporary travel, and not only between the GDR and the FRG, but also, fatefully to "Berlin (West)." This addition, which was initiated without any consultation with the Soviet embassy or with Moscow, clearly circumvented Soviet and Four-Power authority over all of Berlin, a prerogative the Soviets guarded jealously. While the draft law still required would-be travelers to apply and receive permission to leave, it also stated that the new regulations would come into effect "right away." A press release announcing the next draft law was embargoed for November 10 at 4:00 am.

Later that day, unaware of the new draft law, the wording of which rendered the "hole variant" obsolete, and having been unable to reach Shevardnadze, Kochemasov was able to find Deputy Foreign Minister Ivan Aboimov, who told him to inform the East Berlin Politburo to proceed with the "hole variant." Armed with the group of four's text, which he did not read thoroughly enough to understand its significance, and with what he thought was Moscow's approval of the decision represented by the text, even though Soviet approval was for the now-superseded "hole variant," Krenz pushed the document through the Politburo and the central committee that afternoon. He then told Politburo member Günter Schabowski to read the press release at his evening press conference. Schabowski also simply glanced over the text without comprehending its true meaning, fumbling through the text at the press conference. Bewildered journalists couldn't believe what they heard. When would this new regulation take effect? Schabowski again rummaged through his papers and then gave his historic reply: "As far as I am aware it goes into effect right away, without delay."[118] The run on the Wall had begun.

The Berlin Wall was breached suddenly and peacefully late in the night of November 9 without Soviet knowledge, participation or intervention. The Soviet embassy was furious that the travel law included Berlin, which treaded on Soviet authority for the city, yet Soviet diplomats remained passive observers as thousands poured across the open Wall from East to West Berlin.[119] The Soviet Ambassador slept through the night; the deputy ambassador decided against informing Moscow. Krenz waited until the morning of November 10 to inform Gorbachev of the events. He claimed that things were under control, and that only East Germans who had passports and who had applied for and received a visa were being let out, even though masses of people without documents had gone back and forth across the now-open barrier at will.[120]

Writing in his diary, Gorbachev confidante Anatoly Chernyaev captured the moment. When "the Berlin Wall fell," he wrote, "a whole era of the socialist system ended." It meant "the end of Yalta, the finale for the Stalinist legacy," and the "overcoming of Hitler's Germany."[121]

Into the Vacuum Steps Helmut Kohl

"My God, someone has put us in a real mess!" Krenz complained on November 10, only hours after the first East Berliners had crossed over to West Berlin.[122] As the Wall crumbled, so too did the East German communist party's chances to revitalize itself. The regime had botched one of the greatest opportunities imaginable to demonstrate that it was committed to real reforms, and had forfeited its chance at a grand bargain with Bonn, as Krenz's economic advisers had urged. The party was in free fall.

On November 13 Hans Modrow—touted as the Gorbachev of the GDR—was pulled out of provincial exile in Dresden, named successor to Willi Stoph as Chairman of the Council of Ministers, and tasked with building a new government. Modrow's subsequent actions belied his reformist rhetoric, however. His half-hearted attempts at reform were doomed from the beginning. Something fundamental had occurred. The party had proven unable to convince the east German people not only that the government seriously intended to implement reforms, but that an East German raison d'etre still remained. Honecker's carefully cultivated image of the GDR as the one country where socialism had actually produced exploded in a matter of days amidst a string of revelations detailing the extent of the country's insolvent financial situation, repressed inflation, price distortions, uncompetitive industries, scarce consumer goods and widespread environmental degradation. Ordinary east Germans who had previously half-believed government propaganda about socialist economic success were given a severe jolt. The quickly deteriorating situation further robbed many of the hope that they could improve their lives under communism or "improvable socialism," accelerating demands for unification and fueling the continued exodus abroad, as 2,000 people a day fled the country.[123]

East German opposition groups were also caught flat-footed by the opening of the Wall. Having pushed the people into the streets, the East German opposition now began to follow rather than lead the spontaneous, angry revolt from below.

With the SED and the opposition in disarray, the mood quickly changed among the Monday marchers on East German streets. On Monday, November 13 a single placard calling for "Reunification!" was lost among the sea of slogans in Leipzig demanding "Free elections now!" and a variety of other political reforms.[124] Yet only one week later a new message rang out in the political void. In deafening chorus hundreds of thousands chanted "Germany united Fatherland," a phrase from the GDR anthem that had been banned since 1974. The banner cry of the revolution, "We are the people," was suddenly transformed into "We are one people!" The East German people had jumped on the roller coaster of unification.

West German political leaders, alarmed by the intensity of East German anger, were increasingly concerned that the peaceful revolution could turn violent. Politicians urged caution, but the demand for unification threatened to drown out all other voices.

Beyond stuttering steps toward intensified collaboration on practical issues, however, Bonn had no plan, secret or otherwise, to cope with the situation that West German politicians always said they wanted but in reality had not thought about seriously for years: the unification of Germany. In part this was because eager pursuit of such a goal would have raised the suspicions of Germany's neighbors in the East as well as in the West, and also because there seemed to be no realistic prospect of even visible progress toward that end. As a result, West German politicians made ritual proclamations about unity while assuring the world that the Federal Republic, unlike the Germanys of the past, would never go it alone or even do much to bring about unification. Policymakers concentrated on small steps to alleviate the lot of their oppressed countrymen.[125]

Now all this changed. Into the vacuum stepped Helmut Kohl, whose 10-point plan outlined a path to unification that forever changed the context of the East German revolution.

While Kohl was convinced that German-German reassociation was now inevitable, he was anxious that the number of East Germans deserting the GDR for the West might swell to millions, incapacitating the East and sowing chaos and resentment in the West. He was worried that the so far heroically disciplined East German marchers on the streets might get carried away by frustration, provoke the Soviet Union, and spark a dangerous and unpredictable confrontation. He was also concerned that the Bush-Gorbachev summit meeting at Malta might take up the German Question without any Germans at the table. He thus sought an approach that would establish himself as the navigator of German unity by channeling the revolutionary energies in the East in such a way that the historic opportunity that had now appeared would not be squandered by popular chaos or fears, and preempting any possible moves by the Four Powers that might impinge on German interests.[126]

The opportunity came at the end of November. In this atmosphere of anxiety and uncertainty in the face of growing unrest, Kohl's national security advisor, Horst Teltschik, met on November 21 with Nikolai Portugalov, a German expert in charge of the Soviet Central Committee's department responsible for international relations. Krenz would not survive the party congress in December, Portugalov ventured, and would be replaced by Hans Modrow. He handed Teltschik a paper in which the Soviets aligned themselves with the changes in the GDR and, in a bit of revisionist analysis, declared that ever since the "dawn of *perestroika*" they knew the situation in the GDR would have to develop in this way. At the same time, they expressed their concern about the galloping dynamic in German-German relations.[127]

"On the German question we are considering all possibilities, even quasi-unthinkable alternatives," Portugalov told Teltschik. He could even imagine the Soviet Union giving a "green light" to a "German confederation." Teltschik was, in his words, "electrified." He immediately suggested to Kohl that a speech outlining realistic and workable step-by-step plan for unification be prepared for the Chancellor to give during the Bundestag's budget debate the following week. If the Chancellor did not present such a plan soon, Teltschik argued, rival parties would beat him to the punch. Kohl quickly agreed.

To secure the optimal surprise effect, the initiative was kept under wraps. During the weekend of November 24 and 25 an internal working group developed a ten-point plan charting a course via confederal mechanisms between the two German toward an eventual German federation embedded in European structures.[128]

Then, without warning to most of his party compatriots, his coalition partners, his allies in the West, or his neighbors in the East, Kohl stepped to the podium of the Bundestag on November 28 and outlined a ten-point plan for German-German cooperation based on an "ever closer network of agreements in all areas and on all levels." He was cautious not to give any timetables, and emphasized that such a process would have to proceed in harmony with broader European events. "The development of inter-German relations remains embedded in the pan-European process and in East-West relations," he declared. "The future architecture of Germany must fit in with the future all-European architecture."[129]

Nonetheless, the speech awaked hopes by some, and concerns by others, that German unity was now a real possibility. Despite its many caveats, the speech surprised and alarmed Germany's neighbors. It also omitted any reference to German borders. The joy with which non-Germans viewed East German advances was tempered with concern about the pace of change and the uncertain direction in which it was heading. Kohl's speech exposed this raw nerve.

The harshest reaction to the galloping pace of German developments came from Moscow. The initial Soviet reaction to the opening
of the Wall was muted. Gorbachev instructed the Soviet ambassador
to the GDR, Kochemasov, not to interfere and told the GDR leadership to ensure a "peaceful transition"—a signal that there would be
no repeat of the events of June 17, 1953 or the bloody suppression in
Tiananmen Square.[130] Soviet spokesman Gennady Gerasimov repeated
his "Frank Sinatra Doctrine" and hinted that the Soviet Union would
accept a non-communist government in the GDR as long as the GDR
remained a member of the Warsaw Pact, as had non-communist Poland. He dismissed the question of unification as "groundless gossip"
and warned against "recarving the boundaries of postwar Europe." Soviet officials warned that Moscow would not tolerate the demise of its
"strategic ally."[131]

Gorbachev reformers were concerned that the breakneck pace of
change in Germany could overwhelm efforts by GDR authorities to
retain political control of the situation. They feared that Soviet forces could be drawn into the turmoil and that Gorbachev's position at
home could be undermined. Just as Kohl was about to speak to a mass
assembly in Berlin on November 10, the Soviet ambassador in Bonn,
Kvitzinsky, phoned Kohl's adviser Teltschik to relay a message from
Gorbachev, who called on the Chancellor to ensure that "chaos" not
be allowed to erupt at such a delicate time.[132] Kohl and Gorbachev
spoke by phone the next day. Change in Eastern Europe was unfolding much faster than had been expected, said Gorbachev. Each country
must proceed at its own pace; the GDR would require time to implement its reforms. There was no threat or warning, only the request
to let prudence prevail.[133] While Gorbachev's call reassured Kohl that
Moscow would not interfere in the internal developments in the GDR,
it also underscored the Kremlin's concern that events could spin out of
control. Shevardnadze, who had been receiving reports warning that
the situation in Berlin was quite dangerous, asked Genscher directly
about the situation by phone. Genscher replied that while there was
certainly a crush of people visiting the West, the situation was peaceful
and under control.[134]

Although the Kremlin had been engaged in "new thinking" on Germany's future, it was not yet prepared for a historic reversal of Germany's division. In Gorbachev's view, long-overdue reforms in the GDR

were intended to save East Germany, not undermine it; the opening of the Wall, if managed properly, would stabilize German division, not end it. But ordinary East Germans, Poles, Czechs and Hungarians were teaching Gorbachev a lesson he would eventually be compelled to learn at home as well—that the forces of democracy, once released, could escape the party's guiding hand and take off down avenues of their own choosing. The breathtaking collapse of the GDR was particularly shocking. Despite many differences, what united Gorbachev, the Krenz/Modrow leadership and most of the East German opposition was their overestimation of the capacity of "improvable socialism" to sustain the second German state. Their earlier notions of reform were all predicated on change within socialism. Events forced them to realize that freedom of choice could also mean the freedom to reject socialism.[135]

Nonetheless, in the weeks following the opening of the Wall, the internal battle in Moscow raged on. On November 16 the Krenz regime received a written set of recommendations from Moscow as to how to proceed following the fall of the Wall. The so-called "non-paper" praised the fall of the Wall as a "bold and significant action" that demonstrated that the party leadership not only understood the situation but was committed to overcome the growing alienation between the populace and the government. It recommended that Krenz take the high road and characterize the opening of the Wall as a humanitarian decision grounded in respect for human rights. At the same time, the document reiterated the standard Soviet position: "Any attempts to exploit the situation to try to force the reunification of Germany or to revise the territorial order in Europe will unquestionably be doomed to fail." A precondition for closer cooperation with West was "Unconditional recognition of the existence of two German states as a factor of stability in Europe." It warned that "attempts to put the unification of Germany on the current political agenda and to negate the existence of the sovereign socialist state GDR not only affect the interests of the citizens of both German states but also the extremely sensitive security interests of the entire European continent." It affirmed that the GDR could expect continued Soviet support for this position.[136]

The non-paper, which exemplified both a traditional Soviet view of its interests regarding Germany as well as its foreign policy dilemma—as Ambassador Kochemasov told West Berlin Governing Mayor

Walter Momper, Moscow did not want to "occupy" the GDR "a second time"—was one of the last examples of the classical mechanisms through which the Soviet leadership sought to influence the East German communist party. But it also revealed how far behind the political curve Moscow was. The pace of events in eastern Germany was being set on the streets, and the world was racing to catch up.

Another example that Gorbachev had yet to embrace any change in position regarding the two German states came in a message from him to Egon Krenz on November 24. In that message, which was intended to foreshadow his discussions with U.S. President Bush in Malta, Gorbachev indicated that he was ready to move ahead with significant arms reductions, but reiterated the standard Soviet position that such efforts would only be possible if "the foundations of European stability are maintained and strengthened," that "existing borders" could not be questioned, and no "territorial claims" could be allowed, because those were the causes of the two world wars. "Peace in Europe," he wrote, "will last as long as this Pandora's box remains closed." He then went on to state that the "existence and development of the GDR was and is an extremely important underpinning for the European equilibrium, for peace and international stability."[137]

Only two weeks after the opening of the Wall, key Soviet reformers had already given a conditional yes to unification. They argued that the Soviet Union was not in a position to prevent it and could actually use the unification process to harness German energies to propel Soviet reforms. Soviet officials began to call for the transformation rather than the dissolution of the blocs. They started to view the German Question as the lever by which they could pry open the rigid bloc structures toward pan-European security arrangements based on the CSCE.[138]

But there were reservations. Kohl's 10-point plan convinced many in Moscow that Bonn was steering East German developments in a nationalist direction and proscribing the nature and pace of reform. They were genuinely worried about a revival of extreme right-wing activities in Germany and about German attitudes toward the Polish border. Most importantly from their point of view, loose German talk about quick unification would play into the hands of the conservative Soviet opposition. For the dogmatists the GDR had become legend: a model for the viability and effectiveness of a disciplined socialist economy. The shock of Honecker's removal, the fall of the Wall, the arrest of Politburo members and the abolition of the security apparatus by their German communist comrades sparked a conservative revolt. Elements of the Soviet bureaucracy and the army launched a fierce attack on Gorbachev and Shevardnadze for having "lost" Eastern Europe.[139]

The Soviets, deeply concerned over the course of events, called for a Four-Power meeting with the three Western allies—a not-so-subtle signal to Bonn that the still-occupying powers were not to be disregarded or neglected.[140]

The Four React

The rapidity of change within East Germany not only caught the Germans by surprise, it stunned the Four Allied powers who retained rights and responsibilities for all of Germany resulting from their victory in World War II. More than 40 years later, the formal legal framework of the German Question had not changed since the wartime allies split over Germany's future between 1945 and 1947. Since Cold War animosities had overwhelmed efforts, envisioned at the 1945 Potsdam Conference, to conclude a peace treaty with Germany, the four powers still reserved rights and responsibilities for "Germany as a whole," its borders and a peace settlement, despite the creation in 1949 of two separate German states. These rights represented the legal basis of the Four Power role in the negotiations leading to unification.[141]

The initial assumptions in the White House was that unification, though perhaps inevitable, would—and should—unfold gradually.[142] Scowcroft said that Krenz was "buying time for himself, and for the system." He saw no reason yet to presume that either Moscow or East Berlin would allow the east German people to "go their own way and take the state with them." He could not imagine that Gorbachev would allow the GDR to leave the Warsaw Pact. "The basic reality," he said, "East Germany as a Communist state within the Soviet sphere—hasn't changed and probably won't change."[143]

American concerns appeared justified by the initial Soviet response to the opening of the Wall. Gorbachev sent a message to the other three leaders in which he endorsed the leadership change in the GDR but cautioned against any Western attempt to exploit the situation.

Events in Germany were moving at such breakneck speed, Gorbachev warned, that they could still become violent or spin out of control. He repeated his standard line that history had dictated there be two Germanys. He suggested urgent consultations and insisted on being part of any forthcoming decision-making process. "This guy's really upset, isn't he?" Bush said after reading Gorbachev's note. After consulting European allies, Bush sent back a vague reply, emphasizing the importance of German self-determination but not, at this point, accepting the Soviet demand for a role in decision-making.[144]

Soviet attitudes toward unification were also colored by Moscow's changing relationship with Washington. The Malta summit began only four days after Kohl announced his 10-point plan. On the eve of the conclave, Gerasimov's lighthearted quip about a progression of historic events "from Yalta to Malta" contrasted sharply with Kohl's stern admonition that Malta could not be a "status quo summit." Kohl sought to assure both superpowers that the tremendous changes underway in the GDR would neither result in chaos nor in West German attempts to exploit the situation to seek unification "unilaterally." He asked Bush to support his policy when the President met with Gorbachev. Bush was careful to reassure those Europeans who were concerned that Moscow and Washington might cut a deal to decide Europe's fate that there would be "no Yalta at Malta."[145]

Opening the summit in the midst of a raging storm on board the Soviet ship Maxim Gorky, Bush expressed support for *perestroika* and disclosed a variety of initiatives intended to aid Gorbachev, including faster track arms control proposals and U.S. willingness to begin negotiations on trade and investment treaties. In all, 19 initiatives were proposed, partially with the German situation in mind. The U.S. would not exploit Soviet weakness, Bush told Gorbachev. He also tried to persuade the Soviet leader that German unity within Western security structures would be in Soviet interests. Little progress was made on this point. "We have inherited two Germanys from history," Gorbachev replied. "History created this problem, and history will have to solve it." Adopting what he had been told was Bush's favorite word, he said, "Where the question of Germany is concerned, I have a *prudent* and cautious policy." Shevardnadze told Baker during their separate talks that there was "deep unease" within his government about German unification and West German ambitions to regain territory lost at the end of the war, a point underscored in Gorbachev's private talk with Bush.[146] Nonetheless, the U.S. delegation believed that Gorbachev remained open to further developments on the German question.[147]

The new era of Soviet-American relations being charted off of Malta had profound implications for developments in Germany. Whenever the superpowers clashed during the Cold War, the Germans found their margin for maneuver squeezed. A much more cooperative Soviet-American relationship, in turn, was not only likely to facilitate a more forthcoming Soviet approach to developments in Germany, it was likely to free German policy options vis-à-vis both Washington and Moscow.

The day after the NATO Summit Genscher flew to Moscow where he received a tongue-lashing from Gorbachev and Shevardnadze for events in Germany. Both rejected Kohl's 10-point plan as a "*Diktat;*" Gorbachev called it an attempt to "annex the GDR."[148]

On December 4 Gorbachev briefed Warsaw Pact allies on his meeting with Bush. Gorbachev was critical of Kohl's proposal for a German-German confederation. Such a confederation would mean a common defense, common foreign policy, common armed forces. Would this confederation be in NATO or in the Warsaw Pact? Or did it mean a neutral Germany? He said that nothing good could come of Kohl's "immature" idea except more tensions and greater instability.[149]

Soviet alarm over developments in the GDR reached such a peak that it placed some military forces in the GDR on a higher alert status out of concern for safety of Soviet bases and nuclear weapons depots.[150] The primary fear of the Soviet leadership was that German political leaders might take advantage of the street-driven chaos in East Germany to engineer unification as a fait accompli without any regard to Soviet interests. If such a situation were to develop, Gorbachev told Mitterrand in Kiev on December 6, "there would be a two-line report that a Marshall had taken over my position."[151]

This did not mean, however, that Gorbachev objected in principle to unification. Gorbachev had in fact already conducted a radical reassessment of the Soviet position, one much more favorable to a gradual and predictable process of deepening cooperation between the two German states, perhaps even leading to unification, channeled if possible by the Four Powers and "synchronized" with broader efforts to transform East-West relations in Europe. Humiliation of Germany would be counterproductive, Gorbachev told Mitterrand. The Germans had a right to unity, he said. The time had come to develop a framework to channel the process. Soviet officials underscored this approach. Moscow was not trying to brake German unity, they insisted, but rather sought "a synchronization between the political relations among the German states and the parallel development of the renewal of the Helsinki system."[152] The key, they said, was the security arrangements for Germany. They pushed the new line that the German Question, if controlled, could unlock the entire Cold War alliance confrontation and lead to new cooperative pan-European structures based on the CSCE.

Behind the scenes Moscow's hard-line German experts were waging an all-out bureaucratic war with the group of flexible thinkers who had been assembled by Shevardnadze, most of whom had far more experience dealing with the United States than with Germany, to determine Moscow's approach to Germany. Long years of experience with the legalistic and arcane minutia of the German Question had conditioned the Foreign Ministry's "Berlin Wall" to stick to an unyielding position regarding the evolution of the two German states and Four Power rights in Germany as a whole. The Americanists, on the other hand, were accustomed to more flexible opening positions that could be molded and shaped to that "one did not paint oneself into a corner." The conflict of styles between the two groups exacerbated more significant conflicts over substance, and contributed to the erratic picture Moscow presented during most of the unification process.[153] Shevardnadze, who was beginning to believe that unification was inevitable, was concerned that if it came too soon, negative domestic reaction in the Soviet Union could mean the end of Gorbachev's reforms.[154]

Moscow's fear of chaos in the GDR and its hope for controlled change prompted the Soviets to urge the UK, France and the United States to convene an urgent meeting of the Four Powers on December 8. It was the first such meeting since 1972, when they had signed the Quadripartite Agreement on the status of Berlin. Soviet officials told their Western counterparts that if the domestic situation in the GDR erupted into violence, they "would be obliged to use force." Hard-line elements in the military and the KGB were demanding that Moscow intervene militarily to prevent the collapse of the GDR.

The Four Power meeting turned out to be relatively short on substance, apart from an agreement to stress "the importance of stability." Kochemasov welcomed the changes in the GDR yet added that one had to proceed from the realities of the postwar period, which included two independent sovereign German states. To question this would endanger stability in Europe for which the Four Powers were responsible. The Soviet Union was prepared to negotiate Four Power agreements to contribute to the normalization and improvement of the situation "in the affected area." His proposal for regular meetings and the formation of working groups was rejected by the three Western ambassadors, who said that they were only prepared to speak about Berlin. U.S. Ambassador Vernon Walters stressed that even though the Four retained legal authority over Berlin as a result of agreements signed by the Allies after World War II, and that the rights of the Four in Berlin mandated that they be involved in the unification question, they could not simply dictate terms of settlement to the Germans. A further meeting was not agreed upon.[155]

Uncertainty about Germany's future security orientation was compounded by the lack of an acceptable framework in which to balance the German right to self-determination with the right of Germany's neighbors to peace and security, all in a Europe in which the Cold War was rapidly dissolving. Britain, France and the Soviet Union initially preferred that the Four Powers discuss the future of Germany among themselves—and not, at first, with the Germans. The British and French proposed a meeting of the Four alone, to be followed by a conference of the six powers, i.e. Four Plus Two. The Soviets were more interested in Four Plus Zero. The Germans rejected both. "We don't need four midwives" to give birth to unity, snapped Kohl upon hearing in early January that the Soviets had again approached the Americans to hold a Four Power meeting to discuss German issues. Eventually all came around to the U.S. proposal that the Germans had to be in on the negotiations as equal partners from the start. The idea quickly became known as "Two Plus Four."[156]

Debate on both the internal and external aspects of unity remained inconclusive until the furious pace of change on the ground in East

206 EXITING THE COLD WAR, ENTERING A NEW WORLD

Germany forced the German Question to the forefront of the international agenda. On January 28, 1990, with an average now of 3,000 East Germans a day flocking to the West, Modrow announced that he was advancing the date of the GDR's first free elections to March 18, instead of May as originally planned, and would form an interim government that would include members of the opposition. A unified Germany now loomed as an imminent certainty.

The collapse of the GDR wrenched Moscow from its preoccupation with its own internal chaos. On January 26, 1990, Gorbachev and Shevardnadze, meeting with their closest advisors, finally came to the conclusion that "the reunification of Germany was unavoidable." They agreed that the Soviet Union should take the initiative to call a conference among the four powers and the two German states. Contacts with the East German leadership should be maintained, but Soviet policy on Germany should also be more "closely coordinated with London and Paris." Marshall Akromeyev was asked to examine the question of the withdrawal of Soviet troops from the GDR.[157]

Two days after Modrow's announcement, Gorbachev accepted the inevitable by signaling publicly his tentative and reluctant acceptance of unification. "No one casts any doubt upon it," the Soviet leader told journalists just before receiving Modrow in the Kremlin. After meeting Gorbachev, Modrow could only conclude that "the unification of the two German states is the prospect that now lies before us."[158]

The Balancing Act Comes to an End

To the casual outside observer, the German Democratic Republic may have seemed marginal to the world's affairs: a small, loyal and repressive satellite of the Soviet Union. In fact, however, the GDR proved to be pivotal, rather than peripheral, both to the Cold War European order and the eventual breakdown of that order. As the fulcrum of the two central issues that had ignited the Cold War in Europe—the future of Eastern Europe and the German Question—the GDR was the embodiment of Cold War division.

In retrospect, the relative stability of the East German system is as much in need of explanation as is its sudden and dramatic collapse in the fall of 1989. Both the Cold War and East-West détente rested in part on the question of East German domestic stability. Yet this stability was inherently precarious, because the regime was never regarded as just and legitimate. To compensate, the regime sought to sustain a series of delicate balances on three different fronts: to the East, to the West, and at home. The regime could only advance its authority at home if guaranteed support from its patron in the East and a modicum of legitimacy in the West. It could only gain legitimacy in the West by granting greater freedoms at home and receiving greater latitude within the East. And it could only gain latitude and be ensured of continued support in the East if it maintained its authority at home and controlled the destabilizing effects of its relations with the West. The complex, contradictory and fluid dynamic among these three fronts did much to shape the evolution of the German Question and the Cold War order in Europe.

In the end, the regime was unable to sustain this triple balancing act because of shifting dynamics on each front. After Soviet leaders had argued for decades that European stability rested on the division of Germany, Mikhail Gorbachev made the opposite case: stability in Europe was now endangered by continued European divisions, including those between the Germans. At home, the East German people, emboldened by the fresh winds coming from Moscow and the rise of non-communist governments in Eastern Europe, and fearful that their peaceful, democratic revolution could end badly unless East Germany was tied quickly and irrevocably to a stable and prosperous democracy, swept aside the opposition's dreams of "improvable socialism" in favor of rapid unification. And West German leaders, particularly Helmut Kohl, who had neither believed they would experience unification nor had operational plans to achieve it, seized the historical moment to end the divisions of Berlin, of Germany and of Europe. As the unification express sped ahead during the course of 1990, the GDR was becoming the Gradually Disappearing Republic.

Exiting the Cold War, Entering a New World

On January 17, 1991, Helmut Kohl stood before the Bundestag as the newly-elected Chancellor of a Germany united in peace and freedom. The main subject of his inaugural address, however, was war. That very day multinational forces under the leadership of the United

States launched a fierce "Desert Storm" to reverse Iraqi leader Saddam Hussein's August 2 invasion of the oil-rich Middle East sheikdom of Kuwait. The Iraqi crisis built up steam through the late summer and fall of 1990, but German leaders and the German public remained riveted on unification and the subsequent all-German election. As a result, Germans were completely unprepared for the dramatic and violent conflict that now erupted in the Persian Gulf.

For a brief period, the heavens had opened to allow German unity. They now closed with a thunderous clap. Kohl had gotten "the hay in the barn" before the storms came, but the sky had now darkened. Only three days before Desert Storm rumbled, a hail of bullets in the Baltics killed *perestroika* as Gorbachev ordered Soviet military forces to stop Lithuania's bid for independence. Some weeks earlier, Eduard Shevardnadze suddenly resigned, warning of impending dictatorship and bloodshed. Gorbachev suddenly appeared to be the sorcerer's apprentice who, after having unleashed changes of historic scope, now proved not only unable to contain them but likely to be swept away by them. "He who comes too late will be punished by life," Gorbachev once told Erich Honecker. One abortive putsch later, Gorbachev himself was forced to resign as republic after republic asserted its independence. By Christmas Day of 1991, the Soviet Union was no more.

Europe had exited the Cold War. It was now entering a new world.

Notes

1. See Ernst Richert, *Das Zweite Deutschland: Ein Staat der nicht sein darf* (Frankfurt a.M.: Fischer Verlag, 1964); also, Edwina Moreton, *East Germany and the Warsaw Alliance: The Politics of Détente* (Boulder, CO: Westview, 1978).

2. Robert Gerald Livingstone, "United Germany: Bigger and Better," *Foreign Policy*, Summer 1992, pp. 157-174.

3. *International Herald Tribune*, December 13, 1988.

4. J.F. Brown, *Surge to Freedom: The End of Communist Rule in Eastern Europe* (Durham, NC: Duke University Press, 1991), p. 134.

5. A sense of the relationship, even though self-serving, is conveyed by Piotr Abrassimov, the Soviet Ambassador in the GDR from 1962-1971 and again from 1975-1983, termed by many in the West as the "Governing Ambassador." Abrassimov viewed the GDR as nothing more than a test tube baby of Soviet foreign policy: "Strictly speaking, one could compare the GDR with a homunculus from the Soviet test tube. Our influence was unprecedented. Almost half of GDR trade was with the Soviet Union. Without our oil and gas, our metal or our cotton the GDR would not have been able to exist for one single year. KGB advisers—there were more than enough of them—monitored their colleagues One also had a watchful eye on the NVA [National People's Army]—advisors from the Soviet Union were everywhere, down to the level of division commander...above all, we viewed the GDR as our line of forward defense." See the *Izvestia* interview with Abrassimov, reprinted in *Der Spiegel*, August 17, 1992, pp. 20-22.

6. See Peter Przybylski, *Tatort Politburo* (Berlin: Rowohlt, 1991), pp. 101-115.

7. Quoted in "Angst vor den Akten," *Der Spiegel*, August 24, 1992, p. 51.

8. See Michael Sodaro, *Moscow, Germany, and the West from Khrushchev to Gorbachev* (Ithaca, NY: Cornell University Press, 1990), p. 202.

9. Ibid; also Karl Wilhelm Fricke, "Der Verteidigungshaushalt der DDR," *Deutschland Archiv*, No. 2, 1977, pp, 160-168.

10. James McAdams, *East Germany and Détente* (Cambridge: Cambridge University Press, 1985), pp. 152-153; also Michael J. Sodaro, "The GDR and the Third World: Supplicant and Surrogate," in Michael Radu, ed., *Eastern Europe and the Third World* (New York: Praeger, 1981), pp. 106-141.

11. I am grateful to John van Oudenaren for his crisp summary of this position in a presentation at the Aspen Institute Berlin in May 1987.

12. Richard Löwenthal, "Germany Steps Up," *Foreign Policy*, Spring 1976, p. 180.

13. For accounts of the Honecker visit, see *Frankfurter Allgemeine Zeitung*, September 6-12, 1987; Peter Jochen Winters, "Erich Honecker in der Bundesrepublik," *Deutschland Archiv*, October 1987, pp. 1009-1016; *Neues Deutschland*, September 6-12, 1987; articles by Serge Schmemann, *New York Times*, September 7-12, 1987; *Bulletin*, Federal Republic of Germany, September 7, 1987; Erich Honecker, *Reden und Aufsätze*, Vol. 12, pp. 539-540.

14. Quoted in "Who broke down this wall?" *U.S. News and World Report*, November 2, 1992.

15. Quoted in Boris Meissner, "Das 'neue Denken' Gorbatschows und die Wende in der sowjetischen Deutschlandpolitik," in Werner Weidenfeld, ed., *Die Deutschen und die Architektur des Europäischen Hauses* (Cologne: Verlag Wissenschaft und Politik, 1990), p. 54.

16. Ibid., p. 55.

17. The phrase was first used by Konrad Adenauer on June 11, 1961 at a meeting of Germans expelled from Silesia after World War II. "Our goal," he proclaimed, "is that Europe at some point in time will be a large, common house for all Europeans, a house of freedom." The phrase was subsequently used by Brezhnev during his visit to Bonn in November 1981, and by Foreign Minister Gromyko in his January 1983 visit to Bonn, although without reference to Adenauer's "house of freedom." See Michael Mertes and Norbert J. Prill, "Der verhängnisvolle Irrtum eines Entweder-Oder," *Frankfurter Allgemeine Zeitung*, July 19, 1989. Also Daniel Küchenmeister, "Wann begann das Zerwürfnis zwischen Honecker und Gorbatschow?" *Deutschland Archiv*, January 1993, p. 35.

18. William H. Luers, "The U.S. and Eastern Europe," *Foreign Affairs*, June 1, 1987; Sodaro, op. cit., p. 404.

19. Meissner, op. cit., pp. 66-67.

20. Küchenmeister, op. cit., pp. 30-40, which contains numerous citations from the minutes of Honecker-Gorbachev meetings between 1985 and 1989.

21. Central Party Archive of the SED, ZPA, IV 2/1/399.

22. "Aus einem Gespräch M.S. Gorbachevs mit Mitarbeiten vor der Sitzung des RGW, 29. September 1986," in Galkin and Tschnerjajew, op. cit., Aleksandr Galkin and Anatolij Tschnerjajew, eds., *Michail Gorbatschow und die deutsche Frage: Sowjetische Dokumente, 1986-1991* (Munich: Oldenbourg Verlag, 2011), pp. 15-17.

23. Author's interview, February 13, 1993; Vyacheslav Kochemasov, the former Soviet ambassador to the GDR, confirmed that Moscow prohibited Honecker from visiting Bonn. For his recollections, see his interview with *Der Spiegel*, November 16, 1992, p. 148. Gorbachev also spoke of how Moscow's tough line with the Federal Republic also held the GDR in check. See "Protokoll der Sitzung des

Politbüros des ZK der KPdSU, 27. März 1986," in Galkin and Tschnerjajew, op. cit., pp. 1-2.

24. Author's interview with Hans-Dietrich Genscher, February 15, 1993.

25. ZPA IV 2/1/414.

26. Cited in Küchenmeister, op. cit., p. 39.

27. "Attempts to overturn that which it [history] has created or to force it with an unrealistic policy" were labeled as "an incalculable or even dangerous undertaking." See Meissner, op. cit., p. 72. Gorbachev later recounted that he dismissed talk of "German unity" as "far from being 'Realpolitik'." See Meissner, op. cit., pp. 70-71.

28. "The rise and fall of perestroika," *The Economist*, January 19, 1991, p. 40.

29. See Gorbachev's interview, "Es war mein Ziel, eine politische Evolution zu vollbringen," *Süddeutsche Zeitung*, March 10, 1992.

30. Quoted in Milan Svec, "East European Divides," *Foreign Policy*, Winter 1989-1990, p. 49.

31. See Jacques Renard, et al., "Comment le Plan Secret de Gorbachev a echoue," *L'Express*, July 6, 1990; "Hungary: Gorbachev Vows Noninterference," Facts on File, April 7, 1989, pp. 243-244.

32. That same month, in a speech to the Soviet diplomatic service, Shevardnadze repudiated a key principle of Soviet foreign policy: "peaceful coexistence" as a method of class struggle. "Coexistence," Shevardnadze argued, "that relies on such principles as non-aggression, respect for sovereignty and national independence, non-interference in internal affairs and so on cannot be identified with class struggle. The conflict between opposing systems is no longer the decisive tendency in the present age." "19th All-Union Conference of the CPSU: Foreign Politics and Diplomacy," *Pravda*, July 26, 1988.

33. "The rise and fall of perestroika," *The Economist*, January 19, 1991, p. 40.

34. "Shishlin Interviewed on Polish Crisis," FBIS-SOV-88-174, September 8, 1988, p. 31; Hannes Adomeit, "Gorbachev and German Unification: Revision of Thinking, Realignment of Power," *Problems of Communism*, July-August 1990, p. 3.

35. Author's interview with Tarasenko; interview with Dashichev. In his interview with me, Tarasenko chose to emphasize Shevardnadze's Georgian heritage. "As a Georgian, Shevardnadze had the feeling that no one likes a foreign military presence. He said we needed to solve this problem and that we shouldn't abuse our 'friendship' with these countries."

36. In early 1987 Nikolai Portugalov, one of the USSR's leading German experts, implied that the citizens of West and East Germany belonged to a single

German nation: "For every German...the people in the GDR remain Germans who belong to one and the same nation." See Christian Schmidt-Hauer, "Ein Besucher unter vielen," *Die Zeit*, October 21, 1988. In various other statements Portugalov expressed support for efforts at reform socialism in the GDR, welcomed a confederation, but continued to stress that "both Germanys [would] continue to exist as sovereign and equal states." See "Zwei Systeme, Eine Nation," *Frankfurter Allgemeine Zeitung*, November 17, 1989, p. 2; Nikolai Portugalov, "The Soviet View: two Germanys, in Confederation," *New York Times*, December 15, 1989.

37. Author's interviews with Dashichev, Tarasenko and Portugalov. See also Angela Stent, *Russia and Germany Reborn: Unification, the Soviet Collapse, and the New Europe* (Princeton, NJ: Princeton University Press, 1999), p. 71.

38. According to Dashichev, only Yuri Davidov of the Institute for the Study of the USA and Canada agreed with this position. Author's interviews with Dashichev and Tarasenko.

39. See the interview with Dashichev, "Dann erhebt sich das Volk," *Der Spiegel*, January 24, 1991, pp. 136-143; *Die Welt*, June 9. 1988.

40. For accounts of the summit, see *Der Spiegel*, 44/1988; Gerhard Spörl, "Reise mit kleinem Gepäck," *Die Zeit*, October 21, 1988; "Gorbatschow: "Das Eis ist gebrochen,"" *Der Tagesspiegel*, Ocrober 25, 1988; Eghard Mörbitz, "In Moskau fiel Kohl mit der Tür ins Haus," *Frankfurter Rundschau*, October 26, 1988.

41. Author's interview with Tarasenko. See Horst Teltschik, who also quotes Shevardnadze: "Das Konzept vom gemeinsamen Haus," *Frankfurter Allgemeine Zeitung*, December 23, 1988, p. 6.

42. See his interview with DDR Radio II, August 19, 1989. A capitalist GDR would make little sense and would have little reason to exist as a separate state, Reinhold said. Hence the strategy of the East German leadership had to be uncompromisingly aimed at "solidifying the socialist order" in the GDR.

43. Quoted in *Neues Deutschland*, June 3, 1987.

44. In 1988 Honecker told Kochemasov, "we won't use your term 'perestroika' anymore." Quoted in "Jedes Land Wählt seine Lösung," *Stern*, No. 16, April 9, 1987. For Kochemasov's recollections, see his interview with *Der Spiegel*, November 16, 1992, p. 148. For Hager's statement, see Neues Deutschland, April 10, 1987. In October 1988 Hager explicitly rejected Soviet reforms as "not transferable" to the GDR. *Neues Deutschland*, October 29, 1988. See also *Neues Deutschland*, April 11/12, 1987, p. 3.

45. Author's interview.

46. Kochemasov interview, *Der Spiegel*, op. cit. The tendency of COMECON members to dump shoddy, uncompetitive goods in each other's markets led an exasperated Gorbachev to declare in June 1988 that "the socialist economic com-

munity had degenerated into the garbage pail of its member states." Quoted in Jacquelin Henard, "Der Rat der Ratlosen," *Frankfurter Allgemeine Zeitung*, July 8, 1988, p. 13.

47. According to Carl-Heinz Janson, the proportion of the national income devoted to subsidie rose from 7.8& in 1971 to 22.8% in 1987. Carl- Heinz Janson, *Totengräber der DDR: Wie Günter Mittag den SED-Staat ruinierte* (Düsseldorf: Econ Verlag, 1991), p. 81. For the NVA role in the economy, see Jörg Schonbohm, *Zwei Armeen und ein Vaterland. Das Ende der Nationalen Volksarmee* (Berlin: Siedler, 1991), pp. 44, 135, 144-145.

48. As Friedrich Schorlemmer recalls, "Everyone was busy, but only a few had real work." See Schorlemmer, p. 365.

49. *Süddeutsche Zeitung*, May 7, 1987; Janson, op. cit., p. 79; Harry Maier and Siegrid Maier, "Möglichkeiten einer Intensivierung des innerdeutschen Handels," *Deutschland Archiv*, February 1989, pp. 180-191.

50. During the last years of its existence the GDR's ability to repay its debts became its highest economic priority. All economic decisions were affected by the GDR's position on the brink of bankruptcy. Exports were pushed in exchange for whatever hard currency could be gained. Imports were sought on the most long-term credits possible. As Schorlemmer recalls, "in the end everything was being sold—cobblestones for pedestrian passages in the revitalized old cities in West Germany, the best meats, the best wood, the cheapest pots and—when needed—people in prisons." See Schorlemmer, op. cit., p. 365; Janson, op. cit., pp. 68-72.

51. Max Schmidt, "Die Erde—gemeinsames Haus der Menschheit," *Einheit*, No. 2, 1987; Max Schmidt, "New Approaches to Security in Europe," address to the XIV IPSA World Congress, Washington, DC, August 28- September 2, 1988, p. 3, Author's copy; "Militärische Aspekte der Sicherheit—Militärdoktrinen und ihre Umsetzung," *IPW Berichte*, 9/88, pp. 39ff.

52. According to the International Institute for Strategic Studies, GDR defense spending in 1984 was 7.7% of national income, compared with 4% for Czecho-slovakia, the next highest spender. West Germany's defense spending in 1986 was 3.3% of GDP. *IISS Survey*, 1986-1987.

53. Schmidt, op. cit., p. 24.

54. Ibid., pp. 28-29.

55. "We were regularly under the influence of *perestroika*," recalled Jens Reich, co-founder of New Forum two years later. "We read the Soviet journals. There was an expectation of reform." Conversation with the author. See Schorlemmer, op. cit., p. 19; Kucynski, op. cit., p. 35.

56. Monika Maron, "Der Kaiser ist ja nackt," *Zeit-Magazin*, February 18. 1988.

57. For a summary of remarks by Honecker and other leaders at the Vienna CSCE Conference in January 1989, see Bundesminister für innerdeutsche Beziehungen, *Informationen*, No. 2/89, January 27, 1989, p. 2.; also "Die Mauer als Überraschungsthema in Wien," *Süddeutsche Zeitung*, January 21-22, 1989, p. 6; "Honecker: Die Mauer muss unsere Republik vor Räubern schützen," *Frankfurter Allgemeine Zeitung*, January 21, 1989, p. 1; "Schultz: Mauer-Abbau ist Test für die Haltung Moskaus," *Berliner Morgenpost*, January 17. 1989, p. 1.

58. "Concluding Document of the Vienna Meeting of the Conference on Security and Cooperation in Europe," Vienna, January 17, 1989, *Department of State Bulletin*, March 1989, pp. 21-50. The final document was printed with important omissions and changes in *Neues Deutschland*, January 21-22, 1989.

59. Schultz was joined by his Western colleagues. For similar remarks by UK Foreign Minister Geoffrey Howe and FRG Foreign Minister Hans-Dietrich Genscher, see Bundesminister für innerdeutsche Beziehungen, *Informationen*, No. 2/89, January 27, 1989.

60. When asked how he could condemn the Iron Curtain while supporting the Berlin Wall, Shevardnadze replied, "These are two completely different things." Washington Post, January 20 1989, p. A1. See also Daniel S. Hamilton, "Dateline East Berlin: The Wall Behind the Wall," *Foreign Policy*, Fall 1989.

61. "Strafsache gegen Honecker," Przyblski (II), pp. 88-89.

62. See Mary Elise Sarotte, *The Collapse: The Accidental Opening of the Berlin Wall* (New York: Basic Books, 2014), p. 19; "Hinweise zur Reaktion der Bevölkerung," January 27, 1989, BStU, MfS, ZA ZAIG 4246, pp. 1-11; Hans-Herman Lochen and Christian Meyer-Seitz, eds., Die geheimen Anweisungen zur Diskriminierung Ausreisewilliger (Cologne: Bundesanzeiger Verlag, 1992), pp. 7-17, 251-254; "Der Minister, Diensteinheiten, Leiter," January 23, 1989, BStU, MfS, ZA, HA IX 687, pp. 134-136.

63. Interview with author.

64. See Don Oberndorfer, *The Turn* (New York: Poseidon Press, 1991), pp. 318-321, 343-347; Hannes Adomeit, op cit., p. 5; *Pravda*, December 8, 1988; Gorbachev repeated his views in Kiev on February 23. For the West German military's reaction to Gorbachev's speech, See Schonbohm, op. cit., p. 16. On January 23, Honecker announced that the GDR would cut 10,000 troops and trim defense spending by 10%, 600 tanks would be dismantled or refitted for civilian use, and one squadron of 50 combat planes would be disbanded. See Robert J. McCartney, "East Germany Pledges to Cut 10,000 Troops," *International Herald Tribune*, January 24, 1989.

65. Author's interviews with Dashichev, Tarasenko and Portugalov. For an analysis of other views in the Soviet secondary elite, see Michael Sodaro, *Moscow, Ger-*

many, and the West: From Khrushchev to Gorbachev (Ithaca: Cornell University Press, 1990), p. 364.

66. See *Der Spiegel*, February 5, 1990, pp. 142ff. Relations between the GDR and other socialist states were also in a nosedive. On February 1 the GDR raised export tariffs on a range of consumer items, following similar measures by the USSR and Czechoslovakia. Western diplomats were speaking of a "socialist trade war." See Karl-Heinz Baum, "Brüder Im Handelskrieg," *Frankfurter Rundschau*, February 10, 1989.

67. Oberndorfer, op. cit., pp. 358-359.

68. According to *Le Monde* of May 4, 1989, only around 300 people were known to have escaped to Austria by breaching the fences since their construction in the mid-1960s, compared to over 13,000 people who had been apprehended in the attempt; more than 90% of those would-be escapees had entered Hungary from other East European countries.

69. See the secret Stasi report on efforts to disrupt the March 13 demonstrations, MfS, ZAIG, Nr. 122/89, March 14, 1989, "Information über eiene provokatorisch-demonstrative Aktion von Antragstellern auf ständige Ausreise in Leipzig," and an assessment of the popular mood, MfS, ZAIG, Nr. 0/216, April 26, 1989, "Hinweise zur Reaktion der Bevölkerung im Zusammenhang mit der Vorbereitung und Durchführung der Kommunalwahlen am 7. Mai 1989," reprinted in Armin Mitter and Stefan Wolle, eds., *Ich liebe euch doch alle! Befehle und Lageberichte des MfS January-November 1989* (Berlin: Basisdruck Verlagsgesellschaft mbH, 1990), pp. 28-33. As Honecker feared, the Vienna CSCE document was, in Schorlemmer's words, a "powerful" instrument for the domestic opposition: "We devoured every sentence. We searched for everything that legitimized our actions vis-à-vis the state, and finally found that in this document Basket III of Helsinki had been spelled out correctly." See Schorlemmer, p. 21.

70. The *Kampfgruppen*, militia units, 400,000 strong, which had been formed in factories and institutions following the shock of the 1953 uprising, began a new training program geared explicitly to domestic rather than foreign threats.

71. See the secret Stasi report, MfS ZAIG Nr. 286/89, June 9, 1989, "Information über eine Veranstaltung in der Gethsemanekirche im Stadtbezirk Berlin-Prenzlauer Berg am 8. Juni 1989," reprinted in Mitter and Wolle, op. cit., pp. 76-78.

72. See the secret and relatively comprehensive Stasi report of June 1, 1989 on the background and current activities of opposition groups, as well as recommendations aimed at limiting their influence, MfS ZAIG Nr. 150/89, "Information über beachtenswerte Aspekte des aktuellen Wirksamwerdens innerer feindlichen, oppositioneller und anderer negative Kräfte in personellen Zusammenschlüssen," reprinted in Mitter and Wolle, op. cit., pp. 46-71.

73. For accounts, see Meissner, op. cit., pp. 72-73; Thomas F. O'Boyle, "Gorbachev's Visit Boosts Bonn's Standing," *Wall Street Journal*, June 15, 1989, p. 3; Enno von Loewenstern, " 'Gorby' in Germany: The Wall Stays But Anxieties Rise," *Wall Street Journal*, June 15, 1989.

74. See Sodaro, op. cit., p. 361.

75. See Meissner, op. cit. This assessment also reflects my conversations from April-June 1989 with officials from the Soviet Foreign Ministry, including those at the Soviet Embassy in East Berlin, and various members of the Soviet intelligentsia, including Dashichev.

76. See *Umbruch in Europa. Die Ereignisse im 2. Halbjahr 1989* (Bonn: Foreign Office of the Federal German Government, 1990); also Fred Oldenburg, "Sowjetische Europa-Politik und die Lösung der deutschen Frage," *Osteuropa*, 1991, p. 757. Gorbachev reiterated the principles again in a speech before the Council of Europe on July 6.

77. Author's background interviews with Soviet, U.S. and West German government sources. See Oberndorfer, op. cit., p. 360.

78. "East German Hopes and Dangers," *Washington Post*, August 23, 1989, p. A26.

79. Schorlemmer, op. cit., p. 195.

80. Even as late as November 8, the day before the Wall opened, Kohl urged the Germans, "no matter how hard this may be," to "maintain the steadfast patience to count on the path of evolutionary change, the final result of which can only be full respect for human rights and free self-determination for all Germans." Frankfurter Rundschau, November 9, 1989, p. 4.

81. The report, which was intercepted by West German intelligence sources, appeared in *Die Welt*, September 15, 1989 and was quoted in the *Washington Post*, September 15, 1989, p. A22.

82. Author's interview with Sergei Tarasenko. Tarasenko reviewed this incident with me in considerable detail, stressing that the situation in Poland forced the Soviet reformers to come to terms with the true implications of their rhetorical policies.

83. Jackson Diehl, "Poland: The Communists Lose Control of the Process," in special section of the *Washington Post*, "The Turning Points," 1990; Charles Gati, *The Bloc That Failed: Soviet-East European Relations in Transition* (Bloomington, IN: Indiana University Press, 1990), p. 168; "Gorbachev Persuades the Communists," *Facts on File*, August 25, 1989, p. 13.

84. "Walesa, Deutschlands Teilung nicht logisch," *Frankfurter Allgemeine Zeitung*, October 18, 1989; see also Brown, op. cit., p. 57. Adam Michnik said recogni-

tion of the right of Germans to self-determination was "dictated by morality" and was a "precept of the Polish raison d'etre." Adam Michnik, "Liegt die Einheit der DDR im Interesse Polens?" *Der Spiegel*, No. 42, 1989, p. 49.

85. *Die Tageszeitung*, November 4, 1989.

86. Gyula Horn, *Freiheit, die ich meine* (Hambug: Hoffman & Campe, 1991).

87. When asked when this would happen, Horn told them the night of September 3, and said they could use the time to convince their citizens to return home. See the review of Horn's memoirs in *Der Spiegel*, 36/1991, September 2, 1991, pp. 110-126.

88. Quoted in Oberndorfer, op. cit., p. 362. Tarasenko confirmed to me that there had been Soviet-Hungarian discussions.

89. A few days later, Yegor Ligachev, Honecker's conservative ally, traveled to East Berlin, ostensibly to discuss agricultural matters, but in reality to convince the regime that time was running out. See Gedmin, op. cit., p. 94; Oldenburg, op. cit., p. 757; *Neues Deutschland*, September 15, 1989, p. 2.

90. Otto Reinhold, in Radio DDR 2, August 19, 1989; See "Die DDR ist jedoch als kapitalistischer Staat neben der kapitalistischen Bundesrepublick nicht vorstellbar," *Frankfurter Rundschau*, October 13, 1989; *Frankfurter Allgemeine Zeitung*, August 23, 1989; Jürgen Engert, "Sargnagel für den Sozialismus," *Reinischer Merkur/ Christ und Welt*, September 1, 1989, p. 2.

91. *Frankfurter Rundschau*, Ibid; Engert, Ibid.;

92. Authors' interview with Hans-Dietrich Genscher, Frank Elbe, Claus-Jürgen Duisberg and Sergei Tarasenko. According to Tarasenko, Shevardnadze called Gorbachev to pressure Honecker, and then bluntly told Fischer not to "deepen the crisis." See also Frank Elbe, "Die Nacht von Prag," typewritten manuscript given to author of an article written for the *Thüringer Tageblatt*; Cordt Schnibben, "Wie Erich Honecker und sein Politburo die Konterrevolution erlebten," *Der Spiegel*, 16/1990, pp. 72-90; *Die Welt*, September 25, 1989, p. 1. Also Mary Elise Sarotte, *The Collapse*, op. cit., pp. 28-31.

93. Interviews with Sergei Tarasenko, Hans-Dietrich Genscher and Frank Elbe. Also Beschloss and Talbott, p. 132.

94. Gerhard Schürer, Gerhard Beil, Alexander Schalck, Herta König, Werner Polze, Geheime kommandosache b 5—111/89, "Prognose über die Bewegung und Beherrschbarkeit der DDR-Schulden im Zeitraum von 1989 bis 1995 gegenüber dem kapitalistischen Ausland," Berlin, September 28, 1989, p. 4. Reprinted in Przblynski (II), pp. 358-363; Wolfgang Stock, "Die DDR-Führung sah vor der Wende die Zahlungsunfähigkeit am Horizont," *Frankfurter Allgemeine Zeitung*, April 16, 1992.

95. For accounts, see *Die Zeit*, October 13, 1989; Bundesminister für innerdeutsche Beziehungen, Informationen, Nr. 19/1989, October 20, 1989, pp. 7-10; *Time*, October 16, 1989; *Süddeutsche Zeitung*, October 7-9, 1989.

96. Erich Honecker, "Durch das Volk und für das Volk wurde Grrosses Vollbracht," *Neues Deutschland*, October 9, 1989.

97. Günter Schabowski, *Das Politburo*, op. cit., pp. 71-72.

98. Hans Modrow, "Bilanz nach 150 Tagen," *Die Zeit*, April 13, 1990.

99. Schabowski, op. cit., p. 70.

100. A nervous *Neues Deutschland* and the GDR news agency ADN translated Gorbachev's comments about "walls" as "Schranken" (barriers). See Christian Schmidt-Hauer, "Durch Evolution zur Einheit?" *Die Zeit*, November 24, 1989, p. 6; For the Russian text of Gorbachev's speech, see *Pravda*, October 7, 1989, pp. 4-5. In English, see FSIB-SOV-89-194, Soviet Union, October 10. 1989, pp. 29-32. See also *Berliner Morgenpost*, October 7, 1989, p. 1.

101. For the Soviet minutes of the discussion, See "Aus dem Gespräch M.S. Gorbatschows mit E. Honecker, 7. October 1989," in Galkin and Tschnerjajew, op. cit., pp. 187-190.

102. "Aus dem Gespräch M.S. Gorbatschows mit Mitgliedern des Politbüros des ZK der SED, Berlin, 7. Oktober 1989," in Galkin and Tschernjajew, op. cit., pp. 191-197. Also reprinted in *Der Spiegel*, 37/1991, September 9, 1991, pp. 107-110.

103. Schabowski, *Das Politburo*, op. cit, pp. 73-74; Schnibben (II), op. cit., p. 92. For Kochemasov's recollections of Gorbachev's visit, see his interview with *Der Spiegel*, November 16, 1992, p. 148.

104. Shevardnadze later said that the SED leaders had rejected real reforms because they assumed all social problems had been solved and reforms were not necessary. "Thus the time for reforms was irretrievably missed." He added, however, that because he and Gorbachev had been clear about Soviet acceptance of "freedom of choice," they "could not force our position on Honecker." See Fred Oldenburg, op. cit., p. 758, who cites Shevardnadze interview in *Izvestia*, February 19, 1990. Also see Bundesminister für innerdeutsche Beziehungen, *Informationen*, No. 19/1989, October 20. 1989, pp. 7-10.

105. See the article by Stanislav Kondrasov, based on an interview with Kochemasov, in *Izvestia*, April 29, 1990, p. 7, reprinted in translation in *The Current Digest of the Soviet Press*, Vol. XLII, No. 17 (1990), p. 11; Vyacheslav Kochemasov, *Meine letzte Mission* (Berlin: Dietz, 1994), pp. 90-91. Willy Brandt, returning from a trip to Moscow, reported that already in August Soviet troops in Eastern Europe had been told to refrain from intervention in internal unrest, in *Süddeutsche Zeitung*, December 14, 1989. This was confirmed by Tarasenko, who told me that there was

"never any possibility" that Soviet forces could have intervened. Author's interview. Falin also made similar assertions. According to Ekkehard Kuhn, Krenz disputed that there were such instructions, arguing that he would have known of their existence. See Ekkehard Kuhn, *Der Tag der Entscheidung: Leipzig, 9. Oktober 1989* (Berlin: Ullstein, 1992) and Sarotte, *The Collapse*, op. cit., pp. 52-82; Also see the declaration by the Warsaw Pact states in *Izvestia*, September 27, 1989. According to Oldenburg, the official Soviet position appeared to be that the GDR was free to regulate its internal affairs, but that a revision of its borders would not be accepted. Any efforts in this direction would be seen as "revanchist" and thus more open to Warsaw Pact intervention. Oldenburg, op. cit. Also Angela Stent, *Russia and Germany Reborn: Unification, the Soviet Collapse, and the New Europe* (Princeton, NJ: Princeton University Press, 1999).

106. See Peter Przybylski, *Tatort Politbüro: Die Akte Honecker* (Berlin: Rowohlt, 1991), p. 192.

107. *Frankfurter Rundschau*, October 14, 1989.

108. *Wir sind das Volk. Die DDR im Aufbruch*, op. cit., p. 97.

109. See William F. Buckley, Jr., "The Sinatra Doctrine," *National Review*, May 26, 2004, https://www.nationalreview.com/2004/05/sinatra-doctrine-william-f-buckley-jr/.

110. Gerhard Schürer, Gerhard Beil, Alexander Schalck, Ernst Höfner, Arno Donda, "Vorlage für das Politbüro des Zentralkomitees der SED, Betreff: Analyse der ökonomischen Lage der DDR mit Schlussfolgerungen," October 27, 1989. The Politburo accepted the document without changes. Central Party Archive (ZPA-SED J IV2/2/2356). The document is reprinted in *Deutschland Archiv*, October 1992, pp. 1112-1120. See also "Die Wahrheit einfach zugeklebt," *Der Spiegel*, November 9, 1992, pp. 113-119.

111. Sarotte, *The Collapse*, op. cit., pp. 90-92, who cites various internal documents.

112. Quoted in "Er hielt sich für den Grossen," *Der Spiegel*, August 3, 1992, pp. 25-27.

113. Ibid; the East German version of the minutes of Krenz's disussions with Gorbachev are reprinted in Hertle, *Staatsbankrott*, op. cit.; see also "Maueröffnung ohne Befehl," *Frankfurter Allgemeine Zeitung*, November 5, 1990; Uwe Engelbrecht, "Sowjets hätten eine schnellere Gangart gewünscht," *Der Tagesspiegel*, November 11, 1989.

114. On these subjects, there were differing opinions within the party. Most reformers within the party with whom I spoke sought to keep the discussion limited to reforms within the socialist system. When asked about the Wall, there was a surprising range of views. Almost all believed that the GDR could withstand a much

more open interaction with the West, and said that even if the Wall itself "might not come down, it can be made much more porous. This should not frighten us." In early November, the first secretary of the SED in Neubrandenburg, Johannes Chemnitzer, publicly expressed the view that the Berlin Wall "is up for discussion." See "Krenz und die Mauer," *Der Tagesspiegel*, November 2, 1989; Also *Wir sind das Volk*, op. cit., p. 98.

115. The story of this travel regulation, and the miscommunications regarding it that eventually led to the opening of the Berlin Wall on November 9, has been told in detail elsewhere. See, for example, Hans-Hermann Hertle, *Chronik des Mauerfalls. Die dramatischen Ereignisse um den 9. November 1989* (Berlin, 1996); Hans-Hermann Hertle, *Der Fall der Mauer. Die unbeabsichtigte Selbstauflösung des SED-Staates* (Opladen, 1996); Hans-Hermann Hertle and Kathrin Elsner, eds., *Der Tag, an dem die Mauer fiel: Die wichtigsten Zeitzeugen berichten vom 9. November 1989* (Berlin: Nicolaische, 2009); Mary Elise Sarotte, *The Collapse*, op. cit.

116. Author's interview with Gerhard Lauter, at the time chief of the department for passports and registration in the GDR Interior Ministry. See also Walter Süß, "Weltgeschichte in voller Absicht oder aus Versehen?" Das Parlament, No. 46-47, November 9-16, 1990, pp 8-9; Ten days earlier Schabowski had told West Berlin Governing Mayor Walter Momper that the flood of East Berliners going to West Berlin could no longer be channeled through the Friedrichstrasse crossing point. Author's conversations with members of the Senate of West Berlin. As Lauter told me, "anyone who read the November 5 law would know that the Wall would be opened soon." As relayed by Igor Maximychev, in "Was ist bei euch los?" *Der Spiegel*, 44/1994, pp. 43-45; also recounted in Mary Elise Sarotte, *The Collapse*, op. cit., pp. 102; Author's interview with Igor Maximychev. See also Stent, op. cit., pp. 94-95.

117. Hertle, *Chronik*, op. cit., pp. 105-106; Sarotte, *The Collapse*, op. cit., pp. 96-97.

118. Günter Schabowski, *Das Politbüro* (Reinbek bei Hamburg: Rowohlt, 1990), pp. 137-139.

119. Sarotte, *The Collapse*, p. 108; author's interviews with Igor Maximychev and Gerhard Lauter.

120. Gerd-Rüdiger Stephan, ed., *"Vorwärts immer, rückwärts nimmer!" Interne Dokumente zum Zerfall von SED und DDR 1988/89* (Berlin: Dietz, 1994), pp. 240 ff; Hertle, *Chronik*, op. cit., p. 237; Sarotte, *The Collapse*, op. cit., p. 160.

121. Sarotte, *The Collapse*, pp. 162-163; Chernyaev diary, November 10, 1989, MG, 246. NSA online version of the diary.

122. Quoted in Süß, op. cit.

123. David Marsh, "Wind of realism blows through the Wall," *Financial Times*, November 23, 1989, p. 2; "DDR am Rande ihrer Zahlungsfähigkeit," *Süddeutsche Zeitung*, November 20, 1989; *Chronik der Ereignisse*, op. cit., p. 46; "Krenz is Purged by East German Party," *International Herald Tribune*, January 22, 1990, p. 1.

124. See the account by Dieter Strekies in Neues Forum Leipzig, *Jetzt oder nie—Demokratie—Leipziger Herbst '89* (Munich: C. Bertelsmann, 1990) , pp. 239-240.

125. For a summary of these views, see Robert Gerald Livingston, "United Rethought but Not Reborn," *Los Angeles Times*, October 10, 1989.

126. See Elizabeth Pond, *After the Wall: American Policy Toward Germany* (New York: Twentieth Century Fund, 1990)

127. Portugalov presented two papers, one entitled "Unofficial Position," the other "Official Position." The first part of the paper had been initiated by Chernyaev, Gorbachev's foreign policy advisor, and had been discussed with Valentin Falin, former Soviet Ambassador in Bonn and now head of the international department of the Central Committee. Portugalov and Falin had gone over the second part, which concerned itself with questions regarding cooperation between the two German states, unification, the admission of the GDR into the European Community, alliance membership and the possibility of a peace treaty. Author's interview with Nikolai Portugalov and background interviews with senior West German officials; Teltschik, op. cit., pp. 42-45. Portugalov, as usual, was also saying different things to different audiences. In an article in the November 29 edition of the *International Herald Tribune*, Portugalov is quoted as saying confederation would be "impossible."

128. For a description of Portugalov's visit and Kohl's 10-point plan, see Teltschik, op. cit. pp. 43-56; Mary Elise Sarotte, *1989: The Struggle to Create Post-Cold War Europe* (Princeton, NJ: Princeton University Press, 2009), pp. 70-72.

129. As cited in Ferdinand Protzman, "Kohl Sets Out Framework for German Federation," *International Herald Tribune*, November 29, 1989.

130. Author's background interviews with senior Soviet diplomatic officials. See also Oberndorfer, op. cit., p. 365; Teltschik, op. cit., p. 23.

131. *Frankfurter Allgemeine Zeitung*, November 10, 1989.

132. Teltschick, op. cit., pp. 19-20. *Der Spiegel*, November 13, 1989, p. 25 and November 20, 1989, pp. 17-18. See also Gerasimov's comments in the *Washington Post*, November 11, 1989, p. A25; Gorbachev's remarks opposing reunification, *Washington Post*, November 16, 1989, p. A44; Shevardnadze's comments, *Washington Post*, November 18, 1989, p. A17; and Fred Oldenburg, "Sowjetische Deutschland-Politik nach der Oktober-Revolution in der DDR," *Deutschland Archiv*, No. 1, 1990, pp 68-76.

133. For the Soviet minutes of the conversation, see "Aus dem Telefongespräch M.S. Gorbachevs mit H. Kohl, 11. November 1989," in Galkin and Tschnerjajew, op. cit., pp. 229-232.

134. Teltschick, op. cit., pp. 19-20.

135. Gerhard Wettig, "Moskau und der Wandel in Osteuropa," Berichte des Bundesinstituts für ostwissenschaftliche und internationale Studien (BIOst-, No. 25, 1990); M. Skak, "The changing Soviet-East European relationship," Manuscript for the IV. World Congress for East European Studies in Harrogate, Aarhus, 1990, p. 18; Heinz Timmermann, "Die Sowjetunion und der Umbruch in Osteuropa," *Osteuropa-Archiv*, January 1991, pp. 5-6; Nakath, et al., op. cit., p. 23.

136. The paper is reprinted in Nakath, et al., op. cit., pp. 66-69. See also Hans-Hermann Hertle and Gerd-Rüdiger Stephan, eds., *Das Ende der SED*, pp. 87ff.

137. The text of Gorbachev's message is available in Nakrath, et al., op. cit., pp. 69-72. On November 29, Gorbachev reiterated his position that "the unification of the FRG and the GDR is not a current issue" in a conversation with Italian Prime Minister Andreotti. See "Aus dem Gespräch M.S. Gorbachevs mit G. Andreotti, Rom, 29. November 1989," in Galkin and Tschernjajew, op. cit., pp. 245-248.

138. *Pravda*, November 15, 1989; John van Oudenaren, "The Role of Shevardnadze and the Ministry of Foreign Affairs in the Making of Soviet Defense and Arms Control Policy," RAND/National Defense Research Institute R-3898-US-DP, July 1990.

139. Shevardnadze continued to advocate the withdrawal of all foreign forces from Europe, but he moderated his support for the dissolution of the blocs, no doubt in the hope that preservation of the Warsaw Pact could help to maintain Soviet influence and give the USSR leverage in negotiations concerning German unification. Ibid.

140. Kohl also asked Hungarian Prime Minister Nemeth to arrange a meeting with Gorbachev. Kohl wrote to Gorbachev on December 14 in another attempt to reassure him. See Teltschik, op. cit., pp. 76-85.

141. For background, see Lothar Rühl, "The three touchstones of relations between Washington, Paris, London and Bonn," The German Tribune, March 25, 1990; Wilhelm Grewe, *Deutsche Aussenpolitik der Nachkriegszeit*, Stuttgart, 1960, p. 84; Edwina Moreton, *Germany Between East and West*, op. cit., p. 8; Karl Kaiser, "Germany's Unification," *Foreign Affairs—America and the World 1990/91*, Vol. 70, No. 1.

142. Interview with U.S. Secretary of State James Baker on "Good Morning America," in USIS USBER, November 15, 1989, pp. 14-15.

143. Teltschik, op. cit., p. 48; "Der Druck von unten wächst," *Der Spiegel*, No. 48, November 27, 1989, pp. 14-18.

144. See Theo Sommer, "Wem gehört die deutsche Frage?" *Die Zeit*, December 15, 1989, p. 6; Jim Hoagland, "Unification: The Reason for Gorbachev's Retreat," *Washington Post*, February 12, 1990. U.S., British and French approaches to unification and the end of the Cold War are documented in detail elsewhere, including by other authors in this volume.

145. Author's interview with Nikolai Portugalov and background interviews with senior German officials; Teltschik, op. cit., pp. 42-45.

146. Author's background interviews with senior U.S. officials. Teltschik's assumptions about changing Soviet views on unification were supported on November 27 by Andrei Gratchov, Deputy Director of the International Department of the Central Committee, who commented on German television that "the German question is again on the agenda…even if a lot of politicians in the East and West do not want to acknowledge it." See Teltschik, op. cit., p. 55. Also Sarotte, *1989*, op. cit., pp. 77-78; Michail S. Gorbatschows, *Gipfelgespräche: Geheime Protokolle aus meiner Amtszeit* (Berlin: Rowohlt, 1993), pp. 93-129. For the Soviet minutes of the relevant meetings in Malta, see "Aus dem Gespräch M.S. Gorbachevs mit G. Bush, Malta, 2. Dezember 1989," in Galkin and Tschnerjajew, op. cit., pp. 249-254.

147. See Philip Zelikow and Condoleezza Rice, *Germany Unified and Europe Transformed* (Cambridge: Harvard University Press, 1995), p. 130.

148. Author's interview with Hans-Dietrich Genscher. Also Hans-Dietrich Genscher, *Erinnerungen* (Berlin: Siedler, 1995), p. 683; Teltschik, op. cit., pp. 62-64; "Aus dem Gespräch M.S. Gorbachevs mit H.D. Genscher, 5. Dezember 1989," in Galkin and Tschnerjajew, op. cit., pp. 254-265.

149. The GDR delegation's minutes of the meeting are available in Nakrath, et al., op. cit., pp. 74-82.

150. *Washington Post*, December 5, 19989, p. A39.

151. *International Herald Tribune*, December 1, 1989.

152. Robert Kaiser, op. cit.

153. Senate Foreign Relations Committee Hearing, "World War II Final Settlement," Chaired by Senator Claiborne Pell (D-RI). Witness: Robert Zoellick, Counselor, U.S. Department of State, Friday, September 28, 1990. Author's copy of the minutes.

154. As recounted by Pavel Palazchenko, *My Years with Gorbachev and Shevardnadze* (University Park, PA: Pennsylvania State University Press, 1997), pp. 185-191; see also Stent, op. cit., p. 101.

155. Shevardnadze charged that "artificially forcing" the events in Germany could have "unpredictable consequences." See Teltschik, op. cit., pp. 67-70; *Washington Post*, December 6, 1989, p. A20.

156. *Der Tagesspiegel*, January 18, 1990; *Bulletin*, Presse- und Informationsdienst der Bundesregierung, September 1990, p. 63; *Pravda*, December 20, 1989.

157. Others in the meeting included Ryshkov, Jakovlev, Vladimir Kryuchkov, head of the KGB, Falin, Akromeyev, Fedorov, Shachnazarov and Chernyaev. See "Erörterung der deutschen Frage im kleinen Kreis im Arbeitszimmer des Generalsekretärs des ZK der KPdSU, 26. Januar 1990," in Galkin and Tschnerjajew, op. cit., pp. 286-291. Also see Mikhail Gorbatschow, *Erinnerungen* (Berlin: 1995), pp. 714ff; Nakrath, et al., op. cit., p. 28; Anatoly Chernyaev, "Gorbachev and the Reunification of Germany: Personal Recollections," in Gabriel Gorodestsky, ed., *Soviet Foreign Policy, 1971-1991* (London: Routledge, 1994), p. 166; Sarotte, *1989*, op. cit., pp 101-103; Hans Modrow, *Ich wollte ein neues Deutschland* (Berlin: Dietz, 1998), pp. 413 ff.

158. Teltschik, op. cit., pp. 226-235; *Tass*, January 30, 1990; Serge Schmemann, "The Rush to One Germany Starts to Blur Europe's Map of Alliances," *New York Times*, February 4, 1990.

Chapter 8

"Say One Thing and Think Another:" Internal British Debates in the Late 1980s on Germany's Potential Reunification

Liviu Horovitz

During the 1980s, no one within the British government welcomed Germany's probable and irresistible reunification. On this very issue, "we have to say one thing and think another," Charles Powell, the principal foreign policy advisor to Prime Minister Margaret Thatcher, noted already in 1984.[1] He articulated what many within the UK's chancelleries wrote in various memos, reports, and summaries of discussions throughout the decade.

The Cold War status quo suited the United Kingdom well, but British officials concluded it was unsustainable. Soviet power was slowly waning. Without this constraint, the Germans were bound to seek to live together. British planners believed that the Americans, slowly moving away from Europe, were going to become less invested on the continent. Hence, the most likely outcome was a less constrained German state at the center of Europe. Britain's interests would be harmed, and London's leverage to avert such result would be limited. A majority argued that novel, creative, or radical policy solutions were needed. And yet, as newly declassified documents attest, UK policymakers concluded that others would pull Britain's chestnuts out of the fire. Many claimed that France would oppose German reunification. Most important, however, was the mainstream view: the Soviet Union, in spite of its worsening situation, would once again let its tanks roll into Eastern European capitals rather than see Germany unified. In addition, a number of British diplomats concluded that further European integration would anyhow constrain the Germans, despite the fact that London's own political leadership resented the consequences of such deeper European ties.

For all these reasons, throughout the decade, UK policymakers did not foresee either the contours of the ultimate outcome or the swiftness of eventual developments, and so postponed confronting painful choices. To underpin this conclusion, I rely primarily upon recently declassified documents from the Foreign Office and the Prime Minister's Office, both collected at the UK National Archives, as well as upon various other documentary records.

Changed Circumstances: Britain, Europe, and the World in the 1980s

Consigned to the backdrop of international politics throughout the 1970s, the German Question gained increased importance during the 1980s. Massive changes in global and regional politics pushed it back on center stage. Most crucially: the Soviet Union, ever the weaker great power, now faced significant challenges to even sustain its competition with the United States. British planners concluded already during the summer of 1979 that the fundamental contest between East and West was being settled. The Soviets were losing. The menacing size of Moscow's armed forces could not but threaten European nations. Yet things were looking grim from the Kremlin's perspective. In economics, the balance had been firmly tilted. Technologically, the Russians were behind. In military affairs, both economics and technology were weighing increasingly heavy. More important, however, was the fact that the political foundations were crumbling, as Moscow had to rely more and more on coercion to control an otherwise rather pliant population. The British concluded that such Soviet power retrenchment would ultimately eliminate the restrictions under which the two German states had conducted their policies since the late 1940s. And yet, with an attitude that permeated UK thinking from the late 1970s to the final days of the 1980s, the British planners also determined that Moscow would not relax its grip on Eastern Europe, and would rather intervene by force than lose control. As the 1970s came to an end, various UK diplomats wrote that change—in Europe and, implicitly, in Germany—was unavoidable, but assessed that it was not likely "for many decades."[2]

In addition to the transformation of the East-West conflict, technology, demography, and growth were sharpening an economic contest between the advanced industrial centers of Europe, Japan, and the United States—with stark implications for the regional European context. Whereas the United States had been the widely dominant economic power throughout the first decades after the war, both Europe and Asia were quickly catching up—aggressively competing with both the American industrial heartland and between each other. Such commercial rivalry, in turn, was pushing the European Community toward deeper economic and, implicitly, political integration. Within this regional context, the German economic powerhouse was facing fewer security pressures, and was gradually dominating the European Community. "A long-term trend towards normality should not surprise," the British embassy reported from Paris. Four decades had passed since the war. The scars on various Europeans psyches were becoming "less and less visible." Nevertheless, the French still did not trust the Germans "very far." While the British believed growing German concerns for their "purse" to be "perfectly understandable," the French seemed to resent such German assertiveness. Hence, for both structural and ideational reasons, the Federal Republic's closest partners were seeking institutions that limited Bonn's clout.[3]

British planners throughout the Foreign Office concluded in the mid-1980s that Paris, eager to preserve its sway over West Germany and thus influence Europe's future, was prepared to invest significant political capital in its "fellowship" with Bonn. The French feared "greatly" the possibility of a neutral Germany—a scenario that constituted their "*angoisse eternelle*," UK diplomats assessed. Conversely, intent on preserving European stability, the Germans were still willing to "give preferences to France beyond what rational self-interest would suggest." This constellation generated both benefits and costs for Britain. On the one hand, Franco-German amity was greatly preferable to enmity for the stability and prosperity of Western Europe. For instance, Britain often benefited from the "curbs" set on German behavior by deference to France. On the other hand, such fellowship between the two most important continental actors meant less consideration and fewer resources to spare for others' "needs and interests." British officials determined that France's concessions to Germany were limited. In contrast, the privileged attention the Germans gave to French views allowed Paris to punch well above its weight in Europe. Therefore, once common Franco-German positions were agreed upon, they almost automatically became the "European line," a test of loyalty for others and—sometimes—a difficult hurdle for British policies.[4]

Officials in London understood that protecting British sway in Europe—and, indirectly, around the world—required becoming more attuned to continental preferences. On the question of "beat them or join them," all British diplomats concluded that forming a "rival axis" within Europe was neither "responsible" nor "workable." Yet "joining" was anything but easy. France and Germany shared "common attitudes" on "progress towards European unification," Anthony Brenton, a UK diplomat on the Planning Staff, wrote, for instance, in 1985. If Britain was not willing to change its attitude to these questions, it had to reconcile itself with "remaining in the outer tier." British officials concluded that their country's international orientation, its domestic politics, and its allocation of government resources would all need to be altered significantly in order to retain a comparable seat at the Franco-German table. Both French and Germans had made real sacrifices to achieve even the limited amount of unity on display. To put it simply, one diplomat noted, the British people had to become "much more European-minded" than they were. British politicians and officials would have to develop a "more sophisticated" and "indirect" conception of the national interest. Within the bureaucracy, some thought such adjustment would be in Britain's long-term interest. Conversely, even the most committed Europeanists were aware that the country's political and economic inclinations diverged markedly from such a path.[5]

Most important, the Conservative Party of Prime Minister Thatcher loathed all implications—at home and abroad—of such realignment. At home, the Iron Lady was hard at work to free British capitalism of its shackles—and opposed to what she believed were leftist setbacks. In Europe, by the second half of the 1980s the British Prime Minister had succeeded in reducing the UK net contribution to the EC budget. She sought an integrated European market, but resented any concessions on the social, monetary, or fiscal front. As long as the Soviets posed a fundamental threat to democracy and capitalism, as long as Britain remained an indispensable link across the Atlantic, and as long as Germany was divided, Thatcher believed she could achieve her agenda in both Britain and Europe. On top of these political considerations, Britain had been a global power for three hundred years, German Chancellor Helmut Kohl told French President François Mitterrand in August 1986. The British had a "hard time adapting" to Germany being the dominant player in Europe. Both Paris and Bonn had to "hold the door open" for London, Kohl concluded. Mitterrand agreed, but noted that Thatcher was and would remain particularly difficult—an able forecast of problems to come.[6]

Careful Planning: Germany's Eventual Reunification

Against this international and domestic backdrop, UK foreign policy elites realized that Germany's eventual reunification was not Britain's first-best option—but that London could not say this loudly. By the middle of the decade, officials in London agreed that "history [had] not yet spoken its last word" on the German Question, as Julian Bullard, the UK envoy to Bonn, aptly phrased it. Foreign Secretary Geoffrey Howe had "no doubt" that the problem of two Germanys in Europe was "not dead." It was not going to "go away" just because "a politician declares it so." The division had attractions, for almost all the actors on the European scene, Howe noted in January 1985. "But Germany cannot be permanently divided," he recognized, "or at least we cannot tell the Germans that it is to be so," he wrote to his top diplomats. With Germans valuing democracy and capitalism more than unification, such outcome was predicated upon overcoming the division between East and West in Europe. Such "healing" was hard to "visualize," a change "too profound to contemplate." Therefore, Britain could offer a verbal commitment to a goal of self-determination that could only come about in circumstances that could not be foreseen at present, Howe concluded. Nevertheless, a policy of providing assurances of support for an outcome nobody desired raised many questions within the British establishment. A vivid bureaucratic discussion ensued.[7]

By autumn 1987, policy planners in the Foreign and Commonwealth Office submitted a wide-ranging analysis regarding Germany's potential reunification. Its lead author, Mariot Leslie, a promising young diplomat, would become London's envoy to NATO two decades later. The planning paper noted that the imperfect status quo suited Britain "well," and the UK had "no interest in bringing it to an end." Nevertheless, eventual change in Central Europe and thus in Germany was "inevitable." Such change would have profound implications for the United Kingdom, and there was little leverage available in order to prevent it. To reach these conclusions, Leslie and her colleagues assumed that communism was a "spent force." Therefore, Soviet dominance would eventually end. The Americans, more interested in Asia and in their own domestic affairs, would cease their security activities in Europe. Hence, the two alliances would be dismantled. A Europe of free states stretching from the Atlantic to the Black Sea would emerge. At its center would be a united German state, swiftly seeking reconciliation towards an Eastern Europe that would be "inevitably" attracted by "what the Germans have to offer." The British planners argued that Bonn and Moscow would have a "keen interest in each other," but also compete for influence on the European continent.[8]

Such a world would pose great challenges for the United Kingdom. Britain would try to remain one of the "Big Three in Europe," but the relationships would be unequal. Germany would be larger, richer, and uninhibited—a "Central European state which looked East as much as West." The ties binding advanced industrial societies would restrain the Germans somewhat, but the continent's center of gravity would move further to the East—"the tone and style of Bismarck's former capital no doubt rather different from the unpretentious bourgeois comfort of Bonn." On the one hand, both London and Paris would scramble to use their existent links in order to establish a "privileged relationship" with the new Germany. On the other hand, France, the Netherlands, and Italy would worry. Some—or all—would seek reinsurance in the United Kingdom and, perhaps, also in Russia. In the global arena, economic and technological change would render the "developed world" even "more interdependent." And even if Japan was rising on the Pacific rim, the United States would remain the most powerful state on the planet, and retain "the closest interests" in Europe. Still, significant differences in European and American "material interests and international priorities" would render the relationship "much more difficult to manage."

Negative repercussions notwithstanding, most British officials considering Leslie's planning memo concluded that German reunification was not coming anytime soon. On the one hand, the Soviets could break the stalemate in Central Europe. Yet the British thought that the Soviets had no interest in doing so. Moscow would welcome German neutrality and NATO's dissolution. However, to achieve such an outcome, decisionmakers in the Kremlin would have to accept a major confrontation with the West, the loss of their Warsaw Pact allies, instability in the Baltic states and in Ukraine, and a major ideological retreat with unpredictable domestic repercussions. Therefore, Moscow was liable to seek other ways of deploying its "German card" than "laying it bluntly on the table." On the other hand, the West Germans could also elicit change, but only at an unacceptably high price. A small minority within the Federal Republic was ready to contemplate reunification notwithstanding the consequences. Nevertheless, there was a broad consensus around democracy, capitalism, and prosperity in West Germany. Michael Llewellyn-Smith, Howe's personal secretary, summarized what all believed: "Chancellor Kohl (like Adenauer) has given to freedom a higher priority than to unity." Thus, as long as the Soviets controlled Eastern Europe, Bonn would not contemplate forcing the pace of reunification.⁹

Consequently, the crux of the matter rested with correctly assessing the probability of the Soviet Union remaining willing to uphold the Brezhnev Doctrine of intervening militarily to safeguard the status quo. A broad majority within the British establishment could simply not imagine change on this front coming anytime soon. It was far from certain that history would take the course described by Leslie, senior diplomats believed. Gorbachev might fail and his reforms might wither away. The Kremlin's attitude towards Eastern Europe might harden in an attempt to hold on to postwar gains. "Violent convulsions" might shatter Eastern European regimes. The bilateral confrontation between East and West might once again become "fiercer." There were so many uncertainties that predictions had to be "of necessity […] highly speculative," Foreign Secretary Howe concluded. Therefore, the end of such Soviet control was either unpredictable, "many decades" away, or at "the middle of the next century," officials opined. Or perhaps "much sooner," Leslie wrote cautiously in her study, but even she was probably oblivious to how prescient her postscript would end up being. Given these considerations, British ministers and diplomats concluded that London should focus more on improving its relationship with Bonn, but that no radical measures were needed.¹⁰

Bolder Proposal: Advance into Germany, not Retreat into France

Notwithstanding British trust in the immovability of Europe's postwar security architecture, as 1988 progressed change appeared in-

creasingly probable. Developments in the Soviet Union and in Eastern Europe proceeded at a pace that even a year earlier had seemed
"unimaginable." The European Community made very rapid progress
toward a single market, thereby increasing its attractivity towards the
East, giving cause for concern to U.S. planners worried about European protectionism, and challenging Conservative British politicians to
worry about what would come next on the European integration front.
As the Reagan Administration was winding down, the expectation of a
reduced American commitment to Europe became conventional wisdom in London. With Soviet willingness to constrain Eastern Europeans increasingly questioned and the Germans increasingly in a mood
of "national self-consciousness," many concluded that change was in
the air. British officials feared that German political elites were keen to
rush to capitalize on Gorbachev's *glasnost*, were determined to develop
closer relations with the East, and had "little feel for the sensitivities
of allies." Most within the UK foreign policy establishment concluded
that the artificial division of Europe and of Germany could not and
would not continue indefinitely.[11]

For all these reasons, by summer 1988 intrepid planners within
the Foreign Office were challenging their doyens' conventional wisdom. Britain should adopt a strategy that "advances into Germany,
not retreats into France," Donald MacLaren, a young Scottish diplomat within the London FCO, advised. His logic: The barriers were
"coming down." Gorbachev did not want to abandon socialism, but his
economic and political reform efforts were genuine. Britain, Europe,
and the world would all be more secure if the Soviet leader succeeded.
While the Kremlin could still use force to "reverse the foment [Gor-
bachev] knows he is causing" in Eastern Europe, such action could only
be completed with dramatic consequences at home. Hence, the mighty
Germans, "riven with neurosis," were bound to seek "not to remain
dissatisfied forever." Leaders in Bonn had the nationalistic determi-
nation, the strength of purpose, and the economic prowess to achieve
their aims. Moscow would accept a neutral Germany, but not tolerate
a unified German giant in NATO. Therefore, MacLaren assessed that
neutrality was the imperfect but only viable option for the Germans. As
the ideological conflict faded away, Washington policymakers would be
less and less interested in Europe, the planner suggested. Therefore,

the Americans, having "other fish to fry" and "smaller rations of cooking oil," might accept the German neutrality outcome.[12]

Consequently, MacLaren argued that a different strategy was needed. He accepted that the British, like most other Europeans, "shuddered" at the idea of a large united Germany. Confronted with Germany's impending reunification and neutralization, Britain's default policy was to team up with France in restraining the West Germans. In the short term, this was a correct tactic, aimed at preventing the Germans from forcing overly large Western concessions vis-à-vis Moscow. Nonetheless, over the long term MacLaren argued that the policy of opposition "will blow up in our faces." Widely expanding the "Silent Alliance" with Bonn was London's only way to ensure that the Federal Republic's eventual choices would be taken "in accordance with British advice and not over British objections."[13] The memo's bottom-line: it might be possible to cut a deal with the Germans at the expense of the French. Implicitly, MacLaren recognized that his proposed deal would be expensive, and hid the various costs and compromises behind vague formulations. However, his proposal could potentially work, he claimed, in contrast to the other options available on the table—options that simply masked a desire to hedge one's bets and do nothing. The Germans "always have and always will dominate Europe," MacLaren concluded. Britain, for once, should "back a winner."

Senior members of the British government retorted that change was not expected to come so fast. They hoped that Moscow's obduracy would absolve them of confronting uncomfortable policy options. Most within the UK foreign policy elite accepted that the "glue" was "starting to come out" of the Eastern framework and that the Germans might be "tempted." However, a majority did not believe that a neutral unified Germany was very likely—as the Germans themselves would not want it, even if the Americans were to leave. In contrast, most agreed that Bonn's influence in Europe would significantly rise. In terms of solutions, some simply assumed that the Soviet leadership would soon "damp down" the process in Eastern Europe, rendering change anything but "imminent." Others were less optimistic about Moscow's abilities, and believed the key lay in European integration. Deeper and deeper ties were offering a basis for cohesion within the continent's West and a "pole of attraction" to Eastern Europe. In addition, these officials concluded that the "Community bicycle" of European integration had to keep moving forward for the Germans not to "fall off" and choose a path towards neutrality in order to achieve reunification. Yet these Europeanists were fully aware that keeping this bicycle in motion contrasted "rather sharp" with the British government's policy—and, in particular, with Prime Minister Thatcher's objectives. This clear incongruity with British political preferences notwithstanding, other options but for relying on Moscow or pursuing European integration were not considered.[14]

By the end of autumn 1988, after reading the planning exchanges within his own department, Secretary Howe chose to delay and postpone, relying on the Soviets to save the British establishment from disagreeable decisions. Howe told his personal secretary that there were many "striking insights" in MacLaren's paper. Keeping an open mind vis-à-vis the German Question was no longer enough. The British government had to respond "imaginatively" to the German reunification challenge. MacLaren's paper was "provocative," however. Its analysis was "absolutist" and "more challenging than prescriptive." There was "deep-rooted Soviet suspicion of all things German," Howe claimed, following the view of a majority within the FCO. It was therefore "wrong" to put all British eggs today into the German "basket" that might well be the "market leader" in "some years' or decades' time." In terms of action, the Foreign Office should "try to get across" to Prime Minister Thatcher the "sensitivity of the subject," Howe concluded, understanding early on that frontal opposition would be counterproductive. And yet the Secretary determined that London's diplomats in Bonn should only try "filling the role of confessor or candid (listening) friend" when it came to West German officials' views on their own future. Such "confessor" policy was very far from MacLaren's "advancing into Germany" option, and UK diplomats spent the subsequent months doing what they had already done before: observing and worrying.[15]

Conclusion

By not taking any leaps of faith throughout 1988 or during the first months of 1989, the British set themselves up for either accepting Germany's unification without protestation or frontally opposing Bonn's designs. As other scholars have noted, there was little at the end of 1989 and the beginning of 1990 that the British could ask for in exchange for their acquiescence.[16] The Americans were able to remain a European power by ensuring that Germany unified within NATO. The French were able to advance European integration as a means of expanding Paris' influence and constraining Bonn. The Germans, in turn, got to see their country unified and sovereign. Even the Soviets, the true losers of the 1989-1990 affair as they were forced to abandon an empire in Eastern Europe, got some consolation prices and promises from Bonn and Washington.[17] In contrast, anything the British could ask for went against German, American, or French preferences. Having waited for so long, hedging its bets throughout the 1980s, London got nothing. Had the Germans considered MacLaren's proposal, had it been articulated? We will have to wait for a broader opening of German archives to pass judgement on this. Nevertheless, given that London never tried, it wasted even the smallest of chances to have succeeded.

Notes

1. Charles D. Powell, "Note for Thatcher: Memo by Budd," October 11, 1984, The National Archives of the United Kingdom (TNA), Prime Minister's Office Records (PREM) 19/1764.

2. UK Foreign and Commonwealth Office (FCO) Planning Staff, "Planning Paper on Managing Russia," July 11, 1979, TNA, PREM 19/238—available online; UK FCO Planning Staff, "Planning Paper on the Management of East-West Relations," May 2, 1980, TNA, PREM 19/238—available online; Julian L. Bullard, "Letter to Howe: The German Question," October 5, 1984, TNA, PREM 19/1764; and, Colin R. Budd, "Record of a Discussion between the Secretary of State and Chancellor Kohl in Bonn," October 3, 1985, TNA, FCO 33/7992; see also Stephen G. Brooks and William C. Wohlforth, "Power, Globalization, and the End of the Cold War: Reevaluating a Landmark Case for Ideas," *International Security* 25, no. 3 (Winter 2001), pp. 5–53.

3. For instance, Roger B. Porter, "Letter to Sprinkel: Minutes of Economic Policy Council, 17 June 1985," July 22, 1985, Ronald Reagan Presidential Library (RPL), Beryl Sprinkel Files OA17747, box 12, EPC Meeting US/EC; or Alyson J.K. Bailes, "Planning Paper on the UK/French/FRG Relationship," September 18, 1985, TNA, FCO 33/7965. For British assessments of the European framework, Christopher A. D. S. MacRae, "Letter for Munro: On the State of Franco/German Relations," May 7, 1985, TNA, FCO 33/7814; and John W. D. Margetson, "Letter to Jenkins: Visit of the President of the Federal Republic of German to the Netherlands," June 7, 1985, TNA, FCO 46/4469.

4. Colin A. Munro, "Letter for Bailes: The UK/French/FRG Relationship," June 27, 1985, TNA, FCO 33/7814; and "Letter to Dain: Delors," September 18, 1985, TNA, FCO 33/7965. For the second argument, good illustrations are Pauline L. Neville-Jones, "Letter for Dain: Planning Paper on the UK/French/FRG Relationship, RS 021/3/12, DD 1985/380," November 19, 1985, TNA, FCO 33/7816; Colin A. Munro, "Letter to Jennings: Franco-German Relations," December 6, 1985, TNA, FCO 33/7925; or Michael Alexander, "Letter to Boyd: France, Germany and the UK: Bilateralism within the Alliance," October 20, 1987, TNA, PREM 19/3101.

5. Anthony A. Acland, "Letter for Armstrong: Britain, France and Germany," November 19, 1985, TNA, FCO 33/7816. Also, Anthony R. Brenton, "Letter for Bailes: The UK/French/FRG Relationship," June 18, 1985, TNA, FCO 33/7814; and Colin A. Munro, "Letter for Bailes: Planning Paper on the UK/French/FRG Relationship," June 20, 1985, TNA, FCO 33/7814. For the last assessment, I am thankful to Ambassador Rodric Braithwaite for his invaluable insights.

6. For an excellent U.S. assessment, Charles H. Price, "Telegram to State Department: The New Radicalism Eight Years On: Where Is the Thatcher Revolution Now?," February 16, 1988, RPL, Nelson Ledsky Files, RAC Box 9, United Kingdom—1988—Cables (2 of 8); for the German view, Hermann von Richthofen, "Memo for Foreign Office: Political Half-Year Report Great Britain (Politischer Halbjahresbericht Grossbritanien)," September 1, 1988, Politisches Archiv des Auswärtigen Amts (PAAA), B31, ZA 160.037—translated by the author. Horst Teltschik, "Gespräch Des Bundeskanzlers Kohl Mit Präsident Mitterrand in Heidelberg [Conversation between Chancellor Kohl and President Mitterrand in Heidelberg]," August 26, 1986, in Matthias Peter and Daniela Taschler, *Akten zur Auswärtigen Politik der Bundesrepublik Deutschland* (Berlin: De Gruyter, 2017), document 225, pp. 1199-1205—translated by the author. Also, Margaret Thatcher, *The Downing Street Years* (London: Harper Press, 1993); Stephen Wall, *A Stranger in Europe: Britain and the EU from Thatcher to Blair* (Oxford: Oxford University Press, 2008); and Charles Moore, *Margaret Thatcher: Everything She Wants*, vol. 2 (New York: Knopf, 2016).

7. Colin R. Budd, "Letter to Powell: The German Question," October 11, 1984, TNA, PREM 19/1764. The quote is from FRG's Foreign Minister, Hans-Dietrich Genscher, at the United Nations. Also, Michael Llewellyn Smith, "Letter for Bullard for the Secretary of State: The German Question," January 8, 1985, TNA, FCO 33/8083.

8. Mariot Leslie, "The German Question and Europe," September 29, 1987, FCO Planning Staff, declassified in November 2017 at author's FOI Request 1023-17; for an interesting comment on a draft, Stephen J. Wall, "Letter to Leslie: The German Question and Europe," September 8, 1987, TNA, FCO 33/9160; also relevant is Michael R. H. Jenkins, "Telegram to FCO: Whither the US?," November 23, 1987, TNA, PREM 19/2565.

9. Russ Dixon, "Letter to Llewellyn Smith: The German Card," July 17, 1987, TNA, FCO 33/9160; see also Llewellyn Smith, "Letter for Bullard for the Secretary of State: The German Question."

10. For Howe's views on such long-term planning, Lyn Parker, "Letter to Gore-Booth: The German Question and Europe," October 7, 1987, TNA, FCO 33/9160. Also, for instance, the missives by John E. Fretwell, Rodric Braithwaite, Julian L. Bullard, or Jeremy Greenstock, all in autumn 1988, and all to be found in TNA, FCO 33/9160 and FCO 33/9443. For the Franco-German dimension, see Ewen A.J. Fergusson, "Letter to Fretwell: Franco-German Relations," January 15, 1988, TNA, FCO 33/9443.

11. Instructive are Julian L. Bullard, "Letter for Howe: Annual Review for the Federal Republic of Germany (FRG) for 1987," January 11, 1988, TNA, FCO 33/9655; Charles D. Powell, "Letter to Parker: Prime Minister's Meeting with Herr Strauss," July 6, 1988, TNA, PREM 19/3768 and the accompanying

memos and reports; or Timothy Eggar, "Letter to Howe: Fifth Anglo German Round Table for CDU/CSU and Conservative MPs," October 7, 1988, TNA, FCO 33/9777. For the US assessment, see Unknown Author, "The State of the Transatlantic Alliance," February 10, 1988, RPL, Nelson Ledsky Files, RAC Box 5-6, NATO Summit March 1988 Memos-Letters-Cables (2 of 12).

12. Donald MacLaren, "East/West Relations and the Future of Europe: Or, Genscher Looks for Opportunities and We Think We've Got Problems," July 11, 1988, TNA, FCO 33/9777.

13. And not over British "dead bodies," MacLaren's superior morbidly joked in an accompanying memo. David A. Gore-Booth, "Letter to Wright: The German Problem," February 12, 1988, TNA, FCO 33/9777.

14. John E. Fretwell, "Letter to Wall: Brzezinski's Lecture," February 12, 1988, TNA, FCO 33/9777; Mark Lyall, "Letter to Gore-Booth: The German Problem," July 19, 1988, TNA, FCO 33/9777; and Patrick Wright, "Letter to Wall: The German Question," October 24, 1988, TNA, FCO 33/9777. The "bicycle" analogy is attributed to Christopher Mallaby. For the foundations and assumptions of UK diplomats' thinking on Soviet intentions, Ann Lewis, "Letter for Fretwell: East/West Heads of Mission Conference," August 9, 1988, TNA, FCO 82/1947.

15. Stephen J. Wall, "Letter to Wright: The German Question," October 24, 1988, TNA, FCO 33/9777. The Soviet suspicion of "all things German" was "in this connection rather comforting," Tim Eggar, the Parliamentary Under-Secretary for Foreign Affairs, concluded. Richard Makepeace, "Letter to Waldegrave: The German Question," October 17, 1988, TNA, FCO 33/9777. For the conclusions drawn from these discussions by the UK envoy to Bonn, Christopher Mallaby, "Letter for Fretwell: The FRG and the West," October 14, 1988, TNA, FCO 33/9669.

16. Patrick Salmon, "The United Kingdom: Divided Counsels, Global Concerns," in Frédéric Bozo, Andreas Rödder, and Mary Elise Sarotte, eds., *German Reunification: A Multinational History* (London: Routledge, 2017), 153–76.

17. For an interesting debate around this question, for instance Mary Elise Sarotte, "Perpetuating U.S. Preeminence: The 1990 Deals to 'Bribe the Soviets Out' and Move NATO In," *International Security* 35, no. 1 (Summer 2010), pp. 110–37; Kristina Spohr, "Precluded or Precedent-Setting? The 'NATO Enlargement Question' in the Triangular Bonn-Washington-Moscow Diplomacy of 1990–1991," *Journal of Cold War Studies* 14, no. 4 (Fall 2012), pp. 4–54; and Joshua R. Itzkowitz Shifrinson, "Deal or No Deal? The End of the Cold War and the U.S. Offer to Limit NATO Expansion," *International Security* 40, no. 4 (Spring 2016), pp. 7–44.

Chapter 9

1989–1990:
The End of the Cold War
and Challenges for Europe

Markus Meckel

The Difficulty of Remembering—Differences in Assessment

Thirty years after the end of the Cold War and the upheavals and revolutions in Central Europe, it is significant that internationally, German unification counts as a great success story. I can only share this perspective: 1989-90 was the happiest hour for the Germans! Forty-five years after we Germans had brought so much terror and horror to all of Europe, we had the opportunity to live in freedom and democracy, united again, and with the acceptance of all our neighbors. I wouldn't ever have dared to dream that I would experience this!

At the same time, there is currently a discussion in Germany that focuses on dissatisfaction with the way unification has evolved. Particularly in eastern Germany there is a feeling among some that they were "colonized" by the West and that their contribution to German unity remains underappreciated.

Of course, when it comes to describing and assessing events 30 years ago differences are apparent not only in Germany. Poland and Hungary, who blazed the trail for freedom and democracy with the militant slogan "back to Europe" and were the paragons of transformation in the 1990s, have become symbols of a considerable Euroskepticism under their current governments. Anti-liberal politics and nationalist goals are gaining ground and upending European politics—and not just in these countries. How we remember the revolutionary years 1988 - 1991 has become a battleground for values and different points of view.

If 30 years ago Gorbachev's policies were an essential prerequisite for change, in today's Russia he is largely regarded as the gravedigger of former (imperial) grandeur. For current Russian President Vladimir

Putin, "the greatest catastrophe of the 20th century" was the disintegration of the Soviet Union and not, for example, Stalin's crimes or Hitler's destructive war. While the Soviet Union was ready to grant full sovereignty to united Germany in 1990, today's Russia does not accept the sovereignty of its neighboring nations. The annexation of Crimea and the hidden war in eastern Ukraine are only the most obvious examples of this. International law and common values, as they were celebrated in the 1990 Charter of Paris, are under great pressure today. Worries about a new Cold War are circulating.

Therefore, it makes a lot of sense to connect memories of the upheavals at that time with an analysis of current challenges, because our challenge is how the values that were asserted and proclaimed then can be realized today. The situation is made even more challenging by the fact that under President Trump there is now an administration in power in the United States that similarly disparages these values.

In this chapter I will limit myself essentially to events and experiences in Germany and keep things as personal as possible. In the process, however, it is necessary to keep in mind that these German events did not take place separately from their European and global contexts.

The Peaceful Revolution in the GDR in 1989: Opening the Prospect for German Unity

On February 4, 1989, two Protestant pastors, Martin Gutzeit and I, decided to establish a Social Democratic Party in the German Democratic Republic (GDR). This was by no means a spontaneous idea, but rather the logical consequence of a long pre-history and previous joint work.

At the time of our decision, we did not suspect that two days later, round table negotiations would begin in Poland. The result of these was that for the first time in the Eastern bloc semi-free elections took place that led to Tadeusz Mazowiecki becoming Poland's non-communist prime minister.

How much things were fermenting in Central Europe at this time was something that I first experienced first-hand in Hungary in October 1988. I was on my way to Romania, where Ceausescu had begun a village destruction program that was attracting great international attention and generating tensions with Hungary. Hungarian society was starting to change very rapidly. I found this fascinating. In the reigning party (MSZP), János Kádár had been replaced and decisions had been made about economic reforms that were still inconceivable for the GDR. Nevertheless, the economic crisis deepened, which caused polemics against the Hungarian reforms in the GDR press. The democratic opposition was organizing itself; the dissidents had a "network of free initiatives" and founded the "Democratic Forum." Countless associations arose, the historical Hungarian parties and a first free trade union were established. The opposition's *samizdat*, or underground pamphlets and materials, was growing in circulation and was influencing public debate. Starting in 1987 in the *samizdat* newspaper "BESZÉLŐ," a program of the opposition called a "social contract" appeared that put increasing pressure on the MSZP.

The essential background for these Central European developments and also for our own actions were the policies of Mikhail Gorbachev. He had been the General Secretary of the Communist Party of the Soviet Union since 1985. He proclaimed the need for "new thinking," and with *glasnost* and *perestroika* in the Soviet Union he set in motion a reform process that gave us hope, even if it was clear that his intention was to reform communism in order to preserve it. However, at the same time it was perceptible in his speeches that he was not wearing blinders like the communist leaders that we had known. He seemed to really want to solve problems and to have an understanding of global challenges, from the necessary reconfiguration in the security sector with respect to global armament as well as with regard to ecological questions. In his speech to the United Nations in December 1988, he endorsed the "principle of the freedom of choice," which he declared to be "a universal principle to which there should be no exceptions" and dedicated himself to

> the increasing varieties of social development in different countries. (...) This objective fact presupposes respect for other people's views and stands, tolerance, a preparedness to see phenomena that are different as not necessarily bad or hostile, and an ability to learn to live side by side while remaining different and not agreeing with one another on every issue.[1]

This was the rejection of the Brezhnev Doctrine, proclaimed on the world stage: independent developments might be possible in the Soviet Union's own satellite states without having tanks roll again. We slowly began to hope that something could really change. In Poland and Hungary, things had developed further, which gave us in the GDR courage, because the questions with which we were confronted were essentially the same. Our concern was to finally create the prerequisites for enabling the opposition to act politically. The decision to seek new organizational structures outside the church and to establish a Social Democratic Party was a very conscious change of strategy for us. Even after the fact it sounds daring, but we were striving for a basic and categorical change: an overcoming of the communist system. With the founding of the party, we were posing the *de facto* question of power; we wanted a parliamentary democracy of the Western kind.

Up to that point, we had not believed that we could really change anything with our actions, never mind achieve democracy or overcome the division of Germany. It was more a moral action. The concern was to be able to look at ourselves in the mirror in the morning or, as Václav Havel put it, "to live in truth" in the midst of this empire of lies. We had concerned ourselves with the German resistance to National Socialism (NS). We considered this resistance important even if it did not bring down the NS system; to a certain extent, it salvaged Germans' honor. We looked at ourselves in similar vein: we wanted to put an end to our silence and do something! It was important in specific instances to say NO clearly.

Martin Gutzeit and I came from a Protestant tradition. We both grew up with a critical distance from the socialist state and its ideology. There were conflicts when we were in school and we were refused higher education. Both of us rejected military service completely. We did not even join the *Bausoldaten* (a military service without weapons that existed only in the GDR, although each of us also managed to avoid the usual imprisonment. Thus, we received our education only in church institutions independent of the state. We met in 1974 at the *Sprachenkonvikt*, a theological university of the Protestant church in Berlin, where a course of study completely free of communist influence was possible, one that was in no way inferior to Western universities. These theological universities—there were two more in Naumburg and Leipzig—were places of spiritual freedom that were otherwise difficult to find in the GDR.

In addition to these theoretical considerations, starting with a small group in 1976 we began to become politically active in small steps. We duplicated political texts on old printing machines and distributed them to people. These included lectures by Rudolf Bahro about his book *Die Alternative* and the "memory logs" of Jürgen Fuchs about his imprisonment by the *Staatssicherheit*. There had always been such student groups in the GDR. Frequently, participants were imprisoned and—at least in the later years—landed in the West in the end. We were lucky and did not get caught.

I assumed a position as vicar in 1980 and as a pastor in 1982 in a village in Mecklenburg on Lake Müritz. Martin Gutzeit assumed a position nearby. In these years, groups arose in many parts of the GDR that concerned themselves critically with questions regarding peace and the environment. Over the years, the range of topics became ever more varied and fundamental. In my village in Mecklenburg in 1982, I founded such a peace circle. Participants came from all around the region. At the same time, we created networks in order to bring the various groups into contact with one another and to enable cooperation. In Mecklenburg, beginning in 1981 this included the *Arbeitsgruppe Frieden* (Peace Working Group) and the GDR-wide delegate conference *Frieden konkret* (Practical Peace), which had been meeting annually since 1983. Beginning in 1982 we in Mecklenburg organized the *Mobile Friedensseminare* (Mobile Peace Seminars) for a week at the beginning of August. At these seminars, participants from all over the GDR and from abroad formed groups in various locations around the region focusing on different political topics; in the end, there was a larger joint public event commemorating the dropping of the atomic bombs on Hiroshima and Nagasaki. Through these networks and seminars, many opposition activists got to know each other in the first half of the 1980s. This was an essential prerequisite for the Peaceful Revolution years later. These—mostly church—groups sought change in crucial social questions. The topics were broad and varied: the agenda included security questions, parenting and education concepts, environmental problems, human and minority rights, as well as global development strategies. Individuals perceived themselves differently in these groups than otherwise in this communist state; here, they were

244 EXITING THE COLD WAR, ENTERING A NEW WORLD

responsible for the community, they learned and experienced solidarity. Therefore, to a certain extent, these political groups became schools of civil courage and responsibility.

Frequently, people say that these groups arose under the umbrella of the church. However, it is more correct to say that most of these groups arose within the church, were established by politically engaged Christians, who at the same time were open to cooperation with others. Until the end of the 1980s, these groups' networks found their place within the church. At the same time, groups that also emphasized their independence from the church were in intense contact with church-leading representatives and used them as intermediaries as well as their institutional and organizational possibilities.

The churches were the only large organizations in the GDR with their own independent and (for the Protestant church) democratic structures. They had their own facilities and a certain openness, even if it was limited. As becomes clear from Gutzeit's biography and mine as well, the church's own educational resources were also important. The church had people who were trained in its own spiritual tradition and practiced in free communication. Thus, it was no wonder that in many places engaged Christians, pastors, and church employees played an outsized role in the establishment of opposition movements and the moderation of the round tables.

The Soviets gave the churches in their occupied zone of Germany more freedom than in other countries of the Eastern bloc since they recognized the *Bekennende Kirche* (Confessing Church) of the NS era as resistance. Its representatives occupied leading positions in the Protestant church after 1945. The church's social significance was further enhanced by its youth work, which still represented a field of conflict with state authorities who were operating under the rule of the *Sozialistische Einheitspartei Deutschlands* (SED).

In the churches themselves, at the start of the 1980s socio-politically active groups were controversial; this dispute affected all levels, from church communities to the leadership levels. Some people understood this political work as an important dimension of Christian proclamation; others regarded it as foreign infiltration and instrumentalization of the church for political purposes. Acceptance of the political groups increased within the church structures, however, when in 1983 the

Ecumenical Council of Churches in Vancouver called for a "conciliar process for justice, peace, and the preservation of creation"—and thus took up the topics that were the focus of these groups' work. When in 1988-89 the churches in the GDR called an "ecumenical assembly for justice, peace, and the preservation of creation," many representatives of these groups participated and significantly influenced the results. At this assembly, I myself led the working group on development policies and then also had the opportunity to participate in the European Ecumenical Assembly in Basel in May 1989. The substantive results of the assembly in the GDR were incorporated a few months later in various places, among others in the programmatic introductions of the new opposition movements in fall 1989, since a number of their members were among the founders of the various new movements and parties of the opposition.

By 1987, many people in the opposition hoped that the SED "would learn from the Soviet Union (under Gorbachev)" and could make improvements by initiating a step-by-step reform process from above. This perspective dissolved after SED leader Erich Honecker took massive action against the opposition after his visit to Bonn that year. The storming of the *Umweltbibliothek* (Environmental Library) in November 1987 and the imprisonments and deportations to the West at the start of 1988 in connection with the Rosa Luxemburg/Karl Liebknecht demonstration represented a turning point. For Martin Gutzeit and for me, but also for others, it became clear that new forms of opposition were needed. The church alone could no longer form the basis for these activities. We had increasing hope that essential change might be possible—but it would have to be asserted. The church could incite people and encourage them toward freedom-oriented thinking and action—and we had done that for years—but the church could not present programmatic opposition. Therefore, at the start of 1989, we decided to establish a Social Democratic Party in the GDR.

Why didn't two Protestant pastors want to establish a Christian party? I have answered this question frequently: for theological reasons. We wanted to resist any political instrumentalization of Christian belief for political purposes. The Bible cannot really justify practical transport or health policies, it can only provide a basic ethical orientation; no party may claim that it is more Christian than another. Every individual must focus on the dignity of human beings and therefore enable the weak to participate and integrate.

But why did we decide to establish a Social Democratic Party?

In my programmatic lecture upon the establishment of the party on October 7, 1989, the 40th birthday of the GDR, I justified this in three ways.

First, we placed ourselves in the tradition of Germany's oldest democratic party, through which the disadvantaged and downtrodden became the subjects of political action in the 19th century. Accordingly, with this establishment we wanted to leave space so that subjects in the GDR could become citizens, political subjects who assume responsibility for their own reality.

Second, with the establishment of this party, we placed ourselves in an international context in order to do justice to global challenges and overcome the provincialism of the communist GDR. Willy Brandt's report on North-South issues,[2] Olof Palme's report about joint security,[3] and Gro Harlem Brundtland's report about sustainable development[4] were all important orientation points.

Third, by establishing a Social Democratic Party we were withdrawing the social democratic hand from the symbol of the SED party badge (the handshake of Pieck and Grotewohl, KPD and SPD) and withdrawing its ideological legitimation from the SED. This went to the roots of the self-definition of the SED—and it was intentional. We were objecting to the SED's monopoly on truth and power and we wanted it to face up to the need for legitimation from citizens.

With the establishment of this party, we anticipated the break with the dictatorial system of the GDR and at the same time called for the right to define ourselves politically in the framework of democratic plurality—and to fight as an alliance of democratic initiatives for the formation of democratic institutions and structures. In contrast to some others in the opposition, we demanded not just democratic reforms (which would be created by those in power). Our concern was to create the institutional prerequisites to guarantee adherence to human rights and democratic participation through rule of law and division of powers. For this, however, it was necessary to be prepared to assume political responsibility.

During the first half of 1989, I tried, in discussions with various comrades-in-arms in the opposition, to advocate for participation in our project. Of course, this could only happen in secret, but these efforts met with little success. Most people did not want any parties and democracy of a Western kind, but instead were still striving for a basic democracy of any kind. Over the summer, a series of friends in the opposition became aware of our project, including people who themselves later established other movements. Thus, it is possible to say that all groupings that later selected other organizational approaches consciously stepped away from our approach.

I issued our appeal on August 26, 1989, in the final plenary session of a seminar about human rights questions (it was the 200th anniversary of the declaration of citizens' and human rights in the French Revolution). The formal establishment of the party, with elections, took place on October 7. In the course of September, other initiatives of the opposition came to light, such as *Neues Forum* and *Demokratie Jetzt*, which regarded themselves as forums for public dialogue about necessary social changes. On October 4, 1989, the *Kontaktgruppe der Opposition*, comprised of representatives from different opposition groups, met for the first time; important agreements were made here. This is also where the suggestion on November 10 for the establishment of a round table originated, which then met from December 7 to the middle of March and prepared the first free East German election.

Crucial for the success of the Peaceful Revolution were both the common political action of the democratic opposition and the mass demonstrations that lent this action the necessary weight. When 70,000 people appeared on the streets of Leipzig on October 9, 1989, the commanders did not dare to deploy the troops on hand and end the demonstrations with force. I experienced this in Magdeburg, where between 5,000-8,000 people had gathered. We were in the Magdeburg Cathedral. The armed troops were down by the Elbe River, but they did not intervene in the end. From that point on I was convinced: we would succeed in establishing a democracy!

After the fall of the Berlin Wall on November 9, contact between the Social Democrats in the East and West became important. Before then, we hadn't made contact with them. Crucially, this happened entirely on our own authority. However, in connection with the establishment of the party, we turned to Willy Brandt as Chair of the Socialist International (SI) and applied for membership. Willy Brandt reacted quickly and sent Swedish Social Democrats to make contact with us. After the fall of the Wall, he invited us to the SI council meeting in Geneva, where we received status as observers in November 1989.

The Berlin Wall fell on November 9, 1989. It was totally unexpected. The SED had no intention of opening the Wall; it was seeking to render it more transparent. Just beforehand the Central Committee of the SED had agreed to a new travel regulation that would give every GDR citizen the right to apply for travel to the West. Previously such applications required a specific reason, for instance family circumstances. Now no such reasons would be needed in such applications. Poles and Hungarians had long enjoyed such rights; now this was to apply to GDR citizens as well. On November 9, however, when Günter Schabowski, a leading SED spokesman, announced the new regulation to a press conference, he gave the impression that GDR citizens could simply travel to the West without first applying to do so. Masses gathered at the checkpoints to West Berlin and pressed the Wall open; there was no shooting, as there had also been none at the mass demonstrations in the previous weeks.

Suddenly, peacefully, everything was different. Since October 9, we were, as I have just described, increasingly certain that we would succeed in establishing democracy in the GDR. It was also clear to us at the time, however, that two democratic German states divided by a wall would be absurd; it was not a viable proposition. Our belief that we now had a real chance for democracy meant that for us the Wall had already lost its menacing nature. It was not clear what the options would be, but the hope that German unity could be achievable was already apparent.

In October 1989 we did not focus on specific ways we could help make this happen, because Europe and the Soviet Union were in the midst of dynamic changes. Possibilities were likely to become clearer with time—that was our perspective before November 9.

With the fall of the Wall, the realization of democracy in East Germany and the question of German unity were now simultaneously on the agenda. Yet it remained unclear how the process could unfold. The stance of the Soviet Union remained uncertain. Moscow, Washington, London and Paris still retained their Four Power Rights over all of

Germany. Negotiations would certainly also have to take place with the Federal Republic of Germany.

On December 3, 1989, the Executive Board of the East-SPD issued a declaration in which it committed itself to unity, at the same time, however, making clear that this must be designed by both German states, and in such a way that nobody must fear it, neither the socially weak nor Germany's European neighbors. Equally, recognition of Poland's western border was necessary. The first delegates' conference on January 14, 1990 declared:

> The goal of our policy is a united Germany. A government of the GDR led by Social Democrats will take the necessary steps on the path to German unity in cooperation with the government of the Federal Republic. That which is possible immediately should happen immediately. A Social Democratic government will take as its first and foremost task an economic and currency agreement. All steps of the German unity process must be integrated into the pan-European unity process, for we want German unity only with the agreement of all our neighbors. For us their borders are inviolable. We are striving for a framework of European security and peace. We regard as our particular responsibility the encouragement of the democratization process and economic renewal in Eastern Europe.

The round table that had been working since December 1989 had the task of negotiating the conditions for free elections, ensuring the government would hold them, and dissolving the state security services. The government formed after the election on March 18, 1990 under Prime Minister Lothar de Mazière of the *Allianz für Deutschland*, a CDU-led coalition of parties, for which I served as Foreign Minister, confronted the challenge of establishing German unity in negotiations with the Federal Republic. Originally, we had intended to pursue the "merger" of the two Germanys via Article 146 of the Federal Republic's Basic Law, which provided that the Basic Law—essentially West Germany's constitution—would cease to have effect whenever the whole German people adopted a constitution in a free election. With the election results of March 18, 1990, however, it was clear that unification would take place as accession via Article 23 of the Basic Law, by which the eastern *Länder* would accede to the FRG's structures. The large majority of the East German population wanted things this way. It was the legally easier and thus faster way.

In the subsequent coalition negotiations with the East-CDU, we asserted that it would be recorded explicitly that accession would only take place after treaty negotiations in which the conditions of unity were negotiated. It was clear to us that such negotiations were necessary in the interest of East Germans, for it would not be so easy to combine legal and social structures that were so different. At the time, many East Germans underestimated the significance of such negotiations and believed some promises that "immediate unity" would also mean "immediate prosperity" without having to worry about the specific conditions.

For want of space I cannot describe the many details associated with the path to unity and the different positions of the various sides. For us as the East-SPD, contact with the West-SPD was important, yet we faced a growing problem given the great differences within the West-SPD and specifically the positioning of Oskar Lafontaine, the party's candidate for Chancellor. The older generation of West German Social Democrats, led by Willy Brandt, were ardent supporters of German unity. The feeling of belonging to a common nation had diminished among members of the successor generation, however. Oskar Lafontaine felt more at home in Tuscany or in France than in Dresden, Leipzig or Rostock. He treated the idea of the "nation" as a backward-looking concept. This made it hard to develop a common political strategy.

The process of German unity was also burdened by the fact that 1990 was also an election year for the *Bundestag*. Helmut Kohl, whose poll ratings were decidedly poor at the end of 1989, saw—correctly as it turned out—the opportunity to win the election and declined West-SPD leader Hans-Jochen Vogel's offer at the start of 1990 to manage this process in a joint national effort. For Kohl, the unification process was also a great election campaign. Domestic unification politics played a central role in every decision he made. For example, his behavior with regard to the border question with Poland made this abundantly clear: he always kept in mind the opinions and sensitivities of the conservative *Vertriebene*/expellees.

German Unity in the European and International Context

Foreign policy questions did not play a large role in the 1990 election. The immediate concerns were questions of internal unity, such as the role of the Deutsche Mark as a currency for all of Germany, and issues related to economic and monetary union. We Social Democrats wanted to design German unity so that even our European neighbors would not have to fear it. This was not accentuated by the conservative parties, but it was also not really very controversial. Therefore, there was no dispute about the foreign policy passages of the coalition agreement. The government declaration of Prime Minister de Maizière on April 19, 1990 incorporated all the important statements of the coalition agreement.

For us, it was of central importance that we accepted the responsibility stemming from our history. This happened on April 12, 1990 in a declaration of the East German parliament, the *Volkskammer*, during its second session, when the new ministers of the de Maizière government were sworn in. This declaration stated:

> During the time of National Socialism, Germans caused the people of the world immeasurable suffering. Nationalism and racial fanaticism caused genocide, especially for Jews from all European countries, the peoples of the Soviet Union, the Polish people, and the peoples of the Sinti and Roma. This guilt may never be forgotten. From it we want to derive our responsibility for the future.

The SED had always denied such responsibility. In its view, the GDR stood by the side of the illustrious Soviet Union, to a certain extent by the side of the victor of the Second World War and of progress. Because according to its ideology history was always the history of class struggles, it believed itself free of any national responsibility. This is how anti-fascism also quickly became a legitimation ideology for the SED leadership. There was no reappraisal of National Socialism that reflected the incorporation of society and the responsibility of the individual in the Communist GDR. There was no *Vergangenheitsbewältigung* (effort to overcome the legacies of the Nazi past) in the Western sense either. Even in earlier years, only the Protestant churches and various oppositional groups were aware of a responsibility stemming from the nation's guilty history, and they tried to do justice to this through concrete activities.

For the democratic GDR, this admission of guilt on April 12, 1990 was intended to be an essential basis of its policies. Whereas relations with neighboring European countries were previously marked by communist ideology and association with the Soviet sphere of influence within the East-West conflict, they would now be redesigned completely and put on a new basis.

The acknowledgment of responsibility that stemmed from the past for us as Germans, also in the GDR and together with the Federal Republic of Germany, was supposed to make clear on which spiritual and moral basis both the unification of Germany and, until that time, the foreign policy of the GDR, would be founded. This declaration was of special significance for our relations with our eastern neighbors, who had suffered with us under communist dictatorship, but who had also been thoroughly inculcated with the historical amnesia of the GDR.

It was also important to convey that we would not just act as if our only responsibilities derived from the atrocities of the war. We could not suppress the guilt of the communist period; it too had to be incorporated into the national responsibility. This dimension played an important role both with respect to the Jewish people and Israel and with respect to Czechoslovakia. The joint declaration unfurled this responsibility in four different directions and tried to substantiate and update them.

First was the responsibility to the Jewish people. In its depiction of National Socialism, the SED had always minimized the *Shoah* (Holocaust). The *Volkskammer* asked for forgiveness for the "hypocrisy and animosity of official GDR policy with respect to the state of Israel and for the persecution and abasement of Jewish citizens in our country even after 1945." The practical political consequence was that Jewish religion and culture had to be promoted and protected, and cemeteries, synagogues, and memorials maintained and cared for. Even if German unity was about to occur, for symbolic reasons, talks to establish diplomatic relations between the GDR and Israel had to be initiated. Persecuted Jews would be granted asylum in the GDR. To the consternation of the government of the Federal Republic, we implemented this resolution very quickly, with the consequence that even in 1990 and in the years that followed (for the Federal government saw no opportunity to stop this after unification) there was a significant immigration of Jews, which has measurably enriched Jewish life in Germany.

Second, it was also important to us to place future relations with the Soviet Union in historical context. We did not want to identify the Russians and the other peoples of the Soviet Union with Stalin and communism. We wanted to make clear that Russians and the other people of the Soviet Union were largely themselves victims of communist dictatorship, just as Germans were Hitler's first victims. We understood German guilt for the invasion of the Soviet Union and wanted reconciliation. We also wanted to make clear that Gorbachev and the changes in the Soviet Union had made a significant contribution to the victory of freedom and democracy in our country. We believed that this should be considered in the future design of Europe. We believed that peace and security in Europe could only be guaranteed if Germany and the USSR were both be integrated into a pan-European security system. We further declared that the treaties signed by the GDR and the USSR should be adjusted by mutual agreement to the new realities.

Third, with regard to Czechoslovakia, the *Volkskammer* acknowledged the complicity of the GDR in the suppression of the Prague Spring of 1968 by troops from the Warsaw Pact and apologized: "In fear and despondency, we did not prevent this violation of international law. The first freely elected parliament of the GDR apologizes to the peoples of Czechoslovakia for the injustice done." At the time, we did not yet know that, at the last minute, the National Peoples' Army did not, in fact, march into Czechoslovakia in 1968.

Fourth, the relationship to Poland has special significance in conjunction with German reunification. Over the decades of communist rule there was opposition and resistance in all of the Central and East European countries. Particularly since the 1970s, however, that resistance had been broadest and deepest in Poland. The SED did what it could to squash internal dissent and was not afraid to stoke anti-Polish resentment. In the GDR, however, there was great recognition of the independent trade union *Solidarność*, which made the communist regime waver for the first time through civil resistance. Still more important than this historic bond was the need to validate permanently the German-Polish border along the Oder and Neisse Rivers. The *Volkskammer* reinforced this unconditionally:

> In particular, the Polish people should know that its right to live in secure borders will not be challenged by us Germans through territorial claims, either now or in the future. We reinforce the inviolability of the Oder-Neisse border to the Republic of Poland as the basis of the peaceful coexistence of our peoples in a common European house. A future pan-German parliament shall confirm this contractually.

The revolutions and changes in Central and Eastern Europe put many old and new questions on the agenda. It had to be the goal of the Western states to take the initiative after the tumultuous upheaval of fall 1989. The United States had a lot riding on this game—no less than its future role in Europe. As 1990 dawned it was clear that German reunification would come. When and how were still open questions. Of central significance for the United States was NATO membership of united Germany. This was the most important instrument of the leadership role of the United States in Europe. German withdrawal from the Alliance would have greatly reduced the significance of NATO and essentially restricted the influence of the United States in Europe. Thus, President Bush, out of his own national interest, supported Helmut Kohl's concept of as rapid a unification as possible under Article 23 (with the GDR subsumed into the FRG)—naturally under particular conditions.

When after the first free election in the GDR on April 12, 1990 I was selected as Foreign Minister, important international constellations had already been defined. The 2+4 mechanism among the two German states and the four World War II allies had been devised and agreed upon. Hans-Dietrich Genscher described the background to me during a visit to his home immediately after my selection. In fall 1989 in my programmatic lecture for the establishment of the Social Democratic Party in the GDR (SDP), I had still been advocating for a peace treaty to solve the German question. Now, Genscher made clear why such terminology and any such procedures must absolutely be avoided: just fifty years after the end of the war, the Federal Republic's democratic history and its long-term partnership in Western Europe in NATO and the EC could not be abandoned. Germany could not allow itself to become the mere object of four-power talks or even that of a large peace conference. Instead, the Federal Republic had to be regarded as an equal partner among the democracies of the West. Last but not least, it was important to prevent more than fifty former enemies from wanting to have a say over German unification or make new demands for reparations. He emphasized the necessity of having both German states be equal negotiating partners whose agreement was the prerequisite for any settlement. This argumentation illuminated for me that I completely shared these intentions. Furthermore, I felt that we could indicate with pride that we had fought for democracy in the GDR itself. We East Germans had learned from our history. We wanted to help shape self-confidently the design not just of German unity, but also Europe's future.

This urge to shape the future architecture, infused as it was by a strong sense of moral legitimation, nevertheless faced some daunting realities. This became clear to me only little by little. The goal of the freely elected GDR government was the establishment of German unity. Our task was to prepare and execute the voluntary self-dissolution of the GDR into the Federal Republic of Germany, which would offer the legal frame for a united Germany. This alone rendered clear the uneven influence each German state would be able to exercise in the process, regardless of any difference in political experience among the actors involved.

My acceptance into the foreign minister's circle was very friendly. Despite some contrary statements, people did not—and essentially did not want to—count on having a real actor step onto the playing field in the form of the truly democratic GDR. This was abundantly clear when, after the Ottawa agreements about the 2+4 mechanism in February 1990, none of the countries concerned waited until there were democratic elections and thus legitimate representatives of the GDR. The first official meetings of the 2+4 talks, the task of which was to prepare the first meeting on the foreign ministers' level, took place four days *before* the first free selection of the *Volkskammer* in the GDR!

Despite these conceivably poor prerequisites for a truly independent role in the negotiations, we developed our own concepts. The most important positions had already been agreed upon in the coalition agreements. In the following, I will restrict myself to questions relating to the 2+4 talks.

First, we wanted to embed the process of German unification not just in the process of European unification—which was also the goal of the Federal Republic's government—but to design it so that it could also be a catalyst for this. Therefore, with respect to the essentially same goals, our approach to the negotiations was quite different from the very beginning. The Western states, including the Federal Republic, wanted first and foremost the Soviet Union to agree to German unification and sovereignty, dissolution of four power rights, and unified Germany's membership in NATO. Otherwise, they wanted to regulate the future as little as possible. According to this perspective, all other options should be kept open, for it was clear where the center of power in Europe would be in the future—namely in the West. We, by contrast, believed it was important to determine central questions not just of German, but also of European unity and development, at least in rudimentary fashion. We believed there should be transitional rules with respect to various questions in order to keep the process in flux for the future and at least to specify its direction. Precisely such transitional rules were rejected categorically by the West for the reasons mentioned above and, in retrospect, for very justified reasons.

Second, we hoped that after the end of the confrontation of the two blocs in the Cold War that it would be possible to overcome the two camps step by step. Therefore, we strove for drastic disarmament steps and transitional rules for pan-European security structures. In this process we believed the CSCE should have played a central role, which is why we sought ways to strengthen it. We took up a Polish proposal and worked jointly with Warsaw and Prague to develop an initiative for the enhancement and institutionalization of the CSCE (the so-called Trilateral Initiative). At the beginning of March 1990, that is, still before the GDR's free election, I visited Washington for the first time with my undersecretary-to-be Hans Misselwitz and formally to a certain extent in parallel with SPD members of the Bundestag Dietrich Stobbe and Horst Ehmke. During this trip, it became clear to me that a united Germany, at least for a transition period, would have to be a member of NATO. However, we only wanted to agree to such a membership if NATO would also be prepared to make the necessary changes with respect to its function and strategies (forward defense, flexible response and first use of nuclear weapons).

Third, according to our understanding, the recovery of German sovereignty was supposed to go hand-in-hand with sovereign German declarations, taken freely and without pressure, that united Germany would adhere to certain self-restrictions intended to contribute to a European framework for peace. These included, for example, the re-linquishment not just of the manufacturing, possession, and control, but also of the stationing of atomic, biological, and chemical weapons. We would have preferred to have this restriction set down in the Unification Treaty or in the Basic Law. We also wanted to provide an impetus for conventional disarmament and reduction of troop strengths in Europe. The troop strength of unified Germany should be reduced radically. When in June at the 2+4 Foreign Ministers' Conference in Berlin I proposed reducing the number of German troops to 300,000 (or as a compromise to 380,000), this was rejected vehemently by the Western negotiation partners as a "singularization of Germany." A little later, however, this happened anyway at Kohl and Gorbachev's Caucasus summit, even without making reference to my proposal: at the end of August 1990, both German states declared before the Vienna Disarmament Conference of the CFE Treaty that unified Germany would limit its troops to 370,000 men. This declaration became part of the 2+4 treaty.

Fourth, as described above, we felt deeply connected to our Eastern neighbors, who had suffered with us under dictatorship and who had also freed themselves from it. This also included the peoples of the Soviet Union, for they had also started down the path of democratization, which had to be much rockier for them than for us because there was no democratic tradition there. However, not just because of this moral and historic bond, but also especially for basic political reasons, it seemed indispensable to us to reach an agreement with the Soviet Union that it could bear.

Any sense that the Soviet Union agreed to terms of German unification due to momentary weakness could leave a feeling there that they actually did lose the Second World War. This could prove to be a lingering factor of insecurity for the Europe of the future. We wanted to avoid a "Versailles" for the Soviet Union. From our point of view, not just the agreement itself, but real, appropriate consideration of the Soviet Union's interests was in the interest not just of Germany, but of all of Europe. This is why it was important to us that even after Soviet troop withdrawal from Germany the Soviet Union needed to remain permanently bound to Europe—politically, culturally, economically and in terms of security policy. Among other things, it was a problem for the Soviet Union that it would withdraw its troops completely after unification, while not a lot would change for the Western allies.

In order to treat all four allies equally in at least one respect—something that was of great psychological value to the Soviet Union—I proposed at the second 2+4 Foreign Ministers' Conference in Berlin in June 1990 that all four victorious powers leave Berlin as soon as possible. That wouldn't have cost anything from a security policy point of view, but it would have been an important symbol of the equal treatment of the four allies for the Soviet Union. Of course, such a proposal was believed to be completely impossible at that time, even though it has long since been implemented.

Fifth, for us the recognition of Poland's western border was a high priority. It had to be recognized as quickly and easily as possible, in binding fashion under international law and permanently. Only this way could we expect our neighbors to greet German unification and dispel the more or less latent fears of the Polish people. From our point of view, this recognition should have occurred voluntarily. We believed that any impression that we Germans had been forced to do this would be damaging. Nobody was supposed to have to tell us where Germany lies! Germany could prove its maturity by freely recognizing its neighbors' territorial integrity.

We therefore strove for a border treaty that was supposed to confirm in binding fashion according to international law the existing German-Polish border as it was described in 1950 in the Görlitz Treaty between the GDR and Poland and in 1972 in the Warsaw Pact between the Federal Republic and Poland. In the process, we joined with a proposal by Polish Prime Minister Mazowiecki, for we wanted to do everything to avoid doubts and insecurities on the part of the Poles about German behavior. Accordingly, we believed that a treaty between the two German states and Poland should be negotiated and signed immediately after unification by the unified German and Polish governments and ratified by both parliaments. Helmut Kohl vehemently resisted this, so that the talks between the two German states and Poland fizzled out after a brief time.

I believed that the phrase used frequently by Helmut Kohl and Wolfgang Schäuble—that the recognition of the border was the "price of reunification"—was extremely problematic. Anyone who employed such characterizations could not have been surprised when fears arose within neighboring countries that Germany—as soon as unity had been achieved—could have adopted very different positions on the border or on other issues. Nonetheless, in contrast to Willy Brandt, who in 1970 risked a great deal politically when he initiated a dramatic process of reconciliation with Poland and signed the Warsaw Treaty, Helmut Kohl was not prepared to risk losing any votes—even though it was clear he would decisively win the election. Instead, he left Tadeusz Mazowiecki, the first non-communist Prime Minister of Poland, high and dry even though Mazowiecki urgently needed a success with regard to the border issue.

From our point of view, the territories had been lost as a consequence of the criminal war by Nazi Germany. United Germany should recognize it permanently.

The French in particular tried to calm the Poles and carefully influence Helmut Kohl. Later, the Federal Republic agreed to an identical declaration of the German *Bundestag* and the *Volkskammer* in which the existence of the German-Polish border was guaranteed. Soon after that, a solution acceptable to all sides could be found at the July 1990 2+4 Foreign Ministers' Meeting in Paris.

An important prerequisite for this was our proposal to differentiate between a treaty regulating the German-Polish border and a second treaty intended to cover other areas of bilateral cooperation. Originally, neither Poland nor the government of the Federal Republic wanted to accept our proposal, however each for different reasons. Poland wanted to clarify all future questions related to German unity that affected it, not just the border question. The government of the Federal Republic, in contrast, was aware that such an extensive treaty would require a lot of time. This was fine, since it was playing for time due to the December *Bundestag* elections. Thus, in Paris in July 1990 it was agreed that the border treaty should be signed immediately after unification, and that a bilateral treaty covering other aspects of the bilateral relationship would follow later.

In November 1990, however—following unification on October 3—Helmut Kohl walked back from this sequencing, declaring that Germany would only ratify a border treaty with Poland together with the bilateral treaty. This announcement, three weeks before the federal elections, was a signal to the expellee organizations that they could include their claims against Poland in the negotiations on the bilateral treaty. This was pure electoral politics, bought by abdicating solidarity with Poland. This appalled me at the time.

The German–Polish Border Treaty was signed on November 14, 1990 in Warsaw, ratified by the Polish *Sejm* on November 26, 1991 and the German *Bundestag* on December 16, 1991,[5] and entered into force on January 16, 1992. The bilateral Treaty of Good Neighborship and Friendly Cooperation was signed between Poland and Germany on June 17, 1991.

The intent of the Western powers to limit the 2+4 process to a few points of negotiation so as to facilitate quick agreement helped to make prompt German unification possible. It was a great gain for Germany and its European neighbors. Moreover, the "Treaty on the Final Settlement with Respect to Germany" of September 12, 1990 did not just clear the path for German unity, it also influenced the wording of the Charter of Paris for a New Europe, signed by the member states of the CSCE in November 1990. Anyone who reads these texts today can still sense something of the vision of a new Europe founded on common values that motivated us and many people all across Europe at that time.

Because unification proceeded under Article 23 of the Federal Republic's Basic Law, the GDR also automatically and without negotiations became a member of the European Community (EC). From our point of view, the prospect of EC membership was also necessary for the states of East Central Europe. In those days, and in fact for many years following, Western discourse about "Europe" tended to be reduced to considerations affecting only the members of the European Community (later the European Union). We, by contrast, wanted to develop a pan-European perspective and make clear that a stable Europe of the future could only be created with the integration of these

East Central European states and with a binding cooperation with the Soviet Union. Thus, the coalition treaty of the Grand Coalition in the GDR of April 12, 1990 stated that "The GDR wants to develop and deepen its special connection to the people of Eastern Europe, economically, politically, and culturally. It espouses a quick, stepwise expansion of the European Community." For me, these sentences were a mandate and a legacy that inspired me to advocate for the membership of Poland and the other new democracies into the EU and NATO. I joined the NATO Parliamentary Assembly in 1991 and led the German delegation there from 1998-2006.

At the beginning of the 2000s, there was an intensive debate about NATO membership for the three Baltic states. It was not just the German government that hesitated since it feared Russian resistance. In 2001, I organized a statement by European parliamentarians that advocated for including the Baltic states since it was precisely these newly-independent states that urgently needed this solidarity and assurance. We sent this statement to the U.S. Senate, which at that time had not stated a clear position. In my view, we Germans bore special responsibility with respect to this question, given German history, particularly the Hitler-Stalin pact.

Overall, the democratic GDR had little maneuvering room in foreign policy. The reasons for this were many and varied. Certainly, we made some mistakes due to our own shortcomings and inexperience. The lack of unity within our own government did not help. For me, the brief spell as Foreign Minister was my "apprenticeship" as a politician. The most important reason however, was that the East German people voted to accede to the Federal Republic of Germany. The East German people wanted unification quickly. They were not interested in the negotiations that were being conducted on their behalf. They did not see their importance and viewed them as delaying unification. Only later, after unification, did the "mistakes of unification" become a topic of debate.

In February 1990, with a view to the increasingly clear inability of Hans Modrow's communist GDR government to govern, Condoleezza Rice and Philip Zelikow characterized the GDR in February 1990 as "simply a mutating corpse."[6] Yet that was no justification for starting the first official round of 2+4 talks before free elections could be held and a democratically legitimized GDR government could be formed. In essence this was an act of disrespect with regard to the new government even before it could develop a position. Efforts by the Western partners to decide things before there was even a legitimate GDR negotiating partner were highly questionable. We were not being treated any better than we had been under the communist government. The Western partners never considered that the new GDR government would become an equal partner in the negotiations on German unity.

In retrospect, I believe that the 2+4 Treaty was the best path to resolve the German question and achieve German unity. It also created the central basic principles for future European development. In contrast, both the German-German unity treaty and the withdrawal agreement with the USSR for its troops were full of errors and led to many difficult problems.

Even if I believe in hindsight that it was correct not to incorporate into the 2+4 negotiations topics that I wanted to put on the agenda—such as the question of nuclear weapons and their proliferation as well as German responsibility for pan-European security—it is problematic that these topics were sorely neglected in subsequent years, particularly in light of German history. It is no wonder, for instance, that questions about reparations in Greece and Poland have become a current topic. In 2015, German President Joachim Gauck reminded people about the more than three million Soviet prisoners of war who had previously been overlooked completely in German "memory culture." Only recently did Germany's Grand Coalition decide to create a place that tells the story of Germany's war of destruction in the East and that is dedicated to the memory of its victims. Debate continues on this issue as well.

The Path to German Unity as the Process of East German Self-Determination

Even 30 years later we Germans are still far from having a common view of the process of German unity, or even an understanding of the various perspectives that shaped it. Official anniversary events make this clear time and again. For most (West) Germans, Helmut Kohl's image shapes German unity, as if it were his work alone. With all due respect to his important role, this is simply not the case.

For most Germans, the 15 months from summer 1989 to October 3, 1990 have become one event. But I believe that for an appropriate understanding of this time, it is important to distinguish between three important periods.

The first was the culmination of the crisis in summer 1989, amplified by the East German exodus and the opening of the Hungarian-Austrian border; the fall of the dictatorship in the fall 1989 revolution; and the fall of the Berlin Wall. In this phase, the political action and leadership of the new opposition groups and organizations and the powerful pressure on the streets and in the squares produced a symbiotic dynamic that swept the regime from power.

The second phase took place between November 1989 and March 1990. It was the time when the prospect of free elections became real, when opposition groups met with the government of Hans Modrow to address popular concerns and pave the way for elections, and the building pressure that pointed the way to German unity.

The third phase took place between March and October 1990, beginning with the free elections in the GDR on March 18, the decision of the elected *Volkskammer* that the GDR would accede to the Federal Republic of Germany according to Article 23 of the Federal Republic's Basic Law, and the internal and external negotiations on German unification, leading to the currency union on July 1 and the subsequent unification treaty and the 2+4 treaty.

These three phases had one common thread: the path to German unity was driven first and foremost by the actions of East Germans. The dictatorship in the GDR was brought down from the inside, not the outside. The East German people fought for free elections, which became a vote for unity. Accession to the Federal Republic was decided by the freely elected *Volkskammer*. In short, East Germany's path to freedom led directly to German unity. Seen from this perspective, German unification was the self-determined path of the East Germans, who pursued this with their heads held high.

Therefore, I believe that it is not accurate to speak of a victory of the West over the East. It is even dangerous to do this. Anyone who speaks like this is probably referring to the victory of freedom and democracy over the communist dictatorship that ruled Eastern Europe. Referring to this as the victory over the East is mistaken, for people who live there do not feel they were defeated. Throughout East Central Europe, including the GDR, the dictatorships were swept away by the peoples of the East, not the powers of the West. The end of the barriers separating the German people and Europeans East and West was a victory of the people who advocated for freedom and democracy in Central and Eastern Europe.

Of course, the West created basic conditions that were an important prerequisite for this transformation: among others, the successful and magnetic model of the European Community; freedom and democracy; prosperity and peaceful accommodation of various national interests; and the clear position of NATO, which relied simultaneously on deterrence and dialogue. The West was not inactive. On its own, however, it could not bring down the Soviet system without endangering peace. That was the problem. When suppression occurred in 1953 in East Germany, people looked on helplessly—as they did in Hungary in 1956, in East Germany again in 1961, in Czechoslovakia in 1968, and in Poland in 1981. The ultimate breakthrough, the freeing from dictatorship, had to come from within these countries themselves. And just that happened in 1989.

Through these years the Federal Republic could only react and try to influence these dynamics by facilitating people-to-people contacts and influencing East German actors. For the key lay in the GDR. When the revolution finally occurred in the East, it was then incumbent upon the West to bring the ship of German unity into harbor without great shocks, for this is precisely what the East Germans were not in a position to do. This included securing Four Power agreement to unity through the 2+4 talks, ensuring that all parts of a united Germany were included in the EC and in NATO, and reaching broader agreements with the Soviet Union and other European neighbors. This is where I acknowledge the special contribution of Helmut Kohl.

The many-layered nature of the decision-making process has not yet been appropriately researched nor is it present in the public consciousness. However, a differentiated view of this history is important because it is associated with our self-image today.

Legacies

We originally entered the negotiations on German unity intent on forging a unified Germany that would not simply be an expanded Federal Republic in the sense of a "West Germany writ large," but a new joint state in which East Germans would not have to adopt everything that had grown up in West Germany. Some reformers in the West shared this hope. They showered us with reform proposals that we were supposed to incorporate into the negotiations even though they had failed time and again in the West. We were not even in a position to read everything that came across the table! In the end, however, we were unsuccessful. German unity was an acquisition, not a merger. This has led to great disappointments.

The German-German treaty on the internal aspects of unification became a tour de force of the administration of the Federal Republic. It was the generously designed attempt to adapt the completely different social relationships in the GDR to the German Federal legal system so that it would cause as little pain as possible in the East, but also not make changes unless absolutely necessary. As Wolfgang Schäuble, the lead Western negotiator of the internal aspects of unification admitted, "the concern now is unity and not with this opportunity to change anything for the Federal Republic."[7]

One important consequence of this approach is the lingering sense among large parts of the population in eastern Germany that their concerns and contributions were—and are—not really taken seriously. Implementation of unification has also been problematic. Despite massive economic transfers, in many respects the eastern *Länder* represent Germany's *Mezzogiorno*—a region where dim economic prospects are exacerbated by outward migration. 30 years later, east Germans largely feel that their contributions are inadequately recognized. They have yet to arrive in unified Germany.

For some years, the reconstituted communist party, the PDS, reaped the political benefits from this disillusionment. Today, the protest vote is going to the right-wing *Alternative für Deutschland* (AfD). Germany's various grand coalitions have failed to devote the necessary attention to the problems of eastern Germany. Even though Chancellor Angela

Merkel and former President Joachim Gauck are each east German, they did not act on their special identity.

Nobody today denies that mistakes were made. To what extent alternatives at the time could have offered a better approach to the problems, however, is something that is still assessed very differently today.

One important example, which I still believe today was a big mistake, were decisions made regarding the constitution. Even in the constitution commission of the round table and in the *Volkskammer* there was considerable controversy around the nature of unified Germany's constitution. However, the common goal was that unified Germany should provide itself with a new constitution based on the Basic Law. The West-SPD supported this explicitly. In March 1990, in a *Der Spiegel* conversation with Wolfgang Schäuble, I mentioned that for us the concern was not to change so very much about the Basic Law, but rather that all Germans should create a constitution. I still believe today that even if this were a largely symbolic move, it would have strengthened the identification of East Germans with unified Germany as their state and common weal. But that too was rejected. What remained was the constitution commission of 1991-1994, a joint project between the *Bundestag* and *Bundesrat*, the two houses of the German Parliament, which produced meager results.

Thirty years after the Peaceful Revolution and German unity, Germans east and west each face the task of recontextualizing their individual histories and experiences. Most people socialized in the West regarded the East as a "special zone," and in their eyes, German history took place in the West. This overlooks the fact that much of German history in the 20th century was that of a divided postwar country of two different states. It cannot be understood if one fails to examine both halves and their intense relationship.

Thirty years on, the Germans are the people in Europe who know themselves the least. A national conversation is urgently required.

Notes

1. See the transcription of Gorbachev's address at https://digitalarchive.wilsoncenter.org/document/116224.pdf?v=373893a00d59186510e13c0cc7b57141.

2. *North-South: A Programme for Survival*, Independent Commission on International Development Issues, chaired by Willy Brandt, 1980.

3. *Common Security: A Programme for Disarmament*, Commission on Disarmament and Security Issues, chaired by Olof Palme, 1982.

4. *Our Common Future*, World Commission on Environment and Development, chaired by Gro Harlem Brundtland, 1987.

5. In the ratification process in the Bundestag, 13 deputies of the CDU/CSU faction, among them the leader of the expellees, Erika Steinbach, dissented from approval of the border treaty.

6. Philip Zelikow and Condoleezza Rice, *Sternstunde der Diplomatie* (Munich: Propyläen Verlag, 1997), p. 214.

7. Wolfgang Schäuble, *Der Vertrag: Wie ich über die deutsche Einheit verhandelte* (Munich: Deutsche Verlags-Anstalt, 1991), p. 156.

Chapter 10

The International Community's Role in the Process of German Unification

Horst Teltschik

The first half of the 20th century was dominated by two world wars with more than 100 million deaths—soldiers and civilians. As a result, from 1945 on Europe was divided. Germany and its capital Berlin lost their sovereignty. Germany was run by the four victorious powers: the United States, France, Great Britain and the Soviet Union. The political and military dividing line between the three Western powers and the Soviet Union ran through the middle of Germany and Berlin.

The world was divided into a bipolar order between the nuclear superpowers, the United States and the Soviet Union, with their respective alliance systems NATO and Warsaw Pact. The latter was ruled by the Communist Party of the Soviet Union (CPSU) with its ideological monopoly.

In 1945, two militarily devastating world wars were followed by five decades of Cold War. The nuclear arsenals led to a military balance between West and East. The policy of mutual nuclear deterrence did not prevent dangerous political crises—such as the Soviet Berlin Blockade from June 1948 until May 1949, Nikita Khrushchev's 1958 Berlin Ultimatum and the 1962 Cuba Crisis—which brought both sides to the brink of another world war.

In Berlin, fully armed American and Soviet tanks directly faced each other at Checkpoint Charlie. In Cuba, Soviet missiles threatened to attack the United States.

Cold War tensions were compounded by Moscow's bloody military interventions to crush uprisings against its rule in 1953 in the German Democratic Republic (GDR), in 1956 in Hungary, and 1968 in Prague. In 1983 Soviet General Secretary Yuri Andropov threatened World War III if NATO deployed U.S. medium range missiles in Europe.

At the peak of the Cold War—the Cuba Crisis in October 1962—the United States decided to change its strategic approach towards the Soviet Union, which also affected NATO policy. On June 10, 1963, in a speech at American University, President John F. Kennedy announced his "Strategy of Peace." Against the suggestions of most of his advisors, Kennedy entered into personal direct disarmament negotiations with Nikita Khrushchev. On November 28, 1962 they agreed to remove medium-range missiles aimed at each other. The Soviets removed their missiles from Cuba and the United States removed their missiles from Turkey and Italy. Kennedy's lone decision was driven by his realization that "all we have built…would be destroyed in the first 24 hours…Both the United States and its allies, and the Soviet Union and its allies, have a mutually deep interest in a just and genuine peace and in halting the arms race." The Soviet press published his entire speech without any changes.

Kennedy's "Strategy of Peace" profoundly influenced NATO and inspired Willy Brandt's policy of détente. In December 1967, the 15 NATO members agreed on the Harmel Report that stated "NATO and a policy of détente are not alternatives which exclude each other." Security and détente were two sides of the same coin.

In the spring of 1969, half a year after the Soviets had crushed the Prague uprising, Foreign Minister Willy Brandt took up an old initiative by Nikita Khrushchev and initiated a European security conference. He did not want to leave the idea to the Soviets. This turned into the Conference for Security and Cooperation in Europe (CSCE). In parallel, the Brandt/Scheel-government negotiated bilateral treaties in 1970 with Moscow, Warsaw, and Prague as well as several treaties with the GDR.

In 1971-72 they added a Four-Power-Agreement about Berlin. The policy of détente reached its zenith with the signing of the CSCE Final Act on September 1, 1975 in Helsinki.

Nevertheless, the Atlantic Alliance had to learn an important lesson. In spite of the policy of détente and the signing of the CSCE Final Act, Soviet General Secretary Leonid Brezhnev started stationing new medium-range nuclear missiles (SS-20). Because of their range, they were not aimed at Soviet Union's main opponent, the United States but rather at Europeans—such as Willy Brandt—who had most strongly pushed for a policy of détente.

In December 1979, NATO responded with its double-track decision, initiated by Brandt's successor, Chancellor Helmut Schmidt: either the Soviet Union would remove its medium-range missiles or NATO would station U.S. medium-range missiles in Western Europe. U.S.-Soviet arms control talks in Geneva failed.

In 1983 and against massive public protests, the Kohl-Genscher government began stationing American missiles. In January 1983, French President François Mitterrand, a Socialist, gave a speech in the German Bundestag and supported NATO's decision. Soviet General Secretary Yuri Andropov threatened World War III.

The Cold War had returned and reached a new peak. President Ronald Reagan publicly called the Soviet Union an "evil empire." In 1983, he announced his Strategic Defense Initiative (SDI) and thereby appeared to further fuel the conflict. Mikhail Gorbachev, who later became President of the Soviet Union, admitted that both decisions—the stationing of medium-range missiles in Europe and SDI—forced the Politburo of the Communist Party of the Soviet Union (CPSU) to change its ways. The CPSU leadership knew they could not afford a new arms race. They also did not have the necessary technologies to create their own missile defense program.

On October 1, 1982, Helmut Kohl was elected Chancellor of Germany. His foreign policy strategy rested on two main pillars: a strong Atlantic Alliance and close partnership with the United States; and a European Community (EC), which would further integrate, and close friendship with France.

The more stable this foundation, the more leeway the Federal Government would have to conduct a proactive policy of détente towards the Soviet Union and the Warsaw Pact.

Even though East-West tensions were running high, Chancellor Kohl, who had only been in office for a few weeks, announced in a letter to Soviet General Secretary Andropov his interest in improving relations with Moscow. In July 1983, Kohl met Andropov in Moscow. The General Secretary was already severely and visibly ill. The same was true for his successor Konstantin Chernenko, whom Kohl had a chance to meet and talk to extensively at Andropov's funeral. From 1983 until1984, negotiations between the two superpowers had almost come to standstill.

This lack of communications was the reason Chancellor Helmut Kohl travelled to Washington in November 1984 right after President Ronald Reagan had been reelected. He was successful in convincing the President to use all means to restart summit diplomacy as well as disarmament and arms control negotiations with the Soviet leadership. Helmut Kohl was quite satisfied that the President was willing to put this in a joint communiqué. The German Chancellor demonstrated that he was willing to use his influence with Moscow as well as Washington.

In parallel, the Kohl-Genscher government had a core interest in giving political and economic support to reform movements within Warsaw Pact countries. Since 1983, Germany had been giving significant political, economic and financial support to Hungary. In 1989, Hungary started first steps to open its borders. Tens of thousands of GDR refugees had the opportunity to leave Hungary through Austria to West Germany. When Helmut Kohl gave a speech at the Hungarian parliament in December 1989, he expressed his gratitude to the Hungarians for "knocking the first stone out of the Wall" by finally opening their borders on September 10, 1989.

At the same time, the still formally Communist government and its Prime Minister Miklós Németh put Hungary on the path to democratization. In October 1989, Hungary declared itself a Republic and aimed to become a constitutional democracy with a multi-party system. The communist government announced free elections, knowing quite well that they would lose—a historically unique decision.

The German government also secretly supported the banned Polish trade union movement Solidarność. In 1989, I started negotiating with Poland's last communist government about a "Comprehensive Treaty" as a basis for future relations between the two countries. As Chancellor Kohl's personal envoy, I successfully finished these negotiations on August 24, 1989 with Poland's first democratically elected government under Prime Minister Tadeusz Mazowiecki.

For the German government, these talks and negotiations with Hungary and Poland were of decisive importance. We were supporting and experiencing first hand successful transformations of communist systems into democratic governments and societies. We also learned an important lesson: Soviet Secretary General Gorbachev kept his word. Already in 1985 he had promised at a Warsaw Pact summit that the Soviet Union would not interfere any more into the internal affairs of other members. He added that each country would be responsible for its own progress. At this point, there were still Soviet troops stationed in Poland and Hungary that could have stopped any democratic transformation. But for now, they stayed in their barracks. This put an end to the Brezhnev Doctrine, which Moscow bloodily enforced in Prague in 1968 to maintain the communist system.

After the fall of the Berlin Wall in November 1989, Helmut Kohl drew confidence from this experience with Hungary and Poland that Soviet troops in the GDR would also remain in their barracks. At all times, they would have been able to shut down the border between East and West Germany.

The German government was also talking to Bulgaria's President Todor Zhivkov and the Prime Minister of Czechoslovakia, Ladislav Adamec. We were mostly talking about financial aid, but those talks ended without results. Neither was willing to initiate reforms.

In 1983, Chancellor Helmut Kohl had invited Erich Honecker General Secretary of the East German communist party, to Bonn for an official visit. Moscow vetoed the meeting because of the NATO double-track decision.

Most importantly, we wanted to intensify discussions with the GDR leadership on various levels with one clear aim: to reconnect as many Germans from both sides of the Wall as possible; to prevent a further drifting apart; and to achieve improvements for the people in the GDR. Primarily, we wanted the GDR government to lower the age for GDR citizens to travel to West Germany. So far, this was only possible for retirees. The West German government increased its payments to the GDR to allow political prisoners to emigrate to the West. A 2 billion Deutschmark loan to the GDR was quite controversial. Critics called it survival aid for the GDR regime. With this loan, we achieved the removal of trip-wired directional antipersonnel mines from the GDR border fence.

Thankfully, in March 1985 Mikhail Gorbachev was appointed General Secretary of the CPSU. In contrast to his predecessors, he was young, healthy and energetic. In the same year, summit talks between President Reagan and Gorbachev and disarmament negotiations between the superpowers resumed and achieved quick results. In 1987, the INF treaty was signed, which eliminated all ground-based nuclear weapons with a range of 500 to 5,000 km.

In June 1989, Gorbachev visited West Germany for several days. Kohl and Gorbachev signed a joint statement, in which the Soviet leadership for the first time recognized the right of self-determination of all peoples. During long and intense talks, Chancellor Kohl offered as much support as possible for Gorbachev's reform agenda of glasnost and perestroika. Gorbachev soon took him up on that offer.

At the same time, a wave of refugees was leaving the GDR through Poland, Czechoslovakia and Hungary. At the beginning of September, Budapest finally opened its borders.

Simultaneously, mass demonstrations began in almost all GDR cities. On November 9, 1989, the Wall fell and everybody was surprised. Nobody was prepared for that.

On that fateful day, Chancellor Helmut Kohl was in Warsaw. After his return, he called the heads of state or government of the Four Powers. All four responded more or less in the same way: 'We should remain calm and reasonable and prevent chaos.' Nobody had a plan or some kind of strategy. Everybody was surprised by the fall of the Wall.

Chancellor Kohl used the opportunity to announce his objective in an unambiguous keynote address in the Bundestag: to reunite Germany as a federation. At the same time, he outlined his strategy in ten points. Unification was to happen in agreement with the Four Powers and embedded in the European unification process. The Chancellor avoided mentioning a time line.

Chancellor Helmut Kohl did not inform the Four Powers or his own government before the speech. We did not expect the Soviet leadership to support the plan at this point. Nevertheless, several CPSU members publicly talked about possible developments in the GDR and did not rule out reunification. Gorbachev's first reaction followed quickly. He called the Ten Point Plan a "diktat" that he could not accept.

The three Western powers probably would have pushed the Chancellor to discuss strategy before he could go public. This could have led the German government to miss an important, historic chance. In hindsight, all participants should admit that Chancellor Kohl took advantage of the chance for reunification just at the right moment.

One question remains: how did Germany get agreement from all Four Powers? From the very beginning, President George H.W. Bush supported Chancellor Kohl without reservation. In May 1989 in his speech at Mainz, Bush offered Germany "partnership in leadership." During his tenure, he put this into practice.

At the same time, Bush gave a promise to the Soviet leadership: "let the Soviets know that our goal is not to undermine their legitimate security interests." President Bush understood that security was a core Russian interest and responded accordingly. He treated Gorbachev as a partner and equal and never gloated about winning the Cold War. Bush and Kohl agreed early on that this would be important.

From the very beginning, Bush and Kohl also agreed that a united Germany should be a member of NATO and that European borders should remain unchanged. Nobody ever questioned the finality of the Oder-Neisse border with Poland.

George Bush's involvement was particularly useful in getting British Prime Minister Margaret Thatcher's agreement to unification and Britain's participation in the 2 + 4 negotiations between the two German states and the Four Power governments. Margaret Thatcher had great fear that unification could destroy Europe's stable postwar system without knowing what a new European order should look like. She was focused on a united, bigger and stronger Germany as a potential danger for Europe. Therefore, she also insisted on an united Germany that had to be a NATO member.

Chancellor Helmut Kohl was most disappointed about French President Mitterand's initially hesitant support. At a joint press conference in Bonn a few days after the fall of the Wall, Mitterand had spoken quite positively about the German right of self-determination. The

French President was quite worried that a united Germany—larger and economically stronger than France—would not be quite as interested in close bilateral cooperation with France and as the engine of European integration as before.

Helmut Kohl immediately responded. In December 1989, he wrote a letter to Mitterrand and proposed a new joint initiative to deepen European integration by pursuing the goal of a Political Union. Mitterand agreed at once. In April 1990, the European Community (EC) supported this German-French initiative at the Dublin Summit.

In parallel, common preparations for a European Economic and Monetary Union were going on, which had been agreed on in June 1989 at the EC-Summit in Hanover/Germany—long before anyone had even thought of German unification.

One key question remained: what should or must the Federal Government do to get consent from the Soviet leadership? It was quite clear that no single measure would be enough to get over Gorbachev's No. There was only one path to Yes. We had to offer as large a package deal as possible with proposals to support Gorbachev's reform agenda and to improve future cooperation between the two countries as well as between East and West.

In the winter 1989-90, the Soviet Union was experiencing a severe supply crisis. In January 1990, Mikhail Gorbachev reminded Helmut Kohl of his promises to support his reforms and asked for shipments of food and other supplies. The Chancellor and his government immediately came to his help. In 1990, 22 treaties and agreements were signed with the USSR.

Additionally, the German Chancellor used every opportunity at talks with every EC and NATO member as well as summit meetings—including the World Economic Summit—to promote economic and financial support for Gorbachev's reform agenda. In May 1990, the urgency of this aid became apparent. The Soviet government confidentially asked Chancellor Helmut Kohl for a $5 billion loan to safeguard the USSR's ability to meet financial obligations. Otherwise, the superpower Soviet Union would have been bankrupt in the summer of 1990.

Chancellor Helmut Kohl achieved the final breakthrough in the negotiations with Moscow after an April 1990 proposal. He offered to negotiate a treaty under international law between a united Germany and the USSR. It was to be negotiated before unification and would be signed and ratified afterwards. The key offer was unequivocal German security guarantees vis-à-vis the Soviet Union. Mikhail Gorbachev and his Foreign Minister Eduard Shevardnadze responded almost euphorically. In November 1990 after unification, Chancellor Helmut Kohl and President Mikhail Gorbachev signed this "Major Treaty."

German security guarantees were flanked and supported by a NATO Special Summit in July 1990 in London. In the London Declaration, all NATO member states reinforced a message given days earlier stating that NATO no longer saw the Warsaw Pact countries as enemies and extended a "hand of friendship" to Eastern European nations. Since Mikhail Gorbachev was facing a CPSU Party Congress in July 1990, this was very helpful to him—as he later confirmed.

Common security has always been the key issue in finding agreement and cooperating with the Soviet Union and now with Russia. In 1989/90 the German government, the U.S. government and their European partners cooperated very closely at the highest levels, at the 2 + 4 negotiations and within multinational organizations such as NATO, EC and the World Economic Summit.

Nevertheless, in 1990, a number of uncertainties and risks could have derailed the process of German unification. In early January 1990, Mikhail Gorbachev surprised everyone with a press statement cancelling all meetings with his Western counterparts. Chancellor Helmut Kohl was also affected. He was waiting for his first personal conversation with Gorbachev after the opening of the Wall. According to Soviet Foreign Secretary Eduard Shevardnadze, there were intense struggles within the Soviet leadership about whether to use Soviet troops in the GDR. Gorbachev and Kohl personally met for the first time on February 10, 1990. Almost immediately, Gorbachev agreed that it was 'a matter for the two German states to decide if, when and how they were to unite.'

All the same, Mikhail Gorbachev was facing tough arguments within the CPSU. In July 1990, he was the first Secretary General to face more than 1,000 dissenting votes in the Central Committee—a historic precedent. At this point, he could have been overthrown, but he managed to remove his main opponent, Yegor Ligachev, from the Politburo. When

Gorbachev met Kohl a few days later in the Caucasus, he was visibly relieved to have successfully weathered the Party Congress.

In addition, other flash points could have interfered with or even slowed down the process of German unification. On August 2, 1990, the Iraqi army annexed Kuwait. From this point on, the U.S. administration was focusing almost entirely on this new crisis.

Fortunately, the most important decisions concerning German unification had already been taken. When Secretary of State Jim Baker visited Chancellor Helmut Kohl on September 15, 1990 in his private home in Ludwigshafen, they almost entirely talked about Germany's contributions to the war against Saddam Hussein and the development of the region. Jim Baker was very satisfied with Germany's overall contribution of about 3.3 billion Deutschmark. This was more than his government had asked.

The second crisis in the summer of 1990 was brewing in the Balkans. The multiethnic state of Yugoslavia was beginning to break up. From 1991 until 1999, this led to a series of military conflicts. In the final phase of German unification that summer 1990 and considering the run-up to the first Iraq war, nobody saw any urgency in dealing with the rising tensions between the different ethnicities in Yugoslavia. It became clear that administrations have a hard time managing several conflicts at once. In 1991, the first shots were fired in Slovenia and Croatia.

Fortunately, we finished the process of German unification successfully and peacefully on October 3, 1990.

Today, almost 30 years later, the member states of NATO and the European Union (EU) should recall what was changed peacefully and mutually agreed between 1989 and 1991:

In 1989-90, the Soviet Union did not intervene militarily anymore when Warsaw Pact countries such as Poland, Hungary, the GDR, and Czechoslovakia opened the Iron Curtain and started the process of democratization.

Germany was united in agreement with all Four Powers in just 329 days. The Soviet leadership gave up Stalin's most important price from World War II—the GDR and East Berlin—without firing a shot.

The Soviet Union accepted that a united Germany would remain a member of NATO and the EU.

The USSR peacefully withdrew 500,000 troops and their weapon systems from Central Europe—Hungary, Czechoslovakia, Poland, including 370,000 from the GDR alone.

From 1988 until 1992 the most far-reaching disarmament and arms control agreements were signed, limiting or eliminating conventional, nuclear and chemical weapons. Eighty percent of all nuclear weapons were eliminated.

In July 1991 the Soviet military alliance, the Warsaw Pact, peacefully and quietly dissolved.

In December 1991 the Soviet Union peacefully disbanded into 15 independent republics.

Every one of those events could have triggered an internal or external military conflict as briefly demonstrated by the coup attempt against President Gorbachev in August 1991 in Moscow. All of these sensational events happened peacefully and with mutual agreement. Did the West ever realize this?

Let me summarize the reasons for success:

There was mutual trust between all decision-makers. Agreements were kept. Mikhail Gorbachev once said everything could have been different if he had not trusted Helmut Kohl and George Bush.

The Federal Republic and its Western partners were willing to support Gorbachev's reforms economically and financially.

The West took into account Soviet security interests. Washington and Moscow signed far-reaching disarmament and arms control agreements (INF/START/Chemical and Biological Weapons Ban/NRRC Agreement). NATO offered friendship and cooperation to the Warsaw Pact countries. Germany and the USSR signed the Major Treaty with security guarantees.

The culmination of events was the signing of the "Charter of Paris for a New Europe" in November 1990 by all 34 Presidents and Prime Ministers of the CSCE. Its goal was a pan-European framework for peace and security from Vancouver to Vladivostok—the "Common

European House," which Mikhail Gorbachev had envisioned with the same level of security for everyone. What a vision! What a dream!

On May 9, 1991, French President Mitterrand said in Aachen, "For a long time, Europe did not have as many reasons for hope."

Today, everyone in East and West should ask the question: what have we done with this vision?

Chapter 11

Money for Moscow: The West and the Question of Financial Assistance for Mikhail Gorbachev

Stephan Kieninger

Money was a major lever, so some have argued, to "buy" the Soviet Union's consent to Germany's unification and to its membership in NATO. Indeed, West Germany's bilateral financial assistance for the Soviet Union facilitated the negotiations over Germany's unification in 1990. Thereafter, international coordination of Western help for the Soviet Union and Russia failed for a number of reasons: the Soviet Union failed to produce a convincing plan for comprehensive economic and financial reform, to halt support for communist Cuba, or to stop suppression in the Baltic republics; the George H.W. Bush Administration, other Western partners and international financial institutions were not willing to lend substantial funds to Gorbachev under those circumstances; and the Germans could not maintain the level of funds for Moscow on account of the enormous cost of unification.

During the first half of 1990, after the fall of the Berlin Wall but before German unification, the government of the Federal Republic of Germany, led by Chancellor Helmut Kohl and Foreign Minister Hans-Dietrich Genscher, together with West German banks were the only sources of funds for Gorbachev. Helmut Kohl had a precise understanding for the relevance of financial assistance as well as for the importance of its timing. Speaking at a board meeting of his party, the Christian Democratic Union (CDU) on April 23, 1990, Kohl reiterated that "economic relations with the Soviet Union would be of pivotal significance for the process of unification." He pointed out that "for the Soviet Union, the question of future economic ties would eventually matter more than NATO membership for unified Germany." Kohl was convinced that "generous economic cooperation with the Soviet Union would facilitate the resolution of the existing security problems."[1]

Germany accounted for the lion's share of Western financial assistance to the East. From 1990 until 1993, Germany provided 80 billion

Deutschmarks (DM) in assistance to the republics of the former Soviet Union and 105 billion DM to the Central and Eastern European countries. This amounted to 60% of the financial support provided to these countries. In the words of German Defense Minister Volker Rühe, it was "an essential element of Euro-Atlantic security."[2]

This chapter looks into U.S. and German policies and financial aid during the negotiations over Germany's unification.[3] It explores the international process of coordinating financial assistance for Moscow as its economic system crumbled. It examines Western efforts to bolster Mikhail Gorbachev's position trying to tie the disintegrating Soviet Union to the West and to produce a soft landing after the breakup of the country in December 1991.

U.S. President George H.W. Bush's position in 1990 and 1991 was that fundamental reform in the Soviet Union had to come first. His assumption was that the absence of conditionality would result in wasted resources and do nothing to encourage the transition to a market economy. Bush wanted to see Soviet deeds in Cuba and in the Baltics as a precondition for U.S. financial aid. When Mikhail Gorbachev faced a financial meltdown and sought billions of dollars to stabilize the Soviet economy, Bush said he would consider a deal if the Soviets stopped subsidizing Havana's communist regime and if they withdrew their troops from Cuba.[4] Second, Bush wanted Gorbachev to respect the drive for self-determination and independence in the Baltic countries. Last but not least, financial aid would be tied to a halt in the nuclear arms race and to the conclusion of the START Treaty in 1991.

The Kohl administration in Germany was in a different position. Kohl did not worry about Bush's global concerns. Kohl wanted Germany's unification and a new Euro-Atlantic security structure, and he was willing to use unprecedented amounts of financial aid as a catalyst for his diplomacy. Bush made it clear that he expected the Germans to cover the bulk of the cost of whatever aid Gorbachev required to justify the loss of East Germany. Thus, the Kohl government unilaterally funneled massive amounts of assistance to Moscow to shore up the Soviet economy and cover the cost of removing Soviet forces from East Germany.[5]

During the first months of 1990, Helmut Kohl sensed that financial assistance for the Soviet Union was a pivotal way of winning over

Gorbachev.[6] The Soviet Union's economic condition was rapidly deteriorating, Gorbachev could not master his domestic problems without foreign aid and credit, and it was clear that the Federal Republic of Germany was the obvious candidate to provide the kind of financial aid that the Soviet Union needed. Time and again, President Bush indicated that Bonn would bankroll Gorbachev, not Washington. "You've got deep pockets," he told Kohl in February 1990. Kohl understood. "The Soviets are negotiating. But this may end up as a matter of cash. They need money," Kohl said.[7] Indeed, Kohl had long envisaged trade and credits as key components of his *Ostpolitik*.[8] Economics had been an essential part of his rapprochement with Gorbachev.[9]

Kohl was right in his gut feeling about Moscow's priorities. He was right to think that financial assistance would be a decisive element to win over Gorbachev. The price was high. Moscow was seeking 20 to 25 billion Deutschmarks in credit. On May 4, 1990, Soviet Foreign Minister Eduard Shevardnadze asked Kohl for major financial assistance in support of Gorbachev's *perestroika*.[10] By sending Shevardnadze to ask for money, Gorbachev established a link between financial assistance and the solution of the German question. Against the background of its liquidity crisis, the Soviet Union was no longer able to secure loans on its own on the international credit market.[11]

Kohl believed that it was important to lend to the Soviet Union to keep Gorbachev in power and to secure his permission for unification. In May 1990 he convinced two of Germany's financial leaders, Hilmar Kopper of Deutsche Bank and Wolfgang Roller of Dresdner Bank, of this rationale. On May 13, both flew to Moscow with Kohl's chief foreign policy adviser Horst Teltschik. Teltschik's main task on the trip was to convey German willingness for credits in return for Gorbachev's consent to unified Germany's membership in NATO.[12]

Gorbachev was in a tight spot. Presumably in an effort to save face, he told Teltschik that the Soviet Union would not be dependent on any other country. Rather, as he emphasized, the Soviet Union was seeking an investment in its future: "We need oxygen in order to survive two or three years," he explained.[13] A couple of days later, on May 17, 1990, Kohl traveled to Washington trying to convince Bush of the need to lend to Moscow in order to keep Gorbachev in power. Kohl asked, "Do we want to help him or see someone else? I think it is him."

Bush, however, did not endorse the idea that the West ought to loan money to the Soviet Union in the circumstances of May 1990: "On loans, I don't see that without reform," Bush emphasized.[14] Thus, in June 1990, the Kohl government took the decision to funnel unilaterally massive amounts of assistance to Moscow to shore up the Soviet economy. Deutsche Bank and Dresdner Bank gave the Soviet Union a DM 5 billion loan with a government guarantee. Horst Teltschik recalled that Gorbachev reacted "euphorically" on hearing the news.[15] The credit was the ideal stage setter for the Kohl-Gorbachev summit in July 1990.

During their Moscow talks on July 15, 1990, Helmut Kohl recalled the 5 billion DM that he had organized, and he then explained that he needed a plan for Soviet troop withdrawal and agreement that united Germany could enter NATO.[16] The following day, Gorbachev invited Kohl to his home region of Stavropol. Despite the underlying mood of optimism, there was still a debate under which conditions a united Germany could join NATO. Other open questions abounded. How long would Soviet troops be allowed to stay in eastern Germany? How much financial aid would the Soviet Union receive for their withdrawal? Eventually, Kohl and Gorbachev agreed to a three-to-four year withdrawal period.[17] However, there was still no clarity over the kind of financial aid the Soviet Union would receive for the withdrawal. As things turned out, Kohl and Gorbachev had to settle the amount in a number of contentious phone calls in September 1990. The price tag for Gorbachev's concessions: more than 20 billion DM.[18] It was the price for unification and sovereignty, and Kohl paid up.

In the summer of 1990, the next step for Kohl was to coordinate Western help within the G-7 and the European Community. However, he was not successful in either endeavor.

Looking back at the Dublin Summit of the European Community (EC) in June 1990, Margaret Thatcher writes in her memoirs that she "took most satisfaction [...] at this Council from stopping the Franco-German juggernaut in its tracks on the question of financial credits to the Soviet Union."[19] Thus, in August 1990, Helmut Kohl struck a deal with EC Commission President Jacques Delors. Both agreed that Germany had to carry the costs to for unification. There would be no additional costs the other EC countries. It was a move to prevent any possible opposition within the EC, and it was also a means to prevent the poorer EC members from complaints that they would lose out.[20]

In the summer of 1990, before the EC discussions, Kohl tried to get his colleagues at the G-7 summit in Houston to adopt a more generous multilateral approach on financial assistance for the Soviet Union. Prior to the summit, Gorbachev had sent Bush a letter asking for a large-scale assistance program. But at the Houston summit, Bush again emphasized that absence of conditionality would result in wasted resources and do nothing to encourage the transition to a market economy. He argued that "the Soviets have not been very specific in saying what they would do with this money. [...] Without reforms, there will be no growth. Substantial Western foreign assistance to him [Gorbachev] at this time, when market-based reforms are not in place, would not be effective, would not further productivity and growth, and would not increase the Soviet ability to service Western loans."[21] Kohl countered and made the case for a positive approach in an effort to facilitate reforms in the Soviet Union. He argued that "we also have an opportunity to arrive at restructuring of the USSR. If Gorbachev succeeds, then the USSR will be much better in the future. This is a fact. We need to use the opportunity to influence positive developments. [...] We cannot reply in a discouraging way to Gorbachev. I support President Bush's point that our aid should not be mindlessly thrown at the USSR. It must be addressed at a concrete program of reform. Experts, specialists must be provided. We should make our response positive."[22]

In the end, however, the Houston G-7 summit did not produce the results Kohl envisaged. The G-7 could not agree on a common approach for financial assistance. The Bush administration was not in a position to follow Kohl's approach. George Bush and his senior advisers had already discussed the question of guaranteeing loans for the Soviet Union. Bush and his foreign policy team anticipated that there would be no Congressional approval. Bush's National Security Adviser Brent Scowcroft pointed out that "the principal barriers are Lithuania and Cuba—holding up [a] cooperative relationship."[23] While asking for loans, the Soviet Union was still subsidizing Havana's communist regime. The global Cold War and regional US-Soviet conflicts were still alive.[24] Bush believed that the global power competition stood in the way of more substantial U.S. financial assistance. Another chal-

lenge was the fact that the Soviet leadership lacked knowledge and understanding of market economies. Michael Boskin, Chairman of the
Council of Economic Advisors, concluded that there were "very few
people among the top economic policy makers, and perhaps among all
the economists in the Soviet Union, who understand how an economy
really functions."[25]

Against the backdrop of the stalemate at the Houston G-7 summit,
U.S. Secretary of State James Baker suggested that the G-7 needed a
study on the Soviet economy in order to have a basis for decision in the
future. His recommendation was to have the International Monetary
Fund and the World Bank involved. Initially, the Europeans were skeptical as both institutions had the reputation to apply strict criteria for
loans. On the second day of the Houston summit, the G-7 agreed to
have the study prepared under the auspices of the IMF and to also involve the World Bank, the OECD and the newly established European
Bank for Reconstruction and Development (EBRD).[26]

On December 21, 1990 the IMF presented a 2000-page analysis of
the Soviet economy. It concluded that Gorbachev's *perestroika* had just
touched the surface of the Soviet Union's economic problems. The
IMF demanded deep structural reforms as a precondition for loans.
Moreover, the IMF study cautioned against rushed and direct financial
assistance, arguing that "the date on which far-reaching reform will be
introduced is not now known and the requirement for balance of payment assistance will have to be re-evaluated in the light of the prospects
at the time."[27]

Bush stuck to his cautious approach to financial aid. In September
1990, at his summit meeting with Gorbachev in Helsinki, he promised
more long-term aid, but not from his own coffers. "As you know, we
don't have the cash for large economic assistance," he told Gorbachev.[28]
Gorbachev's domestic critics balked at the way he stood firmly at the
side of the United States in the international coalition against Saddam
Hussein giving the United States a free hand in the Middle East. But
Gorbachev remained committed to the alliance with Bush. As Jeffrey
Engel wrote, the deal was "Moscow's compliance in the gulf, as with its
earlier concessions on Germany and NATO, in exchange for Washington's continued blessing and the promise of aid."[29]

Bush tried to normalize U.S.-Soviet trade relations step-by-step, ending trade restrictions and the economic aspects of the Cold War. He was as forthcoming as he could be, given pressures in Congress to tie the normalization of trade relations to increased Jewish emigration from the Soviet Union. In December 1990, Bush suspended the Jackson Vanik Amendment for six months—Congress had passed the amendment in 1974, denying permanent normal trade relations status to the Soviet Union and other countries that restricted emigration of religious minorities. However, Bush still withheld most-favored nation treatment from the Soviet Union. He proposed to grant the Soviet Union associate IMF and World Bank membership so that Moscow could access the financial advice that both institutions could provide.

In January 1991 there were renewed setbacks when Gorbachev sent additional Soviet troops to crack down on the movement for independence in Lithuania.[30] On January 13, 1991, the situation turned into tragedy. Soviet troops fired into demonstrators in Vilnius, killing fifteen. The same evening, January 13, James Baker discussed the issue with British Prime Minister John Major. Baker asked: "Was Gorbachev still fully in control? Or had the military taken the law into their own hands?" Baker's conclusion was: "It would be difficult to proceed on the present path with the Russians if the repression continued or got worse."[31] Following the massacre in Vilnius, the IMF suspended the Soviet Union's application for associate membership, and G-7 Finance Ministers declared that they would no longer discuss new funds for the Soviet Union.[32] The situation only improved after the new Soviet Foreign Minister Aleksandr Bessmertnykh travelled to Washington to assure Bush that "the policy of *perestroika* and new thinking [...] will continue."[33] Ultimately, the Soviet Union recognized Lithuania's independence on September 6, 1991.

The Lithuanian crisis seriously strained U.S.-Soviet relations. The Moscow summit, originally scheduled for February 1991, had to be postponed until late July. The Bush administration was still keenly interested in Gorbachev's political situation, hoping that he would survive long enough to sign the long-awaited START Treaty. In January 1991, Gorbachev demonstrated his willingness for reforms through the Pavlov Plan intended to withdraw money from circulation for reallocation to the production of consumer goods, which were in short supply. On January 1, 1991, under the orders of Soviet Minister of Finance

Valentin Pavlov, the Government freed 40% of prices from state control, and introduced a 5% sales tax.[34] Moreover, in addition to this domestic program, in the spring of 1991 Gorbachev addressed the West through the so-called Yavlinsky plan, a program with the goal to turn the USSR into a normal market economy with a Western structure in the shortest possible time, including macroeconomic stabilization, economic liberalization, private sector development, and a new constitutional structure linking the union and the republics. The idea was to implement the plan under the auspices of economist Grigory Yavlinsky, who spent several months at Harvard where he co-authored the reform program jointly with Graham Allison of Harvard in 1991. In addition, the plan envisaged a redefinition of the relationship between the Union and the republics that choose to participate in it. Last but not least, as IMF analysts pointed out, "envisaged but not stated in the draft program is a request for Western aid of around $150 billion over 5 to 6 years, of which the US would be asked to contribute directly only $3 billion a year."[35]

In these ways, Gorbachev sought to address Western concerns that its assistance could trickle away. By having conservative Yevgeny Primakov sign the program, Gorbachev sought to demonstrate that the program had support among Soviet conservatives as well. Taken together, Gorbachev's initiatives were aimed at a "grand bargain" with the West.[36]

Gorbachev sought to use the Yavlinsky program as a way to convey his willingness for serious economic reforms. The plan was a lever to voice his requests for massive Western aid at the 1991 G-7 summit in London. Gorbachev wanted the industrialized countries of the West to restore the Soviet economy. Bush was not convinced. In May 1991, he told Gorbachev that "in the spirit of frankness, our experts don't believe Pavlov's anti-crisis program will move you fast enough to market reform. If there are more steps toward market reform effort, then we could do more and help especially with the international financial organizations."[37] The question for the London G-7 summit in July 1991 was whether or not the West should prepare a more ambitious strategy promising support for Soviet adherence and implementation of a truly wide-ranging economic reform program.

The U.S. attitude was clear. On June 24, 1991, Bush called Kohl in order to discourage him from seeking a more forthcoming attitude at the G-7 summit. Bush made the point that "we are trying to avoid any talk of a so-called great bargain...We are unanimous that the so-called anti-crisis program is unworkable and that the only good thing would be something like Yavlinsky is proposing. Yavlinsky, however, wants a large aid check up front."[38]

Gorbachev's association with the London G-7 summit raised a multitude of questions: If he was to be invited, it was necessary to give very careful thought to the precise modalities: Would he be invited before or after the summit? How could a precedent be avoided? How could the link between Western help and the necessity for Soviet reform be emphasized?

Eventually, Prime Minister Major invited Gorbachev to come at the end of the summit and to take part in a joint meal. In early July 1991, Bush wrote Gorbachev a letter in order to underscore his interest in the success of Soviet reform. At the same time, he made it clear that he did not want the summit to commit itself to financial assistance: "It will be primarily Soviet sources, not imported sources, which will serve as the basis for a successful turnaround in the economy."[39]

The London G-7 meeting with Gorbachev was indeed a historic one and the first one of its kind. The President of the Soviet Union would address the elite club of capitalist nations asking for financial assistance. Gorbachev introduced his reform program and reaffirmed his commitment to repay debts. Moreover, he did not ask for debt rescheduling, as such a move would have like been perceived as an act of default, thus cutting off the Soviet Union from international credit. Gorbachev's commitment to market reform was remarkable. It would have been inconceivable two or three years earlier. At the same time, Gorbachev still lacked a concise script for reforms. Nigel Wicks, the British G-7 Sherpa, pointed out that "the status of the economic reform program... was not very clear. Gorbachev describes it as 'open-ended and flexible,' but it appears to be little if at all different from the Pavlov plan. It seems to have pushed the more radical element of the Yavlinsky program to one side. But has some thinly disguised proposals for financial assistance."[40]

All G-7 leaders except Helmut Kohl and François Mitterrand asked Gorbachev questions that implied that he should move faster toward a market economy. Helmut Kohl did not want to push Gorbachev at the G-7 summit. He remained silent and tried his best to reassure a nervous Gorbachev.[41] Mitterrand was alone among the speakers arguing that Gorbachev should not move too radically on privatization, but choose a "middle path" and "a happy synthesis between private enterprise and the role of the state."[42] Bush was still opposed to a multilateral G-7 commitment to Soviet aid. He argued that "as for a follow-on mechanism, each nation has its own bilateral problems to work out."[43]

In 1991, it became apparent that the Kohl government had reached the limits of its capacity for additional financial aid. It was questionable whether or not the German economy would prove robust enough to cope with the enormous costs of unification and the transformation of the East German economy. Germany's Council of Economic Advisers frequently warned against the risks involved.[44]

At the same time, Kohl was still willing to help Gorbachev stay in power, even though the future of the USSR was in the balance. The Soviet economy continued to crumble, and the internal battles raged over a new Union Treaty, the introduction of market reform and the independence of the Baltics.[45] The USSR failed to stabilize. In August 1991, a group of hardliners in the Soviet government tried to take control of the country and depose Gorbachev. They were opposed, mainly in Moscow, by a short but effective campaign of civil resistance led by Russian President Boris Yeltsin. Although the coup collapsed in only two days, it signaled Gorbachev's dramatic loss of power. The USSR was on the path toward dissolution. After the August 1991 coup, Brent Scowcroft argued that "the best we can do in this situation is to push hard for the new union and its constituent republics to engage with the IMF and the World Bank in drawing up economic programs which attempt to head off that inflationary spiral."[46] After the August coup, the centrifugal forces in the Soviet Union were at full force. In the autumn of 1991, it was predictable that Gorbachev would not going to be around much longer. On December 1, Ukraine held a referendum in which 70% of the population voted for independence. On December 8, the leaders of Russia, Ukraine and Belarus signed the Belovezha Agreement to dissolve the USSR and create a Commonwealth of Independent States. In December 1991, James Baker went to Moscow for a last visit with Gorbachev. The Soviet Union dissolved that month. Mikhail Gorbachev lost power. Russia's President Boris Yeltsin was the new leader in Moscow—in June 1991 he had defeated Gorbachev's preferred candidate, Nikolai Ryzhkov. The Soviet Union was gone. The future of Russia and the Newly Independent States was uncertain.

Starting in February 1992, Boris Yeltsin asked George Bush and other leaders for more Western support and financial assistance to motivate and facilitate reforms.[47] Western policymakers acknowledged that the collapse of the Soviet Union was a unique opportunity to help freedom take root in Russia and Eurasia. At the same time, there were also enormous risks involved. There was a new sort of world disorder. The single biggest Western fear was the potential of loose nuclear weapons in the Newly Independent States and loss of control over chemical weapons and biological agents.[48] The West worked for a soft landing providing additional financial assistance in 1992 and in the years to come. In retrospect, it easy to argue that more could have been done. But back at the time nobody could have imagined that the Soviet Union would disappear peacefully and with a whisper.

Notes

1. See Horst Teltschik, *329 Tage. Innenansichten der Einigung* (Berlin: Siedler Verlag, 1991), p. 204.

2. Volker Rühe, "Shaping Euro-Atlantic Policies. A Grand Strategy for a New Era," *Survival* 35:2 (1993), pp. 129–137, here p. 130.

3. For the context, see Mary E. Sarotte, *1989. The Struggle to Create Post-Cold War Europe* (Princeton: Princeton University Press, 2009); Hal Brands, *Making the Unipolar Moment. U.S Foreign Policy and the Rise of the Post-Cold War Order* (Cornell University Press, Ithaca/London, 2016); Kristina Spohr, *Post Wall, Post Square: Rebuilding the World after 1989* (London: HarperCollins, 2019).

4. See Memorandum of Conversation between George Bush and Mikhail Gorbachev, 2 June 1990, in Svetlana Savranskaya and Thomas Blanton, eds., *The Last Superpower Summits. Gorbachev, Reagan, and Bush. Conversations that Ended the Cold War* (Budapest: Central European University Press, 2016), pp. 683–694.

5. See, for instance, Stephan Bierling, *Wirtschaftshilfe für Moskau. Motive und Strategien der Bundesrepublik Deutschland und der USA von 1990 bis 1996* (Paderborn: Schönigh Verlag, 1998); Randall E. Newmann, *Deutsche Mark Diplomacy. Positive Economic Sanctions in German-Russian Relations* (University Park: Pennsylvania State University Press, 2002); Tuomas Forsberg, "Economic Incentives, Ideas, and the End of the Cold War. Gorbachev and German Unification," *Journal of Cold War Studies*, Vol 7, No. 2 (2005), pp. 142–164.

6. See Angela Stent, *Russia and Germany Reborn. Unification, the Soviet Collapse, and the New Europe* (Princeton, NJ: Princeton University Press, 1999); Andreas Roedder, *Deutschland Einig Vaterland* (Munich, Beck Verlag, 2009).

7. Memorandum of Conversation between George Bush and Helmut Kohl, 24 February 1990, https://bush41library.tamu.edu/files/memcons-telcons/1990-02-24--Kohl.pdf.

8. For a recent account on the relevance of Soviet trade for the Federal Republic's *Ostpolitik*, see Stephan Kieninger, *The Diplomacy of Détente. Cooperative Security Policies from Helmut Schmidt to George Shultz* (London: Routledge, 2018).

9. See, for instance, Memorandum of Conversation between Mikhail Gorbachev and Helmut Kohl (Excerpts), 24 October 1998, in Aleksandr Galkin and Anatolij Tschernjajew, eds., *Michail Gorbatschow und die deutsche Frage* (Munich: Oldenbourg Verlag, 2012), pp. 122–126. The German record is edited in the *Akten zur Auswärtigen Politik* volume on 1988, published in June 2019.

10. Memorandum of Conversation between Kohl and Shevardnadze, 4 May 1999, in Hanns-Juergen Kuesters and Daniel Hofmann eds., *Dokumente zur Deutschlandpolitik* (DzD), *Deutsche Einheit, Sonderedition aus den Akten des Bundeskanzleramtes 1989/90* (Munich: Oldenbourg Verlag, 1998), pp. 1084–1090; Teltschik, op. cit., pp. 218–221.

11. See Fritz Bartel, *The Triumph of Broken Promises. Oil, Finance, and the End of the Cold War*, PhD Dissertation, Cornell University 2017.

12. See Sarotte, op. cit., p. 159.

13. Memorandum of Conversation between Teltschik and Gorbachev, 14 May 1990, in: *DzD, Deutsche Einheit*, op. cit., p. 115. See Teltschik, op. cit., pp. 230–235.

14. Memorandum of Conversation between Bush and Kohl, 17 May 1990, https://bush41library.tamu.edu/files/memcons-telcons/1990-05-17--Kohl%20[1].pdf, accessed April 4, 2019.

15. Teltschik, op. cit., p. 249.

16. For a most recent account on NATO enlargement, see Daniel S. Hamilton and Kristina Spohr, eds., *Open Door: NATO and Euro-Atlantic Security in the 1990s* (Washington, DC: Johns Hopkins University SAIS/Brookings Institution Press, 2019).

17. See Memorandum of Conversation between Helmut Kohl and Mikhail Gorbachev, 16 July 1990, in *DzD, Deutsche Einheit*, op. cit., pp. 1355–1367.

18. See, for instance, Memorandum of Conversation between Helmut Kohl and Mikhail Gorbachev, 7 September 1990, in *DzD, Deutsche Einheit*, op. cit., pp. 1527–1531.

19. Margaret Thatcher, *The Downing Street Years* (London: Harper Collins, 1993), pp. 762–763. For the background, see Bierling, op. cit., pp. 82–86. On Thatcher's attitude, see Liviu Horovitz's contribution in this volume.

20. Memorandum of Conversation between Helmut Kohl and Jacques Delors, 20 August 1990, in *DzD, Deutsche Einheit*, op. cit, pp. 1479–1481.

21. Memorandum of Conversation, First Main Plenary Session of the 16th Economic Summit of Industrialized Nations, 10 July 1990, https://bush41library.tamu.edu/files/memcons-telcons/1990-07-10--Mitterrand%20[1].pdf, accessed April 5, 2019.

22. Ibid.

23. Memorandum for the Record "Aid to the Soviet Union", 29 May 1990, in: George H.W. Bush Presidential Library (GHWBPL), Brent Scowcroft Collection, USSR-Collapse Files, US-Soviet Chronological Files, Folder

91118-02. Helmut Kohl pursued a different policy towards Baltic independence. In April 1990, in a gesture toward Gorbachev, Kohl and Mitterrand called on Lithuania to suspend application of its declaration of independence from the Soviet Union to facilitate negotiations between the breakaway Baltic republic and the Moscow government. In May 1990, Kohl informed Bush about his talks with Lithuanian Prime Minister Kazimira Prunskienė. Kohl reported he told Prunskienė that "they had done almost everything wrong. I told her that we all sympathize with you, but if you push Gorbachev into a corner you hurt your cause—as in East Germany in 1953 and Hungary in 1956." Memcon Bush and Kohl, 17 May 1990, see https://bush41library.tamu.edu/files/memcons-telcons/1990-05-17--Kohl%20[1].pdf, accessed 10 June 2019.

24. See John-Michael Arnold's contribution in this volume.

25. Memorandum by Michael Boskin, Chairman of the Council of Economic Advisers "Report on my April 7-11 Trip to Moscow," 20 April 1990, in: GHWBPL, Council of Economic Advisers, Michael Boskin Files, NSC Meetings Files, Folder CF 01113-039.

26. Memorandum of Conversation, Second Main Plenary Session of the 16th Economic Summit of Industrialized Nations, 10 July 1990, see https://bush41library.tamu.edu/files/memcons-telcons/1990-07-10--Mitterrand%20[2].pdf, accessed April 5, 2019.

27. See International Monetary Fund/The World Bank/Organization for Economic Cooperation and Development/European Bank for Reconstruction and Development, *The Economy of the USSR. Summary and Recommendations* (Washington DC: The World Bank, December 1990) (Executive Summary), p. 48. For the context, see James M. Boughton, *Tearing Down Walls. The international Monetary Fund 1990-1999* (Washington, DC: The International Monetary Fund, 2012). See https://www.imf.org/external/pubs/ft/history/2012/, accessed March 21, 2018. Starting in August 1990, the IMF started to send out fact finding missions for talks in the Soviet Union. For in depth documentation, see IMF Archives, Alan Whittome Papers, Box 3.

28. Memorandum of Conversation between George Bush and Mikhail Gorbachev, Plenary Meeting, 9 September 1990, see https://bush41library.tamu.edu/files/memcons-telcons/1990-09-09--Gorbachev.pdf, accessed April 6, 1990.

29. See Jeffrey Engel, *When the World Seemed New. George H. W. Bush and the End of the Cold War* (New York: Houghton Mifflin Harcourt, 2017), pp. 424–425.

30. For the context, see George H.W. Bush and Brent Scowcroft, *A World Transformed* (New York: Alfred A. Knopf, 1998), pp. 496–497.

31. Memorandum of Conversation between John Major and James Baker, 13 January 1991, in: The National Archives (TNA), Kew, Prime Minister's Office Files (PREM 19), Vol. 3981.

32. See Bierling, op. cit., pp. 116–117.

33. Memorandum of Conversation between George Bush and Aleksandr Bessmertnykh, 28 January 1991, see https://bush41library.tamu.edu/files/memcons-telcons/1991-01-28--Bessmertnykh.pdf, accessed April 6, 2019.

34. In effect, Pavlov's reform was undermined by the Union Republics who failed to follow Pavlov's orders, along with the widespread existence of local monopolies, which tended to have their own definition of luxury goods and as a result imposed higher prices on such items. See Philip Hanson, *The Rise and Fall of the Soviet Economy. An Economic History of the USSR from 1945* (London: Longman & Pearson, 2003).

35. See Memorandum from Adrienne Cheasty to Massimo Russo, "The Yavlinsky Program for Soviet Reform: A Summary," 5 June 1991, in: IMF Archives, EURAI Country Files, Box 187, File 3.

36. The "Grand Bargain" envisaged a commitment of tens of billions of dollars of aid from Western countries in return for thorough and rapid moves toward a free market by Moscow. The idea was developed by Graham Allison, of Harvard, and Grigory Yavlinsky, a reform-minded Russian policy advisor. See Graham Allison and Grigory Yavlinsky, *Window of Opportunity. The Grand Bargain for Democracy in the Soviet Union* (New York: Pantheon Books, 1991).

37. Memorandum of Conversation between Bush and Gorbachev, 11 May 1991, https://bush41library.tamu.edu/files/memcons-telcons/1991-05-11--Gorbachev.pdf, accessed April 5, 2019.

38. Memorandum of Telephone Conversation between George Bush and Helmut Kohl, 24 June 1991, https://bush41library.tamu.edu/files/memcons-telcons/1991-06-24--Kohl.pdf, accessed April 5, 2019.

39. Letter from George Bush to Mikhail Gorbachev, circa early July 1991, in Savranskaya and Blanton, op. cit., pp. 845–846.

40. Memorandum from Nigel Wicks to John Major "Economic Summit: Handling of President Gorbachev", 15 July 1991, in: TNA, PREM 19/3282/1.

41. See Memorandum from K.A. Bishop to Stephen Wall "Gorbachev Visit 16–19 July: Some Interpreter's-Eye Impressions", 22 July 1991, in: TNA, PREM 19/3283.

42. Memorandum of Conversation, G 7 Meeting with Gorbachev, 17 July 1991, https://bush41library.tamu.edu/files/memcons-telcons/1991-07-17--Gorbachev.pdf, accessed April 6, 2019.

43. Ibid.

44. See Wencke Meteling's contribution in this volume.

45. For the context, see William Taubman, *Gorbachev: His Life and Times* (New York: Norton, 2018).

46. Memorandum from Brent Scowcroft to George Bush "Development in the USSR", 5 September 1991, Savranskaya and Blanton, op. cit., pp. 928–929.

47. Memorandum of Conversation between George Bush and Boris Yeltsin, 1 February 1992, in: GHWBPL, NSC, Nicholas Burns and Ed Hewett Files, Subject Files, Folder CF01421-009.

48. See, for instance, Memorandum from Ed Hewett to Brent Scowcroft "Discussion at the B-C-S Breakfast [Baker-Cheney-Scowcroft] on Planning for Soviet Contingencies, 25 November 1991", in: GHWBPL, NSC, Nicholas Burns and Ed Hewett Files, CIS Chron File / Subject File, CF01599-007.

Chapter 12

Shifting Economic Assessments:
Germany in a Changing World, 1987–1993

Wencke Meteling

For the political economy of the Federal Republic of Germany, the unravelling of state socialism in Central and Eastern Europe, and especially the German Democratic Republic (GDR), posed major opportunities but also huge challenges. Today we know that the German political economy proved sufficiently robust to cope with the breakdown of East German industry as well as agriculture and to stem the enormous cost of reunification. At the time, however, it was open for debate if and how German unity was to be realized and how a reunified Germany would fare economically. Chancellor Helmut Kohl, a Christian Conservative, pronounced his vision in a TV speech on July 1, 1990—the day the Monetary, Economic and Social Union between the GDR and the Federal Republic of Germany was implemented. He announced that the new *Länder* (states) in East Germany would soon turn into "blossoming landscapes."[1] The phrase backfired when euphoria about German unity faded in 1991 and the scale of the economic crisis in East Germany became apparent. The chancellor's words since have become one of the most notorious political statements in the German language, a sarcastic slogan targeting unfulfilled promises of prosperity in East Germany. Taken literally, it pointed to the fact that nature flourished on abandoned industrial sites. East Germans countered Kohl's promise of "blossoming landscapes" with an ironic slogan of their own: "illuminated meadows." It alluded to light installations put in place on empty real estate sites where no production facility ever materialized.[2]

This chapter is about the economic stakes involved for the Federal Republic of Germany during the crucial years before, during, and after reunification when the old national, European, and international order suddenly crumbled.[3] It sets out to convey the economic opportunities, challenges, and risks for the Federal Republic as seen through the lenses of the Kohl government, a coalition of Christian and Social Conservatives and Free Democrats, particularly the Ministry of Economic

Affairs, and the Council of Economic Advisors, an official, independent advisory board to the government.[4] The political decision-making process that led to German reunification and which is often at the forefront of historical research on Germany serves as an important background against which contemporaries' economic expectations and concerns are weighed.[5] There was an obvious dissonance between the government's political rationale for a speedy reunification process and strong reservations by leading economists against it.[6] In a letter to the chancellor in February 1990, the Council of Economic Advisors, the leading national voice in economic matters, fervently warned against the risks for the economy, employment, and state finances.[7] The controversy was—and still is—insolvable because any claim that reunification could have been realized in an economically more prudent fashion remains counterfactual.[8]

"We did not have a masterplan for German unity," Kohl stated in his memoirs.[9] Indeed, the process of German reunification did not follow a political playbook. It was born out of improvisation and crisis management in a complex, volatile historical situation.[10] During the first half of 1990, the chancellor took his chances when a rare window of opportunity for German reunification opened in the domestic and the international political realm. With the exception of British Prime Minister Margaret Thatcher, who fiercely opposed German reunification, and U.S. President George H. Bush, who was Kohl's closest ally in the quest for German unity, international leaders had to be persuaded and nudged in exchange for concessions. Kohl's summit diplomacy succeeded in winning over General Secretary of the Soviet Union Mikhail Gorbachev and French President François Mitterrand. Eventually each of them assented to the prospect of German reunification, including NATO membership of a reunified Germany. Kohl accommodated Mitterrand by consenting to go forward with the implementation of the Economic and Monetary Union in Europe. The German government would have preferred a closer political union, but Kohl saw his bargaining chips confined as his top priority was German reunification. Again and again the German chancellor assured worried leaders that a reunified Germany would be no drag on the future European Union.[11] Gorbachev's acquiescence came at a price.[12] But the bank loan of five billion Deutschmark granted in June 1990 as well as the total sum of German financial support for economic reform in the Soviet Union between

1989 and 1991 proved to be a relatively small price tag, roughly DM 57 billion, when compared to the total cost of reunification, estimated at DM 1.4 trillion until 2006.[13]

Domestically, the Kohl government in 1990 was confronted with acute state failure and rising unemployment in the GDR and a persistent influx of East German resettlers. In February, the German chancellor, supported by his Minister of Finance Theo Waigel, forged ahead and offered a monetary and economic union to the GDR. Signed in May and implemented on July 1, the Monetary, Economic and Social Union between the Federal Republic and the GDR was a major step towards German unity, the internal dimension of which was agreed at the end of August 1990. Kohl's offer prompted an electoral win for the conservative Alliance in the first free general elections in the GDR in March 1990. The offer to the GDR however constituted a major breach against the government's own economic preaching. Previously it had insisted on substantial market-oriented economic reforms in the GDR prior to any kind of federation, let alone a union between the two Germanys. The same was true for the government's position on European integration: it held the view that market-oriented reforms in other member states and institutional reforms of the European Community were a prerequisite for a closer economic union. A monetary union would be the high point of European integration, but nothing to begin with.

In order to explore contemporaries' economic assessments and how they shifted over time, I focus on the perspective offered in annual reports on the German economy published between 1987 and 1993—surveys published each November by the Council of Economic Advisors as well as annual economic reports published by the German government in response each January. Those were compiled by the Ministry of Economic Affairs.[14] I also draw on published documents about German reunification, on Kohl's memoirs, and on formerly undisclosed files from that Ministry that have been released on my request.[15] How did economic assessments shift over time when the division of Germany, Europe, and the world dissolved? To what extent did they move away from the growth optimism of the late 1980s to disillusionment about German unification's economic outcome? What was the government's and economists' respective take on the state of the East German economy before and after unification? Did they see it as an economic opportunity or a liability for the Federal Republic? And how did they evaluate reunified Germany's prospects in the European common market and the emerging global economy?

Section 1 briefly sketches economic assessments of the Federal Republic and the world economy from the late 1980s as they shaped contemporaries' experience and expectations. Against this backdrop Section 2 analyzes reports and forecasts from the crucial months between the fall of the Berlin Wall and the first general election in reunified Germany in December 1990, when the political dynamics of reunification were at full display. Section 3 sheds light on how assessments of reunified Germany's economic prospects in a radically altered national, European, and international framework evolved until 1993.

A Position of Strength: The Economy of the Federal Republic Seen from the Late 1980s

Economic reports from the late 1980s demonstrate a strong belief in the strength of the Federal Republic as a leading industrial and global trading nation.[16] While the Kohl government's annual economic reports reflect self-assurance and growth optimism, the Council of Economic Advisors took a slightly more critical stance, even though in principle the body fully agreed with the government's supply-side oriented approach to economic policy.

The Council of Economic Advisors was founded in 1963 as an official advisory board to the government. Its members, also commonly called the "five economic sages" (*fünf Wirtschaftsweisen*), were renowned German professors of economics. They were nominated by the government and appointed by the German President. According to custom, one candidate was usually chosen by the labor unions and another by the Board of German Employers of Manufacturing (*Gemeinschaftsausschuß der Deutschen Gewerblichen Wirtschaft*). During the 1960s and early 1970s, all members were Keynesians by conviction until the council turned to supply-side economics and monetarism between 1972 and 1976.[17] The Law for the Promotion of Stability and Growth of the Economy from 1967 prescribed that the government responded to the council's survey in its annual economic report, but it was not obliged to follow through on any of the council's policy recommendations—which were actually prohibited by law, but given anyway. Because of the council's function, independence, and reputation, its voice was widely heard in German public and political debate. Usually there was a broad consensus in market-oriented economic policy between the council and the Kohl government, a coalition of Christian Democrats (conservatives) and Free Democrats (economic liberals), but the handling of German reunification produced a rift between them.

After the international deflation crises of the 1970s and early 1980s, the Kohl government's main concerns had been sluggish growth, high unemployment, and rising public debt. The coalition had come into power in late 1982 at the height of the global recession. Since then, the German economy was on a path of recovery. In its reports from 1987, 1988 and 1989, the Ministry of Economic Affairs showed much satisfaction with the economy's trajectory and the seventh year of consecutive growth, rising total employment and shrinking unemployment numbers. It attributed them to the government's market orientation and fiscal consolidation.[18]

The "course is set correctly for the future," the Ministry stated with confidence in its 1987 report.[19] The world economic outlook was also very promising. Remaining risks concerned uncertainty about volatile foreign exchange rates, developing countries' ongoing debt problems, and significant trade imbalances by some industrial countries, which had fueled protectionist demands around the globe.[20] As a global trading nation the Federal Republic relied on smooth international trade and open markets. The Kohl government acknowledged that this role entailed a special responsibility for the world economy, but it argued decidedly against demands by other countries that the German government adopt expansionist fiscal policies. Instead, it stuck to its supply-side credo of "decidedly market-oriented politics," "dynamic competition," and "necessary adjustment."[21] This was in accordance with the Council of Economic Advisors' recommendations. On a European level, the government hoped for a "truly European internal market" as a major opportunity "for more market economy, more internal and external competition, and intensive deregulation."[22] In order to promote open markets, the Kohl government was determined to take action against protectionist inclinations in Europe, Japan, and the United States, and to cooperate with the European Community and the Uruguay Round within the framework of the General Agreement on Tariffs and Trade (GATT).[23] Socialist countries were at the margins in the government's economic reports, with a single reference to the GDR in the very last paragraph.[24]

When the Council of Economic Advisors released its survey in November 1987, the German economy had not fared as well as hoped.[25] The lowest growth estimate of 1.5% had become reality, demand and production were weak, and exports could not make up for these shortcomings. The Council estimated that the German national product would grow by a mere 1.5% in 1988—by international and even by European standards (2%), this was "weak growth" indeed.[26] In order to remedy Germany's slow growth, the Council urged to prioritize a "Politics of Growth."[27] The sages hoped that international cooperation would prevail and help reduce imbalances in the world economy, but they also warned that protectionism was on the rise in almost all countries, including the European Community.[28] The Advisors doubted that the Uruguay Round would be able to pass a new comprehensive system of rules for international trade. Similarly, they thought there was still a long way to go for the European Community to agree upon common economic policies and put into place a single market by 1992. In contrast to the Kohl government's self-congratulatory stance, the Council criticized that neither economic policies nor German businesses had properly adapted to structural change, which explained why growth in Germany was particularly weak.[29]

In its response to the Council's report, the government highlighted two external factors: the stock market crash on "Black Monday" in October 1987 and the depreciation of the U.S. dollar since 1985 (which had caused a currency appreciation of the Deutschmark of 90% within only two years and continued to impede German exports to the U.S.).[30] Despite these developments, the government pointed out, growth in Germany had continued for a sixth year in a row—a result, no doubt, of its market-oriented policies. And in 1990, additional components of its tax reform would take effect. It took the Council's "admonishment very seriously" that growth depended on structural change and that struggling regions and branches such as coal, iron, steel, and shipping would need to adapt to changing conditions on international and domestic markets.[31] Such assessments related to public debates at the time, which focused on how much the government should intervene and subsidize jobs in those branches and regions unable to meet international competition.

The Council delivered a clear answer to this problem in its next report from November 1988: "Jobs in a Competitive Marketplace."[32] In accordance with its supply-side orientation, the Advisors argued that jobs unable to stand up to competition in globalized markets should not be preserved through state intervention. Economic policy was all about making Germany more attractive as a "location for business," so that investment would rise and create profitable jobs. State programs like those in the Ruhr region—a region of struggling steel and coal industries—simply could not provide solutions for structural problems, the sages argued. Regional economic policy had to face market realities.[33] The Advisors' key argument was that investment caused growth, and they took the recent 4% rise in gross domestic product in Western industrialized countries as a case in point.[34] In a world dominated by "international competition between business locations,"[35] Germany had to strengthen its international competitiveness, especially in light of the upcoming European common market: the Federal Republic had fallen behind on emerging markets, it was losing ground in growth, and it was lagging far behind in getting people into jobs. In order to attract business investment, the sages pointed out, countries were forced to constantly review their institutional frameworks. European competition would penetrate the entire European single market.[36]

The government for its part felt fully vindicated in its optimism.[37] Growth had reached 3.4% in 1988, the highest rate since the beginning of the decade. The German political economy was in much better shape than in the early 1980s. Citing the OECD's most recent *Economic Outlook*, the government report stated that the boost in all industrialized countries was more dynamic than it had been since the early 1970s.[38] The Ministry of Economic Affairs agreed with the Council's view of a perpetual increase in competition between business locations in Europe and around the globe, but it rejected the Advisors' critical assessment of Germany's international competitiveness. The government took a very positive outlook on the approaching European internal market, which promised "significant impulses for economic growth" and could turn Europe into a "growth engine for the world economy"—if the European market was based on competition instead of bureaucratic regulation.[39]

On the whole, the Council of Economic Advisors' economic surveys and the government's annual reports in the late 1980s displayed a strong confidence that the economies of the Federal Republic, the European Community, and the world would continue to grow. For market-oriented minds, the task for economic policy on a national, European, and international level seemed clear: to improve supply-side conditions, open up markets, and strengthen a rules-based multilateral international economic order so that foreign direct investment would drive growth, employment, and prosperity for all. This was the recipe for economic success of advanced economies when suddenly demand economies and socialist regimes in Europe faltered.

1989/90: Economic Caveats versus Political Stakes

When the Council of Economic Advisors issued its next survey on November 20, 1989, the Berlin Wall had fallen. The economists could not guess (and the German chancellor at that time either) that only a few months later, on February 7, Chancellor Kohl would offer a monetary and economic union to the GDR.[40] The sages assumed that the Kohl government would stick to its own preaching about the rules and functioning of market economies, just as it did on a European level. According to those principles, a closer monetary or political union between highly disparate political economies—be it the two German economies or the ones within the European Community—seemed unconceivable unless political and economic reforms preceded such a union and lifted the performance of the weaker candidate(s). In the case of the failing GDR economy, this seemed a question of years, not months. It turned out differently. The year 1990 bestowed a political triumph on Chancellor Kohl—and a lot to worry about on economists.

In their preface from November 1990, the sages admitted that during the previous weeks they had focused on the economic consequences of an influx of people from the GDR (over 200,000 East Germans had crossed the border by mid-November), but that in the preceding days, "the rushing events in the interior of the GDR" had further changed the situation. Hopes ran high both inside and outside the GDR. "It is difficult to imagine the tasks that may arise for the Federal Republic's economy."[41] Accordingly, they refused to speculate what might happen next and what challenges might arise for economic policy. Unless the political leadership in the GDR had decided about a new economic order and unless one could conceive how GDR citizens viewed it, the Advisors abstained from any hypothetic assumptions. Only one thing seemed certain: the inadequacies and shortcomings of the economic and political system of the GDR could not be solved by providing capital or by transferring technology. "What is needed is a change in the system. However, it is not up to us to give concrete advice."[42] Feeling unable to predict how many East Germans would decide to abandon the GDR, or how many of those who had left would later return, they assumed for their 1990 report that there were no resettlers at all. And here they moved on to business as usual as if nothing extraordinary had happened and to lay out their ideas on 400 pages.

Their goals remained unaltered: further growth for the Federal Republic and the completion of the European internal market. After a seventh year of growth, the Advisors argued, more economic expansion and employment were to be expected for the Federal Republic if economic policy was pursued in the right way. Once again they beat the drum for improving supply-side conditions. "Setting the Course for the 1990s" was the title of the survey, aiming both at the Federal Republic's economic policy and the European Community's plan to realize an economic and monetary union. Following the "Report on the Creation of an Economic and Monetary Union in the European Community,"[43] the European Council in Madrid in June 1989 had decided to start the first step of implementation—all restrictions on capital and dividend transfers would be abolished—on July 1, 1990. This was the exact date when the future Monetary, Economic and Social Union with the GDR would go into effect, which no one yet foresaw. Uneasy about the speed of the European decision-making process and some member states' monetary instability, the Advisors warned "against hasty steps" which they felt might endanger a smooth completion of the European internal market.[44] Apart from that, they felt confident about the economic development of the Federal Republic, the European Community, and the world.

Responding to the political upheaval in the GDR, the Council in January 1990 published a special survey (*Sondergutachten*) on economic conditions and possibilities to support economic reform in the GDR.[45] It continued to believe firmly that there was only one successful concept for economic reform, "the open border of the market economy with social protections."[46] They went on by laying out how to realize it: the Federal Republic's support for the GDR should be part of broad economic and political cooperation of all European countries.

The government's optimism and confidence were on full display in its report, issued only two days after the Council's special survey. The document is a telling source of West German triumphalism, euphoria, and the government's self-congratulatory stance in view of the demise of command economies and socialist regimes in the GDR and Central and Eastern Europe. The Ministry of Economic Affairs praised supply-side politics, the social market economy, and the "brilliant shape" of the Federal Republic's economy. It branded the economic success mainly as its own achievement, and attributed it only partly to favorable international circumstances.[47] 4% growth in 1989 was the highest real economic growth rate of the 1980s, employment was at a record level with 28 million people employed, unemployment was down, exports were up, and the Federal Republic had become the world's second-largest importer. The chapter ended with a blunt statement:

> The competition among political systems has once again resulted in an impressive display of the Social Market Economy's advantages. It comes as no surprise that this economic and social order receives increased attention from states in Central and Eastern Europe in their search for a more humane order.[48]

In sync with the European Community's commitment, the German government was committed to integrating Central and Eastern Europe with the international division of labor, and to support market-oriented structural reforms in those countries. The same applied to the GDR. "Socialism is dead and does not have a future," the Ministry of Economic Affairs asserted as a firm response to all those who sought to reform socialism.[49] But they recognized the Federal Republic's special responsibility to support the reform process in the GDR. Here the Ministry of Economic Affairs briefly referred to Chancellor Kohl's "10 point program to overcome the division of Germany and Europe" (10-*Punkte-Programm zur Überwindung der Teilung Deutschlands und Europas*) from late November 1989.

With this program Kohl had gone on the offensive in the domestic debate on the future of Germany and laid out the government's strategy for German reunification, albeit stopping short of calling it such.

The program only spoke of a "federation" as goal. Kohl had been careful not to mention German reunification publicly, out of caution not to provoke other state leaders' opposition. Gorbachev especially could have vetoed it. Instead Kohl referred to the right of self-determination for all Germans, which was more difficult for other state leaders to reject. The announcement of the program in the German Parliament was a bombshell and propelled the domestic as well as the international debate on German reunification.[50]

Instead of discussing the 10-point program, however, the report issued by the Ministry of Economic Affairs turned to the Council's special survey on economic reform in the GDR, agreeing with the Advisors' key premise that "there is no convincing alternative to the market-oriented order." Once more the Ministry sent a clear message to the GDR's opposition movement seeking to reform the socialist system: "The federal government considers futile all attempts to reform socialism. The social market economy *is* the 'third way' between capitalism and socialism."[51] Though the full effects of the political and economic upheavals in Central and Eastern Europe could not yet be foreseen, the Ministry of Economic Affairs took an optimistic stance, expecting positive impulses through migrants from the East and through economic cooperation between West and East. At the same time, however, it prioritized establishing the European single market by endorsing a "Europe defined by competition."[52] Given the differing economic conditions in member states and competing aims associated with the prospect of European integration, the German government tried to slow-walk the second step of the Economic and Monetary Union—the harmonization of fiscal and monetary policies of member states in a system of fixed currencies. The French government, in contrast, pressed for a speedy implementation.[53]

The contrast between the German slow-walking at the European level and its simultaneous push for a monetary and economic union with the GDR is striking. Chancellor Kohl had changed his strategy for Germany since the release of his 10-point program in November 1989. Unemployment figures were rising dramatically in the GDR while an increasing number of East Germans were leaving for the West German labor market. Political and economic stakes were high in early 1990, and time was crucial. Kohl gave up any plan by stages which would have taken several years to implement and instead favored a monetary and

economic union with the GDR in the near future. Intensive preparations for such a union were under way in the Ministry of Finance under
Minister Waigel. In a letter from February 7, Waigel substantiated the
government's decision to members of the Christian Democratic Union
and the Christian Social Union in the German Bundestag:

> The daily increasing loss of confidence of our compatriots in econom-
> ic reform in the GDR makes it necessary to present perspectives for
> the period after the election. For this reason, the federal government
> has agreed to negotiate with the GDR over a monetary union.[54]

Chancellor Kohl pursued several goals with his offer to the GDR:
end the exodus of East Germans from the failing economic and political system by addressing their hopes and expectations, have his party's
ally, the Alliance for Germany, win the first free general election in
the GDR in March, and secure German reunification. It was one of
the riskiest decisions Kohl ever took.[55] "I was well aware that a quick
introduction of the Deutschmark in the GDR would entail economic
risks," Kohl wrote in his memoirs. "Above all, it was politically imperative." The offer of the Deutschmark was meant as a "persuasive
signal" for East Germans that living standards would improve soon and
that there was no need to resettle.[56] Chancellor Kohl, Finance Minister
Waigel and their economic advisors in the Ministry of Finance and the
Ministry of Economic Affairs overestimated the East German economy's potential to evolve into a functioning market economy within only
two or three years, and they overestimated business investment from
West Germany. They were not the only ones. The German Institute
for Economic Research also grossly overrated East German productivity, which was in large part due to unreliable and misleading data from
the socialist regime.[57] Kohl particularly was under the misapprehension
that another economic miracle was possible, like the one the Federal
Republic had experienced after the currency reform of 1948, and he
kept musing aloud about "blossoming landscapes" in East Germany.[58]

On February 7, 1990 the Cabinet decided to propose to the GDR
that it enter into a monetary and economic union with the Federal Republic. The offer was fiercely opposed by economics departments, economic research institutes, and the Council of Economic Advisors, and
their concerns were broadly disseminated by the press.[59] On February
9, the Chairman of the Council took the extraordinary step of sending

a letter to Chancellor Kohl, urging him to insist on economic reform in the GDR and to postpone monetary union. The letter has become famous for its precise prognosis of the damaging economic effects of the subsequent union:

> We believe that the swift implementation of monetary union is the wrong way to stop the flow of resettlers. ... The single currency will suddenly make clear the difference in income, demands for a correction will not be long in coming and will be difficult to dismiss. Nominal wages will then increase beyond the increase in productivity. This is to the detriment of the GDR as a location for production, and the urgently needed influx of capital from the West will not be available. ... The pressure on the Federal Republic would increase to reduce the income gap (wages and pensions) by a 'financial compensation' in favor of the GDR. Public budgets would face huge burdens. ... It cannot be denied that the hopes that are attached to the monetary union—and which are deliberately reinforced by it—will be disappointed. However, if the disillusionment goes on, the flow of resettlers will increase even more. ... Emigration from the GDR can only be prevented by giving people a credible perspective for a speedy and sustainable improvement in their living standards. The basic prerequisite for this is the fundamental transformation of the economic system of the GDR into a market-based order.

Kohl had hoped for more support from economists, business, and labor unions, he admitted, but at least the "storm of protest" abated during the following weeks.[60]

On October 3, 1990 German unity was celebrated. When the Council of Economic Advisors finally had an opportunity to address urgent economic issues in detail, it did not hold back on its criticism. In their November survey "On the path toward Germany's economic unity" the Advisors pointed to the economic problems in the former GDR and emphasized that difficult tasks lay ahead for the state, business, employees, social partners, state bureaucracy, and the new state trust (*Treuhandanstalt*). The state trust had been founded to manage the market transition of the formerly state-owned East German businesses by privatizing, reorganizing, or dissolving them.[61] "The transformation of the socialist command economy of the GDR into a liberal market economy is going to be one of the major challenges of the century. It will be unique, without precedent,"[62] the Council rightly stated. Citizens and businesses were to expect great difficulties during the transition period. It did not depend on public funding how quickly living standards in the East would approach those in the West, the Council insisted, but on private investment. Out of concern that the completion of the European internal market might be drowned into the shadows, the economists stressed how primordially important the single market was for the future of the German economy, arguing that the European Community's internal market initiative was a major cause for Europe's economic revival after a period of "eurosclerosis" in the early 1980s.[63] Many European industrial countries had expanded their production levels, whereas growth in the United States, the UK and Canada had nearly stagnated. People in Eastern Europe put high hopes in their countries' integration with world trade. "For the global economy as a whole, a market-oriented readjustment in these countries, and their integration in the international division of labor, will ultimately bring greater wealth," the Council stated.[64] But it issued a warning that those hopes were far from being fulfilled.

Again and again the Advisors argued that the economic transformations would take time and were extremely difficult to implement, while unprofitable production would be closed down very quickly under market conditions. This basic dilemma was especially true for East Germany. With a critical undertone on how German unity had been put into practice, the survey emphasized the huge wealth gap between East and West Germany. The Economic and Monetary Union, implemented without a transition period, had laid open a nearly total lack of competitiveness of the East German economy. Since the introduction of the Deutschmark, production in East Germany had shrunk by a third, privatizations and new businesses had merely started, and Western investors turned to East Germany with hesitation. Those who profited most from the Monetary and Economic Union were West German companies, because they thrived on East German demand.[65]

Given these huge differences between East and West Germany and the lack of reliable data on the East German economy, the Council decided against taking an overall view of the German economy and instead dealt with two separate, highly unequal, but increasingly connected economies.[66] The sages painted a gloomy picture of the ruinous state of the East German economy, which was even worse than anticipated. This negative assessment stood in sharp contrast to their praise of the West German economy, which had grown by 4% in 1990. The economists lashed out at the government's presumably irresponsible fiscal policies, especially the accelerating budget deficit. For 1991, they predicted an ever more divided path for the two German economies: one would continue to rise, while the other had yet to reach its low point, presumably by the middle of the following year.[67]

The Kohl government's endeavor to make a socialist command economy adopt the Deutschmark and the regulative system of the Federal Republic without a longer transition period was a daunting, unprecedented, and large-scale experiment. Politically, it paved the way for electoral wins for the Conservatives and for German unity. Economically, the sudden introduction of the Deutschmark and the exchange rate of 1:1 for wages and salaries exposed uncompetitive East German industry to West German and international competition at a time when their former trade with Central and Eastern Europe literally collapsed. The Monetary Union had the effect of a shock therapy for East German industry, while giving a temporary boost to companies from West Germany, thus widening the economic gap between the two parts of the country.[68]

German Economies Drifting Apart: "Reunification Crisis"

The hopes and expectations underpinning the Kohl government's optimistic stance on East Germany and its economy were dampened in 1991. With ever more companies shutting down and unemployment numbers on a steep rise, it became evident that the productivity level in the GDR had been much lower than estimated, private investment from West Germany was far more difficult to attract than anticipated, in spite of a wide range of government incentives, and the state trust's task to privatize, reorganize or dissolve formerly state-owned companies cost a fortune instead of making profits. East Germany fell into a weary state of what soon became a veritable "reunification crisis." To make matters worse, Western industrialized countries, especially the United States and the UK, slipped into recession.[69]

In its first annual economic report after German reunification, the Kohl government in March 1991 stated as his highest priority to procure equal living standards in Germany. In order to achieve this goal, "a rapid catching-up process" in East Germany was needed. "There is no historical model for this task; never before has a country tried to turn a socialist command economy into a social market economy."[70] Moreover, the Federal Republic faced increasing international challenges: to complete the European internal market, simultaneously realize the Monetary and the Political Union in Europe and make it "a real stability Community,"[71] successfully finish the Uruguay Round within the GATT, contribute to the Gulf War and reconstruction in the Gulf region, and give economic aid to countries in Central and Eastern Europe. These challenges, the report went on, could only be met if the performance of the German economy was further enhanced. In early 1991 there was good reason for optimism in this regard. Gross domestic product in West Germany had risen by 4.6% in 1990—the strongest growth rate next to Japan's during the Federal Republic's ninth year of consecutive growth—and employment numbers were reminiscent of the miraculous 1950s.

In East Germany, however, things looked bleak. Key for economic recovery was private and public investment, which the government tried to stimulate by a wide range of measures. But unsettled property rights, a non-existent modern bureaucracy and an outdated infrastructure constituted major obstacles.[72] The government also issued a warning against wage increases that outpaced productivity levels in East Germany—in vain.[73] One thing was certain: it would take time for investment to become effective. In order to bridge the intervening period, the government set up a *Gemeinschaftswerk Aufschwung Ost*, a solidarity package of 24 billion Deutschmark for East Germany in 1991/92 to stimulate investment and secure employment. It came in addition to the "Fund 'German Unity'" established in 1990. The Fund initially foresaw 115 billion Deutschmark until 1994, but in 1991 alone it had to provide more than 100 billion for the new *Länder* and communities.[74] "German unity also means financial solidarity," the government report appealed to West Germans, just as it appealed to "Western solidarity" for reform efforts in Central and Eastern Europe.[75] As the crisis in East Germany was unfolding, the political pressure on the government rose dramatically to change course in economic policy and intensify state intervention in the East German economy.

Alarmed that the government might depart any further from a market-oriented approach, the Council of Economic Advisors in April issued another Special Survey on economic policy for East Germany. "The crisis of adaptation of the East German economy has brought a total change of mood and expectations. The euphoria tied to the Economic, Monetary and Social Union has vanished; in their place are uncertainty, anxiety and bitterness." While most people were shocked in face of the sudden breakdown of production and employment, the sages felt vindicated in their dire predictions. They still had not digested Kohl's decision for a monetary and economic union with the GDR and the backlash it had conjured not only in East Germany, but to their great dismay also in West Germany. Targeting Kohl's promise of "blossoming landscapes," they insisted that it was "absolutely impossible to convert a socialist economy into a flourishing market economy within only a couple of months." In reference to their own letter to the chancellor from February 1990, they argued that the economic downturn came by no means as a surprise, "there could be differing assessments only about the extent and the duration of the downturn."[76] Four decades of socialist mismanagement were to blame, not the newly introduced market economy which needed "much time" to develop, they told an impatient German public.[77] As far as medium-term growth prospects in East Germany were concerned, though, the Advisors considered them to be "good" and were convinced that the breakdown of the East German economy would not lead to a lasting structural crisis, as some public voices suggested. Therefore, the Advisors saw no need for hasty steps in economic policy. There were "no alternatives to a market-oriented solution," which meant either successfully privatizing companies or closing them down. Affected people were worthy of state protection, not unprofitable jobs and companies. Any policy of conserving them, either by the state or by the state trust, was a horror to the Council.[78]

Though the economy in Western industrialized countries cooled down markedly in 1991, the Council of Economic Advisors did not suspect a recession. The recent slowdown of the West German economy did not cause them much trouble either. Rather, the sages and the Kohl government expected a 2.5% growth rate in OECD countries, headed by the United States, Canada, and the UK.[79] In order to get a better picture of the situation in East Germany, the Advisors undertook an information tour in the summer of 1991. They saw economic development in the new *Länder* "still characterized by the collapse of existing economic structures," and the same was true for Eastern Europe as a whole. Poland, Hungary and Czechoslovakia had made some progress in their reform efforts and fared better than the rest of Central and Eastern Europe, but even in those three countries economic expectations were disappointed. Within a year, employment in East Germany had shrunk by 1.4 million and by almost 3 million since 1989, further boosting the West German labor force. Production levels had sunk to mere 6.7% of West German production, and productivity was less than a third from productivity in West Germany.[80] At the same time, per-capita public spending had already reached 91.5% of West German states' and communities' spending. For the first time since 1983, Germany had recorded a negative balance of current account and had turned into a capital importer. The sages, however, did not ring the alarm bell as they expected the huge gap in economic performance between East and West Germany to shrink, due to heavy investment by the state and West German businesses.[81] Again they were proven wrong.

Any prognosis of how reunited Germany would fare economically was highly speculative at that point. The Ministry of Economic Affairs in early 1992 clearly struggled to come up with rough growth estimates, projecting a growth rate of 1–2% for West Germany and of 5–15% for East Germany. The risk of all growth projections, the report stated, was that they were based on several assumptions: world trade would boost West German exports—the "linchpin" of the German economy, as the Council of Economic Advisors put it; the West German economy would regain former growth rates, and growth in other Western industrialized countries would also rebound.[82] Those optimistic assumptions—and the corresponding growth projections—were disappointed. Western industrialized countries continued to suffer from sluggish growth, and once the reunification boom had evaporated, negative effects started closing in on the West German economy. Labor costs and nonwage labor costs had gone up because of excessive wage settlements and higher social security contributions that were used to co-finance German unity, demand from other European countries shrank, and the ongoing appreciation of the Deutschmark put an additional price tag on German exports. All of a sudden, the West German economy stagnated, and then, "against almost all prognoses" as the Council of Economic Advisors wearily stated, even contracted.[83]

In 1992 and 1993, German economic policy faced a serious dilemma: on the one hand, huge public and private financial transfers were necessary to spur growth in East Germany and to pay for active employment policy in order to keep East German unemployment numbers in check (employment shrunk by 3.5 million [35%] between 1989 and 1993); on the other, the struggling West German economy also needed more investment. The underlying problem in each economy was very different: the West German economy was considered sound, but it suffered from a cyclical lack of demand from other countries, above all from the European Community, where 75% of German exports went. In contrast, the East German economy was utterly uncompetitive (unit labor costs in 1993 were 62.5% higher than in West Germany), and it suffered from a severe structural problem of supply. To make things worse, a heated public debate erupted on the costs of German unity and how to distribute burdens, as taxes, social insurance contributions and public debt were on the rise. Germans began to wonder if economic policy was not up to the task of simultaneously consolidating state finances and securing Germany's economic integration. Uncertainty further fueled a pessimistic economic climate. The Council of Economic Advisors held the view that the state had to lead the way and consolidate its finances. Once again the economists tied national economic policy to European policy, arguing that if Germany wanted the European Community to be based on financial stability and economic competition, the Federal Republic had to prove "that it was able to fix its own house."[84] This seemed less and less the case.

German proponents of a market-oriented economic policy were fighting a two-front battle: they tried to make sure that the Kohl government neither yielded to demands for state intervention and subsidies for failing industries in East Germany, nor to any economic *dirigisme* in the European Community. In the run-up to the Maastricht Treaty, signed in February 1992, a controversy over industrial policy took place, with the French and the German governments on opposing sites: French *dirigisme* in industrial policy clashed with a supply-side approach favored by the Germans. As internal records from the Ministry of Economic Affairs show, the specter of a state-led, active industrial policy "à la française" becoming part of the Maastricht Treaty was haunting German officials and economists alike. The dispute was solved by a compromise which alarmed German advocates of supply-side politics.[85]

Germany was not alone in grappling with contradictory requirements in economic policy. Some Western European countries, facing difficulties to meet the convergence criteria (fiscal and monetary stability) for entering the European Economic and Monetary Union, raised taxes and cut expenditure instead of stimulating their economies. Thus the economic downturn got even worse. One of the main problems, according to the Council of Economic Advisors, was uncertainty: uncertainty about economic policy in Germany and in Europe, about European integration, and the GATT deliberations which had been dragging on for six years already. The economic reform process in Central and Eastern Europe posed major problems, but the transformation crisis of the Commonwealth of Independent States and particularly Russia was even worse. The collapse of the Russian market again exacerbated the breakdown of East German industry.[86]

"For the German economy, 1993 was not a good year," the Council conceded in November 1993. It was a year of disillusionment. The unexpected had become reality: the West German economy had slid into a deep recession, similarly to the one during the early 1980s. Unemployment rose, production and exports shrank, and business investment plummeted. Germany's dependence on exports to Western Europe had turned into a liability as those economies had not yet recovered. All prognoses, including those from international organizations, about Germany and Western Europe had erred again. At hindsight it became clear to the Council that West German growth since 1990 had not been a sign of competitiveness. Rather, the economy had been overheated and fueled by state-induced demand from German unity. The reunification boom had obscured structural weaknesses in the West German economy, which the recession then laid open. This constituted a major reassessment of the German economy. It dawned on economists, politicians, and the broader public that Germany as a whole might be losing its competitive edge, both within the recently established European single market and around the globe.[87]

Conclusion

The aim of this chapter was to dissect how leading German economists and the federal government under Chancellor Helmut Kohl, particularly the Ministry of Economic Affairs, assessed Germany's economic prospects against the backdrop of a radically shifting national, European, and global framework in the late 1980s and early 1990s.

A consideration of the historical development confirmed my initial hypothesis that the costs of German unification replaced the growth optimism of the 1980s with disillusionment. During the 1980s, West Germany's steady economic growth and strong export were nearly being taken for granted. Assessments by economic advisors and the federal government were similar to one another, except that the advisors demanded stricter supply-side politics and warned of subsidies for failing industries while the government claimed economic successes for itself. The global economic situation further fueled a positive economic outlook.

Against this backdrop, Chancellor Helmut Kohl's belief, in 1990, that West Germany could afford to pay for German unification is hardly surprising. In fact, that year became the political and economic apotheosis of the German government. Kohl's offer in February that the GDR could enter into an economic and monetary union with West Germany (which would lay the foundation for German unification) was met with stiff resistance from the Council of Economic Advisors. Their urgent warnings of the economic risks involved in this decision would be proven correct. Unification produced the effects they had predicted. Unification was a shock therapy for East Germany, similar to neoliberal reforms in other formerly socialist states in Central and Eastern Europe.[88] The sages were also correct in emphasizing the government's contradictory stance on economic policy in Germany and in the European Community: while the Kohl government insisted that EC member countries or those applying for membership meet financial stability criteria, it did not insist that economic reform precede German monetary union. The two perspectives that fed the controversy over German unification, an economic supply-side rationale vs. the political goal of national unity, proved to be incompatible. In the end, Kohl's political vision of reunified Germany prevailed over economic concerns. But the two different perspectives have continued to shape the debate since then.

Post-reunification reports and forecasts by the Council as well as the Ministry of Economic Affairs did not conceive of *one* German economy, but of two separated ones, with a massive performance gap between them. While the government's goal was to close that gap as fast as possible, it actually widened before it began to close. The economic advisors struggled to conceptualize the East German economy as a genuine part of the new, reunified Germany, and to develop a positive attitude towards it. The Council considered East German industry a West German liability for years to come. They also feared that massive state subsidies and transfer payments to East Germany could become a model and that the federal government would budge from its supply-side approach, which they considered to be the key formula for self-sustaining growth.

The tides began to shift in 1991 when East Germany underwent a severe transformation crisis. The near total collapse of East German industry and its trade relationships with Eastern Europe and the (former) Soviet Union as well as the rapid rise of unemployment figures did not come as a surprise for the sages. But these developments were a shock for East Germans. They triggered a severe "unification crisis" and put a reality check on West Germany's initial enthusiasm for unification. Many economists and the federal government had underestimated difficulties in transforming the East German economy, on the one hand, and overestimated the strength of the West German economy, on the other.

The years 1992/93 resembled an earthquake in economic reckoning. Unexpectedly, the international recession, particularly in EC member states, lasted longer than anticipated. Massive federal support of East Germany had fueled West German growth, but then international developments caught up with the German economy. Again and again, economic advisors, the federal government, and international organizations were forced to downgrade Germany's economic outlook, abandoning their earlier optimism, which had envisioned an international, and also West German, economic recovery. For Germany, the coincidence was unfortunate indeed. The Federal Republic's economic fortunes worsened at the very moment the federal state, the individual

German *Länder*, and municipalities continued to struggle with the costs of reunification while companies faced stiff competition from abroad and from within the new European common market.

Against this backdrop—a perfect storm of German reunification, national and European recession, and stiff global competition—public and political debates increasingly focused on what came to be identified as Germany's lack of "international competitiveness," the country's inability to attract business investment. With the collapse of command economies and communist rule in Central and Eastern Europe and with the end of the Cold War, a fundamental shift took place from competition between alliance systems to global competition *within* capitalism. It appears that the Council of Economic Advisors was slow in grasping this new reality. Possible negative effects from this shift dawned on them only when the West German economy went into recession and, so it seemed, was in danger of losing its competitive edge. For them, the end of the Cold War had not caused a cognitive dissonance between their pre-1989 experience and their post-1991 expectations. Instead, the sages insisted even more firmly on the need for supply-side politics.

Once the cost of German unity became a contentious issue in public debate, and once the West German economy began to struggle, the Kohl government became concerned that West Germany would consider East Germany a drag. The fierce controversy over the costs of reunification and the state trust showed that German unity was not a given.[89] For the chancellor, it would have been risky to attribute the economic crisis to the costs of propping up East Germany. The debate about Germany's eroding competitiveness and insufficient preparation for the challenges of "globalization" shifted the conversation away from East Germany and unification towards a common, national problem. Boosted by Chancellor Kohl, parts of his government (particularly the Ministry of Economic Affairs), economists, policy consultants, business executives, and national and international media, this paradigm dominated the debate for over a decade. No longer the "poster child," the Federal Republic had become a "problem child" as national and international commentators considered the former "wonderland" the new "sick man of Europe."[90]

Notes

1. TV Speech of German Chancellor Helmut Kohl on July 1, 1990, *Bulletin des Presse- und Informationsamts der Bundesregierung* no. 86, July 3, 1990, https://www.bundesregierung.de/breg-de/service/bulletin/der-entscheiden-de-schritt-auf-dem-weg-in-die-gemeinsame-zukunft-der-deutschen-fernsehansprache-des-bundeskanzlers-zum-inkrafttreten-der-waehrungsunion-am-1-juli-1990-788446.

2. Claas Beckord and Peter Jurczek, "'Beleuchtete Wiesen' oder 'Blühende Landschaften?' Zum Stand der Gewerbeflächenentwicklung und -vermarktung in der Region Südwestsachsen" in *Standort – Zeitschrift für Angewandte Geographie* (2004), pp. 28-58, https://doi.org/10.1007/s00548-004-0181-5.

3. On Germany during the 1980s and 1990s see Andreas Wirsching, *Abschied vom Provisorium. Geschichte der Bundesrepublik Deutschland 1982-1990* (Munich: Deutsche Verlags-Anstalt, 2006); Klaus Schröder, *Die veränderte Republik. Deutschland nach der Wiedervereinigung* (Munich: Bayerische Landeszentrale für politische Bildung, 2006); Jeremy Leaman, *The Political Economy of Germany under Chancellors Kohl and Schröder: Decline of the German Model?* (New York: Berghahn Books, 2009); in a longer historical perspective: Ulrich Herbert, *Geschichte Deutschlands im 20. Jahrhundert* (Munich: C.H. Beck Verlag, 2014); Eckart Conze, *Die Suche nach Sicherheit. Eine Geschichte der Bundesrepublik Deutschland von 1949 bis in die Gegenwart*, (Munich: Siedler Verlag, 2009); for a European perspective, Ivan T. Berend, *Europe since 1980* (Cambridge: Cambridge University Press, 2010); Barry Eichengreen, *The European Economy since 1945: Coordinated Capitalism and Beyond* (Princeton: Princeton University Press, 2007); Andreas Wirsching, *Der Preis der Freiheit. Geschichte Europas in unserer Zeit* (Munich: C.H. Beck Verlag, 2012).

4. Tim Schanetzky, *Die große Ernüchterung. Wirtschaftspolitik, Expertise und Gesellschaft in der Bundesrepublik 1966–1982* (Berlin: Akademie Verlag, 2007); Tim Schanetzky, "Aporien der Verwissenschaftlichung. Sachverständigenrat und wirtschaftlicher Strukturwandel in der Bundesrepublik 1974–1988," in *Archiv für Sozialgeschichte* 50 (2010), pp. 153-67.

5. For a detailed view on the decision-making process see Hanns Jürgen Küsters, "Entscheidung für die deutsche Einheit. Einführung in die Edition," in Hanns Jürgen Küsters and Daniel Hofmann (eds.), *Deutsche Einheit. Sonderedition aus den Akten des Bundeskanzleramtes 1989/90* (Dokumente zur Deutschlandpolitik (Munich: Oldenbourg Verlag, 1998), pp. 21-236. From the vast historical literature on German reunification: Andreas Rödder, *Deutschland einig Vaterland. Die Geschichte der Wiedervereinigung* (Munich: C.H. Beck Verlag, 2009); Dieter Grosser, *Das Wagnis der Währungs-, Wirtschafts- und Sozialunion. Politische Zwänge im Konflikt mit ökonomischen Regeln* [Geschichte der deutschen

Einheit] (Stuttgart: Deutsche Verlags-Anstalt, 1998); Gerhard A. Ritter, *Der Preis der deutschen Einheit. Die Wiedervereinigung und die Krise des Sozialstaates* (Munich: C.H. Beck Verlag, 2nd edition, 2007); Gerhard A. Ritter, "Die deutsche Wiedervereinigung," in *Historische Zeitschrift* 286 (2008), vol. 2, pp. 289-339; Conze, *Suche*, op. cit., pp. 689-746.

6. Grosser, *Wagnis*, op. cit., pp. 149-226.

7. Letter to the Chancellor, February 9, 1990, in Annual Survey of the Council of Economic Advisors (*Jahresgutachten des Sachverständigenrates zur Begutachtung der gesamtwirtschaftlichen Lage*), AS 1990/91 "'Towards Economic Unity in Germany,' enclosed Special Survey January 20, 1990 'Enhancing Economic Reform in the GDR: Prerequisites and Possibilities,'" November 13, 1990, appendix V. Also published in Küsters and Hofmann, *Deutsche Einheit*, no. 168, op. cit., pp. 778-81.

8. See the discussion of counterfactual alternatives in Grosser, *Wagnis*, op. cit., pp. 485-504.

9. Helmut Kohl, *Erinnerungen 1990-1994* (Munich: Droemer Verlag, 2007), 125.

10. Ritter, *Preis*, op. cit., p. 12.

11. Rödder, *Deutschland*, op. cit., pp. 226-78; Herbert, *Geschichte*, op. cit., pp. 1121-7. On Thatcher's opposition see Liviu Horowitz's article in this volume. Among the biographies on German Chancellor Helmut Kohl and his political actions since the fall of the Berlin wall see Hans-Peter Schwarz, *Helmut Kohl. Eine politische Biographie* (Munich: Deutsche Verlags-Anstalt, 2012), pp. 489-618; Henning Köhler, *Helmut Kohl. Ein Leben für die Politik* (Cologne: Bastei Lübbe, 2014), pp. 626-740; Heribert Schwan and Rolf Steininger, *Helmut Kohl. Virtuose der Macht* (Mannheim: Patmos Verlag and Artemis & Winkler Verlag, 2014), pp. 163-270.

12. On "money for Moscow" see Stephan Kieninger's article in the present volume; Küsters, *Entscheidung*, op. cit., pp. 165-73; Herbert, *Deutschland*, op. cit., p. 263.

13. Total sum of net transfers from West to East Germany—or 4-5% of the German gross domestic product every year, Grosser, *Wagnis*, op. cit., pp. 482-3; Ritter, *Preis*, op. cit., pp. 127-9.

14. Council, AS; Annual Economic Reports by the Federal Government (Gvt, AER) (*Jahreswirtschaftsberichte der Bundesregierung*), available online. On the Ministry of Economic Affairs see Werner Abelshauser (ed.), *Das Bundeswirtschaftsministerium in der Ära der Sozialen Marktwirtschaft. Der deutsche Weg der Wirtschaftspolitik* (Berlin: De Gruyter Oldenbourg, 2016).

15. German National Archives, Ministry of Economic Affairs, Dep. IV, General Matters of Industrial Policy 1991-1992, B 102/378614, 400225-30; Competitiveness of German Companies. Hearing of the Christian Democratic Union and the Christian Social Union, German Parliament, on "Germany as a Business Location" 1992, B 102/397005-7. Published documents Küsters and Hofmann, *Deutsche Einheit*, op. cit.; Helmut Kohl, *Erinnerungen* 1982-1990 (Munich: Droemer Verlag, 2005); Kohl, *Erinnerungen* 1990-1994, op. cit.

16. On the German economy and economic policy during the Kohl years see Leaman, *Economy*, op. cit., pp. 43-136; Wirsching, *Abschied*, op. cit., pp. 223-288; Werner Abelshauser, *Deutsche Wirtschaftsgeschichte. Von 1945 bis zur Gegenwart* (Bonn: BpB, 2011); Werner Abelshauser et al. (eds.), *Wirtschaftspolitik in Deutschland 1917-1990*, (Berlin: De Gruyter Oldenbourg, 2016).

17. Schanetzky, *Ernüchterung*, op. cit.; Schanetzky, "Aporien," op. cit.

18. Gvt, AER 1987, January 15, 1987, Printed matter 10/6796; Gvt, AER 1988, January 29, 1988, Printed matter 11/1733; Gvt, AER 1989, January 25, 1989, Printed matter 11/3917.

19. Gvt, AER 1987, no. 1.

20. Gvt, AER 1987, no. 10.

21. Gvt, AER 1987, no. 44 and 46.

22. Gvt, AER 1987, no. 38.

23. Gvt, AER 1987, no. 38-41.

24. Gvt, AER 1987, no. 40 and 63.

25. Council, AS 1987/88, "Priority for Politics of Growth," November 23, 1987, Printed matter 11/1317.

26. Council, AS 1987/88, preface, 2.

27. Council, AS 1987/88, no. 41*-48* and 249-66.

28. Council, AS 1987/88, no. 3*.

29. Council, AS 1987/88, no. 40*-45*.

30. Gvt, AER 1988.

31. Gvt, AER 1988, no. 18.

32. Council, AS 1988/89, "Jobs in Competition," November 18, 1988, Printed matter 11/3478.

33. Council, AS 1988/89, II.

34. Council, AS 1988/89, no. 1*.

35. Council, AS 1988/89, no. 40*. On this notion see Wencke Meteling, "Nationale Standortsemantiken seit den 1970er-Jahren" in Wencke Meteling and Ariane Leendertz (eds.), *Die neue Wirklichkeit. Semantische Neuvermessungen und Politik seit den 1970er Jahren* (Frankfurt/New York: Campus, 2016), pp. 203-37.

36. Council, AS 1988/89, no. 35-8.

37. Gvt, AER 1989.

38. Gvt, AER 1989, no. 1-3.

39. Gvt, AER 1989, no. 15.

40. See Chancellor Kohl's retrospective on the months between the fall of the Berlin wall and his offer of a monetary and economic union to the GDR in Kohl, *Erinnerungen 1982-1990*, op. cit., pp. 964-1059. The most profound study on the Union is Grosser, *Wagnis*, op. cit.

41. Council, AS 1989/90, "Setting the Course for the 1990s," November 20, 1989, Printed matter 11/5786.

42. Council, AS 1989/90, preface, no. I-II.

43. The so-called Delors Report (1988/89) was named after the President of the European Commission Jacques Delors. The Report became the foundation of the Maastricht Treaty of February 1992.

44. Council, AS 1989/90, no. 394-5.

45. Council, AS 1990/91.

46. Council, AS 1990/91, preface and no. 276.

47. Gvt, AER 1990, no. 1. The report contained a special chapter on the Kohl government's economic policy since its inception in 1982.

48. Gvt, AER 1990, no. 8.

49. Gvt, AER 1990, no. 11.

50. On the program see Küsters, "Entscheidung," op. cit., pp. 59-70; Rödder, *Deutschland*, op. cit., pp. 137-42; Kohl, *Erinnerungen 1982-1990*, op. cit., pp. 988-1000. On reactions in capitals see Draft by Ministerial Director Teltschik to Chancellor Kohl, Bonn, November 30, 1989, in Küsters and Hofmann, *Deutsche Einheit*, op. cit., no. 102, 574-7.

51. Gvt, AER 1990, no. 14.

52. Gvt, AER 1990, no. 10 and 70.

53. Gvt, AER 1990, no. 79. On the German-Franco dissent see Draft by *Legationsrat* I Bitterlich to Chancellor Kohl, Bonn, December 2-3, 1989, in Küsters and Hofmann, *Deutsche Einheit*, op. cit., no. 108, pp. 596-8; Letter by Chancellor Kohl to President Mitterrand, Bonn, December 5, 1989, no. 111, pp. 614-15, ibid.; Rödder, *Vaterland*, op. cit., pp. 264-70.

54. Schreiben des Bundesministers Waigel an die Mitglieder der Fraktion der CDU/CSU im Deutschen Bundestag, Bonn, February 7, 1990, in Küsters and Hofmann, *Deutsche Einheit*, op. cit., no. 165, pp. 766-7.

55. See Grosser, *Wagnis*, op. cit., pp. 174-207, 177 (decision).

56. Kohl, *Erinnerungen 1982-1990*, op. cit., p. 1057.

57. Grosser, *Wagnis*, op. cit., p. 264 and pp. 499-500; Kohl, *Erinnerungen 1990-1994*, op. cit., pp. 88-9.

58. Köhler, *Kohl*, op. cit., pp. 773-4.

59. Grosser, *Wagnis*, op. cit., pp. 192-97.

60. Kohl, *Erinnerungen* 1990-1994, op. cit., pp. 80-1.

61. On the state trust see Marcus Boïck, *Die Treuhand. Idee – Praxis – Erfahrung 1990-1994* (Goettingen: Wallstein Verlag, 2018).

62. Council, AS 1990/91, preface, no. 3.

63. Council, AS 1990/91, preface, no. 4 and no. 5*.

64. Council, AS 1990/91, no. 7*.

65. Council, AS 1990/91, no. 11*.

66. Council, AS 1990/91, no. 9*-12*.

67. Council, AS 1990/91, no. 29*.

68. On the economic effects of the shock therapy and of reunification see Ritter, *Preis*, op. cit., pp. 98-140.

69. See Gerhard A. Ritter, "Eine Vereinigungskrise? Die Grundzüge der deutschen Sozialpolitik in der Wiedervereinigung," in *Archiv für Sozialgeschichte* 47 (2007), pp. 527–42.

70. Gvt, AER 1991, March 11, 1991, Printed matter 12/223, no. 1 and 13.

71. Gvt, AER 1991, no. 84.

72. Gvt, AER 1991, no. 21-3.

73. Gvt, AER 1991, no. 34.

74. Gvt, AER 1992, January 30, 1992, Printed matter 12/2018, no. 5.

75. Gvt, AER 1991, no. 14-5 and 87.

76. Council, AS 1991/92, "'The Economic Integration in Germany. Perspectives – Approaches – Risks,' enclosed Special Survey 13 April 1991 'Keeping a Market-Oriented Approach. Economic Policy for the New Länder,'" November 12, 1991, no. 1 and 8.

77. Council, AS 1991/92, Special Survey, no. 1.

78. Council, AS 1991/92, Special Survey, no. 3 (quotes), part III and IV, no. 20.

79. Council, AS 1991/92, no. 1* and 19*; Gvt, AER 1992.

80. Gvt, AER 1992, January 30, 1992, no. 9. East German productivity in 1991 corresponded to the level of West German productivity in 1952/53.

81. Council, AS 1991/92, no. 3*-15*.

82. Gvt, AER 1992, no. 10 and 11; Council, AS 1991/92, no. 234 (quote).

83. Council, AS 1992/93, "For Growth Orientation – Against Crippling Disputes on Distribution," November 16, 1992, no. 213 and 214 (quote); Gvt, AER 1993, February 11, 1993, Printed matter 12/4330, no. 1-3.

84. Council, AS 1992/93, preface, no. 5*, 8*, 42* and 208; Gvt, AER 1993, no. 7 and 9 (employment numbers and unit labor costs for East Germany).

85. Letters by Professor of Economics Joachim Starbatty to the Minister of Economic Affairs Jürgen Möllemann and to Chancellor Helmut Kohl, February 21, 1992, fol. 337-8, German National Archives, Ministry of Economic Affairs, General Questions of Industrial Policy, B 102/400226 vol. 19, February 1-April 30, 1992, fol. 337-8. Starbatty was Chairman of the free-market leaning Action Group Social Market Economy. See also B 102/400225 vol. 18, December 6-January 30, 1992.

86. Council, AS 1992/93, no. 5*.

87. Council, AS 1993/94, "Time to Act –Strengthening the Driving Forces," November 15, 1993, preface and no. 1*-40*.

88. Philip Ther, *Europe since 1989: A History* (Princeton: Princeton University Press, 2016).

89. Marcus Böick, "'Im Säurebad der Einheit.' Die Treuhandanstalt in den medien-öffentlichen Debatten der frühen 1990er Jahre," in *Deutschland Archiv* 43 (2010), pp. 425-32.

90. Roland Czada, "Vereinigungskrise und Standortdebatte. Der Beitrag der Wiedervereinigung zur Krise des westdeutschen Modells," in *Leviathan* 26 (1998), pp. 24-59; Wencke Meteling, "Miraculous Germany: Changing Per-

ceptions of German Economic Performance, in *Renewal: A Journal of Social De-mocracy* 22 (2014), pp. 60-73; Wencke Meteling, "Internationale Konkurrenz als nationale Bedrohung – Zur politischen Maxime der 'Standortsicherung' in den neunziger Jahren," in Ralph Jessen (ed.), *Konkurrenz in der Geschich-te. Praktiken – Werte – Institutionalisierungen* (Frankfurt/New York: Campus, 2015), pp. 289-315.

Part III

Freedom and Its Discontents

Chapter 13

Estonia's Path Out of the Cold War

Mart Laar

In 1940, following the Nazi-Soviet conspiracy of 1939, the Soviet Union occupied and annexed three independent countries on the shores of the Baltic Sea: Estonia, Latvia and Lithuania. In so doing the Kremlin took a bite it never could fully digest. The Western world did not recognize the annexation and continued this non-recognition policy until each Baltic country restored its statehood. Throughout this time, diplomatic representatives of the Baltic countries continued to work in Western capitals. The Soviet Union sought on several occasions to gain from the West *de jure* recognition of Baltic countries as part of the Soviet Union, but without success.

As soon as 1940-41 massive resistance began in the Baltic countries themselves against Soviet rule with the aim to restore statehood. After mass deportations on June 14, 1941 partisan movements spontaneously emerged that helped to push the Soviets out of the country. When the German occupation started, the resistance movement again went underground. By the time the Red Army reached Estonian borders in 1944, Estonians joined the German army, helping to stop the Soviets for eight months. Then in autumn 1944 Hitler decided to abandon Estonia and the Red Army took the country over again.

During the German retreat Estonians attempted to restore the independent Republic and form a new government, but they were crushed by Soviet tanks. Nevertheless, for many people the war was not over. Men and women hid in forests and swamps and continued to fight. They were called forest brothers. Fighting went on for more than ten years, with the last known forest brother killed in action in 1978. Even then their legend lived on. And this legend was much harder to destroy. The forest brothers created a tradition of resistance. They were followed by underground networks of school youth, then by political dissidents. An important role was also played by cultural resistance—keeping up the Estonian language, Estonian cultural orientation and traditions, and most importantly, memory. All this helped to keep the flame of resistance alive, even though for many people it only appeared to be smoldering ash.

Although daily life was strongly influenced by Soviet power, Estonia was still deeply different from the rest of the USSR. The majority of Estonians did not accept the new Soviet identity as their own. In the Baltic countries, where Soviet power had been present one generation less than in the other parts of Soviet Empire, there were many people who remembered lost independence. The time dimension of their world was orientated to the pre-Soviet past. The traditions of free Estonia were kept alive. Estonians remained culturally oriented towards Western Europe and Scandinavia. Everyday contacts with life in the Nordic countries, in particular via access to Finnish television, played an important role in Estonian lives. The Baltic people sympathized with the West and were eager to get any information beyond the Iron Curtain. As a result, Estonians kept their history alive through their memories of independence, while looking at the same time to the future.

In the late 1980s, with a weakening of the Soviet Union and increasing Western pressure, dissident movements everywhere in the Soviet bloc gathered strength, becoming more and more active. The morosity of the Soviet system became clear to more and more people. In addition, the policy of Ronald Reagan and Margaret Thatcher pushed the Soviet Union into a corner. In order to survive and become socio-economically competitive the Soviets would have to reform. As the entire Soviet system was built upon fear and strength, the system of control began to disintegrate. The stagnant economy began to collapse.

I and most other people from the future party *Isämaa* came from the anticommunist resistance. I had been active in independent student movements that tried to preserve historical memory of the nation. I participated in an underground press and published my first works in *samizdat* not under my own name. I was interrogated by the KGB and lost my job at the university.

The collapsing Soviet system opened up new possibilities for my generation; we did not want to heal it, we wanted to crush it. We used every possibility to push boundaries more and more every month. I participated actively in the early demonstrations and played a role in the buildup of the first public national organization in Estonia, the Estonian Heritage Society, which aimed to reestablish Estonia's historical memory. We started to gather oral histories from the communist years. After I published the early results of my work, I was personally attacked and a criminal case was brought against me. I was accused of insulting the Soviet army and security. I almost became the last political prisoner in the Soviet Union. Protests luckily stopped the authorities. During the "singing revolution" the Soviet system practically collapsed in our country.

Seen from one perspective, we lived in a new reality. From another perspective, however, the old Soviet institutions were all still intact and Estonia was still part of the Soviet Union. Popular resistance sought to force former communist leaders from power, but those leaders maneuvered to stay in power by appearing to change their stripes. A second echelon of reform Communists founded the so-called Popular Front that supported *perestroika* and fought both the former nomenklatura and the growing independence movement.

During these developments the economic situation in the Soviet Union deteriorated. In steady decline since the mid-1970s, by 1988 the economy began to worsen rapidly. This gave more strength to independence demands. More and more people began to understand that to get out of the economic crises we needed to start market-orientated reforms rooted in programs of stabilization and liberalization. To do this, we believed we had to get out from the Soviet Union and ditch communism.

Changing Estonian attitudes were documented by polls conducted by EMOR. People were asked what kind of political status they would want Estonia acquire to the future. Possible answers were "a Union republic within the present federation (USSR)," "an independent state in a confederation (USSR)," or "an independent state outside the USSR." In 1988 very few people wanted the current situation just to continue; the options of confederation and independence received roughly equal support. By April 1989, however, 56% preferred independence and 39% preferred a confederation.

Different visions for an independent Estonia emerged. Many were a function of one's perceptions of Moscow's strength. As long as the Kremlin still seemed strong, the idea was presented to make Estonia another Hungary, independent but with "goulash socialism," and still inside the Soviet bloc.

Meanwhile, after the revolutions of 1989 and subsequent electoral changes, the former Soviet satellite states in Central and Eastern European countries each turned their focus to a sustainable transformation into capitalist democracies. Thus, the Hungarian example was no longer relevant for Tallinn. Estonia then looked to Finland, an independent but non-aligned state, even if Estonian perceptions of Finland were somewhat awkward. In the Estonian mind, for instance, Finland's country code SF (Suomi-Finland) translated into Soviet Finland (which of course was not the true political reality).

It quickly became clear that the Soviet Union was so weakened that it could not force the Baltic countries to stay in the Union, and therefore all these ideas fell by the wayside. The Estonian people decided to take their future into their own hands. Since the Estonian Republic still existed de jure—if not de facto—and was recognized by the Western powers, it was merely necessary to seek to "restore" it. For this purpose, citizens of Estonia had to be registered. Then citizens could elect representatives to the Congress of Estonia, which could determine the future of the country. On February 24, 1990 the Estonian Congress was elected, and some weeks later also the Supreme Soviet of the Estonian SSR, representing all inhabitants of the Estonian SSR, including the Soviet army. Each of these bodies declared that it would take steps toward the restoration of an independent Estonia.

The Congress of Estonia was ready to cut connections with the Soviet past more radically, the Supreme Soviet tried to move more carefully. The main difference between them lay in the choice how to restore independence: through restitution of the pre-war Estonian Republic on the grounds of international law; or by gradually taking over the existing organs of state power, seceding from the Soviet Union and proclaiming a new Estonian Republic. The majority of Estonians thought that the two must cooperate: both options for regaining independence should be considered and one of them realized, depending on circumstances.

From the beginning of 1990 these institutions took the lead in restoring the independence of Estonia and to gain international support for/in this process. The Estonian Congress was recognized in the West, but not in Moscow; the Supreme Soviet in turn was recognized as legitimate by Moscow and to some extent also in the West. As the Western powers had continued *de jure* to recognize the existence of an occupied Estonian Republic, it was not necessary to re-recognize the state. One needed only to restore diplomatic relations. And this is exactly what happened in 1991.

During all of these discussions the Soviet Union collapsed in 1991 and then officially ceased to exist. The Baltic countries declared that they were again independent in the wake of the August coup, and the Western world re-established diplomatic ties. Estonia, Latvia and Lithuania also became members of the United Nations and they reentered other international organizations, such as the International Parliamentary Union or the Olympic movement, where their membership had lain dormant for the previous five decades.

Nonetheless, the main question remained: where did the Baltic countries belong? Would they stay in the same orbit with the other former Soviet republics—and in Russia's sphere of influence? Or would they return to the West? Before World War II Estonia had stayed outside of alliances and security arrangements and then lost its independence. In other words, we had once tried to be neutral, and for us (unlike for Finland and Sweden) this was not the best experience. The lesson from the past was clear: Estonia must not stand alone in the future again; it must stay outside Russia's near abroad: it must take sides and become member of security arrangements with countries sharing similar values.

At the same time, we knew perfectly well that an important reason for the survival of our nation during the decades of Communist oppression was its strong moral and ideational connection with the rest of Europe. People expected that the self-evident outcome of political liberation would be their "return to Europe"—that is, to become members of both the EU and NATO. It was clear that this might not be possible immediately. But if we did not start to move toward our goals with urgency, it might be possible that we would never manage to attain the desired outcome for our country.

At the beginning our hopes seemed like empty words, because in reality Estonia had been so bound into to what now was the post-Soviet space. At the start of 1992 Estonia was totally dependent on Russia. 92.5% of trade was with Russia, and most of our energy resources came from the East as well. No one could imagine how Estonia could cut loose by severing so many old ties and creating so many new ones. But if we wanted to join the West, we had to.

As a first step we had to quit the ruble zone. In summer 1992 Estonia introduced its own convertible currency, the Estonian kroon, using currency board arrangements and pegging it to the Deutschmark. After a whole year of economic troubles caused by the ruble's galloping inflation, the misery of empty grocery stores, never-ending queues, food stamps instead of salaries, having in one's pocket a convertible currency with the pictures of national cultural heroes on the bank notes seemed to people to be not less important than to have an Estonian passport, which also came into use that same summer.

The desire to join the West found further ratification by the first free elections of post-Soviet Estonia, which made Lennart Meri president and me Prime Minister. We made membership in both the EU and NATO our priority.

Estonia could have taken several avenues. One would have been to join the Commonwealth of Independent States (CIS). The CIS reminded the Balts too much of the former USSR, however, and there was little appetite for being part of some kind of federal Russia.

A second path could have been to establish special relations with Russia in ways similar to Finland. The Finnish-Russian relationship was also changing, however; the good neighborliness and friendship treaty Finland had with the now-collapsed USSR was dead. Helsinki was moving out of the bear's shadow and, together with Sweden and Austria, poised to join the EU. What's more, Russia understood Estonian independence completely differently than that of Finland: for Russia the former was in no way a normality.

A third path could have been Baltic cooperation or Baltic Union. This had existed at least on paper before World War II and the prospect was raised once again during the struggle to regain independence. Prior to World War II, Estonian experts criticized the Baltic Union because it was in effect impotent and paralyzed. It looked to be more problem than solution. During the restoration of independence, however, it at least seemed to function: Baltic cooperation has become a reality. Actually, since then it has developed into larger Baltic-Nordic cooperation.

At the same time, the world around us in the Baltic region was continually changing. Most important in this regard was the start of the parallel processes of opening the European Union and NATO to new members after the Cold War. With Finland and Sweden joining European Union in 1995 all Nordic countries were now members of either the European Union or NATO or both. In this context the return to Europe became for Estonia the most normal direction. And yet this path to rejoin Western Europe would also be the most challenging.

To take the road toward Europe we had work hard at the painful transition from totalitarianism to democracy, from command to market economy—to make this transition sustainable in the long run. It was a very complicated process, because political and economic reforms had to happen simultaneously.

To really achieve the necessary changes, we had to crush communism, not to heal it. We tried to learn from the experiences of other countries, which had already undergone a similar transition, such as Poland, Hungary, Czechoslovakia and Slovenia. Some lessons emerged. One of these is summed up by the well-known advertising slogan: "Just do it!" In other words, be decisive about adopting reforms and stick with them despite the short-term pain they bring.

We understood that the choice for us was not one of a higher or lower level of equilibrium but either continuing and accelerating decline without systemic change or the introduction of market-oriented reforms. Of course these reforms would temporarily aggravate income problems, but over the longer term they offered the prospect of healthy future growth. During the first reform government of Estonia, then, the dividing line between the parties of the government and opposition was not defined by traditional left-right differences, but rather by the readiness or not to embrace decisive economic and political reforms.

The most basic and vital change, however, had to take place in the hearts and minds of the Estonian people. In the era of Soviet-imposed socialism, most people had withdrawn into some kind of private "quietism." People were not used to thinking for themselves, taking the initiative or assuming risks. Many had to be shaken free of the illusion that somehow someone else was going to come along and solve their problems for them. It was necessary to energize people, to get them moving, to force them to make decisions and take responsibility for themselves. To cut back the overgrown state and get people to step up to greater responsibility, various public functions had to be shifted from the central government to the electorate, to ordinary citizens. Ready to help those who showed a genuine readiness to help themselves, the government in many cases assisted to finance precisely such efforts.

Trying to use this "the window of opportunity" after the 1992 elections, Estonia chose the path of maximum liberalization and launched most of its bold reforms: no tariffs, no subsidies, no regulated prices, no progressive taxation. Soon the private sector boomed and foreign investments grew rapidly. Estonia was presented as the "shining star from the Baltics."

Nevertheless, most crucial for us during this period were relations with Moscow. The more we moved West, the worse relations became with the East. The new Western-orientated government in Estonia was described in Russia as fascist and Russophobe. President Yeltsin as well as the leader of Russia's so-called liberal democrats, Zhirinovsky, made loud angry statements condemning Estonia. We quickly understood, however, that their rhetoric was mostly targeted at their domestic audience. Great barkers are really not biters.

More dangerous was Russia's "near abroad" doctrine, propagated by Sergei Karaganov, adviser to the Russian president. In Karaganov's view, Russia had the duty, even obligation, to keep peace, stability and prosperity in the territories around it. For this, however, Russia had to have special rights in these territories. While it was never clearly spelled out exactly which countries belonged to the supposed "near abroad," it appeared to encompass the territory of the former Russian Empire or that of the former Soviet Union plus Poland and Finland. Soon Poland and Finland were dropped, however.

To exert influence in the "near abroad," Russia felt it needed actively to use Russian-speaking minorities and to present itself as a defender of their rights. In this vein, the "near abroad" doctrine became a real threat for the Baltic countries, opening possibilities to intervene in our internal affairs. They were anyway described as among "former Soviet republics"—which effectively was nearly same being part of the "near abroad." Moreover, at the beginning the notion of the "near abroad" appeared to be connected with the existence of a significant Russian-speaking minority, and then later it became more and more connected with religion: Eastern or Russian Orthodoxy.

The situation was not easy. If we did not want to be part of the "near abroad," we had to get out of it immediately. For this we actually needed three steps.

First, we had to be successful in our transition. Signing an economic treaty with Estonia in 1994, U.S. Vice President Al Gore said that Estonia needed to continue to "just do it!" He added that Estonia's most valuable export product was hope. We needed to demonstrate to other countries how to be successful.

Second, we had to demonstrate that we could manage without Russia. We had to be truly independent. To achieve this, our entire economy had to be turned from East to West. Cheap, low quality products sent to a large eastern market had to be replaced by high quality products suitable for the world market. All energy coming from Russia had to be acquired on a market basis and all energy debts had to be paid.

Third, we had to get Russian troops out of the country. This was most difficult task, as it did not depend just on us. Russia was not interested at all in withdrawing Red Army troops from the Baltics. The Kremlin understood perfectly that by keeping military bases in the Baltics it would be able to maintain its influence. Militarily it would have little significance, but the Red Army presence could sabotage Baltic integration with the European Union, not to mention NATO. The continued presence of Russian troops also hindered foreign investments in the country, which in turn carried repercussions for our stability and economic viability as a state.

Russia, if it wanted to, could just sit and watch. That alone would be obstructive to the Baltics' efforts to join Europe. So the issue of Russian troops overshadowed all others, and bargaining over the conditions for the withdrawal of Russian troops from Estonia was especially painful. The Russian government tried to use the question of the Russian-speaking minority to put political pressure on the Estonian government. Several times the withdrawal was just halted. Estonia at the same time tried to make the stay of the Russian forces as inconvenient as possible. They were not allowed to bring replacement forces from Russia. Their possibilities to move between bases inside of Estonia were strictly limited. In 1994 Estonian police and border guard units took control of the city of Paldiski, where the Russian nuclear submarine training center was situated. Estonia also developed and equipped its military forces with new modern weaponry. All this was done to incentivize Russia to pull back its troops faster.

The reduction of Soviet/Russian military forces—from some 100,000 Soviet soldiers at the height of Soviet power to a few thousand left in the summer of 1994—was a positive development. But these last forces looked as if they had decided to stay there forever. To get these last troops to move, we had to put strong international pressure on Moscow. And to get that we felt we had to prove our worth. That meant we had to be really successful and independent—and to have friends.

Estonia succeeded in finding such friends, not only in the form of support by international institutions such as the United Nations and European Union, but also by key political leaders. For Estonia the most significant help came from Swedish Prime Minister Carl Bildt, German Chancellor Helmut Kohl and President Bill Clinton. Carl Bildt had contacts in Russia and spent lot of time in Russia explaining why troop withdrawal was useful for the Russians themselves. At the same time he held contacts with European leaders, trying to gain more attention for the problem in the Baltics. Helmut Kohl and Bill Clinton in turn used their influence on Russian President Boris Yeltsin, making clear to him that he could not escape the problem and would have to sign the treaty concerning the full withdrawal of former Soviet troops.

Finally, in July 1994 such a treaty was concluded and signed in Moscow. Despite some questions concerning the incomplete moving of the nuclear submarine training center in Paldiski, on August 31, 1994 Estonia celebrated the withdrawal of Russian troops from its soil. Only at this moment was Estonia truly ready to proceed further in its efforts to join Western political, economic and defense structures.

In 1994 the Second World War had ended for us at last. The Cold War, too, was over—but not history. For many countries it actually started—new challenges lay ahead. It was not clear where several countries would or should belong, including Russia itself. For Russia some

Central and Eastern European and especially CIS states belonged to its "near-abroad." But the people of these countries did not necessarily agree. So while the decisive enlargement of the EU and NATO resolved some problems for some countries, a positive denouement could not be witnessed everywhere. In some countries Russia's military presence still continues or has reappeared, creating problems and conflicts. In countries like Georgia or Ukraine, the tensions might even culminate in war. It is crucial to avoid hot war at all costs. The Cold War may be over, but conflicts in Europe can only be a thing of the past once there are not more "grey zones," no more ethnic or religious strife and certainly no territorial or boundary disputes.

Chapter 14

The Baltic Road to Freedom and the Fall of the Soviet Union

Jón Baldvin Hannibalsson

Time Is On Their Side

June 5, 1990. A major CSCE conference on human rights was held in Copenhagen, at the invitation of the Foreign Minister of Denmark, Uffe Ellemann Jensen. In attendance were the foreign ministers of all European states, plus the United States and Canada. This conference was part of a series of meetings laying the groundwork for new relations between European states in the post-Cold War era. The Berlin Wall had been torn down, Eastern Europe had been set free, and democratically constituted governments had been formed in the Baltic states, although they remained within the Soviet Union.

The newly appointed foreign ministers of the then still Soviet Baltic republics, Lennart Meri, Janis Jurkans and Algirdas Saudargas, were in Copenhagen to plead their case for restored independence. The Soviets presented the host with an ultimatum: if they stay, we leave. The Danish hosts caved in and the Baltic foreign ministers were shown the door. When I heard the news, I threw away my prepared text and spoke exclusively on the Baltic issue, because their voices had been silenced. I was the only minister to do so. Here are the relevant excerpts from my spontaneous speech, quoted from the Danish Foreign Ministry's transcript:[1]

> The Berlin walls have started tumbling down. The nations of central- and eastern Europe, who suffered too long from under an alien system, that was imposed upon them by military force, have been set free. The transition from totalitarianism to freedom is a tortuous one. Before things start to get better they may even get worse. But at least there is hope at the end of the tunnel. The main thing is that we see people grappling with pragmatic solutions instead of confrontation behind fortification. There is a longing for

openess and a striving for co-operation. That is the most hopeful change that has occurred.

So far, so good. Since we started on this long journey we haven't suffered any major setbacks. But Tienanmen Square, outbursts of ethnic violence in eastern Europe, within the Soviet Union, in Kashmir, South Africa and elsewhere, are there to remind us how precarious is the peace. And how easily the flames of hatred can flare up again.

We are talking about political leadership. It so happens that the president of the Soviet Union, Mr Gorbachev, is acting out the greatest historical role of any statesman of the post-war era. He has been the initiator of change, a pioneer of peaceful reforms. His refraining from the use of force to halt the democratic revolution in eastern Europe actually made it all possible.

But every step that he takes from here onwards is wrought with dangers. The long delayed economic reforms within the USSR may bring social upheaval in its wake. The use of force in re-pressing legitimate claims to independence of the Baltic nations could destroy our confidence in our unfailing commitment to the universal human values of the rights of nations to independence and sovereignty.

We can not pretend that the problem of the Baltic states can be glossed over or be forgotten, lest we endanger the peace process. The simple fact is: Human rights and the rigths of nations are in-divisible. Those universal human values can not be handed out as privileges to be enjoyed by some of us, but denied to others.

The undisputed historical fact is that the Baltic nations were inde-pendent states, recognised as such by the international community. During the war they suffered the fate of military invasions, occupa-tion and illegal annexation. The illegality of this act of war has by now been recognised by the Soviet congress of deputies.

There can therefore be no solution to this problem that is compat-ible with the Helsinki-Vienna process other than full recognition of the Baltic nations` right to independence. At the same time the legitimate security interests of the Soviet Union in the Baltic sea area should be recognised and negotiated. Any use of force, be it economic or military, to keep those nations illegally and against their will within the Soviet Union, is in contradiction to the new CSCE spirit and will unavoidably put at risk further progress towards a new and stable security order for Europe.

That would be a misfortune, not only for the Baltic nations, but for the Soviet Union themselves and for the rest of Europe as well. Peaceful negotiations, between the Soviet government and the democratically elected governments of the Baltic states, is a *crucial test* of the Soviet Union's commitment to the principles of peaceful reform and fundamental democratic values.

When I stepped down from the podium, a man jumped up and embraced me and exclaimed, "What a privilege it is to be the representative of a small nation and be allowed to speak the truth." This was Max Kampelmann, a renowned Sovietologist and U.S. negotiator. As I headed for my seat, a burly heavyweight shook his fist at me: "Shame on you, Mr. Hannibalsson," he declared. "There was not a word of truth in what you said about the Soviet Union in your speech." This was Yuri Rhesetov, a Soviet expert on human rights in the Geneva negotiations and later Russia's ambassador in Reykjavík. With the U.S. representative ashamed and the Soviet one angry, I felt I was on the right path.

From then on, in every forum where Iceland had a platform and an audience, we insisted on reminding those who wished to forget. We kept the argument running everywhere: at the UN, within NATO, in the European Council, at CSCE conferences, at Social Democratic party leaders' meetings. I wish in this context to pay tribute to my Danish colleague, Uffe-Ellemann Jensen, who soon after Copenhagen joined me in this effort and proved to be an effective champion for our cause, not least within the European Community, where I had no access.

The Baltic Road to Freedom

For almost half a century, the Baltic nations were the forgotten nations of Europe. Their lands had been erased from the map; their national identities and distinct cultures had partly gone underground.

They had simply disappeared from the political radar screen of the outside world. When discussing the Baltic issue with a distinguished foreign minister of a NATO country, he dismissed the subject with a wave of his hand and added, "Haven't these peoples always belonged to Russia anyway?"

Two events that caught the imagination of the outside world did more than anything else to change this attitude. One was the "Singing Revolution" in June 1988. Just about one third of the Estonian nation assembled in the Tallinn Song Festival Grounds, singing patriotic songs and celebrating freedom. Similar events were also staged in Latvia and Lithuania. The world had known cases of Gandhian civil disobedience against injustice before—but singing oneself to freedom was a novelty.

The other event, which made it onto front pages and TV screens around the globe, was the "human chain" of August 1989—also called the Baltic Way. Almost two million people holding hands, from Tallinn in the north to Vilnius in the south, to protest against the Molotov-Ribbentrop Pact and its secret protocols from half a century before. This infamous pact between the two dictators, Hitler and Stalin, had signaled the beginning of the Second World War and gave Stalin a free hand to invade Poland, the Baltic countries and Finland, one of the Nordic countries.

Those inspiring events did not only signal national reawakening. It was a symbol of powerful grassroots democracy. The leaders of the independence movements—the Popular Fronts of Estonia, Latvia and Lithuania—had therefore every reason to believe that they would be welcomed with open arms back into the family of European democracies. After all, most of the West European states had never *de jure* recognized the annexation of the Baltic states into the Soviet Union.

The freedom fighters were in for a rude awakening. When they sent their representatives abroad to solicit recognition of their restored democracies, they were received by polite annoyance. The restoration of independence of the Baltic states—which implied breaking away from the Soviet Union—did not fit in with the scheme of things, within which Western leaders were negotiating in partnership with Soviet leader Mikhail Gorbachev to end the Cold War. Gradually it dawned upon men like Vytautas Landsbergis of Lithuania and Lennart Meri of Estonia that they were being treated as unwelcome intruders into the amiable fraternity of the major powers, which simply had a different agenda.

The Baltic independence movements had unknowingly put the leaders of the big Western democracies upon the horns of a dilemma of their own creation, one from which they couldn't disentangle themselves without outside help. This is a chapter in the story of the endgame of the Cold War, which the major powers in the West understandably want to forget, but which in turn the current masters in the Kremlin are by the same token unwilling to forget.

First, we must acknowledge that the Singing Revolution could not have gathered momentum were it not for Gorbachev's policy of *glasnost* and *perestroika*—his signatory trademarks for opening up and structural reform. Even if the opening up was both timid and limited and effective structural reform never truly materialized, Gorbachev, by ultimately *refusing to use force* to keep the Soviet Union together, made all the change possible.

Second, if through their actions the Baltic states could successfully break away from the Soviet Union, they could signal the beginning of the end of the empire. Not only would such a political tsunami engulf Gorbachev personally, the Communist Party of the Soviet Union would be caught up in its waves as well.

Of course we were all questioning ourselves at the time: Could such a tremendous transformation as the potential breakup of the Union occur peacefully? Or would disintegration unleash a bitter war, with unforeseeable consequences? For a while during the first weeks of 1991, we were teetering on the brink.

Third, the leaders of the major Western powers—George H. W. Bush, Helmut Kohl, François Mitterand and the Iron Lady, Margaret Thatcher—had all staked the success of their policy of ending Cold War antagonism on the political fate of a single individual—Gorbachev. If he were to be deposed, they thought, the hardliners would be back. That would mean a return to the Cold War and—in the worst case scenario—an escalation into full blown war.

Fourth, there was a lot at stake, including disarmament—both nuclear and conventional, reduction in military forces and arms control, the peaceful reunification of Germany and united Germany's continued membership in NATO, the liberation of the nations of Central and Eastern Europe, and mutual hopes for a "peace dividend."

Gorbachev's last line of defense was preventing the breakup of the Soviet Union. If that line wouldn't hold, everything else would be lost.

The leaders of the West found themselves facing a tough choice: should all the aforementioned benefits of ending the Cold War be sacrificed by supporting the small Baltic nations' legal rights and aspirations for restored independence? Or should those small nations —in the name of maintaining peace and stability—sacrifice their dreams, at least for the time being?

There was an almost unbridgeable gap between the official, idealistic rhetoric about the expansion of democracy, human rights and the rule of law—and the coldblooded realpolitik being pursued *de facto* behind closed doors.

This is why President Bush gave his infamous "Chicken Kiev" speech on August 1, 1991, three weeks before the declaration of independence of Ukraine. In it he appealed to the Ukrainians "not to succumb to suicidal nationalism" but to keep the Soviet Union together—in the name of peace and stability.[2]

This is why Chancellor Kohl and President Mitterrand wrote a joint letter to president Landsbergis, urging him to postpone the implementation of Lithuania's declaration of independence of March 11, 1990 and instead to seek negotiations with Lithuania's colonial masters, without prior conditions .[3]

This is why the leaders of the restored Baltic democracies were turned away from conferences where the "New World Order" was being negotiated between the old Cold War adversaries, as potential "spoilers of the peace."[4]

Western Policy:
Keep the Soviet Union Together at All Costs?

When recounting this story more than a quarter of a century later, many questions remain unanswered. One of them is whether the leaders of Western democracy were really so callous as to be ready to sacrifice the legitimate claims of the Baltic nations to restored independence—in return for political gain in dealing with the Soviets. Although it appears to have been so, the real answer is perhaps a little more subtle.

Keep in mind that the Baltic nations had disappeared from the political radar screen for almost half a century. In that sense they had become "forgotten nations." The comment by the distinguished foreign minister of a NATO country that I cited earlier—"Haven't these peoples always belonged to Russia anyway?"—was symptomatic of a way of thinking.

If this was really the accepted view in the chancelleries of Europe, Western leaders were, presumably, not thinking in terms of sacrificing anything. Bear in mind that most of those major powers in the West—the United Kingdom, France, Spain and also the United States—were all ex-colonial powers. The United States suffered a devastating civil war to prevent the breakup of the union. I am not for a moment suggesting that the American Civil War, with the aim of emancipating the slaves, should be compared with imperial aggression with the aim of enslaving free nations. *But preventing the breakup of the union* was the common principle.

The United Kingdom today is in the grip of an existential crisis—as is Spain—in mortal fear of the breakup of the union. Colonial powers—think of the British, the French and the Spanish empires—have fought ferocious wars trying to prevent the breakup of their empires.

The leaders of major powers with a colonial past are not to be expected to be at the forefront in defending the rights of small nations to national self-determination. Rarely have small nations been let free by a benevolent act of major powers. They simply have to liberate themselves. Under such circumstances, the concept of "solidarity of small nations" may have some practical relevance, against all odds.

When it had actually become official Western policy from 1990 onwards to keep the Soviet Union together at all cost—in the name of peace and stability—it should have been obvious that something had gone wrong. What was wrong? Among other things a wrong conception of the political and economic longevity of the Soviet Union under the *status quo*. Despite the rhetoric of reform, the reality was quite different. The economy was totally paralyzed. They couldn't deliver the goods.

The gap between the self-glorification of the Soviet power elite and the reality that ordinary people faced had become too wide. It was absurd for the leaders of the West to put all their stakes on the political fate of a single individual. It was not a given that the hardliners would return, although Gorbachev would be removed from power. Reality turned out to be different, as proven by subsequent events. The analysis was superficial and the policy misconceived.

The Soviet Union was in an existential crisis that the Soviet power elite didn't know how to tackle. The Empire was on the verge of breakdown, as had been the fate of the British and French colonial systems after the war. To me it was outrageous to listen to the leaders of the West, preaching to the captive nations that they should stay in, to hold the Soviet Union together at all cost—in the name of peace and stability. To my ears this sounded like an Orwellian oxymoron. I never saw nor heard convincing evidence justifying this policy.

Recently I have repeatedly been asked by my Baltic friends in leading positions, if there is any truth in what U.S. emissaries are now telling them, i.e. that Iceland's action on the Baltic issue was actually U.S.-inspired and directed; that since the US was in a difficult position to speak up (due to among other things the Gorbachev-partnership and the Gulf War in January 1991) they prompted Iceland on their behalf and with their tacid approval. To tell the truth, it must then have been such a secret U.S. operation that it passed me by.

Why Iceland?

I am often asked why Iceland didn't simply accept the conventional wisdom of the leaders of the West on the Baltic issue? Certainly there was no vital national interest involved. On the contrary, Iceland was dependent upon the Soviet Union for oil and gas—the life blood of any developed economy—since the British placed an embargo upon Iceland during the Cod Wars in the 1950s.[5] And didn't we know that small nations are supposed to seek shelter with and follow the leadership of the major powers?

The truth is that we were reluctant followers. The leaders of the West were obviously pursuing their own agenda. Apart from the envisaged benefits of ending the Cold War, the United States needed Soviet acquiescence for the invasion of Iraq (which was a Soviet ally) in January 1991. For the German government the peaceful unification of their country was naturally paramount. If that agenda did not include the restored independence of the Baltic nations, then that was bad luck for them. There was simply too much at risk, it was believed, by allowing the restoration of independence of the Baltic countries to disrupt the Gorbachev partnership. On that score, Western leadership was more or less united.

We simply disagreed. When it had become the declared policy of the Western democracies on ending the Cold War that the Soviet Union had to be kept together at all cost—in the name of peace and stability—it should have dawned upon thinking persons that something was seriously wrong.

What was wrong? First and foremost, this naive infatuation with Gorbachev was both ill-conceived and downright dangerous. It could not be taken for granted that the hardliners would be returned to power, even if Gorbachev were to be deposed. Subsequent events were soon to prove us right on that score.

We were convinced that the Soviet system itself was in the throes of existential crisis, for which their leaders had no solutions. The empire was in the process of falling apart, just as had been the fate of the British, French and other European empires after World War II. The political life expectancy of the Soviet system was greatly exaggerated.

How come that we dared assume that we had a more reliable take on political reality within the Soviet system than the CIA? Well, it so happens that my elder brother was a graduate of Moscow University and had done graduate work in both Warsaw and Krakow with, among others Leszek Kolakowski, who was a prolific writer on the shortcomings and dangers of the communist regime. Another brother of mine had studied for some time at Charles University in Prague. Both had maintained contacts with dissidents in the Soviet Union and eastern Europe, including the Baltic countries.

I myself as a Fulbright Scholar at Harvard had studied and did research on comparative economic systems. My conclusion regarding the Soviet economy was simple: it didn't work. It had lost its driving force. It was inflexible, wasteful, and inefficient, although it had sectors, mainly connected to the military, which were provided with enormous resources, with some success. In addition, the political elite—the *nomenklatura*—had lost its belief in the system. They had lost their appetite for using force to stay in power, even though the Soviet Union could only be kept together by force.

Contrary to current Russian President Vladimir Putin—who is on record saying that "the fall of the Soviet Union was the greatest geo-strategic catastrophe of the 20th century"—I was convinced in 1989/91—and I still am—that the dissolution of the Soviet Union should be welcomed as perhaps the most beneficial event of the 20th century. If it needed a little push from the Baltic nations, so much the better.

What had the Cold War been all about if not to liberate the captive nations? I was appalled listening to Western leaders preach to subjugated peoples that they should accept their fate as captive nations so that we in the West could enjoy peace and stability. To my ears this was not only a shameful betrayal, it was a blatant mistake.

I personally was reluctant to follow such a recipe. If we could make sure that we could have access to oil from other sources, we would be all right. Remember, the Soviet Union at the time was in steep economic decline. They offered low prices for low quality products. We could secure more profitable markets elsewhere. So we took a calculated risk. And this turned out to be right.

My analysis of the internal situation within the Soviet Union led to a totally different conclusion from the mainstream one. There was no need to sacrifice the rightful claims of the Baltic nations to independence for some greater good in dealing with the Soviet Union. If you are convinced that you are right—and there is a lot at stake—why not follow your conviction?

I have never been beholden by an inferiority complex for being the representative of a small nation. During my political career I have been at close quarters with several great power leaders, who were no more impressive for representing more populous states. I can also cite several examples of how small nations, if they stick together, can change the world.

January 1991: A Turning Point

January 1991 was a crucial time—a turning point. The hardliners in the Kremlin—on whose support Gorbachev increasingly depended—decided to take Western leaders at their word and "keep the Soviet Union together at all costs." That meant to prevent the imminent secession of the Baltic nations from the Soviet Union—by force, if necessary.

The justification given at the time sounds familiar today, in light of current events in Ukraine. The plan was to create incidents to justify military intervention and emergency rule from Moscow, in the name of protecting national (i.e. Russian) minorities; and to restore law and order.

The tanks started rolling. Special troups occupied strategic positions. The killing machine started doing its job. Everything was set for a crackdown on the democratic forces and "regime change"—imposed by Moscow.

I remember vividly being awakened in the middle of the night by a telephone call from President Landsbergis saying in essence: "If you mean what you have been saying in our support, come immediately to Vilnius to demonstrate your personal commitment to our cause. The presence of a NATO foreign minister matters." I was the only foreign minister from anywhere to respond to an appeal to arrive on the scene to demonstrate solidarity in their hour of peril. I visited all three capitals during those crucial days.

I shall never forget those days in the squares and on the streets of Vilnius, Riga and Tallinn. There I personally witnessed nations, unarmed and virtually alone, ready to defy military might, in the name of human dignity, freedom and self-respect. It was a privilege to be allowed to be with them during those fateful days. I came away convinced that if the Soviets would have applied full force to follow up on their original plan of regime change, it would have resulted in a terrible bloodbath.

Would Western leaders have intervened? The leaders of the Baltic independence movements were under no such delusion. In the documentary film *Those Who Dare*,[6] on Iceland's role during the Baltic independence struggle, James Baker, U.S. Secretary of State at the time, makes it absolutely clear that despite a lot of talk, Western military intervention on behalf of the Balts was never a serious consideration. They didn't do it in Budapest in 1956. They didn't do it in Prague in 1968. And it was never a serious option in Vilnius in 1991.

On January 16, 1991, the United States launched "Operation Desert Storm" to drive Sadam Hussein out of Kuwait. It is neither the first nor the last time when oil has turned out to be potent motivation for action. The Soviet Union was an ally of Iraq. To the United States it was imperative that the Soviets would support, or at least not actively oppose, the U.S.-led operation. Soviet cooperation on that score depended on maintaining the Gorbachev partnership. And indeed, Gorbachev's Soviet Union voted in the UN Secruity Council in favor of the resolution to drive Iraq out of Kuwait—with force.

Why did the Soviets back off in the Baltics at the last moment? The tanks had started rolling. Special troops had occupied strategically important places, such as ministries and TV stations. There is no doubt in my mind why they gave up. The reason is the popular reaction: hundreds of thousands of unarmed people flocked onto the streets and confronted the tanks. If the Soviets had used armed force, it could have led to one of the greatest bloobaths in postwar Europe—something for which Nobel Peace Prize holder Mikhail Gorbachev could not take responsibility. It would have meant the negation of everything for which he had stood so far. By stopping at the brink, Gorbachev saved his soul and his reputation. But at the same time the days of the Soviet Union were numbered. The reason why is that when the will to apply violence is weakened, it means the end of a police state. And that's what happened.

It was in the streets of the Baltic capitals that the hard truth was proven: the Soviet Union could only be kept together by force. From then on Western policy on the Baltic issue was in tatters. History has taught us that when the power elite of a dictatorship or a totalitarian police state loses its appetite for violence, it is the beginning of the end.

Violence or the Rule of Law

After my "official" visit to the Baltic countries in January 1991 during the political upheaval, following the Icelandic Government's agreement January 23 to "initiate talks concerning the possibility of strengthening diplomatic relations" with Lithuania, and after the Alþingi (Iceland's national parliament) adopted a resolution on February 11, 1991 calling upon the Government to "bring this issue to a conclusion by establishing diplomatic relations with Lithuania as soon as possible," the Soviet Government at long last showed its displeasure.

First they recalled their ambassador from Reykjavík for talks in Moscow. Then they delivered a strongly worded note of protest against the Icelandic Government's alleged "interference into the domestic affairs of the Soviet Union." Threats to terminate long-established bilateral trade treaties between the countries were repeated more than once to warn the strong shipowners' lobby in Icelandic politics of the consequences of the government's Baltic policy.

We decided to confront the issue, not only politically, but also on the basis of international law. I put together a team of legal experts (with an important input from Estonia) who produced a document, detailing the case of the illegality of Soviet occupation and subsequent annexation of the Baltic states. This was presented to the Soviet authorities on April 12, 1991.[7]

The argument was presented with reference to Soviet obligations under international law (specifically the Helsinki Final Act of 1975) and other major multinational treaties and precedents. We also reminded the Soviet government of the fact, that the Soviet Congress of People's Deputies had itself already accepted the case by declaring the Molotov-Ribbentrop pact of 1939 null and void December 24th.1989.

Here are some key excerpts from the Icelandic legal case:

> It is a well-recognized maxim of international law that no benefit shall be achieved through an illegal act. Refusal by the international

community to recognize illegal occupation and annexation is based on the utter condemnation of the use of force in contravention of international law. Even recent history shows that the international community will not recognize claims that such questions following illegal annexation fall solely within the domestic jurisdiction of the annexing state.

Turning to the situation in Lithuania, it can first be noted that the view that the occupation of Lithuania in 1940 was illegal has been confirmed in a decision of the Congress of People's Deputies of the Soviet Union on 24 December 1989.

Furthermore:

The incorporation of the Baltic States into the Soviet Union, which took place according to Soviet law at the beginning of August 1940, did not represent a voluntary association on a federal basis, but the seizure by force of foreign territory, i.e. an unlawful annexation under modern international law.

On the current situation it stated that

The government of Iceland attaches particular importance to the enactments of 11 March, 1990, restoring the independence of Lithuania and laying down a Provisional Basic Law (Constitution). Those pronouncements allow third states to regard the legal situation in Lithuania as one of continuity. Under this approach the enactments of 11 March, 1990 and their subsequent implementation provide evidence of fulfilment of the classical criteria of territory and population and, on the face of it, an indication of effective government.

Finally we put all this into the context of the changing political landscape, at the initiative of the Soviet Government itself:

The position of the Icelandic government towards Lithuania is to be viewed in the context of the profound changes in European relations which have taken place in recent years. In particular it should be viewed in the context of the democratic revolution that the European political landscape has undergone; a revolution rendered possible primarily by the policies of the Soviet Union.

Finally, the Icelandic government offered its services to act as a mediator between the democratically constituted governments of the Baltic countries and the Soviet government in settling the disputes.[8]

Needless to say, we never received any response from the Soviets to this sophisticated piece of scholarship.

On Gorbachev's Place in History

It should never be forgotten that Gorbachev's decision not to apply military force to maintain Soviet hegemony in Central and Eastern Europe made the peaceful ending of the Cold War possible. Gorbachev was a man of peace. For this he deserved the Nobel Peace Prize.

But in January 1991 he was on the verge of drowning the independence movements of the Baltic nations in a terrible bloodbath. At the last moment he stopped at the abyss and withdrew—again in the name of peace. By doing so he saved his soul and his place in history.

This is the reason why the man of peace, Mikhail Gorbachev—lauded as he is in the West—is less than loved in his beloved homeland, Russia. In the eyes of many Russians, who secretly share Putin's great power dreams, Gorbachev is denigrated as a loser—if not a traitor. He is said to be the man who lost everything that Soviet Russia, in the Great Patriotic War, had won through bloody sacrifices. He is blamed for not having prevented—by force if necessary—the dissoluton and collapse of the Soviet Union. In the eyes of his critics at home, Stalin may have been a tyrant, but he made the Soviet Union a world power. Gorbachev may be a good man, but with this record they deny him any claim to greatness.

To those of us who do not share any dreams of (restoring) the Russian Empire, however, Gorbachev remains the man who made a more peaceful post-Cold War world possible.

Those examples of the role individuals play in history give occasion to compare the fate of two individuals who about the same time faced similar challenges: Chairman Mao's inheritor, Deng Xiaoping, and Stalin's last inheritor, Mikhail Gorbachev. Each came to power in totalitarian states as inheritors of bloody tyrants who had failed to alleviate the poverty of the people.

Deng Xiaoping began by improving the lot of the peasants, allowing them to sell their produce in the cities. Then he opened China up for foreign direct investment and technological transfers in experimental "free trade zones." This limited approach worked. He started the most transformative economic revolution of all times, lifting hundreds of millions of Chinese from poverty to prosperity in the time span of a few decades. Like all Chinese leaders, he was in mortal fear of the dissolution of the Middle Kingdom. Economic reform, therefore, took precedence. Political reform had to wait—if it was ever to come. Hence the crackdown against student protests in Beijing's Tiananmen Square on June 4, 1989.

Gorbachev preached both: structural reform (*perestroika*) and opening (*glasnost*). At home and abroad he was considered a missionary of democratic reform and freedom of expression. But despite a lot of talk of *uskorenie*—acceleration of the economy—it remained mostly empty words. He never managed to present nor implement a comprehensive plan for reforming the Union (or even the bloc). Is it possible to reform a totalitarian police state and a centralized command economy? It turned out that Gorbachev didn't know how to do it. Instead of reform, Russians were exposed to political dissolution, economic chaos, shortages, insecurity and humiliation.

Yeltsin in post-Soviet Russia failed too. Democracy was stillborn, the economy ended up in freefall, the rule of law never took hold, corruption blossomed. Russia remained domestically weak and struggled internationally to refind the place it felt it was due among the other great powers and espcially as an equal of the United States. This is why the revanchist policies of strongman Putin find such resonance with many Russians. But for the rest of us, Russia has again become a country that is by nature dangerous to its neighbors.

This is why Gorbachev's legacy, great as it is, is less than fully appreciated in his home country.

Endgame: Dissolution of the Soviet Union

On August 19, 1991, a sequence of events started that culminated in the recognition by the international community of the restored independence of the Baltic states and the dissolution of the Soviet

Union. The scene began on the barricades in the streets of Moscow; it moved on to a modest ceremony in Höfði-House in Reykjavík less than a week later, on August 25. Five years earlier this modest villa—a former British Embassy in Reykjavík—had been the venue for the Reagan-Gorbachev summit that later turned out to have marked the beginning of the end of the Cold War. Now it was to be the venue for the recognition of the Baltic states' restored independence—a process that turned out to be unstoppable and irreversible. Let me briefly retrace the sequence of events:

- The attempted coup d'état in Moscow began on August 19.

- Two days later the North Atlantic Council met in Brussels. The meeting was held in the shadow of the attempted coup. When the proceedings started there was still some measure of uncertainty as to the question of success or failure of the coup. During an interval NATO Secretary General Manfred Wörner was requested to try to reach direct contact with Boris Yeltsin in Moscow and report back to the meeting. Within less than an hour Wörner returned with the following message from Yeltsin: The coup had failed. He, Yeltsin, and the democratic forces were now firmly in control. Yeltsin urged the NATO foreign ministers assembled in Brussels to do everything in their power to *support the democratic forces* in the Soviet Union.

- After the interval it was my turn for an intervention. Again—just as in Copenhagen a year earlier—I set aside my prepared text. I appealed directly to my colleagues to give serious consideration to the totally changed situation. I reminded them that their former refrain, namely that nothing should be said or done that might undermine Gorbachev and bring back the hardliners, was no longer valid. The hardliners had already tried their hand and failed. President Gorbachev, who had clung to the sole remaining aim to keep the Soviet Union together at any cost under a new constitution—had also failed. The new leader was Boris Yeltsin. As president of the Russian Parliament he had already appealed to Russian soldiers not to use force against the unarmed population in the Baltic countries.

- The Congress of Peoples' Deputies of the Soviet Union had already declared the Molotov-Ribbentrop pact null and void. Thus, the new Russian leader had acknowledged that the occupation and annexation of the Baltic nations into the Soviet Empire was illegal. The Baltic nations had borne the full brunt of Soviet imperial suppression, through repeated deportations and enforcement of a Russification policy. All this was in flagrant breach of the basic principles of international law and the code of conduct in interstate relations that was now in the process of being negotiated. We therefore had a moral obligation to insist on the restoration of justice for those nations, as well as other central and east European nations. The restoration of Baltic independence could be a powerful impetus for the restored independence of other nations that had been incorporated by force into the Soviet Empire.

If I remember correctly, the response to my speech was polite silence.

On my return home I "occupied" the Icelandic embassy in Copenhagen. For many hours and late into the night, I was in telephone contact with Reykjavík and the Baltic capitals. My message was simple: *In politics timing is everything.*

The time to act was right then, while there was power vacuum in Moscow and confusion reigned in the West. I issued formal invitations to the foreign ministers of the Baltic states to come to Reykjavík as soon as possible. There and then we would formally sign the relevant documents restoring full diplomatic relations between Iceland and the Baltic states and appointing ambassadors and general consuls on a mutual basis. This would soon, I argued, be followed up by others. Now was the moment to act resolutely for the sequence of events to gather momentum—*irreversibly.*

The Baltic foreign ministers—Lennart Meri of Estonia, Janis Jurkans of Latvia and Algirdas Saudargas of Lithuania—arrived in Reykjavík on August 25. On August 26 in Höfði-House the four of us signed the relevent documents and made brief statements on the significance of the event. The news had hardly been spread by international media before the invitations started to pour in: could the three foreign ministers— who formerly had been shown the door at all major gatherings of Western leaders—be persuaded to visit European capitals, as soon as possible, to repeat what had been done in Reykjavík? The process had become irreversible. For me that was "mission accomplished." A few months later the Soviet Union had broken up.

The rest is history.

What Can be Learned From All of This?

Looking back over the timespan of more than a quarter of a century, what are the most important lessons to be drawn from the Baltic experience in the aftermath of regaining independence?

The lessons of history are deeply rooted in the psyche of the Baltic nations and their leaders. When the Second World War broke out, they were left alone and unprepared to deal with their fate. That is why after 1991 reinsurance against external threats was uppermost in the Balts' minds . Their aim was to consolidate their fragile independence by "returning" to the European family of nations.

This meant joining the European Union and NATO at the earliest possible opportunity.

During the crucial period of transition from a centralized command economy to a diversified market economy and from a totalitarian state to a pluralistic democracy,—it is invaluable if you can rely on positive external support. When formulating policy and making important decisions, Baltic leaders therefore had an overall guiding principle: Would this policy or that decision fulfill the entrance requirements for the EU and NATO, or not? On behalf of the democratic West this meant firmly rejecting the legacy of Russian imperialism in the form of "spheres of influence" or the so-called "near abroad."

The European Union is not merely a customs union or a free trade area. Its primary purpose, right from the beginning, was political: to prevent war and maintain peace in Europe. The nations of Europe voluntarily apply for membership but undertake the obligation to fulfill the entrance qualifications. They are ready to give up part of their formal sovereignty in order to share in the enhanced sovereignty of the Union itself.

As for the EU internal market, every member state is under the obligation to play by the same rules. The four freedoms of trade in goods, services, financial transactions and the labor market are meant to ensure a level playing field. A win-win situation, as Americans would put it.

Although the EU is not a military organization, nontheless it provides the member states with the "soft power" projected by the most important player globally in international trade.

NATO, on the other hand, is a military alliance, open to democratic societies and providing them with collective defense and security vis-a-vis external threats. During half a century of Cold War, this U.S.-led military alliance for common security proved sufficiently strong to deter any aggression. *I bet it still can.*

This, to my mind, is the most important lesson to be learned from the Baltic post-independence experience. Right from the start, the political leadership stood united, across all political dividing lines, behind the long-term goal of joining both the EU and NATO.

Those ultimate goals enjoyed solid support among the majority of the populations. This unity of purpose gave their domestic politics—despite the political turmoil and social upheaval of the most difficult transition period—the internal discipline needed to push through and stand by difficult and unpopular decisions.

Whenever demagogues or populists wanted to take the easy way out, such moves could be averted if they conflicted with the declared purpose or undermined the capacity to fulfill the entrance qualifications. Steadfastness of purpose and long-term strategy, despite the social upheaval of the transition, helped all three Baltic nations to pull through. This has helped make the Baltic post-independence experience a success story.

Despite ethnic divisions, economic hardship and political strain, each of the Baltic states has managed to build functioning democratic institutions. They have shown the self-discipline required to fulfill the entrance qualifications of both multinational organizations, the EU and NATO. Their economies have successfully been integrated into the inner market of the European Union, including the euro. This has set them on their way of catching up with their more prosperous neighbors.

As fully-fledged members of the North Atlantic Alliance they have the full force of NATO behind them in standing up to hostile military threats to their security. This is a success story from which others can learn a lot.

Unfortunately, the Ukrainian political elite has failed utterly in securing and consolidating their newborn independence by implementing the structural reforms that would make them fit for membership in the Western alliance.

Now it is time that the Baltic leaders exert their influence within the EU and NATO in support of the Ukrainian people, who are engulfed in an existential crisis. They have the knowledge and the experience. They speak the language and share the experience of having had to cohabit with their overbearing neighbor. They are the experts. Now they have to share their post-independence experience with the Ukrainians on how to make the transition from totalitarianism to democracy—successfully.

Notes

1. The unabridged text of my CSCE conference speech in Copenhagen, June 5, 1990, can be found in Jón Baldvin Hannibalsson, *The Baltic Road to Freedom—Iceland's Role* (Lambert Academic Publishing, 2017).

2. The "Chicken Kiev" Speech is the nickname for a speech given by U.S. President George H.W. Bush in Kyiv on August 1, 1991, 3 weeks before the declaration of independence of Ukraine. It was 4 months before the December independence referendum in which 92.26% of Ukrainians voted to withdraw from the Soviet Union. In this speech Bush cautioned against what he called "suicidal nationalism." Exactly 145 days after the speech the Soviet Union collapsed. The speech is said to have been written by Condoleezza Rice, later U.S. Secretary of State under president George W. Bush. It outraged Ukrainian nationalists. *New York Times* columnist William Safire called it the "Chicken Kiev" speech in protest at what he saw as its "colossal misjudgement," very weak tone and miscalculation.

3. The text of this letter of April 26, from President Miterrand and Chancellor Kohl to president Vitautas Landsbergis, is published in the 2011 printed edition of *Baltic Worlds*, pp 8–14, and in a special issue of the 9th Baltic Conference, June 2011.

4. First, the Baltic foreign ministers were shown the door at the CSCE conference in Copenhagen in June 1990. This offensive scene was repeated later that fall when national leaders were gathered for the adoption of the Paris Charter, in the French capital, on November 20, 1990. French foreign minister Roland Dumas, had invited his Baltic colleagues to present their case at the conference. But when the Soviets protested, Dumas capitulated. Again they were shown the door. Danish Foreign Minister Uffe Ellemann Jensen and I tried to make amends by inviting the Baltic ministers to meet the international press as our guests at the conference venue. That helped bring their message to a wider audience.

5. In the latter half of the 20th century Iceland, in an informal alliance with other small coastal states, extended its territorial waters (extended economic zone) in stages up to 200 nautical miles (1954-1976). Great Britain first responded with a trade embargo on Iceland in 1954. Then the Soviet Union intervened and negotiated a bilateral trade deal with Iceland, which gradually grew in importance. In 1958, 1972 and 1975-6 the British sent in the Royal Navy, trying to enforce their fishing rights in Icelandic waters. Iceland responded by guerilla warfare, cutting the gear from behind the British trawlers under the noses of her Majesty's commanders. Iceland won all three Cod Wars. The subsequent Law of the Sea Convention (UNCLOS) was a major step forward in protecting fish stocks and the ecosystem of the oceans.

6. The documentary film *Those Who Dare*, a cooperative Icelandic-Baltic project, tells the story of Iceland's involvement in soliciting support for recognition by the international communtiy of the restoration of independence of all three Baltic states, Estonia, Latvia and Lithuania: http://axfilms.is/those-who-dare/; https://www.youtube.com/watch?v=-4UeJJxNKTc.

7. In response to the Soviet government's protest notes on February 5 and 13, 1991 against Iceland's alleged "interference into the domestic affairs of the Soviet Union," I set up a legal team under the direction of Dr. Guðmundur Eiríksson, the head of the legal department of the Ministry of Foreign Affairs, but with a valuable input from Mr. Clyde Kull, an expert from the Estonian Ministry of Foreign Affairs. After intensive work and consultations the outcome was a position paper that I presented to the Ambassador of the Soviet Union, on April 12, 1991. Landsbergis later told me that this was, as far as he knew, the most thorough and convincing presentation of the legal arguments for the Baltic countries' rights for restored independence under international law. He also meant that it had been useful when Lithuanians were negotiating with the Soviets about the withdrawal of military forces from their territory.

8. The proposal that Iceland should offer its services as a mediator between the Soviet government and the governments of the Baltic countries striving for restoration of independence first came from Edgar Savisaar, Estonia's first prime minister post independence. In light of Iceland's active support for the Baltic countries' restored independence it is perhaps not surprising that the proposal did not appeal to the Soviet government.

Chapter 15

Poland and the End of the Cold War

Janusz Onyszkiewicz

Several processes were essential to bring the Cold War to an end.[1] Among them were the changes of the political situation in Poland, the unification of Germany, a final collapse of communism in Europe, and dismantling of all instruments of Soviet domination, particularly the Warsaw Pact. In this chapter I will concentrate on these three developments.

Polish *Solidarność* ("Solidarity") and the Demise of the Communist System

It would be rather futile to assume that the totalitarian system would collapse by itself in a time of peace.... It is almost impossible to destroy the communist system from within during normal times by a dissident movement or even by the raise of masses of people.

—*Jean-Francois Revel, How the Democracies Perish*

By October 1953, the US Security Council had privately accepted that the eastern European satellite states could be freed only by general war or by the Russians themselves. Neither was possible.

—*C.J. Barlett, Global Conflict*

Soviet domination over Poland is vital to Moscow's control over Eastern Europe. Indeed, controlling Poland has been a 250-year-long Russian objective, first attained late in the eighteenth century after a protracted struggle ... Since then, every Russian government has insisted on Russia's preponderance in Polish affairs ... Control over Poland was presented as central to Russia's security and internal Russian matter... Control over Poland would be the bridge to a decisive Russian role in German affairs.

—*Zbigniew Brzezinski, Game Plan*

Russia finally managed to subordinate Poland at the end of the 18ᵗʰ century. Since then Poles tried to regain their independence at every possible opportunity. The 1794 uprising, the Napoleonic Wars, and uprisings in 1830 and 1863 showed quite vividly that Russia could conquer Poland but it could not digest it.

After many attempts Poland finally regained its independence in November 1918 as an outcome of World War I. Its independence was almost immediately challenged, however, by the Soviet Red Army. As Soviet Marshall Mikhail Tukhachevsky put it, "over the dead body of White Poland there is a path to a worldwide revolutionary conflagration." This time, Russia did not succeed because the Red Army was conclusively defeated by Poles on the outskirts of Warsaw in August 1920.

The situation changed once again as the result of World War II. Russia (as the Soviet Union), managed to regain full control over Poland, which was for Russia one of the most significant gains of the war. For decades, Poland became a part of the external Soviet empire.

During the post-war period the Soviets always considered Poland to be the most troublesome and worrying of all their communist satellites.

First, it was different because of the survival of individual farming, the strong role of the Catholic Church (which managed to successfully defend its independence) and very strong cultural and academic ties with the West, which were partly due to the existence of a strong Polish diaspora which historically had always contributed greatly to the development of Polish culture.

Second, every decade there was a major political crisis, whether the general strike and street fighting in Poznań in 1956, massive strikes and street demonstrations of students in 1968, and more strikes in 1970 in Gdansk, where the army killed several dozen protesters. On top of that, there was a growing movement of discontent among intellectuals demanding more academic and artistic freedoms and protesting against the excesses of censorship.

When in 1976 another wave of strikes was brutally suppressed by the police, leading Polish intellectuals formed a Workers Defence Committee (KOR), which began a process of open institutionalization of the Polish dissident movement. One of the most seminal was the foundation of a completely independent free trade union, albeit small and not recognized by the authorities. (It is worth knowing that according to the Convention of the International Labor Organization, ratified by communist Poland, trade unions could be organized without prior consent of the authorities. Thus, an independent trade union set up after 1976 had a certain degree of legality.)

In 1980 another strike broke out in a shipyard in Gdansk under the leadership of Lech Wałęsa. Soon, many other factories and enterprises followed and the scale of the protest was so great that the communist authorities decided to negotiate.

The agreement signed between the strikers and the government was unprecedented in a number of ways. First, it granted the right to form new trade unions free from communist party control, as well as the right to strike. Second, all political prisoners were freed and censorship was to be seriously limited. Third, it reduced the role of the Polish communist party (Polish United Workers, Party—PUWP) from its "leading role" in all aspects of public and political life to only the "leading role in the State." This freed the trade unions from communist party control.

Thus, for the first time in a communist country, a truly independent trade union—*Solidarność* or "Solidarity"—was born. Within a matter of months it had 10 million members. Under the *Solidarność* protective umbrella a whole range of civic society independent institutions began to function. What initially was only a trade union soon became a national movement aimed at the profound expansion of civil liberties. The powerful Catholic Church, led by Polish Pope John Paul II, openly sympathized with the movement (and often tried to mitigate more radical tendencies within *Solidarność*).

The dilemma *Solidarność* had to face was very serious. It could be reduced to the question how far this process could go without prompting a strong reaction by the Polish communist party and without triggering a direct Soviet intervention like the one in Czechoslovakia in 1968. The prospect loomed constantly over *Solidarność* activities. After all, everyone in Poland knew how critical it was to Soviet interests to have Poland under full control. For *Solidarność* it was absolutely clear that in the case of Soviet military intervention the West would not respond in kind. Memories of the 1956 Hungarian revolution remained fresh.

These were not theoretical speculations. The Soviet Union was ready to intervene militarily in December 1980 to stop a "creeping counterrevolution." That this did not happen was to a great extent due to very strong warnings from the United States and other Western countries. Polish communist authorities also claimed that they would be able to restore full control over the country. A similar danger came to Poland again in March of 1981. Poland's communist leadership was under heavy pressure to restore full control, not only from Moscow but also from even more desperate communist parties such as those of Romania or East Germany who were worried that the "Polish disease" could be contagious and undermine their rule.

Despite these worries, the oppressive political system continued to erode under the pressure of emerging civic society institutions and of nearly-free media operating under the trade union umbrella. In this atmosphere of growing openness, the Communist Party began to crumble. At one stage more than one million members of the Party were members of *Solidarność*.

It became clear that the only structures the communist authorities could really count on were the police and the army. Therefore, the only way to stop *Solidarność* was to implement martial law, which was finally declared on December 13, 1981. Various strikes and demonstrations were crushed by the police and the army, very harsh penalties for every kind of unauthorized activities were introduced, and about 10,000 activists were arrested. *Solidarność* and all other independent institutions were declared illegal.

Despite these harsh measures, civic society survived. This could be seen in the variety of independent cultural or academic activities (often on Church premises), but primarily in the survival and development of an underground independent press (more then 600 regularly published periodicals) as well as an existence of a vast distribution network, linked to numerous underground printing houses publishing hundreds of book titles every year. Incidentally, when in 1980 Czeslaw Miłosz—a Polish poet living in exile—was awarded a Nobel Prize the only books published in Poland with his poems that were available at the Paris Book Fair were those printed illegally outside the reach of the communist censorship.

Despite all odds, *Solidarność* also survived and continued its activities. Lech Wałęsa, the *Solidarność* leader, was interned together with most of other leadership members. Those who managed to avoid arrest set up an underground Provisional Coordinating Committee to serve as the trade union national executive. Despite many efforts by the communist secret police to disrupt it, the Provisional Coordinating Committee managed to survive underground because of a highly decentralized structure and considerable experience accumulated from World War II, when Poles formed a whole range of underground institutions, such as the underground representation of the Polish government in exile, the underground Home Army with partisans units, a schooling system etc.

These activities could not have been developed to such a scale without support from abroad. This was especially important in two areas. First was the material support for the families of those arrested or fired from work. This help took various forms—transfer of cash, legal assistance etc. What was most spectacular was a spontaneous action in many countries like Germany, France, Sweden and others of sending parcels with food, clothing, sanitary materials and medicines, which were distributed by church institutions (not only Catholic) or groups of volunteers acting under the Church umbrella.

The second area of critical importance was the supply of printing machines and printing materials for our underground press. In this respect one should note the great financial support for underground *Solidarność* and various underground institutions of civic society that emanated first and foremost from the United States, through the American trade union the AFL-CIO, as well as from various European trade unions, primarily from France, the UK, Italy, Germany and Sweden, and from Japan.

On the international scene *Solidarność* retained its membership in major international trade union organizations like the International Confederation of Free Trade Unions (ICFTU) or the International Trade Union Confederation (ITUC) and its affiliation to the UN International Labor Organization, which continued treating *Solidarność* as the genuine representative of working people in the Poland.

The dramatic consequences of martial law were augmented by the dire state of Polish economy. The economic crisis loomed over Poland even before martial law. The economic policy of the previous communist Polish leader, Edward Gierek, to embark on a huge investment program based on massive credits from the West had begun to show its weakness, especially at the very end of the 1970s. Gierek's plan to modernize industry and repay the debt through export of products of this industry to the West failed because of poor management and wrong economic assessments.

As a result, Poland's financial needs in August 1980 amounted to $9 billion, which simply could not be met without financial assistance from the West. Default was avoided in 1981 due to the readiness of the West to restructure the debt. These decisions were made to a great extent because the *Solidarność* movement created hopes that U.S. Secretary of State Alexander Haig formulated quite explicitly in his analysis send to President Reagan: "if what had happened in Poland could be consolidated this would be a historic event for the people of Eastern Europe and for Western values."[2]

The fact that Poland depended so heavily on Western financial assistance was an important factor mitigating the harshness of the martial law period. Despite Western reluctance or inability to use fully its economic tools, and because of martial law restrictions, the Polish communist authorities could not stabilize the situation. The country desperately needed far-reaching and painful economic reforms, which could not be carried out without public support and the creation of a measure of confidence and public trust in the authorities. Several attempts were made, but all of them failed, being blocked by strikes and protests organized by the *Solidarność* underground.

It became quite clear that neither the Church nor the West would recognize the artificially created *Solidarność's* poor substitutes, such as new trade unions or various councils, as a true representation of the Polish people. Attempts to reconstruct the government by offering ministerial posts to some prominent people from *Solidarność* failed as well. So at the beginning of 1989 the PUPW Central Committee gave final approval to begin official negotiations with *Solidarność* to break the political deadlock in the country. On Feb 6, 1989 the Round Table Talks began.

Despite the official format of the talks (the round table), in reality there was a clear division of sides: on the one side was *Solidarność* and on the other the Communist Party with its satellites and communist-controlled organizations, such as the official trade unions.

Both sides came to the talks with a similar vision for the eventual outcome of the talks, but each had a completely different view of what would happen thereafter. The common vision was to liberalize the political system (which, thus far, was at least in intention, a totalitarian system) by changing it into a system in which the PUPW would still play a dominant role, but where some areas (like trade union activities) would be free from direct Party control. Roughly speaking, the totalitarian system would be replaced by a kind of a relatively mitigated autocracy. Both sides also knew that due to Gorbachev's *glasnost* and *perestroika* in the Soviet Union there was much greater maneuvering room for political experimentation in Poland than had been the case a decade earlier.

The two sides differed, however, when it came to expectations regarding developments after liberalization of the system. The communist leadership hoped that after the legalization of *Solidarność* the whole movement would be somehow built into the system, and the communist party would be able to maintain overall control over the state. In other words, the system would acquire some legitimacy and self-correcting mechanisms, but would remain the same in its essence. *Solidarność*, in contrast, believed that once the trade union regained its legal status, the whole process of expanding freedoms would start all over again as in 1980-81.

The electoral law for the forthcoming parliamentary elections became one of the areas of major political controversy. The authorities were quite ready to accept a wide representation of the political democratic opposition centered around *Solidarność* to enter the parliament, but on the basis of a common single electoral list of candidates together with the communists. The idea was to have a "non-confrontational election." In the view of the communist party, this would blur the political differences and one common list would be presented under the name of a new version of the Front of National Unity that was so well-known from the past. The carrot was a guarantee that *Solidarność* would be guaranteed 35% of the seats.

Solidarność countered with a proposal to have a completely free and competitive election for the offered 35% of seats, leaving the remaining 65% seats to be filled by the communist party and its satellites.

These proposals were approved, but after a long struggle. The communist side proposed to reinstate the Senate with 100 seats and the position of President, which had been abolished by the communists when they came to power. The president, elected by a National Assembly (both chambers of the parliament), would have very considerable powers, such as the right to dissolve the parliament or to declare martial law. It was quite clear that the election of the president would be determined by a pro-communist parliamentary majority and his very strong prerogatives were intended as an additional safeguard against the situation getting out of control. As compensation *Solidarność* managed to win communist agreement to completely free elections to the Senate, which however had very limited powers.

The final agreement ending the Round Table Negotiations was signed on April 5, 1989. Elections were to take place in June 4. What was extremely important was the clear declaration that the electoral law negotiated during the talks would be applicable to the forthcoming election only. The next elections were to be fully democratic, without any quotas of seats.

The final result of the election was a total catastrophe for the communists. *Solidarność* won, with a crushing majority, every seat except one in the Senate (the only seat not taken by *Solidarność* was won by an independent businessman) and all of the seats in the freely contested part of the *Sejm*, the lower chamber of the parliament.

On top of that, the 65% majority guaranteed by the negotiated electoral law looked much less reliable, because among the members of parliament elected on the communist quota there were many tacit Solidarity sympathizers.

The electoral shock accelerated the process anticipated by the *Solidarność* leadership. There were many signs of dissent and a heightened readiness, especially among the satellite political parties, to desert a communist-led coalition and join the ranks of *Solidarność*.

Finally, the newly elected (by a majority of only one vote) President, the former Secretary General of the PUWP and the de facto ruler of

Poland, General Wojciech Jaruzelski, had no other option but to turn the task of forming a government over to a prominent *Solidarność* activist: Tadeusz Mazowiecki.

The process of forming the government was not easy. To begin with, it seemed important to offer participation in the government to representatives of the communist party. By offering them such critical portfolios as Defense or the Interior Ministry, which was in charge of the police, Mazowiecki wanted to alleviate a possible strong reaction from Moscow. There was also a need to assure the communists a presence in ministries dealing with the economy to involve them in the process of economic transformation.

Finally, on September 12 a new government was finally, and almost unanimously, approved by the Polish Parliament. The communists received 3 of 24 portfolios. Among them were defense and interior, but soon *Solidarność* deputy ministers were nominated in these departments, while the critical Ministry of Foreign Affairs was taken by *Solidarność*. The communist system in Poland came to an end and the process of dismantling this system in Europe began. Something that had seemed quite impossible actually happened in a peaceful, organized manner, without any loss of life or even a single broken glass.

In retrospect, *Solidarność's* contribution to the fall of communism may be summarized in several points.

First, the movement positioning itself in opposition to the Communist Party was of immense scale. Because it encompassed almost the whole of society it showed with compelling clarity that the Party and the system it represented had no democratic legitimacy.

Second, martial law, although implemented with remarkable efficiency and military professionalism, was a political failure. It became clear that tanks on the streets could not save the system.

Third, the Soviet Union was no longer ready to defend the communist system in another country by military means. Clearly with *perestroika* in full swing in Soviet Union one could think that such a military intervention would be very unlikely. But someone somewhere had to put it to a final practical test. That is what *Solidarność* did by forming the first non-communist government in our part of the world.

Finally, *Solidarność* showed quite clearly that in the new, non-communist system even the former communists would not be ostracized or hanged. They would find a place and a role in a new democratic state.

After the historical breakthrough in Poland it became relatively simple for others to follow the Polish way, and they did just that.

Poland and the Reunification of Germany

The East and West Germans share a profound wish to be reunited under one roof sometime in future...though they know there is no chance of it in the presently foreseeable future. It may come sometime in the next century, perhaps late in next century.

—Helmut Schmidt, A Grand Strategy for the West (1985)

Poland's political opposition had a great difficulty with the problem of German unification. For the communist rulers the situation was relatively simple. Only a divided Germany and the existence of the communist German Democratic Republic (GDR) with a powerful Red Army stationing on its territory was a guarantee of the inviolability of the Polish western border along the Oder-Neisse rivers. The communists' justification of this position was not easy to ignore. After all, the German Constitutional Tribunal in Karlsruhe declared that the recognition of Germany's border with Poland, as agreed in treaties between Poland and both German states, would not be binding for a unified Germany. The argument that only Soviet Union was a reliable guarantor of our western border was an important element legitimizing communist rule in Poland.

On the other hand, it was clear for the independent Polish political opposition that Poland would not be able to regain its independence as long as Germany was divided and its eastern part was under Soviet control.

The problem was that the Polish democratic opposition would have liked to see the problem of unification as being central to actual Eastern German policy, whereas for the Germans the issue of unification was absolutely not on the political horizon. Instead, Bonn conducted an Eastern policy known as *Ostpolitik*, which was based on the assumption that cooperation in a spirit of *détente* with East Germany and Moscow might alleviate the situation of the Germans in the GDR and, in a process of "change through rapprochement," eventually undermine the communist government and bring about unification in the long run.

For quite a long time the Polish democratic opposition considered this policy to be interesting and promising. What was very highly valued was not only a treaty between the Federal Republic and Poland that recognized Poland's western border, but also very substantial financial assistance in the form of various cultural and social programs as well as new credits to alleviate Polish financial problems.

Nevertheless, beginning from the late 1970s the *Ostpolitik* began to show its weaknesses. Bonn considered contacts with dissident movements in Poland to be detrimental to the détente process and to perhaps even "set communist parties on a reverse course." The destabilization of communist countries by grass-roots movements would eventually "terminate the peace and détente policy" (both quotes from Horst Ehmke's article published in 1985 in *Frankfurter Hefte*). For the Polish opposition it was very painful to see German Chancellor Schmidt's reaction to the implementation of martial law in Poland. At a press conference on December 13, 1991, held together with the East German leader, Schmidt said only "I am as much dismayed as Mr. Honecker that this was necessary."

Polish opposition criticism of Schmidt's remarks was summarized quite well in a comment published in a leading underground weekly, *Tygodnik Mazowsze*, in 1986:

> It is true that every change in the communist bloc requires Moscow's acceptance. But there is a difference between asking for approval for changes that are only planned and for convincing the Kremlin that it is a necessity to acquiesce to a situation that resulted from the action of some powerful socio-political forces(...)

> The problem is that the unification of Germany cannot be achieved across the dinner table. One can negotiate with the communist rulers the reduction of visa fees, amnesty or passports for some people to travel to the West, but such successes almost exhaust the potential of the present day *Ostpolitik*.

> More ambitious diplomatic initiatives in Moscow or Berlin could
> be seen by the communists as worth considering only if they were
> supported by the authentic, strong and vocal pressure of the GDR
> people. To come closer to the main political goal of unification
> one should work on developing certain civic habits and postures
> in the GDR. In short, a real chance for German unification is not
> in changing Poland into another GDR, but in changing the GDR
> into another Poland.

By 1989 the dramatic and revolutionary developments in Poland
completely changed the political landscape. On top of that, partly because of spillover effects, Central and Eastern Europe began to be engulfed in a wave of social and political turmoil. Hungary opened its
border with Austria and thousands of Germans from the GDR took
the opportunity and escaped. Soon after, the German embassies in
Czechoslovakia and Poland were flooded with refugees from East Germany seeking a transfer to the West. In the GDR street demonstrations
gained strength and the Communist Party was clearly in disarray. On
November 7 the government of the GDR resigned and the following day the Central Committee of the Communist Party changed the
whole party leadership. Finally, in the wide spread confusion and com-
motion, partly as a result of a certain misunderstanding, the Berlin Wall
fell. The unification of Germany was no longer a pipe dream.

The West German leadership was for a very long time completely
unaware of the gravity of the new situation. The day the Hungarians
opened the border with Austria, the CDU national conference in Bre-
men did not see any reason to respond to this event. On the day the
Berlin Wall fell Chancellor Kohl was in Warsaw and had to break off
his visit and fly to Berlin to find out what was going on. His reaction
was swift. Two weeks after the fall of the Berlin Wall Kohl presented a
plan for German unification. Thus, the German government declared
unification not to be a distant, historical goal but a priority of current
German policy.

Kohl's plan, consisting of 10 points, did not answer many very basic
questions. It was not clear what would be the place of united Germany in the newly emerging international order. There were only rather vague references to the European Communities, CSCE and disarmament. What was significant was the absence of any references to
NATO. Moreover, there was no indication what would be the territo-

rial shape of the new, united Germany. This was noticed immediately in Poland and raised a certain concern.

It became quite obvious that the first task for Polish diplomacy would be to "extend" Chancellor Kohl's plan by adding "another point," specifying the question of Germany's eastern borders.

This turned out to be no easy matter. On November 30 the SPD caucus in the *Bundestag* proposed an expansion of Kohl's plan by two points regarding medium-range missiles and Germany's borders. It failed to gain enough support, which understandably raised considerable concern in Poland.

A not very positive scenario of future developments began to be anticipated in Poland. It was a scenario of a united Germany released from entanglements with NATO and the European Communities while keeping open legal questions related to its eastern borders with Poland. It was a scenario of Poland being again sandwiched between the Soviet Union on one side and formally neutral and unconstrained Germany on the other. It was also a scenario in which neutralized Germany might be tempted again to cooperate with Russia to the detriment of Poland, a Germany that could be "a loose cannon."

This is why Poland from the very beginning was against German neutrality and was very much against plans of neutralization of Germany such as those presented by Moscow and by GDR Prime Minister Hans Modrow. Opinions voiced by various SPD politicians that neutrality was a price worth paying for unification were received with equal concern in Poland. Poland's firm support for German membership in NATO was officially confirmed in February 1990 by the Polish Minister of Foreign Affairs during his visit to Bonn.

The Polish position came as a shock to Moscow, which strongly believed that Poland would be particularly sensitive to all German issues and would always share Moscow's views on these matters, The Polish position was soon shared by other former communist countries like Czechoslovakia and Hungary. According to Chancellor Kohl's national security advisor Horst Teltschik, this Polish support was a decisive factor in convincing Gorbachev that his opposition to Germany's NATO membership was untenable.[3] The road to German unification was opened.

The only issue to be decided that was of very special importance to Poland was the problem of Germany's eastern border.

On February 11, 1990 a conference of the Warsaw Pact and NATO countries began in Ottawa. On the agenda was a debate about the "Open Skies" program. Within the framework of the conference several bilateral and multilateral meetings and talks took place. One of them addressed the issue of the unification of Germany. In a communique issued at the end of the meeting, the four powers (United States, UK, France and the USSR) and the two German states announced that talks of the six countries on the "external aspects of the establishment of German unity, including the issues of security of the neighbouring states" would begin. Five month later, in Paris, all controversies on the political conditionalities were overcome, including (as the result of consultations and negotiations with Poland), the satisfactory wording of the final confirmation of German borders, A formal "peace settlement" ending the division of Germany was finally signed by six governments (United States, United Kingdom, USSR, France, GDR and FRG) on September 12 in Moscow. Germany was united again, but not "by blood and iron" as in the 19th century, but by a peace settlement with the full consent of all neighbors and other nations of the Euro-Atlantic area.

The Demise of the Warsaw Pact

There is considerable evidence that the Soviet government has decided in 1989 to allow more beginnings of self-rule in Poland and Hungary and their other satellite states than before. But it is still too early to tell whether this trend ... will be allowed to continue if these satellite states should decide they no longer want to be in the Warsaw Pact. Indeed, the Soviet government said that while they permit Poland to have a non-communist government, Poland "of course must remain a member of the Warsaw Pact."

—Caspar Weinberger, Fighting for Peace (1990)

In 1955 West Germany joined NATO. This was treated by Moscow as a good pretext to form the Warsaw Pact, a military alliance of all European communist countries that was supposed to be a formal counterweight to the North Atlantic Alliance. Until then Moscow could control the satellites through a series of bilateral treaties with extended security clauses and military guarantees. On top of this, great numbers of Russian officers were delegated to the armed forces of other countries to occupy very high positions, which very effectively secured sufficient control by Moscow. However, NATO expansion and integration of West Germany into the Alliance required an additional and more spectacular response. Control exerted through the mass presence of Soviet officers appeared as an overtly crude solution and needed to be replaced by more sophisticated mechanisms.

The new Treaty signed in Warsaw in 1955, known as the Warsaw Pact, stipulated the setting up of a joint military command, which would allow the Soviets to gain direct control of the armed forces of other members of this new alliance. The Treaty also provided a legal framework for stationing of Soviet forces on the territory of other member states.

Although the Warsaw Pact was presented as a copy of NATO and very often treated in the West that way, in fact it was a completely different organization. First, all top Warsaw Pact commanders were Russians. The Supreme Commander of the Pact's United Armed Forces was at the same time the First Deputy of the Soviet Minister of Defense. Similarly, the Chief of the Combined Staff of the Pact Armed Forces was, at the same time, the first Deputy of the Chief of the Soviet General Staff. The Combined Command of Pact Forces was fully subordinated to the Soviet General Staff. On top of this, no one from the national Deputies of the Supreme Commander or the national Deputy Chiefs of the Pact's General Staff had access to an overall war plan, which was available only to Soviet generals. National representatives on the Pact General Staff could be familiarized only with those fragments of the overall operational plan which were necessary for the national planning and commanding. In every country there was a military mission of the Pact Command, but staffed only by the Soviet military. Needless to say, there was no Pact mission affiliated to the Soviet Army. In the Warsaw Pact there was no equivalent to the civilian NATO Headquarters and no regional multi-national commands. There was the Political Consultative Committee consisting of the first secretaries of the communist parties, ministers of foreign affairs and defense but, in reality, this Committee dealt basically with very general and rather ideological issues and had no relevance to real military planning, doctrine and strategy. These issues were worked out by the Soviet General Staff only.

The Polish Army had slightly greater autonomy then the other satellite armies. The Supreme Command Mission to Poland (with Russian staff only) had an office in Warsaw, but unlike in other states it had no permanent liaisons officers allocated to local major army units. Soviet military intelligence GRU (unlike KGB) had no mission in Warsaw. Poland, in case of war, was supposed to deploy three land and one air army, but these forces were to form a separate group of armies (a "front"- in Soviet terminology) which under the Polish command was supposed to capture Denmark and the Danish Straights, northern Germany and the Netherlands.

In the late 1980s, with *perestroika* gaining speed, some attempts to make the Warsaw Pact look more like NATO could be seen. First, Moscow made a vague suggestion that a parliamentary body similar to the NATO Parliamentary Assembly could be introduced, together with some form of more direct political control. Then in 1987, on Moscow's initiative, a Warsaw Pact Reform Group was formed. Discussions at this forum showed significant differences: Poland and Hungary were in favor of democratization of the Pact whereas Moscow, Prague, East Berlin and Bucharest were in favor of increasing its political functions. According to these proposals, the Warsaw Pact was supposed to play a coordinating role not only in military and security matters but also in the area of cooperation in research and development, in the economy and even in cultural affairs. The Group met only a couple of times and turned out to be a forum of general debates only. It soon became irrelevant in view of fundamental political changes underway in Poland and the fall of the Berlin Wall.

The unification of Germany raised fundamental questions regarding the new security system in Europe. The suggestion to dissolve both NATO and the Warsaw Pact, made by Gorbachev in Strasbourg in July 1989, were unacceptable. It was important for NATO was to stay, if only to stabilize the newly united Germany. The GDR ceased to exist, so the Warsaw Pact lost one important member. Although the main strategic documents were to be returned to Moscow, all documentation, data and material assets became available to a NATO country:

united Germany. The Warsaw Pact was no longer covered by the veil of complete secrecy.

Several concepts were presented, such as the "Finlandization" of the area between NATO and the Soviet Union, the creation of a loose federation of the states of the region operating within a democratized Warsaw Pact, or a moratorium on structural changes both in NATO and the Warsaw Pact in order to stabilize the situation. The spectre of chaos in the region emerging from a permafrost of Soviet control and the collapse of Gorbachev loomed very largely on the debates. In May 1989 Zbigniew Brzezinski in Lublin said that "Polish membership in the Warsaw Pact could be seen as something positive providing the Pact will not be an instrument of an enforcement of some orthodox ideology but will be an agent of geopolitical and territorial stability in Europe."[4]

For Poland none of these options was attractive. Regaining full independence and establishing very close ties with the West were the order of the day. Therefore, the dissolution of the Warsaw Pact became an obvious policy. Nevertheless, Poland had to handle the situation with caution. The need to solve the problem of the Polish western border required a very balanced policy towards Moscow. After all, to retain a measure of uncertainty about the final nature of these borders could be seen in Moscow as an element increasing future Soviet leverage on Poland.

Under these circumstances, it was Hungary that took the lead. On July 7, during the meeting of the Warsaw Pact Political Consultative Committee in Moscow, the Hungarian delegation proposed setting up an intergovernmental commission to review the nature, and functioning of the Warsaw Pact, including the option of dismantling all the Pact's military structures. The direction of change was clearly indicated. Soon after that, Hungarian Prime Minister József Antall announced that regardless of the outcome of the debates, Hungary would quit the Warsaw Pact at the end of 1991.

Warsaw took these statements with understanding and sympathy, but decided to take a slightly different course. The idea was not to go for a clash, but to convince Moscow that under political circumstances developing in Europe, even a reformed Warsaw Pact could not serve any positive and constructive purpose and should be dissolved on a consensual basis. For example, in May 1990 Poland declared that Polish troops could be used to defend Polish territory only; any other use of Polish troops outside Poland was completely excluded also in the future.

This imaginative policy, developed and very skilfully carried out by Krzysztof Skubiszewski, the Polish Minister of Foreign Affairs, was soon strongly supported by the President of Czechoslovakia, Václav Havel and by Hungary. Bucharest and Sofia, which had been rather passive for quite a long time, finally decided to follow suit.

Poland and other countries began to withdraw personnel from Warsaw Pact command structures. Soon it became clear that the Pact was in a state of atrophy. In Budapest on February 25, 1991 a decision to dismantle all military structures was unanimously adopted. Three months later, in Prague, the Warsaw Pact was finally dissolved.

Poland's remaining task was to secure a swift and speedy withdrawal of Russian troops from Poland. The negotiations were difficult, but an agreement was finally reached and the last Russian detachment left Poland on September 17, 1993. If one disregards a short period between the two world wars, for the first time since the beginning of the eighteen century there were no foreign troops on Polish soil.

The date of departure of the last Russian soldiers from Poland had also a symbolic significance: on September 17, 1939 Poland was invaded by Russia, at that time an ally of Adolph Hitler.

Notes

1.The term "Cold War" was used for the first time by George Orwell in 1945, but entered the common political discourse after well-known newspaper columnist Walter Lippman published an article analyzing the nature of East-West relations. However, the temperature of these relations began to change over time from a deep frost period, marked by the Korean War and the Stalinist concept of the inevitability of a major war between the "Socialist Camp" and the capitalist West, to Khrushchev's concept of peaceful coexistence, which was presented at the 20th Congress of the Soviet Communist Party.

2.Alexander M. Haig, *Caveat: Realism, Reagan and Foreign Policy*, (New York: Macmillan, 1984) p. 246.

3.Artur Hajnicz, *Polens Wende und Deutschlands Vereinigung* (Paderborn: Verlag Ferdinand Schöningh,1995).

4. Cited in Jerzy M. Nowak, *Od hegemonii do agonii* (Warsaw: Bellona, 2011), p. 163.

Chapter 16

30 Years Ago, a Time of Joy and Hope

Adam Michnik

I remember exactly the evening of November 9, 1989.

Events of great importance were taking place in my country of Poland. In Warsaw a young non-communist government had recently been formed with Tadeusz Mazowiecki as its prime minister. Mazowiecki had been a longtime adviser to Lech Wałęsa, had served earlier as a Catholic activist, and represented an open and post-conciliar Catholicism. That evening an official delegation of the Federal Republic of Germany was paying a formal visit. Leaders included Chancellor Helmut Kohl and Foreign Minister Hans-Dietrich Genscher. I was at a meeting with Minister Genscher. During a very interesting conversation, the minister's colleague entered the room and gave him a small card. Genscher read the card, looked at me and said: "The Berlin Wall has been opened."

I expressed a cry of exhilaration; I said goodbye and ran to the editorial offices of *Gazeta Wyborcza* to write a few words of comment on the first page. Here they are:

> Nobody knows what the consequences will be of the actual destruction of the Berlin Wall. However, something irreversible has already happened: the people were not being shot at. In Berlin, in the heart of Europe, freedom prevailed in the fight between freedom and barbed wire.

It's hard to believe today that it all was a matter of chance. After all, the government of East Germany could still close the borders. Günter Schabowski, a member of the East German Communist Party leadership, declared on television: "We made a decision today. Each citizen can leave through any border crossing" and when asked, he added that this decision came into effect immediately. I think that Schabowski did not know what he was announcing, because right afterwards thousands of Berliners moved towards the concrete wall and pressed it open.

From today's perspective, this process seems obvious. And yet, it was not obvious. In October 1989, Egon Krenz, the leader of the East German communist party, the SED, declared that he understood the "Chinese solution," i.e. the massacre of demonstrators in Tiananmen Square in Beijing who wanted freedom for their country.

That sounded dangerous to a Pole. We did not feel safe. Despite the historic success of the peaceful dictatorship dismantling, we still remembered that communism usually resorted to violence when it felt threatened.

Today there are various responses to the question why Soviet communism fell. Some emphasize the role of West German *Ostpolitik* and the Helsinki CSCE conference promoting relaxation of tensions. Others emphasize U.S. President Jimmy Carter's policy that made a banner for aspirations of freedom out of human rights, or the policy of U.S. President Ronald Reagan, who announced that the Soviet Union was an evil empire and proclaimed a total ideological war against it. Of course, the war in Afghanistan was of great importance; it weakened the Kremlin dictators militarily and politically.

Looking back, however, the most important reason was the significance of *Solidarność* (Solidarity), the Polish confederation of national freedom and independence, whose millions of working-class adherents rendered irrelevant Poland's communist party and its pretense of representing the dictatorship of the proletariat. The Polish proletariat gave the dictatorship a red card.

It seems obvious to a Pole that everything started in Poland. The Polish sequence of events was carried forward by a broad democratic opposition movement comprised of the working class, the intelligentsia, and the Catholic Church with the historic role of John Paul II and his visit to Poland in 1979, a wave of strikes of the summer of 1980 topped by a compromise enforced by the strikers, and the establishment of the Independent Labor Union *Solidarność*. It was then that the first pieces of the Berlin Wall were chiseled out.

The Polish festival of freedom and legal *Solidarność* lasted for several months in 1981, until martial law ended it. An eight-year-long period of resistance by the democratic opposition ensued. It was confined to illegality, discrimination and imprisonment, all the way to the Round

Table negotiations and the election of June 4, 1989. The Round Table talks were a historic achievement of the entire Polish political class, as well as the reformist wing of the ruling communists. They were probably the greatest Polish political achievement of the twentieth century. The June elections were a peculiar referendum; they resulted in a triumphant victory of the democratic opposition over the dictatorship.

Soon after, the domino effect of the fall of dictatorships took place: in Hungary where the revolution of 1956 and its murdered heroes were rehabilitated, the German Democratic Republic, Czechoslovakia, Bulgaria, Albania, and finally Romania. The bloc of satellite states dominated by the Soviet Union fell apart like a house of cards.

Each of these events had its own local background; each had its own internal and external context. The internal context was the economic failure of the command-and-distribution system; the external context was the changes taking place in Russia. These changes surprised many of us, just as they surprised most observers around the world.

For many years we observed the heroism of Soviet dissidents and opposition to the dictatorship, their *samizdat* (self-publishing) and the defense of the civil rights movement. This circle of Russian rebels played a crucial role in the collective consciousness of the Russian intelligentsia; it changed the image of Russian culture. Three Nobel laureates—Andrei Sakharov, Aleksander Solzhenitsyn and Josif Brodsky—came out of this circle. The Russian democratic opposition became an obvious context for the reformist tendencies in the camp of the authorities. Mikhail Gorbachev's *perestroika* is incomprehensible without the knowledge of the activities of Russian dissidents who were persecuted, discriminated, and imprisoned for many years.

The leaders of *perestroika* viewed the dissidents as enemies, but without these enemies the great project of political change would probably have never been created.

*   *   *

This was also a surprise. The 20th Congress of the Soviet Communist Party in 1956 and Khrushchev's report exposing some of Stalin's crimes gave rise to hope for the possibility of "socialism with a human face." This hope gave birth to the changes in Poland and the outbreak of the Budapest revolution that year, which was suppressed bloodily by the Soviet army.

Until 1968, however, many people still hoped that the reforming forces would be able to initiate democratic reforms within the ruling communist regime. This belief in the possibility of political change was historically buried with the Prague Spring and Alexander Dubček's policies. For me, a Pole who was imprisoned for participating in a democratic student protest movement, this was the moment when I lost my last illusions. There were not too many of them, given that military intervention in Poland was supported by brutal police action and an anti-Semitic campaign. Nonetheless, it now became obvious to me: this system cannot be reformed; one must learn how to defend against it.

Gorbachev's *perestroika* revealed our mistake. Historical changes in Moscow started from above—the impulse came from the Kremlin. Moreover, the slogans of openness (*glasnost*) reached extremely fertile ground. The Russian intelligentsia, for years bound by conformism and fear, now became extremely vital, courageous and creative.

However, the open political debates were accompanied by an economic crisis and a crisis of state institutions. From the beginning the general reform movement in the USSR had two faces: in Russia and in the Soviet republics. In Russia, the reform movement had a citizen-democratic face and a traditionalist-nationalist face.

Soviet communism exterminated both democratic attitudes and conservative-nationalist attitudes. It perceived both as threats to its all-encompassing Bolshevik ideology. Debates among Russian dissidents along these lines were well illustrated by the democratic approaches of Andrei Sakharov and the conservative-nationalist views of Alexander Solzhenitsyn. After one hundred years, separation of the nineteenth century into Occidentalists and Slavophiles returned.

These two camps were allies when they fought for the right to vote, but their alliance ended when they actually received the right to vote. This should not come as a surprise—after all, they were completely different voices.

In the nineteenth century, democrats and nationalists jointly opposed the dictatorships of the conservative monarchies of the Holy Alliance. The Spring of Nations of 1848 was their joint accomplishment.

We can say that they were the children of the same mother, who at times had the face of romanticism and at other times that of Enlightenment rationalism. We could also say they were brothers like Cain and Abel; at some point Cain wanted Abel's death.

It was different in the Soviet republics. There, especially in the Baltic countries, the meaning of rebellion was obvious: in these countries, freedom was both personal and national. It was the path to independent statehood. It was similar in the Ukrainian cities, in Georgia or Armenia.

For us in Poland the right to state sovereignty was obvious. *Solidarność*, a great nationwide conspiracy movement for human rights and the rights of the nation, exemplified this. This movement, supported by the Catholic Church and the great authority of John Paul II, harmoniously combined three tendencies: the pursuit of emancipation of the labor world, especially the working environment; a desire to regain and cultivate national identity; and, of course, the pursuit of a political democracy based on human rights.

While every country had its own particulars, this sensitivity to democratic separation existed everywhere. It articulated itself as a return to Europe and national sensitivity that presaged the return of ancestral roots, traditions and beliefs. Some Poles identified with the tradition of democratic independence (the national uprisings of the nineteenth century and Józef Piłsudski). Others looked to the nationalist tradition of Roman Dmowski and national democrats with their ethicist exclusiveness. It was in Roman Dmowski's camp that the mottos "Poland for Poles" and "Catholic state of the Polish nation" were born, along with the violent anti-Semitism that accompanied them. The debates of Hungarians and Czechs, Romanians and Slovaks were similar. These two different mentalities and sensibilities existed both within the anti-communist opposition and within the ruling communist camp.

Gorbachev and Milošević are two classic examples of these different views. If Gorbachev was attracted to a cautious imitation of social democracy, Milošević openly referred to the tradition of Greater Serbian chauvinism. Both of them saw the need for a change. Of course, neither was looking to hand over power; each was trying to find a new way to legitimize his rule. One was looking for a different vision for the future, the other for a new vision within the past.

*   *   *

When the June 4, 1989 elections in Poland resulted a total rout of the communist elite in power, for the first time in a very long time the communists publicly acknowledged their electoral defeat. They did not fake these elections, and after losing, they publicly recognized their defeat.

This was an unprecedented event, and yet even though the elections in Poland were very carefully observed, the news coming out of Poland did not capture world headlines. Front pages around the world were dominated by news coming out of China: protestors for freedom had been massacred in Tiananmen Square. Chinese authorities resorted to violence to maintain their rule. They demonstrated that they would do what it would take, including employing dictatorial tactics, to protect the market mechanisms that were propelling to economic success and a role as a global superpower.

Thus, as early as in 1989 it became apparent that different paths of departure were leading societies away from the Bolshevik model. One path led toward European democracy. Another offered a return to nationalist traditionalism. A third pointed to authoritarianism supported by religious community institutions and religious values. A fourth featured the transition of communist elites and a communist system into a nationalist dictatorship. Some were already observing a renaissance of nationalist and authoritarian traditions from the 1930s.

Yegor Gaidar, an outstanding, prematurely deceased leader of the Russian reformers, noted soberly in his book *Collapse of an Empire*:[1]

> Getting rid of a sense of national greatness and national harm is a nuclear bomb in the politics of countries where the old system is wearing out, but there is no system of developed democratic institutions in place. The problem with a young democracy...is that the slogans that are the easiest to "sell" to politically inexperienced voters become dangerous in practice. During the second half of the 1980s, opposing slogans such as "Serbia should be great" and "We will not let the Serbs be beaten anywhere" in Belgrade, was a political lost cause. The idea that Serbia was and will be great and that the republic's authorities would not allow Serbs to be harmed in other republics and autonomies was easily used on the political

market. Should the Serbian leader not take such a position, there inevitably will be a politician who can use it for his own benefit.

Analyzing the Yugoslav crisis, Gaidar wrote:

> It was not difficult to predict that in Zagreb, Ljubljana and Sarajevo, politicians would enthusiastically take these slogans, replacing the word "Serbs" with the words "Croats" and "Slovenians." The moment the authorities in Serbia adopted a nationalist program as a political and ideological base, the fate of Yugoslavia was sealed. Presenting territorial claims to the neighbors, Serbian leaders opened the door to victory for nationalist ideas in other republics who took advantage of the fear of Serbian domination. Wars became inevitable. A mechanism was launched that cost tens of thousands of people their lives and displaced millions forcefully.

> Political agitation based on the conflicts of nations that previously lived side by side, usually with agreed upon boundaries between them, arbitrarily established by an undemocratic regime, became the prologue of bloody events.

It was similar in the Czech Republic and Slovakia, in Romania and Hungary. In Bulgaria anti-Turkish resentment was used. In East Germany, refugee centers were attacked. In Poland, we heard the slogan "Poland for Poles" and the sinister screams of the homophobes. Nationalism—this poison of our time—entered the center of politics.

This was not the result of a Soviet conspiracy or American secret services. This is what those who subscribe to the conspiracy theory of history seem to believe. They believe that social processes are the work of special services, the CIA, KGB, or Mossad. Their mistake comes from the conviction that society is completely pacified and unable to resist. They are then surprised when opposition unexpectedly appears, when gagged and manipulated people suddenly spit out their gag, when such forgotten values as truth, honesty, courage, dignity and honor—and living according to those principles—come to the fore. They are surprised when cemetery silence is replaced with a tumult of freedom and life. This was the case in 1989, when the first non-communist government was formed in Poland, when the Berlin Wall fell, and when the crowds on the streets of Budapest, Prague, Sofia, Bratislava and Berlin regained their freedom.

At the time, these crowds demanded freedom for everyone. Over the years, however, the crowd has changed its appearance, character, slogans and dreams. It stopped demanding freedom and started demanding bread and games. This was the path that led to violence from humanism through nationalism. And it can still lead to barbarism. The crowd following this path began to transform into a mob.

The first time I got to know the smell and taste of a peasant mob that was let go off the leash was in 1968, when the barriers of decency in public speeches cracked before my eyes. Smarter observers had already offered their diagnosis. The most outstanding Polish humanist, Leszek Kołakowski, wrote about the mob already in 1956, when the liberalization of power—along with the ideas of freedom—was accompanied by a renaissance of anti-Semitism:

> They are separated into various varieties, like malicious insects: some are demanding the Jews to be butchered, they study brochures about ritual murders, others talk about a lower race, and others only about "the cultural strangeness," and others still are content with animosity that is often difficult to find and that, without the help of theory, is easily heard in everyday life. (...) Moderate anti-Semitism in its official form, even if limited to the "economic boycott" of Jewish merchants, sustained and fueled the aura in which the Phalange, and later the Gestapo informers and occupational blackmailers, flourished. As you know, the Nuremberg Laws did not contain the plan for the extermination of Jews, but the principle of racial inferiority...Good-natured anti-Semites give birth to anti-Semites who are thugs, and gentle anti-Semites foster anti-Semites armed with brass knuckles and knives, and passive and abstemious anti-Semites create slaughter organizers. In a suitable environment, the scattered and seemingly non-threatening faint atoms of antisemitism can be instantly focused in a fulminant mixture that explodes as a crime. The tolerance of anti-Semitism in the weakest symptoms of today, is therefore the tolerance of tomorrow's slaughters. You need to grab the shadow of the crime by the throat until it grows meat. We refer the matter to the agenda only because the existence of anti-Semitic outbreaks is an omnipresent open secret which need not be revealed...The mob is the anti-Semitic entity. The mob has no class determination as to the composition, but they have one as to their social tasks. It can be made of elements of the most diverse social affiliation. The mob

updates itself in a mass, and when dispersed, it does not maintain a sense of solidarity, only vaguely aware of the readiness to resume this bond, which is neither class nor national, nor is it a permanent bond of any sorts, but only an occasional bond of variable content. The bond created by the mob is not able to establish a specific program; it is purely negative and destructive, and as a rule, disposes of the class consciousness, it expresses collective dissatisfaction to the confused, and therefore is incapable of rationalized reactions, hates discussion, is subject to suggestion only to the most primitive, is weak-willed when it comes to demagogy, and invaluable as a weapon of crime performed on someone else's behalf.

The mob is the accumulation of collective negative stress, deprived of self-knowledge of its sources and thus, providing itself with virtually an arbitrary direction of expansion, should it be simple enough, concrete, not requiring reflection, self-reliance and releasing all inhibitions, both the reasonable ones, as well as the ones related to the existence of elementary universal rules of morality. The mob may act against the obvious interests of the majority of its participants, but it is usually influenced consciously from the outside. By itself, it is not able to create or organize the form of its activity, because the principle of its existence also represents the denial of internal social discipline.

> The mob tore up scientist Hypatia on the streets of Alexandria, and by slaughtering Jews revealed its action on the night of St. Bartholomew in the Polish anti-multi-faith uproars. The mob can only be a tool for political reactions. It works only in friendly environment of direct effectiveness, only in the environment of quantitative advantage, and it only gives way to violence. Antisemitism is the favorite form that might be assigned to its darkened consciousness."

The answer of the Polish democratic intelligentsia to the anti-Semitic poison—this religion of mobs—was the selection of a different life.

Kołakowski wrote about the mechanisms of communist dictatorship:

> This mechanism assumes a strictly unidirectional dependence within the hierarchy, resulting from the monopoly rule of power; thus, similarly as in all despotic systems, the positive traits in a unitary career (i.e., traits that facilitate climbing the hierarchy lad-

394 EXITING THE COLD WAR, ENTERING A NEW WORLD

der) are servility, cowardice, lack of initiative, readiness to listen to
superiors, readiness to inform, and indifference to social opinion
and public interest. On the contrary, the negative traits are: initiative abilities, care for common issues, and demanding the criteria
of truth, fitness and social benefit, regardless of the interests of
the apparatus. Then, the mechanism of power causes a natural,
negative selection of directorial staff in all areas of the governing
apparatus, and mostly within the apparatus of the party." Practice
shows that the peculiarity of these governments "was systematic
elimination of competent and endowed with initiative people, in
favor of cowardly and submissive mediocrity. The trial which took
place in March 1968—the mass promotion of dunces, informers or
even outlaws ("bedbug invasion," as it was called in Warsaw), was
only the acceleration and intensification of phenomena that was
going on for many years.

At the same time, Kołakowski warned against the fatalism of thinking. He repeated that the idea of full irreformability of the dictatorship

is easily suited for the justification of opportunism and filthiness.
If this is the case, then no individual or collective initiatives aimed
at counteracting the monstrosities of neo-Stalin bureaucratism, no
struggle to perpetuate the respect for truth, competence, reliability, justice and reason in this society, are irrelevant; in short, with
this assumption, any individual dirty trick can be excused, because
it can be simply identified as a component of universal dirty trick,
which is inevitable "temporarily" and is not the work of individuals, but the result of the system. The principle of non-reform-
ability can therefore serve as an advance absolution given to all
cowardice, passivity and cooperation with evil...Those who think
that they pay only with minor concessions for their peace, will be
convinced that the price of this peace will be higher; those who
only pay by seemingly innocent boot-licking, will be forced to pay
for the same commodity tomorrow by denunciation; those who
use their privileges in silence in the face of a crime, which they
can react to, will quickly have to pay for the same privileges by
their active participation in the crime. Moral inflation is the natural right of despotism, meaning that if the social pressure does not
force it to reduce it, it makes one pay more and more money for
distribution of goods.

Kołakowski's words anticipated the formation six years later of the Workers' Defense Committee (*Komitet Obrony Robotników*, or KOR), a Polish civil society group founded to give aid to prisoners and their families after civil protests and an ensuing government crackdown in June 1976.

*   *   *

Václav Havel, the Czech writer, dissident, political prisoner, and later after the fall of the dictatorship the President of the Republic, had similar thoughts. Havel's dissident essays were building the consciousness and value system of the democratic opposition milieus, not only in Czechoslovakia. His biography was a paradox. Like his master, the Czech philosopher Jan Patočka, he wanted to be faithful to the uncompromising attitude of Socrates. And he wanted to remain faithful to it after he became president. At that time, I thought that Socrates had transformed into Pericles.

He never wasted time, even in prison, where he wrote in a letter to his wife Olga: "the moment when an ideological system becomes closed and finite, perfect and universal, this system collapses into debris as a result of a physical breakdown, because reality escapes it."

Such a bust of ideology results in widespread bitterness. A bitter man loses faith in the world and people. And, Havel wrote, he comes to the conviction that "all moral principles and exalted systems and ideals are just a naive utopia. We must accept the fact that the world is as it is, and that is, invariably vile. And yet," repeated Havel, "it is not the wickedness of the world that leads man to resign, and his resignation leads him to the theory of the meanness of the world."

For many of us—for me as well—who were grateful to be Havel's friends—he was one of the most important intellectual authorities in those years.

Havel keenly analyzed the evolution of a bitter man. "As he adapts to the wicked world, this world begins to be a reality, not worse, and certainly better than the subsequent destabilization caused by the actions of naive Utopians who want to make the world a better place." In this way, Havel wrote, "there is a sad end: a moment in which the merciless critic of the world turns imperceptibly into his protector."

Havel said he understood human bitterness: human weakness, lone-liness, and defenselessness all speak for it. Yet he wrote, "I am con-vinced that there is nothing in this vale of tears that could itself take away the person's hope and faith in the life's goals. We lose it only when we fail ourselves."

This poignant confession and definition of the unbending attitude of the dissident conceals dangerous traps. Fanaticism was the most dan-gerous one. Fanaticism was a dangerous disease of many brave dissi-dents. "Fanaticism," Havel wrote to Olga, "is a faith that has betrayed itself":

> The fanatic first believes that he is "responsible for everything"; the more this responsibility is limited, the more defenseless he is against the shock known as the experience of the presence of the world just seen. The faith in the idea is transformed into faith in a specific institution. This is a fatal mistake. The transfer of ideas from the realm of unlimited dream to the ground of real, human acts, makes a person begin to blindly obey the institution in which he sees the fulfillment of his ideals. It is tempting: obedience re-places reflection, man is freed from the command of independent thinking for the service of the institution, in which he sees the way to realize his unlimited dream.

> A fanatic is the one who does not understand that he replaces the love for God and for the religions he created, the love for truth and freedom and justice, with the love for ideology, doctrine, or sect that promised that they will definitely carry them out; the love for people with love for a project that claims that it can—naturally as the only one—really serve the people.

> The greater the fanaticism someone represents, the more he changes the objects of his faith. In one moment of confusion, Mao-ism will turn into faith in Jehovah's witnesses or vice versa, without changing their devotion to them.

Fanaticism can make life easier—but at the cost of destroying life. The tragic fate of the fanatic is that a beautiful human dream to take on the suffering of the whole world eventually turns into multiplying his suffering: in organizing concentration camps, inquisitions, murders and executions.

I have been thinking a lot about Havel's path and the experiences of his life. He is one of the people who symbolize the glory and miserableness of our time, and of the last thirty years. Havel made the Czech Republic a respected and admired country all over the world, but he soon encountered hostility in his own country. He noted it years later. Havel described his presidential election as exile from a fairy tale. He wrote:

> It seemed to us we were all the carriers of ideals of solidarity and normality which in essence was the ideal of mediocrity, banality, and some petty bourgeois ignorance. The dislike for former dissidents was in its heyday.

> Shortly after the revolution and after the regaining of freedom, a very special kind of anticommunist possession became widespread. As if some people who for years were silent and very careful not to get sick, suddenly felt the need to recover from some powerful gesture of prior humiliation or a feeling they did not have before. That is why they aimed at people who least remembered it, the dissidents. They still treated them as a living remorse, as an example of the fact that if someone did not want to, he did not have to completely submit. Interestingly, at a time when dissidents seemed like a group of crazy Don Quixotes, the reluctance towards them was not as significant, as when they got the credit from the history. That was already too much, and this you cannot forgive! And the more apparent it was that the dissidents themselves did not say anything to anyone or accused anyone of anything (and God forbid that they would set themselves as an example), then—paradoxically—the more this anger grew. Ultimately, therefore, the new anticommunist was angrier with them than the representatives of the old regime.

> A special legend about the extreme leftist attitude of dissidents was born out of this, about the fact that it is a closely-knit elite (how can people who spent decades in boiler rooms, or in prisons and who did not elevate themselves think of you as the elite?), who do not have enough respect for the enlightened Western institutions, etc., etc. A certain article about this ideology revealed that dissidents did not have any special merits in the fall of communism, because it was overthrown by normal "regular" citizens, because they cared for their own wellbeing, which probably means that from time to time they removed a brick from a construction site.

This mode of thinking finds therein a strong response in society, which sees the final solution to the rightness of their life choices. Now, when it is possible, we praise capitalism and condemn those who think critically about it, and in the past, when it was not possible, we went obediently to vote for communists to take care of ourselves. And who was the one that disturbed us all the time? Extreme leftist dissidents.

Havel saw "the Czech smallness" and philosophy in all of this: "Do not meddle in affairs that are not your own, bend over and stoop— we are surrounded by mountains, all world's turmoil will fly over our heads, and we will have fun in our own backyard."

"In our history,"—Havel often returned to this thought—"situations are repeated when the society breaks into some action, but then its leaders decide to step back, they give up on something, sacrifice something—it's all in the name of saving the national existence—and the society is initially traumatized, but then quickly gives everything up (that is "understands the reasons of these leaders"), and finally falls into apathy, or even loses consciousness. This was the time after Munich, during the Protectorate, in the 1950s and in 1968 after the Soviet occupation. At first, the following sentences appear: "they betrayed us," "everyone opposed us," and later the sentence "No one has access," ends with a nationalist cry, slogans of national interests, and a quiet consent to persecute minorities. The worst edition of "Czechaczkostwo" wins."

"Czechaczek" is a symbol of ignorance and hate for the people who think differently. The following pleas appear: "Let's get rid of the Jews, then the Germans, then the bourgeois, then the dissidents, then the Slovaks," and who is next? Romas? Homosexuals? All foreigners? Who will stay here than? Pure blood "Czechaczkowies" in their own backyard."

After 1980, the "Czechaczek" reached for a more subtle formula: anti-Europeanism. In Havel's opinion, "this is the same attitude towards the world, why should we ask anyone for advice, listen to someone, why do we have to share power with some foreigner, help someone else, why do we need to have technical standards? We will take care of it ourselves—this is the new face of the "Czechaczkowski's" mentality.

But watch out, Havel cautions: "Czechaczek dares to show the horns and shout battle codes only when he is not threatened by it. However, if he is dealing with a powerful opponent, he pulls his tail in and becomes servile."

This is how Havel revealed the "Czechaczkowski's" vision of the mob.

*   *   *

Today, after thirty years, we are witnessing a crisis of democratic ideas in Europe and in the world. The symbol of this crisis is Brexit and Salvini, Trump and Putin, Orbán and Kaczyński, and the enemies of the European Union in France and Germany. There are various reasons for this shift from democracy to the musty past of nationalism. It is an identity crisis related to globalization and a crisis of thinking about the future; it is a deficit of democratic procedures and customs; it is the theatralization and tabloidization of political life. The answer to this axiological vacuum is the conviction about the defeat of "demo-liberalism," the conviction that nationalism and populism offer a special national path, dangerously similar to the 1930s. Resentments, frustrations and complexes all served to unleash xenophobia against the refugees.

When in opposition, populism and nationalism serve as tools in the power struggle. The cliché about "rising from one's knees" is a clever catchphrase for a ruthlessly conceived sense of nationality of a nationalist. On the other hand, the nationalists and populists who gain power reach for the same clichés to divert attention from the problems related to corruption, destruction of the rule of law, and terrible foreign policy. At that time, enemies in other countries can easily be found (Soros!), and the government is replaced by the special services operations and manipulation of human anxiety.

A Polish psychologist, a participant in many protest actions in the defense of the constitution, civil liberties and the women's rights, says emphatically: "there can be no compromise with the neo-fascists. This is a cruel, inhuman—and forbidden—ideology which was hidden in a plush case in Poland. It is believed that until it uses large-scale violence, it can exist on a par with other ideologies. In no way this is true. I want to take off this case and reveal: look, hence the racism in its pure form, hence the destroying hatred. There is no place in the common space for these views ... You cannot call for hatred on racial grounds, and if you do, you are outside of a civilized society and you have to feel this rejection. There are more and more fascists because they have a sense of impunity."

In turn, a well-known and popular musician says:

"We live in times of widespread destruction. Destruction of people, their achievements, authority, destruction of historical truth, and of putting lies into circulation. The freedom of thought is destroyed, the views are destroyed and removed, and so are the works of art and their authors. Today in Poland, there is no form that has been intact or a social group that has not been abused."

Even if these are exaggerated opinions, they should be considered seriously. They are telling and symbolizing something important to us.

*   *   *

Today the future seems hazy and unclear. Therefore, in conclusion, I would like to present opinions that indicate possible perspectives for a political debate.

Marie Le Pen explained to the French people: "the French were stripped of patriotism, we suffered in silence, but we were not allowed to love our country."

This grim idiocy, aimed for fools who are able to believe that black is white, shows quite well that the disease suffered by such countries as Poland and Hungary, has universal dimensions. All the more so, the French people also need to recall the differences between de Gaulle's patriotism and the patriotism of Petain and Laval. It seems that Le Pen's dream is a France composed of obedient and barracked French Frenchmen, who repeat stupid phrases and are completely liberated from the enslavement by the spirit of Pascal, Montesquieu, Diderot, as well as Camus or Bernanos. A France like this would be very sad, but I do not believe that it will get to this. The society of people who are devoid of will, passive and conformist towards any power, devoid of creative power and doomed to the fate of the infantile-Sołdacka community—no, no one can imagine such a France. France infected the world with freedom and this virus of freedom can no longer be stuffed back inside a bottle.

Liu Xiaobo, the Chinese defender of human rights, participant of protests in Tiananmen Square in 1989, literary critic and essayist, finally the Nobel Prize laureate imprisoned and held in prison until he lost his war with inexorable cancer disease, and released two days before his death so he could die outside of prison, spoke at his trial, looking in the eyes of judges who were not judges but cruel officers of the regime:

> I look forward to the day when my country will become the land of a free zone where the words of each citizen will be treated with equal attention. It is on this earth that various values, ideas, denominations and political beliefs will both compete for each other and peacefully coexist. Here, the views of the majority, as well as the minorities, will be equally guaranteed, and the views incompatible with the government will receive full respect and protection. All political views under the sun will be sent here by citizens, so that they can choose among them, every citizen will be able to express their political views without any fear, and because of differences, no political persecution will happen to them. I seriously much hope that in an endless string of literary inquisitions, I will be their last victim, and from that moment on no one will ever be condemned for a word.

> Freedom of expression is the foundation of human rights, the core of human nature, and the source of truth. An attack on the free speech is a violation of human rights, suppression of human nature, and concealment of truth.

Thirty years after the fall of the Berlin Wall, in a world ruled by a Chinese leader who resembles a cruel emperor of the Mandarin era, in the world of Putin and Trump, in the world of Erdoğan, Orbán, and Kaczyński, I cannot add much to these daring words, which are imbued with dignity and truth.

Note

1. Yegor Gaidar, *Collapse of an Empire: Lessons for Modern Russia* (Washington, DC: Brookings Institution Press, 2010).

Part IV

Reflections

Chapter 17

Why Did the Cold War End When and As It Did?

David C. Gompert

We Cold Warriors—no, Millennials, we are not from "Game of Thrones"—did not expect the conflict of our lifetimes to end in our lifetimes. How wrong we were, to our astonishment and gratification. If not the end of history, it certainly was a fulcrum of history. Much has been written about *how* the Cold War ended, under particular circumstances. But understanding *why* it ended is at least as important, not just for history's sake but for what it may tell us about the behavior of societies and states in times of change and pressure.

The facile answer to why the Cold War ended when it did is that the Soviet Union ended when it did. True, the Cold War can be said to have ended in 1989, when the Kremlin acquiesced in anti-communist revolutions in Eastern Europe, whereas the Soviet Union was formally dissolved two years later. But Gorbachev's main motivation to end the Cold War was to rescue the Soviet Union. Whether he would have sought to end the Cold War if the Soviet Union was not failing is moot.

To redirect the question, then, why did the Soviet Union collapse when it did? Briefly, in the words of an old sailor, the ship of Soviet communism, already listing badly, was capsized by the effects of the information revolution. When its skipper failed to right it, it sank as peacefully as "an old man slipping into a warm bath."[1] By surprise if not default, the West won the Cold War. The end was unpredicted yet, on reflection, not so unpredictable.

The full story is rather complicated. Soviet and Western leaders began working systematically to lower East-West tensions after new General Secretary Mikhail Gorbachev, shaken by the Chernobyl reactor catastrophe, decided that domestic reform and international cooperation were essential. Fundamentally, these events occurred because Soviet communism—a mix of Marxist ideology, economic central-planning, state and party bureaucracy, Russian imperialism, and confrontation with the West—collapsed of its own dead weight. Its ideology could not tolerate truth; its economic central-planning retarded modernization; its bureaucracy was obese; its propaganda was stale; its military was outsized; the arms race drained it of investment capital; and its imperialism, including demands for military intervention, caused bankruptcy and, in Afghanistan, intolerable loss of life. The Soviet Union could no longer compete with the West technologically, economically, militarily, or in the war of ideas. To make matters worse, the price of its principal revenue source, fossil fuel, nose-dived.

In these conditions, the comprehensive reform launched in the mid-1980s by Gorbachev—following alarms sounded and tepid reforms attempted by his predecessor, Yuri Andropov—seemed like a good idea at the time.[2] *Perestroika* would restructure the economy by introducing a modest role for actual demand, market-based pricing, and return-on-capital investing. *Glasnost* would open the Soviet state and communist party by allowing information to move more freely, promote truthfulness, and encourage new ideas. The idea—or hope—was that both communism and the Soviet Union would become humane, accountable, legitimate, innovative, productive and sustainable. "New Thinking" would overhaul foreign policy and produce a negotiated way out of the Cold War. In turn, this would allow access to new technology, which was advancing rapidly and transforming every sector, including the military, in the West.

That Gorbachev believed that these reforms could work suggests that this favorite son of Soviet communism—and to this day a devout socialist—did not understand that it was beyond saving. We now know that *glasnost* and *perestroika* were not just "too little too late" and doomed to fail but would hasten the Soviet end-days. These reforms gave rise to unafraid and interconnected dissent, unfulfillable expectations, unfavorable comparisons to life in the West, and awareness that the glorious story of a successful and harmonious multinational Soviet state was largely fabricated. Revolution swept across Eastern Europe, where communism had been imposed by Stalin's army two generations earlier and still had shallow roots. In parallel, support for communism crumbled in the Soviet Union itself, with the Baltic republics energized to demand independence, separatism on the rise in Ukraine, and Boris Yeltsin's ascent as an anti-establishment—essentially anti-communist— Russian nationalist.

Still, why did the Cold War and the Soviet Union not drag on but instead end *then*? Mainly, the Soviet political-economic system did not—could not—participate in the information revolution. It could not compete either in inventing or using this technology, which depends on free enterprise, consumer demand, and minimal state interference. All along, the West had a profound, if sometimes latent, advantage in innovative dynamism, propelled not by the state but by people and enterprises working to advance their particular interests, usually—not always—producing human progress. The information revolution tapped into this advantage, and it put the West on course to prevail over Soviet communism. While American and fellow Western innovators were not out to win the Cold War (nothing was further from their minds), their role was pivotal.

Communism suffocated innovative dynamism. Soviet scientific and higher-education systems were still excellent. However, because information technology requires initiative, rewards risk-taking, and relies on both consumer and capital markets, state-planned production and resource allocation were anathema. Nor could the Soviet state control the networking, facts, truths, and new ideas this technology offered. Thus, the information revolution would not only bypass but also undermine the Soviet Union. Changes required of the Soviet Union in order to succeed—even to survive—in the information age contradicted its essence.

This contradiction was not well understood at the time in the West because technological upheaval and East-West strategic competition were happening in mutually exclusive realms by entirely separate institutions and by people with unconnected perspectives and agendas. The U.S. information industry was, by its ideological predisposition, divorced from government.[3] It was engaged in fierce international competition, not with the Soviet Union but with Japan. In the author's stint in this sector in the 1980s—a formative time for both the sector and the author—the Soviet Union was literally never mentioned, because it was irrelevant to the opportunities and business at hand. One does recall a speaker at a business roundtable in 1982 stating matter-of-factly that the Cold War was over, and the West had won. By the late 1980s, the U.S. military would harness information technology to transform warfare and give the United States unrivalled superiority. Moreover, globalization of digital infrastructure and, as a consequence, easier access to information would render the Kremlin incapable of hiding the truth and controlling society.

But let's not get ahead of ourselves. The pages that follow cover communism's economic decline (the "listing"), the information revolution in economic, military and political affairs (the "capsizing"), and the cumulative effect of these developments on the viability of Soviet communism and outcome of the Cold War (the "sinking").

Before proceeding, though, the reader is invited on a brief excursion into theories of why certain complex human systems, like the Soviet Union, prove unstable and unsustainable, while others—the Peoples' Republic of China, so far—do not.

Why Some Complex Human Systems May Fail: Fantasies and Rigidities

Two theories concerning the sustainability of complex (socio-economic-political-cultural) human systems bear on our case. The first is that of *fantasy ideology*, which has been ricocheting around the halls of political science in recent decades.[4] Laced with psychology, fantasy-ideology theory tries to explain why groups are drawn and conform to certain all-encompassing and closed closed-minded explanations—predictions *and* prescriptions—of human struggle, progress, and end-states. Nazism offered a racial explanation. Marxism held that human affairs can be explained as a class struggle between owners and workers. Salafism calls on all Muslims to reject modernity, return to 7th-century piety, and do battle with those who disbelieve or get in the way. What such ideologies have in common is that they discount or reject the way people naturally and actually are inclined to *behave*, thus earning the qualifier "fantasy."[5] They are, in a word, impractical. So they require obedience, which dictates coercion, undermines legitimacy and can be sustained only with isolation and still greater coercion. Neither capitalism nor nationalism is such an ideology unless taken to such extremes that it brooks no competing ideas. Liberal democracy is not a fantasy ideology because it is inclusive by definition and therefore resilient. In this regard, what may seem on the surface to be weak states, e.g., democracies, are in fact robust, whereas autocracies may need to rely on power and control to be viable.[6]

States organized around fantasy ideologies tend toward command economies driven by heavy state investment and mobilized labor, which may not be sustainable.[7] Hitler and Stalin drove production with top-down dictates, dedicated cadres, informers, brow-beaten workers, and the prospect of war—all justified by the ideology and by the enemies they saw at home and abroad, such as Jews and democracies. Such economic systems have expiration fates (though unknown dates). In Hitler's case, it led directly to war, extermination of internal enemies, and final destruction. In the Soviet case, it led to collapse because society, along with conquered nationalities, could no longer be mobilized by a failed idea, a bogus economic system based on that idea, or force that became too costly to use.

A different but related theory is that of *complex adaptive systems*—a way of explaining why some organizations thrive and others fail in the face of change.[8] In political-science terms, a complex adaptive system is one in which "micro-level" (fine-grained) sensitivity to a changing external environment guides productive "macro-level" (aggregate) adjustment. Such sensitivity is conditioned by success and failure, possibly cyclical. Because open complex systems are dynamic, they progress better than closed ones. Fantasy ideologies, precisely because they cannot tolerate information that does not fit, are bound to be inflexible and more brittle than they may seem. How long would Nazism have endured had it not been destroyed in the war it started?

A closed system can survive by using brutality, xenophobia, isolation, cult worship of a leader, and acceptance of depressed living conditions: look at North Korea's seventy-year life-span—thirty of them coming after the Soviet Union ended—against stiff odds. Some eventually accept reform and openness when the alternative is increased oppression: look at the spread of democracy in East Asia and Latin America. As for the Soviet system, even after molting its fantasy ideology, under Khrushchev, it did not become adaptive. It did become more complex as its economy diversified, however, which made central planning more tortuous and markets more essential. As we will see, Gorbachev knew what was coming and tried reform—but by then the real choice was between failure and complete transformation.

This leaves us with two questions. First, why did Soviet communism collapse when it did? Second, why has "communist" China not collapsed? The answer to the first question is that these theories could have predicted that Soviet communism would have to be transformed or would collapse, but not *when*. For that, we must examine the particulars, in the pages to come. A brief answer to the China question will come after the Soviet case.

Listing Ship:
Worsening Prospects for the Soviet Economy and Empire

The Soviet economy grew rapidly until about 1970, even allowing for chronic data-fiddling. Then, being a command economy, productivity began to fall. The requirement to meet production targets and avert risk led managers to shun innovation in general and new technology in particular. More fundamentally, Soviet communism discouraged individual initiative, without which sustainable economic progress is impossible in the modern era. Revolutionary technology works only to the extent organizations are restructured in order to exploit it; yet adaptability was not a Soviet quality, at the macro or micro level. Agency resided with the state, not the individual.

The focus of Soviet research and development (R&D) was to improve military capabilities—certainly not to satisfy consumers. The economy depended on heavy industry, and even that was decoupled from demand. Agriculture, so important (and brutish) in earlier times, lacked effective, market-based distribution. Although unsurpassed in arable land and receiving huge state investment, Soviet food-growing was extremely inefficient (except for the 2% in private hands), and the need to import grain and meat sky-rocketed. Modernizing non-military industry was difficult without private capital. Full employment did not improve living standards or reward investment, which was determined by the state, not by markets. Per capital GDP stalled after 1970.

What let Soviet leaders off the hook were rising revenues in what by then had become the economy's main strength (and eventual bane): oil and gas production. Bookended by the energy crises of 1973 and 1979, high prices and gas pipeline deals sustained the growth of an economy that was otherwise in decay. Funds stuffed state coffers, to the satisfaction of officials. Only as fossil-fuel prices plummeted in the 1980s did Soviet economists and leaders—the truthful ones—appreciate their dire straits. Debt to Western banks swelled to pay for imports.

Meanwhile, the global economy was integrating all around the Soviet Union, to the benefit of the United States, its allies, and China, among others. But the Soviet economy remained isolated and uncompetitive except in oil, gas, and other extractive stuff. Trade comprised about 4% of Soviet GDP—compare that to 50% of Chinese GDP today!—and most of that was raw materials and arms. The ruble was not convertible. Soviet workers made little that anyone else wanted to buy. By the 1980s, even Soviet-made arms were less desirable for countries that could afford choice, as they became harder to maintain and fell a generation behind Western competition. While foreign direct investment grew globally, the Soviet economy was not on the list of interesting destinations (compared to, say, East Asia). The inflexible and isolated Soviet economy was trailing by a widening margin in productive enterprise. In the "workers' paradise," health care deteriorated, the mortality rate rose, and cynicism about party and the state grew.

On top of its domestic woes, maintaining the Soviet Union's empire, competing with the West militarily and, to a lesser degree, providing foreign aid comprised a huge economic drain for a weak economy. By 1980, the combined GDP of the alliance arrayed against the Soviet bloc—the United States and its six largest allies—was five times its size and was entering a period of growth based on new technology and globalization. Moscow shoveled more and more resources into the maw of the defense, espionage, and internal security services. By the time Gorbachev introduced *perestroika*, Soviet military spending had climbed to 15-17% of GDP (the highest level in the Cold War). This proved worse than wasteful, as the Soviets' opponents responded with increased military spending from the base of vastly bigger and healthier economies.[9]

The Americans became especially alarmed with the Soviet buildup after the fall of Iran's shah and the invasion of Afghanistan in 1979. With U.S. military outlays on the rise under presidents Carter and Reagan and, as important, emphasis having shifted from Vietnam back to Europe and to Southwest Asia, the Soviets answered with still more tanks, artillery, planes, and missiles. Ironically, this Soviet buildup caused Western intelligence, defense, academic and political figures to overlook the growing inability of the Soviet Union to compete economically, technologically and, eventually, militarily. Recall the Committee on the Present Danger, which supplied thirty-three senior officials of the incoming Reagan administration, where they feasted on CIA assessments of a growing Soviet threat.

The 1980s began inauspiciously for the Soviet Union in its nuclear competition with the United States and its NATO allies. Upon achieving parity in intercontinental nuclear delivery systems, as formalized by the SALT II agreement, the Soviets shifted priority to the nuclear threat to Western Europe, notably in the form of the SS-20 intermediate-range missile. By menacing U.S. allies with weapons that could not reach the United States, the Soviets threatened to "decouple" the U.S. strategic deterrent from NATO's defense.[10] However, the United States and its allies responded by agreeing in 1979 to deploy in Western Europe intermediate-range nuclear forces capable of hitting the Soviet Union. The Kremlin had not only failed in its decoupling scheme, but now it faced the prospect of a new nuclear threat.

There ensued a Soviet propaganda and fifth-column campaign to mobilize the European Left to oppose deployment of NATO missiles and to fracture and paralyze European coalition governments. Though this led to massive demonstrations, it failed. Whatever resonance Soviet ("fantasy") ideology once had in European opinion, it had by then been depleted by revelations of Stalin's crimes and Soviet use of force in Hungary (1956), Czechoslovakia (1968), and Afghanistan (1979), and at that very moment threats against Poland's Solidarity movement. By the time NATO systems were deployed, Soviet leaders had to concede that they could not crack Alliance cohesion or resolve.

Meanwhile, the economic burden of the Cold War was being made heavier by imperial "over-reach."[11] Afghanistan was the tipping point. Although Army Chief of Staff Ogarkov warned that the Red Army had zero experience in counterinsurgency and could not promise success, his aging masters, Gromyko, Ustinov and Andropov—Brezhnev was fading by then—forged ahead anyway. Within two years of a ten-year intervention, it was should have been clear that the war could not be won, was bleeding the Soviet economy, and was fomenting discontent, especially among families whose sons did not come home and who asked "For what?"

When Solidarity challenged communist rule in Poland, the Kremlin first decided to send in troops *only if* the Jaruzelski government requested them. A year later, on further consideration—with war in Afghanistan going badly—it decided against intervention *even if* requested. KGB chief and future party General Secretary Andropov insisted that it was more important to "save our own country" than to maintain communism in Poland.[12] Although the Brezhnev Doctrine was not officially cancelled until 1988 by Gorbachev, forces was no longer an affordable option to save communism elsewhere, including East Central Europe. One reason the Cold War ended when it did was that the Soviet Union became too weak to sustain communism militarily.

Yet, blinkered Western fixation with Soviet military spending and hardware counts, on one side, and misplaced confidence of Soviet leaders in reforming communism, on the other, obscured what was happening. U.S. government institutions regarded the Soviet system as monolithic, robust and increasingly threatening. Western economists and intelligence analysts were guilty—a strong but apt word—of overestimating the scale and growth of the Soviet economy and missing signs that it was in growing trouble. The insatiable appetite and rising costs of the Soviet military added to nominal GDP, economic growth-rate, investment and R&D. The East-West arms race made the Soviet economy look hale when in fact it was sick. Its puny consumer sector was not understood by either side to be a liability, even though consumer demand drives information technology.

Meanwhile, Soviet visibility into the severity of economic weakness was blocked by production-output metrics, which were regularly inflated and anyway ignored that such output was misaligned with real demand, owing to the absence of markets. As noted, productivity was declining, and living conditions were not keeping pace with (misleading) GDP growth. These problems got worse as the economy became too complicated for central-planners to grasp, much less to manage.

Ironically, the Soviets installed some mainframe computers to help them with economic planning and tracking; but rapid progress in computing systems—first mini-computers, then distributed processing—rendered these machines and their clunky software obsolete. There was no mechanism for the Soviets to stay up to speed in information technology. Just imagine if the U.S.-led information revolution had been directed by the government!

In sum, while the Soviet economy was becoming both too sick and too complex to be managed by the state, the information revolution had begun to transform advanced market economies of the Soviets' enemies *and* to integrate the world economy to their advantage. The only role for the Soviet Union was to sell fuel for other's growing economies. A steep drop in energy prices, from $38/barrel in 1981 to $13/barrel in 1987, knocked out the last crutch of the Soviet economy and the chief source of revenue for the Soviet state. Revenue from fossil fuel contracted sharply and could no longer postpone the day of reckoning.

Capsizing: The Information Revolution

The decline of the Soviet economy began before the information revolution did (around 1980)—which could not have helped it anyway because of communism's incompatibility with these technologies. By the time Soviet leaders came to grips with the truths and implications of both economic and political deterioration, in the mid-1980s, the United States and its allies in Europe and East Asia had begun to realize the promise of these (*their!*) technologies. Western economic and, later, military momentum picked up just when the Soviet system began to break down.

As Joseph Nye put it: "At the end of the 20th century, the major technological change was the growing role of information as the scarcest resource of an economy. The Soviet system was inept at handling information...because of its deep secrecy."[13] When Gorbachev came into office in 1985, there were 50,000 personal computers in the Soviet Union compared to 30,000,000 in the United States. That's roughly one for every six thousand Soviet citizens compared to roughly one for every eight Americans. Again, the significance of such a disparity was not understood at the time because the information revolution occurred largely beyond government's field of vision.

While the computer age began in the 1950s, the information revolution did not begin until computers and telecommunications were digitized and linked. In the beginning were computers and, separately, telephones. Certain technological breakthroughs, notably in micro-processing, fiber-optic and satellite transmission, packet-switching and cellular telephony, led to broad-band digital data-networking (or distributed processing). Deregulation of telecommunications and the breakup of the Bell System in 1984 enabled computer-communications integration and competition, which was then propelled by the demands of large Western business enterprises. Voila!—email, the Internet, the World Wide Web, global digital infrastructure, and network-based restructuring of organizations from banks to airlines to utility companies to government agencies, chiefly U.S.-led.

For all the headaches it has caused society—spam, e-porn, unfounded news, hacking, loss of privacy, job-robbing robotics—the ability to share information and collaborate regardless of distance has been breathtakingly positive. For one thing, firms were now able to distribute functions optimally while managing seamlessly, a boon to efficiency and spur to globalization. Productivity increased sharply, as automation allowed humans to do what they do best: think. Education has expanded its reach. Banks have networked. Business-to-business and customer-to-supplier links have been forged. These and many other advancements have been concentrated among the nations that lead in the invention and production of information technologies, which in the latter stages of the Cold War were, first and foremost, the United States, followed by its European and East Asian allies—the same coalition that stood against the Soviet Union.

While the U.S. military was instrumental in supporting early some technologies of the digital revolution, its acquisition red-tape and industrial inertia held it back from the accelerating progress of these technologies in the economy at large. Nonetheless, by 1990, as first on display in the Gulf War, the U.S. military was leading a "revolution in military affairs" (aka "network-centric warfare," aka "targeting revolution") involving conventional forces. The resolution and coverage of sensors were rapidly improving; data networks fused their voluminous products; munitions gained pin-point accuracy at any range; collateral damage was reduced; global-positioning systems gave ships, planes and weapons near-perfect navigation regardless of location; off-board guidance and microelectronics brought per-weapon costs down and lethality up; networking facilitated integrated joint command-and-control and operations.

For a while, U.S. forces had a near-monopoly in applying digital technologies, which were mostly driven by its vast commercial markets, revenues and R&D. Until now—with China's technological and military rise—this military superiority enabled the United States to dispatch joint forces anywhere at will to wage lop-sided combat with few casualties (e.g., liberation of Kuwait and air campaign against Serbia). This pattern was to the consternation yet envy of the Soviets.

Compared to its revolutionary impact on conventional military affairs, the impact of the digital revolution on strategic-nuclear capabilities and competition has been muted. Warning systems, missile guidance, infrastructure for command, control and communications, and computerized weapon-testing have all been modernized, and nuclear weapons themselves have been updated. But core strategic hardware—bombers, bombs, missiles—has endured. Moreover, the need for humans to manage tightly all nuclear operations has inhibited a comparable information-technology "revolution in nuclear affairs."

Although the United States did not seek to achieve strategic-nuclear superiority, the Soviets were alarmed by U.S. work on ballistic missile defense. The Strategic Defense Initiative, dubbed "Star Wars," was little more than a twinkle in Ronald Reagan's eye, for the technologies needed to defend against a large nuclear-missile strike did not—for that matter, still do not—exist. However phantasmagorical it was, Star Wars was seen by the Soviets as a looming threat to their strategic deterrent that would give the United States a potential first-strike capability and, consequently, an advantageous position in geo-politics and crises. In hindsight, we can see that the Soviets were so amazed by U.S. prowess in information technology that they ignored the infeasibility of large-scale missile defense. In any case, this clearly added to their gloom concerning the East-West arms race and their Cold War burdens.

The Soviets were in fact able to maintain rough strategic-nuclear equivalence with the United States, but they were slipping behind qualitatively in conventional capabilities, something bean-counters on neither side could discern. After Vietnam, the Pentagon, led by technologist Harold Brown, embarked on a new "long-term defense program," to which NATO allies signed on, focused on the Warsaw Pact's massive mechanized threat to Western Europe. New technologies—precision-guided munitions, cruise missiles, advanced and extended intelligence, surveillance and reconnaissance (ISR), and broad-band communications—enabled new concepts of operations. The most important of these was "air-land battle," which harmonized ground combat with air strike, and ISR-enhanced targeting of "second-echelon" Pact forces and support. The age of the tank offensive—the Red Army's stock-in-trade—was finished.

Having already been induced by NATO nuclear-force deployments to enter into the Intermediate-range Nuclear Forces (INF) Treaty in 1988, the Soviets—under a leader determined to end the Cold War—entered into a Treaty on Conventional Forces in Europe (CFE) in 1990. The latter imposed equal and lower limits on tanks, artillery, combat aircraft, etc., which the Soviets had long resisted in order to maintain their quantitative advantage. Both these treaties signified the end of the military confrontation and arms race that marked the Cold War. In the analysis here, they reflected the growing inability of the Soviet systems to compete with NATO, even militarily.

For some time, the Soviet military knew what was happening but not how to offset it. Before their American counterparts embraced the network-centric "revolution in military affairs," Soviet military thinkers identified the potential for this in less specific, more intuitive terms. Their vision was fulfilled in the 1980s, not by them but by their opponent. Here again, a fundamental asymmetry ruled: work on information technology in the Soviet Union was concentrated in and for the military sector. In the United States, it was much less in the military sector than in the vastly larger consumer and industrial-goods sectors, owing largely to the R&D budgets of the titans of information technology, e.g., IBM, AT&T, Microsoft, and Intel.

To illustrate: say the United States was spending 5% of its GDP on defense in 1985 and the Soviet Union was spending 15% of its much smaller GDP on defense, and that both were allocating 5% of defense spending to R&D. In that case, the Soviets and Americans were spending about the same amount on defense R&D. However, let's also say that the consumer sector was 70% of U.S. GDP and that 5% of revenue generated in that sector was invested in R&D of new technologies, whereas the Soviets were spending next to nothing on consumer-sector R&D. The net result is that the United States was outspending the Soviet Union in *total* R&D on new technology by ten to one, or by over

$1 trillion during the first decade of the information revolution and last decade of the Soviet Union.

If anything, this illustration is generous to the Soviets, for actual Soviet GDP was less than it appeared to be. And, of course, much of the innovation in information technology came from pony-tailed Americans in garages—a phenomenon as common as unicorns in the USSR. With a small consumer sector, a sclerotic industrial sector, and no way to form, attract or reward venture capital, the Soviet Union had no chance of competing in the information revolution in military affairs as it had in the age of mechanized forces. Instead, it tried to compete by plowing more money into those forces, as well as into its grossly outsized nuclear arsenal. This Soviet reaction, though wasteful, made Western analysts and political critics more worried about the danger of Soviet aggression, when they should have been less worried.

Beyond its effects on economic and military competition, the information revolution disrupted Soviet politics. Here was a state, and an empire, that relied vitally on the ability to restrict and monopolize information available to its subjects. It also went to great lengths to keep dissidents from coalescing. The Soviets depended, in the vivid expression of Hannah Arendt, on the ability to "atomize" the population and thus make it controllable.[14] Until the information revolution, they were good at this. Then, fax machines (remember them?), though much earlier, were able to take advantage of broader telephone bandwidths and thus became a common way of transmitting documents—including dissidents' manifestos and reports of oppression in the Soviet Union and its European satellites. Mass protests were still risky, but state security services could not corral fax-centric collaboration among communism's opponents. Networked dissidence was peaceful—violence would not work anyway against a violent state. State television had to compete with Western satellite stations, and citizens came to doubt what they were told by Soviet mouthpieces.

The mortal danger to the Soviet system of even rudimentary information technology was especially evident in Eastern Europe. The fax was used to organize labor-union strikes, starting in Gdansk and spreading faster than the authorities could manage. By the time *glasnost* was underway, email was available to citizens and dissidents, and the number of personal computers multiplied. Not until well after the

Cold War have authoritarian states, e.g., Putin's Russia and Xi's China, found ways to block email and Web access. (We'll see if they succeed.)

In sum, the inability of the Soviet system to generate, use, or control society's access to information technology added to its economic, military and political failures and set the stage for the final act. Predicting the year and circumstances would have been impossible as late as Gorbachev's introduction of reforms, but it would be sooner than later.

Sinking: The Failure of *Perestroika* and *Glasnost*, and the End

Restructuring the Soviet economy was a palpable failure. The accumulation of fatal weaknesses in central-planning and state ownership could not be rectified by reforms, which tried to make an unworkable system work. Government spending, food prices, and inflation rose sharply. True transformation could not be done quickly. But as Michael Mandelbaum put it, transitioning from a communist economy to a capitalist one was like trying to switch from left-side driving to right-side driving gradually. GDP per capita—as good an indicator as any of economic health—declined by about 1.5%/year from 1986 on. Despite instances of market-based pricing and profits, there were no winners, only losers. The refusal of the United States and European Union to finance *perestroika* before it could be shown to work was out of neither stinginess nor malice. Western sentiment was that investing in what remained of a state-run system would at best fail and at worst keep that system on life-support.

The opening of the political system also backfired. *Glasnost* was seen as a green light to challenge state and party authority. Unsurprisingly, the turn against Soviet control and communist rule would start in earnest in Eastern Europe, where most was known about economic and political conditions in the West. There, Gorbachev was not the target but the icon of opposition and change. The combination of *glasnost* and the end of the Brezhnev Doctrine ignited unrest throughout the satellites, enabled by information technology and free of fear of Soviet tanks. Others in this volume have detailed the spread of anti-communist insurgency across Eastern Europe, from Solidarity's electoral triumph to the opening of Hungary's borders with the West, to Gorbachev's insistence that East Germany's Erich Honecker must go, to the demolition of the Berlin Wall. But these specifics tell how the Cold War ended, not why. The end began in Eastern Europe because communism had no legitimacy there: it had been imposed by a Red Army that was now at bay.

What began in Central Europe quickly infected certain nationalities and republics of the Soviet Union. Soviet communism had no more legitimacy in the Baltic states than in neighboring Poland. They were the most determined to leave the Soviet Union and wanted no part of any post-Soviet commonwealth. Centrifugal forces gained strength as well in western Ukraine and the Caucasus. The union that had been constructed mainly by force could not hold together once force was off the table (certainly after the failed coup). Some old-line communists in the republics changed their colors and stayed on, especially in Central Asia.

In sum, the Soviet economy was in deep trouble on its own terms and incapable of exploiting, much less creating, the most important new technology. This same technology permitted dissent to network and burst in Soviet satellites and some republics. Information technology was also tilting the qualitative military balance in NATO's favor, and that was bound to get worse. All in all, contradictions between the Soviet system and creation and use of the new, dominant technology—the former rejected freedom, and the latter required it—were fatal.

Gorbachev—hero or goat? More than anyone else, he ended the Cold War, which he could see the Soviet Union was losing. To him, ending the Cold War was necessary in order to open the gates to Western technology. But ending the Cold War, he knew, would not be enough: new-found political legitimacy and economic reforms were also needed. The main effect of these steps, however, was to embolden opposition to Soviet communism, which could not be contained at an acceptable, affordable price. Gorbachev's policies brought an end to both the Cold War *and* to the system he hoped ending the Cold War could save.

Did the West win the Cold War? Clearly it did, though less in its end-game diplomacy than in its economic, technological, and military success and superiority, owing in large part to the information revolution that it started and led. A separate yet often conflated question is whether the United States should have *said out loud* that it won the Cold War. Arguing against any such crowing is the belief that it would deepen and prolong Russian animosity toward the West. Arguing in favor of candor about Cold War's winner and loser is the belief that only if Russians accept this bitter truth will they seek a fundamentally different future for their country. What is undeniably important for all to understand is why the Soviet Union capsized and sank.

Concluding Thoughts

Signs of inexorable Soviet decline were visible, to those who knew where to look, decades before the end. Yet, until the failure of the coup and resultant destruction of the "center" in August, 1991, the demise of the Soviet Union did not seem imminent. Moreover, the oxymoron of the Soviet Union in the information age could have lasted for years. But two developments during the middle of the 1980s accelerated the collapse of the Soviet Union, and of the Cold War. First was the sharp drop in fossil-fuel prices, which ripped the bandage off the dismal Soviet economy. The other was the decision by Gorbachev to launch *glasnost, perestroika*, and "new thinking" in East-West affairs. *Perestroika* fell well short of transforming the Soviet economy, but it was probably all the political traffic would bear. It was *glasnost* that invited challenges to Soviet communism in Poland, Hungary, Czechoslovakia, and East Germany by releasing anti-Soviet forces that could no longer be crushed by force, which was no longer an option.

Recalling the discussion of theory at the top of this chapter, the political illegitimacy of Soviet communism, declining economic performance, and inability to compete in or use information technology were symptoms of a complex system rooted in a fantasy ideology and too rigid toto adapt. These factors made the end of the Cold War and the Soviet Union certain, but not how soon.

Why, then, did the Cold War and Soviet Union end when they did? The choice of Mikhail Gorbachev as general secretary, given his predisposition to reform, was clearly a precipitating event. At about the same time, the fall of global oil and gas prices, which was not the Soviets' doing, sent the economy into a steep and final nose-dive. Of course, the full implications of these events were not realized at the time.

Why has the Peoples' Republic of China flourished? For one thing, it has not been in the grip of a fantasy ideology since the death of Mao

Zedong and rise of Deng Xiaoping as de facto top leader starting in 1976. Even before he witnessed the failure of Soviet communism, Deng eschewed "class struggle," opened China to foreign trade, and made sweeping market-based economic reforms, which he then doubled-down on in 1992, right after the end of the Soviet Union. Deng's China avoided nuclear and conventional arms races with either of the superpowers, adopting instead minimal deterrence, nuclear no-first-use, and a military budget of less than 3% of GDP. He also set China's strategic direction and pace with his admonition for China to "bide its time" for as long as needed to build its economy, military strength, and domestic stability.

Since Deng, China been less ideologically rigid; neither its state-heavy market economy nor its rising nationalism excludes other lines of thought. Moreover, its economic success and nationalistic pride has bolstered the regime's legitimacy, thus far. China is also pragmatic: "It doesn't matter whether a cat is black or white; if it catches mice it is a good cat," said Deng famously. It has allowed considerable personal freedom, though drawing the line at questioning the single-party system of government or organizing nation-wide. Being open to the world economically, China is unavoidably exposed to outside information and competing ideas. Instead of resisting information technology, China is determined to become a world leader in it (e.g., artificial intelligence), and becoming such a leader will increase pressure to ease restrictions on information freedoms at home. In these respects, China is a far more adaptive complex system than it once was or than the Soviet Union ever was.

Finally, the Chinese economy is balanced, resilient, and adaptive. Its principal vulnerability is dependence on importing raw materials to sustain its extraordinary, continuing growth. But it has mitigated this vulnerability by diversifying its sources (and has benefited from a long trend of low commodity prices). China is also dependent on Western demand for its manufactures, which have been the locomotive of its economy. It could suffer from a trade war, but not necessarily more than its opponent(s). It could also be susceptible to foreign-policy manipulation by a trading partner. But these exposures do not spell any mortal danger to the Chinese state. Rather, they are part and parcel of integration in the world economy, from which China benefits immensely.

By Gorbachev's time, the Soviet Union was economically, unable to either create or withstand information technology, falling badly behind its competitors, over-spending on its military, and increasingly illegitimate with its population. China is none of these.

Notes

1. *Seinfeld* fans will remember this line uttered by George Costanza to describe the sinking of the Andrea Dorea.

2. The KGB, which Andropov once led, had a better, earlier grasp of the Soviet Union's declining competitiveness than any other organization. Ironically, its subsequent leader, Vladimir Kryuchkov, was a key organizer of the failed coup of 1991.

3. In the United States, DARPA was supportive of data networking in the 1960s and 1970s. But the armed forces, intelligence establishment, and government in general carried on as before until well into the 1980s.

4. Jacques Lacan and Slavoj Zizek being two of the most noteworthy.

5. Reader of Adam Smith's *Wealth of Nations* will recall that his economic theories are based on the non-fantasy of human self-interested "sociability."

6. See Richard Ullman, *Strong States, Weak States*, Foreign Policy Association Headline Series, 2003.

7. In her classic *Origins of Totalitarianism*, Hannah Arendt explained the imperative of increasingly autocratic and brutal rule in order to maintain control. It is arguable whether Soviet communism was totalitarian after the death of Stalin. Hannah Arendt, *The Origins of Totalitarianism* (New York: Harcourt, Brace, Jovanovich, 1973).

8. These ways of thinking were developed mainly at Santa Fe Institute and RAND. Also see nonlinear dynamical systems, heterogenous agents, phase transition, emergent behavior, self-organizing networks.

9. By the end of the 1980s, Soviet GDP was estimated by the CIA to be half of U.S. GDP. This probably understates the gap, given that both the Soviets and the CIA overestimated Soviet GDP. See Marc Trachtenberg, "Assessing Soviet Economic Performance During the Cold War: A Failure of Intelligence? *Texas National Security Review*, 2018.

10. "De-coupling" was a term of the nuclear arts that meant that the United States would not escalate to the use of intercontinental systems if conventional and theater-nuclear defense failed against all-out Soviet aggression.

11. A phenomenon not unique to the Soviet Union, as European empires had also become too costly to keep.

12. Minutes of October 29, 1981 Politburo meeting. Released transcript quoted in Hans Binnendijk, David C. Gompert, and Bonny Lin, *Blinders, Blunders and Wars* (Arlington, VA: RAND, 2014).

13. Joseph Nye, Harvard Kennedy School Belfer Center, "Analysis and Opinions," April 5, 2006.

14. Arendt, op. cit.

Chapter 18

The End of the Cold War: 30 Years On

Anatoly Adamishin

While going through my archived papers dating back 30 years, I came upon this Oscar Wilde quote: "The one duty we owe to history is to rewrite it."

This got me thinking how good it would be to go back in time and replay some actions. Surely something went wrong at some point if Russia is now once again pitted against the United States, has become alienated from Western Europe in a number of aspects and its relationship with some East European nations, including former Soviet republics, is short of hostile.

I anticipate the response: "You have only yourself to blame."

I want to try to prove that the word "only" is wrong.

To be convincing, I have to pay a lot of attention to Russia's eternal vis-a-vis, the United States.

For the United States, the outcome of the Cold War meant global domination. This was something that had probably not happened since the Roman Empire.

There was a positive side to Pax Americana, namely slightly more than a couple of decades of conflict-free relations between the major powers. However, this somewhat forced "calm" could not go on for long, as the entire world was changing dramatically.

One way or another, conflicts between great powers have resumed at a scale that is perhaps even more dangerous than during the Cold War. The dominant school of thought has it that we have not yet reached the peak of tensions.

Against this background, *j'accuse* the U.S. administrations (except Reagan's last years) for one thing in their policies that should have been changed, if we could go back in time: namely, their attitude towards Russia.

But let's put things in proper order.

In March 1985 the Soviet people received a new leader of their country. His name was Mikhail Gorbachev. Now we know what this man did to take the world away from a nuclear catastrophe.

Then, though, very few could hear through the official Kremlin fanfare the first chimes of the bell tolling the end of the Cold War.

Had Gorbachev not come to power, the transformation of the USSR's politics, economy and military known as *perestroika* would not have happened. Or if it had, it would have been much later.

One of *perestroika's* core elements was the cardinal shift in the Soviet Union's foreign policy. Had it remained the same, it would mean postponing the end of the Cold War for an indefinite period.

Gorbachev's predecessors might even have recognized that the USSR's "tail was pinched in Afghanistan, its nose in Poland, and in between there was a mess in the economy." But they couldn't find the strength to break out of the rut of perennial confrontation.

Strictly speaking, the opposing force had no need to rush. The Americans were in a far better position both in geopolitics and economics. In one of the key aspects of the struggle—the arms race—Washington was ahead of Moscow in terms of technology, finance, and integration of the achievements of defense-oriented research and development in the civilian sector.

The Soviet Politburo would later reveal the top-secret figures: the USSR was spending 2.5 times more on defense per capita than the United States.

Trust between the two superpowers was at a low point. Restoring it required proactive measures. This was an important task, yet it was secondary to the main objective: the desperately needed reconstruction of Soviet society.

Gorbachev started implementing his ideas within the first few days of moving into the Kremlin.

Addressing the leaders of the Warsaw Pact countries, who came to his predecessor Chernenko's funeral, Gorbachev said with clear certainty: "We trust you fully, we will no longer make claims for control or command. Your policies are guided by national interests (as opposed to the interests of the global socialist system—author's note), and you bear full responsibility for them before your peoples and parties."

I am not sure that everyone grasped the seemingly evident meaning of his words: we were no longer responsible for the survival of the Eastern European regimes.

Since the beginning of *perestroika*, the leadership was inundated with thousands of letters from ordinary people asking: Why are we involved in the war in Afghanistan? When will it all end? One general was bold enough to sign with his real name: "I am incapable of explaining to my fellow soldiers what an 'international duty' means and to whom we owe it."

As early as in April 1985, Gorbachev put it bluntly to "our" Afghan President Babrak Karmal: "We will pull out." Witnesses' accounts suggest Karmal all but fainted on the spot.

There was no question of whether to stay or to leave. The problem was how to leave. Resolving it took a long time.

For a time, I was at the helm of a working group on Afghan affairs that led negotiations with the Americans. They were slowing down our withdrawal from Afghanistan by providing significant military aid to the Mujahedeen. In the end, however, we managed to achieve a result: the United States and the USSR became the guarantors of the Afghan-Pakistani peace accords inked in Geneva in April 1988.

The last Soviet military officer—who happened to be Commander of the 40th Army General Boris Gromov—left Afghan soil in February of the following year.

People tend to forget that it was Gorbachev's *perestroika*, new thinking and foreign policy that brought relations with China from hostile to normal; led to normalization of the relations with Yugoslavia; and—last but not least—restored diplomatic relations with Israel.

Here is a quote from my diary: "May 30, 1985. Saw Gorbachev in action: four hours of negotiations with Bettino Craxi, Italy's prime minister. Gorbachev is definitely different from the ones we saw before: a confident speaker, who doesn't read from a piece of paper, thinks fast, jokes… He was obviously obliging Andrei Gromyko (then still a Foreign Minister—author's note), giving him the floor. Andrei used that when playing hardball: "Not a single Soviet citizen would understand if we restored diplomatic relations with Israel."

In July 1985 Gromyko, who was minister for 28 years, was replaced by Eduard Shevardnadze. Not a single Kremlinologist could foresee his candidacy; few people knew that Shevardnadze and Gorbachev had long established their like-mindedness.

One year later Shevardnadze made me his deputy, and I was assigned to oversee African affairs and human rights—the latter had just been allocated a separate department within the ministry for the first time in its history.

President Reagan and Secretary Schultz, who didn't trust Gorbachev at first, started warming to him when they saw that we really meant it when we were talking about human rights.

It was we who needed a radical change in this sphere the most. But those changes were a solid bonus when it came to foreign affairs.

My counterpart in this field at the U.S. Department of State was Richard Shifter. We remain friends till today; we even wrote a book together: "Human Rights, Perestroika, and the End of the Cold War."[1] I refer this book to everyone who wants to know how much was done in the USSR domestically and in Soviet-American cooperation in this field.

As for African affairs, the war in the southwest was in the spotlight. The Americans, including my friend Chester Crocker, Assistant Secretary of State for African Affairs, had been trying to stop that war since the early 1980s, notably trying to get the Cubans out of Angola. In December 1988, two and half years after the USSR engaged in the conflict from the position of *perestroika*, accords were signed in New York that put an end to that conflict.

Namibia, the last colony in Africa, gained its independence with South Africa withdrawing from the country as well as from Angola. The anti-apartheid movement rapidly gained momentum in South Africa. Cuban forces left Angola.

That was an unforgettable time for me also because Gorbachev's and Shevardnadze's trust meant that politically my hands were completely untied. It was also due to the fact, perhaps, that Africa was not the primary concern among the mountain of problems with which Gorbachev had to deal. Crocker, similarly, once called Africa a stepchild of the Department of State.

Here's my free summary: if it were not for *perestroika*, Crocker would still be looking for a middle ground between South Africa, Angola and Cuba; Sam Nujoma would have to wait years down the second half of the road for independence, and Mandela and de Klerk for their Nobel Peace Prize; Fidel Castro would still push on with the revolutionary process that had been resistant to move, while Angola would still suffer. (In 1986, Nujoma, the leader of SWAPO, the organization that fought for Namibia's independence, replied in the following way to my question about prospects of his country independence: "We've been fighting for 25 years, and we're probably halfway there.")

U.S. Secretary of State George Shultz, in his book "Turmoil and Triumph," a signed copy of which I have, wrote about the resolution of regional conflicts, including Africa's southwest: "Nothing could be achieved if it weren't for the core changes in Soviet-U.S. relations."

The major core change was in the scope of real disarmament. The Soviet Union and the United States concluded their first ever agreement on the elimination—that is, not on the limitation, as it had been the case in the past, but on the physical destruction—of a whole class of weapons, namely American and Soviet medium-range missiles.

By the way, the Pentagon tried to dissuade Reagan from signing it as the Pershing II and intermediate-range ground-launched cruise missiles deployed in Western Europe gave America a tremendous advantage over the Soviet Union, while the Soviet Pioneer missiles, better known as SS-20, could not reach U.S. territory. One Pentagon hardliner, Richard Perle, even resigned in protest over this.

President Reagan hadn't yielded. Sadly, the end was not happy.

These positive developments, I insist, were triggered by Gorbachev's *perestroika*. But I specifically underline that his words and deeds awoke President Reagan's peace-making nature. The rapprochement between the USSR and the United States began. It was this decisive motion that led to the end of the Cold War in 1988.

But, unexpectedly, a chilly wind came from Washington.

George H.W. Bush, the new U.S. president, decided to change course. He immediately took a pause to radically revise the policy towards the Soviet Union. For the Kremlin, that had a bombshell effect.

Gorbachev, as follows from his memoirs, felt like a bride abandoned at the altar. Experts on the United States from the Foreign Ministry tried to allay fears of Soviet leaders, saying that in the long run Washington would return to the Reagan era interaction. But it never happened.

When talking to Margaret Thatcher in my presence on April 18, 1989, Soviet Prime Minister Nikolai Ryzhkov said in plain terms, "Everything has stopped." Thatcher was trying to comfort Ryzhkov, assuring him that she would "influence George."

I don't know whether or not that conversation played a part, but Thatcher later sounded very dramatic when addressing George Bush, saying that "history would not forgive us if we did not rally to support him [Gorbachev]." François Mitterrand, Giulio Andreotti, and Helmut Kohl told Bush the same, even if less eloquently. All to no avail.

The pause in U.S.-Soviet relations continued almost throughout 1989: Gorbachev and Bush would meet for the first time on Malta only in December. By that time, the cards had already been dealt and the game was actually over. Suffice it to say that the Berlin Wall came down in November 1989, one month before Malta.

Throughout that period, the new U.S. administration behaved in a manner that was clearly anti-Gorbachev, spreading doubts as to the Soviet leader's sincerity, insinuating that he would return to a policy of confrontation once he felt strong enough, and auguring his demise, which is exactly what the U.S. Secretary of Defense Dick Cheney did in an interview with CNN shortly after assuming office.

Six years later, former Secretary of State James Baker would write a book revealing he was frightened of Gorbachev's popularity in Europe (In Italy I even saw mini icons depicting Gorbachev).

A directive completed in the spring of that year revising U.S. policy toward the Soviet Union stated: "American policy must be designed not to help Gorbachev but rather to challenge the Soviets in such a way as to move them in the direction we want."

In parallel with keeping the pause with regard to Moscow, Washington was revising its approach to the seemingly academic question of whether the Cold War was really over.

Thatcher had publicly replied in the affirmative back in November 1988: "We're not in Cold War now." Reagan was of the same opinion. He denounced the Soviet Union's label as the Empire of Evil speaking in its very headquarters—the Kremlin. Outgoing Secretary of State George Shultz was worried that the new administration in Washington "did not understand or accept that the Cold War was over."

That concern was justified. In May 1989, Bush stated that the Cold War would only end once Europe had become "whole and free." Later, to dismiss any remaining doubts, he would add that the unification of Europe should occur "on the basis of Western values."

Bush's National Security Adviser Brent Scowcroft was more explicit: "Our principal goal should be to try to lift the Kremlin's military boot from the necks of the East Europeans."

Now that Washington was urging freedom for the East Europeans, the logical question was how long the status quo between the two German states would last. Until then, Washington's position on the issue was, as Scowcroft wrote in a memo in March 1989, that "no West German expects German reunification to happen in this century."

Those moods should be overcome. In the first few months of 1989, Bush advisers proposed that he reanimate the German issue from a years-long state of anabiosis. He did it even before Germans.

In May 1989, Bush was the first to publicly bring up the topic of reunification, saying "if you can get it on a proper basis, fine."

Instead, West German Chancellor Helmut Kohl's keynote statement to the effect that the German question had been put on the international agenda was made in late August. In late November, Kohl in his famous "Ten points" speech in the Bundestag, openly called for Germany's reunification. (Nota bene: Kohl didn't mention NATO among those points.)

Remarkably, Kohl made that statement only after he got a "hint" from a Russian representative (whose visit to Germany had not been made known to Gorbachev) that the Chancellor of Germany correctly interpreted as the Kremlin's consent to the reunification on some condition (confederation and no rush).

Looking ahead, I should note that German people still view Gorbachev as the one who gave the green light to unification. Back then, both the USSR and Germany hailed the process as part of the historic reconciliation of the two countries. Against the background of today's problems, Russia still enjoys greater cooperation with Germany than with any other Western country.

Margaret Thatcher may have been somewhat late, but she did eventually warn George Bush that hasty reunification would spell the end for Gorbachev. I would add that this also signaled the end of budding democracy in the Soviet Union, which was exactly what happened then.

It was not until January 1992 that George Bush, in what can be viewed as a summary of his achievements, solemnly told both houses of the U.S. Congress that "By the grace of God, America won the Cold War." He reiterated that "the Cold War didn't "end"—it was won."

A year and a half earlier, when the United States needed the Soviet Union's support to oust Saddam Hussein's Iraq from Kuwait, Bush was saying totally different things. Back then, he believed that the Cold War had ended thanks to his cooperation with Gorbachev.

I may witness that the leaders of *perestroika* told the Americans that for the USSR, settling the problems related to the end of the Cold War was a necessary phase which, they expected, would be followed by joint work with the United States to ensure international peace.

Such work was certainly what Ronald Reagan and George Shultz supported. Conversing with Shevardnadze, Ronald Reagan once said: Gorbachev and I are the only ones who can save the world.

Bush, for his part, was not particularly inspired by this perspective. His administration proceeded from the premise that the United States now had an unprecedented chance to become the absolute master of the world, to project U.S. power into the foreseeable future and beyond.

Proponents of a more delicate approach were shouted down by those who believed that the United States would be powerful enough to pull this off. Temporarily, the latter even decided that they had no need for Western Europe as an ally, let alone Russia.

Washington did not conceal the fact that it would resort to any and all means needed to prevent the emergence of a rival that could threaten U.S. interests.

The "we will do what we need to do and to hell with Russia" attitude resulted in preserving NATO as a politico-military alliance, first (despite the Warsaw Pact was dismissed), and then expanding it eastward. U.S. diplomat George Kennan assessed it as the most fatal mistake in the post-war history of the United States.

Still, there was, for a time, a lingering chance for a better future, compared to how it eventually panned out. I mean joint efforts to overcome the split of Europe.

There were also appropriate instruments to start building European security on the new basis of agreements between 35 states-signatories in the 1975 Helsinki Accords and the 1990 Paris Charter for a New Europe.

In 1991, while serving as USSR ambassador to Italy, I was involved in serious discussions with Italian Foreign Minister Gianni De Michelis about the possibility of setting up a European security council as part of the OSCE. De Michelis was dreaming of a "grand treaty" between the Soviet Union and the European Community that would also mean a sort of USSR–West joint venture, and told me that a USSR–EU association agreement could materialize in the near future.

West German Foreign Minister Hans-Dietrich Genscher also took a solid stance. He said that Bonn did not want to leave NATO, nor did it want to see the Alliance expand. What was wrong with Genscher's 'One Germany, One Europe' formula?

In September 2015, I met wheelchair-bound Genscher in Berlin, at an event to mark the 25 years since the completion of the Two Plus Four Group's mission. It dealt with the external aspects of German reunification. I had, at some point, represented the Soviet Union in the group. Genscher said this during an open discussion: "I wanted to overcome the split of Europe, but I did not want to move the dividing lines further to the East."

During negotiations with Gorbachev in February 1990, Kohl said that NATO would "naturally" not expand eastwards, as he thought it went without saying.

U.S. Secretary of State James Baker similarly stated that Germany's reunification would be incorporated into pan-European structures, or would at least run in parallel with the consolidation of those structures. Bush also mentioned the OSCE in the context of Eastern Europe's democratization.

Mitterrand, for his part, called for guaranteeing the Soviet Union's security and proposed setting up a European confederation of West European countries and former Communist states, including the renewed USSR.

There were many voices in Europe calling for a security system on the continent that would be run by Europe with the comprehensive participation of Russia.

However, it took three for this tango. The U.S. administration was firmly committed to building a post-Cold-War Europe around NATO, meaning without Russia.

At the same time Moscow was assured that a new Europe would mean a new NATO. The declaration of July 1990 NATO Summit in London did contain plenty of positive statements by its leaders, and it did incorporate much of what the USSR proposed at the onset of perestroika. Among others, NATO promised not to be the first to use force.

Earlier, in March 1987, Thatcher told Gorbachev that NATO would never use force unless in response to an attack.

Twelve years later, NATO bombed Serbia for 78 days, remaining out of reach for Serbian air defenses. This was done without any approval of the UN Security Council and in direct violation of the UN Charter. NATO members violated their own charter as well by attacking a state that had not performed any acts of aggression against any member state of the alliance.

They had also neglected the 1997 Founding Act on Mutual Relations, Cooperation and Security between NATO and the Russian Federation. This Act symbolized good intentions between Moscow and NATO. Had they materialized, perhaps the Act would have been a breakthrough. But NATO's actions against Serbia were such a blow for the Act that it could not endure.

This came as a great shock to Russia, which was never truly comprehended in the West. Western countries preferred to forget all about the Yugoslavian case as soon as they could, just like they forgot about Kosovo precedent set by the forceful revision of the European borders.

Russian society, formerly quite sympathetic of the West, started to revise its views: apparently, the West says one thing and does another. Nationalism acquired momentum in Russia. In March 2019, the Russian media dedicated a generous coverage to the 20th anniversary of the Belgrade bombings.

Other "initiatives" of the consecutive U.S. administrations—wars in Iraq and Afghanistan, military operation in Libya, withdrawal from the ABM Treaty and from other agreements on curbing arms race (most recently, the United States pulled out of the INF Treaty), claims not to expand NATO eastward (Russian politicians are convinced those were intentional lies), expelling Russia from G8, and so on—all had contributed to the disillusionment of the Russian people in the West.

As for pan-European security, if there ever was a chance to overcome U.S. obstruction by joint efforts of the Soviet Union and a number of Western European countries, it could only emerge in the late 1980s and the early 1990s, under Mikhail Gorbachev.

However, there came the Belovezha Accords whereby Boris Yeltsin and Leonid Kravchuk, President of Ukraine (the main "heroes") dissolved the USSR. For Yeltsin, such a drastic decision was probably the only effective way to realize the main aim: deprive Gorbachev of his office as soon as possible.

Under Yeltsin, who pleaded for U.S. support in his ongoing internal political squabbles, the weakened Russia was not something that Washington cared to reckon with. As a result, the split in Europe was overcome, leaving Russia by the wayside.

This configuration finally has determined the mindset of the Russian people with regard to the West. The initial excitement of belonging to the greater community of nations was replaced with the clear feeling that the West did not need Russia on an equal footing.

A similar change happened in Russia's politics, which had long been aimed at making the country a party of Western structures.

It was, in effect, the United States that sabotaged Russia's attempts to integrate into the West. Unfortunately, a lot of our people think that it was for the better. By way of "compensation," Russia retained (or regained, as some believe) the freedom to operate in an unrestrained manner in the international arena.

During *perestroika*, Bush and Baker were faced with the choice between Gorbachev and Yeltsin.

Gorbachev viewed the reforms as part of the broader context of rejuvenated socialism. In essence, he sought to usher in a socially-oriented economy on the basis of social-democratic ideas, including a free but state-supervised market, and full-fledged democratization of the country.

Gorbachev's reforms produced a fundamental result: the authoritarian Soviet political system had been torn down. Who else but the democratic United States should have been the one to support the Soviet president at this fateful moment?!

The Americans did not care that much about nuances. They favored the anti-communist rhetoric offered by Yeltsin in his bid to win over the sympathies of the West. Indeed, Yeltsin was easier to deal with.

It was not the United States' strategies that played the decisive role in the defeat of Gorbachev's *perestroika*, but rather the entire system of Russia's internal development, first and foremost the escalated struggle for power.

That said, I still believe Washington's choice was inexcusably wrong. They failed to think out of the box of habitual stereotypes. This time, they lacked the strategic vision of Woodrow Wilson, Franklin D. Roosevelt, or Ronald Reagan.

In August 1992, one of the founding fathers of "new thinking," Alexander Yakovlev, told me bitterly that the West had betrayed *perestroika*.

I would like to add color to the picture. When visiting Moscow shortly after the abortive August 1991 coup, Secretary of State Baker wrote back to President Bush: "It is undeniable that the local success of the democrats here is extremely important for us because it would change the world for the better. What is at stake is equal to the post-war revival of Germany and Japan as our democratic allies. The failure of the democrats would make the world much more threatening and dangerous, and I am convinced that, should they prove unable to provide for the population, they will be replaced by a xenophobic, authoritarian leader."

Four months after Baker's visit, a new government came to power in Moscow. As the new leader, Yeltsin suited the Americans just fine. Both sides made numerous statements about strategic relations.

In reality, however, Washington mostly payed lip-service to Yeltsin's "democrats." Significant U.S. assistance was offered only when Yeltsin's position was becoming fragile, and communists could potentially return to power.

While the United States turned a blind eye to the new Russian government's domestic policies (such as the Chechen War and using tanks against the democratically elected parliament) the Kremlin's performance had to be adequate in international affairs.

Under U.S. pressure, Russia gradually lost policy independence. The war in the Balkans provided an example of it, I know this first-hand.

At the same time, Russia was not let in on the decision-making processes. The rule of the day was 'cooperation without participation,' as U.S. political analyst Samuel Charap put it.

Cooperation went out the window when the 'forget Russia' attitude was replaced by one resembling 'the worse for Russia the better,' with little concern for the possibility of this approach backfiring.

Russia's centuries-long vital interests would be repeatedly dismissed and denied until the situation escalated into the armed conflicts in Georgia and Ukraine.

In April 2015, speaking to CNN about the conflict in Ukraine, Baker made a reasonable proposal to the effect that the United States and its Western European allies needed to find a way of returning Russia to the fold of the international community. He also admitted as an afterthought that, following the end of the Cold War and the collapse of the USSR, the United States should have found a way to incorporate Russia into NATO. In Baker's opinion, Russia should have been admitted into the international community, but this did not happen, so the situation is as it is.

In continuation of Baker's thought, I would add, that the United States should have admitted it had played its part in the situation being as it is.

If we are to disregard this, if we think that only Russia—whose actions were often reactive—is to be blamed for all the sins, including those before 2014, then some lessons of the past 30 years will be lost on us.

As far as I know, the first instance of U.S. economic sanctions imposed on czarist Russia was for its mistreatment of Jews. This quickly acquired habit of punishing summarily and unilaterally passing down verdicts is at odds with Russia's nature.

Surviving centuries of the Tatar-Mongol yoke and retaining its status as a great power for three hundred years, Russia has developed a distinct intolerance to being told what to do by foreign states.

We will rather tighten our belts than cave in to a bully. We will identify our own interests and choose methods of protecting them. Is this not what the Americans are doing?

The collision of U.S. dominance and Russian 'mutiny' leaves little room for maneuvering out of the 'Cold War 2.0,' also known as the hybrid war. Just like with the previous Cold War, any possibility to break it off successfully will materialize only after the United States and Russia have found common ground.

This will happen sooner or later, just because there is no acceptable alternative.

Today, I recognize some of the scenarios that I have seen more than 30 years ago. Demands are growing louder in Western Europe and the United States, urging politicians to dare to seek ways out of the confrontation rather than sitting on their hands and waiting for the hammer to fall.

To my great delight, one of those voices belongs to George Shultz.

There is also something new to the current situation. The "urge" to make peace with Russia is coming to the U.S. Western Coast from across the ocean. En passant, I don't quite understand why Washington is doing so much to bring Russia closer to China.

The most convincing reason for a new Russia–U.S. rapprochement is the fearsome fact that a nuclear apocalypse is dangerously close again. This makes me think at times that living in a bipolar world was safer.

Still, it is not easy for the current generation of politicians to get to work in this respect. They are part and parcel of the national egotism, which, thanks to the omnipotent United States, too, has become ubiquitous in the international arena. They are being governed by aggressive domestic lobbies.

Just like during the Cold War, geopolitical disagreements are complemented by ideological differences, this time those related to values.

However, as they said in Ancient Rome, *Dum spiro, spero*. The common wisdom and sense of responsibility of the leaders of three major world powers—the United States, China, and Russia—must prevail.

The paths away from the edge of the cliff are more or less known. This is not the first time we have found ourselves on that cliff, after all.

Certainly, global development, primarily in terms of technological advances, makes the task of finding a consensus more difficult than before. Yet, even this task is manageable.

The problem is lack of goodwill, as the parties involved prefer, for the time being, to play with fire.

There is one thing in which political analysts should rejoice: their profession is, once again, in demand. And not just for analyzing the opportunities missed over the past 30 years, but also for devising possible ways out of the geopolitical impasse. As well as for ranting at the powers that be, who generally ignore our recommendations.

Note

1. United States Institute of Peace Press, Washington DC, 2009.

Chapter 19

Mikhail Gorbachev and the
NATO Enlargement Debate: Then and Now

Pavel Palazhchenko

The purpose of this chapter is to bring to the attention of researchers materials relating to the antecedents of NATO enlargement that have not been widely cited in ongoing discussions.

In the debate on NATO enlargement, both in Russia and in the West, the issue of the "assurances on non-enlargement of NATO" given to Soviet leaders and specifically Mikhail Gorbachev in 1989-1990 has taken center stage since the mid-1990s. The matter is discussed not just by scholars, journalists and other non-policy-makers but also by major political figures, particularly in Russia, including President Vladimir Putin and Foreign Minister Sergei Lavrov. In the West, there has recently been renewed interest in the subject following the publication of some declassified material by the National Security Archive, a Washington, D.C., non-profit organization with a somewhat misleading name.

While some of the aspects of the discussion of the "assurances" are similar in Russia and the West (conflation of fact and opinion, of binding obligations and remarks relating to expectation or intent) the subtext is different. In Russia most commentators accuse Gorbachev of being gullible and naïve and blithely accepting the assurances instead of demanding a binding legal guarantee of non-enlargement. In the West, the subtext is more often of the West's bad faith in breaking what is supposed to be an informal "pledge of non-enlargement" given to Gorbachev. It should be noted, however, that in the eyes of Russian critics of Gorbachev what matters is not this subtext; they use it to support their narrative of Gorbachev's gullibility, or worse.

One example is the preface to the collection of documents published by the National Security Archive in December 2017, which begins with the following:

U.S. Secretary of State James Baker's famous "not one inch east-ward" assurance about NATO expansion in his meeting with So-viet leader Mikhail Gorbachev on February 9, 1990, was part of a cascade of assurances about Soviet security given by Western lead-ers to Gorbachev and other Soviet officials throughout the pro-cess of German unification in 1990 and on into 1991, according to declassified U.S., Soviet, German, British and French documents posted today by the National Security Archive at George Wash-ington University.

The documents show that multiple national leaders were con-sidering and rejecting Central and Eastern European membership in NATO as of early 1990 and through 1991, that discussions of NATO in the context of German unification negotiations in 1990 were not at all narrowly limited to the status of East German ter-ritory, and that subsequent Soviet and Russian complaints about being misled about NATO expansion were founded in written contemporaneous memcons and telcons at the highest levels.

The documents reinforce former CIA Director Robert Gates's criticism of "pressing ahead with expansion of NATO eastward [in the 1990s], when Gorbachev and others were led to believe that wouldn't happen." The key phrase, buttressed by the documents, is "led to believe."[1]

That indeed is the key phrase. Not so much for a Western reader, who may not regard Robert Gates as the best arbiter in the debate on NATO enlargement, but for a Russian steeped in the anti-Gorbachev narrative, who will read it as "Gorbachev was naïve/stupid enough to believe." This, indeed, is how it was "interpreted" in most of the Rus-sian commentary of the publication.

So what was said and what was agreed on Gorbachev's watch, and what were the alternatives?

I have discussed the subject with several Russian and Western par-ticipants in the political and diplomatic processes of 1989–1991. None of them recalls that there was any substantive discussion of a possi-ble NATO enlargement to countries of Central and Eastern Europe during those years. This is regardless of their evaluation of NATO en-largement as such, i.e. whether it was a good or a bad idea in the first place and whether it was properly managed.

At my request two participants in the process gave me access to their correspondence discussing the subject. They are Ambassadors Jack Matlock and Rodric Braithwaite. Matlock was the United States Ambassador to the Soviet Union in 1987–1991 and he has continued to comment on U.S. and world affairs since then. Braithwaite was the UK's Ambassador to the Soviet Union and Russia until 1992.

I will first quote from Ambassador Braithwaite's letter of April 24, 2011:

> Russians say they were given oral assurances by Western leaders in 1990-1991 that NATO would not be enlarged beyond united Germany. They regard the subsequent enlargement of NATO as a breach of faith. They criticize the Soviet government of the day for not having insisted on getting binding assurances in writing.
>
> Western officials and historians say either that that no assurances were given, or that they were without significance, or that they have to be seen in the context of a rapidly changing situation.
>
> Despite the passage of twenty years, the issue still crops up as a burden on Russia's relations with the West.
>
> **The assurances**
>
> Russians point to the following:
> Assurances given in 1990:
> * James Baker, US Secretary of State, 9 February 1990: "We consider that the consultations and discussions in the framework of the 2+4 mechanism should give a guarantee that the reunification of Germany will not lead to the enlargement of NATO's military organization to the East";
> * Helmut Kohl. German Chancellor, 10 February 1990: "We consider that NATO should not enlarge its sphere of activity."
>
> Assurances given in 1991:
>
> * John Major. British Prime Minister, Speaking to Defence Minister Yazov, 5 March 1991: "He did not himself foresee circumstances now or in the future where East European countries would become members of NATO;
> * Douglas Hurd, British Foreign Secretary, speaking to Foreign Minister Bessmertnykh, 26 March 1991: "[T]here were

no plans in NATO to include the countries of Eastern and Central Europe in NATO in one form or another;"

- Francois Mitterrand, speaking to Mikhail Gorbachev, 6 May 1991: "Each of the [Eastern European] countries I have mentioned will seek to ensure its security by concluding separate agreements. With whom? With NATO, of course. ... I am convinced that is not the right way forward for Europe." This was, of course, a prediction, not an assurance.

[*Author's note*: recently declassified material published by the National Security Archive contains some additional references to similar "assurances.']

This factual record has not been successfully challenged in the West. The remarks by Major and Hurd are confirmed by British records. I was present on both occasions.

A distinction needs to be drawn between the assurances given in 1990, and those given in 1991. The earlier assurances were given before agreement was reached in the "2+4" negotiations about the status of united Germany and its position in NATO between the Soviet Union, the United States, Britain, France and the two Germanies.

American officials later argued that James Baker's remarks referred only to the possibility that NATO forces would be introduced into Eastern Germany after reunification. As they stand, however, the remarks are ambiguous, and it is not surprising that they have been interpreted as referring to a wider expansion. In the event, Baker's point was dropped from the US negotiating position in the 2+4 negotiations, because his lawyers advised that it was not sustainable. A tortuous form of words concerning the deployment, exercising or stationing of non-German as well as German NATO forces in East Germany following reunification was agreed in the last hours of the 2+4 negotiations in Moscow on 13 September 1990.

The situation had, however, changed radically by the time John Major and Douglas Hurd spoke six months later, by when it was clear that the Warsaw Pact was on its last legs. Their remarks related specifically to expansion beyond German into Eastern Europe. They followed a speech by the Czech President Havel arguing that Czechoslovakia, Hungary and Poland should all be brought into NATO.

German and Americans leaders do not appear to have given the Russians similar assurances. Given the care with which the British normally clear statements on common issues of policy, especially with the Americans, it is barely conceivable that the two British statements should not have reflected a common Allied understanding. However the relevant documents have not yet emerged from the British archives.

The Context

Western officials now argue that given the turmoil at the time— Germany reunified much more rapidly than anyone had expected, the ending of Communist governments all over Eastern Europe, war in Iraq, and the impending tragedy in Yugoslavia—it was not surprising that Western leaders failed to consider the issue of NATO expansion more systematically: at that time the possibility seemed remote. The argument is plausible, even if it is not very respectable.

Nevertheless, the Russians were entitled to take seriously the repeated high-level assurances they were given. They were bound to feel that they had been dealt with in bad faith when the push for NATO enlargement began not long afterwards under President Clinton. It is easy to imagine how the West would have reacted if the positions had been reversed.

An Alternative?

Primakov and other Russians have since argued that the Gorbachev government ought to have got Western assurances about NATO expansion in writing. Some argue that this was one more example of Gorbachev's failure to stand up for Soviet interests.

This is unrealistic. If the Russians had demanded that the West give them written assurances, Western governments would have had to consider much more carefully whether or how they wished to bind their hands for the future. It is highly unlikely that they would have agreed. The chances of the Russians getting written assurances were close to zero.

Regardless of what assurances were or were not given, some people in the West argue that it was a major error of policy to alienate Russia by enlarging NATO into Eastern Europe without providing for a wider European security arrangement in which Russia was included. But the uncertainty following the collapse of the Soviet Union, and the unsurprising concerns of the East European countries including the Baltic States that they would be left to deal with the consequences on their own, were powerful motives for NATO to move into a vacuum. The expansion of NATO into Eastern Europe was almost inevitable in the circumstances, even though it was badly tainted by Western triumphalism and sloppy Western diplomacy.

The subsequent push to expand NATO into Ukraine, the Caucasus and even Central Asia has stalled, probably permanently.

How far the deterioration of relations between Russia and the West in the 1990s would have been slowed or prevented if NATO had not expanded must remain an open question. There were plenty of other sources of friction at the time. Expansion is now a fact, to which all are having to adapt. Russia and its Western partners seem to be settling into a more pragmatic relationship, in which both Western triumphalism and Russian bitterness play a lesser role. The question of who said what to whom in the early 1990s will eventually become a matter of concern only to historians."[2]

Ambassador Matlock, who disagrees with Braithwaite on some points, particularly on the wisdom of NATO enlargement, gives his perspective on the "assurances" in his reply to Ambassador Braithwaite:

As yet, the Bush Library has not declassified many of the documents involved in the 1990 negotiations. However, what was said by Baker in his February, 1990, meetings with Shevardnadze and Gorbachev has been reported accurately both in Gorbachev's memoirs and in the book on German unification by Zelikow and Rice (*Germany Unified and Europe Transformed*, Harvard Univ Press, 1995, p. 187). It is quite possible that there was no formal discussion among the allies on this point—strange as it may seem. I was told subsequently that Baker picked up the idea from Genscher, whom he saw on his way to Moscow, and floated it with Gorbachev. It was not a formal proposal and, clearly, what he had in mind regarding expansion of NATO jurisdiction to the east was the territory of the GDR. (The Warsaw Pact was still in existence at that time and though one might have suspected that its days were numbered, nobody was thinking of NATO taking on new members in the East.)

Baker was trying to persuade Gorbachev that it would be in the Soviet interest to have a united Germany in NATO—as assurance that it would not in the future make an attempt to dominate Europe or to acquire nuclear weapons. He advanced the argument with a comment to the effect that he did not expect an immediate answer, but wanted Gorbachev to think about it. Gorbachev's answer was sufficiently forthcoming that I advised Baker when we were riding back to the embassy that "he is going to buy this, because in fact it will be in the Soviet interest to have Germany tied to NATO and some U.S. military presence in Europe as a guarantee." (Not a direct quote, of course, but a paraphrase from memory.)

When Baker returned to Washington from his Moscow trip, he was told by State Department lawyers that there was no legal way to exclude the territory of the GDR from "NATO jurisdiction" if that territory was part of a NATO member state. So the idea was dropped from subsequent negotiations. That is probably why it was never formally discussed in NATO. Subsequently, in the two plus four negotiations, it was agreed that foreign troops would not be stationed on the territory of the erstwhile GDR, so in fact that territory was excluded from the full force of NATO jurisdiction.

This latter point is relevant because, subsequently, the Clinton Administration refused to consider bringing the East European countries into NATO with restrictions on stationing foreign troops there. "We will not have second-class NATO members!" it was argued, ignoring the fact that France was not part of the military structure at that time.

It should also be recalled that the February 1990 conversations took place just a few weeks after Bush and Gorbachev had met in Malta harbor, at which time Gorbachev pledged not to use force in Eastern Europe and Bush assured him that the U.S. would not "take advantage" of the rapidly changing situation there. It was not yet obvious in early December 1989 that German unity would occur so rapidly, or on the terms it did. But when it became clear that the East Germans had no stomach for a separate state, U.S. policy was to make sure that a united Germany stayed in NATO. If we could have done so legally, we would have been pleased to exclude the territory of the GDR from NATO jurisdiction. As it was, we all agreed that only German forces could be stationed there.

In my view, the subsequent expansion of NATO by the Clinton Administration, was an error of the first magnitude, but not because it violated promises given earlier. It was an error because it militated against bringing Russia into the European security community, which should have been a strategic goal of our countries in the 1990s. And it was a reversal of the Bush policy of not "taking advantage" of the democratization of Eastern Europe.

Matlock strongly disagrees with the critics of Gorbachev's "gullibility:"

> It is easy to say that Gorbachev could have gotten a formal com-
> mitment not to expand NATO if he had asked. Nobody in the
> senior ranks on our side was thinking of taking in new NATO
> members and all would have been eager to reassure Gorbachev.
> But I am not sure what concrete form such assurances could have
> taken, other than an oral agreement that the Bush Administration
> would not approve new members of NATO in East and Central
> Europe. (A promise which, though never made, was in fact kept.)
> Attention was not paid to this issue. From August 1990 it was Iraq
> and Kuwait, then concern about the Soviet Union itself breaking
> up, and Yugoslavia showing even more distressing signs, plus a
> desire to get START nailed down while there was still a coher-
> ent Soviet government. To the best of my knowledge, nobody
> in a decision-making level of the U.S. government was thinking
> of expanding NATO or preserving the right to do so. But how,
> practically, could binding assurances have been given? Would the
> U.S. Senate have accepted a treaty that removed this option for
> future administrations? Not very likely. Gorbachev was probably
> wise not to open that potential can of worms with everything else
> that was going on.
>
> Therefore, my position remains that the decision to expand
> NATO was a cardinal political error. It was bad policy for the
> reasons I have given—and gave at the time. But it is a stretch to
> say that, so far as the U.S. is concerned, it broke a promise made
> earlier.

If there is anything that contemporaneous public statements of
Western officials and recently published documents prove, it is that
the United States and NATO countries did not, at the time, have the
policy of encouraging East European countries to seek membership in
NATO. Another reason, in my view, for Gorbachev "not to go there."

It is arguable that refraining from enlargement of NATO continued
to be the West's intent for a certain period of time after the breakup
of the Soviet Union. Whereas Poland and some other countries raised
the possibility of joining NATO, it was not enthusiastically received by
NATO's key members.

As late as August 1993, when the possibility of NATO's enlargement and Poland's membership was first mentioned at the summit level

during Russian President Boris Yeltsin's visit to Warsaw, Washington's attitude to the idea was described by the *New York Times* as cautious:

> The incorporation into NATO of former Communist countries, particularly Poland, Hungary and the Czech Republic, has been talked about among the alliance's members and theoretically welcomed.
>
> But Washington has been cautious about bringing former Warsaw Pact countries in too quickly, for fear of antagonizing Moscow.[3]

Therefore, Yeltsin's response to President Lech Wałęsa's raising the possibility during the negotiations surprised his interlocutors. In hindsight, it may be argued that it gave a boost to those favoring enlargement:

> But in an appearance in the gardens of the presidential residence here, Mr. Yeltsin and President Lech Walesa issued a joint statement that repeated Poland's desire for NATO membership and pointed to Mr. Yeltsin's "understanding."
>
> Afterward, the Polish Defense and Foreign Ministers and members of Mr. Walesa's inner circle took Mr. Yeltsin's acquiescence as an occasion to push the West to open up NATO's membership."[4]

It is not clear why Yeltsin reversed the previous Russian position, described by the *New York Times* as one of "reservations about Poland's ambition to join the alliance." It is possible that he was not properly briefed by the foreign ministry or his staff before the visit, or that he just improvised, given his desire to build a new, positive relationship with Poland.

Yeltsin's attitude of "understanding" was, however, reversed after his return to Moscow. On September 15, 1993 he sent letters to Western leaders—Clinton, Major, Mitterrand and Kohl—stating Russia's official position on possible NATO enlargement in much stronger terms than it was ever stated before.[5]

Commentators at the time noted that Yeltsin's letter was sent at a time when he embarked on a collision course with the opposition, thus sharply changing the domestic political landscape and requiring him to show a strong stance in his foreign policy. It is noteworthy that, according to *The New York Times*, President Clinton at the time had not yet made the decision to endorse NATO enlargement. Ambassador

Matlock believes (private conversation) that Clinton did so during the 1996 election campaign, also for domestic political reasons—to get the votes of Polish Americans in key states.

> The overall impression of the letter was expressed by a Western diplomat who said: "Yeltsin calls it an elaboration of his position, but I'd describe it as furious backpedaling."[6]

Though the original assessment by Western diplomats, as reported by *The New York Times*, was that "the result … is that NATO expansion is certainly further off than it could have appeared even a month ago," it may be argued that the letter actually speeded the process as East European nations began to apply increased public pressure in favor of enlargement.

As the momentum of enlargement intensified, Russia's position became more rigid and the coverage in the media more strident. In mid-1990s, Russian leaders began to criticize Gorbachev for failing to get "written guarantees" of NATO's non-enlargement and articles appeared in the Russian media blaming him for the situation.

A typical example is an article by Alexei Pushkov published in early 1997 in *Nezavisimaya Gazeta*. Pushkov was then a TV commentator and later a member of the State Duma. He is currently member of the Federation Council (the upper chamber of the Russian parliament). (An interesting detail: in 1991 Pushkov was working in the international affairs section of Gorbachev's executive office). I was not able to find his article on the Web but his message is I think clear from the rebuttal I was able to publish in the same newspaper a few days later:

> Alexei Pushkov believes that "the current collision between Russia and NATO could have been avoided if not for yesterday's omissions." Now, however, Russia won't be fooled: in "the document now being prepared" about relations between Russia and NATO there must be legally binding assurances that preclude the membership of the Baltic countries and Ukraine in NATO.
>
> The criticisms of Gorbachev, so much in fashion now among the current Russian "elite," are in this case groundless. Talks with Baker and Kohl [*author's note: brief passages from which are cited in Pushkov's article*] took place in February 1990, when the Warsaw Treaty was still in existence. For that reason alone, any attempt by

the Soviet leaders to "give concrete expression" in this way to the assurances of Western leaders would look ridiculous. And, somewhat later, they would be accused of speeding the disintegration of the Warsaw Treaty Organization by doing so. What was being discussed in 1990 was just that the structures of NATO and the military exercises of the alliance must not extend to GDR territory and that nuclear weapons not be deployed there. To that effect not only were assurances obtained but a special clause included in the Treaty on the final settlement with respect to Germany.

Of course, the subsequent decisions of the United States and NATO to admit East European countries in the alliance violate the spirit of those assurances. But conditions for that arose much later, when not just the Warsaw Treaty but the Soviet Union, too, disintegrated. However, not only did not Russia demand legally binding guarantees of NATO's non-enlargement; initially, it did not even object to the idea of enlargement.

But even that is not the most important thing. Any country has the right to decide to be or not to be a member of any alliance. Its neighbors have a right speak about it and to make political objections. This matter, in essence, is a political rather than an international law issue. Had Russia been able to avoid self-weakening— almost self-destruction—had it been able to build normal relations with its neighbors, there would be no question of their joining NATO. This is the real "lesson of recent history."

It's useless to chase the chimera of "codification of intent" (Alexei Pushkov's language). As any law student knows, you can only codify domestic or international law. A treaty that would transform NATO into a "closed company" that rejects aspiring candidates is no more than a fantasy, a utopia, which would have come to nothing then and will equally fail now. Indeed, this is a harmful utopia, since by demanding "legally binding guarantees" the Russian leadership has already painted itself into a corner from which it would be difficult get out. Selective printout of "excerpts" from archive documents will certainly not help.

From the distance of over twenty years I might add that the obsession with "legally binding guarantees" looks even more naïve now that the United States has withdrawn from both the ABM and INF treaties. What could be more legally binding than a treaty duly signed and ratified? And, since Pushkov believed that a piece of paper could have prevented the membership of Baltic states in NATO, it is easy to understand his—and Russian policy makers'—frustration when the exact opposite happened a few years afterwards, on Putin's watch.

As the pace of NATO enlargement intensified, this frustration became more intense and more obvious. Whereas Yeltsin and, initially, Putin mostly refrained from publicly blaming Gorbachev, this changed later—paradoxically, during the Obama years, when the United States slowed the pace of enlargement and the possibility of Ukraine and Georgia becoming members was, for all practical purposes, taken off the table.

Putin chose the American film director Oliver Stone to give a condensed assessment of his view of what he sees as Gorbachev's mistake:

> When the issue of unification of Germany and of the subsequent withdrawal of Soviet forces from Eastern Europe was being decided, both the U.S. officials and the NATO Secretary General, all of them, were saying that the Soviet Union could be sure of one thing—that the Eastern border of NATO would not move farther than today's Eastern border of the German Democratic Republic.
>
> "It was not recorded on paper. Now, this was a mistake on the part of Gorbachev. In politics, you have to record things. Even recorded things are often violated. But he just had a conversation and decided that it's over. That was not so," Putin replied.[7]

So how does Gorbachev respond to such criticism?

Some of his remarks, taken out of context from interviews containing "leading questions," may give the impression that he agrees that he was "taken for a ride." In part, this is because the issue of "assurances" is often conflated with Gorbachev's attitude toward enlargement, which is of course negative. However, in more detailed discussions of the issue his response has been forceful.

Following the Stone interview, Gorbachev was asked by the Interfax news agency to comment on Putin's criticism:

> Today, many international news agencies have echoed Russian President Vladimir Putin's remark made to the American film director Oliver Stone about Soviet President Gorbachev's "mistake" of not raising the subject of guarantees of NATO's non-enlargement to the East.

Gorbachev replied:

> It is hard to understand what may have caused such a statement of
> the President of the Russian Federation. It seems to set aside all
> that was done in the sphere of international security, i.e. normal-
> izing relations with the United States and other countries of the
> world. Historic meetings of the heads of the USSR and the United
> States were held in Geneva, Reykjavik and Malta, which eventu-
> ally led to creating prerequisites for and signing of the treaty—of
> unlimited duration—on the elimination of all intermediate and
> shorter range missiles (INF Treaty), the treaty on the limitation
> of strategic offensive weapons (START-1), the Treaty on conven-
> tional forces in Europe, the unification of Germany and finally the
> end of the Cold War.
>
> As for Gorbachev's "mistake," under those circumstances it was
> not even possible legally to discuss such an issue. Until July 1991,
> two politico-military alliances existed—NATO and the Warsaw
> Treaty Organization. The Warsaw Treaty countries did not raise
> the issue.
>
> To conclude, let me also remind that the process of new mem-
> bers joining NATO began in 1995 and gained momentum since
> 2000, long after I had stepped down from the presidency of the
> USSR.[8]

Gorbachev's most extensive explanation of his position regarding
NATO enlargement and its antecedents is contained in his recent book
In a Changing World published in Russian in late 2018.[9]

Citing Secretary of State James Baker's remark in their conversation
on February 9, 1990:

> We understand that it is important not only for the Soviet Union
> but also for other European countries to have guarantees that if
> the United States continues to be present in Germany within the
> framework of NATO, there will be no expansion of NATO juris-
> diction or military presence one inch in the Eastern direction.

Gorbachev goes on to say:

> Later, these words of Baker and other documents reflecting that
> period's discussions on the problem of politico-military status of
> a united Germany became the subject of a lot of loose talk and

speculation. Some say: Gorbachev was given assurances of NA-TO's non-enlargement. Others: Gorbachev was unable to obtain guarantees of NATO's non-enlargement, he should have pushed harder—and then there would be no problems subsequently related to the accession of Eastern and Central European countries to NATO. Some say such things because of lack of knowledge or misunderstanding, but there are also those who do it in bad faith. So, as the phrase goes, from here on out let's go into detail.

Baker stated, "We consider that the consultations and discussions in the framework of the 2+4 mechanism should give a guarantee that the reunification of Germany will not lead to the enlargement of NATO's military organization to the East.

Hence, the guarantees were provided exclusively in connection with the unification of Germany. What is more, as a result of enormous amount of work conducted at the political and diplomatic level, those guarantees were expressed in treaty form (the Treaty on the Final Settlement with respect to Germany of September 12, 1990). They include non-stationing of nuclear weapons and their delivery systems in the territory of the former GDR and a substantial reduction of the FRG's armed forces (to the level of 370 thousand men). All provisions of that Treaty have been fulfilled and even more: at present, the numerical strength of the FRG armed forces is 185 thousand men.

Should we then have raised the issue of NATO's non-enlargement to the East in more general terms, rather than just with respect to the territory of the former GDR? I am sure that raising it in such terms would have been simply foolish. Given that not just NATO but also the Warsaw Treaty Organization continued to exist at the time (the decision on the self-dissolution of that organization only entered into force on July 1, 1991), if we had started talking about it then, on top of everything else we would now be accused of "suggesting" the idea of NATO enlargement to Western partners as well as speeding the process of disintegration of the Warsaw Treaty Organization.

Quite a different matter is the process of NATO's enlargement to the East that began several years after I had stepped down from the presidency of the USSR. Without a doubt, it violated the spirit of the agreements reached during the Germany's unification and undermined the mutual trust that had been built through arduous efforts and was later severely tested. [It is interesting that the same argument, though phrased somewhat differently, is used in Yeltsin's letter of October 15, 1993: The spirit of the treaty on the final settlement with respect to Germany, especially its provisions that prohibit the deployment of foreign troops within the Eastern lands of the Federal republic of Germany, precludes the option of expanding the NATO zone into the East.—Note added by me. PP]. Let me add: I am sure that had the Union been preserved the enlargement of NATO would not have happened and both sides would have taken a different approach to creating a system of European security. What is more, the North Atlantic Treaty Organization would have been different in nature if they hadn't consigned to oblivion, particularly more recently, the provisions of the London Declaration, adopted in the summer of 1990, concerning evolution of NATO into a mostly political organization, contributing to overcoming the legacy of the Cold War and strengthening the role of the CSCE.

Even though Gorbachev has been treated unfairly by the current government-directed propaganda and often by high-ranking Russian officials, including the president, he has remained generally supportive of Russia's position on NATO enlargement, i.e. its criticism of it as ruinous for relations between Russia and the West and for European and global security. Therefore, the two things—Gorbachev's defense of his foreign policy decisions during the final years of the Soviet Union and his evaluation of the subsequent NATO enlargement process and Russia's response to it—should be treated separately, instead of being conflated as is often done in by interviewers and commentators.

An example of Gorbachev's effort to strike a balance between "defense" and "offense" can be found in his forthcoming book, to be published in Germany in 2019:

> Membership of a unified German state in NATO—an organization born in the years of the Cold War—was perceived by many in our country with much apprehension. We said that frankly to our negotiating partners and proposed options for solving the problem. After long and arduous discussion we agreed that Germany, as a sovereign nation, should itself decide in which organizations and alliances it would participate. But our agreements included more than that.
>
> First, we agreed that the territory of the former GDR would have a special politico-military status.... Secondly, and that was of fundamental importance, the Germans pledged to reduce the personnel of their armed forces by almost fifty percent.
>
> At the same time, within both NATO and the still existing Warsaw Treaty, military doctrines were being revised. There were

plans to increase the political component while reducing the military component in their activities....

Proposing then ... some kind of a "legally binding agreement" on NATO's non-extension to Eastern Europe, as my critics are now demanding in hindsight, would have been absurd and ludicrous. We would have been accused of ruining the Warsaw Treaty with our own hands.

Under the circumstances we did our utmost. Russia was fully entitled to demand observance not just of the letter but also of the spirit of those agreements. The decision, taken a few years later, to enlarge NATO was a step toward undermining trust that had emerged in the process of ending the Cold War.

Russia had to draw appropriate conclusions from that.

*   *   *

Why go through all this now, when the enlarged NATO is a fact of life that cannot be reversed? Certainly the subtext of "Gorbachev's gullibility" does nothing to contribute to the debate on the wisdom of NATO enlargement and on whether the problem of European security could have been handled differently in the 1990s. It is a mystery to me why some Western scholars are willing to provide backup vocals to this narrative.

Yet it is always useful to establish the facts and then to study what the perception of those facts was in the countries involved. Even today, when the damage caused by both sides" mishandling of European security issues has been done, there is some value in discussing what different actors intended or believed at different points from 1989 to the late 1990s.[10]

While the prevailing view in the West today is that the enlargement of NATO was almost certainly inevitable, I believe that the issue, once it arose, could have been handled differently. It remains poisonous today on both sides because Russia and the West have not been able to build a constructive relationship. Was it because of bad faith or ill will? My personal view is that both sides tried, often sincerely but unfortunately with little success.

We should now look for a way forward while learning from lessons of the past. The dysfunctional policies firmly entrenched today on both sides have to be reconsidered. A good place to start would be arms control and arms reduction, as suggested in recent articles by George Shultz, William Perry, and Sam Nunn and by Mikhail Gorbachev.

Notes

1. https://nsarchive.gwu.edu/briefing-book/russia-programs/2017-12-12/nato-expansion-what-gorbachev-heard-western-leaders-early?fbclid=I-wAR0txTibkSxUqqX-vjnqwS-_YtZxRNWzY2IMx6Q73MjZCt8NOBCE_JeHwnU

2. http://www.pavelpal.ru/node/874.

3. Jane Perlez, "Yeltsin "Understands" Polish Bid for a Role in NATO," The *New York Times*, August 26, 1993, https://www.nytimes.com/1993/08/26/world/yeltsin-understands-polish-bid-for-a-role-in-nato.html.

4. Ibid.

5. The letter to Clinton has been declassified and the full text can be found here: https://nsarchive2.gwu.edu//dc.html?doc=4390818-Document-04-Re-translation-of-Yeltsin-letter-on. See also https://nsarchive.gwu.edu/briefing-book/russia-programs/2018-03-16/nato-expansion-what-yeltsin-heard.

6. Roger Cohen, "Yeltsin Opposes Expansion of NATO in Eastern Europe," *New York Times*, October 2, 1993, https://www.nytimes.com/1993/10/02/world/yeltsin-opposes-expansion-of-nato-in-eastern-europe.html.

7. https://www.bbc.com/russian/news-40257219.

8. See http://www.gorby.ru/presscenter/news/show_29766/.

9. Михаил Горбачев. В меняющемся мире. Издательство АСТ, 2018.

10. See https://www.novayagazeta.ru/articles/2015/11/02/66215-adam-daniel-rotfeld-171-na-zapade-net-planov-izolyatsii-rossii-187.

Chapter 20

Turkey's Changing Role After the Cold War: From Ideational to Civilizational Geopolitics

Cengiz Günay

The two years between November 1989 and December 1991 radically changed international politics. The fall of the Berlin Wall, the collapse of the Communist regimes in Central and Eastern Europe and the disintegration of the Soviet Union set the beginning of the end of the post-World War II order, which had been characterized by deterrence and bipolarity. The end of the Cold War ushered in a new era in world politics. The removal of the Iron Curtain in particular fuelled hopes about a democratic future and the end of bloc thinking. Francis Fukuyama enthusiastically proclaimed the "end of history" in Europe and the beginning of a liberal era.[1] A year later, as German unification was being wrapped up, President George H.W. Bush declared the beginning of a "new world order," one characterized by international cooperation. By 1995, discussions on the "end of the nation state" and the beginning of a "borderless age" became popular.[2]

In ensuing years, however, it became increasingly clear that borders had not disappeared and the divisions of the world had not been overcome. Instead, boundaries were being redefined. Geopolitical considerations became influenced by debates on ethnic and religious identities, gradually replacing political ideology and bloc thinking.

Turkey was among the countries significantly affected by the end of the bipolar world system. With the end of the Cold War, Ankara not only suddenly found itself in the center of a destabilized neighborhood ridden by various ethnic conflicts, it also struggled with the redefinition of its own identity and place in international politics.

The tectonic shifts in Turkey's immediate neighborhood between 1989 and 1992 confronted Ankara with multiple challenges. In 1989, Turkey had to deal with an influx of more than 360,000 ethnic Turkish refugees fom Bulgaria who were expelled by the communist Zhivkov regime. In 1990 the conflict between the Soviet Republics of Azerbaijan and Armenia over Nagorno-Karabakh broke out. In August of the same year, Saddam Hussein invaded Kuwait. As a neighboring state, Turkey was key for the implementation of the international embargo imposed on Iraq. In January 1991 the Gulf War broke out. Turkish air bases were crucial for the anti-Saddam coalition's air strikes against Iraq. In March 1991, more than 450,000 Kurds fled from Saddam Hussein's retaliation to the mountainous border region between Turkey and Iraq, leading to a major humanitarian crisis in Turkey's border regions. In summer 1991 Yugoslavia fell apart and the Balkan wars began. Turkey was confronted with an influx of Bosnian refuges. In December 1991 the Soviet Union collapsed, leaving Turkey with three newly independent and politically instable neighbors; Georgia, Armenia and Azerbaijan.

Turkey initially had trouble adapting to this rapidly changing international environment. Removed from the enthusiasm of the Western allies about Europe's imminent reunification, Turkey became increasingly isolated and estranged. Once a Western military outpost at the borders of the Soviet Union, Turkey was now forced to redefine its own international role. In this regard, the 1990/1991 Gulf War marked a turning point. The months leading up to the 1991 international intervention redefined Turkey's geostrategic importance in a new area, not only in the eyes of its Western allies but also those of Turkish decision makers themselves. Developments in the immediate neighbourhood compeled Turkey to become active and more assertive in multiple regions.

Turkey became at the same time active in the Balkans, the Middle East, the Black Sea region, tha Caucasus and in the post-Soviet Republics in Central Asia. As Turkey was lacking economic and political capacities—the country was ravished by hyperinflation, political instability and the military fight against the Kurdish separatist PKK—Ankara's neighborhood strategy sought to capitalize on a common Ottoman history, common religious traditions, cultural affinities and kinship ties. Moreover, supported by the United States, Turkey tried to export its own secular and pro-Western model to the newly independent Turkic Republics of Central Asia.

The emphasis on kinship, religion and secularism in the neighborhood strategy further fueled Turkey's simmering domestic identity questions. A rising Kurdish movement and an emergent Islamist movement increasingly challenged the Kemalist (named after the founder of the Republic Mustafa Kemal Atatürk) notion of nationalism and secularism.

Whereas most of the literature on the end of the Cold War deals with the repercussions on Central and Eastern Europe, this contribution puts the focus on a country at the European periphery. I argue in this chapter that in the era after the Cold War, the notions of "East" and "West" were being redrawn along civilizational lines. Turkey, a country with a Muslim majority but part of the Western bloc, has struggled with redefining its own identity as well as relations with its neighborhood and its Western partners. I argue that while the emphasis on Turkey's Muslim–Turkish but secular identity first seemed to increase Turkey's role in the neighborhood and also leverage its importance in the eyes of its Western allies, in the mid- and long run identity politics further increased estrangement between Turkey, Europe and the United States.

Turkey During the Cold War:
A Frontier State Against Communism

The founding of the Turkish Republic in 1923 entailed a radical break with the country's Ottoman past. The young Republican regime of Mustafa Kemal Atatürk implemented an authoritarian modernization program that aimed at reconstructing state and society. Republican Turkey was modeled on the ideal of Western European nation states. Comprehensive political, legal and cultural reforms such as state-imposed secularization, the introduction of the Latin alphabet, and a language reform were accompanied by a foreign policy that was strongly orientated towards France and Britain. This Western orientation entailed a conscious turning away from the country's Eastern neighborhood.

Tevfik Rüştü Aras, one of the first foreign ministers of the young republic, declared that "Turkey is now a western power—the death of a peasant in the Balkans is of more importance to Turkey than the death of a king in Afghanistan."[3] As much as the young republic's foreign policy orientation towards Europe was ideologically driven and aimed at establishing Turkey as a European power, it also represented a pragmatic adaptation to the realities of the post-WWI era. After all, most parts of the neighboring Middle East had come under direct or indirect European rule and most of the policies affecting the region were made in Paris or London.[4] Parallel to the restoration of relations with former adversaries France and Great Britain, the young republican regime was careful to preserve friendly relations with its large neighbor, the Soviet Union. However, at the same time the Republican regime was eager to prevent any advancement of communism in Turkey.

At the end of WWII the Turkish government felt threatened by Stalin's call for a revision of the Montreux Convention Regarding the Regime of the Straits and claims on the two Turkish border provinces of Ardahan and Kars. The fear of a Soviet intervention drove Turkey closer to the United States. The Turkish government tried hard to be integrated into the emergent Western bloc. Washington first remained caucious, as it was wary of Turkey's reliability and also feared that any intervention in Turkey's favor could jeopopardize the postwar peace settlement. However, efforts of the Turkish government proved successful when Soviet-American relations deteriorated in 1946. The same year, the Turkish government decided to introduce a transition from single party rule to multiparty democracy. In 1947, Turkey received a first grant of $100 million under the Truman Doctrine to develop its military capacities.[5] In 1949, Turkey became a member to the Council of Europe and in 1952 it became a member of NATO. Integration with the alliance and European institutions was seen as an important guarantee against the Soviet Union and the threat of communism, but at the same time, it was seen by the Kemalist elites as a confirmation of the country's aspired Western identity. Despite the fact that at that time Britain and France saw Turkey's role for the alliance mainly in a Middle Eastern defence context.[6]

From the perspective of NATO allies, Turkey's geographic location is what mainly counted. As the only NATO member bordering directly on the Soviet Union, controlling the Bosporus and the Dardanelles straits and commanding a large standing army, Turkey represented an important outpost at the Alliance's southeastern flank.

Turkey's relations with its communist neighbors such as Bulgaria in the West and the Soviet Union in the East were restricted by the framework of the Cold War. Relations with the Middle East remained rather weak. Ankara acted as a status-quo power in the Middle East. The Baghdad Pact signed in 1955 between Turkey, Great Britain and the pro-Western governments of Iraq, Iran and Pakistan was to establish a defensive regional organization to contain leftist revolutionary regimes and to preserve the status quo in the region. Turkey was motivated to contain Arab nationalism at its doors, because Arab nationalist regimes were seen as providing a gateway for Soviet influence. Ankara also believed that cooperation and alignment with the policies and the security interests of the United States and Great Britain would establish Turkey's credibility as a reliable ally. Alignment with the West went so far as that Turkey voted in 1956 in the UN General Assembly against Algeria's independence.[7]

Alignment with Western interests, however, neither leveraged Turkey's importance within NATO nor furthered its role in the Middle East. Many allies still doubted Turkey's commitment to Western security and most Arab regimes thought that Turkey acted like a "henchman of Western imperialism."[8]

The 1962 Cuban missiles crisis highlighted Turkey's dilemma. The Kennedy administration's secret deal with the Soviet Union in order to de-escalate the crisis included a swap. In return for the withdrawal of Soviet nuclear weapons from Cuba, the United States removed nuclear missiles based in Turkey. The fact that decisions concerning Turkey's security were made over its head increased the feeling of being a second-class NATO member and raised suspicions about Washington's commitment to Turkey's security. But Ankara hardly had any alternatives.

In view of the rise of leftist tendencies within Turkey, right-wing parties regarded NATO membership as an instrument to contain communism and Soviet influence in the country. The fear of communism also helped build peculiar domestic alliances in favor of NATO. Even Islamists and right-wing nationalists joined the domestic pro-NATO front. In the 1960s the fear of communism went so far that Islamists accused anti-NATO protesters as of being un-Islamic and of spreading communist thought.[9] One can argue that throughout the Cold War, Turkey's role as a NATO member shaped perceptions of national interest and in a broader sense national identity.[10]

Changing Priorities in a Radically Evolving Neighborhood

The chain of events beginning with Mikhail Gorbachev's policies of *glasnost* and *perestroika* that led the dissolution of the Warsaw Pact and the eventual disintegration of the Soviet Union radically transformed Turkey's immediate neighborhood. Once the most Eastern outpost of the Western bloc, Turkey now found itself in the middle of a region in flux—one characterized by various political crises and ethnic conflicts with major repercussions for Turkey's own stability. Thus, for Turkey the end of the Cold War entailed the end of a certain predictability and regional stability. What came was just the opposite: a rise of uncertainty and regional instability.

Parallel to the rise of instability in and around Turkey, NATO allies seemed utterly fixated on the stabilization of Central and Eastern Europe. Turkey had drifted to the margins of their agenda. As a result Ankara feared a downgrading of Turkey's geostrategic role. In view of these developments many Turkish policy makers felt nostalgia for the days of the Cold War when Turkey had its clearly defined role and "when the East was East and the West was West and never the twain should meet."[11] Ankara entered a difficult process of soul searching, assessing alternative geostrategic options.[12]

Iraq's invasion of Kuwait in August 1990 challenged the emergent, yet fragile post-Cold War world order and at the same time represented a historical moment for its configuration. In retrospect, America's response to Saddam Hussein's naked aggression represented an important opportunity for Turkey to redefine its geostrategic role. In this process, President Turgut Özal played a crucial role. Appointed by the military after the coup of 1980 as minister of economy, Özal had been in charge of neoliberal reform policies and Turkey's transition to liberal market economy. In the first elections after the coup, held in 1983, Özal won with his newly established Motherland Party an overall majority. In 1989, he was elected by parliament as president of the republic. Turgut Özal was the first to break with Turkey's foreign policy tradition of a cautious and restrained approach towards the neighborhood. He was ready to take risks. Against the advice of the Turkish military leadership, the foreign ministry, the resistance of cabinet ministers and strong public opposition—according to a survey 70 percent of the people asked opposed Turkey's active involvement in a war—Özal decided to place Turkey at the forefront of the emergent international coalition acting against Saddam Hussein. Despite of high inflation and the negative effects of an embargo, Özal reassured President Bush of Turkey's support for the embargo imposed on Iraq and even offered to provide troops.[13] In the months leading up to the military intervention, Özal became a frequent interlocutor of Bush—giving the president insights and assessments about developments within Iraq, the capacities and the motivation of Iraqi armed forces and Saddam Hussein's psyche. In that time, Turkey also opened an informal channel between Washington and Tehran. Özal was able to assure Bush of Iranian President Rafsanjani's approval and even indirect support for the war on Saddam Hussein.[14]

As Iraq's neighbor and a major trading partner, Turkey was crucial for building economic and military pressure on Baghdad. Turkey joined the embargo and closed the two oil pipelines leading from Iraq into the Turkish harbor of Yumurtalik, deployed military forces at the border and opened the Incirlik base for air operations from Turkey. While the closing of the pipelines increased the economic pressure, the provision of the air bases to the U.S.-led international coalition enabled the opening of the northern front and enhanced military pressure on Saddam Hussein.

After the war, in spring 1991, faced with a growing number of Kurdish refugees at the Iraqi-Turkish border, Ankara mobilized Washington. Together with British Prime Minister John Major, Turgut Özal was able to convince President Bush of the humanitarian crisis at the Turkish-Iraqi border, and that a "massacre of the Kurds by the Iraqi army could turn the victory in the war into a debacle for the West."[15] In April 1991, the UN passed resolution 688 which enabled the allied forces to establish safe havens on Iraqi territory. The ensuring Operation Provide Comfort started protecting Iraqi Kurds and delivering aid. This also entailed the establishment of a no-fly zone north of the 36th parallel, enforced by U.S., British and French air forces. President Özal suggested to send Turkish troops into northern Iraq, but Bush, who was critical of any boots on Iraqi ground, turned down his offer.[16] Operation Provide Comfort laid the basis for the establishment of the Kurdish Autonomous Region in Northern Iraq (KRG).

Özal's active role in the Gulf War highlighted Turkey's new geo-strategic role and initiated a more assertive Turkish neighborhood policy. In contrast to its role during the Cold War, when Turkey was a backbencher of international politics, it suddenly became catapulted to its forefront.[17] Turkey began to reimagine its geostrategic importance. In contrast to the Cold War, its new role was no longer that of playing a "military obstacle" vis-a-vis a Soviet offensive into Europe, but one of fulfilling such a task in regard to aggression emanating from the Middle East.[18]

President George H. W. Bush's visit to Turkey in July 1991, the first of a U.S. President since that of Dwight D. Eisenhower in 1959, was to honor Turkey's new role. Bush's visit was to be later followed by Bill Clinton's visit in 1999, that of George W. Bush in 2004 and Barack Obama in 2009 and 2015. The sequence of visits of U.S. presidents highlights that from the Gulf War on, Turkey gradually came to play a central role in U.S. strategies towards the Middle East.

Turkey's new activism in the region initially remained within the confines of Western policies. Turkey only became assertive where its assertiveness was in line with its Western allies, and especially the United States. This was also the case in the Balkans—even though the bloody Yugoslav wars of secession posed a new and different challenge to Turkey.

The Rise of Identity Politics

The end of the Cold War signaled a shift from ideology based to identity-based politics. The crisis in the Balkans caused by the violent falling apart of Yugoslavia represents one of the most important developments in this shift. Slobodan Milošević's speech in Kosovo in 1987, where he incited Serbian nationalism with references to the Ottoman conquest and at the expense of the autonomy of majoritarian Muslim Albanians, set the beginning of the end of Yugoslavia.

In the beginning, Turkey refrained from any direct involvement in the developments in the Balkans. Ankara waited and watched what positions Europe and the United States would take.[19] However, the Turkish public became increasingly concerned with the fate of Muslim communities in the Balkans. Many Turks had family ties with Muslims in the Yugoslav Republics of Bosnia, Macedonia, and Kosovo, as well as Albania. Passivitity in regard to the massacres on Muslims in Bosnia incited indignation among many Turkish citizens. Moreover, the events became instrumentalized by an emergent Islamist movement. The Refah Party's discourses depicted the sufferings of European Muslims in civilizational terms, as part of a new world order that is characterized by Western (Christian) hegemony and the repression of Muslims. The pictures of the genocidal massacres had a deep effect on Turkish society, much beyond Islamist constituencies. Fundraising for the Muslim brethren in Bosnia and demonstrations for Turkey's active involvement were expressions of solidarity with developments in the Balkans. President Özal also pressed for a more active Turkish foreign policy towards the Balkan crisis, however meanwhile his party had lost the majority in parliament and the president and his foreign policy positions became rather isolated. Despite growing pressure, the new Turkish government's stance towards the Yugoslav wars in general and especially Bosnia remained observant and cautious.

Turkey's policies changed only when Western policies shifted in 1992. The Turkish government only recognized the independence of the former Yugoslav republics of Slovenia, Croatia and Bosnia-Herzegowina after the United States and the European Community did in April 1992.[20]

Later, the Turkish air forces participated in reinforcing the no-fly zone over Bosnia and deployed 100 soldiers to Zenica.[21] Between 1992 and 1995, Ankara contributed troops to the UN Protection Force (UNPROFOR), as well as to its successor the Implementation Force (IFOR), between 1995 and 1996 and then between 1996 and 2004 to the Szabilization Force in Bosnia and Herzegovina (SFOR). Turkey was also actively involved in NATO operations in Kosovo.

On the domestic level, the Balkan wars and the sufferings of Bosnian Muslims certainly supported the rise of the Islamist Refah Party (RP), which won the municipalities of Istanbul and Ankara in the local elections of 1994. The Islamists also capitalized on growing social disparities and the decline of leftist parties. From the mid-1980s on, competing discourses of ethnic and religious identities, had gradually begun to replace economic struggle as the defining factor in political organization and protest.[22] The Refah Party combined in its political

messages the fight against inequality and injustice with religious references and a language of moral principles.[23] The RP propagated social
justice based on Muslim solidarity. Their discourse moved religious
references to the center of political debates.

In retrospect, one can hold that the sufferings of Bosnian Muslims
during the Balkan Wars and the international community's inertia triggered a political discourse that would later position Turkey as a champion of the rights of oppressed Muslims in the world.

Since the early 1990s Islamism and an emergent Kurdish separatist
movement were two identity-based political movements that would increasingly challenge the Kemalist political settlement.

The rise of the Welfare Party and the Kurdish question were not
only expressions of the politicization of supressed religious and ethnic
identities, but they were also a result of the distorted distribution of
wealth, resulting from a developing capitalist economy. The Islamist
movement was supported by lower income groups and the Kurdish
question emerged in Turkey's poorest and economically underdevel-
oped provinces.[24] The military conflict between the Turkish army and
the Kurdish separatist PKK had flamed up in the 1980s and reached a
climax in the 1990s. Most of the country's eastern and south-eastern
provinces were under a state of emergency.

At the same time, the collapse of the Soviet Union in 1991 provided
Turkey with three new neighbors to its east: the independent former
Soviet Republics of Georgia, Armenia and Azerbaijan. Ethnic conflicts
among and within these countries and beyond had an immediate, destabilizing effect on Turkey. Many Turkish citizens are of Abkhaz, Cir-
cassian, Chechen or Georgian origin. Many of them have sympathized
with the different conflict parties. Due to common ethnic origins, Turkey openly sided with Azerbaijan in the Nagorno-Karabakh conflict,
but refrained from getting actively involved in any military conflict.

The newly independent Turkic Republics in Central Asia provided
another new arena for Turkish foreign policy. Encouraged by the United States, Ankara entered with Russia and Iran into a race over influence
in the region. Ankara hoped to capitalize on common ethnic grounds
and expand its economic, cultural and political sphere of influence in
Central Asia. Another objective was to explore new sources for energy

and decrease Turkey's dependence on Russian gas supplies. However, Turkey's ambitious Central Asia policies failed. Ankara underestimated Russia's continuing presence in the region, that is geographically and historically rather disconnected from Turkey and overestimated Turkey's own economic and political capacities as well as the strength of ethnic communalities.

At the same time, one can assert that Ankara's emphasis on ethnic and religious commonalities with neighboring regions reinforced domestic debates on Turkey's identity. However, the political scientist Hakan Yavuz rightly emphasizes that despite the fact that the emergence of new independent states in Central Asia and the war in Bosnia have played a role in the re-imagination of Turkish identity, during the 1990s, Turkish foreign policy continued to be mainly influenced by debates in Washington and in major European capitals.[25]

The Shift Towards Civilizational Geopolitics

In his famous article on "The Clash of Civilizations," Samuel Huntington argued in 1993 that the divisions of the Cold War into a First, Second and Third World were no longer relevant. Instead, he predicted that the majority of conflicts in the new, post-Cold War world would occur between nations and groups of different civilizations. Samuel Huntington defines civilizations as "the highest cultural grouping of people and the broadest level of cultural identity people have short of that which distinguishes humans from other species. It is defined both by common objective elements, such as language, history, religion, customs, institutions, and by the subjective self-identification of people."[26]

"The fault lines between civilizations will be the battle lines of the future."[27] In contrast to "class and ideological conflicts where the key question was 'Which side are you on?' and people could and did choose sides and change sides in conflicts between civilizations, the question is "What are you?" That is a given that cannot be changed'.[28] Although Huntington held that a civilization is defined by various core elements, religion was the constitutive factor in his conception. He contrasted a rather vaguely defined Western civilization with non-Western ones such as Confucian, Islamic, Hindu, Slavic-Orthodox that are all defined by religion. Moreover, the reduction of different traditions and histories to a common religious background suggests monolithic and homogeneous cultural blocks and does not allow any kind of liminality and hybridity.

The political scientist John Agnew has highlighted that discourses on civilizational geopolitics categorize the world along the cultural civilizations to which people who inhabit these regions are thought to belong. These discussions have had a huge impact on Turkey's self-perception and its perception by others.

I argue that from the 1990s on, the Turkish political establishment began to position Turkey as a liminal state, underscoring its hybrid identity and its unique geography between the civilizational concepts of East and West as a meeting place for different cultures. As much as this strategy aimed at increasing Turkey's economic and political influence in these regions and guaranteeing energy supplies, it also hoped to leverage Turkey's strategic importance for its Western and especially European allies. An example of Turkey's conscious re-positioning in the framework of emergent civilizational geopolitics as a country that guarantees for European security and at the same time links the East to the West was President Özal's address to the Western European Union Parliamentary Assembly in Paris in 1991. In his speech he defined Turkey as "a drawbridge of Europe's fortress of contemporary civilization and its gateway to the Middle East."[29]

Özal's statement largely was in alignment with Washington's views. The Clinton Administration (1993–2001) saw Turkey as part of the European security architecture. Turkey was considered to be important for Europe's security, but in light of rising Islamism and Kurdish extremism it was also considered to be instable. It's secular character should therefore be stabilized through the anchoring within the EU. Consequently, the United States became an important advocate and promoter of Turkey's integration with the European Union. Ian Lesser argues that from Washington's perspective Turkey's integration with the EU was about more than its place in Europe and its positive effects on Turkey's stability, "it was about regional security and the development in the European periphery—and beyond."[30]

The European Union Summit of Lisbon in 1992 acknowledged Turkey's new geostrategic importance for the EU and called for the deepening of relations. Behind the scenes, the Clinton administration strongly urged allied EU members to send positive signals towards Turkey. Within Europe, views on Turkey differed. While the UK and Italy supported Turkey's membership in so far as it would strengthen Europe's Atlanticism, others such as Greece, France, Denmark or Germany were rather critical of Turkey's potential accession.[31]

At the same time, Turkey failed to undergo a profound democratization process. Turkey had experienced the transition to the market economy at the beginning of the 1980s, but economic liberalization was not accompanied by more political freedom. Turkey had difficulties in adapting to the emergent liberal democratic order. Turkish democracy still functioned within an authoritarian secular Kemalist framework guarded by the powerful military, supressing Kurdish, Islamic and leftist political identities. The rise of Islamism and Kurdish nationalism even further hardened Kemalist authoritarian secularism.

While NATO allies often overlooked undemocratic developments in Turkey during the Cold War, Turkey's democracy deficit increasingly strained relations with the West in general but specifically with the EU in the post-Cold War era, when most former communist countries experienced the transition to democracy. In its ambition to become a member of the EU, Turkey fell behind the Central and Eastern European reform states.

The critique of Turkey's accession to the EU soon attained a culturalist notion highlighting Turkey's different, Islamic nature as the major obstacle for membership.

Whereas during the Cold War, the perception of political Europe had been identical with "free Europe" as opposed to "communist Europe," with the end of the bipolar world system, the conceptual definition of East and West changed.[32] Europe's boundaries were slowly redrawn along civilizational lines. In the following years, debates on civilizational geopolitics would increasingly overshadow other pro and con arguments in regard to Turkey's accession process.

Opponents as well as supporters of Turkey's membership to the EU would mainly refer to Turkey's Muslim identity and distinct geopolitical place and weaken Ankara's positioning as a hybrid country that bridges East and West. Whereas opponents referring to Turkey's Muslim identity doubted its Europeanness and problematized its location, supporters highlighted Turkey's strategic importance for European security and its ability to combine Islam with democracy and market economy as strategic asset.

In 1997, European Christian Democrat parties, the major opponents of Turkey' accession, issued a joint declaration claiming that "the European Union is a civilization project and within this civilization project Turkey has no place."[33] In view of the negative messages emanating from European capitals regarding Turkey's accession, most parts of the Turkish public became convinced that the "the 'Iron Curtain' that once divided Europe was being replaced by a "cultural/religious iron curtain."[34] This time, however, Turkey seemed to have moved behind that curtain.

Conclusion

The end of the Cold War marked a turning point for Turkey's international role. Although Turkish foreign policy continued to be influenced by policy strategies and debates in Washington and major European capitals, with the end of a bipolar world order Ankara gradually discovered its neighborhood. From the early 1990s on, Turkey tried to become more active and developed strategies toward multiple regions. Since Turkey lacked financial and political capacities, Turkish foreign policy emphasized emotional links through culture, kinship and religion. The strong emphasis on identity, had the effect that Turkey also gradually re-discovered its own Ottoman heritage. This did not take place without tensions. From the 1990s on Turkish domestic politics have been characterized by high polarization around identity issues. Debates revolve around the role of religion and the inclusion of non-Turkish ethnic identities such as Kurdish identity. Foreign and even more so the neighborhood policy have on the one hand mirrored these debates and on the other hand they have reinforced them. This also explains various contradictions in Turkish foreign policy.

While in the wake of the Cold War Ankara's foreign and neighborhood policy tried to present Turkish secularism as a model for Turkic states in Central Asia, this strategy was undermined by Ankara's own policies towards the Balkans, emphasizing a common Islamic and Ottoman heritage with local Muslim communities. From the early 2000s on, Islamic and Ottoman references became dominant, while the promotion of Turkey's secularism lost traction.

On the one hand this reflected the power shift within Turkey—in 2002 the Islamic conservative Justice and Development Party came into power—on the other hand it also resonated with civilizational discourses in the wake of the 9/11 attacks. After 9/11, Turkey and its reformed Islamist ruling party served as a democratic anti-thesis to Islamist extremism á la al-Qaeda.

As much as civilizational geopolitics seemed to work in Turkey's favor—Turkey played a major role in the policies of both George W. Bush and Barack Obama towards the Middle East —it also gradually alienated Turkey from its Western allies. Turkey's accession to the EU seemed less and less likely and Turkey became increasingly active in the Middle East. However, Turkey's growing involvement in the Middle East was less the consequence of a strategic turning away from the "West," but rather an inevitable result of the fact that Turkey became increasingly isolated from European integration processes.

Ahmet Davutoğlu, the architect of Turkish foreign policy after 2002, positioned Turkey as the center of a cultural geography defined by the Ottoman Empire. Besides more economic and political activism in the Middle East, this also entailed increased cultural diplomacy. Ankara financed the renovation of Ottoman architectural sites across the region. This also included a stronger emphasis on Ottoman legacy witin Turkey. The Islamic conservative government's neo-Ottoman policies were reflected in education, architecture, music, clothing and political rhetoric, causing many domestic controversies and furthering domestic political polarization.

Tarık Oğuzlu speaks in the context of Turkey's ever stronger involvement in the Middle East of the "Middle Easternization" of Turkish foreign policy. Oğuzlu highlights that not only Turkish foreign policy has been increasingly informed by political developments in the Middle East, but that internationally, Turkey as a country became increasingly defined through its importance for policies towards the Middle East.[35]

Therefore one can conclude that the end of the Cold War and the rise of civilizational debates had a huge impact on Turkey's self perception as well as on its relations with others. From 2010 on, Turkey's relations with its Western partners and allies have been increasingly overshadowed by Tayyip Erdoğan's and the ruling Justice and Development Party's pan-Islamist, culturalist and populist anti-Western rhetoric. References to Ottoman grandeur and the emphasis of a common heritage with Muslim communities have been important to boost Erdoğan's and his party's international image as in the voice of a marginalized global Muslim community and such discourses have also shored up his and the party's support within Turkey. Today, thirty years after the end of the Cold War, Turkey has been hardly associated with a Western or European country, although still a NATO member and an official candidate for EU membership, Turkey has moved over the last years to the East. From the perspective of civilizational geopolitics, it has been perceived as a Middle Eastern power and a Muslim state.

Notes

1. Francis Fukuyama, "The End of History?" *The National Interest*, No. 16 (Summer 1989), pp. 3-18.

2. Kenichi Ohmae, *The End of the Nation State: The Rise of Regional Economies* (New York: The Free Press, 1995).

3. Aras in Feroz Ahmad, *The Making of Modern Turkey* (London: Routledge, 1993).

4. Nicholas Danforth, "Ideology and Pragmatism in Turkish foreign policy: From Atatürk to the Akp," *Turkish Policy Quarterly*, Vol. 7, No. 3 (2008), pp. 83-95.

5. Senem Üstün, "Turkey and the Marshall Plan: Strive for Aid," Yearbook University of Ankara (1997), pp. 33-34, retrieved from: http://www.politics.ankara.edu.tr/yearbookdizin/dosyalar/MMTY/27/3_senem_ustun.pdf.

6. William Hale, *Turkish Foreign Policy 1774-2000* (London: Routledge, 1997) p.119.

7. Eylem Yılmaz and Pinar Bilgin, "Constructing Turkey's "Western" Identity during the Cold War: Discourses of the Intellectuals of Statecraft," *International Journal*, Vol. 61, No. 1 (2006); "Turkey: Myths and Realties" (Winter,2005/2006), pp. 39-59, p 41.

8. Meliha Benli Altunışık & Özlem Tür, "From Distant Neighbors to Partners? Changing Syrian–Turkish Relations," *Security Dialogue*, Vol. 37, No. 2 (2006), pp. 229–248, DOI: 10.1177/0967010606066172.

9. Cengiz Günay, *From Islamists to Muslim Democrats? The Trajectory of Islamism in Egypt and Turkey against the Background of Historical, Political and Economic Developments* (Saarbrücken: VDM, 2008), p. 92.

10. M. Hakan Yavuz, "Turkish identity and foreign policy in flux: The rise of Neo-Ottomanism," *Critique: Journal for Critical Studies of the Middle East*, 7:12 (1998), 19-41, p. 21/22.

11. Agnew in Pınar Bilgin, "A Return to 'Civilisational Geopolitics' in the Mediterranean? Changing Geopolitical Images of the European Union and Turkey in the Post-Cold War Era," *Geopolitics*, Vol. 9, No. 2 (2004), pp. 269-291, DOI: 10.1080/14650040490442863, p. 269.

12. Nathalie Tocci, *Turkey's European Future. Behind the Scenes of America's Influence on EU-Turkey Relations* (New York: New York University Press, 2011), p. 3.

13. Clyde Haberman, "War in the Gulf: Turkey's Role in Air Assault Sets Off Fear of Retaliation," *The New York Times*, January 20, 1991, retrieved from: https://www.nytimes.com/1991/01/20/world/war-in-the-gulf-turkey-turkey-s-role-in-air-assault-sets-off-fear-of-retaliation.html.

14. Memcon, August 20, 1990, Nicholas Burns, G. H. Bush, Telephone Conversation with President Turgut Ozal of Turkey, Bush Presidential Library [online available].

15. Strobe Talbott, "Post Victory Blues," *Foreign Affairs*, Vol. 71, No. 1 (1991/92), pp. 53-69, p. 65

16. Memcon, April 16, 1991, Nicholas Burns, Telcon with President Ozal of Turkey, Bush Presidential Library [online available].

17. Kemal Kirişçi, "The End of the Cold War and Changes in Turkish Foreign Policy Behavior," Foreign Policy Institute, November 29, 2016, retrieved from: http://foreignpolicy.org.tr/the-end-of-the-cold-war-and-changes-in-turkish-foreign-policy-behaviour-kemal-kirisci/.

18. Ibid.

19. Şaban Çalış, "Turkey's Balkan Policy in the Early 1990s," *Turkish Studies*, Vol. 2, No. 1 (2001), pp. 135-146, DOI: 10.1080/14683849.2001.11009177, p. 136.

20. Ibid.

21. Ibid, p. 140.

22. Jenny White, *Islamist Mobilization in Turkey: A Study in Vernacular Politics* (Seattle: University of Washington Press, 2002), p. 191.

23. Günay 2008, op. cit., p. 148.

24. Binnaz Toprak, *Türkiye'de Laiklik, Siyasal Islam ve Demokrasi*, unpublished manuscript (Istanbul: Bosporus University, 2004)

25. Yavuz, 1998, op. cit., p. 22.

26. Samuel Huntington, "The Clash of Civilizations?" *Foreign Affairs*, Summer 1993 Issue.

27. Ibid.

28. Ibid.

29. Turgut Özal, Turkish Stand on the Gulf Crisis, Middle East and Europe, Address to the WEU Parliamentary Assembly in Paris on May 5,1991, published in the Foreign Policy Quarterly, *Foreign Policy* Vol. 16, No. 1-2, re-

trieved from: http://foreignpolicy.org.tr/turkish-stand-on-the-gulf-crisis-middle-east-and-europe-turgut-ozal/.

30. Ian O. Lesser, "US Policy Towards Turkey and Implications for EU-Turkey Relations," in Nathalie Tocci (ed.), *Talking Turkey in Europe: Towards a Differentiated Communication Strategy* (Rome: Quaderni IAI, 2008), p. 219.

31. Hanna Ojanen, "The Impact of Transatlantic Relations on the European Debate on Turkey" in Tocci, Ibid., pp. 244-245.

32. John Agnew, *Geopolitics: Re-Visioning World Politics* (London: Routledge, 1998).

33. Hale, op. cit., p. 239.

34. Öymen in Bilgin 2004, op. cit., p. 270.

35. Tarık Oğuzlu, "Middle Easternization of Turkey's Foreign Policy: Does Turkey Dissociate from the West?" *Turkish Studies*, Vol. 9, No. 1 (2008), pp. 3-20, DOI: 10.1080/14683840701813960.

Chapter 21

Reflections on "The End of the Cold War?"

Joachim Bitterlich

Towards a (New) Cold War Without a Reliable Order ?

"It's official. We lost the Cold War," the title of a *Washington Post* column by Dana Milbank on December 21, 2018, and "A new kind of cold war," the title and main story of *The Economist* of May 18, 2019, are just two examples of current debates nearly thirty years after October 3, 1990, the day of German reunification, that historic moment when we thought the Cold War was over. Really?

October 3, 1990 was a marvelous moment after an incredible year that saw the first rather free elections in Poland, the opening of the Iron Curtain in Hungary, peaceful protests in the GDR and intensive negotiations with regard to the reunification of Germany. It was the beginning of new era in Europe.

Veteran U.S. diplomat William Burns opens his remarkable article "The Lost Art of American Diplomacy"[1] by returning to the year 1991. The United States had just triumphed in the Cold War, overseen the reunification of Germany and handed Saddam Hussein a spectacular defeat in Iraq. Everything seemed to point to a period of prolonged U.S. dominance in a liberal order the United States had built and led after World War II. Russia was flat on its back, China was still turned inward.

Did the Cold War really end at that moment, especially in Europe? My answer at that time was clearly no. But we were hoping to reach that moment very soon.

In a conference in Harvard in January 1993 I reaffirmed that after the end of communism and the Warsaw Pact, after the fall of the Iron Curtain and the Berlin Wall, and after the reunification Germany, Europa was in a period of "radical change." A strategic vacuum was emerging.

After 40 years in which Europe was bound together by the East-West-conflict, we had entered into a new strategic situation that I summarized as follows: "the postwar period meant threat but hardly risks, while the post-postwar period means great risks, but less direct threats." I spoke about "uncertainty"and the need for "control" and "step-by-step-adaptation." Some observers were even calling it "the new world disorder."[2]

We had entered into a period of transition characterized by growing volatility, uncertainty and complexity. It was a period marked by both foreseeable and unexpected crises and conflicts, by a tendency towards greater use of power —and by an accumulation of erroneous assumptions due to lack of strategy and a limited number of responsible forward-looking actors.

Today, nearly thirty years later, the situation is perhaps even more difficult and even less predictable. We may characterize current developments again as a sort of new Cold War, partly between the classical actors, partly with new ones, and partly because many have lost the capability for strategic thinking and acting.

In May 2019 I spent some days engaged in intensive talks in Moscow. Russian and European participants in an off-the-record meeting spoke openly about the return of Cold War mentalities. The cover story of *The Economist* that same week, assessing U.S.-Chinese relations, was entitled "A new kind of Cold War."[3]

Today we are very far away from a reliable "world order." It is more a certain disorder offering risks and dangers that are potentially more dangerous than during the period of the Cold War.[4] Geopolitics are suddenly back on the agenda.

After retiring as France's Permanent Representative to the United Nations in June 2019, Ambassador François Delattre concluded that "We are now in a new world disorder. The three main safety mechanisms are no longer functioning: no more American power willing to be the last-resort enforcer of international order; no solid system of international governance; and, most troubling, no real concert of nations able to re-establish common ground."[5]

To understand and assess this situation we have to look at the last thirty years in a comprehensive and inclusive way. It is necessary to consider this development as a whole, going back to its origins in the first years of transition, in those years where many of us had real hope, where some of us were dreaming of the "peace dividend."

We may distinguish two periods. The first was characterized by hope despite growing uncertainties, the second by fading hopes and the return of geopolitical risks and challenges that until now we have been unable to control and master. The appropriate slogan to describe the actual situation of the world seems to be "VUCA," a world full of volatility, uncertainty, complexity and ambiguity.

The 1990s: First Hope, Then Growing Uncertainties

At the end of the 1980s we experienced an unexpected window of opportunity due to the collapse of the Soviet Union and of its political and economic satellite system in Central and Eastern Europe: Czechoslovakia, Hungary, Poland and finally the GDR became the falling stars. The Soviet economic system was breaking down. The door was suddenly open to the reunification of Germany and the launch of democratic regimes in Central and Eastern Europe.

All this happened amidst a growing acceleration of events, but despite the anxiety or resistance of some politicians the people promoting the peaceful revolution of those days in East Germany, Poland, and Hungary never let things get out of control. The same was true for the rational yet visionary actions of leading authorities during that period.

It is widely forgotten but important to remember that in the crucial year 1989 President George H.W. Bush had proposed to Germany a "partnership in leadership." What appeared at first glance to be an honor for Germany was in reality at the same time a poisoned gift to Germany in this unsettled Europe. The U.S. offer was met with suspicions from France and the UK, as the main U.S. allies in Europe, as well as from smaller countries fearing an overweight Germany. The answer of Chancellor Helmut Kohl was therefore diplomatically positive, but in fact embarrassed, reluctant, and defensive. He was thinking much more in terms of further anchoring West Germany (and later reunified Germany) within reinforced structures of European integration, both via the Franco-German tandem and with the support of smaller partners, to achieve greater political acceptance of Germany's role in Europe. Nonetheless, as the dynamic events of 1989 and 1990 unfolded, President Bush did in fact become our most important ally on the path to reunification.

In 1991 we negotiated and finalized the Maastricht Treaty, a real achievement and step forward in European integration, but the nascent European Union was still a "limping union" due to the resistance of the UK and others. The time was not yet ripe to reach a break through to a common foreign and security policy and a common policy on internal security (including migration). Some even rejected Franco-German proposals on security policy for fear of weakening the Atlantic Alliance. Our American allies were among those reluctant to support the renaissance of this European idea, even though it was an attempt to re-integrate France more closely into the overall European and transatlantic security domain.

Chancellor Helmut Kohl accepted the Maastricht compromise with the European partners, being convinced that the introduction of the euro would reinforce the pressure to build a strong "Political Union." For Kohl, the euro was the necessary "cement" to bind the EU tighter and indissolubly together. His credo was that Economic and Monetary Union—and Political Union—would make the European integration "irreversible."[6]

This goal was one of Kohl's guiding principles: "German policy must be clearly oriented to the principles and aims of European union. By the same token, my government's objective is to resolutely promote the integration process and make it irreversible."[7] He was convinced that the common Home and Justice Policy and the common Foreign and Security Policy, for the moment still the weaker elements of the "Political Union," would follow this path of engagement.

He said to me often: "I will sign all the initiatives you are preparing with your comrades-in-arms on Foreign and Security policy, but the completion of this area will be the very last step of European integration because of the remaining traditions and the history of some of our important partners such as France and the UK. You will have to remain flexible and use new paths to reach progress."

He knew that European integration was among united Germany's most important vital interests. It would enable the new Germany to be better accepted by its partners in Europe and to help overcome finally the reflex of at least some of our partners to control Germany—Europe's historical trouble spot, the country in the middle of the continent with the greatest number of borders.

From 1991 on Western Europe took prudent, hesitant steps toward the reunification of Europe. The leading ideas and reflections were intent, on the one hand, to ensure that the future "security architecture must make allowance for the legitimate security interests of every country," and on the other hand that the "the European Community must and will remain open—open to the reformist countries of Central, Eastern and Southeastern Europe. The Community will not stop at the Elbe." These were literal extracts from Chancellor Kohl's reflections about the future development in Europe in February 1990 in Davos. [8]

The Western European nations thought that process would happen first via the EU, without saying when or how, while it was becoming clearer that some of the new democracies in Central and Eastern European that wanted to become part of the EU and NATO were focused much more on the protection offered by the Atlantic Alliance.

The EU needed three years to develop its fundamental approach with regard to its enlargement, which was agreed in Copenhagen in June 1993. We then needed four more years to prepare the phase of concrete negotiations with a first group of candidate countries, and then later with a second wave of applicants. We Germans had to be cautious, since most EU member states had not favored any enlargement. Even the accession of Austria, Finland and Sweden had been more than difficult.

EU enlargement to the East was ultimately realized later in a technocratically nearly perfect way. The candidate countries merit respect for the transformation of their economic and financial systems. At the same time, however, we forgot politics. Looking at today's situation, which some observers describe as a schism between East and West, it has become clear that the new member states first had to recreate their national identities—and we had to support them much more on that path—before adding the "European idea" into their politics. The result is a European Union with less coherence and therefore in urgent need of further consolidation.

Despite the growing pressure from some of the former member states of the Warsaw Pact, NATO also only slowly opened its door. The United States was as least as hesitant as the European members of the Alliance. Until the middle of the 1990s there was not a majority in favor. Most Europeans waited for a decision in Washington. In public speeches until early 1993 I even avoided the word "enlargement," as the situation was still extremely fragile with regard to the majority of our European partners.

Chancellor Kohl shared this view entirely. Only Defense Minister Volker Rühe was pressing for early NATO enlargement, knowing well that the Chancellery disagreed. This positioning did not enhance his credibility, but put "us" under greater pressure. The response from the Chancellory was clear: "It is the personal opinion of the minister, not that of Chancellor." Kohl clearly reserved his right to take the necessary decisions on this crucial question once it became "mature."

Our political priority was on the one hand to protect the former members of the Warsaw Pact by being their defender and supporter in Moscow. For the past 50 years they had been under Soviet control; especially in Poland and in the Baltic states the fear was widespread that Russia would look for ways to win back control of its "near abroad."

Chancellor Kohl spent hours and hours with Russian leaders, in particular President Yeltzin, to ensure the freedom of the Central and Eastern European countries. At the same time we were trying to contribute to the stabilization of Russia. Political Moscow had difficulties digesting the end of the Soviet Union and its empire, and seemed to be under pressure by the military leadership, which considered developments since 1989 as a pure defeat.

In the 1990s Germany had to become the main financial contributor to the stabilization of Russia and of Central and Eastern Europe. Within the frame of the G-7 the Canadian government distributed at one point a sort of "ranking" of the assistance to Russia and to the states of the fromer Soviet Union. This paper underlined that Germany was paying between 1990 and 1995 ten times more than France and thirty times more than the UK.[9] While this was a useful documentation of reality, for us it was also a double-edged sword in terms of domestic consumption and EU policy. To some extent it was even dangerous, as it could have been used by domestic critics to support their claim that

Germany had become "the paymaster of Europe." Therefore we were hesitant to use figures documenting our significant financial efforts in the public debate. I remember that in one of these papers we prepared regularly for the Chancellor's international discussions we wrote that our financial support in favor of the reform states in Central and Eastern Europe and of the successor states of the former Soviet Union between 1990 and 1994 totaled DM 146 billion (€74 billion) or DM 1,800 (920 €) per capita.[10]

Our problem was that that most of our partners and allies were not really interested in this complex of ultra-sensitive questions. The general feeling was "*sollen doch die Deutschen ausbaden, was sie uns da eingebrockt haben*" ("the Germans should pay for what they have brewed"), and they were waiting for the United States.

We knew that the Pentagon was skeptical of NATO enlargement and that the State Department in principle was in favor, but unclear about who, how and when. In 1994 the Pentagon offered the Partnership for Peace (PfP) as a compromise formula, as cryptic reflections swirled in Washington about various possibilities, for instance enlargement without Article 5 guarantees or a possible neutral status for the Baltic states or Romania. Taking into consideration the U.S. political calendar and developments in Russia, the Clinton administration preferred to take decisions on enlargement in 1997 or 1998.

After returning from one of the regular trips to Washington in early October 1994, I was sufficiently alarmed by the inconsistencies and of the various approaches that I recommended to the Chancellor to intensify his contacts with President Clinton so that they together could develop the appropriate concept. We Germans were not against expansion to the East, but we insisted that we should not destabilize the fragile situation in Russia.

The Chancellor agreed. He was convinced that it was important to address these questions with circumspection and under no time pressure. He also thought we should first develop the Partnership for Peace program with all interested countries in Central, Eastern and Southaastern Europe, thereby contributing toward necessary confidence-building in Europe, not least with regard to Russia. At the same time he believed we should avoid a public or semi-public debate about

NATO expansion due to the sensitivity of these questions. In his letter to President Clinton of mid-October 1994 he added that

> as enlargement of NATO is intended to contribute towards security and stability in the whole of Europe, we must also discuss this issue quite frankly with Russia. An important element will be Russia's greater integration into the European security structures.[11]

More than one year later and having met and agreed with President Clinton on the general orientation, Chancellor Kohl, opening the traditional Munich security conference in February 1996, continued to insist publicly on this political line:

> It is only right that our Eastern neighbors should want to join the Alliance...We must approach NATO's enlargement with care and political discretion since this is a matter of fundamental importance to the Alliance itself and to Europe's future security. It is vital to us Germans and Europeans that NATO should retain its stability and scope for action. It is also essential for us to develop a good relationship based on partnership with Russia and Ukraine.[12]

When we arrived at the NATO summit in Madrid in July 1997, there was not yet an agreement on the concrete design of enlargement. President Clinton, President Chirac and the Chancellor tasked their national security/diplomatic advisors—Sandy Berger, Jean-David Levitte, and me—to resolve the question in the night before the discussion of potential summit conclusions. The compromise we achieved in the early morning consisted in proposing an enlargement in two phases in order not to destabilize Russia. First we would invite three countries—Poland, Hungary and the Czech Republic. Later, in a second stage, we would invite the Baltic countries, Slovakia, Bulgaria and Romania.

The Baltic countries, particularly Estonia, had difficulties understanding the German position and especially Chancellor Kohl's strategy. They felt left alone with their large Russian neighbor. They were more sensitive and anxious that others about Russia's unstable development. They took note of but had limited confidence in our deliberate actions in Moscow. Years later, during my short period as NATO Ambassador in Brussels, I had an intense personal exchange with the first President of Estonia, Lennart Meri, trying to explain to him that our actions in Moscow, as in Washington, had been in their vital interest.

The Russians had agreed to German reunification, the end of the Warsaw Pact, and the independance of the Baltic states and the republics of the former Soviet Union. But they did not expect that the West would expand NATO to the east. In 1990/91 this question was not on our agenda. In 1991/92 then the idea of a "European Confederation" launched by the French further accelerated the reflex of the Central and Eastern European nations to request to the Western world security reassurance against Russia and any risk from that side by asking for their integration into the Atlantic Alliance.

In that period relations with the former Soviet Union and its successors were characterized by a real uncertainty about how to deal with Russia. Efforts on the Western side did not go far enough. Our U.S. friends were convinced of the need to reach out to the Russians, but at the same time kept on the brake. Presidents Bush and Clinton understood the challenges and the risks and were helpful as far as possible—but American neo-cons were trumpeting the "final victory" over Russia. That left the Germans once again to try to help, much more than others, to stabilize the fragile situation in Russia and its neighbors.

To us it was becoming clear in the 1990s that Russia's red line was not the Baltic area, it was Ukraine—and the stationing of nuclear weapons and troops at their border.

In these years I traveled regularly not only to Moscow, but also to Kyiv, leading a German delegation with the instruction to do our best to stabilize Ukraine. It was slowly becoming clear that we were faced with "mission impossible." Diplomatically expressed, we discovered a country with limited "statehood." We slowly began to believe we were all underestimating Leonid Kuchma's successes in constructing a deeply corrupt oligarchic system. During my missions to Ukraine I met the Russian Ambassador in Kyiv, Viktor Chernomyrdin, he explained several times to us Russia's highly paranoic sensitivities, particularly their fear that the United States could take over this delicate relationship.

During these negotiations we discovered the AN 70 project, a nearly ready military transport aircraft, a project that would have helped to stabilize the armament industry in eastern Ukraine. The German government supported the project, but it failed due to the lack of interest of our successors and to resistance from Airbus and our friends on the other side of the Atlantic.

After Yeltsin's departure the attention of the West towards the situation in Russia was slowly diminishing, September 11, the interventions in Afghanistan and in the Middle East changed the compass. Moscow—and the blessed soul of the Russians by the end of the Soviet-Union and the difficult transition years - did not seem to be any more in the centre of our preoccupations.

The United States and other Western allies were driving steadily towards Russia's red line: the offer of the George W. Bush administration to invite Ukraine and Georgia to join NATO at the 2008 NATO Summit in Bucharest. This initiative was stopped in a common effort by Nicolas Sarkozy and Angela Merkel, at least by postponing for some time any decision.

The same development characterized attitudes within the G-7. While Germany sought to integrate Russia, the United States hesitated until 1994. During these years we even were reflecting with Chancellor Kohl about the usefulness to integrate in the longer run China as well as other representatives from Asia, Africa and Latin America in this frame of informal worldwide coordination.

During the 1990s Germany provided considerable international assistance to Russia, to the CIS and the Central and Eastern European countries. These efforts were—with regard to Russia—only partly due to German reunification, the real charges went clearly beyond those commitments, their aim was to contribute actively to the stabilization of Russia and of the neighbors in the East in a phase of critical development of all these countries.

The civil war in Yugoslavia constituted a critical moment within the Western alliance—and with regard to Russia. The United States hesitated, hinting to the Europeans they should settle this conflict on their doorstep. During this period Serbia stuck to its aggressive position. It was convinced that its former allies—France, Britain, the United States and Russia—would recognize its indispensable role in the Balkans. Serbia therefore agreed only to a limited solution to the conflict in Bosnia, an agreement *a minima*, through the Dayton Agreement.[13]

Chancellor Kohl had doubts of the viability of this agreement, but, in loyalty to his Vice Chancellor and Foreign Minister Klaus Kinkel, who had been among the driving forces of that agreement, tried to help to stabilize the fragile result with regard to Bosnia. At the same time he maintained his distance from Franjo Tuđman's Croatia.

In autumn 1997 Serbia tried through confidential channels to establish a direct contact to Chancellor Kohl. He asked me to sound out confidentially with the Serbian leadership ways and means to stabilize the Balkans, in particular Bosnia, and especially to avoid the nascent Kosovo conflict. Our offer consisted in integrating Serbia and the whole Balkans in the longer run in a specific way to be developed into the EU. Despite several intense meetings we failed. Serbia felt too much on the "safe side" and indirectly protected by its former "friends and allies" in Russia. Miloşević and his people did not feel the political necessity to renounce their goals in Kosovo.

The Kosovo conflict and the NATO intervention in Serbia was then the hard core of my year as German Ambassador to NATO in 1998/99. With regard to this conflict, I was more than surprised in Spring 1999 to get to know the Kosovo separatist leader Hashim Thaçi in the U.S. NATO compound in Brussels.

During the second half of the 1990s the political regime in Moscow had become weaker and proved unable to join the main Western allies to resolve the growing Kosovo conflict. Western intervention in Serbia—and probably even more the recognition of Kosovo—constituted a setback in efforts to integrate Russia in the evolving European security architecture.

Nonetheless, even if the end of this first decade was overshadowed by growing divergences and conflicts, at the end of the 1990s the situation was still characterized by hope and a sense that we had a certain control over evolving dynamics. We still seemed on track toward a final end to the Cold War and the beginning of a new order.

The Second Decade Had to Be Worse: The Return of Geopolitics

How should we best characterize the second decade? More than a decade of permanent crisis management followed that first period. Are Europe and the world on their way out of the tunnel or back into the Cold War?

Europe and the Western world succeeded to some degree in pragmatically mastering the financial and economic crisis that swept down upon a liberal and increasingly unregulated globalized system. Yet this was done without any clear common view or vision for the longer-term sustainability of the system.

With regard to foreign and security policy, however, the assessment must be far more critical. including geopolitics. Hubert Védrine underlined often that during these years the West—Europe and the United States—had lost its capacity for statecraft and statemanship in foreign and security policy. He called the current state of affairs in Syria a prime example of how the West has lost its hegemony and ability to steer events because of policies guided by moralism rather than vital interests. Europe today is surrounded by crises rather than friends.

The turning point probably came with the terrorist attacks on the United States on September 11, 2001 (9/11), which prompted a major change in the policies of many critical actors and which uncovered some real misunderstandings regarding a number of geopolitical issues. Why did this come about?

Looking at the arc of crisis, especially in our near neighborhood, we have to begin with Afghanistan. Today we know that the Americans hesitated about whether they should respond to the 9/11 attacks with an intelligence operation backed by special forces or a classical military intervention. But the United States and the West did not listen to those, like the British or the Russians, who had solid experience with this country. The Allies did not even include Pakistan in their evaluation.

The Germans made their very special experience. The government of Gerhard Schröder and Joschka Fischer felt obliged to support the United States and decided to participate in the military intervention, after the Balkans for Germany the second active experience in a miltary intervention. Still today I have some doubts whether it has been reasonable for Germany to engage in an underestimated "learning corner" in Kundus in northwest Afghanistan instead of reinforcing Western troops in different areas. The German intervention has been met with divided views among our allies and friends, with some allies believing the German effort has been partially successful, although loaded with too many caveats, and other allies thinking it has been a certain setback.

We began an unwinnable war with a contestable strategy. How do we view the future of this country, the condition of which has direct consequences for the regional neighborhood?

Looking eastward, Russia and Ukraine are the other showcase(s) for the future of our foreign policy. The alienation between Russia and the West began in the 1990s. It was ignited by the Kosovo war, but was sparked by two other events. The first was European Commission President Romano Prodi's decision not to conclude and to sign the EU-Russia agreement in 2003/2004, despite a clear mandate to do so. Some sensitive questions, such as visas, still had to be settled, but seemed solvable. Who prevented him from signing? Two West European heads of government asked me desperately in the last years, who phoned him? The second spark was the U.S. push to integrate Ukraine and Georgia into NATO and the unfortunate positioning of the EU.

The Russians woke up and reacted negatively. Why did the West fail to react either to Medvedev or to Putin's mixture of a last warning/call for help in his Munich speech of February 10, 2007? Even with regard to Cold War this speech constitutes a reference:

> Only two decades ago the world was ideologically and economically divided and it was the huge strategic potential of two superpowers that ensured global security. This global stand-off pushed the sharpest economic and social problems to the margins of the international community's and the world's agenda. And, just like any war, the Cold War left us with live ammunition, figuratively speaking. I am referring to ideological stereotypes, double standards and other typical aspects of Cold War bloc thinking.[14]

Why did the West make these fundamental errors in assessing Russia, the state and the place of Georgia and even more that of Ukraine? And where is our common assessment of current Russian foreign policy? Is Moscow just a "bad cop" pursuing aggressive policies, or is it just trying to be recognized on the same level as Washington and thus in reality conducting defensive policies? The relationship with Russia seems to me too important to leave it in the sorry state it is in today [15]

A key case for the Europeans and the Americans has become again the relationship with Turkey. After forty years of hesitation the EU in 2003 launched accession negotiations with Ankara, but with no real conviction and in the knowledge that the time was not ripe for Turkish membership in the EU. Was this hypocrisy or realpolitik? It is astonishing that we did not express our doubts, starting in 2005-2006, about the real background of Recep Tayyip Erdoğan's approach to the EU—did he really seek membership or did he use Europe as a tool to advance his efforts to replace Turkey's secular governance a la Atatürk by a fundamentally different regime, as well as a re-ordering of Turkey's relations in its region? We understood rather well Turkish sensitivities regarding the Kurdish question, but it is rather incomprehensible that the United States and the EU did not have any feeling from the beginning about the sensitivity and risks of the "Gülen"-case, Erdoğan's former ally who fled to the US. During these years Turkey failed partly in its attempts to assert a leading role in the Middle East. Other contenders—Iran, Saudi-Arabia, Egypt, Israel—treated Turkey with a certain mistrust. Another sensitive question of Turkey's foreign policy has always been its relationship with Russia—Erdoğan seems at least to have stepped back from Washington while looking for common ground, perhaps even a partial realignment, with Russia.

Under these circumstances EU leaders, at the latest by 2010, should have been re-examining the entire relationship with Turkey and put at least as a first step an alternative offer to accession on the table, for instance membership in the Single Market.

The U.S. intervention in Iraq and its consequences has been the other critical leading subject in the last two decades. Looking backwards at the development of the region it is more than astonishing that the United States and Europe supported Saddam Hussein's ugly war against Khomeini's Iran.

The two misled U.S.-interventions had three consequences: a failed state, the rise of the IS, and the re-opening of the unsettled Kurdish question, which is explosive for Iraq, Turkey, Iran and Syria.

With regard to the civil war in Syria I remain convinced that the United States and Russia could together have stopped Bashar al-Assad in the first phase of unrest. I am not the only one to suspect that the Israelis were involved in this assessment.

The Europeans have largely been spectators of these developments, and have been targets of terrorism and refugees. In those years in particular France missed different opportunities for a real comeback in the region. Twice it proved unable to respond to the call from Damascus asking for stronger cooperation to relaunch its influence in the region. In fact, Paris and its leading politicians felt blocked by the situation in Lebanon and the strong implication of Syria in the killing of Hariri in 2005. Today only the involvement of Russia and the United States, seconded by the regional powers, may help us find a way out of the highly risky situation in the Middle East with its various conflicts that could easily lead to an open war.

In the second half of the 1990s the last real attempt was made to reach a solution to the Israeli/Palestine-conflict. In 1999 the last serious U.S. attempt failed in the aftermath of Rabin's assassination. Since then, it seems to be even more insoluble.

In that period there was for the first time strong coordination between the United States and Germany—and through Germany with the EU—in which Europe actively supported the U.S. lead in attempting to reach a breakthrough in the peace process. In Chancellor Kohl's regular contacts with Israelis, Palestinians and Jordanians, discretely supported by the European Commission, the idea of a regional community for water, natural resources and infrastructures had been developed, outlined and accepted by the partners in the region. To our regret this project ended abruptly soon after the asassination of Itzhak Rabin because of the growing mistrust between the parties involved.

Many today are waiting anxiously for the peace plan the Trump administration has announced that it is developing. Some first elements have been leaked, but what will be the concrete content and goals? The decisive question is whether President Trump will take the risk to present the plan in a moment where the political situation is unstable in Israel. As far as is known, one of the elements of the plan would consist in the "exchange of areas" ("huge real estate exchange plan"), but what are the other elements necessary to form a viable concept? Jordanian friends have expressed to me the fear that such a plan would only destabilize Jordan. And there is another open question: would there be any coordination with or at least implications for the other guarantor of Israel, Russia?

With regard to Egypt the Europeans and the West have committed major errors. One of these fundamental errors was to support the Muslim brotherhood as a democratic force while giving up on Mubarak. The result is a Arab winter, not an Arab spring.

The same diagnosis applies to Libya and North Africa. The West seemed to have made an unenthusiastic yet rational peace with the Ghaddafi regime, only to see France (and Britain) push this country back to its former tribal state. In my view this was a huge Western error with risks and consequences for the neighborhood, in particular for Tunisia, which does not receive enough support from us at a crucial time. Tunisia tried to reach an Arab spring by ousting its dictator. Today the country feels left alone. And in the Maghreb, Algeria and even Morocco have become unstable. These countries have numerous links to Europe and instabilty there means serious risks for Europe.

The other key case in our Middle Eastern neighborhood is the relationship with Saudi Arabia and the Arab Peninsula. The case and the country which divides us most from the United States is Saudi Arabia, which has become a more visible active regional power over the last decade.

Concentrating on its oil exports, Saudi Arabia has in reality never been neutral. The kingdom has been the main supporter of groups and movements close to or at least compatible with Saudi Salafist religious convictions. The expansion of one of the sources of terrorism in Europe is a consequence of the Saudi presence in Belgium, which has grown due to invitation of the Belgian government to promote the training of Imams by salafists. The 2015 attacks in France were directly linked to this; Molenbeek, a suburb of Brussels, was the terrorists' base of operations. This development has been underestimated by European security authorities for too long. In addition, Saudi Arabia has been financing Islamist groups in Algeria (FIS) and Palestine (Hamas—before Qatar), and is active in the war between two groups close to Iran and themselves in Yemen. The murder of Saudi journalist Jamal Khashoggi in Istanbul seems forgotten and without our side imposing any consequences.[16]

Saudi Arabia, one of the strongest U.S. allies in the region and one of the most important oil suppliers, and at the same time a threat to our security, has become under the U.S. umbrella one of the new regional powers in the Middle East. For the moment Saudi Arabia has even developed new and strong cooperation with Israel. Together they seem to have become the U.S. deputies in the region. Two open questions remain: will Saudi Arabia step back from its extreme behavior through internal reforms? Can Saudi Arabia achieve a sustainable model of development given that the importance of oil is diminishing?

Iran is in many ways the "bad cop" in the game, but part of a sort of "G-4" of the Middle East. Four leading nations or four plus one who would like to be the leading force(s): Turkey, Saudi Arabia, Egypt, Iran—and Israel. Until now there is no winner. In this open political game, Israel occupies a special place in the policies of all of these actors and those of its two guarantee powers, the United States and Russia.

Iran is a highly complex regime marked by internal divisions and partly dangerous autonomous groups. But it would be a real political mistake to refuse dialogue or avoid efforts to integrate the oldest civilization in the region into the "concert of nations," however difficult that may be. Its nuclear aspirations are not new; they have existed since the time of the Shah, who at that time was supported by Israel, France, Germany and the United States.

What Europe and the Western world lack is a real permanent dialogue with the leading forces of the region and a common assessment and policy towards the region and its main actors as a way to attain some degree of "strategic influence" in this potential powder keg.

Invoking our southern neighborhood we have to integrate in our assessment the Sahel zone and Africa. It is strange that we are beginning to reflect now on this region, and not thirty years earlier. Africa seems to be a deep mixture between failed states and astonishing developments, it is not black and white, it is not a clear picture, but China is everywhere, and where are we? The EU is trying to set up a new strategy of partnership, but these are only first steps.

How to evaluate China? It is a stabilizer, a commercial partner, and at the same time a competitor. It seeks to advance its vital interests through a strategy of conquest through the Silk Road concept by acquiring strategic assets in the European neighborhood and in Europe itself. China seems to follow a long term strategy consisting of four vectors: achieving a predominant role in Asia; establishing a relationship on equal footing with the United States; building ties to Europe as a supplier of technology; and developing relations in Africa/Middle East as critical suppliers of natural resources. At first glance this is a brillant strategic concept. It still to prove its sustainability and coherence, however, with regard to domestic Chinese developments.

Asia as a whole has a prominent place in European reflections , but do we have a real Asian strategy ? I fear we do not. What is our assessment of the role and potential of Japan, India and Indonesia, the evaluation of cooperation bodies in the region and their relations with China, the United States, Russia and Europe?

The United States and Europe

During the period of East-West-conflict following World War II, the United States was Europe's protector, perhaps "controller," even promoter of European integration as long as it did not bother U.S. influence and interests. At the same time the United States remains until today the easiest and best possible scapegoat of all.

In the last decade, however, we have been observing two major changes in U.S. perceptions and tendencies with regard to the orientation of its foreign and security policies.

Over the last decade the American *leitmotiv* has become "Asia first." For some Europeans the United States seemed on track towards an unpredictable "G-2" with China, which some thought might lead to a clash of civilizations. Others speak now about a new type of "cold war," or a bilateral truce at European expense, or a bit of both. This struggle has to do with more than trade hostilities. It is about predominance and control.

President Trump has added to this first goal a second: "America first." This is not a new American policy goal—Roland Reagan pursued comparable objectives in the early 1980s. What is new, at least for some Europeans, is that the United States has become a more unreliable and unpredictable partner than was the case under Reagan.

Europe's limited international role

In 2003 the EU in its first strategic review fully subscribed to the idea of being surrounded by a peaceful and friendly neighborhood. It charted a bright future for an effective multilateral system. These were the years of the "peace dividend," a description that we would consider today as a romantic illusion as the EU faces an arc of crises both to the east and to the south. On the other hand the EU has been able to manage and consolidate the banking, financial and economic crisis. While the EU still seems to be working in "crisis management mode," it also looks to be on track on its way out of the tunnel.

During these years Europe has looked more inward, as classic differences between north and south loomed. What is new is the growing rift between east and west; eastern EU member states do not feel that their western neighbors understand them. EU achievements also seem much weaker with respect to its Neighborhood Policy and its Foreign and Security Policy. More than ever we are far away from the goal of a common policy.

Consequences and Perspectives: Who Are The Winners?

It is astonishing that the European Union has been relatively stable in recent years. The threats to its financial and economic stability and the Brexit challenge even been helpful in some ways, particularly by reinforcing EU cohesion. The EU, in fact, seems to be in a better shape than the majority of its member states, but this does not mean at all that Europeans can feel reassured. The EU faces a number of key challenges, including internal security and migration, security and defense, and the self-assertion of its economy. The slogan "A Europe that protects" seems to be the common denominator in order to consolidate the EU's role and future.

Europe is facing a growing vacuum in its neighborhood. The dissolution of previous structures that provided a certain degree of order is generating serious dangers for stability, peace and progress. One consequence is the risk and reality of greater migration flows and the resulting need to identify and implement ways to regulate such flows. A second consequence is the challenge of terrorism being imported from the neighborhood, which in part is also due to the lack of comprehensive immigration and integration policies.

While the European record of the last fifty years has been remarkable, its performance during the last two decades has been much weaker. Europe is not (yet) in dangerous waters, but it must adddress these challenges if it is to retain its sense of security and prosperity and its place in the world.

China has emerged as the primary winner of developments over recent decades. At least in Europe its importance has still been recognized only by a minority. The question remains whether China's extraordinary development of the last forty years is sustainable.

Russia is not a winner. It has been losing its place as one of the two superpowers in the world. Russia remains the second nuclear superpower, but it has lost ground in in most other areas of endeavor. Since the middle of the first decade of this new century having lost any belief in a cooperation with the West on the basis of equal footing, the Russians are trying to win back its former position, at least with the aim of being respected as an equal player to the US. Their actions seem to be at first sight for a Western observer assertive, but in reality the Russians try to defend their positions with regard to positions they consider as strategic (Ukraine, Syria). Furthermore part of this strategy consists in disturbing Western cohesion whereever possible.

The winner is not the United States. The Trump reflex—"America first"—is not a new one in recent U.S. history; remember Ronald Reagan's policies in the early 1980s. The difference seems to be that Reagan was at the same time a reliable partner, whereas Trump seems to be much more difficult and unpredictable.

The Necessary European Action

There is strategic urgency for European reflection and action—without, but not against the United States, and not without the UK, even after a possible Brexit.

The answer until now seems to be only Macron—with a "modernized" French approach to Europe and the world, especially in European foreign and security policy. But nothing decisive has been achieved until now, although basic cornerstones exist.

The problem more than ever is Germany—the necessary partner, the reluctant economic hegemon, but a country without any strategy or consensus in foreign and security policy. Germany has become characterized as "a dangerous pacifist" or NATO's biggest "freeloader."

Germany's weakness, its contradictions and its lack of any strategy have become serious problems for its partners.

It is true Angela Merkel has been a pragmatic leader, and effectively managed the European response to the financial crisis, but she has no clear medium-term compass or vision. Germany needs a real national debate about its role in foreign and security policy and with regard to its European and international responsibilities. Until now the Germans are reluctant to accept fully the expectations of their partners, who ask them to accept more concrete international responsibilties even if linked to real risk. In the eyes of its partners German policy seems to pay a certain lip-service, a permanent "yes, but" to the demands of its European partners.

France and Germany remain the fundamental partners in Europe, but there are still essential cultural differences between them, especially concerning the military, security and defense. Germany needs assistance in order to reach a really compatible approach—Paul Taylor in his study says Germany needs to "jump over its own shadow."[17] A must for France and Germany is therefore a frank discussion of such fundamentals as cooperation in intelligence, planning, transport and logistics, equipment, procurement (and control), export of armament, common units, specialization of forces and ensuring a strong technological basis for of armament industries.

We are at the beginning. The real difficulties are ahead of us. But there is urgency and no alternative. For the first time there is a real chance.

Cold War II: The Way Out

Fareed Zakaria has stated that "we find ourselves in a post-American world order, the United States is withdrawing from a world it has dominated economically and by power over the last hundred years—and no one is taking its place."[18] This seems clear, but the situation seems to me a bit more complex.

In the spring of 2019 I took part in a seminar of the "Club of Three" - a Franco-German-British brainstorming launched more than twenty years ago by Lord George Weidenfeld—in Moscow. The central agenda should have been the question how to overcome current "non-rela-tions" between Moscow and the West, how to launch the renaissance of the relationship between Russia and the EU despite of all the obstacles.

The concordant view of the European "operating actors" in Moscow was clear: "we are farther away than ever from a common policy; we must develop such a policy." The same applies to the relations between Europe and the United States. Different attempts have been made but none has been successful.

Bearing in mind the growing uncertainties and risks it is a vital ne-cessity to act. It is not up to me to advise the United States, but the main elements of a European answer to get out of Cold War II could be made up of the following.

First, the EU should concentrate on "essentials" and main challenges.

This means on the one hand a comprehensive approach to great-er European "self–assertion," the long term survival of the European economy in the face of its main global competitors, the United States and China. This has to include the completion of the internal market, including the review of the tools at our disposal to defend our vital interests in international trade and investment and a radical new ap-proach to innovation and research, including using the methods of the DARPA-model. The last elections to the European Parliament have underlined the importance of a holistic and engaged approach to cli-mate change.

The 19 members of the eurozone are called to enhance and complete the euro: this includes in particular the question of a specific eurozone budget where finance ministers have reached a common orientation still be worked out in detail, and furthermore the transformation of the European Stability Mechanism (ESM) towards a sort of European Monetary Fund.[19]

Another major subject has to be a common policy on internal se-curity and migration. Such a program—as the necessary counterpart to the opening of the internal borders by the Schengen system—was proposed by Chancellor Kohl in 1991 (!), but member states seem only to have taken it seriously since the 2015 terrorist attacks and the migration waves. Until now we have reached only about 40 percent of what is really necessary; this is alarming.

A specific challenge will be a "reset" towars a totally rebuilt common foreign and security policy, including defense and development policy. If we are honest with ourselves we have to admit that we are far away from a common policy; progress reached in the last decades has only scratched the surface. I argue therefore in favor of a radically new approach including establishment of priorities and especially real cooperation between national capitals and "Brussels," including joint actions led by a lead nation and reflections about a EU "security council." Part of a sound review will have to be EU development policy, which for instance is unfolding in Africa without any clear coordination among EU member states and the Commission. The review of the Cotounou Agreement with the ACP-countries in 2020 should offer opportunity for a thorough reform, introducing a serious coordination effort with clear priorities.

Last but not least we should not forget the reinforcement of the European framework. This includes a new reflection about improved legitimacy by integrating national parliaments more in the decision-making and oversight. Furthermore there is a need to actually apply the principle of subsidiarity when it comes to the role of "Brussels." Our citizens want our major problems to be solved; they do not want endless declarations and poorly applied directives. We should be guided by what is possible and efficient, rather than waste time hunting for the ideal approach. If intergovernmental approaches are feasible, we should engage in this way, and not wait for the implementation of the classical communitarian approach.

And we should try to improve EU governance. Europe has to be led by the tandem—Commission and European Council—but we should reflect whether a "EU Security Council" could be a useful instrument in order to enhance decision-making.

Second, we have to rebuild a sustainable transatlantic and in particular EU-U.S. relationship.

Our first reflection should deal with a renewed transatalantic Alliance, a "new NATO" in which the Europeans take greater and more visible responsibility[20]. This should be based on a common structure and on a European (EU plus?) caucus.

At the same time the U.S.-EU relationship and dialogue will have to be adapted to a situation which has deeply changed. The aim has to remain a modern TTIP-or CETA-type agreement with regular high- level consultations of major issues of common interest. The U.S. Congress and the European Parliament should be involved, perhaps by setting up a small permanent U.S.-EU committee.

Third, we need a deep "reset" of the relationship with Russia.

The very first step has to be the settlement of a core question—the future of Ukraine. I do not think it is too late for a negotiated solution. We have to be aware that the independance of Ukraine has been from the outset an "agreement to disagree" with the Russians, for whom Ukraine due to history has always been a specific case. I agree with Dimiti Trenin, who is right to push in favor of a face-saving compromise asking for the withdrawal of Russia from the East while maintaining the Crimea. This could be a first step towards developing again a common agenda.[21]

In parallel a discussion should take place regarding the relaunch of a common European security architecture, a development that has stalled since the 1990s. These discussions should integrate in particular the future of the OSCE or that of the relationship between NATO and Russia and of the NATO-Russia Council, which never found a real place in the heart of the relationship. I understood well Russian NATO Ambassador Sergei Kisljak expressing to me his feeling being alone, isolated, not at home in a circle where the other 19 members had coordinated their positions before hand and no real discussion was possible. A parallel process should focus on EU-Russia relations.

In this overall context it could be helpful to set up common lines to develop a permanent discussion about subjects of common interest such as economy, migration, extremism, cyber, Middle East, Black Sea, de-conflicting of areas of tension.

Fourth, the relationship with China.

This should be based on a broader, permanent dialogue with the aim of a more balanced relationship including a permaent structure and regular high-level consultations. At the same time the EU should reflect how to reinforce our relationship with India, Japan and Indonesia at the bilateral as the multilateral level (review of the ASEM-concept).

Fifth, improvement of worldwide cooperation.

Last but not least, the EU and U.S. should examine major common issues: A "G 2" or a "G 4" (U.S., China, Russia, EU) seem to be unrealistic. The G-7 is a structure of the past, reflections should favour a sustainable "G 16+1" bringing together the major nations as future core beyond the UN-Security Council.[22]

Instead of a Conclusion

Neither the EU nor the Western world as a whole have been following the compass opened in the transition in the 1990s with the aim of overcoming definitely the period of Cold War. After hopeful beginnings and attempts in the 1990s we have been leaving this line and entering into a period of conflicts and unforced errors. Only under crisis management auspices has it been possible to avoid the worse. But today's general situation is more than ever characterized by a volatile, uncertain, and risky environment worldwide. Therefore the justified thesis has arisen about a (new) cold war or a fallback into the cold war which we had not seriously overcome. Therefore it has become today much more difficult and complex to reach the necessary turn and reset towards a safer and cooperative world where Europe and the U.S. are natural allies, where Europe and Russia need a good neighbourhood, where Europe and China and Asia can be strong partners. This goal is certainly very ambitious, but it seems still possible with political courage and a certain vision bearing in mind our mutual dependance and responsibilities.

Notes

1. William J. Burns, "The Lost Art of American Diplomacy," *Foreign Affairs*, March 27, 2019, https://www.foreignaffairs.com/articles/2019-03-27/lost-art-american-diplomacy.

2. Speech at the Minda de Günzburg Centre for European Studies January 31, 1993.

3. *The Economist*, May 17, 2019.

4. The aim of this outline is not a new theory on the order of the world (see the excellent article of Hanns Maull, "The Once and Future Liberal Order, in *Survival*, Vol. 61, No. 2, p. 7-32).

5. See François Delattre "The world grows more dangerous by the day", *New York Times* June 13, 2019 (Delattre is the future Secretary General of the French Foreign Ministry, the Quai d'Orsay).

6. See for example his speech in Madrid on May 21, 2002.

7. Extract from his speech in Munich on February 3, 1996.

8. Statement ("Europe—Every German's Future") of Chancellor Kohl, 3 February 1990, Davos (German Information Center NY, Statements & Speeches, Volume XIII No 4).

9. Personal archives of the author.

10. Personal archives of the author.

11. Translation of the letter of mid-october 1994 to President Clinton, personal archives of the author.

12. Translation of Chancellor Kohl's speech of 3 February 1996.

13. See the remarks of Richard Holbrooke, *To End a War* (New York: Random House, 1998), p. 361 ff.

14. Text following *Washington Post*, December 12, 2007.

15. See the interview of Horst Teltschik in *Der Spiegel* Nr. 11/2019, pages 24-26.

16. See the Report of UN Special Rapporteur on Extrajudicial, Summary or Arbitrary Executions Agnes Callamard of 19 June 2019 (A/HRC/41/CRP1).

17. See Paul Taylor's outstanding studies of the future of France, Germany, Poland and Italy in the European defense and security scene (edited by Friends of Europe, Brussels).

18. Zakaria in Bulletin Crédit Suisse 1/2019, Page 15 ss.

19. See in detail Miranda Xafa, Euro-area Governance Reform, The Unfinished Agenda, CIGI-Papers No 203, November 2018.

20. See among many other contributions to "NATO at 70" Experts view in *Politico*, April 3, 2019.

21. Dmitri Trenin, "It's Time to Rethink Russia's Foreign Policy Strategy," Carnegie Moscow Center, April 25, 2019; see William H. Hill, "Russia's Search for a Place in Europe," *Survival* Vol. 61, No. 3 (2019), p. 93.

22. G16+1= (1) America: U.S., Canada, Mexico, Brazil; (2) Asia : China, Japan, India, Indonesia; (3) Europe: France, Britain, Germany, the EU-Commission; (4) Turkey, Egypt, Nigeria, South Africa; plus the UN Secretary General.

Conclusions

The Exit from the Cold War:
Lessons and Warnings

Kristina Spohr

Destiny, it has been said, is not a matter of chance; it's a matter of choice. It's not a thing to be waited for; it's a thing to be achieved. And we can never safely assume that our future will be an improvement over the past. Our choice as a people is simple: We can either shape our times, or we can let the times shape us. And shape us they will, at a price frightening to contemplate, morally, economically, and strategically."[1]

These were George H.W. Bush's words on December 15, 1992 in a speech at Texas A&M University, five weeks before he left office. He had just lost the election to Bill Clinton, and was trying to come to terms with political defeat and the humiliation of going down in history as a one-term president. Using the speech to offer some reflections on history and leadership, Bush was seeking perspective on all that had happened to the world during his whirlwind four years in the White House from 1989 to 1993.

The challenge that faced Bush remains with us today, because the dramatic upheavals he was struggling to come to terms with in December 1992 still preoccupy us, three decades later. In some ways, Bush's generation of international policymakers did shape change. But in other ways those times shaped them—and still shape us today, in the era of Trump, Putin and Xi.[2]

The Power of the People and the People in Power

During Bush's first three years in office, the map of Europe was completely redrawn. In 1989, the bicentenary of 1789, an equally momentous surge of revolution swept away the *ancient régime* of communist dictatorship and command economics, melting the Soviet bloc that had been frozen in place since the 1940s.

The great symbolic moment was the fall of the Berlin Wall on November 9, 1989. Over the next year divided Germany became one.

Eastern European states underwent total economic and political transformation, seeking to render their new capitalist democracies viable and sustainable (with Western aid). The Warsaw Pact and COMECON dissolved and the Red Army began to withdraw from the former Soviet satellites—a process to be completed within four years.

By 1991—as the Soviet Union disintegrated relatively peacefully and Yugoslavia exploded violently—the European Community was metamorphosing into the European Union at Maastricht and NATO had established a "North Atlantic Cooperation Council" so that "West" could embrace "East" in what was billed as a new community of "free nations" extending from Vancouver to Vladivostok.

During Bush's final full year as President in 1992, "post-Wall Europe" was also in a process of "reunification" as the Central and Eastern countries (CEE), Baltic states and many former Soviet Republics, including Russia, looked west for financial support of their transformation and even aspired to "integration" in formerly "Western" structures: EU, NATO and G7, all of which would undergo consequential changes.

Meanwhile, the GATT—forged after the Great Depression of the 1930s and World War II—was being re-formed under U.S. pressure into a more open World Trade Organization (WTO). The new WTO (1995) would eventually include a communist-capitalist People's Republic of China (PRC) and a post-Soviet Russia—both of which had been keen since the late 1980s to enter the global market.

All this, many contemporaries believed, was a reflection of an overall trend towards some kind of Westernization—both across Europe and on a global plane. The spirit of America's 28th president was invoked as pundits talked anew about "Wilsonian" values. There were even predictions that the 1990s would be a "unipolar moment"[3] in which the United States would shape a more peaceful, norms-based world.

How had such rapid and peaceful change in the global order come about? Why was there such optimism about the future? What were the new order's weaknesses and flaws? What are the problems still with us today?

On one level the upheavals had stemmed from major structural shifts in geopolitics and in the global economy. On another, they had been propelled by people power—mass protest and electoral revolution—and magnified by transnational diffusion.

But Bush was not alone in believing that it was leaders who mattered—especially at such a critical juncture in history. Kohl and Gorbachev articulated similar views. In fact, the exit from the Cold War and the entry into what I call the post-Wall, post-Square era, must be understood as a process—"managed" by a group of historical actors who navigated the dramas of 1988-1992 together, each seeking to influence and even direct events.

People power, therefore, was not an uncontrollable protean force; it could be channeled by politicians who dared, like Bush, to "shape" events rather than be shaped by them, politicians who, to quote Kohl, saw history as opportunity, not fate. Each saw themselves as operating at a decisive moment in history.

All these leaders had to make choices.[4] In doing so, they contributed to outcomes that none of them had planned or even foreseen. To avoid anarchy or even conflict, this moment of decision-making required co-operation between leaders. Yet these were men (and one woman) with very different ideological outlooks, historical baggage and domestic constraints.

Such a challenge was, of course, not unique in modern history. In 1814-15 in Vienna and again in 1919 in Paris, leaders had met *en masse* in an effort to manage historical change. But these were gatherings of the victorious to make peace after hugely destructive wars. After the Second World War, no general peace treaty was ever negotiated. And the summit of victors at Potsdam in 1945 prefigured a shift from wartime cooperation to Cold War confrontation.

In the wake of 1989, however, there was neither an international conference, nor a conclave of the victorious. Post-Wall was a *process*, involving a plethora of summits, discussions and phone calls over the next two years that cumulatively negotiated the exit from the Cold War and the coming together of former enemies.

The core group of "managers" in 1989-1991 comprised the leaders of the Western alliance, many of whom had worked together for years.

Bush, as U.S. president, was not only pre-eminent but had been personally close to the center of policy for two decades. As a result, he was also well acquainted with veterans of the European scene, especially Thatcher, Mitterrand, Delors and Kohl. He also managed to build a rapport with Gorbachev, whom he "liked," and he was a *lao pengyou* (an old friend) of Deng Xiaoping.

These leaders' style of management could be termed "conservative," in the literal sense of that word. Politicians like "known knowns." Rather than risk creating total novelties, for the sake of stability and predictability they normally prefer to cling onto what already exists and has been shown to work, while adapting and modifying where it seems necessary. This was certainly true in 1989-91. Despite their anxieties, these leaders came to embrace transformative change. But, at least initially, they tried to cloak it in garments from the past—even if in some cases they were later forced to reinvent.

When it comes to the change of the global order and what the conservative managers did, three key stages in the transformative processes can be identified. I call them conserving, adapting, and re-inventing.

This is no rigid template. Some of the leaders—notably Gorbachev—never got to the stage of successful re-invention.

The designs for the future that emerged in 1990-1991 were not so much products of conceptually pre-conceived schemes. They grew out of choices made at what were seen as historically decisive moments. And they evolved while the upheavals lasted—settling into a reinvented and lasting form from early 1992.

There was no pre-made grand strategy—either in Europe, or in the Kremlin or the White House. To be sure the leaders fed off intellectual capital from past success—and while some were more conceptual (Mitterrand, Genscher, Delors), others were more practical problem-solvers working on the basis of political instinct and particular principles (Kohl, Bush).

All had to show some flexibility amid constantly novel situations. But they did not always find it easy to adjust. The bureaucracies worked in overdrive producing situation reports, option papers and blue sky thinking—but it was the leaders who would have to take the ultimate decisions.

At a time of flux, when each leader fixated on national interest and international opportunities (all the while juggling their domestic electoral agenda), they also found it challenging to view things from the other side of the fence. And yet this skill was needed to forge compromises and find a way into—what they hoped—would be a more peaceful post-Cold War world.

The cooperative spirit of 1989-1992, in which agreements were hammered out and decisions made, was a particularly striking feature of these "hinge years." Indeed, the overriding fixation (of America and the West at large) was ensuring stability and peace, collective action instead of unilateralism.

Marketization and democratization in the Central and Eastern European countries and Eurasia were driven less by ideological zeal (which some ascribed to Wilsonianism[5]) than as a Western reaction to the desires emanating from the transforming states, including the USSR and Russia.

It was in this light (and to counter Gorbachev's "Common European Home" rhetoric[6]) that Bush spoke in May 1989 in Mainz about a "Europe whole and free" and "a commonwealth of free nations."[7] The same pragmatic approach was evident in Bush's engagement with Communist China where hopes for better relations were dashed after Tiananmen. He held on to dialogue "to preserve some kind of relationship"[8] while abstaining from vocally pushing any political "liberalization" or human rights agenda.[9]

Political Improvisation and Management

As regards the process of political improvisation and management, let me draw on a few concrete cases to illustrate the stages of conserving, adapting and reinventing.

One example is Mikhail Gorbachev, who set out to preserve the Soviet Union and to make it more viable. He sought to reform and revitalize the USSR and thereby reposition it for continued but now peaceful competition with the West. He had clear, broad goals, but had little idea how to achieve them. Having started with partial economic reform, he quickly became more radical, persuaded that true restructuring could only work if combined with political liberalization. *Perestroika* went hand in hand with *glasnost*. This was part of the adaptation process.

His vision for Europe was a common European home. His vision of future U.S.-Soviet relations was superpower cooperation and partnership despite ideological differences; relations that went beyond literal peaceful coexistence, undergirded by arms reductions (notably the Conventional Forces in Europe (CFE) and START treaties in 1990 and 1991).

He promoted a policy based on universal, common, democratic, Eastern European freedom of choice, Soviet opening to the world economy and a desire to work through the United Nations (as evident in the international diplomacy of First Gulf War).

However, the more he adapted and modified at home and abroad, the more he lost control—on the periphery and in the heartland. He finally swung right to the hardliners in the winter of 1990-91. As he zigged and zagged, Gorbachev undermined the command economy and the communist monopoly of power without creating stable alternatives. And thus, he wound up presiding over the destruction of the Soviet multinational state. He never got to the stage of re-inventing the Soviet Union.

A second, contrasting example is offered by the People's Republic of China. Deng Xiaoping and the communist party leadership had originally embarked on a path of deliberately gradual economic reform. They could not prevent bouts of soaring inflation, which by the late 1980s triggered political protest and demands to change the system. But faced with an escalating domestic crisis and sobered by the erosion of communist authority in Eastern Europe, the Chinese Communist Party regime cracked down vigorously in June 1989 and reasserted its control.

Communism and one-party rule were thereby conserved. Secessionist nationalism would be stamped out. And after a brief reactionary phase imposed by Premier Li Peng, the process of economic (but not political) liberalization resumed in 1992 under reformist party boss Jiang Zemin. The economy would thus continue to be adapted and modified for entry into the global market.

The Chinese, in their mind, had learned lessons from what they regarded as Gorbachev's mistakes—excessive modification and loss of managerial control. The legacies of China's cautiously managed long-term transformation—from an insular Maoist state into an authoritarian communist-capitalist powerhouse with global reach—are still being played out in the 21st century. From developing country to world power: this has been China's communist re-invention. Post-Square was not like Post-Wall.

In sum, whereas Gorbachev failed in remaking his Union, Deng succeeded and his PRC was remade.

A third example of the management of change by conserving and adapting existing frameworks was evident over the "German Question." Here, re-invention was particularly fruitful.

First, Chancellor Helmut Kohl facilitated unification by using article 23 of West Germany's 1949 Basic Law to incorporate the eastern *Länder* in the Federal Republic. Likewise, he brought them into the Deutschmark (DM) zone on the argument (being made daily on East German streets) that if the Deutschmark did not come to the East Germans, they would come to the Deutschmark. The March 1990 East German election result confirmed that the GDR would effectively be absorbed into the old West German structures.

Second, adaptation and reinvention were also evident on the European plane. Once the GDR was part of the FRG, that meant it would automatically become part of the European Community—avoiding the danger of endless haggling with Germany's European partners about admitting a new, socio-economically weak state and, potentially, setting a precedent for admitting others from the former Soviet bloc.

Kohl could not quell dyspeptic mutterings in London about the "Fourth Reich," but his European solution to the German question did manage to assuage French fears about German revanchism and continental dominance. The DM—cornerstone of the German "economic miracle" since the 1940s—would now be subsumed into a common currency, as the heart of a new European Economic and Monetary Union (EMU). This in turn would realize the long-cherished integrationist aim of Jacques Delors—to dramatically deepen the Single Market instigated in 1986 while ensuring that it could not be dominated by newly unified Germany.

Other key Western European institutions were also adapted and re-invented to address the new German question. In regard to the emerging post-Cold War European security order, Bush was quick to insist that a unified Germany must remain a member of the Atlantic Alliance and Kohl fully agreed. This meant that NATO would outlive the Cold War for which it had been created. The Alliance would be adapted territorially to include the GDR and re-invented doctrinally through the 1990 London Declaration. NATO's perpetuation would ensure a continued American military presence in post-Wall Europe and there-by continue to fulfill its key purpose of guaranteeing mutual security. While satisfying Mitterrand and even Thatcher, this NATO solution to the German problem also helped reassure Moscow about the dangers of Teutonic revanchism. Ironically it ultimately suited Mikhail Gor-bachev as well—because the German settlement, in combination with the CFE treaty, would take care of the military balance in Europe.

Cumulatively, Germany was unified and the Europe surrounding it transformed on essentially Western terms—incorporating the central features of post-war liberal international order in successfully modified and reinvented form.

Where Leadership Mattered: The Triple Axis of Cooperation

These major structural changes were made possible because of dip-lomatically creative political friendships, or what we might call axes of cooperation. Three stand out: Bush-Kohl; Kohl-Mitterrand; and Gor-bachev-Bush/Kohl.

The warm accord between Bush and Kohl was rooted in four de-cades of successful "transatlantic partnership" within NATO. Kohl built on the Adenauer tradition of *Westbindung*, and indeed moved it onto a higher level as Bush welcomed unifying Germany as America's preferred new "partner in leadership."

Kohl and Mitterrand could find common ground in fostering the European integration project—despite Mitterrand's neuralgic spasms about German power and despite the two men's divergent priorities about the precise forms of economic and political union. They renewed the Adenauer-de Gaulle relationship for a new generation and a new era.

Against all odds, Gorbachev was able to develop a real rapport with both Bush and Kohl. This happened on a personal level but it was cemented by Gorbachev's fixation with "universal values," a "common European home" and the principles of the Helsinki Final Act.

As a result, these three men were able not only to transcend the ideological antagonism of the Cold War but also to heal some the scars of WWII, leading to real peacemaking in Europe. Adroit "checkbook diplomacy" on Kohl's part helped smooth Gorbachev's pullout of the Red Army from GDR soil, one of the most vivid—and livid—legacies of Soviet victory in 1945.

These axes of cooperation, built on political friendships, were essential to facilitate the threefold process of conserving, adapting and reinventing that lay at the heart of German unification. They were, however, less successful when it came to re-invention on the European plane. Two exogenous events in 1991—neither foreseen in 1989—proved critical obstacles: the dissolution of the Soviet Union, albeit peacefully; and the violent implosion of Yugoslavia, which quickly descended into bloody wars of secession. The challenges created by both break-ups would reveal the limits of conservative management and the problems with reinvention under even less predictable and more hostile circumstances. The stability of the post-Soviet space was an issue of long-term concern, but the ferocious Yugoslav wars prompted immediate reactions and laid bare some serious structural flaws in the Europe now being remade.

Reunifying Europe: The Dream, and the Problems, of Western Institutional Reinvention

The new European Union—despite its assertive rhetoric—was never up to the task of restoring peace in the Balkans. It was not able to speak with one voice, or to move beyond the EC's "civilian" tradition[10] of trying to mediate and help keep the peace, without developing a real European military capability. Ever since, post-Maastricht Europe has struggled to re-invent itself in the guise of foreign-policy actor and political "superpower" to which it aspired.

NATO, too, struggled with its reinvention after 1991. U.S./NATO military operations in Yugoslavia only became possible after the Alliance shifted its focus from "collective defense" to "collective security" in order to justify and allow NATO "out of area" operations.[11] This process took four years—from NATO's "new Strategic Concept" (1991) to the first UN-sanctioned NATO bombing campaign in Bosnia. The outcome of these operations was the Dayton peace accords. But NATO's doctrinal and military reinvention was deeply flawed. Dayton proved only a partial solution to the wide-ranging problems of the Balkans. And this U.S. spasm of peace enforcement exposed the power asymmetries between America—the only ally with the necessary firepower and lift-capacity—and the Europeans, still haunted by historical ghosts from their dark 20th century. The United States, in turn, struggled between "isolationist" tendencies and its global leadership role—now energized by Clinton's 1994 national security strategy of "engagement and enlargement."

Crucially, NATO's "out of area" reinvention made the Alliance in the long run also more problematic for the Kremlin. America's show of force in a Slav space (even if under NATO and UN auspices) threatened Moscow's geopolitical position—and a similar ideological challenge was posed by Clinton's rhetoric about exerting America's global weight to promote the nation's values. Although there was no disagreement with Russia over the Bosnia operation, the 1999 Kosovo bombing campaign by what was then an enlarged NATO (without UNSC authorization) brought these differences into the open.

In the view of many Russians, NATO's second reinvention through enlargement to the east (in 1999 and 2004) made matters worse.[12] The task of what Bush called "building a Europe whole and free" through a solid security framework had been fraught from the outset. Despite efforts of transforming the pan-European Conference on Security and Cooperation in Europe (CSCE)—the so-called "conscience of the continent"[13]—into an organization (OSCE) that would serve as a tool for greater transparency, for upholding rights, for monitoring elections and in dispute resolution, it failed to develop into the type of muscular mechanism that could put a stop to such atrocities as in former Yugoslavia. Likewise, the North Atlantic Cooperation Council (NACC) that first met in December 1991 was really just a loose forum for East-West liaison and information exchange spanning the Atlantic area and across Central Asia to the Pacific. It was later transformed into the Partnership for Peace (1994) and the Euro-Atlantic Partnership Council (1997) as a means of moving beyond information exchange with a then-defunct Warsaw Pact to operational mechanisms for cooperative military activities, including with Russia.

But it was NATO itself that was crystallizing as the only historically successful organization to provide hard security on the continent. And so East looked West—for membership.

In early 1992—as Russia assumed the Soviet seat on the UN Security Council—even Yeltsin declared Russia's partnership ambitions with the United States and NATO. Yet no seat for Moscow would materialize at the table *inside* the core of the Euro Atlantic community.[14]

Undoubtedly Western leaders did try to sustain the Russian state as a second key player in the international system. They became deeply involved in Russia's flawed transition into a market democracy and both Bush and Clinton made conscious efforts not to "isolate Russia" or turn it "from potential friend to potential adversary." But over the long term it became clear that it was not possible to keep Russia on side (not least because Russia had no intention of giving up even an iota of its sovereignty in order to integrate into what was effectively a US-led club) *and* to address the desire of the Central and Eastern Europeans and the Balts for full membership of NATO as well as the EU (as they sought to escape the fate of remaining as part of Russia's "near abroad").[15]

For its part, the United States—feeling it had "won" the Cold War—became increasingly assertive in its "unipolar" moment. The terrorist attacks on the United States on September 11, 2001 (9/11) were, of course, a turning point, but the early 1990s were of critical importance. Bush '41's campaign in 1991 to drive Saddam Hussein out of Kuwait was characterized by alliance cooperation and operational self-restraint: the President would not go "all the way to Baghdad." The Bosnian war was also a limited mission and had Russian approval. But the Kosovo war and a growing feeling that the U.S. could and should have finished off Saddam for good fed into the post-9/11 passion for liberal interventionism—an expansive policy direction increasingly resented by the Kremlin.

Indeed, during Putin's reign (from 2000), and especially since his return to the presidency in 2012, Russian alienation from the West has intensified and a heightened nostalgia for the country's great-power past, back to the glory days of defeating Napoleon after 1812 and overcoming Hitler in the Great Patriotic War, has re-emerged with a vengeance.

So, while re-inventing NATO (and the EU) as a Europe-wide entity was always going to be problematic, the combination of Russian *amour propre* and American ideological self-assertion made matters toxic. These issues could probably never have been resolved, even by the most sensitive diplomacy. But it is true that the confrontation became undoubtedly more direct and more dangerous in the Putin era.

Conclusions

What conclusions may America and the West draw from the story of global transition and international management that we have explored in this book?

Today we live in an era of erratic U.S. behavior and a changing balance of power with both a revisionist Russia whose president claims that "liberalism is obsolete" and an ambitious post-Square China und Xi Jinping challenging American leadership.[16] To quote Russian Foreign Minister Sergei Lavrov, they are seeking a "post West world."[17] We also have a U.S. president who seems unwilling to lead—or at least to do so as part of an alliance, rather than throwing his weight about unilaterally. Indeed, he claims that America "must as a nation be more unpredictable."[18]

The effect has been to unsettle the Atlantic Alliance. Can America afford to become isolationist, turning its back on Europe? And is it worth throwing away allies that are run by norm-governed regimes? Trust is easily broken. Re-establishing it is much harder and takes much longer. The same goes for arms control regimes.

Examining the end of the Cold War yields a few pointers for the future:

First, given the difficulties in creating new international institutions, there is much to be said for the process of conserving, adapting and reinventing those that work. This was particularly efficacious in facilitating German unification.

Second, this process depends for its success on fruitful axes of cooperation between leaders. In 1989-91 the relationships between Bush, Kohl, Mitterrand and Gorbachev stood out.

Third, reinvention seems to have been much less successful when it came to NATO's out-of-area role and the process of NATO's and the EU's eastern enlargement. But these processes did help to bring much of the former Soviet bloc into Europe "whole and free" and thus served to stabilize a highly volatile part of the old continent. And arguably NATO's traditional "containment"[19] role remains applicable in the Putin era. In other words, the jury is still out—it's too early to judge.

Fourth, as regards the future, a new process of adapting and reinventing will be necessary to address the challenges of right-wing populism to democracy, the digital age and new forms of aggression, notably cyber warfare.

Fifth, the crux is to sustain the cooperative relationships on which consensually-based leadership must rest. George H.W. Bush understood that; Donald J. Trump does not.

Some of Bush 41's words in that farewell speech in Texas now look strikingly prescient when he warned that "economically, a world of escalating instability and hostile nationalism will disrupt global markets, set off trade wars, set us on a path of economic decline." Future challenges, he believed, "must be met with collective action, led by the United States, to protect and promote our political, economic, and security values." And, he added, "A retreat from American leadership, from American involvement, would be a mistake for which future generations, indeed our own children, would pay dearly."

Notes

1. Remarks by President George H.W. Bush at Texas A&M University, College Station, Texas, December 15, 1992.

2. I reflect on this at length in my global history of 1989-1992, *Post Wall Post Square: Rebuilding the World after 1989* (New York/New Haven: HarperCollins, October 2019 & Yale University Press, March 2020)

3. Charles Krauthammer, "The Unipolar Moment," *Washingon Post*, July 20, 1990; idem, "The Unipolar Moment," *Foreign Affairs* 70, 1 (1990/1991) [America and the World 1990/91] pp. 23–33; idem, "The Unipolar Moment Revisited," *The National Interest* 70 (Winter 2002/3) pp. 5–18. Cf. Hal Brands, *Making the Unipolar Moment: US Foreign Policy and the Rise of the Post-Cold War Order* (Ithaca, NY: Cornell University Press, 2016); Odd Arne Westad, "The Cold War and America's Delusion of Victory," *New York Times*, August 28, 2017

4. See Philip Zelikow and Condoleezza Rice, *To Build a Better World: Choices to End the Cold War and Create a Global Commonwealth* (New York: Twelve Books, 2019)

5. John A. Thompson, "Wilsonianism: The Dynamics of a Conflicted Concept," *International Affairs* 86, 1 (2010) pp. 27-48.

6. Mikhail Gorbachev, *Memoirs* (New York: Doubleday, 1996), p. 428.

7. Bush's Remarks to the Citizens in Mainz, Federal Republic of Germany, May 31, 1989.

8. TNA UK PREM 19/2597, PS Charles Powell to Stephen Wall (FCO) Memorandum re: Bush-Thatcher telcon on "China," June, 5, 1989, pp.1-2, MTF.

9. Cf. Strobe Talbott, "Post-Victory Blues," *Foreign Affairs* 71,1 (1991/92) [America and the world 1991/92], pp. 68-69.

10. Jan Orbie, "Civilian Power Europe—Review of the Original and Current Debates," *Cooperation and Conflict* 41, 1 (2006), pp.123-8; Karen E. Smith, "Beyond the Civilian Power EU Debate," *Politique européenne* 2005/3 (No. 17), pp. 63-82.

11. See David S. Yost, "The New NATO and Collective Security," *Survival* 40, 2 (Summer 1998), pp.135-160; Daniel S. Hamilton and Kristina Spohr (eds), *Open Door: NATO and Euro-Atlantic Security after the Cold War* (Washington, DC: Johns Hopkins University SAIS/Brookings Institution Press 2019), p. xv. See also Tarcisio Gazzini, "NATO's Role in the Collective Security System," *Journal of Conflict & Security Law* 8, 2 (Oct. 2003), pp.231-63.

12. For various views on NATO enlargement, see Hamilton and Spohr (eds), op. cit.

13. GHWBPL, NSC, Gompert Files, ESSG (CF01301-009), US Security and Institutional Interest in Europe and Eurasia in the post-Cold War era (undated, ca. Feb. 1992), p. 2 [with Cover note from Gompert to Zoellick et al. 19.2.1992]; US National Security Interest in Europe and Beyond the NATO Area (undated, ca. Feb. 1992) pp. 1-4 [with Cover note from Gompert to Zoellick et al. 7.2.1992]; NACC—CSCE Relationship (undated, early 1992 by EUR/RPM: SMcGinnis) pp. 1-4.

14. William H. Hill, *No Place for Russia: European Security and Institutions Since 1989* (New York: Columbia University Press, 2018).

15. GHWBPL, NSC, Gompert Files, ESSG (CF01301-009), Memorandum from Lowenkron to Howe—Subj.: ESSG Mtg 30 Mar. 1992 SitRoom 26.3.1992, p. 2 ('Handling Russia'). See also Hamilton and Spohr (eds), op. cit.

16. Cf. Stephen Kotkin, "Russia's Perpetual Geopolitics: Putin Returns to the Historical Pattern," *Foreign Affairs* (May/June 2016) online; Bobo Lo, *Axis of Convenience: Moscow, Beijing, and the New Geopolitics* (Washington, DC: Brookings Institution Press, 2009); Graham Allison, *Destined for War: Can America and China Escape Thucydides's Trap?* (New York: Mariner, 2017); Odd Arne Westad, "The Sources of Chinese Conduct: Are Washington and Beijing Fighting a New Cold War?," *Foreign Affairs* 98, 5 (Sept./Oct. 2019) [Autocracy Now], pp. 86-95. ; "'Liberalism Is Obsolete,' Russian President Vladimir Putin Says Amid G20 Summit," *Time*, June 28, 2019.

17. Joel Gehrke, "Russia Calls for "post-West World Order,'" *Washington Examiner*, February 18, 2017; "Russia: "We Are in the post-West World Order,'" *Washington Examiner*, June 29, 2018; 9.6.2018; Nicole Gaouette, "Russia, China Use UN Stage to Push Back on a US-led World Order," *CNN*, September 21, 2017. See also "Xi says China must lead way in reform of global governance," *Reuters*, June 23, 2018; Did Tang, "Xi Jinping sets out China's ambitions as world power," *The Times*, December 18, 2018.

18. "Transcript: Donald Trump's Foreign Policy Speech," *New York Times*, April 27, 2016. See also Michael H. Fuchs, "Donald Trump's Doctrine of Unpredictability has the World on Edge," *The Guardian*, February 13, 2017.

19. Cf. Nicholas Burns and Douglas Lute, "NATO at Seventy: An Alliance in Crisis" Report—Belfer Center/Harvard Kennedy School (February 2019) online; Michael Mandelbaum, "The New Containment," *Foreign Affairs* (March/April 2019) online.

About the Authors

Anatoly Adamishin is Honorary President of the Association for Euro-Atlantic Cooperation. He served as Deputy Minister of Foreign Affairs of the USSR from 1986-1990, as Soviet/Russian Ambassador to Italy from 1990-1992, as First Deputy Minister of Foreign Affairs of the Russian Federation from 1992-1994, Russian Ambassador to Great Britain from 1994-1997, and Minister of the Russian Federation for CIS Countries Cooperation from 1997-1998. He was Vice President, International Affairs for "SISTEMA" Joint-Stock Financial Corporation, Moscow, Russia from 1998-2005. He served as a Guest Scholar of the Jennings Randolph Fellowship Program at the U.S. Institute of Peace in Washington, DC in 2006-2007.

John-Michael Arnold is a Visiting Professor of International Relations at the George Washington University. He was a DAAD Post-Doctoral Fellow at the Johns Hopkins School of Advanced International Studies (SAIS) during the 2018-2019 academic year. He holds a Ph.D from Princeton University's Woodrow Wilson School of Public and International Affairs and his research interests include U.S. foreign policy, strategic studies, transatlantic relations, and NATO. During his doctorate, he was a graduate fellow at Princeton's Center for International Security Studies (CISS) and he completed a pre-doctoral fellowship at the George Washington University's Institute for Security and Conflict Studies (ISCS). Prior to enrolling at Princeton, he worked as special assistant to the president of the Brookings Institution. He also has a master's degree in International Relations from Yale University and a BA in Philosophy, Politics, and Economics (PPE) from the University of Oxford.

Joachim Bitterlich currently serves as a professor at ESCP Europe business school in Paris. He is a Member of the Independent Historical Commission to the Ministry of Food and Agriculture in Berlin; Chairman of the Franco-German Business Cercle Berlin; and a Senior Advisor to Eutop Brussels, BGA-Berlin Global Advisors, and CogitoPraxis, Paris. He also serves on a number of boards, including those of Ecole Nationale d'Administration ENA Paris, Institut Jacques Delors Paris, Friends of Europe Brussels, and the Bosporus Institute Paris/Istanbul. He served as European, International and Security Policy Advisor to German Chancellor Helmut Kohl, as German Permanent Representative to NATO, and as German Ambassador to Spain. He was

Executive Vice-President International Affairs and Chairman for Germany of Veolia Paris.

Sir Rodric Braithwaite spent much of his career in the British foreign service dealing with the Soviet Union and East-West relations. He was ambassador in Moscow in 1988-92, and then adviser to the Prime Minister and chairman of the Joint Intelligence Committee (1992-93). He has written four books, three on modern Russian history, the fourth (*Armageddon and Paranoia*) on the nuclear confrontation.

David C. Gompert served as the acting Director of National Intelligence (DNI) and Principal Deputy Director of National Intelligence between 2009-2011. In between government and academic tenures, he has worked in senior executive positions at Unisys, AT&T, and as a senior fellow at RAND. Before that, he was a distinguished research professor at the National Defense University's Center for Technology and National Security Policy. From 2003 to 2004, he was the senior adviser for national security and defense to the Coalition Provisional Authority in Iraq. From 1975 to 1983, he held numerous positions at the U.S. Department of State, serving as deputy to the Under Secretary of State for Political Affairs, deputy director of the Bureau of Political-Military Affairs, and special assistant to former Secretary of State Henry Kissinger. Following these capacities in the Ford, Carter, and Reagan administrations, he was appointed Special Assistant to President George H. W. Bush. He received a bachelor's degree in engineering from the U.S. Naval Academy, where he later served on the faculty, and a Master of Public Affairs from Princeton University's Woodrow Wilson School of Public and International Affairs.

Elias Götz was a DAAD Post-Doctoral Fellow at the Foreign Policy Institute of Johns Hopkins SAIS in 2018-2019 and is a researcher at the Institute for Russian and Eurasian Studies (IRES), Uppsala University. He holds a Ph.D in Political Science from Aarhus University (2013). His main areas of expertise are security studies, international relations theory, and Russian foreign policy. He has published on these topics in journals such as *International Studies Review*, *International Politics*, *Foreign Policy Analysis*, *Global Affairs*, and Contemporary Politics. He is currently working on a book project entitled *Russia's Quest for Regional Primacy*.

Cengiz Günay is the Deputy Director of the Austrian Institute for International Affairs (oiip) and lecturer at the University of Vienna. He was an Austrian Marshall Plan Foundation Visiting Scholar at the Foreign Policy Institute of Johns Hopkins SAIS in 2018-2019. His research interests are neoliberal interventions and the transformation of state and statehood, European Neighborhood Policy and the rise of authoritarianism. His regional focus lies on Turkey, and the Arab Middle East. Recent publications include *Border Politics:*

Defining Spaces of Governance and Forms of Transgressions (Berlin: Springer, January 2017); "Decoding the authoritarian code: Exercising 'legitimate' power politics through the ruling parties in Turkey, Macedonia and Serbia," *Journal for Southeast European and Black Sea Studies*, 16 (4) 2016; "Foreign Policy as a Source of Legitimation for 'Competitive Authoritarian Regimes' – the Case of Turkey's AKP," *Georgetown Journal of International Affairs*, 2016; "Challenging the EU's Liberal Peace Model in the Mediterranean" in, Heinz Gärtner et al. (eds.) *Democracy, Peace, and Security* (New York: Lexington Books, 2015); "Turkey: A Model for Continuity Rather than Change," in Larbi Sadiki (ed.) *The Routledge Handbook of the Arab Spring* (London: Routledge, 2015).

Daniel S. Hamilton is the Austrian Marshall Plan Foundation Professor and Senior Fellow at the Foreign Policy Institute of Johns Hopkins University's Paul H. Nitze School of Advanced International Studies (SAIS). From 2002 to 2010 he was the Richard von Weizsäcker Professor at SAIS, and is Richard von Weizsäcker Fellow at the Robert Bosch Academy in Berlin. He was the Founding Director of the School's Center for Transatlantic Relations, and for fifteen years served as Executive Director of the American Consortium for EU Studies. He has served as Deputy Assistant Secretary of State for European Affairs, responsible for NATO, OSCE and transatlantic security issues, U.S. relations with the Nordic-Baltic region, and stabilization of Southeastern Europe following the Kosovo conflict; U.S. Special Coordinator for Southeast European Stabilization; Associate Director of the Policy Planning Staff for U.S. Secretaries of State Madeleine K. Albright and Warren Christopher; Senior Policy Advisor to Assistant Secretary of State and U.S. Ambassador to Germany Richard C. Holbrooke. In 2008 he served as the first Robert Bosch Foundation Senior Diplomatic Fellow on the policy planning staff of German Foreign Minister Frank-Walter Steinmeier. Between 1982 and 1990 he was Deputy Director of the Aspen Institute Berlin, where he engaged with many of the protagonists, East and West, who feature in this book. His book *Rule-Makers or Rule-Takers: Exploring the Transatlantic Trade and Investment Partnership*, was named "#1 Global Policy Study of the Year" in 2016. Selected publications include *Beyond Bonn: America and the Berlin Republic* (Washington DC: Carnegie Endowment for International Peace); *Advancing U.S-Nordic-Baltic Security Cooperation; The Eastern Question: Russia, the West and Europe's Grey Zone*; and *Alliance Revitalized: NATO for a New Era*; and (with Kristina Spohr, eds.) *Open Door: NATO and Euro-Atlantic Security in the 1990s*. He has been presented with Germany's Federal Order of Merit (Bundesverdienstkreuz); named a Chevalier of France's Ordre des Palmes Académiques; and awarded Sweden's Knighthood of the Royal Order of the Polar Star. He was presented the State Department's Superior Honor Award for his work to integrate the Baltic states into Euro-Atlantic structures.

Jón Baldvin Hannibalsson is an Icelandic politician. He was leader of the Icelandic SDP from 1984 to 1996. From 1987 to 1995 he served as Minister of Finance and then as Minister for Foreign Affairs and External Trade. As Finance Minister he is remembered for reorganizing the entire revenue and tax system of Iceland. As minister for Foreign Affairs and External Trade he led Iceland´s negotiations with the European Union on the European Economic Area (EEA, 1989-1994). As Foreign Minister he persistently solicited support for the restored independence of the Baltic states, within NATO and elsewhere. In recognition of his support he has been awarded the highest honors of all the Baltic states and made an honorary citizen of Vilnius. He studied at the Universities of Edinburgh, Stockholm and was a Fulbright scholar at Harvard. He is a prolific writer on economic policy, education and international affairs. His autobiography became a best seller in Iceland in 2002. His most recent books are *The Baltic Road to Freedom: Iceland's Role* and *The Nordic Model vs. The Neoliberal Challenge*.

Liviu Horovitz is an SNF Postdoctoral researcher at the Institute for European Studies of the Vrije Universiteit Brussel. He was a DAAD Post-Doctoral Fellow at the Foreign Policy Institute of Johns Hopkins SAIS in 2018-2019. He is currently writing a book on the United States' desire for military preponderance within the current international system. He has served as a research fellow at Harvard University's Belfer Center for Science and International Affairs, a senior researcher on nuclear policy at the Center for Security Studies in Zurich, a consultant for the Preparatory Commission for the Comprehensive Nuclear-Test-Ban Treaty Organization in Vienna, and a research associate at the James Martin Center for Nonproliferation Studies in Monterey. His work has been published in, for instance, the *Journal of Strategic Studies, European Security, International Spectator, RUSI Journal, The Washington Quarterly, Nonproliferation Review*, and *Bulletin of the Atomic Scientists*. He holds a doctorate from ETH Zurich.

Stephan Kieninger was a DAAD Post-Doctoral Fellow at Johns Hopkins University SAIS in 2018-2019. He received his Ph.D in Modern History from Mannheim University in 2011. His current research looks into Western financial assistance for the Soviet Union and its impact on the peaceful end of the Cold War. He is the author *The Diplomacy of Détente. Cooperative Security Policies from Helmut Schmidt to George Shultz* (London: Routledge, 2018) which explains how East-West trade and the Helsinki process fostered cooperative security policies despite recurring crisis in international relations. His first book, *Dynamic Détente, The United States and Europe, 1964–1975* (Lanham: Rowman & Littlefield, 2016) investigates the emergence of détente and the origins of the Helsinki Final Act in 1975.

Mart Laar is an Estonian historian and politician. He has served twice as the Prime Minister of Estonia, from 1992 to 1994 and from 1999 to 2002. He was Estonia's Minister of Defense from 2011 to 2012. He has multiple orders from Estonia and other countries. He was awarded the Cato Institute's Milton Friedman Prize for Advancing Liberty in 2006. He has written several books on politics and history, including *War in the Woods: Estonia's Struggle for Survival, 1944–1956* and *The Power of Freedom: Central and Eastern Europe after 1945*. He holds a Ph.D in history from the University of Tartu.

Sir Roderic Lyne was a member of the British Diplomatic Service from 1970 to 2004. He served at the British Embassy in Moscow from 1972-74 and again from 1987-1990, and was Head of the Soviet (subsequently Eastern) Department in the Foreign Office from 1990-93. From 1993-6 he was the Private Secretary for Foreign Affairs, Defence and Northern Ireland to Prime Minister John Major; and from 1997-2000 he served as the UK Permanent Representative to the international organizations in Geneva. Sir Roderic became the British Ambassador to the Russian Federation in January 2000, retiring from Moscow in August 2004. He has since worked as a company director, business consultant, and lecturer. He was a co-author, with Strobe Talbott and Koji Watanabe, of "Engaging with Russia," a report to the Trilateral Commission (2006). From 2009-16 he served on the Committee of Inquiry into the UK's involvement in the Iraq conflict.

Markus Meckel is a German politician and former Protestant pastor who was a prominent critic of the East German (GDR) regime. In 1989 he initiated the creation of the Social Democratic Party (SDP) in the GDR. From February 23, 1990 until the merger with the West German SPD on September 27, 1990, he was deputy SDP party chairman, and acting chairman from March 26 to June 10, 1990. After the first free democratic elections in the GDR, he served as Foreign Minister and negotiated German unification in the framework of the 2+4 talks. Between 1990 and 2009 he served as a Member of the German Bundestag, where he focused on European politics, security issues and the Eastern Partnership. From 2000-2002 he was Vice President of the NATO Parliamentary Assembly. He was Vice-Spokesman of the Social Democrats for foreign policy and Spokesman in two commissions dealing with the SED dictatorship and its consequences. In October 2013 he was nominated President of the German War Graves Commission.

Wencke Meteling was a DAAD Post-Doctoral Fellow at the Foreign Policy Institute of Johns Hopkins SAIS in 2018-2019. She was Assistant Professor at the History Department and Research Group Leader at the Collaborative Research Center "Dynamics of Security," Marburg University, and a Humboldt Post-Doctoral Fellow at Wolfson College and the History Faculty, University of Cambridge. She holds a doctorate from Tübingen University and wrote an award-winning book on Germany and France during the Franco-Prussian War and World War I. She has written or edited five books and numerous articles. Her fields of expertise include international competitiveness in a globalizing world, neo-liberalism, transatlantic economic and social policies after the Second World War, historical approaches in Critical Security Studies, and European Military and War History. Her current book project focuses on economic competitiveness in the United Kingdom and Germany and transatlantic discourses on statehood and market freedom.

Adam Michnik is a Polish historian, essayist, former dissident, public intellectual, and editor-in-chief of the Polish newspaper *Gazeta Wyborcza*. Reared in a family of committed communists, Michnik became an opponent of Poland's communist regime at the time of the party's anti-Jewish purges. He was imprisoned after the 1968 March Events and again after the imposition of martial law in 1981. Between 1977 and 1989 he was the editor or co-editor of underground newspapers published illegally, and a member of the management of NOWa, one of the biggest underground publishers. In the years 1980–1989 he was an adviser to both the independent self-governing trade union *Solidarność* in the Mazovia Region and to the Foundry Workers Committee of *Solidarność*. He played a crucial role during the Polish Round Table Talks, as a result of which the communists agreed to call elections in 1989, which were won by *Solidarność*. He has received many awards and honors, including the Legion of Honor and European of the Year.

Janusz Onyszkiewicz was a member of Poland's democratic opposition beginning in the mid-1960s. After martial law was imposed in Poland on December 13, 1981, he was imprisoned for over one year, then rearrested several times. He was National Spokesman of Solidarność until 1989 and a member of its National Executive (Presidium). He was the spokesman of the Solidarność delegation to Round Table negotiations with the communist authorities between February and April 1989, and a Member of the Polish Parliament from 1989 to 2001. He served as Deputy Minister (1990-1991) and Minister of National Defense (1991-1993 and 1997-2000). Member of the Democratic Party (previously- Union for Freedom) and its President in 2006-2009, member of the European Parliament (2004-2009) and its Vice President, and Vice President of the Foreign Relation Committee of the European Parliament. He has served as President of the Council of the Euro-Atlantic Association of Poland, Member of the Advisory Board of the Security & Defence Agenda in Brussels, member of the European Leadership Network, Senior Fellow in the Centre for International Relations in Warsaw, adviser to the Minister of National Defense from 2010-2015, and Chairman of the Defense Industry Cooperation Committee of the Polish-Ukrainian Chamber of Commerce. He is a speleologist and alpinist, and was President of the Polish Mountaineering Association from 2001 to 2016. He has been decorated with the Great Cross of Order of Gedymin (Lithuania), Officer of the Legion of Honour (France), Manfred Wörner Cross (Germany), Terra Mariana Cross (Estonia), Commander of the Polonia Restituta Cross (Poland) He holds a Ph.D in pure mathematics and a Doctor Honoris Causa from the University of Leeds (UK).

Pavel Palazhchenko is Head of International and Media Relations for the Gorbachev Foundation. He also serves as an analyst, spokesperson, interpreter and translator, as well as the president of the Russian Translation Company. As Principal English Interpreter for Mikhail Gorbachev and Soviet Foreign Minister Eduard Shevardnadze, he participated in all U.S.-Soviet ministerial and summit meetings and talks leading to the end of the Cold War. He writes on international politics, U.S.-Russian relations, arms control, and related topics in multiple Russian and international newspapers. His memoir, *My Years with Gorbachev and Shevardnadze: The Memoir of a Soviet Interpreter*, was published by Penn State Press in 1996.

Condoleezza Rice was the sixty-sixth U.S. Secretary of State and the first black woman to hold that office. Prior to that, she was the first woman to serve as national security adviser to the President of the United States. She is a professor at Stanford University and cofounder of RiceHadleyGates LLC. She is the *New York Times* bestselling author of *No Higher Honor: A Memoir of My Years in Washington* (2011), *Extraordinary, Ordinary People: A Memoir of Family* (2010), *Democracy: Stories from the Long Road to Freedom* (2017), and *Political Risk: How Businesses and Organizations Can Anticipate Global Insecurity* (2018).

Thomas W. Simons, Jr., was a U.S. Foreign Service Officer from 1963 to 1998. He served in Warsaw, Bucharest, and Moscow, and in the State Department's Bureau for European and Canadian Affairs in Washington as Director for Soviet Union Affairs (1981-1985) and as Deputy Assistant Secretary responsible for relations with the Soviet Union, Eastern Europe, and Yugoslavia (1986-1989). In the 1990s he was U.S. Ambassador to Poland (1990-1993), Coordinator of U.S. Bilateral Assistance to the New Independent States of the former Soviet Union (from Washington, 1993-1995), and U.S. Ambassador to Pakistan (1996-1998). He has been a Visiting Scholar at Harvard's Davis Center for Russian and Eurasian Studies since 2002.

Kristina Spohr is Helmut Schmidt Distinguished Professor at the Henry A. Kissinger Center on Global Affairs at Johns Hopkins University's School of Advanced International Studies (SAIS) and a member of the International History Department at the London School of Economics and Political Science (LSE). She studied at the University of East Anglia, Sciences Po Paris, and Cambridge University, where she earned her Ph.D in History and then held a post-doctoral fellowship. She also worked as a Research Fellow in the Secretary General's Private Office at NATO headquarters in Brussels. She has authored several books, most recently *The Global Chancellor: Helmut Schmidt and the Reshaping of the International Order* (Oxford University Press, 2016) – also in extended German edition *Helmut Schmidt: Der Weltkanzler* (WGB/Theiss, 2016) – and co-edited *Transcending the Cold War: Summits, Statecraft, and the Dissolution of Bipolarity in Europe, 1970-1990* (Oxford UP, 2016). Her newest book, on the global exit from the Cold War, is *Post Wall, Post Square: Rebuilding the World after 1989* (HarperCollins/UK; Yale University Press/US, 2019/2020), with a German edition entitled *Wendezeit: Die Neuordnung der Welt nach 1989* (DVA, 2019).

Horst M. Teltschik currently serves as an international consultant and expert on foreign policy and security affairs. He is Member of the Board of the German – Russian Raw Material Forum, Member of the German–Korean Consultative Group on Korean reunification, Honorary Professor at the Faculty for Economics of the Technical University in Munich, Honorary Professor at Gorny University in St. Petersburg, Russia, and an Advisory Board Member of various German inter–governmental institutions and charitable organizations. He previously served as Chairman of the Munich Conference on Security Policy; President of Boeing Germany; Member of the Executive Board of the BMW Group, Munich; Director-General, Central and Eastern Europe, Asia and Middle East of the BMW Board, Munich; Chairman of the Executive Board of the BMW Foundation Herbert Quandt; and Executive Director of the Bertelsmann Foundation. He was Director General, Foreign and Domestic Relations, Development Policy and Foreign Security in the Federal Chancellery, where he served as National Security Advisor to Chancellor Helmut Kohl, and was Deputy Chief of Staff at the Federal Chancellery in Bonn. He served as Chief of Staff of the Chairman of the Christian Democratic Union/Christian Social Union (CDU/CSU) Parliamentary Group in Bonn, Executive Undersecretary in the State Chancellery of Rhineland-Palatinate in Mainz, Director General for Foreign, German and Security Policy of the CDU Federal Office, and as Assistant Professor for International Affairs at the Free University Berlin.

Philip Zelikow is the White Burkett Miller Professor of History and J. Wilson Newman Professor of Governance at the Miller Center of Public Affairs, both at the University of Virginia. His books and essays focus on critical episodes in American and world history. A former civil rights attorney and career diplomat, he has served at all levels of American government. He was the executive director of the 9/11 Commission and, before that, directed the Carter-Ford commission on federal election reform. He has also worked on international policy in each of the five U.S. administrations from Reagan through Obama.